Religion in History, Society, and Culture

Edited by
Frank Reynolds
and
Winnifred Fallers Sullivan
The University of Chicago, Divinity School

A Routledge Series

RELIGION IN HISTORY, SOCIETY, AND CULTURE
edited by Frank Reynolds & Winnifred Fallers Sullivan

Lest We Be Damned
Practical Innovation and Lived Experience among Catholics in Protestant England, 1559–1642

Lisa McClain

Routledge
New York & London

Published in 2004 by
Routledge
29 West 35th Street
New York, NY 10001
www.routledge-ny.com

Published in Great Britain by
Routledge
11 New Fetter Lane
London EC4P 4EE
www.routledge.co.uk

Routledge is an imprint of the Taylor & Francis Group
Printed in the United States of America on acid-free paper.

10 9 8 7 6 5 4 3 2 1

Library of Congress Cataloging-in-Publication Data

McClain, Lisa, 1965–
    Lest we be damned : practical innovation and lived experience among Catholics in Protestant England, 1559–1642 / by Lisa McClain.
        p. cm. — (Religion in history, society & culture ; 6)
Includes bibliographical references and index.
    ISBN 0-415-96790-2 (alk. paper)
    1. Catholics—England—History—16th century. 2. England—Church history—16th century. 3. Catholics—England—History—17th century. 4. England—Church history—17th century. I. Titles. II. Series.
    BX1492.M37 2003
    282'.42'09031—dc21

                                                            2003014634

For Doug, Anna, and Will

Contents

❖

Series Editors' Foreword

R ELIGION IN HISTORY, SOCIETY, AND CULTURE BRINGS TO A WIDER
audience work by outstanding young scholars who are forging new
agendas for the study of religion in the twenty-first century. As editors, we have two specific goals in mind.

First, volumes in this series illuminate theoretical understandings of
religion as a dimension of human culture and society. Understanding religion
has never been a more pressing need. Longstanding academic habits of either
compartmentalizing or ignoring religion are breaking down. With the entry of
religion into the academy, however, must come a fully realized conversation
about what religion is and how it interacts with history, society, and culture.
Each book in this series employs and refines categories and methods of analysis that are intrinsic to the study of religion, while simultaneously advancing
our knowledge of the character and impact of particular religious beliefs and
practices in a specific historical, social, or cultural context.

Second, this series is interdisciplinary. The academic study of religion is
conducted by historians, sociologists, political scientists, anthropologists, psy-
chologists, and others. Books in the series bring before the reader an array of
disciplinary lenses through which religion can be creatively and critically
viewed. Based on the conviction that the instability of the category itself gen-
erates important insights, "religion" in these works encompasses and/or
informs a wide range of religious phenomena, including myths, rituals, ways of
thought, institutions, communities, legal traditions, texts, political movements,
artistic production, gender roles, and identity formation.

In this, the sixth book in the series, Lisa McClain provides an engross-
ing narrative about the struggle of a religious community to survive in the face

of a powerful, state-supported effort to destroy its inherited sense of identity and to eradicate its influence. The story that McClain recounts occurs in England during a time when Protestant reformers, strongly supported by the monarchy, sought to forcefully impose their version of Christianity on a population that included a significant Roman Catholic component.

In the story itself, McClain focuses attention on the popular side of Catholic religion. She describes the creative partnership of the lower, pastoral clergy with the engaged segment of the laity as the locus of innovation through which the Catholic community was able to maintain and adapt its liturgical practice on the one hand and its inherited sense of identity on the other. At the same time McClain artfully evokes an appreciation for the kind of lived experience that she associates with ordinary believers and practitioners who combined a firm commitment to their Catholic heritage with a practical flexibility that enabled them to adapt to a radically changed religio-political order.

As editors we are pleased to include within the *Religion in History, Society, and Culture* series a book that brings a fresh perspective to a familiar topic—early modern Catholicism—using the new theoretical and methodological approaches being developed by cultural historians and historians of religion.

Winnifred Fallers Sullivan, The University of Chicago, Divinity School
Frank Reynolds, The University of Chicago, Divinity School

Acknowledgments

THIS BOOK COULD NOT HAVE BEEN COMPLETED WITHOUT THE AID OF numerous professional colleagues, friends, and family members who supported me throughout the various phases of the process. Thank you in particular to Brian P. Levack and Ann W. Ramsey whose guidance and commentary have proven invaluable. I also extend my appreciation to those scholars who have reviewed parts of the work at various stages of the process and from whose learned advice I have benefited immeasurably: Myron Gutmann, Alison Frazier, Christopher Ellison, Shelton Woods, Todd Shallat, Charles Odahl, Sharon Arnault, Geoff Clayton, Rob Stephens, Clayton Whisnant, Paul Hagenloh, and Andrew McFarland. My thanks to Fr. David Wettstein for his insights into the relationships between clergy and laity. In the editing stages of this book, the aid of Frank Reynolds, the series editor, and of Doug Sims proved invaluable.

I would also like to extend my appreciation to the various institutions whose assistance made the completion of this study possible: Boise State University for the time to write provided by a Faculty Research Associateship, the Woodrow Wilson Fellowship Foundation for the Charlotte W. Newcombe Dissertation Fellowship, the Philanthropic Educational Organization for the P.E.O. Scholar Award, and the University of Texas for the Bess Heflin Endowed Fellowship and the David Bruton Fellowship.

Professionals at many archives in the U.S. and the U.K. also justly deserve acknowledgment for their advice and ability to retain a sense of humor throughout my investigative quest, in particular Pat Fox and the staff at the Harry Ransom Humanities Research Center at the University of Texas at Austin, and also the archivists at the British Library, the Public Record Offices at Kew, Truro, Chester, and Newcastle, Durham Cathedral, York Minster Library, Chester City Archive, and the National Archives of Scotland, as well as the staff at the Borthwick Institute, York, particularly Christopher Webb. Additionally I would like to thank Paul Johnson and Christine Campbell at the Public Record Office, Kew, and the British Library respectively for their assistance.

Many others in the U.K. provided guidance and assistance at various stages of this project and merit recognition. Thanks to Deborah Bennetts of Ponsanooth, Cornwall, for her aid with Cornish language and history. And to Leonard Lockwood of Cornwall for access to his personal archives which provided specialized information I was unable to locate elsewhere. Andrew and Sheryl Lebman introduced me to the archives in Edinburgh and in particular to the Benedictine archives at the University of Edinburgh.

On the personal side, I extend my gratitude to my husband, my children, and the rest of my family and friends for their daily love and support throughout this indescribably exhilarating yet exhausting process.

List of Figures

List of Abbreviations

A	Visitation Acts Books, BIY
AD	Additional/Miscellaneous Accessions, CRO
AR	Arundel, CRO
BIY	Borthwick Institute, York
BV	Bullar Family of Morvel, CRO
CBorderP	*Calendar of State Papers Relating to Scotland*
ChRO	Cheshire Public Record Office
CN	Carlyon of Trehegan, CRO
CRO	Cornwall Public Record Office
CSP Dom	*Calendar of State Papers, Domestic Series*
CSP Rome	*Calendar of State Papers, Rome*
DD/CY	Coryton Muniment, CRO
ECC	*English Catholic Community*
EDA	Proceedings of the Royal Commissioners, ChRO
EDC	Diocesan Records Consistory Court, ChRO
EDV	Visitation Correction Books, ChRO
EN	Enys Family, CRO
FS	Facsimiles of documents, CRO
HCAB	High Commission Act Books, BIY

HCCP	High Commission Cause Papers, BIY
Lanc	*Reformation and Resistance in Tudor Lancashire*
R	Rashleigh Family of Menabilly, CRO
RP	Rogers Family of Penrose, CRO
RS	Rashleigh Family of Stoketon, CRO
SP Dom	State Papers, Domestic Series
SP Scot	State Papers, Scotland
T	Tremayne of Heligan, CRO

Introduction

I N 1586, MARGARET CLITHEROE FOUND HERSELF ON TRIAL, CHARGED WITH harboring Catholic priests in Protestant England. If found guilty, this butcher's wife from Yorkshire faced death. Thinking to offer Clitheroe a way to save her soul and her life, Protestant magistrates and ministers attempted to convince her to attend Protestant services at least once. Again and again, she refused. "Answer me," a frustrated minister demanded. "What is the church?"[1] It was a simple question without a simple answer for many Christians following the Catholic and Protestant reforms of the sixteenth and seventeenth centuries. And although more than 400 years have passed since Clitheroe's trial, the minister's query is not any easier to answer today, whether one is Catholic, Protestant, or a practitioner of any faith.

Prior to Protestant reforms of the sixteenth century, the late medieval English church was visible, and it was vital.[2] English Christians shared common sets of diverse norms and behaviors regarding their relationship with the divine and their opportunities for salvation. They participated to varying degrees in a religious culture peppered with priests, sacraments, and a cornucopia of public ceremonies, festivals, and holy places designed to knit together public communities of believers. Rituals such as Mass, rushbearings, church ales, and public processions through town and countryside joined the faithful to one another as they worshiped side by side.

All of this took place under the institutional umbrella of the church based in Rome. The English church had been organized according to the Roman model into bishoprics, dioceses, and parishes. Through this structure, the church was administratively subordinate to Rome. The church was also legally subordinate to Rome, with ecclesiastical courts in England taking their place in a hierarchy reaching to the papal see. The Roman Church decided issues of doctrine and ritual and communicated its decisions through this chain of command.

Most pre-reform English Christians defined "the church" and their membership in it through their experiences within this institutional setting. The presence of priests, the centrality of the sacraments, the availability of physical locations of worship, the importance of material objects, and the prominence of performance and action taken by both the clergy and laity combined to make ritual, communal experience meaningful for members of a congregation. For example, the main ritual of the Roman Church—the sacrament of the altar—required a priest's presence to celebrate the Mass, the ritual sacrifice of Christ's body. Physical location proved important. Priests usually celebrated Mass upon an altar in a church or chapel. Central to the sacrifice were material objects, such as the eucharistic bread, the chalice, the wine, the book from which the priest read the service, the priest's garments, and various ornaments and linens. The activities of both the laity and the clergy combined to help the faithful participate in the ritual. As the priest performed his Latin prayers before the altar, the laity could listen to his words, knowing their meaning if not their precise translation. Or individuals might pray their own prayers, perhaps the *Pater noster* or their own private devotions. A layperson might read from a religious work or simply contemplate the book's illustrations. Even without a text, a layperson could consider the pious images decorating the walls or stained glass windows of the church. Such lay activities did not ignore the priest and his performance at the altar.[3] Instead they provided a separate but equally important means for laypersons to participate in the ritual with their own pious acts.[4] All eyes eventually returned to the priest's gestures as he consecrated the host and elevated the body of Christ above his head so that all could see Christ and visually adore him together, thereby providing the highlight of the ritual. Priest, sacrament, physical location, material objects, and religious gestures and actions combined to join a congregation into a religious community.

In 1559, less than a year after Elizabeth I ascended the throne, the first Elizabethan Parliament passed the Act of Uniformity that effectively prohibited Catholic worship. Through this act, Parliament prescribed one form of Protestant worship for the entire realm. England had been fluctuating back and forth between Catholic and Protestant forms of worship for almost 30 years. Following the vacillations between Catholicism and Protestantism during the reign of Henry VIII, the strict Protestantism of Edward VI, and the subsequent reversion to Catholicism under Mary I, England was once again a Protestant nation under Elizabeth I. The new monarch insisted that all subjects adhere to her new 1559 Prayer Book, attend Sunday and holy day services, and participate in Protestant communion three times yearly.

At first glance, Elizabeth's initial changes to religion do not appear to have radically altered many of the rituals used by pre-reform English Christians, yet their effect upon the religious identity and sense of community of those who refused to accept her reformed church was profound. The public organization and sacramental structure of the church was no longer tied to Rome. Under Elizabeth's direction, the Church of England removed Catholic priests from their cures and reduced the number of sacraments from seven to two, retaining only baptism and a newly interpreted communion.[5] The physical sites of Catholic worship were also transformed as Protestant ministers took control of Catholic churches and cathedrals. Most of the material objects which had played an integral role in Catholic ritual and worship were seized by Protestant authorities or demolished by angry crowds seeking to remove any vestige of what they considered to be idolatry from the church. Finally, the new laws banned most of the ritual actions and performances familiar to English Catholics, including traditional services, processions, and the celebration of Catholic saints' days and feasts. The penalties for violating these dictates ranged from loss of liberty and possessions to loss of life.

Some individuals—such as Margaret Clitheroe—who adhered to the Catholic faith were willing to lose their lives rather than accept these changes. Most, however, engaged in variations of a dangerous balancing act. They attended Protestant services (thus adhering to the letter of Protestant law) while simultaneously remaining Catholic at heart (and attempting to fulfill the spirit of the Catholic Church's dictates). But why were ties to Rome so critical to some? Why were the relatively small changes in ritual deemed so important? As the Yorkshire minister asked the future martyr Clitheroe, "What is the church?" Was it a physical location? A particular set of rituals and beliefs? A gathering of like-minded believers? Loyalty to church leaders? Adherence to a particular set of doctrinal beliefs as the only correct path to salvation? There was no agreed-upon answer for English Catholics in the sixteenth and seventeenth centuries, yet some were willing to lose their lives, livelihoods, or peace of mind over the issues involved rather than fully embrace the Protestant version of "church."

Such questions were hardly unique to England. During the vast religious and cultural shift commonly known as the Reformation, both Protestant and Catholic reforms produced a climate in which such issues were debated by theologians, monarchs, parish clergy, and the laity. And while such questions regarding church, salvation, and relationships to the sacred exist as fascinating theoretical issues, many ordinary individuals of both lay and clerical status grappled with such concerns on a daily basis. They struggled to construct religious experience that was spiritually meaningful and personally comforting as they worked toward salvation in an environment of religious, social, cultural, economic, and political change.

The best way to understand religion as lived experience is to examine religious culture at the popular level—at the level of Margaret Clitheroe and the many other English Catholics who chose to continue in the Roman faith (although certainly not to the extent of sacrificing their lives as Clitheroe did). In the face of Protestant change, how might such ordinary Catholics have practiced their faith and understood the Catholic Church in England in new ways? Three key issues emerge. First, how did such Catholics redefine their relationship with the sacred? Second, what made such Catholics continue to identify with one another as members of a Catholic Church when the public organizational and administrative structure of the church and the fundamental sacraments, symbols, places, and objects previously so central to their faith were seemingly denied them? And finally, how did such Catholics maintain their sense of religious community when they often could no longer worship side by side?

The answers to such questions lie in the ability of English Catholics to adapt traditional practices, beliefs, and expectations of the Catholic faith to meet the demands of this new environment. I argue that Catholics attempting to remain Catholic within Protestant England experimented with a variety of new alternatives for worship, religious identity, and communal religious experience. This study examines the choices that English Catholics possessed, reasons they made such choices, and how they understood their choices within the framework of the Roman faith. Innovative pastoral clerics in conjunction with flexible, engaged laypersons living in England—facing the daily challenges of practicing Catholicism illegally in a Protestant country—labored to provide such choices, accommodating them to the particular needs of different segments of English Catholics.[6] For example, some English Catholic clerics and laypersons reinterpreted the traditional practice of various sacraments, such as the sacrament of the altar, to allow Catholics who could not find a priest to experience the benefits of these sacraments through non-traditional means. In the absence of cathedrals and churches, Catholics claimed new locations such as prisons, execution sites, homes, and even their own bodies as places to worship and experience Catholic fellowship. Clerics and laypersons infused the few religious objects remaining to them, such as the rosary, with new meaning and power to compensate for perceived losses in other areas.

Providing such options did not involve a challenge to the essential tenets of the Roman faith. These clerical and lay English Catholics saw themselves as fulfilling a pastoral need rather than challenging doctrine. They attempted to quell Catholic fears regarding the possibility of salvation in the absence of priests and sacraments, and they viewed their actions as negotiations between Catholic orthodoxy and practical necessity.

An inquiry into English Catholic efforts to promote and adopt alternatives to traditional, late medieval and post-Tridentine[7] ritual, identity, and community is new. I intend this study as an addition to scholars' recent efforts to define the subtle variances and complexities of the doctrinal and liturgical spectrum being lived daily by a religiously diverse population within England and throughout Reformation Europe. Many scholars have previously examined various aspects of English Catholic history during this period. Eamon Duffy and Christopher Haigh, for example, persuasively demonstrate that many English laypersons revered traditional pre-reform religious beliefs and practices, that Protestant reforms produced dramatic—in many ways insurmountable—shifts in religious culture, and that religious change thus occurred slowly in post-reform England.[8] Comprehensive studies of the entire post-reform English Catholic population, such as Haigh's and John Bossy's,[9] as well as numerous county analyses, such as J. C. H. Aveling's investigation of Yorkshire, S. J. Watts's examination of Northumberland, and A. L. Rowse's work with Cornwall,[10] make substantial contributions to our understanding of English Catholics by describing and quantifying various socio-demographic aspects of Catholic life in a Protestant state. More recently, scholars such as Patricia Crawford have attempted to refine these general depictions of Catholic community by focusing on women's unique experiences and contributions to the maintenance of English Catholicism.[11]

These authors, however, limit the scope of their works to a particular set of concerns about Catholics. Such studies seek to locate, quantify, and explain the geographic distribution of Catholics across England. They identify community as the social ties binding Catholics to one another. They document these social ties and attempt to understand Catholic relationships with Protestant authority. They chart the advances and declines of the various institutionalized aspects of the late medieval Catholic Church, such as priests, Mass, public worship, images, the church calendar, and traditional sacraments. And, unavoidably, they chronicle Protestant persecution of Catholics through the penal laws.

While these scholars' queries remain important and tell a significant part of the story of English Catholics, they overlook vital dimensions of the English Catholic experience—the changing interpretation and use of Catholic rituals themselves along with changing self-perceptions of Catholic identity and community among ordinary believers who chose to remain Catholic. Previous scholars either looked for evidence of English Catholics engaging in devotional practices as they would have in late medieval England when the

Roman faith was the state religion, or they expected to find proof of Catholics conforming their beliefs and pious practices to the uniform standards of doctrine and liturgy insisted upon by the Council of Trent (1545–63). When they did not find much evidence of either phenomenon, scholars often depicted English Catholicism as slowly withering either by losing its late medieval vitality or by failing to adequately take advantage of Catholic renewal on the continent.[12] Such characterizations overlook the success of the Catholic Church's centuries-old *modus operandi* of accommodating itself to different, often hostile, environments in its efforts to perpetuate the Roman faith.[13]

Other valuable studies of English Catholics concentrate on theological, doctrinal, intellectual, or propagandist issues debated by English Catholic immigrants on the continent.[14] Such issues, however, were being argued by English Catholics who did not have to practice their religion under daily Protestant restrictions. Although this subgroup of English Catholics certainly produced a great body of casuistry literature and theological treatises worthy of analysis, such texts are frequently out of touch with and seldom reflect the common experience and beliefs of Catholics practicing within England during these years.[15]

Recently, the most enlightening scholarship on Catholics practicing within England has been produced by scholars such as Alexandra Walsham, Peter Lake, and Michael Questier. These scholars agree that previous portrayals of Catholicism as "fading" or "withering" are based on an understanding of Catholicism that is too narrow in scope, a view popularized earlier by Haigh. Walsham suggests there were a "wide range of responses to the moral predicament in which adherents of the Church of Rome ineluctably found themselves—responses characterized by various degrees of partial, occasional, and qualified conformity." Walsham's greatest contribution to our understanding of the impacts of reform on ordinary individuals lies in her attempts to define and categorize where people fit into this new spectrum of conformity with great sensitivity to the subtle nuances of the doctrinal issues involved.[16] Questier agrees with such an approach, broadening Walsham's stance as he argues that, ". . .Catholicism might have been not only not so straight-jacketed as to be confined to a few Counter-Reformation zealots but also not so lazy and vague just as to sleepwalk into a 'parish Anglicanism' for lack of anywhere else to go. Instead it might have actively participated in the shifts of ecclesiastical emphasis in the early seventeenth-century Church."[17]

But in effect, scholars such as Walsham, Lake, Questier, and more recently Norman Jones, are largely looking at reclaiming active roles for Catholic-inclined English within the Protestant Church, not the Catholic Church. None choose to investigate how ordinary Catholic-inclined laypersons understood or helped shape their own ideas about religious identity and community within the Catholic faith, nor do they deal with changing experiences and understandings of rituals and pious practices of those committed to remaining within the Catholic belief system.[18] For example, in *Church Papists: Catholicism, Conformity, and Confessional Polemic in Early Modern England*, Walsham notes that although Catholic clerics recognized church papists as members of the Roman Church, the subjects of her study "are perhaps best assessed as a congregational component of that inclusive and eclectic institution—that effective umbrella organization—the Church of England."[19] When she recognizes a "Catholic community," she does so in the singular and confines her inquiry into such a community to that which priests attempted to construct through the interplay of their theological, pastoral, and casuistry writings. While valuable, her analysis provides little sense of how ordinary Catholics would have received such clerical messages and incorporated them into any adaptations they might be making to pious practices and understandings of Catholic ritual or to their self-perceptions of Catholic religious identity and community outside of the issue of Catholic participation in the Church of England. Walsham largely portrays the English *Protestant* Church as a church in evolution. Lively debates took place. Rituals and doctrine were slowly solidified. A diversity of beliefs and practices was acceptable. Walsham concludes that Catholics who chose to attend Protestant services participated in and significantly influenced the development of the Anglican Church.[20]

This work looks in a different direction. I argue that a process of evolution similar to that taking place within the Anglican Church was occurring within the Catholic Church in England.[21] Whereas Walsham describes English Catholics as "a diffuse and amorphous dissenting group," I suggest we explore how diffuse and amorphous English Catholics considered themselves to be by exploring their changing perceptions of religious ritual, identity, and community.[22] Assuredly, Catholicism became a vigorous minority faith in late Tudor and early Stuart England. But as decades passed, this ceased to be the same Catholic faith that Elizabeth I suppressed with the Act of Uniformity in 1559. Catholicism practiced illegally within a Protestant nation cannot be expected to recreate the religious experiences possible within the state-sponsored, sacramentally based Catholicism of late medieval England, nor to conform to the uniform standards insisted upon by the Council of Trent. Instead, we must look for something new. Lively religious debates occurred among Catholics as well as Protestants (although often less publicly), and Catholic laypeople and clergy modified rituals and accepted a diversity of beliefs and practices too. Moreover, many ordinary English Catholics sought to keep these new understandings of their faith separate from the Anglican Church rather than gradually integrating traditionally Roman forms of ritual, identity, and community into the Church of England.

Understandably, evidence of this evolution does not exist in any quantitatively demonstrable form, nor can it be expected to, considering the dangers involved. English Catholics often did not publicly proclaim their Catholicity. They did not wish to incriminate themselves by leaving concrete documentation of their particular brand of piety by discussing it in letters or journals. But although meager and at times obscure, what evidence there is can be put to the best possible use to provide what Joyce Appleby, Lynn Hunt, and Margaret Jacob have described as a "reasonably true description" of the patterns of religious behaviors and experience, and the range evident among English Catholics' sense of their religious identity and community.[23]

To provide qualitative confirmation of such a shift in understandings of ritual, identity, and community, I have adopted the role of cultural historian, sifting and integrating information from the standard government documents, judicial records, pastoral literature, martyrologies, letters, and journals with analyses of architecture (such as the distinctive design and decoration of Cornish churches), material culture (such as rosaries, bench ends, gravestones), art (such as stained glass windows and religious artwork commissioned by English Catholics living in England during this era), and English Catholic poetry and balladry, to name a few examples. Such media are, of course, small pieces of a larger puzzle that must be reconstructed within many layers of context.[24]

In recent years, the tools for examining such contexts have been provided by religious history's increasing contact with a vigorous new cultural history, itself animated by social history from below, cultural anthropology, textual criticism, and women's history. I attempt what Roger Chartier encouraged, which is to examine not just the historical artifacts themselves but how people would have used and manipulated their understandings of ideas, objects, and experiences to fulfill their own often individualized and ever-changing needs.[25] I explore these sources looking for manifestations and metamorphoses of the *functions* of Catholic priests, rituals, physical sites, and symbols rather than searching for the traditional, formal, institutionally established forms mandated by Rome. Furthermore, I also approach such artifacts for clues to personal religious identity and collective associations among Catholics. As Natalie Zemon Davis so well reminded us, accounts of activities as diverse as street demonstrations and festive celebrations may be studded with rich evidence of individual and collective mentalities if historians are sensitive to the clues.[26]

In employing such an approach, new evidence emerges that Catholicism remained vital, popular, innovative, flexible, responsive, and orthodox within Protestant-governed England.[27] Such an interdisciplinary approach reveals English Catholic loyalty to a church that was neither late medieval nor post-Tridentine in character, although it certainly drew from both traditions whenever possible. Instead, the Catholic Church in England was evolving in new directions. This study explores change in three areas—alterations in beliefs, rituals and devotional practices; changes in English Catholics' self-perceptions of their religious identity; and alternative forms of religious communities arising among Catholics within England and the connections between such communities and with Rome.

English Catholics sought to remain loyal members of their faith while at the same time exploring their options. They pushed the limits of orthodoxy, all the while remaining within the rather flexible bounds of the multi-faceted interaction between the institution of the Roman Church and the needs of believers. English Catholics did not accept every new option or reinterpretation offered to them regarding their pious practices, identity, or community. Furthermore, the options and interpretations that were available to them changed over time. The capacity to make adaptations depended upon a particular Catholic's perceived religious needs, level of piety, access to remaining priests and sacraments, and geographic location within the country. The ever-changing domestic and international political situation, particularly from 1587 to 1590, played a dramatic role in influencing which alternatives Catholics both suggested and adopted. Fluctuating levels of diligence exercised by local Protestant authorities in curbing Catholic practices were also a significant factor. Catholics might pick and choose one or more options or reinterpretations to best fit their needs, either as individuals or as groups, at any given time and felt free to change course if the situation warranted. To satisfy their religious needs, English Catholic men and women depended upon choice and flexibility. These concepts were at odds with post-Tridentine continental Catholicism, but many English Catholics believed such ideas were necessary to sustain the faithful in England.

God in the eyes of man is never static, and despite characterizations of the Reformation-era Roman Church as doctrinal, orthodox, and traditional, the Church remained, as it always had been, defined by interplay between the rules handed down by the institutionalized hierarchy based in Rome and the reception of these rules by ordinary believers. To best understand how religious rules translate into lived religious belief, experience, and action, we must examine the reception of such rules at the popular level—at the level of Margaret Clitheroe and the many other English Catholics of varying levels of conformity whose stories are told throughout this book.

The foundations of such an inquiry lie in the theoretical underpinnings of a variety of disciplines such as sociology, cultural anthropology, and literary criticism, as well as history. As the sociologists Peter Berger and Thomas Luckmann argued two generations ago, despite the appearance of institutions as normative, reified sources of authority, institutions are created by individuals. They exist as reflections of human priorities and experiences. Institutions such as the Roman Church or any organized faith thus act as backgrounds for lived religious experiences and for further negotiations and innovations as human needs change.[28] Religion is dynamic and adaptable. But how do individuals "experience" religion, decide what they need, and put it into practice within a larger institution such as a church, particularly as conditions change?[29] For ordinary believers such as the English Catholics in this study, practical knowledge and need, informed by—but not necessarily in strict conformity with—abstract theories contained in theology and doctrine, constitute what is "real" in lived religious experience.

Such an investigation into the lived experience of religion illuminates the shifting balance between clergy and laity, between institution and individual, that exists within most organized religions and that produces the daily conditions and experiences of active faith and worship. This balance is a continual process rather than an end result. Earlier scholars such as Davis, Chartier, and Carlo Ginzburg, in their path-breaking case studies, described a reciprocal, cyclical relationship between high and low, dominant and subordinate cultures. More recently, scholars such as Robert Scribner, John C. Olin, John W. O'Malley, R. A. Markus, Jonathan D. Spence, and Catherine Bell have analyzed how clergy and laity enjoy a similar on-going, give-and-take partnership in shaping religious environment and experience, particularly as the environment in which a religion is practiced changes.[30] The dynamics of this partnership are not simple. The interests of the clergy are not uniform or constant, nor are the interests of the laity. In subsequent chapters, I hope to paint in broad strokes while remaining attentive to the tensions inherent within these groups and their relations to one another. For example, there are differences between clergy who serve the organized church primarily as upper-level administrators and clergy who work locally, primarily as providers of pastoral care. Clergy involved with administering the institution of a church are frequently involved with theological and doctrinal decision-making and the eventual enforcement of those decisions. Such clergy often chart the long-term future of the faith in light of a myriad of religious, political, social, and economic opportunities and challenges that may or may not be apparent to lower-level clergy and the laity.

These lower-level clerics, whom I will term pastoral clergy, are typically engaged with communicating, teaching, and enforcing doctrine, performing the liturgy, and providing pastoral care, including sacraments, to the laity at a more localized level.[31] The activities of these clerics are often assumed to be in accordance with the decisions of the hierarchical institution of the church. Whether a particular faith has a large bureaucratic operation, such as the Roman Catholic Church, or a more locally based organization, such as a Congregational Church or a Baptist Church, there are typically basic sets of understandings about the faith and the running of a larger organization in which local clergy are expected to take part and support. But, as Theodor Klauser has described, when there are tensions between the priorities of high-level, administrative clergy and laypeople, local clergy are often placed in the middle of disputes.[32] Such clergy must then attempt to balance conflicting priorities, caught between their responsibility to obey the mandates of their hierarchical superiors and do what may be best for the organization of their church and their responsibility to provide the best pastoral care to their flocks. English priests working within Protestant England were certainly caught in just such a conflict as they attempted to enforce Rome's rather unrealistic mandates (which showed little significant accommodation to the day-to-day realities of English laypersons attempting to remain Catholic) at the same time as they attempted to provide the best pastoral care possible under restrictive conditions. Depending upon the motivations of a particular cleric (or religious order or organization within the greater whole), the needs and mandates of a larger institution might take a back seat to the immediate, localized needs of parish and parishioners. This may occur as a matter of blanket policy or on a case-by-case basis, as clerics use their consciences and best judgment to steer a course that best meets their interpretations of the needs of both church and laity. The institutional hierarchy of the church can, officially or unofficially, be somewhat flexible in such situations. As John C. Olin has pointed out, although various sixteenth- and seventeenth-century popes, beginning with Paul III, attempted to coordinate liturgy and reform through efforts such as the Council of Trent, the Roman Church frequently allowed flexibility in priests' interpretations of liturgy. This was especially true in regions where the Catholic Church did not possess a strong foothold in religion, which was precisely the situation in England.[33]

The laity exists as the final piece of this loosely-based partnership, although it grossly oversimplifies the laity to describe them as a monolithic group. Laypersons are members of a faith who do not possess clerical status. They are believers in doctrine, participants in liturgy, attendees at church. For some believers, religion is relatively black and white. These believers comfortably accept a faith's theological precepts and liturgy without challenge. In fact, attempts to innovate or to deviate from established norms of religious understanding and practice meet strenuous resistance from such laypersons.[34]

Others within the same faith, however, interact with doctrine and liturgy to participate with clergy in shaping their religious environment and experiences. I will describe such laypersons as more "engaged." Such laypersons—those who tease out the shades of gray, the subtleties, the amount of "wiggle room" within a given doctrinal understanding or liturgical activity—do so for many reasons. They frequently have different priorities for their own spirituality, their relationship with God, their salvation, and their vision of what their church is and what role it should play in their lives and in the lives of their communities. Finding and interpreting evidence of lay participation in and impact on organized religion is difficult. Whether in the past or present, evidence of lay activity, belief, and influence is often oral or indirect in nature. It takes place in conversation among believers or in the way a lay reader receives a text, inscribing new meanings upon an author's intended message. And while perhaps some evidence can be found in official church records, investigators must be careful not to view information about the laity provided through the filter of the clergy as an accurate representation of lay attitudes or practices. More often than not scholars have to search in other, more neutral locations for evidence of lay belief, interpretation, and practice—their lived experience of religion.

Through the conjunction of the clergy with the laity, religion becomes lived experience for the majority of a faith's adherents. For the purposes of this study, I would argue that the pastoral clergy working with the more flexible, engaged sector of the laity provided the majority of the new options for worship, identity, and community that became the crux of lived experience for England's Catholics following reforms.

One might ask why a creative English Catholic laity needed the clergy at all, considering clerics were frequently in short supply and clerics in Rome seemed unsympathetic to the challenges inherent in practicing Catholicism illegally in a Protestant nation. Within the Roman faith in particular, laypersons need the clergy in order to obtain salvation. Relationships between clerics and laypersons might be renegotiated and communication among members of these groups might take on new forms, but the clerical hierarchy is an indispensable part of the equation. According to the Roman Church's doctrine of apostolic succession (and the subsequent modification known as the Petrine Doctrine), Christ ordained the first priest when he provided his apostle Peter with the keys of heaven and called Peter the rock upon which he would build his church.[35] Christ instructed Peter to ordain other priests to carry out God's work and conferred the power to save or damn souls upon Peter and his successors. Through the sacrament of ordination, Catholic priests take their place as links in this chain of succession, serving as Christ's literal representatives on earth and as channels of saving grace. Sever the links, and the chain would be broken. Priests of the Roman Church exist as a separate order of human beings, providing the sacraments to believers and mediating between God and the laity, much as Christ mediated between God and humanity.[36] During the Reformation era, the Council of Trent confirmed the status of the priesthood as the primary channel through which Christ dispenses saving grace.[37] For an English Catholic layperson to carve out alternative means to participate in the Catholic faith without consultation with clergy and without a prominent role being played by clergy in whatever re-conceptualizations were arrived at was tantamount to denying oneself access to Christ and salvation. The clergy must play a role in whatever alternatives are created.

That being said, we can see the working out of a new balance between clergy and laity most clearly in English Catholics' negotiations of new understandings regarding ritual, self-perceptions of religious identity, and alternative types of religious communities. All three issues are inextricably linked. Anthropologists such as Clifford Geertz and Victor Turner have pointed to the power of ritual in the hands of ordinary individuals both to construct and reconfigure communal ties. In the absence of an institutional church, this is precisely what many English Catholics sought to do.[38] Sociologists such as Philip Selznick have explained liturgical ritual as a mechanism through which laypersons debate larger questions of religious authority and community.[39] And as Michel de Certeau has affirmed, the environment of secrecy in which ritual was conducted by many English Catholics would have been no hindrance to such a debate since the element of secrecy creates a "play between actors" and, in essence, organizes a social network, a type of communal relationship.[40]

I will explore many of the recent historical innovations in the study of ritual in detail in later chapters. At the outset, however, it is important to emphasize a particular quality that all ritual holds for Roman Catholics. Ritual possesses an ontological power to make something exist that does not exist. It has the ability to alter reality, to transcend time, and to make that which is absent, present. This substantively creative capacity of ritual was increasingly placed within the hands of English Catholics cut off from the institutional church. English Catholics manipulated their understandings and performance of the tools of ritual to build new relationships with the divine, their church, and with one another. They thus made what at first appears absent—God, priests, the sacraments, a fellowship of believers, a church—present. They could use ritual to help construct a new domain in which they could both shape their religious identities and communities and create new lived religious experiences.

A study of English Catholics' changing interpretations and uses of ritual highlights the larger contention made above. The institution of a church, such as the Roman Church, does not enjoy a monopoly on the performance or interpretation of religious ritual, no more so than it unilaterally defines the sense of religious identity a believer will hold or the experiences of fellowship and community a believer will create. To understand English Catholics' practical innovations and lived experiences in all three areas is to gain a greater understanding of what Margaret Clitheroe and other English Catholics envisioned their church to be after their traditional, institutional church setting became inaccessible during this period of upheaval.

An introductory chapter sets the stage by introducing the major players and issues concerning English Catholics. Subsequently, this study is divided conceptually into three parts. First, I provide specific examples of how both English Catholic pastoral clerics and engaged laypersons reshaped their traditional understandings regarding religious rituals and other pious practices to create devotional alternatives. The examples—the carving out of new places for worship, new uses of material objects such as the rosary, and reinterpretations of the efficacy of sacraments such as the Mass—suggest that the availability of options was key to Catholics' ability to worship in the frequent absence of priests and traditional sacraments.

In the second part of this study, three case studies—London, Cornwall, and the northern shires bordering Scotland—reveal how Catholics in each area combined new devotional options in different ways, both as individuals and as communities. Previous scholarship has tended to examine Catholics in particular counties of England in isolation from one another or to lump English Catholics together as a monolithic group, often characterized by Protestant persecution. Instead, I demonstrate that many different types of Catholic communities were possible, and that although subject to Protestant persecution, the members of these communities did not entirely define themselves by that persecution.

The third and final aspect of this study examines how Catholics such as those in London, Cornwall, and the northern shires perceived themselves and their relationships to other Catholics, their sovereign, and to the institutional Roman Church—in other words, how English Catholics defined their Catholic communities at the local, national, and international levels. English Catholics possessed many choices when building new religious communities. These communities were fluid, and a Catholic could participate in multiple communities. Some such groups are relatively easy to discuss. They are defined in large part by location or physical proximity to other Catholics. Not all communities, however, are based on such contact, and this section pinpoints some alternative communities with little or no physical contact between community members, such as those organized around prayer, ritual, or common usage of a text. While such communities are difficult to define and quantify, they did exist and were no less real or important to believers than the Catholic communities defined by physical proximity.

This final chapter defines the interconnections between English Catholic identity and community by examining English Catholic relations with Rome. These two concepts of identity and community are related but not identical. I define Catholic identity as a self-perception of sameness, likeness, or oneness with other Catholics. Catholic community, on the other hand, considers the relationships between those who identify with one another. Both concepts will be discussed in more conceptual detail in the final chapter. Such an inquiry sheds light on how ordinary English Catholics mediated between their sense of oneness and continuity with their church and their willingness to be tied into hierarchical relations with that church.[41] In short, while devotion to Rome remained stronger in the first decades following the Act of Uniformity, English Catholics eventually began to think about accommodation with their Protestant sovereigns. When the papacy refused to consider any type of accommodation, many English Catholics, including pastoral priests, began to make their own distinctions between the spiritual unity of the Catholic faith, institutional unity with Rome, and a subject's loyalty to a monarch. In their own minds, believers simultaneously remained good subjects and heirs to the primitive church—wedded to the sacraments, traditions, rituals, and beliefs of their faith. They refused, however, to conduct their relationships with one another along the lines defined by Rome. In other words, many English Catholics maintained a strong sense of Catholic identity while redefining their sense of community. In doing so, they opened up new, but not necessarily unorthodox, experiences within Reformation-era Catholicism. Most English Catholics— including martyred Margaret Clitheroe—considered themselves part of a larger Catholic Church that had, in the words of an anonymously authored prayer of 1649, been scattered "and a remnant preserved" while those among the remnant struggled to glorify God and remain "upright" in the midst of challenge.[42]

By rethinking the Reformation in such ways we open a window onto the English Reformation in particular and on the study of religion more generally in the past and in the present. This study focuses upon the maintenance of the *functions* of spirituality, rather than upon strict adherence to *institutional forms*. Catholicism in Protestant England did not wither. It did not get subsumed into the Church of England. It evolved. English Catholics might maintain traditional practices when possible, but they did not shy away from molding religious values, rituals, symbols, and sites to fit new circumstances and needs. While scholars such as Eamon Duffy and Miri Rubin have explored such issues in pre-reform England, and scholars such as Robert Scribner, William Christian, Ann Ramsey, and Susan Karant-Nunn have expanded our understanding of the popular experience of the Reformation era by examining such issues in post-reform continental Europe, such questions have really not been asked of England's Catholics after 1559 when reform finally began to solidify.[43]

Interpreted more broadly, this study adds to the investigation of the continual struggle among virtually all faiths to balance the dictates of doctrine and tradition with the ever-changing, immediate, and often individualized needs of believers. Both sides press against one another as the institutions of religion attempt to structure the day-to-day lives and belief systems of adherents while individuals test the boundaries of institutional rules to make religion more personally meaningful.

This work offers the lived experiences of English Catholics as a means of addressing such timeless issues common to most religions of the past and present. It distinguishes between religion as a system of belief and ritual as opposed to religion as a reified, institutional authority. It focuses attention on whether individuals have a right to define themselves as members of a religion based on belief and practice, or whether religious institutions exclusively maintain the right to recognize members. English Catholics often defined themselves against the official mandates of Rome, yet the Church generally continued to encompass them as members of the Roman faith. Additionally, this study explores the possible interrelationships between an individual's personal identification as a member of a certain faith and membership in communities with others of the same faith. I also suggest that the religious communities formed informally by laypersons may have as much impact on individual and communal spiritual development and satisfaction as those formally organized by official religious institutions.

Finally, this study also makes a contribution to the study of the negotiations between spiritual and secular authority, a conflict that grew heated and deadly during the Reformation era. I examine the re-negotiation of the relationship between God and government—and between individual and church—at the popular level in England.[44] In doing so, this work adds the popular viewpoint to a discussion that typically is portrayed as taking place among religious and governmental leaders. In addition, by entering into this debate, this study explores larger issues of separation of religious and political authority that have been dealt with by many of the world's faiths and which continue to be negotiated today.

We tend to think of contemporary Western society as having moved beyond the scenario of religion as a dominant force permeating every aspect of daily life. We are secular, rational, tolerant, modern. It seems antithetical to the last few centuries of "progress" that government policies be dictated by religious priorities or that individuals be so consumed with their faith that they are willing to give their lives for it. Such situations seem overly zealous, even irrational, in light of what we like to think of as twenty-first-century priorities.

Yet we live in a world in which the drives for religious toleration and religious persecution exist side by side. As recent events have reminded us, issues of religious belief can be as mobilizing and the strength of religious intolerance as riveting in the twenty-first century as they were hundreds of years ago in Reformation Europe. Religion continues to play a staggeringly important role in many individuals' lives, from the political and economic to the moral and ethical. From the zeal of religious martyrs who bring down airplanes, buildings, trains, buses, and those within them, to the public that flocks into churches, synagogues, mosques, and temples in record numbers in the days and weeks following attacks, religion (and how one chooses to practice it) matters just as it did decades, centuries, and millennia ago.

Such contemporary events raise questions about religion and the way in which people understand it and assign it importance in their daily lives. Do believers adhere to the tenets of their faith precisely as expounded in religious texts and by religious leaders? To what extent do laypeople interpret religious beliefs, writings, and doctrines for themselves? And what impact does this have on the laity's understanding and experience of religious ritual, identity, and community? How and under what circumstances does religion evolve in new directions, both acceptable and unacceptable to the institution and the rest of believers? This book attempts to look at another period of crisis, centuries past, and ask such questions. Such queries are timeless, and this study provides a basis from which to answer them, not just for the sixteenth and seventeenth centuries, but for the present era as well.

CHAPTER 1

Knitting the Remnants

Catholic Challenges and Priorities
in Protestant England

O hear me for thy Son Jesus sake. That it may please thee to look compassionately on this persecuted part of thy church now driven from thy public altars into corners and secret closets; that thy Protection may be over us wherever we shall be scattered and a remnant preserved among us by whom thy name may be glorified, thy sacraments administered and the Souls of thy servants kept upright in the midst of a corrupting and of a corrupt generation.[1] (*anonymous Catholic prayer*, 1649)

T HE FIRST PARLIAMENT OF ELIZABETH I PASSED THE ACT OF UNIFORMITY in 1559, returning England to Protestant worship after five years of Catholic rule under Mary I. With this act, which reintroduced the Protestant Book of Common Prayer,[2] Protestant leaders sought to do more than restore their own faith to power. Their goal was to drive Catholicism out of England by cutting off access to Catholic clergy, holy sites, sacraments, and symbols. For example, the Act of Uniformity abolished the Mass, the most frequently performed sacrament of the Roman faith. The law also banned the further ordination of any Catholic priests, a measure aimed at gradually depriving lay communities of Catholic priests and sacraments. Over time this is just what happened in many areas. The government hoped that its efforts to wipe out any vestiges of the Roman Church's presence in England would also end the practice of Catholic recusancy—the refusal of Catholics to attend Protestant religious services—and eventually result in a unified and unchallenged Protestant Church of England.

There was a gap, however, between expectations and reality, between the letter of the law and the often reluctant spirit with which officials enforced it, and those among the laity who favored the Catholic faith accepted it. This lax enforcement was particularly common during the first decade of Elizabeth's reign. Traditional Catholic practices persisted in many nominally Protestant parishes.[3] In 1567, the Bishop of Bangor reported that Catholic altars and images were still being used in Protestant churches and that parishioners still worshipped with relics and rosaries.[4] And two years later, in 1569, the government faced an outright Catholic rebellion in the north of England—the Northern Rising.

Still, by 1570 many government leaders felt that their anti-Catholic policies were working. The Northern Rising of 1569 lacked widespread support and was easily quashed. There had been no large-scale efforts to revive Catholic religious institutions in England.[5] Officials kept a closer watch on suspected Catholics after 1569, but to many Protestants, their hopes for the eventual demise of Catholicism in England seemed justified.

In the 1570s, however, Protestant officials faced a new set of challenges. The most prominent of these was the emergence of a growing Catholic missionary effort in England. English Catholics trained for the priesthood at seminaries on the continent and returned to England as missionaries to replace the dwindling number of Marian priests.[6] The mission began after William Allen, a Lancashire priest and emigrant, founded an English College attached to the University of Douai in the Spanish Netherlands in 1568.[7] Seminary priests began arriving in England in 1574. Jesuit priests first landed on English shores in 1580. Dominicans, Benedictines, and Franciscans arrived in smaller numbers in subsequent decades. The number of priests on mission in England increased steadily from 1580 to 1642—the latter date marking the beginning of the English Civil War.[8] Estimates of the size of the clerical population vary significantly. John Bossy estimates that between 700 and 800 priests labored on the mission in the whole of England on the eve of the Civil War.[9] Contemporary Protestant authorities, although undoubtedly prone to exaggerate, placed the number much higher, claiming that in 1624 there were 2,400 seminary priests and Jesuits in London alone.[10] Because of the need for secrecy to protect the identities of missionaries, the true number will never be known. Regardless, the efforts of the missionaries dealt a blow to the Elizabethan government's hopes that Catholicism would fade away as the priests remaining from Mary Tudor's reign died.

Other threats to Protestant control of the nation emerged as well. In 1568, Mary Queen of Scots arrived in England and was promptly imprisoned by her cousin, Elizabeth I. The Catholic Queen Mary, who briefly claimed the English crown during her marriage to Francis II of France, was considered by most English Protestants and Catholics to be next in line for the English throne. Many Catholics hoped that upon Elizabeth's death, Catholicism would return to England with the Scottish queen. Pope Pius V stirred up this already volatile situation of mixed loyalties by excommunicating Elizabeth with his papal bull *Regnans in Excelsis* in 1570. This raised a crucial question—if events forced Catholics to choose, would their allegiance lie with their excommunicated monarch or with the Pope?

A CHANGING RELIGIOUS ENVIRONMENT: PENAL LAWS AGAINST THE PRACTICE OF CATHOLICISM

In response to these three events—the founding of the English College at Douai, the presence of Mary Queen of Scots in England, and the excommunication of Elizabeth I—Parliament passed new penal laws in 1571. Claiming that previous acts against treason were insufficient, the new laws made it a treasonable offence to question the validity of the monarch's religion, to challenge her right to the crown on religious grounds, or to aid those who did so. It also became treason to "reconcile anyone to the Catholic Church, bring or receive papal bulls, crucifixes, rosaries, or an *agnus dei*." Abettors and harborers of Catholics or priests were liable to loss of goods and life imprisonment.[11] This act significantly hampered priests' efforts to find safe houses and means of support, to physically administer the sacraments, to distribute the material symbols of the Catholic faith, and to perform and encourage traditional rituals among Catholics.

For the next thirty years, the severity of the penal laws and their enforcement fluctuated as the threat of foreign invasion or domestic insurrection ebbed and flowed.[12] In 1580, two royal proclamations denounced English Catholics living abroad, especially students, and demanded their return to England. These efforts were aimed at preventing English Catholics from studying for the priesthood on the continent and returning to England to minister. In 1581, the Act of Persuasions decreed that anyone withdrawing an English subject from his natural loyalty to the queen or her religion would be charged with treason and subject to execution. Moreover, this act raised the fine for non-attendance at Protestant services from one shilling per week (the penalty imposed by the 1559 Act of Uniformity) to £20 per week for four successive absences. Anyone who heard a Mass could be fined 100 marks (£66, 13s, 4d) each month, and any priest found celebrating Mass could be fined 200 marks and imprisoned for one year.[13] Under the act, few Catholics could afford to avoid Protestant services without risking financial ruin.

The Act of Persuasions struck fear in the hearts of many Catholics, as the Jesuit Robert Persons described. In the early 1580s, Persons served as a missionary in England. While hiding in Catholic homes and performing his duties, Persons witnessed first hand the stress and danger faced by the Catholic faithful. Persons wrote to his superiors in Rome:

It is the custom for Catholics to take to the woods and thickets, to ditches and holes even, for concealment, when their houses are broken into at night. Sometimes when we are sitting at table quite cheerily . . . it happens that someone rings at the front door a little more insistently than usual so that he can be put down as an official. Immediately, like deer that have heard the voices of hunters and prick their ears and become alert, all stand to attention, stop eating, and commend themselves to God in the briefest of prayers: no word or sound of any sort is heard until the servants report what is the matter; and if it turns out that there is no danger, after the scare they have had, they become still more cheerful. It can truly be said of them that they carry their lives always in their hands.[14]

By 1585, the threat of invasion by Catholic Spain increased. New penal laws reflected the government's increased suspicion of Catholics who, officials feared, would support a Spanish invading force rather than defend their Protestant queen.[15] According to these laws, any priest found in England ordained beyond the English shores was automatically guilty of treason. It was now illegal and punishable by death just to *be* a priest ordained after 1559 in England. Harborers and helpers of priests were to "suffer death, loss, and forfeit as in cases of one attainted of felony."[16] Protestant authorities increased financial pressure upon English Catholics as well. After 1587, civil officials could seize two-thirds of all income derived from land held by those who refused to pay the fines for non-attendance at Protestant church services.[17]

In 1588, the threat of the Spanish Armada forced counties to hold inquiries to determine which of the queen's subjects could be depended upon to defend the realm. The government ordered the lord lieutenants of the counties to imprison any Catholics considered to be "incorrigible" since they were seen as threats to national security.[18] Many of Elizabeth's Catholic subjects greatly feared for their lives. Recalling the terror engendered by France's St. Bartholomew's Day Massacre in 1572, William Weston, a Jesuit priest on mission in England, described the apprehension of the English Catholics during the year of the Armada:

In London sometimes—I witnessed this myself and listened to Catholics groaning and grieving over it—a report would go round and be confirmed as certain fact, that the Queen's Council had passed a decree for the Massacre of all Catholics on this or that night. Then many people would abandon their homes and lodgings and pass the night in fields; others would hire boats and drift up and down the river. And a rumor was afoot, supposed to have come from the lips of Cecil himself, that he was going to take steps to reduce Catholics to such a state of destitution that they would be incapable of helping one another and, like swine, would be grateful if they could find a husk on which to appease their hunger.[19]

Priests and the lay Catholics who harbored them lived with the greatest fear and risk. In his autobiography, the Jesuit John Gerard described an event that occurred in the autumn of 1591 at 5 a.m. in Warwickshire.

> Father Southwell was beginning Mass and the rest were at prayer, when suddenly I heard a great uproar outside the main door. Then I heard a voice shouting and swearing at a servant who was refusing him entrance. . . . Father Southwell heard the din. He guessed what it was all about, and slipped off his vestments and stripped the altar bare. While he was doing this, we laid hold of all of our personal belongings; nothing was left to betray the presence of a priest. . . . Some of us went and turned the beds and put the cold side up to delude anyone who put his hand in to feel them. . . . Outside the ruffians were bawling and yelling, but the servant held the door fast. They said the mistress of the house, a widow, was not yet up, but was coming down at once to answer them. This gave us enough time to stow ourselves and all our belongings into a very cleverly built sort of cave.[20]

English Catholics suffered additional periods of repression in 1591, 1593, and 1599 as the Spanish threat advanced and declined. Priests and lay Catholics claimed that they had nothing to do with the political forces of continental Catholicism, but Elizabeth could not take that chance. The government, fearing invasion, continued to view English Catholics as a pro-Spanish "fifth column," ready to destabilize England internally to return the country to the "Romish" religion.[21] Prior to 1590, the government took bonds from Catholics to guarantee their appearance before the courts if necessary. In 1591 and 1599, the government imprisoned many Catholics who had previously posted bonds. As soon as the immediate Spanish threat passed, Elizabeth allowed the Catholics to return home, still under bond to appear before the courts when called. The Act of 1593, however, placed further restrictions on Catholics' movements by requiring them to remain within a radius of five miles of their homes unless specially licensed to travel further. Those found in violation of this law risked forfeiture of all they owned.[22]

Many Catholics hoped that James I's ascension to the English throne in 1603 would ease such restrictions and penalties.[23] James, Elizabeth's cousin, was the son of the Catholic Mary Queen of Scots and a man many expected to promote greater toleration of Catholicism. James I quickly made it clear that he would not restore Catholicism as the state religion, though he did waive the steep financial penalties against Catholics who refused to attend Protestant services. This respite quickly ended following the Gunpowder Plot, the attempt by Catholics to blow up the Houses of Parliament on November 5,

1604. James reimposed the Elizabethan fines and punishments and added a few more for good measure.[24]

In a particularly controversial decision, James also required all subjects to take the Oath of Allegiance, recognizing him as sovereign of England to whom all subjects owed their ultimate loyalty. If a subject refused this oath, the government could deprive the subject of lands and imprison him for life.[25] By requiring the oath, James could simultaneously assure himself of the loyalty of many of his Catholic subjects while sowing division between the oath-taking Catholics and the remainder of English Catholics who refused the oath.

Despite the seeming increase in severity of the penal laws under James, scholars generally agree that most of these laws were poorly enforced. James's own foreign policy agenda was often to blame. For example, James wished to marry his son Charles, Prince of Wales, to the Spanish Infanta.[26] During the marriage negotiations, James suspended enforcement of the penal laws against English Catholics to appease Catholic Spain. When these negotiations fell through in 1624, James reissued many of the penal laws, particularly against priests and Jesuits, and encouraged judges to enforce them.[27] When James entertained the possibility of a match between Charles and the Catholic princess Henrietta Maria of France later that year, he again stayed prosecutions against Catholics.[28] In 1625, shortly after his ascension, Charles I reissued the existing penal laws against Catholics.[29]

When James was not rescinding his own penal laws for political purposes, Protestant lawmakers faced another fundamental challenge to their efforts to enforce the penal statutes: the inefficiency of local law enforcement mechanisms. Numerous studies have proven that the penal laws against Catholics as a rule were poorly enforced under Elizabeth, James, and Charles. There was little Protestant leaders could do in the absence of a more coordinated, efficient judicial system.[30] Grand juries, commissions, and the councils set up to find recusants were, to a great extent, composed of local gentry. When those gentry possessed familial and community connections to Catholicism, it often proved difficult to secure their dedicated efforts to root out the old religion.[31]

In addition, the lack of coordination among many officials within the judicial system allowed many Catholics to slip through the cracks. In general, there was little cooperation among the civil courts, ecclesiastical courts, and local officials charged with enforcing the recusancy laws. In addition to the courts, the judicial system included a morass of "Sheriff's deputies, gaolers, parish and head constables, churchwardens, the sworn men of many juries of presentments, sureties to recusant bonds (and) searchers at the ports," all of whose cooperation was necessary to prosecute Catholics.[32] Local administrations paid many of these positions poorly. As a result, many officials accepted bribes to make ends meet. Local officials also worried about burdening the parishes with the cost of imprisoning Catholics who could not pay their jail costs because the government had stripped them of their livelihoods.[33] In their own self-interest, the local authorities often failed to bring the full weight of the law against Catholics.[34]

The challenge of effecting cooperation between courts and officials proved difficult to overcome. In July of 1598, for example, Sir Francis Knollys attempted to take legal action against an admitted recusant, a suspected priest, and other "papists." He soon became frustrated at local authorities' lack of effort to help him pursue his prosecution. He complained in a letter to Lord Burghley, the Lord High Treasurer: "But, my good Lord, to be plain with you, I do stand almost discouraged to serve her Majesty faithfully against these popish traitors, and traitorous recusants, because I do not find my self well backed nor countenanced."[35] Without the cooperation of local authorities, the government could make little headway against locally based Catholicism.[36]

As a result, Catholicism might remain well entrenched in counties where those sympathetic to Catholics controlled the legal system. Catholics living in other counties might be subject to constant searches, imprisonment, and fines if devout Protestants held the majority of local public offices. Additionally, since the religious balance between Catholics and Protestants often changed decade by decade if not year by year in the same county, local Catholics might find themselves relatively free to practice their faith at certain times but restricted in their movements and worship at other times.

HOW MANY CATHOLICS WERE THERE?

Many historians have attempted to estimate the number of Catholics practicing in England or in a particular county in the century following the Act of Uniformity. Since it is not the purpose of this study to attempt another counting of Catholics, I will provide such estimates with the caution that they underestimate the number of Catholics who continued to practice the faith. Previous historians often based their approximations on the diocesan visitations and returns of recusants (those who refused to attend Protestant services). Such records, however, could only be as accurate as the authorities' willingness to locate or prosecute Catholics at any given time and place. Such figures also regularly failed to take into account many of those who considered themselves Catholic but who nominally conformed to avoid the penalties. The best known of this group were the "church papists," those who occasionally attended Protestant services to avoid the penalties attached to the penal laws.[37] When these Catholics refused Protestant communion, they were frequently recorded as "non-communicants." Furthermore, estimates also overlook those dissimulators who still practiced the Catholic faith but attempted to hide their religious views from the authorities. Such individuals quietly attended Protestant services and took communion without any overt show of papistry while remaining faithful in their hearts and homes. Given such circumstances, any calculation of the total population of Catholics in England, no matter how carefully compiled, must be considered low.

John Bossy, in his landmark study, *The English Catholic Community, 1570–1850*, estimates the total number of Catholics in 1603 as approximately 40,000. By 1642, he estimates the population had grown by half to approximately 60,000.[38] Bossy multiplies the number of recusants and church papists by certain factors to account for inefficiency in reporting and for the children of the recusants and non-communicants. Whether one accepts Bossy's figures or not, scholars tend to agree that the number of Catholics increased rather than decreased over the period between 1559 and 1642. Of course, such an increase was not linear. Certain periods of particularly intense enforcement of the penal laws, such as occurred in the late 1580s and early 1590s with the threat of Spanish invasion, no doubt hindered the growth rate of the Catholic population, but taken as a whole, the number of Catholics was rising, particularly after 1600.[39] But numbers are not really the issue.

WHO WAS A CATHOLIC?

Rather than attempt to quantify the size of the Catholic population, I examine the evolving beliefs, pious practices, and self-perceptions of Catholic identity and community among ordinary Catholics practicing within Protestant England. Simply defining who or what can be termed Catholic for purposes of such an inquiry is problematic for a variety of reasons. Admittedly, pigeon-holing individuals by assigning a label of "Catholic" or "Protestant" by any criteria erects a more strict and artificial boundary between Catholics and Protestants in England than actually existed, yet the problem must be addressed. Rome, for example, offered one definition of a true Catholic and the Church of England another. Moreover, contemporary historians of English Catholicism have imposed a variety of their own definitions in an attempt to organize the scraps of information about individual Catholics into a coherent picture of a larger community.[40]

For the purposes of this study, a belief in the sacraments and rituals of Catholicism and the desire to participate in the spiritual life of that faith—however difficult to quantify—determine who or what is Catholic, regardless of the level of accommodation shown to Protestant authorities. In other words, open recusancy, what Michael Questier has termed the "gold standard" of Catholicity, is not a requirement for inclusion as a Catholic in this study nor is public accommodation to Protestant authority necessarily a disqualification. Few followers of any religion are willing to sacrifice their lives or the futures of their families solely for their religious beliefs. Martyrs are ideals and symbols. Those martyrs celebrated in most faiths for their willingness to sacrifice all for their beliefs are considered notable precisely because they are rare. Neither institutional churches nor historians can reasonably hold a body of believers to the same standards applauded in such exceptional individuals. For the average person and many of the English Catholics addressed in this study, decisions about family, faith, and sacrifice are rarely so clear-cut.

Just as with most individuals today, English Catholics of the late sixteenth and early seventeenth centuries possessed many priorities in their lives. Religion assuredly was one, but competing with religion on a daily basis were other considerations, such as family, friendships, personal finances, career advancement, and social position.[41] The experience of Walter Montague illustrates the many issues Catholics balanced in their personal and public lives. Montague was raised Protestant by his family but converted to Catholicism in adulthood. Montague wrote a letter to his Protestant father in 1635 trying to explain his reasons for conversion and conveying his confusion and frustration at being pulled in different directions by his conflicting roles and obligations as son, subject, and Catholic. At first, Montague dances around the issues as he admits he has debated in his mind the duty he owes to his father against the duty he owes his God. Should he remain silent and allow his father to continue to think of him as a loyal Protestant son, deferring to his father in matters of faith? Should he afflict his father with the truth, causing him pain and anger?

Montague finally admits he converted to Catholicism and announces, "in her [the Catholic Church] I resolve to live and die as the best way to salvation." Montague declares to his father that he considers his primary loyalty to be to God and to the salvation of his soul and his second fidelity to be to nature, or his sovereign and father. In discussing his obligations as a subject of Charles, Montague contends that the king, being rightly informed in all things, surely recognizes that "the Catholic faith doth not tend to the alienation of the heart of a subject." In his own mind, Montague has reconciled the seemingly conflicting religious dictates of the Catholic Church and his English monarch. Regarding his family, Montague assures his father that his change in religion in no way obviates his duties as a son, and describes himself as "Your loving and obedient son" and "Your lordship's most obedient son" despite his obvious disregard of his father's wishes. He states that even if he incurs his father's displeasure over this conversion to Catholicism, such anger will in no way deter him from his faith. Yet, in the end, he requests his father's blessing of his choice of religion.[42] In other words, both as a subject and as a son, Montague tries to balance his spiritual obligations as a Catholic with his secular responsibilities as subject and son. Although he has chosen to privilege Catholicism, he needs the understanding of his sovereign and his father because he has duties to fulfill to them as well.

While Montague decided to privilege his identity as a Catholic above his other roles, not all Catholics chose to do so.[43] Most notably, many Catholic priests and laypersons renounced Catholicism shortly before their scheduled executions out of fear. And John Good, a Member of Parliament and a secretly self-defined Catholic, came up with a very different balance between spiritual and secular obligations than did Montague. Good wrote in the early 1600s that only the desire to preserve his social, financial, and political lifestyle "and fear to incur those penalties which the rigor of the laws imposed, not only by loss of goods, lands, and liberty, but also of life . . . were the true and only motives, that kept me in the practice of Protestant religion."[44]

Good was hardly unique. Many other Catholics, particularly during the Oath of Allegiance controversy under James I, balanced their religious and worldly priorities in similar fashion. During the controversy, many Catholics opted to swear loyalty to James I rather than pay exorbitant fines for refusing. In 1611, John Nelson, an English priest, wrote to Rome that "men (in England) stick not to say that none of them would lose lands or liberty for (not taking the oath) if the case were theirs: and many say that they see not why they should lose their lands and goods for an oath which no man will take pen in hand at home or abroad to defend."[45] To save their livelihoods, many English Catholics, in other words, were willing to take the oath, which obligated the taker to defend the monarch and country from all invaders, even the Pope.

Such individuals did not see the swearing of the oath to defend their Protestant-governed country and sovereign as a conversion to Protestantism. They still considered themselves Catholics and continued to raise their families as Catholics. Though they did not give top priority to their faith in every decision they made, these individuals, based on the patterns of a lifetime's worship, should still be considered Catholics and will be for the purposes of this study.

We can see the value of such an inclusive definition by examining how the level of persecution often determined the degree of conformity adopted by English Catholics. In the Field in the diocese of Chester in 1595, Catholics habitually refused to attend Protestant services for the majority of every year. A few weeks before the assizes, however, these Catholics conformed and went to Protestant services, becoming church papists: those who attended services but refused communion and whom everyone knew to be Catholics. The Catholics maintained this practice until 1603 or 1604 during the transition between the reigns of Elizabeth I and James I. Believing that James I would support greater toleration for Catholics, many of these Catholics elected to avoid the Protestant church altogether. In this transition period ending in late 1604, the number of recusants increased from roughly 2,000 to 3,500. Church papists numbered approximately 500. By 1613, however, following James I's attempts to strengthen the laws against Catholics following the Gunpowder Plot, there were 2,000 recusants again, just as there had been near the end of Elizabeth's reign. The number of non-communicating church papists rose from 500 to 2,400. Apparently, many of the Catholics who adopted recusancy between 1603 and 1604 in hope of greater toleration elected to return to nominal conformity when such hopes ended.[46] Does this mean they were any less Catholic because they feared persecution?[47]

Rome's official position was yes. Rome vehemently prohibited any type of conformity with Protestants throughout the century following the Act of Uniformity.[48] Rome feared that any concessions allowing English Catholics to outwardly conform to Protestant practices might be interpreted as relinquishing Roman jurisdiction over England. As will be discussed in the last chapter, Rome's reluctance to work with English Catholics to accommodate their special circumstances would alienate many of England's Catholics from the papacy although not the Catholic faith.

Many of the English Catholics who emigrated to the continent to worship freely supported Rome's prohibition against concessions to the Protestant faith. Many instructed Catholics remaining in England to suffer and die for the faith rather than conform.[49] As will be seen throughout this study, emigrants' writings often display a striking naiveté regarding the day-to-day realities of trying to remain a practicing Catholic in England. Emigrants' instructions to attend Mass weekly, maintain all feasts and processions, and confess frequently to a priest simply were not practicable in England. There were powerful reasons for emigrants to conform to Rome's position. Many of the English exiles enjoyed pensions from the Pope or from Catholic leaders such as Philip II of Spain and the powerful Guise family of France.[50] Exiled English writers would not have wanted to risk angering their patrons by voicing opinions contrary to Church policy.

Like Rome and the English emigrants, modern scholars have established their own definitions of "Catholic" too. This study's definition of Catholicity modifies and builds upon these previous definitions. John Bossy, for example, insisted that historians primarily look at behavior as opposed to belief when determining who was Catholic. By his standard, only those Catholics who refused any sort of compromise with the Church of England and broke away to form their own "sectarian" communities ministered to by Catholic priests should be considered Catholics for the purpose of defining a Catholic community.[51] Other historians, such S. J. Watts on Northumberland, J. A. Hilton on Cumbria, William Hunt on Essex, and Peter Clark on Kent have accepted this definition of Catholic community and have structured their conclusions accordingly.[52] Historians led by Christopher Haigh and more recently by Alexandra Walsham and Michael Questier have argued for a wider interpretation of non-recusant Catholicism.[53] As Roger B. Manning has pointed out in his study of Catholics in Sussex, most "avowed Catholics" conformed at least once, under pressure of family or career. "Human nature is frail. It is not the weakness displayed in a difficult moment, but rather the pattern of a lifetime that gives the best indication of a man's religious views."[54] In other words, the degree of conformity to Protestantism should not be used as a gauge of Catholicity, only as a gauge of fear. And Walsham extends this logic further, arguing that "Conformity needs to be seen as a positive option rather than a form of spineless apathy or ethical surrender."[55]

By allowing English Catholics, through their spoken or written words and through their documented actions, to define themselves as Catholics, this study raises the universal question, "Who determines membership in a religious body?" The institutional administration? A believer? A congregation? Catholicism in England was in flux, and as such, the power of institutional rules and judgments of co-religionists were less effective in determining who or what was Catholic. As such, individuals had more ability to define their own religious identity and community. In the eyes of the Roman Church, some individuals might no longer be Catholic and faced eternal damnation; by English law some also avoided the Catholic label. But as will be seen throughout this work, individual Catholics often determined for themselves that they could remain good Catholics while protecting other aspects of their identities and lives at certain times.

CATHOLIC PRIORITIES

Although those who defined themselves as English Catholics certainly lived in a world in which the penal laws and local law enforcement efforts were prominent, Protestant attempts at repression in no way defined the totality of how Catholics lived their daily lives, practiced their faith, and understood their relationships to God and to one another. Because of their faith, Catholics also lived within a set of understandings about how the world worked, how their relationship with God was structured, and what priorities came first. In order to understand how English Catholics created particular devotional alternatives—which are the crux of this study—it is necessary to understand the core beliefs comprising the Catholic worldview. These include the immanent nature of the world, the importance of saints, priests, and the sacraments, and the desire for salvation.

Immanence

English Catholics of the late sixteenth or early seventeenth centuries believed that the divine was immanent in the material world. In other words, that which is sacred could inhere in physical matter.[56] The material and spiritual spheres overlapped, and at the points of intersection, individuals in the material world could interact with God, Mary, saints, angels, and even the spirits of the dead on quite intimate terms.

The sacrament of the Mass provides an excellent illustration of Catholic belief in sacred immanence. Catholic sacraments are ritual behaviors that through their symbolic performances in the natural world produce results in the supernatural world.[57] (The sacramental structure of the Catholic Church will be discussed in more detail in chapter 4 on the Mass.) A Catholic priest performs the gestures and words of the Mass to reenact the crucifixion in which Christ's body was broken and blood was spilled for remission of sins. Reformation-era Catholics understood the performance in the material world to be a real sacrifice, transforming the bread and wine into the physical body and blood of Christ. The ritual procured actual remission of sins in the spiritual world at the specific point in time in which a particular priest said the Mass, thus gaining the same saving grace that occurred at the original event.[58] The immediate, physical act in the natural sphere brought forth concrete spiritual results in the natural and supernatural spheres. Catholics could, therefore, impact both the material and spiritual worlds through bodily actions, use of material objects, and resort to particular places.

This contrasts with the prevailing Protestant worldview that emphasized that ritual lacked the capacity to change one iota of reality.[59] For example, Anglican Eucharistic liturgy did not explicitly deny the corporal presence of Christ in the Eucharist, however Anglican clergy were not believed to be recreating Christ's death on the cross over and over again through the power of the priesthood.[60] There was no cause-and-effect relationship between an Anglican priest's words and the presence of Christ in the Eucharistic elements. To allow ritual to transform reality would grant powers to humanity which only God possessed.

In reality, the distinction between an immanent Catholicism and a transcendent Protestantism is not so simple. For the purposes of this study, however, the most important working distinction between the two worldviews was in the way each religion taught believers to access the sacred. The Catholic Church maintained that believers could open a two-way channel of communication and effect change in both the physical and spiritual worlds through their ritualized actions (such as celebration of the sacraments, processions), use of material objects (such as the consecrated bread and wine, saints' relics, and rosaries), or resort to sacred locations (such as the altar or saints' shrines). On the other hand, the Church of England taught that believers could open a channel of communication with the divine through prayer. Although Protestants believed that they could discern God's influence in the material world by observing natural phenomena and the work of providence, they could not use the physical world as an opportunity to influence the divine to effect change.[61] God's presence in the world was active but not necessarily *interactive* as it was for Catholics.

Saints, Priests, and Sacraments

One of the primary ways in which Catholics believed they could bridge the permeable divide between the natural and supernatural spheres was by accessing saints, priests, and the sacraments provided by priests. The Catholic Church of the late sixteenth and early seventeenth centuries believed in a religious hierarchy of mediators that reached its apex in God. In order to gain God's favor, believers had to work through this network, asking mediators on levels higher than themselves to intercede with God on the believer's behalf.

There were two main groups of mediators to whom the faithful might turn: Mary and the cadre of saints and Catholic priests. Believers accessed each group differently, and each group served a different, but related, purpose. Saints were individuals, recognized either by the institutional church or the religious laity, whom God singled out and blessed for their holiness. Saints were divine intercessors in heaven whom believers called upon by prayer and ritual addressed to the saint. Having been specially recognized by God, the Church and laity believed saints possessed special efficacy in presenting petitions to God.[62] Catholics of this period accessed the saints primarily through individual prayers, contact with saints' relics, or pilgrimages to shrines dedicated to a particular saint. Because of their belief in the immanent nature of the sacred in this world, words, objects, and locations could all be used as opportunities to connect with the sacred.

Priests, however, provided a different quality of mediation. Priests were earthly mediators who believers accessed through ties with the institutional church. Believers did not pray to the priests as they did to saints. Instead, they asked priests to mediate between themselves and Christ through the priest's prayers and performance of the sacraments. Priests served as Christ's representatives on earth. Christ ordained the first priest when he provided his apostle Peter with the keys of heaven and called Peter the rock upon which he would build his church.[63] Christ instructed Peter to ordain other priests to carry out God's work and conferred the power to save or damn souls upon Peter and his successors. According to Catholic belief in apostolic succession, any priest in the Catholic Church can trace his lineage of ordination all the way back through the apostles to Christ. As Christ's representatives on earth, priests, therefore, possess a direct channel of authority through which to deliver God's grace in the natural world.[64]

When Protestantism became England's state religion in 1559, most Catholics perceived that they had lost contact with both groups of mediators. Protestants discouraged the Catholic cult of the saints, defacing saints' images, destroying saints' relics, and tearing down saints' shrines. In addition, the penal laws against priests hampered clerical ability to provide the sacraments to a Catholic population spread widely over the English countryside. The Jesuit Robert Southwell, writing to his superior Claudio Aquaviva in December 1586, lamented the loss of priests and sacraments, particularly the Mass. He claimed that, "Of a truth, one remaining solace of the Catholics amid all this trouble and turmoil is to refresh themselves with the bread of heaven, which if it be taken away, it cannot be but that many will faint and grow feeble, whose piety and constancy was heretofore nourished and increased at his table."[65] Before 1590, Catholic missionaries such as Southwell had difficulty conceiving that they might maintain the faith by means other than those used by the late medieval or post-Tridentine Catholic Church.

Lay Catholics perceived a difference between what the Protestant church offered and what they had experienced previously with Catholic saints, priests, and sacraments. The Catholic Church recognizes seven sacraments and, with few exceptions in cases of extreme necessity, a priest is necessary to perform and administer these sacraments. As explained previously, sacraments—such as the Mass, Baptism, Penance, and the Last Rites—are ritual performances that procure some measure of God's grace simply by virtue of the ritual performance having taken place. The purpose of this sacramental system is primarily "soteriological," or designed to help believers attain the salvation of their souls.

Protestant priests were not, in the minds of Catholics, capable of participating in this sacramental system to save souls. Protestant priests were not Christ's representatives on earth, lacking the direct lineage traceable to Christ and Peter. Catholics believed that the English Protestant Church severed these links by denying that the ordination of priests was a sacrament. The Catholic Church severed these links as well by excommunicating the Protestant ministry. Lacking the sacramental inheritance of clerical authority passed from priest to priest from the mouth of Christ himself, Catholics perceived that Protestant priests could not be effective mediators with God in the way Catholic priests could. Similarly, the Protestant sacraments could not aid salvation in the way Catholic sacraments did. Protestant communion, for example, differed from the Catholic Mass in that Protestant celebrants did not effect the transubstantiation of the elements of bread and wine into Christ's actual body and blood. It was a memorial of Christ's sacrifice, not a recreation. The Protestant sacrament, therefore, did not bring about the same remission of sins.

Laypersons without advanced degrees in theology or access to books discussing the doctrinal differences between the Protestant and Catholic churches could understand these basic differences. For example, in 1576, Agnes Weddell, wife of the butcher John Weddell, testified before the Ecclesiastical Commission in York that she refused to come to the Protestant services because "there is neither altar, priest, nor Sacrifice." The locksmith William Bowman agreed, citing his reason for nonattendance as being that "there is neither priest, altar, nor sacraments." Others presented before the commission, such as Elizabeth Wilkinson, Catherine Wildon, Lucy Plowman, Margaret Taylor, and Thomas Pearson, expressed similar concerns over the absence of proper priests and sacraments.[66]

Catholics went to great lengths and undertook substantial risks to access Catholic priests to provide the Roman sacraments. Whenever a Catholic priest traveled through a community, he would perform a variety of services, including Masses, confessions, marriage ceremonies, baptisms, the last rites, and even exorcisms.[67] If priests failed to travel to certain areas, some Catholics would leave home to find a priest, such as the midwife from Standish who traveled about the countryside with children searching for Catholic priests to perform baptisms.[68] Some Catholics kept one or even two priests in their homes to ensure they did not die without receiving the last rites.

Salvation

Catholic concern over saints, priests, and sacraments was primarily due to overriding concern over the salvation of the soul. Both the Catholic and Protestant churches taught that there was only one road to salvation—theirs. English Catholics wanted to make sure they followed the right path, lest they be damned. The late medieval English church had long preached the paradise that awaited souls reaching heaven and the everlasting torments awaiting the damned in hell. For example, in the Corpus Christi plays common throughout Coventry and other English towns in the fourteenth and fifteenth centuries,

> Hell mouth was characteristically a painted set of gaping jaws, perhaps on a separate smaller wagon wheeled in front of the main pageant; the unfortunate victim could then be seen to be devoured alive to the sound of pipes, drums and gitterns. . . . The Corpus Christi play was not an historical entertainment but a statement of the eternal truths and episodes of the faith.[69]

Ensuring they were doing all that was necessary to merit salvation proved to be the key issue concerning English Catholics. Various types of evidence ranging from wills, interrogations, poetry, petitions to the Roman

Church, prayers, letters, art, and pastoral literature reveal the deep-seated concern many Catholics experienced over the fate of their souls and the souls of friends and family members. Thomas Freke, a Catholic originally from London but residing in Seville in 1606, wrote home to his uncle, George, imploring him to return to the Catholic faith for the health of his soul. Thomas expressed concern that George, who was evidently advancing in years, take responsibility for his soul before "that certain approaching of that day wherein God will demand of you upon what ground you have left that religion wherein your forefathers and progenitors were glad to die and in which you yourself were baptized and brought up in."[70] The recusant layman Thomas Pounde, jailed at least 16 times for his religion, reminded Catholics that they would all be called to account for their lives on Judgment Day, where the Lord will "devour unstable souls like bread."[71]

The Catholic laity believed their church's teachings that God had laid down certain conditions which must be met in order for a believer to be saved and enter heaven. The church instructed that man must obtain God's grace. Grace was God's gift to humankind, freely given and indispensable to the soul's deliverance to heaven and participation in the divine life with Christ and the Father.[72] But how does a soul receive this grace? God gives grace freely, but man must accept grace, largely through his faith and participation in the Catholic Church.[73]

The pre-reform English church, the Council of Trent, and the most popular English post-Tridentine catechism advertised that the primary way God conferred sanctifying grace upon mankind was through the sacraments of the Catholic Church.[74] The sacraments were both a sign of God's grace and the means of conferring grace upon the recipient. Grace was viewed not only as God's personal gift but as part of an economy of salvation in which each soul maintained an active account and attempted to increase the account balance of grace. Continual participation in the sacraments, therefore, could be viewed as making continual deposits of grace into one's personal account in this "bank of salvation."[75]

Fear of everlasting agony spurred many lay Catholics to reject Protestantism and continue seeking particularly Catholic means to procure eternal life through the Catholic economy of salvation. Some Catholics tried to continue the traditional medieval practices of seeking Masses and priests' prayers and purchasing indulgences.[76] Sir Thomas Stuckley, for example, an English exile living in Louvain, arranged in 1575 for the Pope to bless a number of crucifixes to be sent to England with indulgences attached. All an English Catholic had to do to earn 50 days indulgence was to gaze upon one of the crucifixes with reverence and devotion. By saying prayers and bowing to the crucifix, a penitent could gain even greater indulgences.[77]

English Catholics continued to obtain indulgences, despite their prohibition, and valued them highly. John Harrison of Shropshire was captured in London in March 1596 with an indulgence upon his person, as well as with pictures of the Pope and various saints, relics of bone, and rosary beads. Incarcerated and examined in Bridewell prison in London, Harrison claimed he found the indulgence two days previously in the "street at Crooked Lane's end in London in the evening."[78] Was he lying? Had he purchased or earned the indulgence himself to aid his own quest for salvation? It would have been very dangerous for Harrison to have admitted that the indulgence was his. Considering that England's fear of invasion by Catholic powers was perhaps at its height in the late 1580s and 1590s, evidence of loyalty to the Pope could be considered treasonous. But even if Harrison did not originally procure the indulgence, the fact that he kept it, knowing what it was and what dangers he assumed by carrying it about with him, demonstrates the value he placed upon the document. The power of an indulgence to remit the pains of the soul's punishment in Purgatory could be transferred to someone other than the original recipient. Harrison might easily have assumed "finders, keepers," and that the benefits of the indulgence now fell to him.

William Goodwyn and Bridgett Palmer obviously valued the saving powers of indulgences highly. When Protestant authorities searched the couple, they reported finding nine indulgences, absolutions, and testimonials granted to the twosome. Each one was dated after 1580, long after the Act of Uniformity. One indulgence, entitled *Indulgentia concessa a Gregorio 13 pro grano Benedicto & pro Medallis*, offered indulgences attached to the praying of the rosary. Also found in the search were a pair of beads wrapped in paper upon which Goodwyn and Palmer might pray to acquire this indulgence. But perhaps the item most telling of the couple's apprehension or zeal over their salvation was the whip of five cords found in the search. Each of the five cords had attached to its end pieces of brass resembling "the Rowells of Spurs."[79] Either Goodwyn or Palmer, or perhaps both, were flagellants. They would have used such a whip to mortify their flesh and punish and cleanse their bodies of sins, a ritual practiced in Christianity from the days of the desert fathers such as St. Anthony in the third century.

Yet as these more traditional avenues of attaining salvation—intercessors, sacraments, prayers, Masses said by priests for the health of souls, and the purchasing of indulgences—became more difficult to achieve, many English Catholics required alternatives. As previously noted, in 1586 the Jesuit Robert Southwell feared that the lack of priestly-administered sacraments would equal the decline of the faith. He could not conceive of Catholicism being nourished in any other way. However in 1587, after the execution of the Catholic Mary Queen of Scots, Southwell was amazed to report to his superiors, "And yet the faith is still alive! . . . The families are not falling away. . . . Only priests are lacking. It is clear and certain that, whatever storms are raging . . . very many are seeking access to (the Church)."[80]

But, with limited access to priests, sacraments, saints, and indulgences, what was this "church" that English Catholics sought? Would Catholics remain faithful to a church that was not providing them with the traditional tools necessary to follow the only road to salvation? Or did English Catholics begin using different tools?

MEETING CATHOLIC PRIORITIES

The first decades following Elizabeth's Act of Uniformity witnessed the beginning of Catholics' attempts to adapt to the new religious environment under Protestant rule. At first, Catholics either struggled to maintain late medieval practices unchanged or to adopt the more stringent recommendations of the Council of Trent (1545–1563). This Council attempted to channel Catholic worship through the sacraments and the priesthood, neither of which English Catholics had reliable access to.[81] As the years passed, however, most Catholics recognized the impossibility of such efforts. In approximately 1590, following the execution of Mary Queen of Scots in 1587 and the failure of the Spanish Armada in 1588, Catholic goals changed—from maintaining strict adherence to pre-reform or Tridentine practices in direct defiance of the Protestants to finding ways to duplicate the *functions* of traditional or Tridentine practices while reinterpreting the *forms* such practices might take.

Catholic clergy and laity labored together to devise new ways to keep English Catholics on the right path to salvation. The largest concerted effort of clergy and laity was the English mission. Both the Catholics and the Protestants viewed the arrival of continentally ordained English priests on English shores as an aid to beleaguered English Catholicism. The type of aid, how it was to be delivered, and how effective the priests were at delivering it are all hotly contested issues. Much of the historiography of the mission characterizes it as a failure due to the disproportionate concentration of priests among wealthy families in southeast England where there was little opportunity for missionary work. According to historians such as John Bossy and Christopher Haigh, priests were assigned to gentry families. The priests lived in the manor homes of their hosts and neglected pastoral duties elsewhere, preferring to sit in luxury and minister to select groups of wealthy Catholics. According to these interpretations, the missionaries ignored the poorer Catholics and the Catholics of the northern regions where there was plenty of opportunity to convert people and minister to existing Catholics but where there was little money. When communities no longer enjoyed the regular serv-

ices of a priest and could not receive the sacraments, Catholicism faded.[82] Is
this an accurate depiction of the mission, its goals, and its accomplishments?

Scholars such as Bossy and Haigh saw the purpose of the mission as the
formal reconciliation of large numbers of people in poor, remote regions of
England to the Catholic Church, thereby increasing the number of recusants
and saving Catholicism from extinction. Increasing numbers of recusants, for
these historians, would be the sign of a successful mission.[83] But perhaps what
is implied by the word "mission" does not accurately describe the activities of
the seminarians and Jesuits in England. "Mission" in the singular form seems
to imply one coordinated effort. Yet England at this time was not linked by a
communications system that would have allowed a centralized effort to distribute priests. Letters were dangerous to send. Few knew where to send
them. Traveling was even more perilous. By expecting the mission to be a coordinated effort, historians have underestimated the logistical difficulties under
which the mission operated.

In reality, there was not just one mission. The Jesuits' attempts to coordinate missionary activities from London are by far the best known, but theirs
were not the only efforts. Priests who entered England from the South and
passed through London certainly would have benefited from Jesuit efforts at
coordination but were under no obligation to participate in such a network. An
increasing number of seminary priests chose to enter England from the North,
either on the northeast shores of England around Yorkshire or Durham or
across the Scottish border. Especially during the decade of the Spanish
Armada, these were considered the safer routes. It is most unlikely that these
priests chanced the perilous journey to London just to enter the Jesuit network
of safe houses. As the Jesuit William Weston points out,

> Every road, cross-way and port was watched day and night, and sealed off
> so effectively that no person could pass without the most rigorous exami-
> nation. Lodging houses, private homes, rooms were searched and exam-
> ined with minute thoroughness; neither friend nor acquaintance could
> escape without being forced to give an account of himself. In this way,
> many priests were captured, and Catholics filled the prisons throughout
> the country.[84]

Instead of using the Jesuit network, many priests used locally established networks, such as the one the seminary priest Thomas Bell set up in
Yorkshire and, later, in Lancashire. Bell organized an "underground railway"
system to transport priests from remote northern ports to areas where they
were needed in these counties. Patrick McGrath and Joy Rowe have found evidence of these networks in counties in all regions of England, such as
Lancashire, Yorkshire, Sussex, Hampshire, Oxfordshire, and Durham.[85]

Thinking of the mission on this smaller scale of localized networks allows the historian to question the characterization of the mission as poorly coordinated and of the priests as "gentrified," socially pretentious, overeducated men who enjoyed living the manor-house lifestyle.

Through these local networks, clerics and laypeople of all ranks cooperated to provide pastoral care to English Catholics. John Gerard's autobiography provides many details about the daily activities of priests and laity which suggest that such broad-based cooperation was necessary to minimize the risks assumed by all Catholics. Gerard, born in Derbyshire, attended the English College of Douai and later Rheims before arriving at the English College in Rome where he joined the Jesuits. He returned to England on the mission in 1588. A successful organizer of the Jesuit mission in East Anglia, Gerard experienced first-hand the difficulties associated with finding safe places for priests to reside on their journeys and to live once they had reached the area where they would work.

Although a valuable document, Gerard's autobiography must not be taken at face value. It was meant to motivate young priests about their future work. As such, Gerard's depiction of his success rate in converting Catholics is questionable. Virtually every person he converted was wonderfully pious and desperately happy as a Catholic despite the Elizabethan persecutions.[86] Not one of Gerard's contacts ever betrayed the Catholic cause, even under torture.[87] Elizabethan court records suggest that Catholic loyalty was not quite as unwavering as Gerard's tale suggests.

Despite these constraints, Gerard's narrative of the dangers of life as a hunted priest makes it clear that previous scholars' characterizations of the mission fail to adequately recognize the hazards with which the mission was fraught and which necessitated certain working and living habits. Considering that approximately half of all priests were imprisoned at some time or another during their missionary careers and that approximately 125 were executed, the dangers were great indeed. A priest could not simply enter a community and begin ministering to Catholics. He must have a cover. The gentry were the group best suited to provide that cover. Their homes were the sites of frequent gatherings, and they often entertained visitors.[88] The homes were large enough to accommodate "hiding holes" where a priest could conceal himself, his books, and his vestments in the event of a search. Homes were often situated near orchards or woods which offered priests the ability to come and go virtually unnoticed.[89]

Protection was clearly a key concern of priests coming on mission, and here laypersons of all ranks worked with the clergy to contribute to the success of pastoral efforts. If a priest's identity was not well disguised and protected, he could not provide pastoral care to many. George Gilbert was the founder of the

Catholic Association in England, a group of laymen that directed priests to those in need of pastoral care and escorted the priests around the country-side.[90] Gilbert expressed his concerns in a memo of 1583:

> As soon as any father or learned priest has entered an heretical country he should seek out some gentleman to be his companion. . . . He (the gentle-man) should be knowledgeable about the country, the roads and paths, the habits and disposition of the gentry and people about the place, and should be a man who has many relations and friends and much local information. He should associate himself with a man of this sort so as to be able with his aid to appear and mix freely everywhere, both in public and in private, dressed as a gentleman and with various kinds of dress and disguises so as better to be able to have intercourse with people without arousing suspi-cion.[91]

As Gilbert suggests, a gentry disguise was often best, as shown by the experience of Father Ingleby in 1586. A contemporary account reveals that Ingleby was dressed as a poor man and leaving York on foot at the time of his arrest. A Catholic gentleman of York accompanied Ingleby to the gate and stayed to speak with him for a few moments before departing. Unfortunately, the spot where they conversed was underneath a window of the Bishop's Palace. Two chaplains looking out the window witnessed the exchange between Ingleby and his companion. When saying good-bye, the gentleman repeatedly showed Ingleby greater marks of respect, such as doffing his hat, than were due to a man dressed such as Ingleby. The chaplains, after making inquiries, had Ingleby arrested. He was later executed.[92] Since Catholic priests com-manded great respect, it was expedient that they occupy a social station to which such respect was owed.

Priests also developed strong connections with non-gentry lay Catholics. This can be seen in the efforts made by the non-gentry to accom-modate priests in their homes, to serve priests by performing various jobs for them, and to educate their children in the continental colleges recommended by the priests. These lay efforts were complemented by priestly commitment to leave the manor houses to visit the non-gentry.

When a safe environment was available in non-gentry homes, priests would stay there as well. Several poor laymen undertook the construction of safe hideouts for priests so that they might harbor them nearby. Richard Jebbe, a farmer, constructed a small safe house measuring approximately seven feet in width, ten feet in length, and eight feet in height. He located this sanctuary in a spot surrounded by many bushes in the middle of his field where it would not be noticed. Priests lodged there, and Jebbe went into the field to converse with them.[93] Another lay Catholic, William Napper, leased a portion of his land at

Cowdray to a mason, known as Badger, who built a similar structure to hide priests or any Catholic who needed a place to hide.[94] Other Catholics below the rank of gentry who harbored priests include "George Baylie, a Clerkenwell glover; a Yorkshire yeoman called Bickerdike who harbored John Boste; the former schoolmaster Swithen Wells and his wife . . .; and Margaret Clitheroe, the wife of a York butcher."

Although the priests frequently stayed in non-gentry households when it was safe to do so, it was not always safe for the poorer families who housed them. For example, John Green and his wife, poor residents of Yardley in Warwickshire, allowed a priest to hide in their home for three days and say Mass. When the priest was captured, he betrayed them. And when a poor, illiterate Catholic in Winchester, the father of 10, harbored a priest in 1599, he was discovered, arrested, and executed.[95]

There were many other roles that those below gentry status filled in order to help the mission, and pockets of yeoman and middle-class recusants emerged. They served as "housekeepers" for priests' residences. They worked as factors, or business agents, for recusant families. They guided priests through the countryside and delivered messages throughout the counties.[96] They helped operate the secret presses that published illegal English Catholic pastoral literature.[97] The non-gentry also played a valuable role in maintaining Catholicism by sending their children to the seminaries on the continent, thus providing a significant portion of the clerical workforce.[98]

Within these local networks of priests and laity, priests often resided in manor houses, though many of these homes simply served as bases from which the priests operated. A canonic prohibition discouraged priests from living vagabond lifestyles.[99] The priests established a residence as their base of operations, but they were not confined to this base. Priests' ministries radiated out in two ways. First, the yeomen, peasantry, and lesser gentry from the surrounding area could come to the base to attend Mass, talk to a priest, and generally partake of Catholic ritual and fellowship even though they did not live at the manor house.[100] Second, priests were not confined to the manor house. They frequently left the house and walked nearby, stopping to visit the homes of those they knew to be Catholic.[101] William Weston would even stop in the shops of Catholics for discussions during the workday.[102]

Priests also left their bases on long journeys throughout the countryside. As J.C.H. Aveling points out, many priests operated on circuits, traveling from community to community. This was a practice instituted early in the mission. The first English Jesuits on mission, Robert Persons and the martyr Edmund Campion, made frequent trips into the countryside, splitting the counties between them. On one such excursion, Persons took Gloucestershire, Herefordshire, and Worcestershire while Campion ministered in Berkshire,

Oxfordshire, and Northamptonshire.[103] Campion describes the lifestyle of the
traveling priest:

> I ride about some piece of the country every day. . . . On horseback I med-
> itate my sermon; when I come to the house, I polish it. Then I talk with
> such as come to speak with me; they hear with exceeding greediness, and
> very often receive the sacrament, for the ministration thereof we are ever
> assisted by priests, whom we find in every place, whereby the people is
> well served.[104]

Campion returned to London following this journey, but left again for the
countryside once the winter had passed, traveling to 11 other shires.[105]

The Jesuits were not the only peripatetic priests. Seminary priests frequently left their home bases to travel, as James Sharpe did. Although his base
was in Osgodby, he spent most of his time traveling and ministering.[106] John
Chapman made his base in Somersetshire, yet he made journeys to
Dorsetshire to minister.[107] Robert Kirkman journeyed throughout the northern
regions, providing pastoral care to the resident Catholics, before he was captured in 1582.[108] The priest John Boste, a native of Westmoreland, traveled
throughout the northeast for three years.[109] Ralph Sherwin, a Derbyshire
native, maintained a base in London with a schoolmate of his from Oxford, the
Cornishman Nicholas Roscarrock. Despite his London address, Sherwin spent
six months traveling and preaching throughout various counties in England.
These seminary priests have left fewer personal accounts of their travels than
the Jesuits did, but the time they spent traveling in order to provide pastoral
care and their contact with laity of middling and lower ranks was no less pro-
nounced.

Evolving Goals

The efforts of these clerics and the laypersons with whom they labored
changed over time in response to the changing needs of English Catholics and
the changing environment in which Catholicism was practiced. From the
beginning of the mission to approximately 1590, the mission's purpose was not
to swell the ranks of recusant Catholics but to sustain Catholicism until its
hoped-for restoration. Recent history indicated that Protestantism was by no
means guaranteed its hold as the state religion. Henry VIII vacillated between
the Cromwellian Protestant faction and the Howardian Catholic faction
throughout his reign and included many *de facto* Catholic practices under the
label of Protestantism. The Edwardian years ushered in a strict form of
Protestantism for approximately six years. Mary re-established England as a
Catholic country for the following five years. Elizabeth converted the country

to Protestantism at the beginning of her reign, but both Protestants and Catholics evinced uncertainty about England's religious future. Many Catholics hoped the winds of religious change would blow in their favor with the next king or queen.[110]

The Jesuit Robert Persons wrote in 1581, "At my first entry into England, I cast my eyes around so far as I could to determine which portion of the kingdom was in greatest need of our help, and which portion as time went on would be best able to further our cause."[111] Peter Holmes, in his analysis of non-resistance propaganda in the middle Elizabethan years, offers insight into what Persons and other members of the mission felt were their needs and those of the country. Holmes concludes that the English on the continent believed that the persecution of Catholics was only a temporary affair and that tolerance was "an interim measure to save the faithful" until God intervened and punished the heretics.[112] If the émigrés viewed the period of Protestant domination as only temporary, perhaps the mission's goal was not so much to increase the number of Catholics throughout the country as it was to preserve a solid core of Catholicism that would withstand the storm. As such, the mission would have concentrated its energies on those segments of the population most likely to further these short-term efforts or who would most likely be lost irrevocably to the Protestants.

John Gerard indicates, for example, that the mission was not very worried about losing the loyalty of Catholics in the north, the very population that Haigh and J. A. Hilton view as so under-served by the mission. In the northern counties, such as Lancashire, Gerard perceives the populace as having strong Catholic inclinations and being easy to convert to his religion. Considering the strong evidence uncovered by Aveling, Haigh, and Hilton regarding the persistence of Catholic ritual and the non-enforcement of the penal statutes in the north, Gerard's viewpoint appears reasonable. Gerard comments that, while the northerners tend to fall away from Catholicism at the moment of persecution, they return to Catholicism as soon as the crisis is past.[113]

Before the late 1580s when hope of a national re-conversion filled the hearts of many Catholic priests and laypersons, the priests counseled Catholics to make every effort to maintain Catholic worship as Catholics did on the continent and to make no accommodation to the Protestants. These were the orders of the Roman Church, and the English priests strove to ensure compliance.[114] Representatives of the pope commissioned Laurence Vaux, a former fellow and warden of the collegiate church at Manchester, and an exile living on the continent, to carry this directive into England, which he did in 1566. When English Catholic priests and laypersons expressed some uncertainty about the intent of these instructions, Vaux clarified in no uncertain terms that

I am charged to make a definitive sentence that all such as offer children
to the baptism now used or be present at the communion or service now
used in churches in England, as well the laity or the clergy, do not walk in
a state of salvation; neither we may not communicate nor sociate ourselves
in company with schismatic or heretic in divine things; there is no exception or dispensation can be had for any of the laity if they will stand in a
state of salvation. [115]

Vaux spread the news of this directive through *A catechisme or A Christian
doctrine, necessarie for children & the ignorant people*, perhaps the most popular catechism circulating in England for several decades. Vaux instructed
readers that to deny their Catholicism or not to confess it openly equaled a
breaking of the first of the Ten Commandments. Furthermore, Vaux insisted
that all Catholics must hear Mass every Sunday and holy day and receive the
Eucharist at minimum once yearly. Vaux's form of confession required a priest
to be present.[116] Vaux, of course, living on the continent, had never experienced the day-to-day difficulties of English Catholics trying to worship without
regular access to priests or sacraments.

Missionaries before approximately 1590 also saw their primary duties as
providing the sacraments in the traditional manner and allowing no alternatives to institutionally approved Catholic practices. Most missionary priests
working within England during this early period insisted that Catholics must
not outwardly accommodate the established religion or their own religion to
their special circumstances. For example, the Cornish priest Cuthbert Mayne,
martyred in 1577, ordered Catholics to shun even the appearance of conformity with the Protestant church. "Any that is a Catholic," he asserted, "may not
in any wise receive the sacraments, come to the church, or hear the schismat-
ical service which is established in the same here in England."[117] Many English
Catholics adhered to this advice and attempted to recapture their recently lost
traditions exactly as they remembered them or to keep in step with contemporary reforms of the Roman Church. The results, however, were generally dis-
appointing, resulting in cycles of guilt and frustration on the part of Catholics
who failed to meet their religious obligations.

Father John Cornelius, chaplain to the Arundel family, clarified the
dangers of conformity and cooperation with the Protestants. Lady Elizabeth
Arundel's son, Lord Stourton, conformed outwardly to Protestantism so that he
could attend court. Still a Catholic, he kept two priests secretly in his household as insurance, so that if he were in danger of dying, he could be reconciled
to his true faith before death. After Stourton's death, Lady Elizabeth requested that Cornelius perform a Mass for Stourton's soul. After completing the
Mass, Cornelius told how during the Mass (in between the consecration of the
holy bread and wine and the prayers for the dead) he had a vision of Stourton

being tormented in the afterlife for his dissimulation at court and for his role in condemning Mary Queen of Scots. John Carey, a server at the Mass, admitted that he saw this vision too.[118] Clearly, the message delivered was that outward conformity endangered the soul. Priests counseled Catholics to endure all persecution for the faith and await their rewards in heaven.[119]

In approximately 1590, however, the goals and counseling of many missionary priests began to change. The turbulent final years of the 1580s witnessed two events that dashed Catholic hopes for England's re-conversion: the beheading of Mary Queen of Scots, Catholics' best hope for the reestablishment of Catholicism in England, in 1587 and the failure of the Spanish Armada to forcibly reconvert the island in 1588. As the chances of a nationwide return to Catholicism withered, the mission's original goal of holding out until the Catholic cavalry arrived no longer seemed practicable.

Many missionary priests and laypersons began searching for alternatives for Catholic worship at approximately this time.[120] After 1590, English Catholics still centered their efforts around providing pastoral care and comfort to English lay Catholics who feared for their salvation, but these efforts became more focused on fulfilling the *functions* of traditional Catholic sacraments and rituals than in providing the traditional Catholic forms. They recognized that the small number of priests providing limited access to the sacraments now represented the long-term environment in which English Catholics would have to practice. Holmes, when examining the many Catholic casuistry manuals written to instruct seminary priests on how to handle the challenges faced by the laity in England, has discovered that the English Colleges encouraged practicality and flexibility among their missionary priests. Accommodations might be made. Mass might be said without vestments or with tin chalices. Priests might equivocate when questioned by the authorities.[121] Most importantly, priests could offer confession and the sacraments to those who practiced occasional Protestant conformity out of fear.[122] Holmes argues that close cooperation between laity and priests developed a small, flexible, and vibrant core of Catholic ritual and belief in England.[123] William Allen, the "founding father" of the mission, wanted to train men to become catechists, confessors, and pastors who could work effectively within this new English environment.[124] Trained to be pragmatic and to work within a challenging environment, as Holmes suggests, missionary priests were capable of suggesting new options that the organizers of the mission on the continent did not foresee.

It is important to make the distinction between the efforts of missionary priests working within England and the stated goals of the English mission and Roman Church for England. English missionary priests juggled the dictates of the institutional church which they loyally served with their desires to provide realistically for the pastoral needs of the English Catholics whom they also served and whom they saw fearful and frustrated over their inability to worship traditionally.[125] We must view their efforts to provide devotional alternatives with an open mind and understand their desire to satisfy their often-competing institutional and pastoral responsibilities.[126] The written evidence of efforts to provide new options for devotion must be read with these considerations in mind. These writings—primarily pastoral literature, letters, journals, and even poetry—have their own logic, shaped by the historical circumstances of the day-to-day difficulties of Catholic worship within Protestant England. As such, we must read them differently from the apologetical, doctrinal, controversial literature written on the continent. These priests did not seek primarily to debate, challenge, or create doctrine. But they did push orthodox doctrine to its limits to provide realistic opportunities for English Catholics to worship and find comfort regarding the fate of their immortal souls. For example, in 1617, the priest William Stanney, in his translator's preface to *A treatise of penance . . .*, advocated membership in the Third Order of St. Francis, a continental lay order established in 1221 which sought a return to the more austere religious observances originally advocated by St. Francis of Assisi. He recognized that the original treatise had been written in a "Catholic country [France] (where all virtuous actions, and pious devotions are freely practiced)" and that it would be impossible for Englishmen to engage in the same activities. Stanney freely admitted that he altered some of the original author's prescriptions and claimed his goal was to eliminate all doubts and difficulties English readers might experience in adopting the practices of the order and to "accommodate it in abstinences, fastings, and all other austerities unto the convenience of the persons, time, and place of our Country."[127]

The French version of the treatise, for example, stipulated that a wife must gain her husband's permission to join the order. Stanney translated this stipulation from the original work but then added his own advice. Whereas in a Catholic country, no Catholic husband would act against his wife's best interests and deny her membership, the same might not be true in England where many Catholic wives were married to Protestant husbands. "God forbid that such devout souls, which have great need of aid and consolation, should for want of their husbands' consent be deprived of so many and great comforts as this holy order of penance doth afford unto all such as are admitted thereunto."[128] Stanney released Englishwomen from this requirement, thus accommodating the counsel of the original treatise to fit English circumstances. Similarly, Stanney recognized that the custom of fasting on Mondays and Wednesdays might make Catholics too conspicuous to Protestant authorities, so he counseled readers to make their fasts less obvious, using some restraints in their diet, either abstaining from those meats which are most pleasing at their table, or at the least to take a more sparing diet than on other days and instead of strict fasting, to redeem it with alms deeds or prayer, saying at the least . . . 5 *pater nosters* and *aves* in all such days as they cannot conveniently fast.[129]

Stanney's promulgation of the idea of a trade—one devotional act replacing another but with the same result—recurs frequently in the pastoral literature of this period that I examine in the next three chapters.

Understanding that priests and the sacraments were rare in England, pastoral authors after 1590 asked English Catholics to adopt different ideas about where, how, and under what circumstances to worship. They suggested different interpretations of religious space, images and objects, the sacraments, and how souls achieved salvation. What these authors counseled was not innovative, but what they emphasized as the means to salvation was. Roman doctrine had always allowed that God could confer grace in the absence of priests and the sacraments in times of emergency.[130] Midwives might baptize dying babies if a priest were not available. A man dying alone might make a last confession of his sins and cleanse his soul without a priest's final absolution.[131] The distinction between Roman doctrine and the English examples, however, is that what the Roman Church had hitherto taught as the exception only to be used in isolated cases of extreme necessity now became the day-to-day rule in England. The *continual* situation in England was one of extreme necessity.

Steering Catholic focus away from traditional practices might be perceived as bypassing traditional church hierarchy by decreasing the laity's reliance upon priests and promoting lay-directed worship, but such was not the case. Authors such as Stanney who encouraged accommodation in traditional understanding and practice insured the presence of a non-embodied priest through their texts.[132] As will be seen in the next three chapters, authors typically provided intensely detailed directions for specific thoughts and actions. Though there is no priest present, by adhering to the instructions the supplicant receives *per verbum* the functional contributions of a priest. The text becomes a proxy intercessor, a "virtual" priest, attempting to educate, minister to, and provide a channel toward God's grace for English Catholics who had restricted physical access to a priest.[133]

The authors whose works will be examined throughout this study encouraged and adopted new understandings of the sacraments and promoted new devotional alternatives. They did not, however, challenge the sacramental or sacerdotal doctrines of the church. Examined carefully, such writers did not attempt to annul the reception of the sacraments or the use of priests. They supported the frequent celebration of the sacraments when the realistic opportunity arose. They supported the necessity of priests and the maintaining of all honor due to the sacerdotal office, as shown in Robert Southwell's *Shorte Rule of Good Life*:

> love him as a parent or father . . . reverence and honor him as the vicere-
> gent of god and consider Christ in his person, and do my duty to him (the
> priest) as if in him I did see Christ . . . always carrying myself with due
> respect to his function and office . . . to obey him in all things . . . taking
> his words when he counseleth, commandeth, or forbiddeth me anything
> . . . persuading myself that though the man be imperfect, yet god whose
> viceregent and instrument he is never will deceive me.[134]

Although Southwell is orthodox in his reverence for the priesthood, he makes no mention of attending upon a priest to make confession or to hear Mass, a priest's two most important contributions to the lives of laypersons. Could it be that he saw little use in discouraging his readers by advising them to do the improbable? And yet, by urging Catholics to accept priests' words of counsel, Southwell implicitly asked Catholics to reverence the written words of priests—such as those contained in English Catholic pastoral literature—in the absence of a priest's spoken words.

These writers also avoided doctrinal statements explaining how Catholics received the merits of the sacraments or what was sufficient to attain salvation. They were not entering the theological debates engaged in by Catholics and Protestants regarding justification and salvation. Their mission remained pastoral. They comforted English Catholics by reminding them that those who had no access to priests and sacraments could still gain God's saving grace. These authors accepted orthodox doctrine and encouraged adherence to traditional forms of worship *whenever possible* but provided alternate inter-pretations and forms of devotion when traditional avenues were no longer available.

Overall, a shift in how Catholics were advised to view the sacraments and achieve salvation occurred after 1590. The sacraments were important since they were instituted by God, but their absence need not impair the soul's chance of salvation as much as might be feared. Instead, English Catholics shifted the emphasis on how Catholics achieved salvation to alternative, yet orthodox, means to obtain God's grace.

While these writings reveal much about changing interpretations of the sacerdotal and sacramental system, they only provide hints of what Catholics thought would fill the void left by the absence of priests and sacraments and help souls on their journeys to salvation. How did an individual gain God's grace to save the soul now? How did an individual identify with Christ now? How might a Catholic proactively work to assure the soul's salvation? The answer lay in what Catholics still possessed—limited access to physical locations, material objects, certain sacraments, and ritual actions—the building blocks of faith that Catholics might use and reinterpret to meet their religious needs. These foundations will be examined in greater detail in the following three chapters.

BOOK TRADE

An important means of communication between the priests and the lay audience they considered their flocks was through pastoral literature. Such literature could be read independently or read aloud to others. Or the ideas contained in the books could be disseminated orally and discussed among larger groups.[135] Although an examination of such literature (as occurs in chapters 2, 3, and 4) is profitable, it remains incomplete without evidence that such literature reached its intended audience (and even then, it is difficult to determine how readers received the information). It is not possible to know for certain how many Catholic books were printed, imported, traded, or possessed due to a lack of records. Barring exact figures, however, it can be demonstrated that enough pastoral literature was produced and distributed to have had significant success in reaching English Catholics.[136]

The types of books that English Catholics possessed included but were not limited to manuals, primers, psalters, missals, breviaries, and prayer books. Many Catholics kept a range of such books, as did Mistress Hampden of Stoke, Buckinghamshire in 1584. When a group of Protestants searched Hampden's home, they took from various chambers of the house a copy of Vaux's *Catechism*, 3 Jesus psalters, "a book called a manual of prayers," a book of Masses to particular saints, a basket filled with "papistical books," an Office of the Blessed Virgin Mary, a Rheims Testament, what is possibly a treatise of St. John Chrysostom, and various other "popish books." When they searched the stable, they found a further cache of Catholic books in the quarters of the stable staff. In addition to the books, the searchers also found religious pictures, tablets, rosary beads, letters of reconciliation written by the Pope, holy bread, copes, and pieces of religious needlework. As this search progressed, a man rode up to Hampden's house and, realizing it was being searched, turned and rode away, thus arousing the suspicions of the searchers. Some members of the search party followed the man and captured him. They found upon him an old printed Catholic service book and an Office of the Blessed Virgin Mary, as well as a copy of a papal letter granting indulgences and a relic of hair.[137]

In a similar example in December of 1583, the Bishop and Mayor of Winchester heard rumors that Winchester's Catholics intended to gather to hear Mass. These two officials obtained a warrant from the Privy Council to search the homes of suspected Catholics. Upon searching the residence of

Lady Mary West, widow of Sir Owen West, authorities discovered "diverse new and old papistical books printed and written." Hidden separately, the searchers also found a chest bound with iron filled with the following items: Massing apparel, a tin chalice, finely embroidered altar linens, *agni dei*, a pax, singing cakes, rosary beads, and books, particularly new Mass books, manuals of prayer, and catechisms. West's servant, Frances, confessed that the same chest had been in Lady West's chamber earlier that morning and was only hidden when the household learned of the search of Catholics in the city. That West kept these books so close at hand implies that West and other Catholics probably used these new books with some regularity. In a further hidden location in West's home, searchers located a further cache of approximately 40 old Mass books and Latin service books.[138]

The books found in West's home numbered far more than the immediate household would need for worship. West obviously provided access to Catholic books for those who might not possess their own copies. As the searches of the West and Hampden homes reveal, a wide variety of books formed an integral part of Catholic religious devotion. As evidenced by the variety of objects discovered with the books, these texts were only part of a much wider culture of material objects and worship in which ordinary Catholics might partake, yet the information contained in such books directed and influenced the way in which Catholics might use these other items.

Previous scholars have suggested that the influence of books upon English Catholics was limited to members of the gentry classes who were more likely to be able to read and to afford books.[139] Such a characterization is perhaps too limited.[140] Some individuals of yeoman rank and below could read at a rudimentary level and possessed books,[141] and authors purposefully wrote many of these works in very simple language to appeal to the widest audience possible. Devotions in these books included short exercises and easy-to-remember prayers. The seminary priest John Radford, for example, in his 1605 work *A Directorie Teaching the Way . . .* stated that "I have accommodated myself as much as I could to the plain man's understanding, using plain words, and now and then often repetition of things." Radford encouraged the unlearned to try his exercises, saying that "an unlearned man, may easily by himself or another find out sufficient authority to satisfy his mind."[142]

Unlearned Catholics, such as William Edmonds, a servant in Great Torrington, possessed such simple books and used them. One of Edmonds's fellow parishioners reported him to the authorities in 1594 for using a copy of Vaux's *Catechism* in his parish church during Protestant services. The examination of Edmonds's fellow parishioner, Alexander Barry, reveals that Barry:

did see in the hand of the said Edmonds a little book, to whom the said Barry said, I pray you, what new book have you, and the said Barry prayed him to leave it that he might peruse it. The said Edmonds answered it is a catechism and delivered him the book, whereof the said Barry perused and read a little part, and perceived that it contained popish doctrine.

Barry refused to return the book to Edmonds "because it contained matters against the queen's proceedings," and Edmonds became quite upset, telling Barry, "You will not use me so, I pray you deliver me my book." After Edmonds unsuccessfully attempted on numerous occasions to convince Barry to return his catechism, Barry reported the book to the mayor of Great Torrington. Edmonds's employer, Thomas Chappell, when examined, testified that Edmonds could "read badly, for the said catechism the said Edmonds did confess that he brought it from London with him." Edmonds disappeared before the authorities could arrest him for possessing a Catholic text. A friend of Edmonds, Humfrey Reynolds, also a servant, told the authorities that he had seen Edmonds with the catechism long before Edmonds's encounter with Barry at the church. Reynolds claimed that he spoke with Edmonds just prior to his disappearance and that Edmonds "feared lest that he should have trouble for the book and therefore he would shift for himself."[143]

Those involved in producing and disseminating pastoral literature refused to ignore those English Catholics who were unable to read even the most rudimentary pastoral works. Some shipments of pastoral literature also included books teaching the ABCs to increase the size of the pastoral books' audiences.[144] Additionally, many books contained images—even pictorial catechisms—that the unlearned might contemplate to increase their devotion.[145] Authors also frequently encouraged their literate audience to read to others from such books.[146]

Despite laws against the importing, printing, selling, or buying of "any Popish primers, lady's psalters, manuals, rosaries, Popish catechisms, missals, breviaries, portals, legends, and lives of saints,"[147] Catholics continued to obtain books from a variety of sources. As seen from the booty found in the Hampden and West homes, many still owned Catholic books from pre-Reformation years.[148] In addition to using pre-Reformation Catholic books, English Catholics also began to distribute and use new texts. Authors and printers provided post-Reformation Catholic books in four forms: manuscript copies, books printed secretly in England, books printed abroad and smuggled into the country, and books printed legally in England which masqueraded as non-Catholic texts. This final category consisted of dissimulating works which still delivered a powerful and recognizable Catholic message. Within England, both lay and clerical Catholics set up *scriptoria* and secret printing presses, primarily in London and its environs but also throughout the country. Scriveners and printers ideally preferred remote locations so that their scattered manuscript copies or the noise of the presses would not betray their presence, but some printers risked printing books in dangerous locations—for example, within London's prisons—in their attempts to provide an adequate supply of Catholic books.[149]

Although it is impossible to estimate the total output of the scriveners or secret presses, scattered evidence provides insight into the quantities produced and the demand that existed for such works.[150] The Jesuit Henry Garnet, undoubtedly exaggerating but clearly pleased with his efforts, claimed that the disseminators of Catholic pastoral literature had "filled the kingdom with catechisms and other pious works." The size of an average print run for an edition numbered approximately 1500 books. In certain years, such as 1599 and 1604, print runs were often much larger.[151] Printers also produced many editions of certain popular books over short periods of time, such as between 1591 and 1595 when printers published no fewer than 10 editions of the writings of the Jesuit priest Robert Southwell.[152]

Printers frequently moved their presses to avoid detection by the authorities,[153] but informers who worked for the government often located either the presses themselves or stockpiles of books printed illegally in England. For example, the Protestant informer William Udall located presses and seized thousands of Catholic books during the first decades of the seventeenth century. In 1608 he reported that he had recently seized 800 books and shut down five printing presses and could not understand why his government did not reward him more handsomely.[154] Jean-Baptiste Van Male, the agent of the Archduke to the English Court, described that in 1617 he witnessed an enormous public bonfire lit at St. Paul's to burn "an extraordinary quantity of Catholic books such as Breviaries, Offices of Our Lady, and similar other (books) of devotion which had been discovered at the house of a certain Catholic printer."[155]

In addition to books printed within England, English Catholics could also procure books printed abroad and smuggled into the country.[156] Continental printers produced many such books in the vernacular to appeal to a broad audience.[157] Methods of smuggling books into the country included nighttime drops along remote coasts and the carrying of books across the Scottish border, as well as smuggling efforts by many foreign Ambassadors.[158] In late July and early August 1609, for example, John Wilson, a priest at the English College of St. Omer in France (which ran a prolific printing press for English Catholic literature) sent a shipment of at least 600 books into England[159] where they were stored at the residence of the Ambassador of Venice. An inventory of the books stored in the Ambassador's house included 25 titles, among them instructions for the rosary, martyrologies of English saints, and pastoral works, such as *The Rules of Good Life* and *The Rule of Perfection*.[160] Although the authorities attempted to halt such illegal importation of Catholic books, their efforts could not stem the flow, as the Earl of Leicester complained in 1640/1:

> The officers of the ports are very negligent in their duty; for all kinds of persons pass and re-pass without difficulty and great quantities of Popish books are carried into England, from (France) and other parts, contrary to the laws. . . . I am sure that some great persons have known of it long since, from me, but no remedy has been applied.[161]

Finally, an English Catholic might acquire a book printed legally within England that provided Catholic counsel. By writing an apparently secular treatise, open Catholics could gain permission to publish in Protestant England while including and disguising Catholic messages in their texts. Such books dissimulated, appearing not to be what they really were—Catholic pastoral efforts—much as English Catholics dissimulated in many aspects of their daily lives.[162]

The number of Catholics captured in possession of such religious texts shows that many such books made it into the hands of English Catholics.[163] Merchants sold Catholic works in their shops,[164] and Catholics could even purchase books publicly in places such as St. Paul's churchyard in London.[165] Some individuals sold such works privately from their homes[166] or bequeathed them in their wills to other Catholics.[167] Priests also delivered books as they made their peripatetic rounds of neighborhoods.[168] Catholics frequently lent their own books to others[169] and copied printed books by hand[170] so that many works received even greater exposure than the print runs might indicate. Books were sent into prisons[171] and across the country to friends and relatives.[172] Even staunch Protestants were caught reading Catholic books.[173] And often, when many of the more unscrupulous informers and searchers found Catholic books in Catholic homes or upon a Catholic's person, they would fine the Catholic for possessing the books but then sell the books back to the Catholic and pocket the profit.[174]

As will be seen in the three following chapters, these pastoral texts provide some of our best clues regarding how priests and laypersons developed and adopted devotional alternatives to traditional Catholic practices, but they are only one of the sources used. These chapters examine various reinterpretations of Catholic symbols, material objects, physical sites, gestures, and sacraments which many English Catholics would have been familiar with and capable of using. This body of literature and the ideas which it spread contributed to the formation of Catholic communities as various Catholics practiced these new options both as individuals and in groups. Such Catholics understood that the strong spiritual bonds engendered by a commonality of faith and ritual could still bind Catholics to one another—knit Catholics together, making them as one in faith—even in the absence of the administrative ties, priests, sacraments, holy places, and the cornucopia of public ceremonies and rituals of the institutional Catholic Church, now prohibited in England.

Chapter 2

A "Church" without a Church

English Catholics' Search for Religious Space[1]

I n Golborne, Lancashire, during Easter week of 1604, English Catholics met secretly at the home of Peter Croncke the elder. The guests included people from diverse backgrounds, such as a laborer, a shoemaker, a husbandman, a miller, and a tailor. On the floor of one of Croncke's rooms, the Catholics laid an ordinary basin. On top of the basin, they placed a broken cross.[2] The faithful then got down upon their hands and knees and "did creep" across Croncke's floor to the broken cross. This ritual is rather easily recognizable as the traditional creeping to the cross, an activity typically performed in a Catholic church on Good Friday. But these Catholics performed this ritual upon an unconsecrated floor in a private home and included everyday household objects, such as the basin, in their celebration. How did English Catholics shift their understanding of sacred space and the centrality of the physical church to allow religious rituals to take place regularly outside a church?

Following Protestant reforms, many English Catholics found themselves without their traditional places of ritual, worship, and fellowship. Sporadically throughout the reigns of Henry VIII and Edward VI, and even into the reign of Elizabeth I, Protestant authorities and groups of zealous Protestant laypersons tore down or defaced the many images which filled churches and chapels and the many shrines which dotted the English landscape.[3] After 1559, Protestant ministers permanently moved into Catholic churches and cathedrals, performing the new Prayer Book rites in these formerly Catholic places of worship.

As the Yorkshire martyr Margaret Clitheroe was asked, what was this church to which English Catholics adhered? Certainly it was more than a place or a building, yet choice of space *was* important. In a religion of Catholic immanence, physical locations were more than simply places to gather or conduct ritual. By an individual's mere physical presence at such sites, the individual came closer to God. Prayers and rituals performed at such a spot became more effective because of the supplicant's proximity to the divine and the two-way interchange between the material and spiritual worlds that characterized the Catholic worldview.[4]

In the absence of places such as churches, cathedrals, and shrines, English Catholics had to find new locations to worship, maintain their Catholic identity, enjoy a sense of community, and come closer to the holy. In this chapter, I explore English Catholics' creative attempts to find alternative places to meet such religious goals.[5] The chapter begins with an explanation of how an individual or body of believers experienced a physical site in a religious way. Following will be a detailed exploration of particular locations where English Catholics might gather to foster identity and/or community. (Both functions need not be served in every case.) Such locations generally fall into two categories: places where those known to be Catholic gathered as Catholics and places where Catholics gathered while dissimulating. In the latter case, English Catholics congregated together publicly in groups while knowing only among themselves that they were enjoying Catholic worship or fellowship. Both attempts to reclaim space for Catholic ritual, identity, and community allowed Catholics to worship God, engage in Catholic behaviors, and enjoy Catholic fellowship, regardless of whether it was done openly or secretively.

THREE DEGREES OF SEPARATION

Despite Protestant presence in the old churches and cathedrals, some English Catholics remained loyal to the buildings and the lands once belonging to the Catholic Church. Such Catholics refused to give up their traditional spaces, believing that Catholic identity, community, and a connection to the divine were best sustained through worship, ritual, and congregation at these familiar sites. Some attempted to take over Protestant churches and conduct their familiar rituals. Others continued to frequent the ruins of holy shrines and holy wells.[6]

Some English Catholics, however, began to search for new Catholic spaces. These Catholics believed that fidelity to the older, formerly Catholic locations was not as important as finding spots where they could engage in devotions, maintain their identity as Catholics, and enjoy communal fellowship with more regularity. But how would Catholics find such locations?

Catholics converted ordinary space into religious space through their ritualized use of that space. Such ritualized action did not necessarily involve the formal religious rituals of the Catholic Church or the presence of a priest.

Instead it comprised any conscious attempt by English Catholics to set aside space or use space in a manner that would fulfill their religious goals for worship, identity, or community. Ritualized action, therefore, could assume a multiplicity of forms.[7] Richard Broughton, in his 1617 work, *A new manual of Old Christian Catholick Meditations & praiers*, suggested that such action began with a separation:

> If because of misbelievers, we cannot go to the Church, but the wicked occupy the place, thou must flee from that place, because it was profaned by them. For as the priests do sanctify holy things, so the impious defile them. If the true believers cannot assemble together neither at home nor in the Church, let everyone by themselves sing, read, pray, or two or three gathered together. For where there be two or three gathered together in my name, there am I in the middle of them (*Matthew 16*).[8]

In general, such detachment from the "misbelievers" can be classified into three categories. It might be a *physical* separation, with each side occupying a different space. It might be a *ritual* separation, with each side performing different gestures or speaking different words in either a shared or separate space. Furthermore, such division might be *imaginative*, occurring in the minds of believers either in a shared or separate space.

For believers, these three types of separation—physical, ritual, and imaginative—distinguished what was Catholic and sacred from what was Protestant, ordinary, or even defiled. It erected boundaries between that which was identifiably Catholic and that which was not. More than simply a response to persecution, such separation was also an active attempt to reinforce Catholic identity and create new opportunities for community and worship.[9]

Inclusion was based upon adherence to Catholic traditions, rituals, and/or beliefs. For example, a Catholic attending a Protestant Prayer Book service might carry a pair of rosary beads in her pocket and recite Latin prayers throughout the service, thus *ritually* separating herself from the Protestants with whom she shared the church. Moreover, as has been amply demonstrated in previous scholarship, Catholics *physically* separated themselves into communities when they used their homes as religious sites to hear Mass, receive priests, make confession and penance, and congregate with their Catholic friends and neighbors. Even a spot as seemingly defiled as a barn could become a spot at which to practice the faith, for example, as it did for the Benedictine Ambrose Barlowe and the Catholics to whom he ministered in Lancashire in the 1620s and 1630s.[10]

But not all religious spaces need be characterized by the presence of priests, the performance of the sacraments, or the gathering of large numbers of Catholic laypersons. Instead, as the Jesuit Robert Southwell suggested in his

A Shorte Rule of good lyfe, English Catholics could reconceptualize how they thought about the ordinary spaces of their everyday lives in order to create sacred spaces in which to practice the Catholic faith. Southwell agreed with Broughton. He counseled that the goal of a good Catholic was to differentiate himself from the heretics in faith and in action, even if the Catholic was the only one aware of the difference. One way to do this was to set aside Catholic space from Protestant space. To do so required an *imaginative* separation wherein the actual separation of Catholic from Protestant, or sacred from pro-fane, occurred mainly in the minds or imaginations of believers creating the space.

Southwell advised his readers that they could turn one room or all the rooms in their own homes into chapels and churches. Southwell described the sort of action necessary to turn any location to sacred use.

> I must in every room of the house where I dwell, imagine (in some decent place thereof) a throne or chair of estate, and dedicate the same and the whole room to some saint, that whensoever I enter into it I enter as it were into a Chapel or Church, [tha]t is devoted to such a saint. And thus having in every room settled a several Saint, and in mind consecrated the same unto him, and decked it in such furniture as is fit for such an inhabitant, the whole house will be to me in manner a paradise. . . .[11]

Such a transformation need not be effected by redecorating with new furniture, pictures, or icons. In addition to being beyond the financial means of most Catholics, such refurbishing could be dangerous to the householder if Protestant authorities ever made search of the home. Instead, the believer could leave his rooms just as they were. All he needed to do was re-conceptu-alize the purpose and meaning of each room. A family member could look at one corner of a room where a chair sat. Although in the past, he would have looked at the corner with the chair as a place to rest after a hard day's labor, he might now imagine the corner as a small shrine to St. Anne. He could mental-ly construct a niche in the wall holding an image of the saint, richly decorated, perhaps as it had been in his local parish church prior to Protestant reform or perhaps as he would like to see St. Anne arrayed if given the means and oppor-tunity. He might now use his usual chair as a place to sit and contemplate the works of the saint. He might kneel in the corner to pray to the saint to inter-cede for him. The corner still appeared to any observer as the same corner of the room it always had been, but the function of the corner changed to fulfill the Catholic resident's need for religious space.

Southwell's directions allowed enough flexibility so that Catholic indi-viduals or families could create religious space within their own homes that best fit their needs and preferences. For example, although the author at first suggested that the believer dedicate each room to just one saint, he undoubtedly recognized that some families had very few rooms. He therefore allowed each room, particularly if it were the most used room in the house, to be dedicated to two or three saints, as long as each saint occupied a separate space in the mind of each individual. As an additional option, Southwell suggested not consecrating a space to a particular saint but to a religious event, such as one of the mysteries of Christ's life as contained in the rosary.[12] By making such creative adjustments in thought and imagination—by concentrating on the function of space rather than on material form—"the whole house will be to me in manner a paradise," as Southwell described earlier. By following Southwell's instructions, each member of the household could live simultaneously in his own home and in a religious space carefully constructed to meet his needs. English Catholics could find the sacred in the ordinary.

This rededication of ordinary physical space to religious use did not end with the rooms of the house. Southwell also suggested that Catholics redefine the outdoors: orchards, woods, fields, and gardens. Locations in the natural world could become churches and chapels dedicated to saints just as the rooms of the home could. Southwell directed his readers "to make (your) walks as it were short pilgrimages to visit such saints as are patrons of the place (you) go unto."[13] Whereas the ritualized act of dedicating or consecrating such natural locations sanctified the spots for religious use, the further ritualized act of pilgrimage renewed belief in the sacrality of the location and emphasized the element of choice involved in Catholics' creation of these new religious spaces.

Although by its nature, evidence that Southwell's suggestions were being followed is difficult to find, we do have indications that some Catholics were attempting to re-dedicate the ordinary space of their homes or lands for religious use in a manner similar to that which Southwell advised.[14] In the example with which this chapter began—the creeping to the cross in the private home in Lancashire—we see household space being dedicated to and representing a religious event: the crucifixion of Christ. The laypersons participating in this ritual crept across Peter Croncke's floor as they would have crept around the stations of the cross in the parish church. Instead of kneeling before the images of the stations of the cross, they kneeled or crawled around an ordinary basin and a broken cross imagining the events of Christ's imprisonment, death, and burial. They created sacred space out of what they had available.

In a further example, in a letter of 1605 to Sister Elizabeth Shirley, an English nun at Louvain, the Jesuit Henry Garnet reported that he and a group of about twenty-five Catholics commemorated Corpus Christi day and the octave by making a procession around a garden outside a private home.[15] Normally, this procession would have begun in a church and taken the participants on a circuit throughout town as they bore the Eucharist in a reliquary.

Instead, this procession began and ended in a private Catholic home and took the faithful in a small circuit outside upon Catholic-controlled land. There is no mention of the Eucharist being carried about the garden, yet Garnet does describe the celebration as having been conducted with the proper solemnity, even including music.

Furthermore, in approximately 1620, the Catholic laywoman Dorothy Lawson practiced a dedication of the space of her own home to religious use in a manner similar to that which Southwell counseled. Lawson and her extended family prepared to move into a new home at St. Anthony's on the Tyne River. Her biographer records that when the house was completed, she dedicated the whole home to St. Anthony and St. Michael and that each room of the home, save the chapel, "was nominated and publicly known by the name of some particular saint."[16] In both this instance and the two described above in the garden on Corpus Christi day/octave and in Croncke's home, Catholics turned private homes and lands into Catholic space through their re-conceptualization of that space and the ritualized behavior conducted within it.

In addition to the rooms of the home and the land surrounding the home, Southwell suggested one further location that Catholics might re-conceptualize and dedicate to pious use: the bodies of those who lived in the home. For Southwell, the body existed as a physical space which could be manipulated and reinterpreted just as the space of a bedchamber or an orchard might be.[17] Southwell recommended that Catholics allow each person living in the household to represent a saint. Southwell was not asking each person to try to imitate a particular saint. Instead, he intended that everyone by their presence would inspire the memory of a saint,[18] just as the imagined niche to St. Anne would inspire remembrance of and devotion to her.

As will be discussed in more detail in later chapters, the body as a physical location provided a space where Catholics could perform ritualized gestures to bolster their sense of Catholic identity or help join themselves and others into Catholic communities. For example, Catholics could offer their bodies to be executed for their faith in front of crowds containing many English Catholics. Such Catholics might climb the ladder to the gallows with crosses stitched onto their backs, awaiting hanging with their arms outstretched in the form of the cross. Or English Catholics might discipline their bodies, thereby sanctifying them unto God and joining in a penitential tradition perpetuated by a community of many Catholics worldwide, just as Mary Ward did in the early 1600s. When still a laywoman, Mary Ward, founder of the Institute of the Blessed Virgin Mary, lived the life of a well-to-do woman of fashion in London while wearing a hair shirt beneath her gowns of velvet and satin.[19]

The body was also a canvas whereupon Catholics could earn God's favor and strengthen their faith, identity, and sense of Catholic community using a palette of less fatal, less austere gestures. Individuals or groups of Catholics could ritually fast, denying themselves certain foods on certain days. In the Catholic world of immanence, this simple act of fasting could move God to act on behalf of the righteous. As William Stanney professed in his 1617 *A treatise of penance*, "What overcame and overthrew the army of the Assyrians? The fasting of Judith (*Judith* 9). What did deliver the people of Israel from the sentence of death that was given against them? Hestor's fasting. . . ."[20]

Even the act of crossing oneself—using the hand to make the sign of the cross across the front of the body—was a ritual intended to designate the body as a separate site dedicated to God. In 1577, the Earl of Derby caused such a stir by crossing himself in church that the act was recorded for posterity in the Liverpool Town Books.[21] Even the phrase used to record the Earl's deed, that he did "mark himself unto God" reveals that the laity understood the act of separation involved in making such a ritualized gesture. The Benedictines Arthur Crowther and Thomas Vincent discussed the power of crossing oneself in their 1657 work *Jesus, Maria, Joseph . . .* , wherein they persuasively argue:

> . . . who looks upon Christ more faithfully than he who frequently imprints his Cross upon his heart and forehead? . . . (it) exhorts all Christians to remember at how dear a rate they are bought and to glorify and carry God in their bodies. . . . It defends us from all our enemies. . . . It drives away the Devils . . . is a comfort to Christians. . . . Since therefore this sign is of so great power and efficacy . . . Let us . . . be careful to arm ourselves therewith."[22]

English Catholics interpreted the ritual separation of their bodies through the act of marking themselves unto God as an armament of protection, as did the laywoman Anne Line who "made the sign of the cross upon her" as she faced the gallows in 1618.[23] English Catholics' bodies could serve as religious spaces upon and within which believers could bolster their religious identity, participate in religious community, and actively shield themselves from the evil influence of both demons and Protestants (two groups between which some of the more zealous Catholics seldom differentiated).

Converting private homes, gardens, and one's own body to pious use allowed English Catholics to enjoy ritual and fellowship—such as the creeping to the cross or the Corpus Christi procession discussed above—far from the prying eyes of Protestant authorities. Hidden behind closed doors or walls, these locations were sites which, to a large extent, Catholics could be said to control. There were no Protestants present. But were all the places where Catholics created new religious spaces necessarily so secretive? Did the restrictive environment in which Catholics attempted to worship dictate that

Catholics must hide themselves away in order to worship, congregate, and foster their religious identity and sense of community?[24]

PRISONS

Ironically, the prominent locations where Protestants most hoped to quash Catholic spirit and opportunities for worship—the prisons—were the sites where English Catholics gathered most prevalently to maintain their rituals and their sense of identity and community. Although the government's efforts to punish Catholics enjoyed questionable success, many scholars have demonstrated that the state's attempts to capture seminary priests proved quite fruitful and there were many priests in the jails. For example, Patrick McGrath and Joy Rowe's analysis of Godfrey Anstruther's data on seminary priests revealed that 471 seminary priests were active at one time or another during Elizabeth's reign. Of these, approximately 285 were arrested and imprisoned. Prisoners in Elizabeth's, James's, and Charles's reigns frequently spent long years in jail, even if they were sentenced to be executed.[25] As will be discussed below, their jail time was punctuated with periodic examinations by the authorities and by Protestant ministers who hoped to convince the priests to apostatize. Prisoners also appeared in public at their trials and, if it was their fate, at their executions.

This concentration of so many priests in the prisons provided English Catholics with a reasonably accessible and reliable source of spiritual counsel and the sacraments. Additionally, the prisons allowed Catholics to congregate for fellowship and form mutually recognized communities. Free priests entered the prisons to minister to imprisoned Catholics and walked out the gate when they were finished. Free lay Catholics entered the prisons to receive the sacraments from imprisoned priests and left the jail unmolested. Imprisoned priests provided pastoral care to imprisoned lay Catholics. Imprisoned priests also left their jails to minister to free lay Catholics in surrounding areas and subsequently returned to their cells without punishment. The prisons, the supposedly impenetrable bastion of state dominance over the individual, became a focal point for Catholic individuals—lawbreakers—to continue breaking the law.

To understand how this could be so, it is necessary to examine the government's system for imprisoning Catholics. The authorities housed priests in some fifty prisons throughout England.[26] The government did not administer the majority of these jails. Instead, the running of the prisons was contracted to jailers. The government did not pay the jailers; the Catholic prisoners paid the expenses of their imprisonment. The jailers, hoping to recoup their investment of capital and time, received payments from the prisoners for their food and upkeep.[27]

Many jailers resented having to perform an office that promised little remuneration.[28] Understanding the reality of the prison system, one jailer joked that:

> The Keeper of the Clink . . . had priests of several sorts sent unto him. As they came in, he asked them who they were. 'Who are you?' to the first. 'I am a priest of the Church of Rome.' 'You are welcome,' quote the keeper, 'there are those who will take care of you. And who are you?' 'A silenced minister.' 'You are welcome too, I shall fare the better for you. And who are you?' 'A minister of the Church of England.' 'O, God,' quote the keeper, 'I shall get nothing for you. I am sure you may lie and starve and rot before anyone will look after you.'[29]

Because the keepers sought to make a profit, prisoners who had funds could enjoy many privileges while in jail. An open purse opened prison doors.[30] Many prisoners even possessed the keys to their own cells.[31] Those who did not have keys frequently enjoyed unrestricted entrance into and exit from their cells and a freedom to roam the prison grounds and receive visitors.[32] Prisoners sent and received letters. They hid caches of Catholic books. Priests possessed clothing and the accoutrements necessary to perform a Mass, and often kept holy pictures, rosary beads, wax candles, and holy water.[33]

The laxity uncovered at the Winchester Jail in 1599 illustrates both the challenges jailers experienced trying to turn a profit and the benefits imprisoned English Catholics could enjoy in an accommodating relationship with their jailers. Richard Brewning appeared before the Bishop of Winchester and other ecclesiastical commissioners in 1599 to explain conditions at the jail. The former jailer of Winchester, Anthony Uvedale, had died recently, and Brewning inherited the jail. Brewning admitted that upon assuming responsibility for the jail, he discovered that many Catholics supposedly imprisoned there were at large. Seven of the poorer recusants had been released "for charity's sake" to a living by their labor. More likely, motivated by profit and not by sympathy, Uvedale had not wanted to shoulder the expense of their upkeep.

Those Catholics who remained incarcerated at Winchester Jail enjoyed substantial privileges. Andrew Valence, a tanner imprisoned for debt, reported that a priest, Edward Kenyon, regularly dined with the deputy jailer. Valence testified that during Kenyon's stay Catholics typically kept the keys to their own cell doors. They "went out at their pleasure, and let out whom they listed and when they listed; these all kept Kenyon's company, and dined and supped with him, and no man was denied speaking with him if they would." Furthermore, the deputy jailer's wife, accompanied by various Catholic wives of the neighborhood, would visit the priest for walks in the garden.

Imprisoned Catholic laypersons enjoyed freedoms similar to those the priest Kenyon possessed. Thomas Abraham, for example, was a prisoner at Winchester Jail for recusancy for ten or eleven weeks prior to escaping. Valentine Noyse, the underkeeper of the jail, testified that during those weeks, Abraham "often lay at his house in Hyde St. and had a door open out of the jail, by which he went in and out when and where he would until a week before his departure." Another prisoner for recusancy, Robert Joy, testified before the investigating commission that he was supposed to reside in the jail, but Uvedale had given him leave to go back to his house seven years previously, and Joy had not been back to the jail since.[34] Brewning, the new jailer, requested that the commissioners grant him time to seek out and retrieve such absent prisoners.

All of this is not to suggest that conditions for many English Catholics in the jails were not unpleasant or even dangerous at times. Some prisoners were tortured. Some prisoners were placed under close confinement, during which time any type of human contact was restricted.[35] Such confinement could prove particularly dangerous for Catholic women. Anne Bellamy, for example, entered the Gatehouse prison in London in January 1592. After three months of close confinement, she was pregnant, most likely by the notorious jailer Topcliffe, a man in his sixties.[36]

But despite these realities, many opportunities existed for English Catholics to manipulate the prison system for their own purposes. First, priests knew that imprisoned lay Catholics would be concentrated in certain places and in need of succor. Despite the danger of arrest, free priests entered the prisons to provide pastoral care. Some went in to minister to a known individual, as John Brushford, a priest from the west country, did when he entered the Gatehouse in London in the mid-1580s to visit and comfort the recusant Sir John Arundel.[37]

Usually, however, free priests sneaked into prisons hoping to minister to as many incarcerated Catholics as possible. Robert Southwell reported that during a visit to London, he "managed in the meantime to do a good deal of work for our prisoners and was able to help and console those who were not in too strict confinement."[38] In their furtive attempts in the prisons, priests cared for both wealthy and poor Catholics alike, as did the seminary priests William Hart and William Lacy who frequently visited poor Catholics imprisoned for the faith in York.[39]

Conversely, free Catholic laypersons would visit certain jails, knowing that priests and laypersons would be concentrated there, willing and able to provide spiritual comfort and companionship. At a time when priests were not consistently available, this relatively reliable source of spiritual guidance sustained Catholicism among members of all classes, especially the poor. Among those free Catholics of the lower ranks who entered jails to visit priests was Katherin Sleepe, the wife of a serving man, who in 1593 claimed she never knew any seminary priest except a priest named Clifton who was imprisoned at Newgate.[40] A Hampshire husbandman, Richard Dowse, maintained that he had no access to priests, "saving those as are and have been in prison."[41] In 1593, Robert Page, a servant in Lincolnshire, admitted that he "hath known diverse seminary priests, for that before his (own) imprisonment he hath resorted to them in prison."[42] In 1595, William Freeman, a seminary priest whose territory included Warwickshire and Worcestershire, mentioned a Catholic friend's visit to him in prison, during which he recalled that they "joked merrily about the bolts on his legs."[43]

Many free lay Catholics took advantage of prison laxity to congregate together in large numbers to enjoy both the services of a priest and the fellowship of other believers. In 1602, for example, the Chief Justice's men and a group of pursuivants—hunters of priests and lay Catholics—raided the Clink in London. With drawn swords, they rushed into a room and found an altar prepared for Mass. Three priests stood before the altar ready to perform the sacrament. Nearly forty laypersons, mostly women and poor people from the city, stood ready to receive.[44]

In a world in which one's prison accommodations were only as good as one's ability to pay the jailor, lay visitors contributed to the upkeep of the incarcerated priests while enjoying many of the religious benefits of a community of believers. In 1596, Edward Hall, a prisoner at the Gatehouse, reported that while he was imprisoned at Wisbech Castle, a part of the see of the bishop of Ely, he witnessed many free Catholics visiting and maintaining incarcerated priests. A Mr. Newton, Hall testified, visited the priests of Wisbech two or three times yearly. Newton was, "a great friend of the whole company . . . bring[ing] them a greater part of their maintenance . . . [and] making great cheer, having plenty of wine" with the detained priests.[45] In such an environment, lay Catholics such as Newton could enjoy the company of the priests and other Catholics and build an informal Catholic community. They would talk and perhaps trade books with one another. Laypersons would even send their children into the prisons to be educated by the priests. Protestant authorities referred to Wisbech Castle as a "seminary to corrupt youth" after discovering that the sons of Catholic gentlemen entered Wisbech under the guise of serving the priests.[46]

In addition to the spiritual commerce between imprisoned and free members of the Catholic community, imprisoned priests ministered to the imprisoned laity, both Catholic and Protestant. David Ringsted, a clothworker from Winchester, claimed that he never knew any seminary priests or Jesuits "but such as have been prisoned with him."[47] Robert Jackson, a merchant residing in Newcastle-upon-Tyne, when asked what priests he knew, answered that "he hath not had conference with any but such as were prisoners with him in the Marshalsea—and that during the time of his imprisonment there."[48] The Devonshire yeoman John Hewes insisted that "he hath not been acquainted with any Jesuits nor with any seminary priests but in the prison where they were likewise prisoners. . . ."[49]

Priests imprisoned for long periods of time in the same prison could develop an impressive list of prison parishioners from a wide range of social backgrounds. A priest known as Corbet resided in a cell at Newgate in London in the 1590s. Among the other Newgate prisoners who admitted to consorting with Corbet were Christopher Roche, an Irish scholar from Washford; Thomas Tindall, a Sussex-county gentleman; John Collins, a mercer from Winchester; William Thornbury, a servant from Staffordshire; Christien Ringsted, the wife of a Winchester clothworker; and Richard Webster, a Yorkshire schoolmaster.[50]

Catholic priests ministered to Protestant prisoners as well as to those who were already Catholic. Jailers placed two priests, Anthony Middleton and Edward Jones, amidst the throng of common thieves in the Clink in London, and the priests acted as disciples for their faith, ministering to Catholics and attempting to convert all who were not.[51] The Jesuit William Weston described a similar interaction with Protestants at Wisbech Castle:

> At one of these Assizes (at the Isle of Ely) two men and a woman were brought to trial for some offense or other and condemned to death. . . . Some of us, taking the opportunity to meet the criminals, were able, in the short time available, to persuade them to become Catholic and expiate their sins by confession. . . . It was more difficult, however, to get access to the woman. But here the two men were of great assistance. Their cell adjoined hers and, through a grating in the dividing wall, they were able to make her understand all. . . . Time was very short, but with God's help, a means [for the woman to make confession and receive absolution] was devised. All cooperated and great ingenuity was shown, and she achieved her desire.[52]

Weston related this story to explain how he and his allies saved three souls from dying outside the Catholic faith, thus saving them from hell. Just as interesting, however, are the obstacles that imprisoned priests and laypersons overcame by cooperating with one another.

Finally, imprisoned priests could even leave their prisons to minister to free Catholics in the areas surrounding the jails. For example, the priest Thomas Bluet received a prison furlough for 10 days in 1602. He left the castle at Framingham, his place of imprisonment, and traveled to London to visit and minister to the Catholic population. As Bluet explained, "In England, a priest, even in danger of his life [scheduled for execution] is often released on his word. . . ."[53]

The Protestant authorities knew of this practice but were seemingly ineffective at halting it. In 1617, for example, a Protestant spy, Arthur Saul, gained the confidence of the Catholic population in the Clink. He reported to his superiors, Secretary Winwood and the Archbishop of Canterbury, not that Catholic prisoners crept away secretly from the prison, but that they were "allowed to go abroad" by the prison authorities.[54] As always, a well-placed bribe opened many doors, including the one to the prison itself. Even though the government branded priests as criminals, most Englishmen and women so trusted the authority and integrity of Catholic priests that when those priests promised to return to their cells if allowed outside the prison, the keepers trusted them to keep their word (as they pocketed their money).

The government fumed over the liberties taken by Catholics in prisons yet could do little to correct the situation, especially in prisons located far from London. Protestant authorities understood the challenges involved in incarcerating Catholics within such a potentially corruptible system,[55] and the Privy Council and other governing bodies issued strict instructions to the keepers explaining how to restrict and monitor prisoners' activities. The council wanted to ensure that Catholics were isolated from their fellow prisoners and outsiders. The guidelines especially cautioned jailers not to allow prisoners to converse with strangers, except in the presence of the keeper or other authorized personnel.[56] Protestants also sent spies into jails to monitor Catholic activities, as mentioned previously.[57]

Such efforts to restrict Catholic activities met with little success. For example, Wisbech Castle housed many seminary and Jesuit priests during the Spanish threat and afterwards. The keeper at Wisbech, Thomas Gray, angered the Privy Council when he relaxed discipline and allowed a constant stream of visitors in to see the priests. Weston, imprisoned at Wisbech, reported that:

> As soon as it became known to Catholics that we had been given freedom to see and speak with people outside, practically no day passed without some visitors. There was an almost continuous stream of them—heretics as well as Catholics—to get our advice or dispute with us. . . . The throng of Catholics from every condition of life was so unending that it gravely alarmed the Queen and her Councilors. They duly upbraided the keeper for allowing it. However, the place was a long distance from the capital, the events did not take place under their eyes, and once a way had been broken through the barrier, it could be blocked by the keeper only with greater trouble. They came from every part of the kingdom, some as to a holy place, undertaking a kind of pilgrimage, others, as if they were cele-

brating a solemn feast, came for Communion, Mass, and the sacraments so
that the prison was scarcely if ever empty.[58]

Although Weston's account perhaps exaggerates the omnipresence of Catholic
visitors, the Acts of the Privy Council verify the government's dismay with the
lax security at Wisbech. They issued orders for the arrest of Catholics known
to be regular visitors at Wisbech, and they called the keeper, Gray, to task
about the flow of visitors, as well as for other freedoms taken by the Catholic
prisoners.[59] Yet as Weston reports, Wisbech was located far from the prying
eyes of government officials. Gray was trying to make a return on his capital
investment, and therefore, visitations continued unabated. Wisbech remained
a "college of priests" for decades to come.[60]

But what exactly was occurring during all of these comings and goings
within the prisons? How were these prisons becoming *religious* spaces for the
Catholics? First, as Richard Broughton and Robert Southwell suggested, a
process of separation occurred. Catholic priests and laypersons met with each
other one on one or in groups in an environment physically separated from the
majority of the Protestant population. Ironically, Protestant efforts to cordon
off the Catholics in jails assisted Catholic attempts to separate themselves from
the Protestants so that they could perform Catholic rituals, maintain their identity as Catholics, and join in Catholic communities. Even when not joined in
ritualized worship, so many Catholics meeting together openly as Catholics
within the prison walls defined the character of the space they inhabited. This
was especially important for poorer Catholics who had fewer opportunities to
act openly as Catholics. For these believers, the prisons may have offered
some of their only chances to worship and congregate openly with their co-
religionists.

Catholic sacraments conducted within prison walls also transformed
the ordinary spaces of the jail cells into Catholic spaces. Priests could perform
many of the sacraments within the prison walls. Priests celebrated the sacrament of the altar as often as possible.[61] Although prison security often
remained somewhat lax, Catholic prisoners still took precautions. They scattered Massing apparel, books, chalices, and other items used to perform the
Mass throughout the prison to minimize the chances of their discovery.
Weston illustrated the subterfuge that was often necessary to perform the ritual properly:

> . . . sometimes also we were able to fix a time and place for Mass [within
> the prison]. Then secretly in the middle of the night we would lower a rope
> to the room below . . . and draw up the sacred vestments. Early in the
> morning, when Mass was over . . . we would let the rope down again in the
> same way.[62]

To celebrate Mass at some prisons, such covert means were unnecessary. In Gloucester Jail, jailers allowed the priest Pibush a special space in which to say Mass. Pibush enjoyed a "sort of a separate cell" within the common jail. When Catholics came by to visit, Pibush would frequently say Mass within this chamber.[63] Sometimes, jailers who permitted Mass to be said inside their prisons charged a fee to outsiders who wished to attend.[64]

Priests administered other sacraments within the prisons as well. Priests heard confessions and absolved Catholics of their sins inside the prisons.[65] For example, William Baldwin, a priest arrested at sea and imprisoned, described how he found a Catholic youth in prison who had been tortured and was upset because he had confessed to lies under the torture. Baldwin waited until the Protestant prisoners fell asleep, then he listened to the youth's confession and absolved him, thus comforting the young sufferer.[66] Priests might join two Catholics in marriage as well. As the number of Marian priests declined, Catholic couples turned more frequently to the seminarians and Jesuits, many of whom were imprisoned, to perform the marital rites.[67]

Many other types of non-sacramental rituals were possible within the jails, thus further transforming ostensibly Protestant-controlled space into Catholic religious space. Priests and laypersons could engage in self-mortification in the privacy of their cells to comfort and cleanse their souls.[68] Catholics also held banquets, observed feast days, and organized informal clerical councils within jail cells.[69] Catholic priests might even undertake St. Ignatius Loyola's *Spiritual Exercises* and become Jesuits while incarcerated.[70]

Prisons also served as religious space in which to educate, catechize, and convert souls. As mentioned in chapter 1, prisons served as valuable distribution points for Catholic pastoral and educational literature.[71] Such literature could be taken home and used by visiting Catholics. Often, however, education and conversion occurred within the jails themselves. As mentioned above, Catholic priests educated and sometimes converted their fellow Protestant prisoners. Other Protestants within the penal system were also susceptible to the persuasive efforts of these priests. Those most vulnerable were the Protestant servants of the prisoners. Ordinarily, Catholic priests and the better-off recusants were allowed one or two servants while in prison. Servants tended to be poor boys between the ages of thirteen and eighteen who lived in the towns surrounding the prisons. Priests took this opportunity to instruct these boys in the tenets of Catholicism. Some servants actually converted from Protestantism and even traveled to the continent to become seminary priests themselves. Thomas Dowlton, who had been a servant to priests incarcerated at Wisbech Castle, was one such boy. He returned to England as a priest and was captured in 1595. The mayor of Rye and church officials tried to persuade him to return to his original Protestantism. Dowlton refused, saying, "But although I am but a poor lad I am not so far to obey you [to go to Protestant services], having a soul to save as well as any other Catholic."[72]

Catholic priests also converted their Protestant jailers and their families. Many such families lived on prison grounds and were in frequent contact with many Catholic prisoners who enjoyed substantial freedom to roam about prison property. The Wisbech priests, for example, converted their warder's daughter.[73] In a similar incident years later, Richard Cooper, a priest incarcerated in Newgate in 1615, "grew too familiar with the wife of Haughton, the keeper, whom he perverted in religion." After Cooper escaped from Newgate with two or three other priests, Protestant authorities suspected that Haughton's wife aided their departure, possibly procuring the key to the prison door for them.[74]

In sum, Catholics transformed portions of these jails into Catholic spaces where Catholics could worship, reinforce their sense of Catholic identity, and create new forms of Catholic community and fellowship. Such Catholics provided themselves with new spaces in which to practice their religion by separating themselves physically and ritually from the Protestants. The supposedly impenetrable stone walls of the English prisons became gateways through which Catholics passed *in both directions*, entering and exiting the jails. Prisons served as gathering points for many Catholics. Jails provided many lay Catholics with their best opportunities to locate priests, receive the sacraments, and enjoy companionship. Previous scholars have even suggested that priests may have preferred prison life to life on the run.[75] Rather than viewing incarceration solely as a restriction upon their religion, English Catholics made the best of a bad situation. They used opportunities provided by their changed circumstances to pursue their faith.

EXAMINATIONS, TRIALS, AND EXECUTIONS

Prisons were but one site open to Catholics searching for locations where they might create or sustain a sense of identity and community. Opportunities for ritualized action to build such identity and community were also available at Catholic examinations, trials, and executions. English Catholics transformed the churches, courtrooms, and gallows where such events were held into religious sites by separating themselves from the Protestants. Such separation could be overt, as in Catholics physically separating themselves into one corner of the room. More likely, however, the separation would be imaginative. It was dangerous to single oneself out publicly as a Catholic, especially with the authorities so near. Instead, although their appearance and actions did not necessarily distinguish them as Catholics, individuals visited these places *as Catholics*, knowing themselves to be different from the Protestants who stood nearby. In their minds, these Catholics separated themselves from their heretical neighbors and experienced the examinations, trials, and executions differently than did the Protestant witnesses. Public, Protestant-controlled space was thus reconstructed into Catholic religious space and created Catholic community for those Catholics in attendance.[76]

For example, Protestant ministers frequently examined imprisoned priests and tried to convince them to apostatize, or renounce the Catholic faith. An ordained Catholic priest who renounced his religion in favor of Protestantism was a valuable weapon in the propaganda war for the public's allegiance.[77] Protestant churchmen expended great effort in debates to convince Catholic priests of the errors of their ways. Sometimes these conferences would be held in private. At other times, the debates would be held in front of an open audience, with both Protestants and Catholics in attendance.[78]

The results were not always what the Protestant examiners planned. Although the Protestants hoped that their superior arguments would sway the Catholics in the audience, a Catholic could just as easily have his faith reinforced when a Catholic priest's arguments countered a Protestant priest's contentions effectively.[79] The efforts of the English colleges on the continent to instruct priests in rhetoric often paid off in this way.[80]

The courtrooms that hosted the trials of imprisoned priests and lay Catholics provided another venue for Catholics to separate themselves from their Protestant neighbors and appropriate space to bolster Catholic identity and community. Priests and laypersons often argued their cases persuasively in front of the bench, as Robert Southwell did during his trial that attracted a crowd of onlookers from both religions.[81] In front of the courtroom, English Catholics such as Southwell justified their religion, tainted the government with charges of religious persecution, and strengthened the resolve of the Catholics in attendance. People often pressed forward so that they could hear what the accused had to say and perhaps be spoken to in return.[82] At other times, moving forward was unnecessary, as during the trial of the laywoman Anne Line in 1601. When asked to declare herself guilty or not guilty of the charge of harboring priests, Line, rather than offer a simple plea, shouted out, "My Lords, nothing grieves me more but that I could not receive a thousand more." This, despite the fact that Line was so weak she had to be carried into the courtroom on a chair.[83]

Trials offered Catholics the opportunity to speak with priests as they passed nearby. Some Catholics offered encouragement to the priests.[84] Others asked priests for their blessings.[85] Richard Thirkill (or Thirkeld), a Durham priest who frequently worked near York, served Catholics in this way during his trial in 1583. For example, four Catholics passed him on their way to the bar as Thirkill waited for his turn. The Catholics asked Thirkill for his blessing and begged his prayers. Thirkill complied. When Thirkill himself was at the bar, an old woman who had also been summoned to court that day approached him. She asked for his blessing in open court, which he gave her.

Thirkill also used his trial as a forum to strengthen the resolve of his co-religionists. After his own hearing, while Thirkill remained in court, he watched a lay Catholic couple approach the bar. The authorities presented the twosome on charges of recusancy, and the couple's goods were about to be confiscated. Their kinsmen pleaded with them to conform. Thirkill chimed in and asked the couple what mere goods were compared with the fate of their souls. The judges commanded Thirkill to be silent, but Thirkill responded that it was a great joy "to see the courage and constancy of these Catholics in maintaining so good a cause, and that it was his duty to exhort and encourage them upon these occasions."[86] Not surprisingly, the authorities executed Thirkill soon afterwards. After the execution, so that Catholics might not gather any of Thirkill's blood for use in relics, the authorities ordered a fire to be made from straw on the place where the executioner disemboweled the priest.[87]

The places of executions provided another opportunity for Catholics to convert ordinary space to Catholic use. The state executed 112 priests, both seminary priests and Jesuits, in the first twenty years following the beginning of the English mission.[88] In the seventeenth century, executions decreased as the government realized it was creating martyrs around whose example and memory many Catholics rallied.[89] Despite a decrease in the total number of deaths, executions did continue in the seventeenth century. Seventy priests died for their religion between 1601 and 1680. The state executed the majority of these between 1601 and 1615, 1641 and 1652, and 1678 and 1680, times of domestic political upheaval.[90]

By hosting the martyrdoms of English Catholics, execution sites existed as potent Catholic spaces. On one hand, these sites might appear to be Protestant-controlled locations. Protestants forcibly drew unwilling Catholics through the streets and took their lives publicly, violently, and painfully upon the scaffold. On the other hand, Catholics could claim the execution sites as their own, accepting and even seeking out martyrdom and maximizing their opportunities to turn the events into positive expressions of piety. In his 1611–1612 travel diary, Sir Charles Somerset explained how Catholics viewed martyrdom and how martyrdom consecrated ordinary spaces into sacred ones. When in Rome, Somerset contended that what made Rome holy was the blood of martyrs. So many had been put to death:

> only for the confession of the name of Christ and profession of Christian religion; insomuch as one can hardly tread upon any one foot of ground there, but that it is holy; in respect it hath been embrued with the blood and entombed with the bodies of so many blessed martyrs of the primitive church that suffered there, not only to the wonder of us that live after

them and read their lives and martyrdoms, but also for the edification of
the whole Christian world.[91]

The deaths of the martyrs helped consecrate English execution sites in a similar manner. In the minds of English Catholics, English martyrs died as the
primitive martyrs of Rome did: for confessing the one true faith. In doing so,
their blood consecrated the ground and inspired those who watched or learned
about the events afterwards.[92]

Catholics—both those witnessing executions and those being executed—used the places of executions as Catholic spaces in a variety of ways.
Whereas some might expect the executions to have had a demoralizing effect
on English Catholic witnesses, many Catholics who attended the executions
used their experiences of group suffering to enhance their sense of identity and
community and to express their unity and strength. At the execution of the
priest George Haydock in 1584, for example, Haydock asked the Catholics
present to pray with him before he died. Someone in the crowd reportedly
shouted, "There are no Catholics here!," after which another voice in the
crowd retorted, "We are all Catholics!"[93]

Coordinated refusal to attend or conduct an execution could also imply
Catholic control over the execution site. In 1586, when the authorities in
Gloucester needed an executioner to carry out the death sentence upon the
seminary priest John Sands,[94] no one wanted the job. Furthermore, no one in
the town would rent their tools and knives to be used in the job. Even if the
town could not save the priest, they could refuse to support the death sentence. By cooperating to deny the Protestant authorities the means to carry out
the execution, the residents of Gloucester resisted Protestant attempts to force
them into religious conformity. When at last the authorities persuaded and
paid a very poor man to carry out the execution, the man blacked and disfig-
ured his face so his neighbors would not recognize him when he performed the
deed.[95]

Catholic attempts to disrupt ongoing executions could also turn an execution site into Catholic space to promote identity and unity. Onlookers
observed such an effort at Catholic solidarity in 1612 when authorities brought
a priest named either Latham or Molyneux to Tyburn in London to be executed. Isaac Wake, John Chamberlain, and Dudley Carleton, all Protestants, later
corresponded with one another about the disruptions caused by the Catholics
present at the execution. Wake complained that so many Catholics attended
that they spoke of attempting to rescue the priest from the gallows. Although
Catholics never carried out their threat, they were able to build a sense of unity
in the face of yet another martyrdom by recognizing their potential strength in
numbers. Wake revealed his frustration over Catholic efforts at solidarity and

community when he pointed out to Carleton that the Privy Council had recently held meetings to suppress assemblies of Catholics "who speak too boldly" as the Catholics had done at Tyburn. Chamberlain agreed that such goings on at executions created much mischief.[96]

As many Catholics flocked to these execution sites, some interpreted their journeys through the streets and their presence at the gallows as acts of piety. As the hurdles drew the condemned Catholic prisoners through the streets toward the gallows, each avenue could become a *via sacra* along which the faithful and the scornful would gather, mimicking the crowds that gathered to witness Christ carrying the cross to Golgotha.[97] Such events provided Catholics with the physical and psychological space they needed to experience the executions as opportunities to witness to their faith. The execution of the priest John Boste in York in 1594 illustrates how Catholics might interpret martyrdom as a positive aid to their own devotion. Father John Cecil, present at Boste's death, reported that approximately 300 women followed the condemned priest through the streets toward the execution site. When asked why they trailed Boste to the gallows, the women reportedly answered, "To accompany that gentleman, that servant of God, to his death as the Maries did Christ."[98] The "Maries" refer to Mary, Jesus's mother, and Mary Magdalene. These two disciples remained with Christ throughout his death and cared for his body following its removal from the cross.

Through their ritualized action, these women of York temporarily claimed the streets and the gallows as their own religious space. To do so, they walked through it, they stood in it, and they watched while in it. As they walked and stood and watched, they imaginatively separated themselves from the rest of the crowd by interpreting their actions as devotional gestures through which they served Christ as they simultaneously served Christ's representative on earth: the priest. These women ritualized their own actions to find more than a passive role for themselves in the execution. They could be more than demoralized Catholic women helplessly witnessing yet another of their blessed priests go to his death. They could be disciples. They could be Mary or Mary Magdalene, revered by their church and by God for their efforts on Christ's behalf. Their attendance at Boste's death could be holy, sanctified, and meaningful—to themselves, to God, and to the rest of the crowd at the execution.[99]

Many other Catholics claimed the execution sites as religious spaces by speaking to and being blessed by future martyrs. Thomas Alfield, a seminary priest from Douai, and Dolman, a law student studying at Gray's Inn in London, witnessed the execution of Edmund Campion and two other priests in 1582.[100] They took notes, recording the crowd's interactions with the priests:

They were drawn from the Tower to Tyburn there to be martyred for the Catholic faith and religion. Father Campion was alone on one hurdle and the other two (priests) on another, all molested by ministers and others calling upon them by the way for their subversion, and by some others also, as opportunity served, comforted, and Father Campion especially consulted by some in cases of conscience and religion, the mire wherewith he was all spattered most courteously wiped off his face.[101]

Catholics in the crowd also called upon Robert Southwell before his execution in London in 1595. On the way to the gallows, Southwell's procession halted before descending a steep hill in front of the church of St. Sepulchre. The way was rough with rocks and pits, and a fast-flowing brook fed by recent rains rushed at the bottom of the hill. As the group waited, plotting the best course through the stones and brisk waters, a young woman, possibly named Margaret Gage, slipped through the crowd and knelt beside Southwell to receive a last blessing.[102]

Priests who as yet had not been captured by the government frequented executions just as the laity did. The reason for their presence, however, was quite different. The priests who were about to be martyred relied upon priests in the crowd to give them absolution before the hangman's noose tightened. Free priests, disguising themselves, worked their way through the crowds to be near the scaffold to perform this service.[103]

Catholics in the crowd were not the only Catholics present at the executions who grasped at opportunities to transform the scaffold into Catholic space. Those about to be executed often used the gallows as a pulpit, one of the most potent religious spaces. The condemned individual often left observers with a sermon, a blessing, or statement of belief, as the Franciscan Thomas Bullaker did in 1642 when he preached a sermon at the foot of the gallows prior to his hanging.[104]

Condemned clerics and laypersons consoled themselves with words as they were drawn to ugly deaths. In 1615, the Protestant authorities spoke with some degree of respect for a priest imprisoned at Newgate named Ainsworth. Ainsworth, they said, "is a marvelous active priest full of bitterness and sauciness," who was trying to convert all the condemned prisoners at Newgate to Catholicism prior to their executions. After a successful conversion, Ainsworth reportedly instructed the condemned person that "going from the prison and at the Gallows they should with a loud voice cry out, 'All Catholics pray for us.'"[105] By asking for prayers from the Catholics in the crowd, the condemned individuals comforted themselves. The prayers of others would assist the salvation of their souls. Catholics believed that prayers said on behalf of the soul of the deceased eased the soul's torment in Purgatory and helped it ascend to heaven.

Those who spoke at the scaffold also attempted to unite the crowd with a lasting message about the strength of the Catholic faith in the midst of adversity.[106] By asking all Catholics present for their prayers, these condemned Catholics joined the Catholics in attendance into a community of believers both during the time of the execution and afterwards as such Catholics continued to pray for the souls of the new martyrs. Catholics in the crowd would know they were not alone in their faith even if they could not identify exactly which other individuals in the crowd were their co-religionists. And by praying for the new martyrs at the moment of martyrdom, Catholics also joined themselves to the martyrdom itself, hoping to gain the martyr's powerful intercession before God.

Some Catholics who attempted to speak upon the scaffold were silenced by the authorities. Priests and laymen alike, however, persisted in their efforts to communicate, and they frequently used their last moments to make nonverbal statements about their faith. A small group of lay Catholics slated to die wanted the crowd to know they were Catholics and intended to die in the faith. They wore their shrouds to their execution, placing the garments around their necks and bringing them down in "transverse folds over the breasts in the form of a cross. To make the gospel of the cross more apparent still they had stitched a black strip of cloth down the full length of their burial robes."[107] In a similar nonverbal gesture, the priest Anthony Briant carried a cross of his own making at his execution.[108] Both Catholics and Protestants in the crowd could hardly fail to notice the strength of faith of those about to die and to consider the religious implications of such gestures. The execution became a site of spiritual reflection and strengthening, both for the condemned individual and the observer.

Witnessing executions deeply affected some observers, causing them to strengthen or change their beliefs or actions. In 1582, Henry Walpole, a young law student at Gray's Inn, witnessed the execution, discussed above, of Edmund Campion and the two other priests at Tyburn. Walpole would have watched as Campion countered the arguments of the Protestant ministers who tried one last time to convince Campion of the error of his ways. Walpole would have observed Campion conversing with and blessing certain Catholics in the crowd as his hurdle drew nearer to the gallows. As the executioner dismembered Campion's body, Walpole stood close enough to be spattered with the blood of the new martyr. After returning home, Walpole decided that the day's events were a sign. He left Gray's Inn and traveled to the English College at Rheims to study for the priesthood. He later became a Jesuit and returned to England on mission. He was captured, tortured, and martyred in York in April 1595.[109]

Similarly, Dorothy Arundel changed the course of her life because of the execution of Father John Cornelius in 1594. Cornelius, Arundel's family priest, was a very strict Counter-Reformation Catholic cleric who fervently adhered to Rome's instructions not to have any contact with England's heretics. He even refused to say grace if a Protestant were present at table. Evincing his desire for martyrdom, Cornelius once wrote in a book of his, "Would that I might be despoiled of this my flesh, whether by the rope, the cross, or the torture." Condemned for high treason in Dorchester, Cornelius refused an offer to ransom him out of prison, preferring to await his impending death.

Dorothy Arundel visited Cornelius in prison in the days prior to his execution. During this time, Cornelius promised Arundel that if she would join the Bridgettine order in Lisbon, he would present her vow to St. Bridget. He was already looking past his physical martyrdom to his future role as intercessor. Arundel attended Cornelius's execution. Watching the priest standing upon the gallows, the gallows suddenly appeared to Arundel as if surrounded by rays of light. Cornelius's death was surely blessed by God, Arundel opined. Arundel left soon afterwards for a convent in Brussels. Cornelius's spirit appeared to her in the convent to direct her actions. Even in death, Cornelius remained her priest. Arundel later wrote down Cornelius's acts.[110]

English martyrdoms were highly publicized,[111] and English Catholics placed high religious value on them, as indicated by the confession of Marwood, a servant to Anthony Babington, in 1586 following the Babington Plot. When asked "what had become of Zwinglius, Jerome of Prague, Luther, and Calvin [the Protestant reformers], [Marwood] answered with a full voice that they were all damned; and as to Campion, Sherwyn, Throgmorton, and others [all Catholic martyrs], answered ragingly and repiningly that they were saints in heaven."[112] Martyred saints in heaven possessed potent power as Richard Verstegan confirmed in his 1615 translation of the prayer *Rex gloriose martyrum* for inclusion in an English prayer book:

They, for thy sake, with stout contempt have borne
The causeless rage of men and torments fierce
And cruel hooks which have their bodies torn
But had no power their souls to pierce . . .

Thou conquering in thy martyrs pains
Confessors sav'st in threatening times
So vanquish sin, which in us reigns
Forgiving our ungrateful crimes.[113]

English martyrs endured extreme torment and death for the sake of other English Catholics. And after death, such martyrs might intercede for English Catholic souls, protecting them from threats, saving them from sin, and garnering forgiveness before the throne of God.

Overall, although the examinations, trials, and executions were intended to discourage Catholics and decrease the number of practicing priests, the events likely had the opposite effect. Like the prisons, each of these locations provided an additional site at which Catholics could nurture their piety and buttress their Catholic identity and union. Catholic priests and laypersons consoled onlookers with the steadfastness of their faith during examinations and trials. Accused priests offered prayers and blessings to onlookers, and laypersons bore witness to their faith. Free laypersons attended trials to seek out the advice and company of these Catholics. Even if the Catholics on trial eventually died for their faith, they became heroes of the Catholic cause, motivating other Catholics to continue in their faith. Some Catholics even altered the courses of their lives to more fervently witness to the faith, as did Henry Walpole and Dorothy Arundel. As the northern priest John Boste exclaimed before his death, "My head and quarters will preach every day on your gates and walls the truth of the Catholic faith."[114]

After 1559, English Catholics found themselves without churches, cathedrals, and shrines—the locations at which they had practiced their religion for centuries. Despite their guilt, dismay, and remorse over the loss of such sites, Catholics began to search for new places to gather for worship, ritual, and community. Some looked no further than their own bodies. Some, such as Dorothy Lawson and Peter Croncke of Lancashire, looked no further than their own homes. Some refused to accept the Protestant "takeover" of what had traditionally been Catholic buildings and lands, while some like Robert Southwell used the woods, fields, and orchards as their sacred spaces. But still others searched for new religious spaces in the most unexpected places, even the places which at first glance appeared controlled by Protestants. Locations such as prisons, trials, examinations, and executions could become spaces where Catholics might gather openly or covertly to attend a Mass, receive a blessing, hear the advice of a priest, collect a martyr's relic, or recreate a familiar Catholic world of unity.

All space possessed the potential to be used by English Catholics for religious purposes: for worship and ritual, for maintaining Catholic identity, and nurturing a sense of Catholic community. To tap into this potential, all Catholics need do was engage in some type of ritualized action which physically, ritually, or imaginatively separated the space from ordinary use and dedicated it to attaining one of these purposes. This activity could be as simple as the Earl of Derby's gesture of crossing himself to mark his body unto God. It could require the mental action of consecrating a certain corner of the room as a shrine to a saint. Or it might be a Catholic's attendance at the examination, trial, or execution of a priest. One's mere presence at a site was sufficient to transform the space into religiously potent space as long as the Catholic consciously separated himself from the surrounding Protestants to experience and interpret the space and the event through Catholic eyes. Chapters 5, 6, and 7— the case studies of London, Cornwall, and the northern shires—provide ample examples of English Catholics using space in just such ways.

CHAPTER 3

Using What's at Hand
English Catholic Reinterpretations of the Rosary[1]

S OME TIME BEFORE HIS EXECUTION IN 1577, THE CORNISH PRIEST AND martyr, Cuthbert Mayne, received a gift of a homemade rosary as a "thank offering" from a Cornish Catholic whom he had reconciled to the Roman Church. The craftsman had collected brightly colored stones which he strung together and secured with small hoops of metal. Protestant authorities discovered this handcrafted rosary upon Mayne when they arrested him.[2] In a sharp contrast of styles, the Langdale Rosary, belonging to Lord William Howard of Naworth in the early seventeenth century, was crafted of gold. The artist engraved both sides of each bead either with an image of Christ or of a saint, identifying each saint with an inscription around the bead's edge.[3] Whether a simple handicraft or an ornate work of art, a rosary can assume many forms. Moreover, a rosary is both a material object and a set of prayers.[4] Just as the beads are worked by the hands of the supplicant or the vision of the craftsman, so too may the prayers of the rosary be manipulated to meet the needs of the user.

In this chapter, I argue that material objects such as the rosary played a key role in English Catholics' quest for salvation given the frequent absence of traditional avenues to grace. As discussed in chapter 1, many English Catholics feared for their souls as the number of Catholic priests and access to the sacraments gradually declined or became increasingly irregular. Yet in the midst of this changing religious environment, the rosary appears to have maintained, if not increased, its popularity among English Catholics. This occurred despite prohibitions against possessing the beads.

A partial explanation lies in the physical and spiritual manipulability of the rosary. Rosaries are small, portable, and easily concealed. It is relatively easy to worship with a rosary, either praying at home or praying silently in public with the beads concealed in a pocket or the folds of a skirt. Although initially consecrated by a priest, rosaries do not rely on the immediate presence of a priest for their effectiveness. Once ritually blessed, the laity can carry away rosaries, distribute them freely, and use them independently or in groups. The Roman Church does not attach a prescribed set of prayers to the rosary, so worshippers can adapt the prayers to their own needs each time they pray the beads. In other words, in the absence of an institutional church setting or priests, an English Catholic could use what was at hand—a rosary—as a fairly reliable, accessible, and flexible medium through which to worship according to the traditions of the Roman faith.

But the significance of the rosary as a religious tool goes beyond its convenience. Material objects such as rosaries had long played an integral role in Catholic religious culture. Catholics in Protestant England lived in a world where many traditional tools used to procure salvation were officially prohibited. Under such circumstances, it is not surprising that believers invested the objects and symbols that remained with new meaning and ritual power. Examining the evolving uses of objects such as the rosary opens a window through which to view new intersections between piety and material culture within English Catholicism in particular and within religion more generally. Changes that English Catholic clerics and laity negotiated relating to the rituals, symbolism, and effectiveness associated with rosary worship offer clues as to how lay needs drive religious practice and experience to evolve in new directions to adapt to changing social and political environments. The result is not necessarily unorthodox but reflects the manner in which religious practice is not simply dictated to believers but shaped jointly by laity and clergy to meet the needs of believers.

In addressing such issues, this chapter first will demonstrate how popular the rosary continued to be with English Catholics in the late sixteenth and early seventeenth centuries despite penal laws banning possession of such items. Next, contemporary instructions for and encouragement of rosary use written by English Catholics will be examined for evidence of any changing interpretations of the rosary. Finally, to emphasize the distinctive nature of the English innovations, this type of rosary use will be compared with pre-reform English and post-Tridentine continental Catholic beliefs and practices in the late sixteenth and early seventeenth centuries.

Overall, English Catholic authors, most of them priests, were offering English Catholics a menu of options, much as they had done in encouraging English Catholics to find new religious spaces. Broadly interpreted, these options appear to address English Catholics' main priority: the quest for salvation. Authors exhorted English Catholics to pray their rosaries independently or in groups—most often through the Society of the Rosary. Authors advertised that by participating in such group efforts, believers could worship together, garnering saving grace in a variety of ways while simultaneously rebuilding communal ties with other Catholics within England and around the world. Additionally, to help attain salvation, believers were to use their rosaries to appeal to a reinterpreted, strong, warrior-like Virgin Mary who fought for believers' souls. In sum, English Catholic authors promoted the rosary to gain back much of what had been lost by those with Catholic loyalties after English reforms: worship assisted by palpable, material objects (the beads); access to a powerful intercessor in the figure of Mary (in the absence of priests, images, and relics); soteriological benefits of the sacraments (which priests were not always readily available to perform); the solace of working to ensure one's own salvation (through performing the prayers with beads); and worship conducted communally (in a Society of the Rosary). In these particular efforts, clerical authors did not seek to debate doctrine. Their mission remained pastoral. They did, however, push orthodox Roman doctrine to its limits to provide realistic opportunities for English Catholics to worship and find comfort regarding the fate of their souls.[5]

PRAYING THE BEADS

As mentioned above, the rosary was both material object and set of prayers. English Catholics in the late sixteenth and early seventeenth centuries probably conceived of no separation in meaning, and they used the term indiscriminately to refer to either the material item or the liturgical exercise. A basic rosary or chaplet, also called a pair of beads, or grains,[6] consists of fifty small beads separated in intervals of ten (called a decade) by a total of five larger beads (one large bead, ten small beads, one large, ten small, and so on) joined to make a circle. A large bead signals the rosarist to say a *Pater noster* and each small bead an *Ave Maria*.[7] The five large beads, often called *Pater noster* beads, represent the five wounds of Christ and signal the devotee to pray upon one of the larger "mysteries:" the miraculous or significant events in the lives of Christ and Mary. Each of the ten small *Ave* beads following allows for more detailed meditation upon the larger mystery. In addition, a large *Credo* bead and a crucifix were often hung separately from the circlet of beads, marking the beginning of the rosary and signaling the solicitant to pray an Apostles' Creed at the beginning of each journey through the beads.

In a convenient, easy-to-use package, the rosary might perpetuate what Catholic catechists were unavailable to continue to do in post-reform England: teach a large portion of the doctrine of the faith to a large group of believers. English priests such as the Jesuit Henry Garnet, superior of the Jesuits in

England from 1586 until his execution in 1606, in his 1596 work *The societie of the rosary*, claimed the rosary was particularly valuable, because it provided a

> certain sum or abridgement of the New Testament and Christian doctrine. . . . [The] beads therein contained do serve to renew the memory of all the mysteries of the life of Christ and the blessed Virgin, and of the principal parts of the Catholic religion as of the Blessed Trinity, the Incarnation, and Passion of Christ, the worship of God & his Saints, the 10 commandments, Justification, and life everlasting. [8]

English priests of this period diligently documented a powerful lineage for the rosary, linking it to the best-known and most powerful figures and scriptures within Christendom. These authors intended such a pedigree to increase English Catholics' confidence in the strength and efficacy of the rosary. Arthur Crowther and Thomas Vincent, two English Benedictines writing from exile on the continent, advertised in *Jesus, Maria, Joseph, or the Devout Pilgrim of the Ever Blessed Virgin Mary*, that the rosary

> undoubtedly as to its substance is of equal standing with the sacred Gospel, since the Lord's Prayer, and the Angelical Salutation[9] (the material parts of our Rosary) are the very Evangelical words and sentences: And as to its use, is also of equal antiquity with our primitive Christianity, since (according to the general Maxim of our School Divines) when in Ecclesiastical matters by the Church Universally embraced, no certainty can be found of their first beginning, they must be believed to have proceeded from the Apostles.[10]

Anthony Batt, another Benedictine living on the continent, agreed with this interpretation of the pedigree of the prayers of the rosary in *A Poore mans mite . . .* , published in 1639. Batt sent his sister in England a rosary with instructions detailing its proper use and benefits and included a particular set of prayers called the Golden Rosary with the material beads. He explained to her that the prayers of the rosary in general were particularly ancient and efficacious since the *Pater noster* was given by Christ, the *Ave Maria* by the angel Gabriel, and the *Credo* by the Apostles.[11]

Batt's translation of a particular type of rosary illustrates that prayers attached to the rosary were by no means uniform. Nor did English priests' efforts at promoting worship through the rosary appear coordinated.[12] At a basic level, most authors agreed that the purpose of the first journey through the beads (one circle around the rosary = one *Credo*, five *Pater nosters*, and fifty *Ave Marias*) was to meditate upon the five joyful mysteries of the lives of Christ and Mary. The second journey was to consider the sorrowful mysteries, and the final cycle of prayers celebrated the five glorious mysteries. But authors often disagreed as to exactly which five mysteries were the most joyful, sorrowful, or glorious, and thereby deserving to be prayed upon in the rosary.[13] These alternatives, rather than provoking competition between different forms of the rosary, allowed rosarists to choose the form of prayer which best suited their needs, and all of the variations upon the prayers could be performed using the one sacramental object, the beads.

SACRAMENTS VERSUS SACRAMENTALS

The sixteenth-century Catholic Church recognized the rosary as a sacramen*tal*. Sacramentals are related to, but not identical to, the church's sacraments. A sacrament is a ritual behavior instituted by God.[14] A sacramen*tal*, however, is either an object or ritual instituted by the church.[15] Sacramental objects were usually material objects used in Catholic liturgy, such as holy water, *agni dei*, Palm Sunday palms, hallowed candles, and rosaries. A priest would ritually bless the items to consecrate them for sacred use.[16] Then the laity would remove the objects from the church for private use.

As Robert Scribner has observed, the distinctions between the efficacy of sacraments and sacramentals were key to the Catholic Church. Sacraments served primarily as direct *(ex opere operato)* aids to salvation, immediately conferring God's saving grace. The performance of the ritual of a sacrament, such as the sacrament of the altar, baptism, or the last rites, automatically produced soteriological results. Sacramentals, on the other hand, were effective by reason of the church's intercession: by the church's use of Christ's power given to the priesthood *(ex opere operantis Ecclesiae)*.[17] They were not as powerful as the sacraments, but they were more effective than individualized private prayer. Sacramental objects such as the rosary might be aids to salvation but only indirectly and only if they were used in the right manner.[18] It is this "right manner" which English priests felt free to reinterpret in order to comfort English Catholics fretting over their salvation in light of their decreased access to priests and the sacraments.[19]

Most commonly, priests produced sacramentals to provide pastoral comfort and aid in a variety of circumstances.[20] Sacramentals were used to encourage devotion, aid believers in temporal matters, or provide protection in adversity. The English priest Thomas Wright, for example, concluded that material objects made persuasion "more forcible and the passion more potent" in the minds of believers. Access to spiritually charged objects encouraged cultural memories and delivered believers from fear, "thereby conceiving the infallible assistance and protection of God over them."[21]

Priests may create sacramental items, but the laity and clergy can then remove the items from the original setting and institutional control. This lack of supervised usage contributes to one of the most important defining features of sacramental items: their ability to accommodate priestly and lay efforts *to redefine the items' usage and meaning* as the environment in which the items are used changes. As discussed in chapter 2, English Catholics' pious needs changed in this century. English clergy and laity reconceptualized traditional ideas about religious locations or "sacred space" to fill such needs. Could priests and laypersons accomplish a similar reinterpretation of material objects used in worship, with sacramentals such as the rosary?

OBTAINING THE BEADS

Despite legal prohibitions against possessing beads and other sacramental objects—including penalties ranging from loss of land to loss of freedom[22]— rosary beads remained common items in late Tudor and early Stuart England. Beads seem to have been readily available to most Catholics with half a mind to locate a pair. Many Catholics possessed at least one pair,[23] and beads were among the first objects the Protestant authorities searched for as evidence that a suspect was a practicing Catholic.[24] Beads were often distributed among Catholics, as occurred in 1584 in Norwich. The future Catholic martyr Montford Scot brought numerous hallowed beads into Norwich and delivered them to many of the city's Catholics with instructions to wear them and to absent themselves from Protestant services, saying such services were "damnable and heretical." Unfortunately for Scot and for the men and women such as Thomas Bozomer, his wife, Martha, and James Nelson who received beads from Scot, the authorities surprised the Norwich Catholics at Mass, took their beads, and discovered Scot's activities. Scot and most of the Catholics who received beads from him were apprehended and indicted.[25]

English priests working within England frequently possessed ready supplies of beads to distribute to the laity. In 1615, a Protestant spy, Christopher Newkirk, infiltrated a group of Catholics in the North. Two priests operating in Doncaster named Winter and Digby believed Newkirk to be sincere in his desire to practice Catholicism and provided him with "an altar, devotional books, beads, etc.," from a chest full of them.[26]

We find Englishmen and women using beads in activities as diverse as while walking along roadsides and while in church during Protestant services.[27] In 1598, Margarita Hornebie and an unnamed blind woman were presented in the deanery of Amounderness in Lancashire for carrying their rosaries in their hands when they were about to receive Protestant communion from the minister of their parish.[28]

Records often show beads being brought back from the continent by priests or lay Catholic travelers.[29] Catholics sent rosaries through the mail,[30] left them in bequests to family members,[31] and even occasionally had the opportunity to buy them in rural markets or on the streets. In 1639, authorities arrested Darby Bantre, an Irishman, at Euston upon the charge of begging. In Bantre's knapsack, however, they discovered £3. 11s. Bantre must have been quite a persuasive beggar that day. Or perhaps the large sum is better explained by the remainder of the contents of the knapsack. Bantre's pack also contained 31 strings of rosary beads "with pictures and crosses at them" as well as five copies of the *Office of the Blessed Virgin,* a work that contains the prayers of the rosary. Obviously, there were more beads and books that any one man would need for his private use. Was Bantre truly a beggar? Or might he have been selling and distributing the rosaries and books in the London area?[32]

Rosary beads were even on sale in prisons, both to prisoners and to visiting Catholics interested in purchasing such sacramentals. John Tendring, the provost marshal of Middlesex, presented a scathing report to the House of Commons on conditions within New Prison in 1626. Among a variety of complaints about Catholic liberty-taking within the jail, Tendring accused both priests and laity in the prison of being "agents and factors for the Pope" by keeping "open trading," selling many types of sacramental items, especially beads and *agni dei* "freely without denial or controlment."[33]

Catholics even carried their beads into prison and meditated upon the mysteries of the rosary to comfort themselves in their adversity. Mary Queen of Scots apparently used her beads while imprisoned by Elizabeth.[34] Philip Howard, Earl of Arundel, imprisoned for religion for 11 years, asked for a book upon the rosary to be brought to him in prison. Reportedly, he spent the night before his death in 1595 praying his beads and repeating those psalms and prayers that he knew from memory.[35] And when the priest Thomas Worthington, imprisoned in the Tower of London, found himself without beads or prayer books, he created his own form of the rosary consisting of the appropriate number and types of prayers and meditations, divided by decade "whereby as well the just number of prayers may without beads be exactly observed."[36]

Even lay Catholics less illustrious than a queen or an earl carried beads and other sacramental items into prison. In 1583/4, sheriffs at the prison of Kidcotes upon Ousebridge, York, searched the chambers of recusant prisoners. The lawmen discovered beads, holy pictures, holy water with strencles to cast it, and wax candles, in addition to Mass books and vestments.[37] And Francis Eyerman, writing to his brother who had been imprisoned for religion, comforted his brother by recommending the prayers of the rosary to him. Eyerman consoled his sibling with the advice that even if he was allowed no books in prison, he could still gain comfort by praying the meditations of the joys and sorrows of Our Lady, especially those on the passion of Christ.[38]

And if by chance a Catholic was so isolated as to have no opportunity to buy beads, obtain them from a priest, have them brought back from the continent by a traveling friend, arrange for them to be mailed by a family member, be left a pair in a relative's will, or even have a pair kept hidden from pre-reformation years, he was not necessarily out of luck. He could always make his own pair of beads, as the Cornish Catholic who handcrafted the rosary of brightly colored stones for Cuthbert Mayne did in the 1570s or as a carpenter and mason named Greene did in 1595.[39]

Finally, if a Catholic was not so artistically inclined, one further option remained: a *picture* of a rosary could be used to say the prayers. John Bucke, an English priest living in exile in Louvain and serving Anne, Lady Hungerford, sister to the Duchess of Feria, provided such an image in his *Instructions for the use of the beades.* (See Figure 1.) This detailed image depicts a rosary, complete with crucifix and with each bead marked to signal the rosarist that it was time to pray a *Credo*, a *Pater noster*, or an *Ave Maria*. Bucke conveniently surrounded the image of the rosary with the words to the *Ave Maria*, additional pithy Marian prayers, and pictures of the Virgin's life and Christ's crucifixion.[40] Just as might have been accomplished by providing wooden, glass, or stone pairs of beads, this priest supplied English Catholics with a rosary for their use. It was still a physical object, and both a tactile and visual aid, used to help laity and clergy procure the benefits of the prayers of the rosary and aid their souls' salvation.[41]

Authors promoted the regular use of the rosary beads, presumably in whatever form, as fruitful for every Catholic—man and woman, learned and unlearned, and for those of any estate, including "the husbandman in the field . . . the laborer with his toiling."[42] Garnet and other priests, such as Bucke,[43] enthusiastically advertised the facility with which one could reap all the profits of the rosary. It required no more knowledge than the ability to say the *Pater noster* and the *Ave Maria*. It incurred no more cost than that of procuring the beads. Furthermore, Catholics could pray with the beads without necessity of a church or altar or priest. Bucke suggested that Catholics might pray the rosary either in word or in thought while traveling, conducting business, or plowing their fields.[44]

According to such authors, a Catholic could remain an active, practicing Catholic and work toward salvation at the same time he or she participated in the wider, multi-dimensional society of which he or she was a part. This need was common to many English Catholics who struggled to balance their families' social and financial well being in Protestant England with their fears for the fates of their souls.

However, while all indications are that English Catholics enjoyed access to the rosary in the century following Elizabeth's Act of Uniformity, such evidence does not reveal the manner in which individual Catholics used these

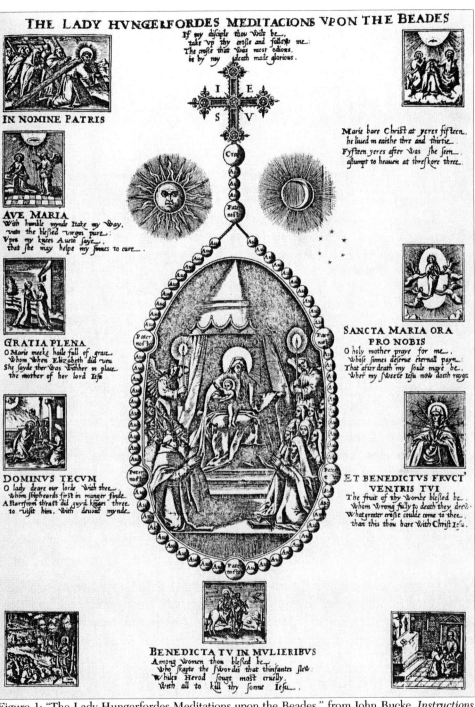

Figure 1: "The Lady Hungerfordes Meditations upon the Beades," from John Bucke, *Instructions for the use of the beades*, orig. 1589 (Menston, Yorkshire: The Scolar Press, 1971), insert. Reproduced by the permission of The British Library.

objects. What can be examined, however, are the new teachings about the rosary being written by English priests both at home and on the continent. Books providing written instructions on how to use the rosary were often among the most numerous works contained in shipments of Catholic literature captured by Protestant authorities.[45] These books typically encouraged rosary worship through the Society of the Rosary, advertised the indulgences available to those who would use the beads, and touted the rosary as a powerful aid to salvation.[46]

Moreover, an analysis of such writings indicates that interpretations regarding the nature of the rosary's power were changing to allow the rosary to fulfill English Catholics' new devotional needs. Garnet signaled that it was time to reinterpret the efficacy of the rosary when he stated that although the rosary's usage had been embraced with "great devotion" in England in times past, "yet neither hath it hitherto been so generally used neither the nature and profit thereof so perfectly known as for so great a good were required."[47] In other words, the spiritual needs of Garnet's countrymen had changed, prompting a reconceptualization of the benefits of the beads to meet the urgency.

We cannot, of course, definitively prove that English Catholics widely accepted such reconceptualizations of the rosary. Evidence of this sort does not exist in any quantitatively demonstrable form nor can it be expected to exist considering the dangers involved. Yet the continued popularity of the rosary provides an important indicator that it was perceived as satisfying a necessary function, so much so that English Catholics went to great lengths to transport rosaries, hide them, distribute them, smuggle them, even craft them with their own hands in order to obtain them. A perpetuation of late medieval beliefs regarding the comforting and solely pastoral benefits of these items seems inadequate to explain these activities. Instead, these material, sacramental objects and the prayers that went with them were manipulated according to the needs of the English Catholics. As mentioned above, English Catholic authors promoted the rosary to gain back much of what had been lost by those with Catholic loyalties due to Protestant reforms: worship with material objects, access to intercessors, soteriological benefits of the sacraments, the comfort of working to ensure one's own salvation, and worship conducted communally. Moreover, by opening a channel by which Catholics communicated with the divine while taking positive action to procure their salvation, rosaries provided evidence of divine concern for, and presence and action in, the natural world.

SOCIETY OF THE ROSARY[48]

Any English Catholic could, of course, use a rosary independently and in the manner taught by the Roman Church prior to reforms in England. Following

1559, however, new messages about rosary worship and how to gain the utmost saving merit from the beads began circulating among English Catholics. For example, English authors of new literature on the rosary stressed that Catholics could do much more to work toward salvation by becoming members of the Society of the Rosary and joining other Catholics in communal worship with the beads. Anne Winston-Allen, in *Stories of the Rose: The Making of the Rosary in the Middle Ages*, describes the organization as a "self-help association providing supplementary insurance . . . against the pains of purgatory."[49] The Society promoted the regular saying of the rosary as a particularly effective and orthodox means to glorify the Virgin and receive her intercession. English Catholic authors and Rome, however, manipulated the general messages and advertisements about membership in, and the benefits of, rosary worship through the Society of the Rosary in order to meet English Catholics' special circumstances and quell English Catholic anxiety over salvation.

But in a country in which communal Catholic worship and the beads themselves were illegal, how did either the papacy or English priests realistically expect the Society of the Rosary to take root? Many benefits for believers' souls might be available for rosarists joined in such a confraternity, but unless English Catholics possessed the opportunity and willingness to join, new messages about the rosary and its powers provided few concrete benefits or comforts regarding salvation. For this reason, English authors modified the rituals and practices of the Society of the Rosary for England. English priests pushed at the boundaries of the institutionally established ritual structure to provide opportunities for English Catholic worship, and they did so with the papacy's tacit approval.

As a Dominican-led confraternity, all branches of the Society of the Rosary, including those established during the late Tudor and early Stuart periods, had to be instituted with the approval of the General of the Dominicans.[50] Yet in England we find it was the Jesuits (such as Henry Garnet), the Benedictines (for example, Arthur Crowther, Thomas Vincent, and Anthony Batt), and the secular priests (such as William Allen, John Bucke, and John Wilson) who took the lead in propagating the use of the rosary and membership in this society.[51] These English priests, with Dominican approval,[52] modified many of the original Dominican rules in order to allow English Catholics realistic opportunity to become members of the society. For example, the original Dominican rules specified that for admission into the society, the prospective member must participate in a special set of rituals with a priest present. Crowther and Vincent described this initiation ceremony in some detail in *Jesus, Maria, Joseph*. Following the writing of the potential initiate's name in a "Register book of the Rosary," the initiate knelt down, holding a rosary and a candle in his hands, in front of an altar and image specially dedicated to the

Society of the Rosary. Following special prayers and a benediction by a priest, the initiate would lay his rosary upon the altar. The dean (of the chapter) would place a stole about his neck and specially bless the beads and subsequently bless wax candles for the rosarist to use at the hour of death.[53]

English authors, however, realized that most English Catholics had no altars, little access to the services of a priest, and would be wary of signing their names to a Catholic document, thereby potentially incriminating themselves if the registers were discovered by Protestant authorities. Cardinal William Allen, a secular priest and the founder of the English College at Douai, wrote to English Catholics in 1592 encouraging them to enter the Society of the Rosary, saying they might do so "without any limitation of a particular altar . . . (and that) there needeth no writing of names at all, but only (a bare) admission without solemnity" and that these English initiates would still receive the plenary indulgence attached to entrance into the Society.[54]

In 1596, Garnet, in his treatise *The societie of the rosary*, agreed with Allen's easing of the rules of admission into the Society. Garnet required no special altar or image for the initiation rite. A priest was not necessary to perform the benediction or bless the beads, as long as the beads had been blessed before. And the Jesuit comforted potential initiates, saying that "This manner of enrolling (in a register) being not convenient in our country for respects too well known: it sufficeth that after the names be once taken of such as enter, they be torn."[55] Garnet advised members that if safe, convenient opportunity ever offered itself to be enrolled in writing, they should avail themselves.[56] Garnet assured English Catholics that nothing more was necessary to enter the Society of the Rosary and that if anyone thought otherwise "requiring either ordinary prayers or frequenting of sacraments or any solemn procession" then that person was confusing the Society of the Rosary with another organization.[57]

Just as membership requirements were eased to encompass the special needs of English Catholics, so were accommodations made in how communal rosary worship through the Society conferred benefits to members' souls. Rome's *general* stance on the Society of the Rosary was that it promoted the regular saying of the rosary as a particularly effective and orthodox means to glorify the virgin and receive her intercession. The message advertised to English Catholics by Rome and by English priests was somewhat different. Wilson, Garnet, Batt, Crowther, and Vincent all advocated the use of the rosary and encouraged membership in this Society. In addition to the benefits of Mary's intercession, such clerical authors—with Rome's approval—heavily touted the indulgences attached to society membership and stressed the relaxation of requirements necessary to earn the indulgences. Moreover, English priests told their readers that they were the beneficiaries—through spiritual

reception—of the benefits of the Mass and prayers for Mary's intercession performed by Society members throughout Christendom. Most English Catholics,
recall, feared for their souls in the frequent absence of priests and the sacraments. They were now being informed of an opportunity to gain some of the
saving benefits of the Mass and of communal prayer that they felt had been
lost.

The papacy and English clerics thus worked jointly to make such communal rosary worship accessible and attractive to English Catholics.[58] Popes
eased the rules, making it simpler for English members of the Society to gain
indulgences attached to the rosary. In 1579 and 1583, for example, Gregory
XIII modified the conditions under which the plenary indulgence for visiting
the altar of the rosary might be received. He allowed that, "Such Brethren and
Sisters of the Rosary who by reason of sickness, a journey, Imprisonment,
Persecution, Service, distance, danger, or any other lawful impediment, cannot
be present at the Processions (of the Rosary) aforesaid, nor visit the altar of the
rosary; may notwithstanding gain all the indulgences as if they were present"
by confessing and communicating, or by saying the rosary, or by saying the
seven penitential psalms before either some devout picture or altar.[59] And in
1586, Sixtus V renewed all previous indulgences attached to the Society and
granted an additional plenary indulgence to those lawfully hindered from fulfilling societal obligations, such as celebrating the feasts of the rosary, marching in processions of the rosary, or visiting churches or chapels dedicated to the
rosary to which other indulgences were attached. English Catholics, if nothing
else, could gain the indulgences offered by either of these popes simply by
praying the rosary, which even their limited circumstances could usually
accommodate.

English Catholics were aware of such plenary indulgences attached to
rosary worship.[60] Papal bulls were frequently smuggled into England by missionary priests. Lay Catholics abroad would write to their friends and relatives
in England advertising such news, sometimes sending pairs of beads along in
an effort to persuade the recipients to engage in such worship to the benefit of
their souls, as William Gifford, a fellow of the English College at Rome, did
when he dispatched four rosaries to his friend, William Middelmore,[61] in
England. Gifford carefully mentioned that the four pairs of beads had been
blessed by priests and that he did not doubt but that Middelmore would recognize the great pardons attached to their use.[62]

Catholic pastoral literature also spread the news of this benefit of rosary
worship. In 1617, an anonymous work entitled *A chayne of twelve links*
appeared in England, translated from Italian. The translator, the English secular priest John Wilson, in a preface written in 1605, lauded the efforts of various popes to attach indulgences to the use of certain sacramental items, par-

ticularly rosary beads, medals, and crosses. The popes did so, according to Wilson, in consideration of the "desolation of our country" and in order to animate and succor English Catholics and to inspire Catholics of other countries to pray for England's return to Catholicism. Wilson claimed that he was inspired to translate *A chayne of twelve links* into English at that time because Pope Paul V had just renewed all indulgences attached to these sacramental items which so benefited his countrymen.[63]

English authors stressed the great number of indulgences available through membership in the Society. Crowther and Vincent told their readers that Society members could gain a plenary indulgence for every day of the year by saying a daily rosary.[64] Garnet attempted to quantify for his readership the years of indulgence available for a Society member who said the rosary weekly. He estimated that in generations past it was 77 years and 240 days. With the new indulgences recently granted, he was certain that this number had greatly increased.[65]

Certainly, Rome advertised such indulgences and they were attractive to non-English Catholics as well, but the issue is one of emphasis. Catholics living in Catholic countries would have regular access to the sacraments and other tools to procure saving grace and thus not need indulgences to as great a degree as would a Catholic in England. As André Vauchez and Richard Kieckhefer have argued, the attraction of this organization to continental laypersons was due largely to a lay desire to imitate monastic practice.[66] For English Catholics considering membership, salvation was the overriding priority, and indulgences thus came to the forefront in English Catholic writings on the Society. With the shortage of most other avenues to saving grace, English Catholics magnified what opportunities remained, refocusing the message regarding both the availability of membership and saving benefits to believers.

English Catholic authors, however, suggested an additional way in which society membership could accrue salvific merit: through the spiritual participation of Society members in the benefits of the Mass. According to such priests, group worship through the rosary served the functions of the sacrament albeit packaged in a different, yet completely orthodox and acceptable institutional form. Crowther and Vincent stressed that members of the Society of the Rosary would also have a share in the merit of "so many divine sacrifices of the Mass celebrated yearly, monthly, weekly, daily" wherever there was an established Society of the Rosary. The Brothers and Sisters of the Society of the Rosary "being anywhere receiv'd are everywhere priviledg'd" and would benefit from the spiritual sacrifices and prayers of all other members "who are registered in Rome, in Paris, in any place in the whole universe."[67] Anthony Batt supported Crowther's and Vincent's assertions. After sending his sister in England the set of beads with instructions, he comforted his sister, who was unable to attend Catholic services, by telling her that all Catholics reap the spiritual benefits of Mass and prayers conducted "throughout the world" even if they are not corporally present.[68]

Garnet agreed. Although he admitted it would be desirable if each Society member took the sacrament, "yet that this is not altogether necessary, the very Practice of the Society doth show, which receiveth those who are absent, and not in care or possibility to receive holy Sacraments." Although ordinarily non-reception of the sacraments might hinder the reception of the benefits of the Society, Garnet carefully pointed out that "yet doth it not hinder but that so long as one remaineth in the unity of holy Church, and sayeth his Rosary . . . every week" if he could conveniently do so. As long as an English Catholic received the sacraments when he was able and said the rosary when he was able, then the common prayers and sacraments of the entire Society were applied to him as a member thereof.[69]

What these priests assert is that English Catholics received the benefits of the Eucharist spiritually rather than corporally, an issue that will be explored in greater detail in the next chapter on reinterpretations of the Mass. God still conferred the saving benefits of the Mass without a priest present or Mass having been said before the Society member. How do we interpret this language so tantalizingly close to making a dramatic doctrinal challenge to the Church? Examined closely, such claims by English priests do not challenge the Council of Trent. They do not attempt to annul the use of priests or the reception of the sacraments. They support the frequent celebration of Mass and reception of the Eucharist whenever possible. Nor do such authors ever attempt a definitive doctrinal statement as to how Catholics receive the merits of the Mass or what is sufficient to attain salvation. They are not entering into the theological debates engaged in by Catholics and Protestants regarding justification and salvation. Their mission remains pastoral—as efforts to provide sacramentals typically were, as discussed above. Such clerics comforted English Catholics by reminding them that those who have no access to the Mass are beneficiaries of the merits of the Mass through their membership in a body of believers, whether or not they see or ingest the host. This understanding of the efficacy of the Mass was used in the Middle Ages to justify the celebrants' reception of the Eucharist for the laity. Paradoxically, priests such as Garnet, Crowther, Vincent, and Batt employed this orthodox explanation of "one receiving for all" to justify spiritual lay reception of the Eucharist in the absence of priests.

Moreover, by making the rosary the vehicle by which English Catholics could aid their own salvation and accrue the benefits of prayers and sacraments, authors such as Garnet, Crowther, Vincent, Bucke, and Batt might be perceived as bypassing the traditional church hierarchy by decreasing the laity's reliance upon priests and promoting individual worship. After all, the rosary seems largely a solitary exercise. The focus rests upon the individual supplicant. This is one of the reasons it works so well for English Catholics. It can be done privately in one's room without a priest. It can be said silently while one works. It remains difficult for the Protestant authorities to detect rosary worship. Yet Garnet, Crowther, Vincent, Bucke, and Batt and the author of *The chayne* ensured that a non-embodied priest was present at each praying of the rosary. Each author provided detailed instructions regarding how to use the beads, how to achieve a proper mental disposition before saying the rosary, and how to meditate upon the events described within the rosary. These directives were often intensely detailed.[70] Garnet asserted that he had included "whatsoever is necessary for devotion" through the rosary in his instructions.[71] The supplicant obtained his beads, confessed his conscience, prayed his rosary, meditated upon the mysteries of Christ and Mary, made direct supplication to Christ and Mary for his needs, and received the saving grace of the church for doing so, all with the direction of a priest. While the clerical author is not physically present, his voice carries out *per verbum* the traditional functions of a priest, attempting to educate, comfort, minister, and provide a channel toward God's grace.

CHANGING ROLE OF THE ROSARY AND MARY

English Catholic authors attempted to further comfort English Catholics by providing yet another channel to saving grace through rosary worship by reconceptualizing the type of aid provided by the Virgin Mary. The rosary is the most popular devotion centered around the Virgin Mary promoted by the Catholic Church. Although the rosary is considered a Marian devotion, the rosary traditionally is intended to offer access through Mary to Christ, the source of all saving grace. By calling upon Mary through the rosary, English Catholics hoped to obtain grace through her intercession with Christ. This grace was what English Catholics perceived to be in short supply in the absence of priests and the sacraments.

In the decades following Elizabeth's Act of Uniformity, English authors changed their emphasis on the rosary, advertising this sacramental object as an important means to call upon Mary, encourage her presence and action in the material world, and achieve saving grace. In the process, they also promoted a different image of Mary than was predominant in pre-reform England, in Protestant England, and on the continent. They glorified Mary as a powerful warrior, capable of protecting the souls of those who venerated her through the rosary.

While the rosary was certainly available and popular in late medieval England, it was but one among a variety of options used to appeal to the Virgin. English Christians dedicated many cathedrals to Mary.[72] Many churches contained images and altars to the Virgin. Marian shrines, such as the ones at Walsingham and Willesden, were among the most popular pilgrimage sites in pre-reform England. Holy wells associated with Mary dotted the countryside.[73] If a pre-reform Christian wanted to pray to Mary, a rosary was available but not necessary.

Such images and shrines played an important role in making Mary's presence felt in the hearts and minds of believers and in stressing Mary's presence in the material world of pre-reform England. As Robert A. Orsi has noted, material representations of Mary are not received solely as "signs" of Mary but also as containing the presence of the very thing signified.[74] Mary was *there*, with believers. By viewing images of Mary, by touching icons, by praying at one of these Marian altars or shrines, believers called on Mary to be present with them.

Protestant reform gradually curtailed all forms of Marian worship and thus minimized the perceived, palpable presence of Mary.[75] In the absence of cathedrals, churches, altars, images, relics, shrines, and public prayers invoking her aid, Catholics possessed few traditional channels to request Mary's presence and her powerful intercessory abilities.[76] But they often still possessed their rosaries. Authors began to magnify the rosary as one of the only channels remaining to contact Mary and request her presence and aid. They placed many of their spiritual hopes, so to speak, in this well-known basket.

By invoking Mary through the rosary, English Catholics attained two valuable comforts: 1) Mary's presence and protection through her role as the powerful Mother of God, and 2) her intercession with her son, Christ, to procure his saving grace and forgiveness of sins. English priests presented Mary as accessed through the rosary as a warrior, defending English Catholics and their souls. Garnet described Mary's aid:

> From this bow there goeth none but chosen arrows taken forth out of the quiver of God himself, yea arrows of the salvation of Our Lord, arrows of salvation against Syria that is, arrows of salvation both in tranquility of the Church; and also against all enemies of Israel and the Church of God in the time of temptation and disturbance.[77]

Garnet lauded Mary's immediate relationship and, hence, powerful intercessory ability with God. He stressed that Mary received her weapons and power from God's own quiver, to which she was so close as to be able to reach in with her own hand.

When English Catholic authors such as Garnet depicted Mary as a powerful warrior, they drew upon primitive church traditions of militancy dating to the centuries following the reign of Constantine.[78] Such traditions largely had been supplanted in the later medieval years.[79] However, while the post-

Constantinian church had been militant, Mary had not necessarily been portrayed as such. For example, an image of Mary from about 500 AD, after the Council of Ephesus, shows her sitting on a throne. She is flanked and protected by two warrior saints, but Mary herself is not depicted as a warrior as she was by English Catholics in the century following the Act of Uniformity.[80]

In post-reform England, the rosary became a weapon for English Catholics to call upon this warrior-like Mary. Garnet continued by asserting:

> So the beads must be to our afflicted brethren, in stead of all manner of armor or weapons: for the weapons of our warfare are not carnal, but mighty of God . . . for therefore is she (Virgin) called a well settled array of a pitched army, because she mightily overcometh, not only her own, but also her devout clients' adversaries. [81]

Since the English Catholics possessed no armor or weapons for use in this spiritual war with the Protestants, the rosary became viewed as a weapon because its use brought the power of Mary onto the side of the Catholics.[82] Mary was thus an active participant in the religious conflicts of the times. Rosarists became her clients. Mary carried weapons, fought, protected, and overcame both the enemies of the faith and the enemies of salvation.[83]

Arthur Crowther and Thomas Vincent supported the portrayal of the beads as an effective means to garner the support of this powerful, protective Mary.[84] They described Mary as an "Instrumental Partner with the most sacred Trinity."[85] Mary was a partner with Christ. They called her the "Mother of Power." Crowther and Vincent agreed with Garnet that England's emergency circumstances necessitated the greater use of the rosary by English Catholics. They emphasized that "forcible reasons" induced English Catholics to turn to the rosary and such a powerful protector as Mary. By turning to the rosary, believers would gain her "powerful patronage, prayers, and protection . . . (and she will) give us a certain kind of hopeful confidence." The authors portrayed fervent devotions to Mary upon the rosary as "proper for such Catholics as live in Heretical countries" and who were "liable to persecution."[86] They advertised that Mary possessed unique abilities to destroy heresy "and so to terrify all the Satanical Armies of her Sons and his Church's adversaries that they are put to flight, at the sole appearance of her formidable presence."[87] Mary was very much an active participant in the troubles of the English, and a sacramental item—the rosary—could be used to make her presence felt in this world.[88]

More than providing protection, English authors emphasized the rosary as an important aid to salvation. Praying the rosary implored Mary to intercede with Christ for sinners. Garnet explained the relationship of the rosary with such a request as he wrote, "And to every [Lord's] prayer we do adjoin 10 *Ave Marias* . . . that by the intercession of the Blessed Virgin through the merits of our Lord's Passion we may attain full remission of sins which is signified in holy Scripture. . . ." [89] The believer requested such aid from Mary through the last line of the prayer, "Holy Mary, Mother of God, pray for us sinners." Garnet comforted distressed Catholics by urging them to use the rosary to pray to Mary, exhorting them

> If thou beest troubled with the enormity of crimes, confounded with the uncleanness of conscience, frighted with the horror of judgment, & beginnest to be swallowed into the gulf of sadness, or into the depth of despair, think upon Mary. In dangers, in distresses, in doubtful cases, think upon Mary, call upon Mary. Let her not depart from thy mouth. Let her not depart from thy heart. . . . Following her thou strayest not; calling upon her, thou despairest not: thinking upon her thou errest not: she holding you, thou fallest not: she protecting you thou fearest not. . . . [90]

By putting oneself under Mary's protection by praying the beads, the supplicant was assured of walking the proper path to judgment, not straying, not erring, and obtaining salvation through her guidance. Garnet advocated that Catholics become Mary's clients and pupils. [91]

Mary's powerful presence was portrayed dramatically in an anonymous seventeenth-century English manuscript of praises to the Virgin. The book details a dialogue between Mary and a petitioner. Mary specifically asks the solicitant to recite Marian prayers, and the first prayers Mary calls for are those of the rosary. [92] In contrast to all the previous works discussed, this pastoral work does not merely inform the reader about Mary, but allows Mary to speak directly to the supplicant. In addition to her reconceptualized English role as powerful warrior and intercessor through the rosary, Mary is now fully present in the text and prayers, speaking and expressing herself on earth, and a petitioner could engage in a two-way dialogue with the Mother of God. [93]

Throughout the manuscript, Mary establishes an inviolable pedigree *for herself*, just as the English priests were wont to do, by asking her petitioner to serve her faithfully throughout life, as had many named primitive churchmen, martyrs, saints, and reformers. [94] In return for the petitioner's devotion and service, Mary promises to cleanse and intercede to protect the Christian's heart and soul. "Give me your heart my dear Child and if it be as hard as flint I will make it soft as wax, if it be more foul and loathsome as dirt I will tender it more clear and beautiful as crystal." [95] Mary offers the solicitant the example of her acts on behalf of St. Charles:

> Wherefore at his death I was attending for the going out of his soul . . . to conduct and lead it into Paradise, and I will do the like for you my dear Child [the penitent]. . . . I will be present at your death and although you

had one foot in hell, yet would I draw you out and defend you against your enemies. [96]

The author of this prayer pushes the limits of Marian doctrine to make some very powerful statements about Mary's ability to aid salvation. Doctrinally, Mary helps sinners by interceding on their behalf before Christ. Yet here there is no specific mention of Christ or of Mary interceding with him to wipe clean the penitent's sins or to save the penitent's soul. Instead, Mary is depicted as reaching down to save the sinner herself, reminiscent of Garnet's portrayal of Mary reaching into God's own quiver to pull out arrows of salvation.[97] Undoubtedly, this author was not challenging doctrine specifying exactly how Mary helped sinners. He or she was, however, trying to portray Mary as powerfully as possible to emphasize her ability to aid English Catholics' salvation at a time when they needed every help that was at hand.[98]

ONE OF MANY EMERGING VIEWS OF MARY

This change in emphasis regarding the use of the rosary to request Mary's intercession on behalf of sinners and to make present a warrior-like Mary was new to English Catholics.[99] English authors began by taking orthodox—yet rather obscure—depictions of a powerful Mary and adapting them to English needs. A tradition of a powerful Mary did exist in the Christian Church, however it was primarily an Eastern tradition at this time, rarely seen in Western Europe.[100] While the Roman Church did associate Mary with the Christian victory over the Muslims at the Battle of Lepanto in 1571, the view of Mary as helpful in assuring military victory over heretics and, more importantly, the image of Mary as warrior, were not the predominant portrayals of Mary on the continent in this period.[101]

The authors of English pastoral literature, however, took this depiction of Mary that was popular with the Eastern Church and applied it in new ways to combat their own threat from heretical forces and to meet their own soteriological needs. Rome did not suggest that English Catholics use Mary in this way. Nor did Rome help advertise Mary as the new "Mother of Power" in England as English Catholic authors were doing.

Pre-Reform Use and Interpretation of the Rosary in England

Pre-reform English Christians prayed the rosary, certainly, but they did not use it to ask for Mary's intercession in the same way as Catholics after 1559 did. Moreover, the English Catholic portrayal of Mary as warrior-like protector contrasts sharply with the more popular late medieval and post-Tridentine continental portrayals of a meek Mary or of Mary as remote Queen of Heaven. Both developments are evidence of the many new interpretations of Mary emerging in the West among both Protestants and Catholics during the years of reform.[102] Just as the rosary beads and prayers could be handled to suit the various needs of the users, so too was Mary a flexible symbol, and both clergy and laity could manipulate her physical and spiritual image as they used the rosary.

Late medieval English Christians, although passionately devoted to Mary, did not use the rosary to petition Mary directly as a powerful intercessor. Prior to reform, the *Ave Maria* traditionally used in England did not contain the last line, "Holy Mary, mother of God, pray for us sinners."[103] The experience of an English Catholic merchant named Frampton illustrated the extent of English knowledge of the use of the rosary to ask for Mary's intercession. Frampton, trading in Spain in 1560, was brought before a Spanish bishop, Juan Gonsalius, and interrogated about his religion. Frampton related:

> [H]e asked me if I could say my Ave Maria. I told him, yea. 'Then say it,' says he. I said it: 'Ave Maria, gratia plena, Dominus tecum, benedicta tu in mulieribus et benedictus fructus ventris tui Jesus Amen.' 'Say forth,' said the bishop. 'I have said all that I can say.' 'There,' he said, 'herein thou dost deny the intercession of the saints.' I answered that I had never knew more nor heard more. 'Then,' saith he, 'there lacketh "S. Maria, Mater dei, ora pro nobis peccatoribus."' I told him I never heard it till then.[104]

The *Ave Maria* as the pre-reform English Christians knew it glorified Mary and instructed Catholics about the Annunciation, a valuable tenet of Catholic belief, but it only *implied* a request for intercession if a rosarist knew the final line of the prayer existed. Even then, the force of the prayer was considerably weakened without the actual petition being made. Lawrence Vaux, the author of one of the most popular catechisms written by an English Catholic following the Act of Uniformity—*A catechisme or a christian doctrine, necessarie for children & the ignorant people*—asked in his 1567 edition of this work, "Why is the *Ave Maria* used so often to be said for a prayer, seeing there is no petition in it?"[105] This is not to imply that the English never asked for Mary's intercession for the remission of sins prior to the Act of Uniformity. Certainly they did so, but they did not use the rosary to ask for such intercession.

Moreover, when pre-reform English Christians prayed to Mary, it was not to the powerful warrior Mother of God to whom English Catholics were later instructed to pray. Instead, they addressed their requests for aid to one of two representations of Mary: either to a milder medieval Mary or to the Queen of Heaven.[106] The former representation was most common in prayers. English Christians addressed Mary primarily as the "Gentle Lady" of heaven, the mother who held her son's lifeless body at the foot of the cross (the *Pietá* or

Mater dolorosa).[107] In this guise, Mary primarily served as an exemplar of humility, service, piety, and suffering.[108]

Medieval prayers (those not attached to the rosary) address such a Mary as a help to souls, but the tone of the prayers differs from the post-reform prayers to Mary cited above. Mary is a mediator rather than a protector. She mediated by bringing Christ into the world through the incarnation, and she mediated by interceding at the throne of God.[109] For example, the Steeple Ashton manuscript *Book of hours of the blessed Virgin Mary* from the early fifteenth century included a typical request to Mary.

> Blessed lady Mary, virgin of Nazareth
> And mother to ye mighty Lord of grace
> That his people saved hath with his death
> From ye pains of ye infernal place:
> Now, blessed lady, kneel before his face,
> And pray to him my soul to save from loss,
> Which with his blood hath bought us on the cross.[110]

This prayer addresses Mary as virgin and mother of God, not as a warrior. This medieval English Mary humbly kneels before the throne of God to plead for sinners.[111] She does not reach into a quiver to pull forth arrows of salvation. This prayer may invoke Mary's aid, but the thrust of the prayer is Christocentric, emphasizing Christ's protective ability rather than Mary's.[112]

Alternatively, many of the best-known images of Mary in English shrines portrayed her as the Queen of Heaven. For example, the popular Marian shrine at Walsingham depicted an enthroned, regal Mary. Although this is a more powerful image than that of the humble Mary contained in medieval English prayers, the nature of Mary's power is different than that of the warrior Mary of the post-reform years. The exquisitely robed Queen of Heaven acts on behalf of believers from her remote throne situated in heaven. The later, armed, bellicose Mary exerts much of her influence in the material world with a less regal, more urgent passion.

The earlier Mary was often objectified in inanimate metaphors by the church. When building a pedigree for the rosary based upon the writings of church fathers, Crowther and Vincent repeated the primitive church's metaphors for Mary. The ancient authors referred to Mary as a treasury, a cabinet, a fleece of wool, a bridge, the root of a flower, a robe, a furnace, a mirror, a chariot, and a lamp. Mary was rarely portrayed as an actor.[113]

Crowther and Vincent consciously maintained this ancient imagery but made subtle changes in the metaphors used. Instead of being an inactive "treasury," as the primitive church fathers described Mary, the English priests depicted her as the "charitable Dispensatrix of [her son's] treasures" of salvation, capable of repaying the devout prayers of her petitioners with greater real rewards than the most powerful earthly sovereign could dispense. "The Glorious Virgin (say our Doctors) is the Treasuress of the celestial riches. . . . [S]he carries the keys of the divine coffers: All power is given to you . . . so that you have leave to do what you please in Heaven and Earth."[114] Mary now makes choices as to how to distribute her son's saving grace from a treasury instead of being the inactive receptacle itself. She acts with few or no limits.

In Contrast to Post-Tridentine Continental Portrayals of Mary

This English Catholic representation of a powerful Mary contrasted sharply with more popular sixteenth and early seventeenth century continental portrayals of Mary as either the traditional Queen of Heaven[115] or, more lately, as meek, self-sacrificing, humble servant of God and role model for Catholic female docility. For example, the Council of Trent promoted Mary as a quiet learner. Trent upheld this image of Mary to encourage Catholic mothers to teach their children their catechism at home. In continental annunciation scenes of this period, the angel Gabriel often finds Mary sitting and reading.[116]

The characterization of the Virgin as mild and modest dominated post-Tridentine Marian literature written on the continent.[117] These authors attempted to persuade readers to conform their lives to the devout example set by Mary. As the Italian Luca Pinelli opined in *The Virgin Marie's life, faithfully gathered out of auncient & holie fathers* (orig. 1594), "she taught by example how everyone ought to behave himself as well in time of prosperity and favor as of adversity and tribulations. . . . [s]he did humble herself with all her heart. . . ."

Pinelli divided Mary's life into three periods, the descriptions of which provide insight into the needs continental authors were trying to fulfill with their characterizations of Mary. From age three to fourteen years, Mary stayed in the temple of Jerusalem with other virgins, abhorring vanity. Pinelli portrayed her as the model for young women. From age fourteen to forty-five, Pinelli glorified Mary as a "mistress to married women and such as have care of households." Pinelli painted her as obedient, honorable, and respecting of her spouse. From age forty-five until death, the author hoped Mary would serve as an example to widows and poor women to live "dead to the world, (living) wholly unto God. . . ."[118]

Continental authors perpetuated the primitive church's comparisons of Mary with inanimate objects, such as when the Italian Jesuit Gasparo Loarte, in his *Instructions & advertisements how to meditate upon the misteries of the rosarie of the most holy Virgin Mary*, requested readers to meditate upon Mary, as God's "temple, and the sacred tabernacle of the holy Ghost." The continental Mary frequently remained a vessel rather than an independent actor.

Indeed, Loarte wrote of Mary, "Verily the Almighty hath done great matters *to* thee. . . ."[119]

While continental authors did not deny Mary's usefulness as an intercessor, they certainly downplayed this role, in contrast to English Catholic authors' emphasis upon it. Pinelli's meditations, for example, stressed chastity and modesty over protection, strength, or mediation.[120] In continental works, Mary had her eye on believers' salvation, but there was little sense of Mary down in the trenches with the sinners as in English works. These prayers did not ask Mary to walk into battle to protect believers from heresy or damnation.[121] Mary as exemplar was depicted as retired from the world. Mary as intercessor was frequently depicted in similar fashion.[122] She may have reigned in heaven, but she was removed from the down and dirty business of daily life on earth.

We can grasp even more clearly the distinctiveness of English Catholic appeals to Mary through the rosary by contrasting them with representative continental works that depict the rosary as primarily a Christocentric exercise rather than a Marian one. Continental authors instructed rosarists to meditate upon Mary's life but only in so far as necessary in order to meditate upon Christ's life.[123] According to Loarte, the goal of praying the rosary was to meditate upon Christ's examples: to walk as he walked, lowly and meek.[124] Loarte suggested that by praying the rosary, Christ became spiritually present "by means whereof he even at this day illuminateth, guideth, & teacheth us as though he were present, with that he before did (wandering corporally in this world) speak, work, endure, and teach." Whereas English Catholics were being told to pray the rosary to become Mary's clients, Loarte and other continental authors such as the Spanish Jesuit St. Francis Borgia and the French Jesuit St. Francis de Sales instructed believers to pray the rosary to become Christ's clients.[125]

English Catholic authors certainly would not dispute that the rosary is a Christocentric exercise. Rosarists meditate upon the lives of both Mary and Christ, and they pray to Mary to access Christ's grace. It is, as always, an issue of emphasis, and English Catholic authors placed a much greater emphasis upon Mary than did continental authors. In general, continental authors did not promote the rosary as an important tool to gain salvation nor was there any real need for them to do so. Continental authors wrote for readers with ready access to priests and the sacraments. Mary could serve primarily as an exemplar for female behavior, and sacramental objects, such as the beads, could provide only pastoral comfort when no greater need impelled priests and laity to expand the scope of their power or effectiveness.[126]

Mary and the rosary were flexible symbols for the Roman Church, both in England and on the continent, and were continually employed in a variety of ways to meet diverse and ever-changing needs.[127] English Catholics' emphasis on rosary worship and their reinterpretation of the type of aid Mary offered through the rosary were, therefore, just some of the many views regarding worship with material objects and on Mary developing during the age of reform. As English Catholic needs for comfort, protection, and saving grace grew, so too did reliance upon Mary as protector and intercessor. As English Catholics' ability to invoke Mary's aid through Marian cathedrals, chapels, altars, shrines, images, relics, and public prayers decreased, so too did their reliance upon the rosary to access Mary increase, as suggested during the execution of the Jesuit John Ogilvie (*c.*1580–1615) in 1615. Ogilvie met his death upon a scaffold in Glasgow. He was executed for treason. According to an observer, young Baron Idus of Eckelsdorff, then a Protestant:

> When Ogilvie, before his death, was bidding farewell to the Catholics from the scaffold, he threw amongst the people a rosary of the blessed virgin as a memorial of himself. That rosary—thrown as it appeared at random, fell on me. . . . In a moment there was such a rush of Catholics upon me, requesting the rosary should be given up to them, that, not wanting to be assaulted violently, I was obliged to throw the rosary out of my breast. [128]

Of all the things he might have taken with him to the scaffold, Ogilvie took his rosary. Of all the gestures that Ogilvie could have made his last, he chose to throw his rosary. Why? Was it, as Eckelsdorff postulated, simply meant as a memorial gesture? What might it mean both to possess and give away a rosary at the liminal moment between life and death?[129] As John Ogilvie flung his rosary from the gallows, he caused a stir as Catholics scrambled to retrieve it. In addition to uniting Catholics in the crowd and motivating religious fervor, Ogilvie may also have been emphasizing the rosary's evolving role in the quest for salvation, particularly at the nexus between life and death. Through its connection to a powerful, protective, warrior-like Mary and her intercessory abilities, the rosary offered English Catholics options in both its use as material object and in its interpretation as prayer, ritual, and symbol so English Catholics could aid the health of their souls.

Pastoral literature on the rosary written by English clerics embodies changes in understandings of Catholic ritual, identity, and community that are the crux of this study. By reinterpreting the saving benefits of the rosary, authors manipulated the experience of the ritual itself. By encouraging the prayers of the rosary and the use of objects traditionally used in worship, authors reinforced Catholic identity among believers albeit in new ways. And in promoting the Society of the Rosary, clerics urged English Catholics to build new communal ties to one another and to believers worldwide.

As the resources of a religious community change, the religion itself must alter to fulfill believers' needs. Symbols, rituals, physical locations for worship, even the telling of the religion's history might evolve in new, but not institutionally unacceptable, directions in such circumstances.[130] In all probability, this is what occurred with the rosary in England. Many English Catholics could still acquire rosaries, whether of the homemade variety, such as Cuthbert Mayne's thank offering, or of the superior craftsmanship of Lord William Howard's engraved golden beads. As authors reinterpreted and advertised the salvific benefits of one of the most widely recognized symbols of the Roman Church—the rosary—some segments of the English Catholic population found solace in adopting these instructions of their spiritual fathers regarding the beads, membership in the Society of the Rosary, and the re-interpreted Virgin. English priests took imaginative possession of the rosary and invested it with new capabilities, such as the beads' ability to make present a strong, weapon-wielding Mary on the side of the English Catholics.

English Catholics, after losing regular, reliable access to priests and physical contact with most sacraments of the Catholic Church, required alternatives to work toward the health of their souls. English priests strove to provide them with such alternatives. These options were not radical challenges to Catholic orthodoxy but were changes in emphasis and re-conceptualizations of existing doctrines necessitated by the pressures of attempting to practice Catholicism within Protestant England. The attempted redefinition of the usage and efficaciousness of the rosary—a sacramental item—was one such option.

But the rosary was just one among a number of sacramental items available to English Catholics, as an inventory of a large "fardell" taken by D. Fletcher, working in Lewes in 1582, revealed. Among the list of catechisms, Bibles, and books of Catholic controversy were also nineteen large pictures and twenty-seven small pictures, all in silk, and "a little green box containing certain white cakes broken printed with *agnus dei* and written within the box *agnus dei* of Mr Bell." Also inside, Fletcher found a small collection of crucifixes, tablets, and other brooches wrapped in paper, a pair of broken rosary beads, "a little paper with a piece of old satin and written upon Queen of Scots," four pairs of rosary beads wrapped in a paper inscribed with the name of John Sherman, another twenty-one pairs of beads wrapped in another bit of paper with no name, and a further package of eleven pairs of small beads and one pair of large black beads, again with no addressee. Completing his inventory, Fletcher described a last paper-wrapped bundle containing three saints' relics: "*de vestes Edwalli* (or Cedwalli)," a piece of bone of St. William, and a piece of bone of Mary Magdalene.[131]

Evidence of English Catholics obtaining, trafficking in, and using such sacramental items is widespread. As the contents of the package indicate, sacramentals such as hallowed crosses and crucifixes remained popular items,[132] as did *agni dei*.[133] Palm crosses, pictures, and images were also common, as were saints' and martyrs' relics,[134] including blood, bone, and hair. Holy water was widely distributed as well.[135]

The presence of so many sacramental items underscores the fact that the rosary was but one flexible material object among many that were central to Catholic worship. One of the most important defining features of such sacramental items, recall, is their ability to accommodate priestly and lay efforts *to redefine the items' usage and meaning* as the political and/or ecclesiastical environment in which the items are used changes. As the religious environment within England altered, English Catholic authors changed the emphasis of the rosary—increasing its efficacy and its ability to contribute to the salvation of believers—to compensate for Catholic losses elsewhere. The same redefinition or reconceptualization of the benefits of sacramental objects as occurred with the rosary may also have been possible with other sacramentals, such as holy water, candles, and *agni dei*, and merits further inquiry.

CHAPTER 4

Reclaiming the Body

Receiving the Benefits of the Mass in the Absence of Priests

W HEN THE ECCLESIASTICAL COMMISSION AT YORK ASKED HER WHY she refused to come to Protestant services, Elizabeth Wilkinson, a miller's wife, claimed that she would not come because "there is neither priest, altar, nor sacrifice." The weaver Thomas Pearson concurred, saying that the new service "lacketh the Sacrament, the priest, and the altar."[1] Again and again, laypersons brought before the commission in 1576 stated that they refused to attend Protestant services because of what the Church of England could not provide: access to the sacrament of the altar which, stated another way, is access to Christ's body sacrificed for remission of sins.[2] In pre-reform England, believers witnessed a Mass at virtually every church service. The Mass served as the primary vehicle by which Christians worked to save their souls. It was also the primary medium by which Christians identified with their Savior, experiencing sensory contact with Christ—seeing Christ and perhaps even touching and tasting him through the Eucharistic bread.[3] In Protestant England, without "priest, altar, or sacrifice," how would souls be saved? How would grace be attained? How would English Catholics come to know closeness with Christ?

This chapter begins to address these large and complex issues. Following the Act of Uniformity and particularly after 1590, authors of English Catholic pastoral literature began to emphasize different understandings as to how a believer might receive the body of Christ and thus attain grace and create a perception of unity between the believer and Christ. To achieve these objectives, Catholics were encouraged to shift their focus from duplicating the traditional rituals of the Mass to fulfilling the *functions* for which the sacrament was intended. In general, three characteristics distinguish these authors' strategies: first, a belief in the spiritual rather than corporal reception of the sacraments; second, a focus on the physical, crucified Christ rather than the Christ embodied in the host; and, finally, a willingness to equate believers' bodies with Christ's body which they felt they had lost. Authors often turned to late medieval pious practices, such as mysticism, for inspiration. Or they fell back on what the church had taught was acceptable in cases of extreme necessity. In sum, they seldom failed to manipulate older practices to meet current needs. Such efforts were not radical breaks with the Catholic past. The English possibly viewed their emphasis on alternative ways to receive the benefits of the sacrament as a return to older, still acceptable church positions regarding the sacrament.[4]

As when creating new religious spaces and reinterpreting the rosary, such Catholics did not seek to challenge Roman doctrine regarding the Mass. Challenging church doctrine was heresy and would have only served to further distance English Catholics from their faith. Moreover, if lay and clerical authors wanted to appeal to the widest possible segment of English Catholics, they needed to make use of the symbols, rituals, and beliefs with which English Catholics were most familiar.[5] They could, however, endow these familiar symbols, rituals, and beliefs with new messages about the Mass.

FUNCTIONS OF CATHOLIC SACRAMENTS

The Catholic Church recognizes seven sacraments.[6] The purpose of these sacraments is primarily soteriological—or designed to help believers attain the salvation of their souls. In the late sixteenth and early seventeenth centuries, the Eucharist, or sacrament of the altar, was the most frequently performed sacrament within this soteriological system.[7] This sacrament is created when, during a Mass, a priest reenacts Christ's sacrifice of body and blood upon the cross to procure the salvation of humankind.[8] As discussed in chapter 1, this ritual action does not merely commemorate a past sacrifice made centuries previously but repeats the original sacrifice in the present time. Catholic doctrine teaches that a priest's actions in consecrating the bread and wine used in the ritual transform the substance of the bread and wine into Christ's physical body and blood.[9] By making Christ's sacrifice immediate, a priest aids the salvation of souls immediately and effectively *each time he celebrates a Mass.*

Prior to reform in England, Christians learned how to understand the sacrament of the altar from their parish priests and from a growing body of devotional works intended for the laity.[10] Both priests and literature emphasized the necessity of physical attendance at Mass to attain God's saving grace. A believer's presence at Mass fulfilled two purposes.[11] First, according to the Catholic Church's basic doctrinal position, attendance at Mass confers God's grace as an aid to salvation. Priests and literature extolled the benefits to the soul of hearing the Mass and seeing Christ's body contained in the host, or Eucharistic bread. Second, Mass brings believers to a closeness, an identification with Christ.[12] For example, the prayer *"salve salutaris hostia,"* typically found in sixteenth-century primers, allowed believers to greet Christ, welcoming him in the host as they prayed.[13] Clerics and authors of this literature taught that the Mass joins and "incorporate[s] the worthy receivers unto Christ." It links the believer not only to grace but to the "Author of Grace" himself.

In order to earn both these benefits of the sacrament of the altar—saving grace and closeness with Christ—pre-Elizabethan literature emphasized the necessity of priests and the presence of the body of Christ upon the altar.[14] Lay people understood a priest's presence to be integral to their ability to gain the benefits of the Mass. Priests consecrated the bread and wine into Christ's body and blood. Moreover, a priest typically ate the consecrated bread and drank the consecrated wine while the lay audience did not.[15] A layperson need not "communicate"—in other words, ingest either the bread or wine—to receive the benefits of the sacrament of the altar. Priests' reception of the Eucharist was considered sufficient to accrue the benefits of the sacrifice of the altar for all present. Without priests, there would be no sacrament, no benefit to the soul, no identification with Christ.

When the laity did not receive the body of Christ corporally, they experienced the sacrament of the altar in a variety of ways, many of which were tied to a priest's actions. For laypersons, *seeing* the host—when the priest elevated the consecrated bread above his head—was the key to salvation and to perceiving a closeness with Christ.[16] In pre-reform years, it was not uncommon for laypersons to go from altar to altar and from church to church to witness many elevations on the same day, to see Christ over and over again.[17]

Priests' actions were considered "points of departure," intended to trigger certain lay experiences of the Mass and bring attendees closer to Christ's saving grace and to a nearness with Christ.[18] For example, the pre-reform *Lay Folk's Mass Book* and Lydgate's *History of the Exposition of the Mass* offer meditations for the laity to accompany specific actions of the priest as he celebrates Mass. There are meditations for when the priest ascends and descends the altar steps and for when he turns to face the congregation. There are meditations for when he raises his arms, intended to spark the experience of Christ's arms outstretched upon the cross. Despite the many possible ways to participate in the Mass through the senses, meditation, and prayer, a priest's physical presence and actions were intended to structure and direct each experience.[19]

The pre-reform English liturgy also stressed access to Christ's *body* as integral to obtaining the benefits of the sacrament of the altar. Pre-reform Christians understood Christ's body to be physically present upon the altar following the priest's consecration of the Eucharistic bread. For example, the 1536 edition of the *Horae Eboracenses*, the Church of York's official Book of Hours, asked Catholics to pray to Jesus:

> O glorious Jesus, o meekest Jesus, o most sweet Jesus, I pray thee that I may have true confession, contrition, and satisfaction or I die, and that I may see and receive thy holy body God man Savior of all and mankind, Christ Jesus without sin, and that thou wilt, my Lord God, forgive me all my sins for thy glorious wounds and passion. . . .
>
> The holy body of Christ Jesus be my salvation of body and soul. (Amen.) The glorious blood of Christ Jesus bring my soul and body unto everlasting bliss. (Amen.)
>
> I cry God mercy, I cry God mercy, I cry God mercy. . . .[20]

By repeating prayers such as these, generations of English Catholics learned to equate physical experience—such as seeing and receiving—of the body of Christ with forgiveness of sins and ultimately with salvation. The body equals salvation. The blood equals heavenly bliss.

Although seemingly focused primarily upon Christ's body, the Mass emphasized the bodies of believers as well.[21] The Roman Church instructed Catholics to be physically present at Mass as frequently as possible, and Catholics were to receive the body of Christ into their own bodies at least once a year, typically at Easter.[22] The Frenchman Louis Richeome explained the necessity of reception to readers of his *Holy Pictures of the Mystical Figures of the Most holy Sacrifice and Sacrament of the Eucharist . . .* , published in English in 1619. Christ's body feeds believers

> . . . not to sustain us after the fashion of corruptible meats, which are converted into the substance of our bodies, but rather to convert our bodies into it, imprinting in them his divine qualities, and giving them a living spring of immortality; according to which our Savior hath said 'He that eateth this bread shall live eternally: He that eateth my flesh and drinketh my blood, he hath life eternal, and I will raise him up in the last day' (*John* 6.51.44).[23]

Contact with Christ's body as contained in the Eucharist, in other words, changes the physical body of the believer. It transforms the substance of the mortal body, making it more Christ-like and bringing it closer to salvation.

Finally, the sacrament of the altar knit the faithful into what the church called a body of believers, or the mystical body of Christ. The sacrament joined Catholics into a community, effectively preserving the community's memory, while simultaneously sending that memory forward to future generations.[24]

The priest and the body of Christ upon the altar were perceived as integral to this community. The church provided a location for the faithful to assemble into this one body to adore God publicly through the priests' celebration of the Mass. Without this sacrifice, Louis Richeome claimed the church would be a "body without a soul."[25]

Pastoral literature written after the Act of Uniformity linked the absence of the sacrament of the altar to perhaps the worst soteriological fear— the loss of one's soul and the impossibility of ever entering heaven to share in eternal happiness. Without a priest, there can be no Mass. Without the Mass, Christ's body is not present. Without Christ's body, there is no saving grace. As suggested by the testimony before the Ecclesiastical Commission at York, even laypeople understood what was at stake. What was the point of attending Protestant services if salvation was not available there, if they could not meet Christ there?[26] Southwell described this worry as a "sacred hunger." Catholics, he maintained, "refreshed themselves with the bread of heaven" and nourished their piety and constancy at God's table. How long could English faith remain strong, he wondered, without the sustenance of the body of Christ as provided in the Mass?[27]

FILLING THE NEED

As discussed in chapter 1, fear over the fate of their immortal souls was perhaps the greatest anxiety looming in the minds of English Catholics. For centuries, the Christian Church had attempted to focus lay efforts to achieve salvation on the sacrament of the altar. Loss of the Mass threw English Catholics into a state of apprehension over the future of their souls in the absence of their greatest aid to salvation.

Catholic priests attempted to meet the demand for the sacrament by traveling secretly throughout the English shires, celebrating Mass whenever possible. Such efforts, however, were hardly sufficient to provide regular, reliable, satisfying access to the Mass. The Jesuit William Weston, imprisoned for years in Wisbech castle, recalled both the practical difficulty and the danger of discovery inherent in priests' efforts to provide the Mass when he remembered the years of his itinerant priesthood:

> It used sometimes to happen that in Catholic houses there were no altar breads for celebrating Mass, and for that reason the principal benefit of our ministry was lost, for we could neither celebrate Mass nor distribute Holy Communion. As a precaution against this, I thought it would be well to obtain some altar-breads and carry them about with me. As we had no suitable case to put them in, my companion arranged them, and wrapped them up, quite securely as he thought, in a linen cloth which he happened

to have with him. With the constant jogging of the horse, however, they shook their way out and gradually, first three or four, then a large number dropped out and lay scattered on the public road for the space of nearly half a mile.[28]

Weston and his companion, made dangerously conspicuous by the Hansel-and-Gretel-like trail of unconsecrated communion wafers spreading out behind them, were forced to retrace their path, finding and retrieving every wafer. Imagine their fear and dismay as they discovered the large pile that had dropped in front of the Protestant pastor's house! Luckily, it was harvest time when most inhabitants of the area were off working in the fields. Either no one noticed the altar breads or no one chose to report them to the authorities.

Weston's account also illustrates some of the practical obstacles hindering the regular provision of Christ's body to believers. How was a Catholic to receive the benefits of the sacrament of the altar if there was no bread for consecration? Even if a priest could be located to celebrate a Mass, he often was unable to do so if some of the proper accoutrements were unavailable. Some sort of alternatives were needed, and English Catholic priests and laity faced quite a challenge learning to see the sacrament of the altar on new terms.

In the absence of the traditional rituals of the Mass, English Catholics, particularly after 1590, began to search for alternative means to reap the benefits of the sacrament—saving grace and a connection to Christ (especially to the body of Christ). Prior to 1590, English Catholics relied primarily on literature written by Catholics on the continent to instruct them how to understand and receive the sacrament of the altar.[29] In general, continental authors conformed to Tridentine teachings on the Eucharist.[30] This literature, written mainly by French, Spanish, or Italian Catholics or by English Catholics living on the continent in exile, reveals a distinct desire to preserve all seven sacraments without any accommodations to the realities of Catholic life under a Protestant government. Most of these authors had never experienced first hand the challenge of practicing Catholicism in such an environment. As discussed in chapter 1, many of the English Catholic exiles who wrote much of this literature were financially dependent upon the Pope and the continental Catholic princes who maintained them in exile. Exiled English writers would not have wanted to anger their patrons by voicing contradictory opinions about Church policy and risk losing these pensions. There were powerful reasons to conform one's writings to orthodox Catholic teachings.

Writers on the continent insisted upon frequent reception of the Eucharist and attendance at public Mass and worship services. They stressed two key issues: the need for a priest to administer the sacrament and that the sacrament benefited only those present at its performance. Laurence Vaux, the

English exile in Louvain and author of the most popular catechism used by English Catholics, *A catechisme or a Christian doctrine, necessarie for children & the ignorant people*, was one of the strongest advocates for maintaining the sacraments in the traditional manner.[31] Although Vaux would later travel to England on the mission, Vaux had no knowledge of the real restrictions on English Catholic worship at the time he wrote his catechism. He left too soon after the Act of Uniformity to experience the progressive legal curtailment of English Catholic pious practices.

Vaux revealed the limitations of his experience when he commanded English Catholics to attend Mass every Sunday and holy day to help assure their salvation.[32] The sacraments, Vaux instructed, were "a visible form of an invisible grace, which is instituted of God for our sanctification."[33] The sacrament of the altar was particularly efficacious, Vaux claimed.[34] According to Vaux, just as Adam and Eve ate the apple and "brought everlasting death and damnation, so this blessed Sacrament is a pledge, to bring us everlasting life. . . ."[35]

Although Vaux did not deny the existence of other means to achieve grace, absolution, and everlasting life, he offered no such tools in his catechism. In the absence of the sacrament of the altar, how would English Catholics believe themselves to be saved? Or would they think themselves damned? When Vaux discussed the sacrament of the altar, he did so in terms that made no allowance for English circumstances. For example, Vaux's explanation of the sacrament of the altar emphasized the priest's role, focusing upon the body and blood of Christ:

> which is consecrated upon an altar by a lawful priest at Mass. . . . The form of this sacrament is the words of Christ wherewith this sacrament is made wherewith the Priest speaketh in person of Christ. . . . The effect of this sacrament is to knit, join, and incorporate the worthily receivers thereof unto Christ. By the worthy receiving of this blessed sacrament, grace is increased, virtue is nourished . . . the merits of Christ's passion are received in us, our bodies and souls are spiritually nourished with this blessed sacrament (being the blessed fruit of holy Mass). . . .Who is the Minister of this Sacrament? . . . the Priest.[36]

As in pre-reform years, the priest was an integral part of the lay experience of the sacrament of the altar around whom the action flowed and through whom those in attendance received saving grace. English Catholics had an insufficient number of priests, altars, and Masses. Would English Catholics therefore conclude that an insufficient amount of grace was being deposited in their accounts of salvation?

Non-English writers on the continent, such as St. Francis Borgia, show a similar desire to keep the traditional rituals and obligations of the sacrament of the altar without concessions to English circumstances. In his pastoral treatise *A Short Rule how to Live Well*, the Spaniard Borgia counseled Catholics that it is good, commendable, and profitable to the soul to hear Mass every day because

> by that oblation the merits of our Savior's passion be applied to us. Thereby also we receive the remission of our venial sins and pardon of part of the pains that we have deserved for them. We obtain many graces and favors. . . . We must hear Mass with great reverence and devotion both inward and outward, observing what is said and done both by words and actions. . . . We must together with the priest, offer unto God the holy sacrifice of the Mass for the very same intention which he offered it to the divine majesty.[37]

Borgia wanted his readers to hear, see, feel, and even offer the Mass in all its components along with the priest in order to gain the benefits thereof.

For continentally based authors such as Vaux and Borgia, believers' physical attendance at Mass was absolutely necessary for the remission of sins, and priests were absolutely necessary to the celebration of Mass. The Italian cleric Antonio Possevino's *A Treatise on the Holy Sacrifice of the Altar, called the Masse*, translated into English in 1570 by Thomas Butler, an Englishman living in Rome, advised readers that the benefits gained by Christ's sacrifice on the cross "availeth nothing for the remission of their sins" unless Catholics received the sacraments, particularly the sacrament of the altar, from the Church.[38]

Continental writers either assumed their readers enjoyed access to churches and the services of an adequate number of priests, or they did not wish to recognize or accommodate the special needs of the English. Louis Richeome, writing from France, insisted that there should be "a public worship of Supreme honor, by which men assembled in one body, and society, might profess their faith and duty towards him [God]." Richeome still required priests to administer the sacraments ". . . under the forms of bread and wine which he shall offer, even until the end of the world by his Priests and Vicars. . . ."[39] Possevino agreed, asking his readers to recall that the priesthood had always been required for fulfilling the commandments of God.[40] Indeed, Possevino likened the priesthood and God's commandments to two halves of a whole, each imperfect without the other half.

Perhaps more importantly, Richeome stressed that all sacraments profited only those who directly participated in them, either by being present or receiving them from a priest.[41] Continental worshippers could congregate before a priest and hear a Mass and go home afterwards comforted in the knowledge that they had done their duty to the Church and for their souls' health. English worshippers could not. Yet these were the primary instructions being read by English Catholics in the first decades after 1559. How frustrating and worrisome to be told how to save your soul only to lack virtually every one of the means advertised to help do it.

SPIRITUAL RECEPTION OF THE BODY OF CHRIST

After 1590—after Catholics' best hopes for England's re-conversion to Catholicism failed—English writers began to reinterpret the reception of the sacrament of the altar to comfort Catholics over the fate of their souls. Modifying strict church doctrine on the sacraments in response to emergency circumstances was not entirely new. For example, Laurence Vaux admitted that although ordinarily a priest is required at the sacrament of baptism, a layperson can perform the rite in times of necessity, such as when a newborn child's life is in danger.[42] English Catholics now began to stretch this principle of "times of necessity" more widely to offer various options to duplicate the two functions of the Mass, for they faced not a passing challenge but a time of daily crisis whose end was not in sight.

In order to accrue the first benefit of the Mass—God's grace to aid the salvation of souls—English authors argued that English Catholics could spiritually receive the saving benefits of the sacrament of the altar even if they could not attend Mass themselves or partake of the Eucharist. Several spiritual guides published in the Elizabethan years point in this direction. Although most writers of such guides attempted to educate readers about the Mass at a basic level, such works were not intended to explain complicated doctrinal truths of the Mass or to convert non-believers to Catholic beliefs. Instead, authors worked to allow this sacrament—the laity's primary tool to achieve salvation and identify with Christ—to remain accessible to the laity in the absence of churches, altars, and priests. Their goal was to preserve Catholicism as a viable, workable faith in England.[43] As discussed in chapter 1, evidence that lay English Catholics adopted such reinterpretations is understandably slim. English Catholics often did not wish to incriminate themselves by writing letters or journals discussing their faith. Inventories of captured shipments of books and of private Catholic libraries, however, indicate that English Catholics possessed such pastoral works in significant numbers.

These guides first claim that although the Church's sacraments, particularly the Mass, contain God's grace and saving merits, God is not so bound to them that he cannot confer grace in other ways. A seminary priest from Derbyshire, John Radford (alias Tanford), steered Catholics in this direction. His 1605 work, *A Directorie Teaching the Way to the Truth in a Briefe and Plaine Discovrse against the heresies of this time*, is a brief treatise, written in plain English and devoid of complex theological justifications or arguments, for

the English laity.[44] Through his experiences growing up in England and studying on the continent, Radford was exposed both to the difficulties experienced
by the English Catholic laity in maintaining their rituals and to the Tridentine
push for conformity and hierarchy in religion on the continent. Radford
instructed readers that the sacraments contain God's saving grace and confer
such grace upon those who receive them. God could, however, bestow his
grace to achieve salvation even in the absence of the sacraments.

> These sacraments do contain in them, and confer, grace to the worthy
> receiver: Though Christ is the author of his Sacraments, neither is God so
> bound to his sacraments, but that he can bestow his grace without them,
> yet because he ordained that by means of his sacraments we are to obtain
> his grace, we neither with contempt of them, nor without will and affec-
> tion, when necessity offereth itself and just opportunity is given to receive
> them can be partakers of his grace.[45]

Radford's teachings conform to the Roman Church's traditional catechism regarding the sacraments, but they also accommodate English fears
about the frequent absence of the sacraments. Radford supported Tridentine
doctrine by instructing the laity to seek out a priest for reception of the sacraments when a reasonable opportunity was offered to do so.[46] The church typically promoted the Mass—complete with church, priest, and physically present parishioners—as the primary sacrament through which to work toward salvation. Additionally, however, the Roman Church had long assured Catholics
that God provided everything that was necessary to procure these rewards. If
Mass were unavailable, it is not a large leap for English priests and laity to conclude that if God provided sufficient accommodation to save all souls, then he
would naturally accommodate the Church's requirements regarding the Mass
to the special needs of English Catholics.

Radford counseled that God created many channels through which he
could offer salvation. Radford taught that while the Mass remained the primary
vehicle God used to confer this grace, receivers benefited from the Mass by
spiritually receiving rather than *corporally* receiving the Eucharist. Radford
counseled his readers that:

> . . . the real eating of Christ's flesh according to the worthy eating thereof
> which Christ commanded, doth make us all free from the pain of everlast-
> ing death, & the children of grace & glory. But as every man did not eat
> the prohibited apple in his own person & by his own act . . . so it is not
> needful that every man in his own person eat the flesh of Christ which is
> given to us in the Sacrament to be eaten. But it is absolutely needful that
> some or other eat it. . . .[47]

The concept of spiritual reception was not new. Theologians had long debated the exact manner in which a believer received the body of Christ.[48] Building upon older arguments, Radford claimed that just as all men share in original sin since one man ate the apple, so do all men share in the benefits of the Mass if just one or a few partake of the host. English Catholics who did not ingest the host or who had no access to a Mass were beneficiaries of the merits of the Mass through their membership in the body of believers. This ancient understanding of the efficacy of the Mass was used in the Middle Ages to justify the celebrants' reception of the Eucharist for the laity.[49] Ironically, Radford attempted to accommodate the sacramental structure of the Roman Church to the immediate needs of English Catholics by employing this orthodox explanation of "one receiving for all" to justify lay reception of the benefits of the Eucharist in the absence of priests.

William Stanney unequivocally declared that individually partaking of Christ's body as contained in the Eucharistic bread, either by viewing the Mass or ingesting communion, was not necessary to personal salvation. Published in 1617, Stanney's *A treatise on penance* . . . advocated membership in the Third Order of St. Francis, a continental lay order established in 1221 which sought the return to the more austere religious observances originally advocated by Francis of Assisi. Stanney taught that God's grace does not depend on "the common use of natural things but upon the benediction and will of God."[50] To join together in church for a public Mass complete with all ornaments and accoutrements for the common reception of the Eucharistic bread, therefore, would not be absolutely necessary. Stanney comforted English Catholics, equating them with the biblical Israelites whom God provided with plenty of water from the hard stones when they were ready to perish from thirst, perhaps in much the same way English Catholics presently hungered for the sacrament of the altar. "Whensoever, therefore thou shalt see thyself, in never so great distress, either without bread, or anything else, wherein thou mayest have any hope, call to mind, and firmly believe that he can as well without bread as with it sustain and nourish thee."[51] Stanney concludes that even without physical access to the body of Christ in form of bread, God will provide whatever is necessary for salvation.

Stanney was not questioning the validity or necessity of the Mass, just as Radford had not. Instead he, like Radford, advocated spiritual reception instead of the corporal ingestion of the Eucharist or sensory contact with Christ's body through the Mass. Stanney advised those who lacked the opportunity to receive Christ's body to first examine their consciences thoroughly. This mirrors the Roman Church's requirement that potential communicants confess and be absolved of their sins prior to receiving. In the absence of a priest, English priests believed that a private examination was the next best option. After such preparation, believers should instill within themselves "a fervent desire, to receive spiritually their Sweet Savior, in the Holy Sacrament of the Altar." Spiritual reception, the author advertised, could gain the believer almost as much merit as if he had received corporally. Stanney appears uncomfortable with an exact substitution of spiritual reception for corporal, but he clearly comforts Catholics that they would make progress toward salvation by receiving spiritually in the absence of the Mass.

As the necessity of personally receiving the body of Christ by viewing the Mass or ingesting the Eucharist declined in emphasis, it was accompanied by an increased confidence that God offered himself in sacrifice to everyone, everywhere, and not just on the altar through the Mass. This can be perceived in works of English Catholics such as William Perin, a Dominican priest from Smithfield, who intended his spiritual guide to be used both by the Catholic laity within England and by members of the English religious orders.[52] Perin recommended private contemplation of the place of God in an individual's daily life, and he downplayed the role of the priest and of the sacraments as intermediaries between God and man. Instead, he asked his readers to identify themselves with the crucified Christ.

He exhorted his readers to "Consider what thy lord god is, who he is, what manner and how great he is, *not in body*, but in might, power, goodness, wisdom & mercy."[53] The body of Christ as contained in the Eucharist was not stressed and was, in fact, downplayed.[54] Instead, Perin accentuated the omnipresence of God in every aspect of daily life as suggested in this prayer to his readers:

> Grant me most merciful and loving Lord, grace to perceive and remember always with ghostly joy and thankfulness that thou . . . dost offer thy self unto me everywhere, specially in my soul, more verily present, than I am with my self, being always and everywhere, ready to conserve, to govern, to save me, and to bring me to thy bliss.[55]

In other words, Christ made his offering to redeem humankind everywhere in the world, regardless of a priest's reenactment of Christ's sacrifice on the altar. And in the absence of priests, altars, churches, and bread, in the absence of all the sensory experiences of the Mass contained in the rituals advocated by the institutional church, Christ continued to sacrifice himself to procure man's salvation. Christ's sacrificed body remained with believers, residing in their hearts and souls and bestowing saving grace, regardless of whether they witnessed the elevation of the host, or whether the body as Eucharistic bread entered their stomachs or their priest's.[56] Perin's interpretation echoes the early Christian practice of priests who reserved a piece of the consecrated host so that it could be dropped into the chalice at the next Mass to act as a starter, or leavening agent. The church instituted this custom to remind the faithful that despite the amount of time lapsed between services, each Eucharist was one in the same with all other Eucharistic celebrations, without beginning and without end.[57] Perin interprets this belief quite liberally, but still within orthodox boundaries, to show that Christ's sacrifice was without beginning or end, provided continuously with unity and universality in all times and in all places.

A sonnet written by the English Catholic poet William Alabaster echoes this confidence in an omnipresent sacrifice, accessible to all. Alabaster likely wrote this sonnet between 1597 and 1598 when he undertook an intense, private period of prayer and meditation and completed St. Ignatius Loyola's *Spiritual Exercises*.[58] Alabaster clearly identified Christ's body as his subject in the sonnet's title, "Incarnatio est Maximum Dei Donum" ("God's Greatest Gift Is the Incarnation"):

> Like as the fountain of all light created,
> Doth pour out streams of brightness undefined,
> Through all the conduits of transparent kind,
> That heaven and air are both illuminated,
> And his light is not thereby abated:
> So God's eternal bounty ever shined
> The beams of being, moving, life, sense, mind,
> And to all things himself communicated.[59]

Alabaster played on the double meaning of the word "communicated" to highlight the totality of God's penetration into the lives, bodies, and souls of believers. God's perpetual gifts of salvation and grace do not lie stagnant, waiting for a priest to activate them through the Mass. God communicates himself. He both advertises knowledge of his gifts and he delivers them, or "communicates" them, in a manner similar to, but not limited to, the communion that occurs during the Mass. God thus imbues his saving gifts with "being," motion, feeling, and consciousness, communicating these gifts to humanity by his own luminous nature.

FINDING THE BODY

But, in the absence of the traditional rituals of the Mass, what did it mean for English Catholics praying alone or in small groups to receive Christ's body *spiritually*? Would it be the same as hearing and watching a Mass in which the priest communicates but the parishioners do not? Perhaps, but there was no priest physically present to read the Eucharistic prayers, to hold up the cup of wine and bless it, or to break the consecrated wafer to reenact the breaking of Christ's body upon the cross. Alternatively, would English Catholics imagine themselves to be ingesting the bread, recreating the taste and feel within their mouths, chewing and swallowing just as they would if they were corporally communicating? While questions such as these are useful, they are also limiting. They all presuppose a sameness between spiritual reception and sensory reception, in which the believer regretfully imagines the precise events of a Mass he cannot attend and attempts to remember them to recreate what he has lost. Such attempts, while at first fruitful, would likely become frustrating as a greater amount of time passed between the last sensory experience with the host. Memories typically recede, and as the images of the Mass faded, so might faith, as Southwell feared.

Alabaster's and other authors' promotion of an omnipresent communication of saving grace fulfilled the first function of the sacrament of the altar—delivering the saving merits of Christ's sacrifice. But replacing the second function of the sacrament—an identification and closeness with Christ—was harder to achieve. Reinterpreting how God delivered the benefits of the Mass did not address the missing sights, sounds, tastes, and touching of Christ's body that constituted such large measure of the lay experience of this sacrament. Pre-reform Christians felt they *knew* Christ through the Eucharist. How would English Catholics *know* him now?

RECLAIMING THE BODY: CHRIST'S AND ONE'S OWN

Some English Catholics tried to fulfill the second function of the sacrament of the altar—to know and identify with Christ—in new ways and not all of these ways focused upon the Mass itself. As Perin and Alabaster suggested, they had to trust that Christ would be omnipresent and make himself known, regardless of the availability of the Mass. This did not, however, mean that English Catholics should sit around waiting for Christ. English Catholics went to find him. Through meditative and performative acts, English Catholics constructed connections with Christ, emphasizing the crucified Christ, rather than Christ as contained in the host. And they drew parallels between Christ's suffering and English Catholic suffering to create shared experiences so that they might better know Christ.

When discussing the spiritual reception of the fruits of the Mass, authors such as Alabaster and Perin taught that Christ's sacrifice and communication permeated all things. A consequence of such teaching is that daily life, as opposed to the church and the sacraments, can become the focus of piety. Relatively commonplace events could turn into opportunities to experience the sacred in daily life, to identify with Christ, and to attempt to reclaim the body. In essence, Catholics could reclaim two bodies: Christ's and their own. By inscribing Christ's suffering into their own minds and bodies, they renewed the experiential connection to Christ's body that was absent without the sights, sounds, touches, and tastes of the Mass.

English Catholics could regain this connection in a variety of ways. Forging a bond with Christ could mean physical proximity, through touching with the skin, seeing with the eyes, or tasting with the tongue, as Catholics has once connected with Christ's body via the Eucharistic bread. But these connections could take other forms as well. These included imagining a conversation with Christ, imagining touching Christ's body,[60] witnessing the events of Christ's life, imagining oneself to be sharing the same thoughts, emotions, and physical pains as Christ suffered in his life, or even imagining oneself being Christ. Any Catholic anxious over losing access to Christ's body need only choose one of many ways to reclaim a connection to and sensory experience with that body. English pastoral literature advertised the means to do so.

English Catholics were also regaining the religious use of their own bodies. Protestant reform in England restricted Catholics from congregating in churches, processing on holy days, speaking to priests, and touching religious images. In other words, the penal laws restrained Catholics from using their bodies to worship in a myriad of traditional ways. By making daily life, instead of the institutional church and its sacraments, the location where sacrality could be identified and experienced, English Catholics could endow a variety of bodily experiences with religious meaning.

To identify with Christ, English Catholics tried to tap into Christ's suffering, either by meditating upon it or by equating it to their own sufferings. English Catholics' equation of their suffering with Christ's did not immediately follow from the loss of the Mass. During a period of transition, some of the pastoral literature first began to alter the focus of contemplation upon Christ— from Christ as embodied in the bread and wine of the Mass to Christ as understood as the physical, crucified Christ without reference to the Mass. While still a powerful symbol, the Eucharistic bread could no longer resonate as powerfully with English Catholics since they could typically no longer see it, taste it, or touch it. In the absence of Christ's body on the priests' altars, English Catholics may have been intimidated by the prospect of trying to develop new means to join with Christ as Son of God. How does one bond with a God?[61] They might have found it easier, however, to bridge this awesome gap by relating to Christ as suffering man—Christ as the medieval Man of Sorrows, broken upon the cross.

The contemplation of Christ's sacrifice was a familiar theme to English Catholics. The scene of the Crucifixion is commonly portrayed in late medieval English books of hours. Often, however, the crucifixion is depicted in these books as a host adorned with a crown of thorns.[62] Christ's body as contained in bread and wine was emphasized rather than the corporal body of Christ.

Following the Council of Trent, the Roman Church also depicted Christ as contained in the Eucharist as an earthly prince who held court within the church walls.[63] English Catholics in the late sixteenth and early seventeenth centuries possessed limited access to the consecrated host or to churches and thus placed greater emphasis upon the physically suffering Christ. This corporal image would have reinforced the images of the physically suffering English Catholic martyrs who were incarcerated and/or publicly executed. It would also have reinforced the feelings of loss, suffering, and persecution experienced by many Catholics who did not decide to make the ultimate sacrifice for their faith.

Pastoral literature written by English Catholics succeeds in evoking powerful mental images for readers to meditate upon to identify with the suffering Christ. These are often intense, graphic images of Christ's bodily suffering, intended to make readers feel as if they are present with Christ at the crucifixion. If Catholics could not see Christ upon the altar in the host, they could see him in their minds and with their spirits, just as their spirits received the saving benefits of the sacrifice of the altar in the absence of attendance at Mass or corporal reception of the Eucharist. John Bucke, an English secular priest and author of a book of instructions for using the rosary, *Instructions for the use of the beades*, published in 1589, prompted his readers to meditate upon Christ's crucifixion by acting as their tour guide, walking them step by step through each phase of Christ's suffering.

> And here behold how the cruel tormentors do boisterously pull off his clothes fast cleaving to his flesh which procured a new torment. Mark how they stretched him along and nailed hands and feet with rough and blunt nails to the cross. Consider what huge torture he endured in every member and part of his body, through all his senses in one instant while they hoisted him up thus hanging upon nails by his hands and feet, with all the weight of his body, having no other thing to rest upon.[64]

Bucke placed his audience in the midst of the action. Bucke included the well-known events, such as the nailing of the hands and feet to the cross, in his tour. He also attempted to stimulate readers' imaginations by including minute details as to what Christ's human body was enduring, something to which Bucke's readership of mortal humans might relate. For example, Christ's clothes adhered to his skin, attached by the drying blood from his previous scourging. You understand, Bucke seems to intimate, what it would feel like to have that fast-stuck cloth ripped off, reopening the fresh wounds, causing the blood to flow again. And imagine not only the pain of the penetration of the rough, rude nails into the tender flesh of the palms of the hands and soles of the feet, but consider the all-encompassing pain of supporting the entire weight of a full-grown man's body on those ripped hands and feet, the flesh tearing further as the burden pulled the body downward.

A brief, seventeenth-century manuscript entitled "A Meditation on our Savior's Passion" also focuses on Christ's physical suffering, simultaneously reestablishing the lost connection to Christ's body and his sacrifice and reminding readers of the sufficiency of Christ's sacrifice for the salvation of their souls. The unnamed author guides the reader through the suffering and gore of the crucifixion as Bucke did, asking his audience to "Behold him fastened to a cross accursed," and witness the stretching of Christ's arms and hands to be nailed to the wood. His head bleeds and lolls to one side without anything to prop it upright. Streams of blood flow from Christ's body, as he hungers and thirsts in his agony.[65]

> Then think what love he had that bore this pain
> And even for love sit down and weep again
> But as thou weepst look upon the Cross[66]
> And count what gain thou hast by his Life's Lost
> Look up and reckon over his griefs again
> And thou shalt find great comfort in his pain
> Behold he dies, but dies that thou mayest live
> He loses strength, thee greater strength to give
> He sleeps in Death to give thee greater light
> And by his wounds, thy wounds are healed quite . . .
> This Doom thy quital nakedness and blows
> Both health and righteous garments on thee throws.
> His Curse did bless the mourning, give thee joy
> His thirst and hunger thine did quite destroy.
> Those precious fountains powered out for thy good,
> Are wells of life in thee, sprung from his blood.[67]

By emphasizing the crucified Christ rather than Christ as contained in the host, this author redirected English Catholic anxieties away from that to which they had no access. Christ's suffering on the cross delivered life to humanity just as the Eucharistic bread sustained souls.

It is simply a question of where authors place their emphasis. Christ's body and the Eucharistic bread are one and the same. The sacrifice is the same, whether upon the cross or upon the altar. This author even refers to Christ's body dying upon the cross as bread. As Christ's life force ebbs, he pens, "The Bread is hungry, dew of heaven doth thirst."[68] But here the bread is suffering man on a cross rather than consecrated wafer on an altar. The author suggests an alternative way for the faithful to experience Christ's body and receive the benefits of the Mass without the performance of the sacrament itself.

The author of this meditation bridges the gap between man and an awe-inspiring God that might intimidate English Catholics seeking to form new spiritual connections with Christ. He does so by alternating the imagery of his verse between God's great deeds and Christ's suffering as a human on the cross. The same God who gave meaning to all things bridged the gap between God and man through the incarnation. He was now fastened to a cross, just as any man might be. The same hands and arms that created the heavens and the earth were now nailed to a tree. The same deity who gave homes to birds, beasts, and men and who created the kingdoms of the world now lacked a place to rest his bleeding head, crowned with thorns.[69] Catholic men and women knew this pain, fear, and the sense of not fully belonging. They experienced these physical sensations and emotions in many facets of their day-to-day lives. As Bucke phrased it, they bore their *own* crosses.[70] Through Christ's incarnation and sacrifice, Christ and these Catholics shared common experiences of suffering that would allow English Catholics to feel a greater unity with their deity in the absence of the Mass.

In a related exercise intended to establish connections between the believer and Christ, priests such as William Perin suggested that readers imagine themselves not just watching Christ's crucifixion but participating in a similar event themselves wherein their own bodies were crucified. While prayer and meditation are normally thought of as "interior" or "transcendental" activities, Perin stressed the visual and tactile aspects of the experience. In doing so, he followed the lead of Ignatius Loyola's *Spiritual Exercises* and other lay prayer books that frequently advocated vivid imagery. Perin's exercise, however, differs dramatically from Loyola's in its focus on the crucifixion and detailed instructions to recreate imaginatively the marks of the crucifixion upon the believer's own body.[71] Perin exhorted Catholics to *pull* sin out of themselves so that they might be "knit and made one spiritually with [Jesus]."[72] Perin became graphic in recommending spiritual crucifixion when he ordered:

> These foresaid virtues of our Lord Jesus Christ thou must ask of him and labor to print them in to thy body and soul (as much as in thee lieth) all thy life time . . . beholding by devout contemplation, the image and memory of his crucified life and death . . . stretching and nailing thy self . . . unto his cross, so that to what so ever thou turnest thy self, either on the right hand, either on the left hand thou mayest behold, on that part of thy body and on that side, one of these virtues in Jesus set before thine eyes to behold and to follow. For our Lord Jesus will make no one partakers of his death that refuseth to crucify for his sake, his own flesh with vices and lusts, and to mortify the same.[73]

Now Perin's reader must meditate upon the memory of crucified Christ (not on the host). He must mentally stretch and nail himself unto Christ's cross. He must regard himself as Christ's wounded body with great deliberation and thoroughness, beholding the wounds of Christ when he looks at his own hands and sides that have been pierced just as Christ's body was pierced. The believer's identification with Christ crucified, rather than with Christ as salvation recreated through the Mass, could hardly be more clear.

Priests such as Perin and Henry Garnet brought their readers closer to Christ by asking them to use their own minds and bodies to mentally and physically experience what Christ had suffered. In his prayers dedicated to the Five Wounds of Christ, Garnet begged God to wound him in body and soul, in memory of Christ's Passion, so that he would "melt" into Christ's love. He prayed "Sweet Jesus, imprint in my heart a continual memory of thy Passion that may incessantly move my mind to compunction, wound and wholly swallow up my mind melting and consuming it in the love. . . . O Passion most noble, of my Lord and Savior, wound my soul."[74] Strikingly, such authors did so by barely mentioning the primary sacrament, the Eucharist, through which identification with Christ was traditionally achieved and to which priests traditionally controlled access. These priests manipulated the symbols of the most important Catholic ritual in the ongoing creation of new understandings about the ritual to meet the need of Catholics to feel a connection to Christ in an ongoing emergency situation.

In addition to identifying with Christ through meditation upon his suffering, English Catholics also recreated their bonds with the body of Christ by comparing their own bodily hardships at the hands of the Protestant government with Christ's sufferings. The recusant Thomas Pounde summarized his thirty years of distress and imprisonment in an appeal to Christ written in 1606. He discussed his sacrifices openly with God, reminding him that

> Thou hast accepted me to lie for thy Catholic cause in prison and three times therefore to be put in irons. . . . (I have endured) so many committings and many fold afflictions so many years for my zeal of thy holy truth and the honor of thy house, sweet Jesus, send me some special comfort in thee at my last hour against all enemies of my soul for thy accepting of me so oft and so long to some partaking with thee in thy sufferings.[75]

Pounde perceived that he had suffered so long and so much for his Christ that he partook of some of Christ's own sufferings. As a result, Pounde felt "accepted" by Christ. He assumed Christ watched his incarcerations, interrogations, and sacrifices and found them pleasing. He felt free enough in his relationship with his God to discuss these issues in a respectful yet informal way, unbound by the conventions of the Church's institutional prayers. Sharing the hardships of Christ linked this man to his God.

Francis Eyerman wrote to his brother who was imprisoned for the faith in London and attempted to comfort him with a similar comparison of suffering. He advised his brother that each time he felt burdened under his sufferings to imagine that suffering was instead "some such like grief that Christ himself received for you and what great comparison (there) is between your two persons and there shall you find yourself well comforted."[76] In this telling phrase, Eyerman refers to his brother and Christ as two persons, not as one mortal man and his God. English Catholics could use their own sufferings—their incarcerations, their interrogations, and torture, the searches of their homes, the arrests or emigrations of friends and family, anything causing them mental or physical distress—as opportunities to identify with Christ as suffering man. This did not diminish English Catholic respect for or worship of their God, but it was a mindset that reinforced a connection to Christ.

Perhaps the strongest efforts to identify with Christ came by equating Christ's suffering at the crucifixion with English Catholic experiences at executions and burials. Those who practiced such symbolism intended to advertise their commitment to the Catholic faith, but they also attempted to identify with and participate in Christ's sacrifice. And prior to journeying into the afterlife, they hoped to tap into any grace available from linking their deaths to Christ's. Such bonds could take a variety of forms and were often overt and highly publicized.

The priest John Mush draws a powerful connection between persecuted Catholics and the persecuted Christ in his account, written about 1600, of the sufferings of the Yorkshire martyr Margaret Clitheroe, the same martyr whom Protestant authorities asked the question with which we began this study, "What is the church?" Mush coordinated missionary efforts in Yorkshire and other northern counties in the decades around the turn of the century.[77] He witnessed Clitheroe's arrest and sentencing and was probably one of the last Catholic priests to visit her before her execution.

Protestant authorities arrested Clitheroe, a butcher's wife, in York in 1586. After discovering "priest stuff" in her house, they confined her and accused her of entertaining Catholic priests. Upon being arraigned, Clitheroe refused time and again to enter a plea to the charges, claiming she had committed no crime by receiving good, virtuous men who wanted nothing other than to save her soul. She was sentenced to death.[78]

Clitheroe herself apparently did not try to advertise publicly the similarities between her ordeal and Christ's. She clearly saw herself as dying *for* Christ. She claimed she was "joyful to be bound for Christ's sake."[79] In the days before her execution, she fasted and prayed fervently. Each time she walked through town to face her accusers, she gave alms to the poor. By such endeavors, she attempted to fulfill the obligations of a good Catholic preparing for death.

Whereas Clitheroe thought of herself as dying *for* Christ, Mush clearly portrays her as dying *as* Christ when he draws parallels between the events of Christ's crucifixion and Clitheroe's martyrdom. During her arraignment, Clitheroe's judges appear reluctant to pass judgment on her, recalling Pontius Pilate's reluctance to sentence Jesus, whom Pilate felt had committed no crime. However, just as a group of unnamed rabbis and Jewish leaders pushed for Jesus's conviction, so did a group of unnamed Protestant ministers "which most greedily thirsted for her blood" come to the judge, exhorting him to sentence her. Clitheroe, they reminded him, had broken the queen's law and if she were allowed to live, more Catholics would refuse to acknowledge the queen's authority. The judge "thinking to wash his hands with Pilate" turned over the decision to the city council, just as Pilate allowed a boisterous crowd the option of saving Jesus by giving them authority to free one criminal that day. The York counsel, like Pilate's crowd, elected to carry out the execution.[80]

Sustained only by bread and brackish water, Clitheroe spent her last three days fasting and praying. When the time for her execution arrived, a sheriff, Gibson, led her from her place of confinement through the streets of York. Clitheroe arrived at the Tollbooth prison where she was taken to the lowest level. As the men turned their backs, the women present took off Clitheroe's clothes, laid her on the ground, and placed linen over her face and over her "secret parts." Two soldiers each took one of Clitheroe's hands and bound them with string "so that her arms made a perfect pattern of a cross." A sharp stone, approximately the size of a man's fist, was positioned beneath her back. A weight was then placed upon her chest. Clitheroe, approximately 30 years of age, finally died as she was crushed beneath the weight, estimated to be between 700 and 800 pounds, which broke her ribs, "causing them to burst forth at the skin." Attending her execution were magistrates, soldiers, and a few beggars to place the weights on Clitheroe's body. After her death, her clothes were distributed.[81]

The similarities Mush draws between Jesus's death and Clitheroe's are unmistakable. Clitheroe waits three days to join her God, just as Jesus waited three days before ascending into heaven. During these three days, she accepted her death, just as Christ recognized and accepted the necessity of his death. She spent her time kneeling alone in prayer, just as Jesus knelt by himself in the garden at Gethsemane asking for the courage to endure his fate. Recalling Christ's journey through the streets, bearing his cross in front of the crowds, Clitheroe walked barefoot and barelegged to the place of her execution in the Tollbooth through a "street which was so full of people that she could scarce pass by them." Like Christ, she was stripped naked prior to her execution, a particularly humiliating experience for a respectable sixteenth-century woman. In the absence of a wooden cross, Clitheroe's body formed her cross, as her outstretched arms tied to posts resembled the desired symbol. The dressing and laying out of Clitheroe's body in linen by the women is reminiscent of the care shown to Christ's corpse after it was removed from the cross as Mary and other female disciples of Christ anointed the body and wrapped it in strips of linen before laying it in the tomb. The witnesses to Clitheroe's crushing bear similarities to Christ's audience of magistrates, rabbis, soldiers, and thieves. After her death, Mush writes that Clitheroe's clothes and possessions were distributed, as Christ's clothes found new owners following his decease. Clitheroe's clothes likely served as martyr's relics for many who received them. In the final parallel to Christ, Mush revealed that the authorities executed Clitheroe on a Friday, just as Christ perished on Good Friday.[82]

Because the events of Clitheroe's death were so contemporary, physically proximate, and available, the equation of her sufferings with Christ's provided the type of immediate, sensory, and experiential connection to Christ's sacrifice that English Catholics were seeking in the absence of the Mass. Such options, recall, need not necessarily involve the Mass itself but rather the fulfillment of the *functions* of the Mass, the second function of which is to create connections to Christ. Other English writers were telling Catholics to visualize vividly the events of the crucifixion to create bonds with Christ. They walked readers through Christ's arrest, imprisonment, trial, and execution. Here was a Christ-like arrest, imprisonment, trial, and execution right before their eyes. Mush's implicit and explicit parallels allow those aware of Clitheroe's ordeal to reenact and relive the events of Christ's sacrifice as if they were physically present. Of course, Mush was not claiming that Clitheroe was Christ or that her death obtained the same saving grace as Christ's. But the execution did offer actual observers and those who read or heard about her martyrdom the realistic opportunity to witness something so similar to Christ's ordeal that they could forge emotional bonds with the suffering Christ in the absence of the sensory experiencing of Christ's body at Mass. Instead of the challenge of trying to connect to events occurring 1600 years previously, English Catholics could use the immediacy of the Christ-like martyrdom of a middle-class English Catholic woman in Yorkshire to spark their imaginations and enhance their experience of Christ's sufferings. If it could happen to Christ and it could happen to Margaret Clitheroe, it could happen to them.

And there is evidence of English Catholics drawing parallels between Christ's and Clitheroe's deaths and their own experiences. The recusant laywoman Jane Wiseman, accused of maintaining Catholic priests, was "very much aware of the powerful example of Saint Margaret Clitheroe" as Wiseman was brought before her judges. Like Clitheroe, she refused to enter a plea, knowing what the consequences would be. She was sentenced to be crushed to death. According to John Gerard, she wanted to follow in Clitheroe's footsteps "rejoicing that she had not been thought unworthy to suffer for Jesus's sake the form of death she had hoped to be hers." When she heard that she was to be placed on the ground with her arms extended in the form of a cross as Clitheroe was, Wiseman reportedly drew parallels between such a death and Christ's as she commented, "Now, blessed be God that I shall die with my arms a cross as my Lord Jesus." [83]

Although Clitheroe herself did not draw the parallel between her own death and Christ's, many other executed Catholics drew much more explicit parallels between their martyrdoms and Christ's, often employing the symbol of the cross in a variety of ways. The Venerable Anthony Briant carried a cross of his own making as he was drawn through the streets toward Westminster to his condemnation in November 1581.[84] And the Jesuit priest William Weston, in his autobiography, described how a small group of lay Catholics, slated to die, arrived at the gallows wearing their shrouds. They placed the garments around their necks and brought them down in "transverse folds over the breasts in the form of a cross. To make the gospel of the cross even more apparent still they had stitched a black strip of cloth down the full length of their burial robes."[85] These acts will be placed in a broader context of martyrdom in chapter 8.

Executed Catholics were not the only Catholics to use the cross overtly to connect their deaths to Christ's: ordinary burials of lay Catholics exhibited this same desire to imprint the cross upon their deaths. Visitation Correction Books of this period include the presentations of many lay people for placing cloths in the forms of crosses upon the dead, similar to the manner in which the lay Catholics described by Weston arranged their shrouds in the shape of crosses and stitched crosses onto their clothes prior to their executions. The cloths placed upon bodies were often the same cloths that had been placed upon the high altar of the church before reform. By placing items connected with the Mass upon their dead, these lay Catholics made a conscious effort to connect Christ's sacrifice and body with the deaths of loved ones. In 1611, Jacob Darne, of the deanery of Blackburn in Lancashire, was presented "for bringing his Daughter to the church to be buried with a cross of towel to the evil example of others."[86] Richard Proctor of Caton parish in Lonsdale deanery created quite a commotion in his parish church during the burial of his father in January of 1622/3 when the churchwarden removed the cross made of towel which Proctor had placed on the corpse's breast. Proctor apparently retrieved the towels, made another cross, and replaced them upon his father's body "to the disturbance of the minister and congregation."[87] In 1600, the suspected recusant Ralph Hitchmough, a husbandman of Much Wooten, made it impossible for church officials to remove the crosses from his wife's corpse. He attached a large red cross to the sheet covering her body, but he also burned two more crosses onto the sheet with an iron. Even if the officiating minister had been able to remove the stitched-on cross, he would have had to unwrap the corpse and change winding sheets if he wanted to remove the other two.[88]

English Catholics also attempted to place their own bodies in proximity to Christ's sacrificed body upon the altar. Protestant clergy taught that the location of one's body after death was of little importance and had no impact upon one's salvation. English Catholics, however, continued to show concern over the places their bodies were buried. Many insisted in their wills that they be buried in sacred ground.[89] Some Catholics, however, wanted to associate their deaths more strongly with Christ's crucifixion and the salvation procured thereby. At St. Mary Cray in Cornwall, for example, there exists a grave dating from 1604 containing the body of Richard Manning. The grave is located inside the communion rails.[90] By placing one's body inside the special boundaries of the communion rail, a person is asking to be perpetually associated with Christ's sacrifice. Such concern with the location of the grave signals a continued belief in the immanentist traditions of Catholicism, particularly of holy spaces and a desire to bond with Christ crucified and obtain his saving grace.

A final, more radical option to create intimate bonds with Christ and obtain the saving grace earned at the crucifixion was that suggested by Arthur Crowther and Thomas Vincent in *Jesus, Maria, Joseph. . . .* The two Benedictines advocated ways for a believer to assume both the role of priest and of the Eucharistic host within his own person, sacrificing his own body as if upon an altar. This involved transforming oneself by prayer into the Eucharist and offering oneself to Christ rather than having a priest transform the bread into the body of Christ and offer it to the believer. Truthfully, this was probably not an option adopted by many English Catholics. It is significant, however, in that it reflects the strong desire of Catholics to fulfill the two primary functions of the sacrament of the altar and the extremes to which English Catholic authors might go to offer options to satisfy this need. The authors intended *Jesus, Maria, Joseph* to promote worship upon the rosary, but the Christocentric prayers containing the language for laypersons to transform themselves into Christ were included separately from the prayers of the rosary. Crowther and Vincent specifically informed their readers that these new prayers were not part of the rosary nor were they mandatory.[91]

Crowther and Vincent recalled the earlier efforts of priests such as Radford, Stanney, Perin, and the layman Alabaster to advertise that God was so powerful that he could provide all the benefits of his sacraments in the absence of the sacraments themselves. Holiness and grace, they believed, issued forth from the "Essence and Person" of the divine, not necessarily from any gestures or material forms that may have been joined with this essence and person.[92]

Crowther and Vincent differed from these earlier priests, however, by suggesting that laypersons can gain the salvation and the closeness with Christ provided by the Mass not by spiritually receiving the benefits of the sacrament of the altar celebrated elsewhere but by, *in effect, performing the sacrament upon themselves.* By this, I mean that Crowther and Vincent seem to advocate that the supplicant use his own body as the material substance, similar to the unconsecrated bread, which will act as the Eucharistic host. The human body will be consecrated and have its substance annihilated and replaced with the body of Christ. The intent to connect with Christ by vividly experiencing Christ's sufferings and equating them with English Catholics' own hardships takes on a new form. In this most intimate of acts, Catholics could perhaps experience the closest connections, connections of substance, that they had ever achieved even when the sacrament of the altar had been available.

Crowther and Vincent phrase in a variety of ways this desire to become one with Christ through the transformation of the substance of the supplicant's body into Christ's body. They called these prayers "Elevations," reminiscent of a priest's elevation of Christ's body when he raises the consecrated bread over his head. The authors began the 8th Elevation by having the supplicant litanize all that humankind owes to Christ's sacrifice and stressing how supplicants already enjoyed a close connection to Christ by this debt.

> Your Divinity (as it were) Incarnated, is my substance, and my subsistence: your humanity (as it were) divinized, is my health and my life: your Body is my diet and your Blood is my Bath, your Death is my life, your weakness is my strength, your Cross is my quiet, your suffering is my rejoicing. Thus I am yours and you are mine.[93]

Yet the supplicant appears to want to forge even closer links:

> Let me forget myself, for you forget Your self for me: Let me leave and lose myself, for you annihilate Your self for me: Let me be yours, for You are mine; let me be all yours, for You are all mine; Let me be all yours for-ever, for you are all mine forever.[94]

The supplicant then asks God to act as priest and consecrate the supplicant, much as a priest consecrates the bread and wine. The supplicant, like the bread and wine, becomes filled with Christ and thereby becomes a part of Christ himself.

And I am yours (O my loving Savior!) by your *self*, and by a means so noble
. . . by so many sorts of ways which give you unto me, which *consecrate* me
to you; and which even draw and drain you all out for me . . . you are not
only mine and I yours, but I am in you . . . by your Incarnation, you establish a new manner of gracious favor in the world, which makes me in the
Order of Grace, not only existent by you, but existent in you. So that by
this manner of Grace . . . I am not only yours, not only by you, but I am in
you; I live in you, I make a part of you; I am bone of your bone, and flesh
of your flesh; let me also be spirit of your Spirit, let me live by your life, let
me participate of the Interior, of Grace, of the Estate, of the Spirit of your
Mysteries.[95]

Christ empties himself to fill the supplicant, sharing the supplicant's body and
mind, much in the way that Christ embodied in the Eucharistic bread nourished and filled the body and spirit of the communicant. But this supplicant
takes this sharing further and posits a two-way exchange between God and
man. Man becomes part of the divinity, being "in" Christ, living in Christ, and
being a part of Christ. The supplicant considers himself bodily connected to
Christ through bone and flesh but desires a further intimacy. To become one
with Christ implies a sharing of Christ's interior, his essence, his grace, his spirit. Man as man cannot hope to achieve such participation with the divine. But
man consecrated and substantially transformed into Christ might. In the 9th
Elevation, the supplicant perceives that his consecration by God placed him in
the order of Grace which was a condition specially suited to allow the reception and forbearance of God's sacred operations and which allowed a more
"strict and inward Communication."[96] Crowther and Vincent suggest that these
prayerful Elevations lead to a special, interior communion or Mass between
believer and God.

    Crowther and Vincent's subtle allusions to the actual transformation of
the supplicant into Christ occur in the 12th and 13th Elevations. The supplicant, through the special manner of grace recognized earlier, has been separated from himself and "united and incorporated" into God, as a "parcel" of
God. This grace has "annihilated" a part of him, but simultaneously established
God within him and he within God.[97] The supplicant now, instead of asking
God to act as priest to consecrate him, acts as his own priest, causing the annihilation[98] of his own substance and its replacement with the divine:

In the strength and virtue of this Grace which hath its origin in you, and in
your new estate of God-Man; I annihilate myself in my own self, to be in
you; and I will carry in my soul a death to all things, that I may live in you:
And I will that my Being be reduced to be nothing else than a pure
Capacity of you filled up with you. . . . *I will transform myself into you.*[99]

Crowther and Vincent identified the mechanism through which the supplicant could effect such a transformation as love, and they further clarified that this transformation takes place at the level of substance:

> . . . Love puts you on the cross, and placeth us in Glory; and, finally, this Love transforms us into you, not only by a communication of qualities, but even by a communication of substance, O Son of God! I love you, and I adore you in this love, in this annihilation, in this powerful transformation.[100]

By coupling with humankind, God does not just make believers more Christ-like in humility, selflessness, and goodness, mimicking Christ's actions during his incarnation. This communication does not allow believers merely to act like Christ and hope therefore to be saved by divine grace that would recognize a similarity of good works. Such good works were important, certainly, but Crowther, Vincent, and their readers wanted to achieve more than this. They wanted to share themselves with Christ and for Christ to share himself with them at the level of substance, or of what each was essentially. No deeper bond with Christ could be forged.

ORIGINS OF THESE OPTIONS

All of these methods—spiritual reception of the sacrament, meditation upon the crucified Christ, equation of personal suffering to Christ's suffering, and the radical suggestion of transforming the believer's substance into Christ's—were alternatives to traditional experiences of the Mass. Faced with an inability to provide Mass for all believers or to attend Mass, English priests and laypersons developed these alternatives. What these efforts share is the desire to re-conceptualize a believer's relationship to Christ and the salvation available through his sacrifice in the absence of the Mass. Beginning in approximately 1590, the clergy and laity began to realize they needed such options. As discussed in chapter 1, Catholics' realistic hopes of reestablishing their religion as the state-sponsored religion faded in the aftermath of Mary Queen of Scots' execution, the failure of the Spanish Armada, and the inability of the papacy to provide adequate priests and sacraments to completely satisfy English Catholic soteriological needs. It did not necessarily follow, however, that Catholic faith faded with this realization.

Re-conceptualizing the sacrifice of the altar was hardly new to the sixteenth and early seventeenth centuries. English clerical and lay efforts to mold the experience of the Mass to fulfill the functions of the sacrament were part of a series of negotiations over the meaning of the Eucharist that had been evolving for centuries. As one of the Church's most potent sacraments and symbols, theologians, clerics, and laypersons continually argued about the celebration of the Mass and the symbol of the Eucharist as each group attempted to gain access and control over both and the freedom to interpret both. Despite the institutional church's efforts to regularize access to and the experiencing of Christ's sacrifice, both clerics and laypersons continually searched for opportunities to experience the sacrament of the altar in ways that fulfilled their own religious and perhaps even secular needs.[101] In the twelfth and thirteenth centuries, for example, the Roman Church attempted to design a blueprint for the Mass, dictating the clothes to be worn, the language to be used, and the gestures to be performed by the priest. The institutional church instructed the laity how they wanted laypersons to experience and interpret what they were seeing and hearing during each ritual moment.[102] It tried to control the rituals and symbols surrounding the creation of Christ's body as tightly as possible. The Council of Trent attempted to regularize access to and the experiencing of the Mass even further.[103]

The Roman Church, however, was striving to control access to what many clerics and laypersons traditionally considered their own most powerful tool for salvation and link to Christ. As Miri Rubin has argued, the institutional church might control the creation of Christ's body through its control of the Mass, but once created, the laity and clergy could reclaim some control over the body of Christ.[104] It is in this tradition that English clerics and laypersons reinterpreted the *functions* and reception of the Mass to meet their needs, thus illustrating the two-way interaction between institutions of religion and ordinary believers that is commonplace in most faiths, regardless of official doctrines.

To reinterpret the reception of the Mass and an individual's relationship with the divine, Catholic authors drew upon many diverse strands within late medieval Catholic lay piety, reshaping them to fit the particulars of their situations. Elements of late medieval mysticism can clearly be seen in Radford's, Stanney's, Perin's, and Alabaster's exhortations to readers to forge a direct channel to God's grace in the absence of priests.[105] Mystics such as Teresa of Avila, Julian of Norwich, and Margery Kempe built one-on-one relationships with Christ that were characterized by high levels of conversational intimacy, emotion, and even physical sensation.[106] English priests and laymen attempted to create similar experiential knowledge and spiritual affection with Christ through vivid, experiential, individualized contemplation of the physical body of Christ and his suffering. Crowther and Vincent's creation of a substantial coexistence with Christ follows these mystical efforts to their most radical conclusions.

In late medieval England, the English Christian Church viewed mystics as potential threats to the public fabric of the church. In bypassing priests' roles as intermediaries, by claiming direct access to the divine, mystics challenged the foundation of the Church hierarchy.[107] The Church, while tolerating many mystics, channeled mysticism into approved roles and behaviors so that Church authority and the unity of Catholic community were not undermined.

Paradoxically, the English priests discussed above (the men whose professional role in the Church was perhaps most threatened by individuals' direct access to God's grace) appear to recommend bypassing the traditional Church hierarchy. They encouraged individual relationships with God similar to those which late medieval mystics practiced. Yet, akin to the late medieval church's efforts, these priests attempted to regulate individuals' direct access to the divine. They directed each stage of the believer's mental processes. They acted as non-embodied priests, directing the reader's thoughts and feelings and providing proper prayers. Most, such as Radford, commanded readers to go to priests whenever they were available. Experiencing the benefits of the sacrament of the altar *in absentia* was only permissible when no realistic opportunity existed to obtain access to a priest. The difference was that now, instead of seeing personal connections with Christ that have been achieved without direct sacerdotal mediation as a *threat* to the Catholic Church, these English priests viewed one-on-one interactions with the divine as *one of the only ways to sustain* the English Catholic faith.

Another strand of late medieval lay piety from which these priests drew their inspiration were the many spiritual guides written touting how a believer could receive the benefits of an act of piety by spiritually experiencing it rather than physically performing it. The Church, for example, allowed pilgrims to make pilgrimages for the deceased or for believers who were too ill to make the pilgrimages themselves. Catholics rather freely interpreted this leniency, however, to mean that all benefits of pilgrimage could be gained without leaving home. This helped spur the fifteenth-century growth of devotional literature that explained to readers how to follow an imaginary pilgrimage in their own homes and gain all the indulgences and benefits as if the pilgrim had made the actual journey.[108]

English priests and laypersons accepted these earlier traditions regarding the accrual of spiritual benefits by contemplative action, but we must also confront the changes English priests and laypersons made in these traditions. By extending the application of these traditions to the sacraments, Catholics such as Radford and Stanney reinterpreted the efficacy of the Mass. And Perin's, Crowther's, and Vincent's readers, for example, no longer *followed* Christ's sacrifice. Instead, the reader *experienced* the sacrifice in her own body, mentally crucifying or substantially transforming herself, in order to create the intimate identification with Christ that was unavailable elsewhere.

Overall, the English Catholic clergy and laity provide some continuity with church tradition. These Catholics, however, reinterpreted these old forms to allow Catholics the opportunity to fulfill the functions of the sacrament of the altar in the midst of a changing environment that denied them their traditional access to Christ's body and its saving grace. Despite the lack of priests and access to the Mass, Catholics could earn Christ's saving grace. They could also identify with Christ, experience closeness with Christ, and even *become* the suffering Christ to stave off what Southwell called "sacred hunger" for Christ's body as formerly experienced in the sacrament of the altar. This sacrament recreated Christ's incarnation in this world and duplicated his sacrifice of his human body upon the cross. Christ came in the body, flesh of our flesh, and bone of our bone. English Catholics believed that Christ walked among us, wept for us, ate with us, served us, touched us, and finally died for us. Is it surprising that in the absence of one of the only physical intimacies Catholics retained with him—the celebration of the Mass and the viewing, touching, and eating of Christ's body as contained the Eucharistic bread—they should search for other ways to walk with him, weep with him, serve his needs, and feel his immediate presence? Or that the connections of sacrifice and bodily suffering should bind them? As the examinants at York revealed in their testimony, they understood what was missing at Church of England services: an altar, a sacrifice, the body of Christ itself. The opportunity to endure hardship for Christ, with Christ, and in Christ allowed English Catholics to reclaim Christ's body and reclaim the use of their own to fulfill their pious and soteriological needs.

Catholics anxious over their own salvation had long understood salvation to be achievable through the frequenting of priests and the sacraments provided by priests, particularly the sacrament of the altar. An examination of the options offered for English Catholics to reinterpret the efficacy of the Mass exposes just the tip of the iceberg of the menu of choices being offered to help English Catholics attain saving grace and build new forms of closeness with Christ. Other sacraments could also be reinterpreted to provide such benefits. Perhaps one of the most fruitful inquiries that could be made would be a similar exploration of the sacrament of penance. Priests were frequently unavailable to perform the sacrament of penance so that laypersons could obtain forgiveness for their sins. Recognizing the challenges inherent in such an environment, many English Catholic authors began counseling those burdened by the weight of their sins to construct one-on-one relationships with God so that they might confess directly to God (instead of to a priest). These lay Catholics could then judge their own actions and impose penance upon themselves for their sins. Authors advertised the multifold benefits of such a practice—a closer relationship with God, an imitation of Christ's sacrifice on the cross, and ultimately the improved health of one's soul. Examinations of conscience were not new, but these authors, typically English clerics, now emphasized them instead of the traditional reception of the sacrament of penance. Self-judgment and self-imposition of penance, however, were new. In comparison to this exploration of the sacrament of the altar, such a study of penance likely would confirm a continuity in the approach taken by English clerics to re-conceptualize the benefits of sacraments—concentrating on *function* rather than *institutionally prescribed form*—so that their countrymen might receive their benefits.

Such re-conceptualizations expose the willingness of English Catholics to de-emphasize or reinterpret traditional rituals regarding the sacraments, much in the same way some Catholics willingly reinterpreted their use of religious space and material objects such as the rosary. In doing so, English Catholics promoted as common, day-to-day practice what the Roman Church allowed only in cases of extreme necessity. But English Catholics perceived most days in Protestant England to be ones of extreme necessity. The following three chapters explore Catholics' experiences in three very different areas of England—London, Cornwall, and the northern shires—and provide ample examples of English Catholics acting in just such ways.

CHAPTER 5

Lawyers, Jailbirds, Grocers, and Diplomats

Catholic Options for Piety and Community in London

T HE SAGA OF WEALTHY CATHOLICS IN AND NEAR LONDON IS A FAMILIAR one. Prominent families flaunted the penal laws, continuing their own Catholic practices and encouraging others to do the same. Such families, like those of William Wiseman or the Arundels, owned or rented houses both in the city and in the countryside—houses peppered with convenient hiding places for Catholic clergy and laypersons evading Protestant authorities. These families received and maintained priests who celebrated the Mass and provided the other sacraments for family members and Catholic friends and neighbors. They sent their children abroad to be educated in Catholic colleges, seminaries, and convents. They gave money to support the English mission. They occasionally involved themselves in international Catholic intrigues.[1]

But the lives of London's "seigneurial" Catholic community are only part of the story. London in the late sixteenth and early seventeenth centuries boasted a diverse set of Catholic communities formed among an array of institutions, neighborhoods, and occupations. Catholics of many backgrounds— prisoners, the poor, tradespeople, foreigners, and priests—contributed to maintaining Catholic rituals and identity. This hodgepodge of London Catholics sustained thriving underground communities amid the city's sprawling landscape. Just as importantly, London served as a focal point for various communications networks that connected Catholics within the city, throughout England, and on the continent.

This chapter explores new types of communities that Catholics created within the heart of Protestant authority in England. An examination of some of London's institutions and geography reveals that Catholics often clustered within areas that provided some measure of the privacy needed for religious expression. Catholics used the ordinary space within institutions such as the Inns of Court and within their own neighborhoods as a means of sustaining and creating Catholic identity and community. Furthermore, in London more than anywhere else, the prisons provided a focus for Catholic worship, identity, and fellowship. Moreover, many Catholics were executed in London. These executions, rather than deterring traditional religion, often bolstered the courage of Catholics and established communal bonds among the witnesses. In a related phenomenon, communities of relic takers also emerged, uniting London Catholics in their efforts to recognize martyrs' contributions, preserve their relics, and advertise the stories of and miracles associated with the new martyrs.

London's unique economic and political status within England allowed certain Catholic individuals or groups of individuals to play key roles in contributing to Catholic identity and community. Due to the amount of trade in and out of London, the city's merchants or tradespeople were able to smuggle Catholic people, objects, and information throughout London, the countryside, and even the continent. The city's role in international affairs enabled foreign Catholics—such as diplomats and members of their households—to aid English Catholics on a daily basis. Such assistance took forms as varied as providing Masses, starting informal Catholic religious orders within England, and spiriting Catholics into and out of the country.

It is important to emphasize that these diverse groups of individuals did not comprise one monolithic Catholic community in London. They do represent, however, the diversity of Catholic communities that were possible within England's largest city. A London Catholic might enjoy communal ties with one or a number of these groups. Moreover, these varied communities built links to one another within London and with Catholics in the British Isles and on the continent.

INNS OF COURT

The four schools of law that comprised London's Inns of Court provided valuable opportunities for Catholics in London to engage in ritual and build religious communities. The Inns of Court—the Inner Temple, Middle Temple, Gray's Inn, and Lincoln's Inn—were professional institutions with many privileges that protected the privacy of their members. For example, the Inns possessed the right to administer their own chapels, which were largely exempt from any episcopal oversight. The Inns also lay outside the jurisdiction of city and suburban authorities. In addition, the bustle of "lawyers, clients, students, and servants" (as well as the location of the Inns near woods and fields) allowed for many Catholics to pass through the Inns unnoticed.[2] As Norman Jones has described, the Inns adopted an unofficial policy of "live and let live, so long as no one made a point of thrusting his religious persuasion on fellow members."[3]

In a confession written by the Cornish seminary priest John Hambly, it is clear that Catholic rituals were conducted inside the Inns of Court, thus maintaining a sense of Catholic identity among some of the gentlemen of the Inns and helping cement communal ties among them. Hambly confessed to serving as priest at Gray's Inn for approximately 12 months. Hambly reported that when he arrived, the lay Catholics provided him with a Mass book and "all other things incident and appertaining to the (Mass)," including vestments, stole, altar ornaments, singing cakes, and superaltar—everything needed to maintain the Catholic sacraments within the Inns of Court.[4] Clearly, Hambly's were not the first Catholic rituals conducted at the Inn, nor were they expected to be the last.

Hambly described how he had celebrated Easter during his year at Gray's Inn. Despite bans on public acts of Catholic devotion, Hambly and a group of nine or ten laymen staged an Easter procession through the streets of Holborn and back to Gray's Inn where Hambly performed Mass.[5] To the average eye, they were simply about a dozen gentlemen, each dressed in Inn robes, walking through the streets.

What was the significance of this public yet seemingly innocuous act? Examining the actions of the laymen suggests that in their *own* eyes, they were acting as a small community of Catholics. It was Easter, the most important holiday on the religious calendar. They celebrated by publicly walking through the streets of London as a group. The priest and laymen chose a route through one of the most Catholic sections of town, Holborn, and ended their journey at a location seen as tolerant of and safe for Catholics.[6] On their journey, they clothed themselves distinctively in their Inn robes, clearly identifying themselves as a special group, separate from other pedestrians.

The walk through the streets was not simply a prelude to later Catholic rituals but part of the ritual itself. By joining together in the ritual, these Catholics formed a community, however temporary. As Michel de Certeau suggests, the very secrecy of such actions creates a type of communal relationship, a "social network," among the participants.[7] By marking themselves off from other Londoners on the streets, the participants in the procession privileged their Catholic identity. As they processed, they ritually renewed Catholic claim to the streets of London, the neighborhood of Holborn, and the space of Gray's Inn—all areas ostensibly under Protestant control.

When they arrived back at Gray's Inn, the Catholics solemnized the occasion with a Mass during which most attendees received communion. In addition to consecrating the Eucharistic bread, Hambly also created holy water—a sacramental item—which the laymen could use later for their own devout purposes. One attendee, a Mr. Good, chose to be reconciled by Hambly to Catholicism after the Mass. Hambly reconciled Good in a room at the Inn.[8]

The Inns of Court so jealously guarded their customs and privileges that they preferred to allow their members substantial religious freedoms rather than accept outside intervention in their affairs that might decrease their corporate independence. As Hambly's Easter celebrations exemplify, Catholics took advantage of such freedoms to conduct rituals and sacraments to enhance Catholic identity and community. Although Cecil ordered that the Inns be purged of Catholics and that all Catholics be prohibited from using the Commons, lodging at the Inns, counseling, or appearing before the bar, no Inn made a concerted effort to comply. Recusant lawyers such as Edmund Plowden were allowed to remain and continue practicing both their Catholicism and the law right under the noses of the Privy Council in London.[9]

PRISONS

London's prisons became another set of institutions through which Catholics could engage in ritual and foster their sense of religious identity and community. As discussed in chapter 2, prisons brought together Catholic priests and laypersons to share common space. In doing so, prisons offered both free and imprisoned English Catholics places in which they could hold religious services, celebrate and receive the sacraments, maintain a sense of Catholic identity, and enjoy the fellowship of other Catholics.

London's prison community deserves particular attention because of the number of prisons clustered within a small geographical area, the great number of Catholics imprisoned therein, and the communication possible among the Catholic populations of the London jails. Of the approximately fifty prisons in which the Protestant government incarcerated priests, thirteen of these were in London. The largest of these were Newgate, the Clink, Marshalsea, and the Tower of London.[10]

Catholics of many ranks and offenses were well distributed among London's many jails. The recusant layman Thomas Pounde—incarcerated approximately sixteen different times over a forty-year span—took a veritable odyssey through London's system of prisons. At various times, he resided in the Tower, the Fleet, the Marshalsea, the Gatehouse, and the Counter.[11]

Prisons formed the crux of a network of Catholics within London, thus becoming a key site in evolving Catholic communities in and around the city. Prisons often provided London Catholics of the poorer ranks with some of their only opportunities to meet with priests, receive the sacraments, and enjoy a fellowship of believers.[12] As described in chapter 2, incarcerated priests were sometimes allowed to leave confinement, at which times they likely ministered to Catholics in the surrounding neighborhoods.[13] Visitors to jailed Catholics were frequent, carrying news back and forth between the outside world and the prisons. Moreover, families of prisoners often took up lodgings near the prisons, creating small pockets of Catholics throughout London.[14]

Even those Catholics who could not actually get in to see jailed Catholics found other ways to contact them. In 1595, for example, the Jesuit Robert Southwell was kept in the Tower prior to his execution. Two Catholics, both women, sought his blessing but had no authorization to enter the Tower to visit Southwell. Instead, they got approval to pick some flowers from the Queen's Privy Garden that was located inside the Tower walls. Once inside, the women walked past Traitor's Gate toward the garden. Looking up at the tower in which they thought Southwell resided, they saw a hand extended between the bars of one of the windows. It blessed them. They hoped it was Southwell, but they could not be sure, so they walked by the same tower again. Again, the priest blessed them, and this time they recognized him as Southwell.[15]

London's prisons also served as information centers for Catholics throughout the country, serving London's Catholics as well as those just arrived in or traveling through London. Catholics would go to the London prisons to find out where there were safe places for them to lodge, where they might find a Mass, or where they could tap into a pre-existing community of Catholics who could provide guidance, community, and perhaps financial assistance. When the priest Robert Persons arrived in London on mission in 1580, one of his first orders of business was to visit the Marshalsea where he met the recusant Thomas Pounde. Pounde provided Persons with the names of reliable London Catholics whom he should contact. Several years later, when Henry Garnet and Robert Southwell were preparing to enter England on the mission, Persons advised them to visit London's prisons. They were "excellent information centers" for Catholics, Persons counseled.[16] The Lancashire seminary priest Thomas Cottam agreed. When he returned to England from the English College at Douai in 1580, he immediately headed for London to make plans for his missionary work. As soon as he arrived in the capital, he sought out a fellow Catholic in prison to begin his labors.[17]

And when the imprisoned priest Thomas Bluet received a prison furlough for ten days in 1602, he left the castle at Framingham, his place of imprisonment, and traveled to London to visit the Catholic population. As Bluet explained, ". . . I came to London, which I had not seen for twenty-four years, and knowing no Catholic, went to a prison where were seven priests to consult how to act. One of these seeing me, joyfully exclaimed, 'It is Father Bluet!'"[18] Knowing no one in London, Bluet understood that a prison offered him the best opportunity to tap into an established network of area Catholics. That a London priest he had never met knew of Bluet reveals that some communication existed between imprisoned populations even outside London.

This is not surprising considering the wide variety of methods for prisoners and free Catholics to connect, as discussed in chapter 2.

In their role as information centers, London's prisons proved to be clearinghouses for many Catholic books. Prisoners both possessed and distributed books. In 1614, for example, Protestant authorities searched the cells of Catholic prisoners in various London jails. In the priest Ainsworth's cell in Newgate, they found eleven books including a breviary and various books of spirituality and religious disputation. In a Mr. Browne's cell in the Gatehouse, searchers found a breviary and a translation of St. Francis de Sales's *Introduction to a Devout Life*. In cell after cell of Catholic clerics and laypersons, government agents discovered all manner of Catholic books, despite prohibitions against the possession of such literature.[19]

Furthermore, in 1607, Protestant authorities compiled a list of books found to have been delivered predominately to Catholics in London's prisons. This list confirms the importance of prisons as distribution centers for Catholic texts. Some books were sold in prisons for personal use. Mr. Webster, a lay Catholic prisoner in the Clink bought a missal and breviary. Mr. Penkerell in Newgate purchased "one memorial, resolution, and meditation." Mr. Pim, who just happened to be visiting the Catholics at Newgate, acquired a work by Thomas Aquinas.[20]

The authorities also inventoried large numbers of single works received by individual prisoners. Mr. Brunele, a prisoner in the Marshalsea, for example, received 150 Jesus Psalters, two "great primers," one "little primer," two copies of Richard Broughton's *Resolution of Religion*, and a gilt copy of Luis de Granada's *Memorials of a Christian Life*. A Mr. Wigges, likely the Cornish recusant William Wigges, resided at Newgate when he accepted delivery of 100 copies of Broughton's *Resolution*, bound, and perhaps as many as twenty-five more, unbound, as well as ten copies of Granada's *Memorials*.[21] Such prisoners obviously had no personal need for so many copies of a single work. Instead, they served as cogs in a larger machine of distribution of which the London prisons were an important part.

Prisoners might even set up their own *scriptoria* and printing presses within the London prisons and sell and distribute books throughout the country. John Tendring, the provost marshal of Middlesex, bemoaned the abuses in New Prison in a complaint to the House of Commons in 1626. In addition to Catholic prisoners possessing keys to their cells, the freedom to leave the prison without a keeper, the liberty to receive Catholic visitors, and the license to visit taverns "where upon excess of drink they unmask their thoughts by railing on the king and state," they also operated a press inside New Prison! Tendring alleged that they printed and bound all manner of Catholic books. The books were then "freely vended and uttered to all parts."[22]

In sum, London prisons, more so than prisons in other English towns, provided an environment in which Catholic efforts to preserve Catholic identity and community could be loosely coordinated. London prisons were centers of ritual and community for those Catholics without social connections to the wealthier Catholics who retained their own priests and practiced Catholicism behind the closed doors of private homes. Prisons were information centers for Catholics throughout the country and for Catholics arriving from abroad. They served as clearinghouses through which people, information, and books passed. The size and importance of London made this possible. As England's largest city, it had the most prisons, accompanied by a large population of free and imprisoned Catholic priests and laypersons. As the country's center of government and trade, London housed the strongest lines of communication to other parts of England and to the continent. London Catholics capitalized on such strengths in their efforts to build Catholic identity and community.

CATHOLIC GEOGRAPHY OF LONDON

But a London Catholic did not need to walk through the doors of a prison or a protected institution such as the Inns of Court to experience a sense of Catholic identity or of belonging to some form of Catholic community. Reminders of London's Catholic past were difficult to erase. Catholic influence had not confined itself to the myriad of churches dotting the city. Catholicism permeated the everyday culture and landscape of London. Streets retained names such as "Pope's Head Alley," located from Cornhill to Lombard Street. Taverns with names commemorating cardinals, bishops, monks, as well as popes continued to operate with their signs providing vivid pictorial reminders of a Catholic history, identity, and community not long past.[23]

Although Catholics lived throughout London, they were most concentrated in the neighborhoods of Holborn and Fleet Street. Chancery Lane connected the two areas and also boasted a large population of Catholics. The Inns of Court were also located nearby. These neighborhoods were the focal point of Catholic activity in London.[24]

Holborn in particular became a gathering place for Catholics from around London and around the country. Catholics who made the journey to London typically stayed at homes or inns in the Holborn area, such as the Red Lion or the White Swan.[25] Priests frequented these houses. The sacraments could be found here, and a Christian could be reconciled to the Catholic Church.[26] Such places also served as meeting points to plan strategy and discuss political issues impacting English Catholics. The Gunpowder Plot allegedly was planned at just such an inn in Holborn.

EXECUTIONS

Holborn also became a *via sacra*, a martyrs' way, for many Catholics on their way to executions at Tyburn. Condemned Catholics imprisoned at Newgate Prison had to walk through Holborn under guard to reach the scaffold at Tyburn.[27] In 1608, when the priest Thomas Garnet learned he was to be executed, he allegedly responded, "My Lord, I am not only ready for Newgate, but to be dragged through Holborn to Tyburn; and death to me is my highest ambition, that I may wholly possess my Jesus, to whom long ago I have given my whole heart."[28]

Protestant authorities did not re-route this type of traffic, perhaps hoping that marching those who were soon to die past Catholic neighborhoods would frighten Catholics into conformity. This was not always the result. Executions, as discussed in chapter 2, provided condemned English Catholics with spaces—the streets and the gallows—wherein to plead their cause. They simultaneously provided Catholics with communal spaces in which to gather individually or in groups. Such communities would likely be informal, temporary, and "imaginative" in nature. That is, they would exist largely in the perceptions of those Catholics witnessing the execution.[29] It was dangerous to single oneself out publicly as a Catholic with Protestant authorities so near. Yet in silent ways, Catholics at these execution sites separated themselves from the Protestant onlookers and experienced the executions differently than did Protestant witnesses. Although their appearance and actions would not necessarily have distinguished them to onlookers as Catholics, individuals attended executions with their identities as Catholics in mind. This imaginative recognition of religious identity—and through it, community—mirrors the manner in which John Hambly and his companions created an Easter procession without publicly declaring their Catholicism.

Perhaps nowhere more than in London were Protestant executions of Catholics used to further Catholic sense of community. Possibly this was due to the greater number of Catholics executed in London, the greater numbers of Catholic witnesses to the executions, or the close proximity of London's Catholics in areas such as Holborn, Fleet Street, and Chancery Lane to the execution sites. Regardless, news about the executions—and the legends and miraculous stories that arose about the martyrs and their relics—provided a focus for Catholic loyalty in London more so than did executions in other, more remote locales.

During an execution, the opportunities to create Catholic communities were many. Two complementary dynamics were often involved: the *overtly* Catholic communal gestures that took place in Catholic neighborhoods en route to the execution site and the more *covert* expressions of identity and community that took place at the actual site. For example, the typical experience of an execution probably began as Catholics heard a commotion and came out of their houses or watched from their windows as condemned priests or laypersons rode on hurdles or walked through Holborn or some other Catholic neighborhood to the gallows. These Catholic neighbors called to the condemned priests, begging for their blessings and asking them to speak. They grasped at the condemned person's clothing, trying to rip off something that might be used as a relic.[30] These moments would have been infused with religious significance. The men and women about to die were to be martyrs, especially blessed by God and having the ear of God in heaven. A martyr's journey to the gallows may even have seemed like a recreation of Christ's last walk through the streets on his way to Golgotha to be crucified.[31]

Condemned Catholic priests or laypersons possessed many opportunities to speak to onlookers before their deaths. Many condemned Catholics prayed at the gallows.[32] Others preached sermons about theological issues, such as the Franciscan Thomas Bullaker's lesson on the real presence of Christ in the bread and wine of the Eucharist, delivered at Tyburn in October 1642.[33] Alternatively, the captive might criticize the Protestant monarch and encourage loyalty to Rome as did the first of the Elizabethan martyrs, Blessed John Felton. The government executed Felton in 1570 for having nailed the papal bull, *Regnans in excelsis*, which excommunicated Elizabeth I, to the door of the Bishop of London's palace near St. Paul's Cathedral.[34] As the authorities led Felton out of Newgate prison on the morning of his death, he told the crowd of onlookers that "he was going to die for the Catholic faith, and because he acknowledged the primacy of the Sovereign Pontiff and denied the pretended Queen to be the supreme head of the church."[35]

Perhaps the execution of the priest Thomas Holland on December 12, 1642, best exemplifies the religious and political impact that could be drawn out of one of London's well-publicized executions. For two days prior to his execution, Holland received Catholic prisoners at Newgate. He spoke with many of them and celebrated Mass. As a future martyr, his counsel, his company, and his personal effects were considered extremely valuable.

On the gallows at Tyburn, Holland used every opportunity to create a sense of Catholic identity and community and advertise the truth of the Catholic faith. Upon the gallows, he asked for and was granted permission to speak. If the eyewitness's report is accurate, Holland at first launched into a heated attempt to prove his innocence. He raised his voice to call for the crowd's attention. Then he expostulated, "Let us begin with the sign of the cross, which the Calvinists heartily detest. . . . Is there any one in the audience who is scandalized by this sign?" He paused for a reply. With one simple question, Holland attempted to draw a boundary around those who were Catholics and those who were not, thus creating a sense of identity and community among the Catholics present and himself to the exclusion of any "Calvinists."

Receiving no reply from the crowd, Holland continued. He defended himself, citing texts and points of law, attempting to show that the government convicted him without any proof. Rather than simply lecturing to the crowd, he involved them in his defense. "Is there any one in this assembly," he asked, "who has seen me do an evil deed, either against God or the king?" Again, he received no reply from the onlookers. "Here our common proverb is exemplified," Holland claimed. "'Silence gives consent.' Then all of you confess that I die innocent and against the law, without juridical proof."

Holland knew that his spirited defense of his innocence would not excuse him from the gallows that day. So why did he take the time to plot out a literate, erudite defense? Had he been denied the right to defend himself in his trial? Having been convicted of treason, might he have been concerned about his personal reputation? Or could he not perish without the last word?

In all likelihood, Holland hoped to prove his innocence and dispel his public image as a traitor to lend credibility to the second half of his message to the crowd, a message of faith. After telling the crowd that by their silence they were judging him innocent of any crime, he informed them that he was a Lancashire native and had been a Catholic since birth. Then he defended his faith, not his personal reputation.

> Because as there is one only God, so there is one only faith in which is salvation; this is the Roman faith which our forefathers for so many years professed, with a wonderful and continuous succession of marvelous and miraculous events, as so many English annals testify. . . . I have studied very seriously all the fundamental principles of true religion; and I have found that the fundamental principles of contrary [religions] were false, that those of the Roman faith were the only true ones, and that in it alone could salvation be had.[36]

Holland carefully constructed his last words to leave the greatest possible lasting impact on the crowd to further the Catholic cause. In previously defending his innocence, Holland had already proven to his audience that he could use texts and laws skillfully to argue a point to its logical conclusion. Now he told them he had done the same thing with historical and religious texts and proven that the Catholic faith was the one true faith.

At this point, a Protestant minister stopped Holland's speech. One wonders what took him so long. The executioner hanged Holland, cut him down half dead, and "cut open his breast and tore out his heart." But before Holland died, he availed himself of many opportunities to create a spirit of community among Catholics witnessing his execution. The eyewitness who wrote this account of Holland's martyrdom drew a parallel between Holland's death and Christ's death when he claimed that two thieves died with Holland at Tyburn that day just as two thieves died with Christ at Golgotha. As discussed in chapter 4, English Catholics continued to identify their sufferings with Christ's, hoping to comfort themselves, bring themselves closer to salvation, and feel a bond with the Christ.

Contrary to Protestant intentions, many Catholics—both the condemned and the witnesses—used the executions to enhance this spirit of community and to express their unity and strength. As discussed previously, for example, at his execution in 1584, the priest George Haydock asked Catholics in attendance to pray with him before he died. Allegedly, when someone in the crowd yelled, "There are no Catholics here!", another voice quickly called out, "We are all Catholics!"[37]

Such community-building efforts within London could be spread to Catholics in other areas as well. The London executions and the speeches of the priests upon the London gallows were particularly influential because of the speed with which news of these events was spread both at home and abroad. Diplomats based in the city sent reports of the London executions back to the continent. Family members and eyewitnesses disseminated the news quickly within England using London's superior channels of communication, just as Thomas Dolman, a Gray's Inn student, and Thomas Aulfield, a newly arrived seminary priest, did after Edmund Campion's execution in 1582. These two young men attended the execution, took notes of what they saw and what Campion said, and immediately delivered the notes to a printer in Smithfield named Rowlande, who printed the account for quick production and distribution.[38]

Most common, however, were the ever-expanding martyrologies of the English Catholics. Typically printed abroad, the martyrologies were frequently found in shipments of Catholic books captured in England. As the pursuivant William Udall complained to Sir Julius Caesar, Catholics continually updated such martyrologies to include the newest English martyrs, a disproportionately large number of them being the London martyrs. In 1608, for example, Udall captured a shipment of books containing *The Lyves and Deaths of English, Irish and Scottish saynts and martirs*.[39] The book had been edited and the stories of priests recently executed in London—such as Henry Garnet and Edward Oldcorne—had already been inserted.[40]

Alternatively, rather than reading about the new martyrs, English Catholics who could not attend executions could experience the power of the event in a traditionally Catholic manner by taking a pilgrimage to the execution site later. Tyburn, the execution site for many London martyrs, became a sacred part of London geography.[41] The site of the gallows was located at the intersection where Watling Street bisected Tyburn Road en route to Westminster, near Marble Arch in twenty-first-century London.[42] The ground itself became holy for Catholics. Even Charles I's queen, Henrietta Maria, reportedly visited Tyburn in pilgrimage.

> The Friday next after St. Peter's day being the _____ of _____ 43 . . . the Queen, having according to custom and opinion gained the Jubilee in her chapel at St. James, went forth thence in coach accompanied with 30 persons . . . and upon the way to Hyde Park descended from her coach and went on foot directly through Hyde Park to Tyburn. One of the company, Mr. F. demanding . . . whither the Queen went, (another) answered, to Tyburn to pray to God that he would give her grace with the like constance to die for her religion that those martyrs had done before in that place and named one of their sacrifices there martyred, a friar Minim . . . Arrived there in the highway, the Queen with her company . . . upon their knees before Tyburn's gallows prayed. . . . this was done about 3 of the clock in the afternoon, and here the Pilgrimage ended.[44]

By offering Catholics new opportunities to engage in traditional pious activities such as pilgrimage, execution sites further bolstered Catholics' sense of their own religious identity. Henrietta Maria appears to have planned her afternoon carefully to obtain the most salvific merit for her efforts. The Queen arrived at the gallows as a pilgrim typically would have, on foot and as part of a group of faithful people. She made her pilgrimage on a Friday, a day commonly recognized as religiously significant since it was the day of the week on which Christ was crucified. She also chose to make her pilgrimage the Friday after the feast day of St. Peter, the keeper of the gates of heaven, the saint entrusted to bind and lose souls. Although the pilgrimage site at Tyburn was a relatively new one, she used the site in a traditional manner. As a queen, she enjoyed the freedom to do so. For the majority of English Catholics, the experience undoubtedly would have been different.

RELIC TAKERS

An unintended consequence of executing Catholics for treason was that new relics were being created with every execution. These new relics filled a void in Catholic devotional life created when Protestant iconoclasts destroyed many of the saints' and martyrs' relics that the late medieval Christian Church had treasured for centuries.[45] Stories of the miracles associated with the new relics circulated widely, and Catholics gathered relics in the hope of procuring the new martyrs' intercessory aid.

A community of relic takers formed. Relic takers were often bold, creative, and, at times, zealous, in their collection of the martyrs' bodies and personal effects. [46] Of course, English Catholics were executed throughout the country, but the greater number of Catholics executed in London and the greater number of Catholics concentrated in London ensured a greater supply of and demand for relics in a limited location. Relic hunters thus clustered in greater numbers here.

The importance of these relics was enhanced by the vivid memories of the onlookers who had watched the violent suffering of the Catholics for their faith. Executions emphasized the physicality of not only the individuals to be executed but also of those observing the horror. The execution flooded the senses of the victim and the observers with images, sounds, smells, and emotions. As the executioner performed his grisly tasks, blood flew, bits of bone scattered, and the victim screamed. Those who watched were spattered with gore at the same time as they heard the sound of rent flesh and disjointed bone as the executioner quartered his victim. These same witnesses would later smell the flesh of the victim as the executioner boiled his victim's quarters. The witnesses, however, did not shrink from this onslaught upon their senses. They participated in it and used it to enhance their understanding of the Catholic immanence of the holy in the flesh and to strengthen their commitment to their religion.

The very act of engaging in traditional relic taking buttressed a Catholic community of collectors. After an execution was complete, the many London relic takers would descend on the gallows to collect relics, seeking material reminders of the great sacrifices made for their faith and concrete links to the intercessory power of the new martyrs. They were engaging in an act begun centuries earlier during the martyrdoms in the first centuries of Christendom. They were preserving Catholic history, building channels between the material and spiritual worlds and ties to one another.

London Catholics could be quite resolute in their zeal for relics. Mrs. Lucy Ridley obtained a particularly choice relic following the execution of the priest Edmund Jennings in 1591. An observer, JJ, reported that Ridley was upset when she could not find a means to obtain a relic from Jennings's corpse. But her luck turned when the hangman stopped at the door of Newgate where the priest's quarters were to be boiled. The hangman showed the crowd one of Jennings's quarters, and apparently the arm dangled so that Jennings's hand lay upon the ground near where Ridley stood. Ridley claimed she only meant to touch the hand reverently, but when she grasped the dead flesh, the whole thumb came off in her hand. Immediately tucking it out of sight, she kept it as a relic.[47]

Anything was fair game. When the hangman wiped the mud from the Jesuit Robert Southwell's face prior to his execution in 1595, he threw the dirty handkerchief into the crowd where Catholics retrieved it as a relic. Following Southwell's hanging and disemboweling, Catholics gathered to claim other spiritual remembrances:

> Meanwhile the hangman went on methodically with his work, chopping off members, hacking at joints, and tearing back the ribs to grope for the heart. . . . A few men and women, seeming to pass by him casually, dipped handkerchiefs in the sprayed blood, and offered [the hangman] money for a piece of bone or a lock of hair.[48]

The power of the purse apparently worked as well at executions as it did in the prisons. Catholic families collected and protected relics, passing them down from generation to generation.[49]

Competition among this community of collectors became fierce. Occasionally, relic takers did not wait for the death of a London martyr before taking relics. Once a Catholic was condemned to die, his personal effects could become coveted items. After all, the Protestant authorities would attempt to prohibit relic taking at the execution site, so why not take clothing, books, or even locks of hair before the future martyr was hauled away on a hurdle? These items would not possess any power until after the martyrdom, but after the execution they would serve as powerful material channels through which to solicit the intercession of the martyr. Thomas Garnet, a Jesuit priest and nephew to Henry Garnet, was imprisoned in Newgate and tried for treason in 1608. After receiving the death sentence, Garnet returned to his cell to await his execution. London Catholics visited Garnet to receive the blessing of the future martyr. They also "strove to carry off whatever they could lay hands upon, to reserve as precious memorials and relics of the martyr." Garnet was not even dead yet! He grumbled about the thefts, complaining that the relic hunters even took his girdle.[50]

As such competition reveals, relic takers were part of a mutually recognized community of Catholics within London. Although not organized or formally associated, relic takers clearly knew of one another's existence, hence the zeal to beat the other relic takers to the punch by taking relics from future martyrs. They gathered in close physical proximity at the jails and at the executions, sometimes jostling one another for position near the gallows or near the site of the dismemberment. Although somewhat unusual, such a community was actually based on some of the oldest traditions within Christianity.

Stories of miraculous events surrounded the London martyrs' relics and circulated widely. Miracles may have been associated with English martyrs' relics taken in places other than London, but the London miracles received greater notoriety, with news reaching even the continent. After Thomas Garnet's death, for example, a "wildly dressed man of the woods" clothed in green and with mussed hair approached the executioner as he hacked Garnet's body into quarters. The woodsman—in reality, the priest William Atkinson in disguise—claimed to be among Garnet's poor relations. The family, Atkinson claimed, wanted Garnet's clothes and pieces of his body as memorials. Atkinson paid the executioner a small sum and took what he wanted.

Garnet's relics quickly gained fame for their healing powers. Soon after Garnet's execution, Atkinson fell dangerously ill. Physicians could do nothing. In a last-ditch effort, Atkinson placed certain of Garnet's relics upon his chest to help invoke the martyr's aid. Allegedly, Atkinson felt immediate relief from his illness and was up and about the next day.[51]

The relics of Thomas Garnet's uncle, Henry Garnet, who was similarly executed in London just two years earlier, also reputedly possessed miraculous abilities.[52] Reminiscent of medieval descriptions of saints' relics, Henry Garnet's severed head reportedly failed to decompose properly.

> [It] appeared in that lively color as it seemed to retain the same hue and show of life which it had before it was cut off . . . being cast into hot water, it received no alteration at all; as neither it did after it was placed upon London Bridge and set up there upon a pole [for six weeks, and it] never waxed black, as usually all heads cut from bodies do.[53]

In addition, Henry Garnet's death gave rise to what was called the "miracle of the straw." A relic taker, John Wilkinson, attended the execution. He took up his position close to the block upon which the executioner was dismembering Garnet's body, hoping to mop up a stray drop of martyr's blood. After the executioner severed Garnet's head, he held it up so the crowd could see it. Then the executioner threw it into a basket of straw. When the head dropped into the basket, a piece of blood-saturated straw allegedly "leapt" out of the basket and into Wilkinson's hand. He happily walked away with his relic.

Soon afterwards, the miraculous nature of the relic revealed itself. Wilkinson gave the straw to a Catholic gentlewoman, Mrs. Hugh Griffin, who placed the straw in a reliquary. A few days later, a Catholic gentleman came to view the relic. When gazing at the straw, he claimed he saw a face upon part of the husk, as if it had been painted there. Catholics claimed the face was "the image of Father Garnet drawn by the hand of God." The straw allegedly cured illness. It reportedly saved a woman in childbirth who had been unable to bring forth her child until the straw was "brought and applied with great reverence." A woman suffering from a fit was also cured by the straw after traditional medicine proved ineffective.[54]

Quickly, news of the miracle of the straw spread both in England and on the continent. In February 1607, the English ambassador to Brussels, Thomas Brookes, wrote to Cecil that rumors of Garnet's relics were circulating in Brussels. Two Catholic Englishwomen, he reported, had recently arrived, intending to become nuns. The two women were telling everyone how they had seen Garnet's straw fourteen times and "that it doth grow in show more angelical together with an appearance of wings more than was before seen."[55] Additionally, portraits of Garnet's face in the straw were made and circulated both in England and on the continent (See Figure 2). The portraits portray Garnet's head, topped with a martyr's crown, upon an ear of wheat. The face of the infant Jesus was also reputed to be visible in the straw as the lower part of the martyr's face, as can be seen in the illustration.[56]

Stories of Garnet's well-preserved severed head and miracle-working straw spread like wildfire largely because the executions and relic taking occurred in London. Well-known Catholics such as Garnet drew many Catholic witnesses to the executions. Religious excitement was high, encouraging relic taking and stories of miracles among many of these Catholics. The printing presses, distribution networks, lines of communication, and contacts with the international Catholic community were all more prevalent in London than elsewhere, helping ensure that the news of the executions and the powerful relics would spread. Through the London executions and relic taking, more so than at executions and relic taking elsewhere, English Catholics bolstered their identity as Catholics and joined together in reverence and belief over the London martyrs and their miracles.

As Catholic experiences at executions, prisons, and the Inns of Court illustrate, finding places to practice ritual, reinforce Catholic identity, and build Catholic community were important to London Catholics. Equally as important, however, were differing groups of individuals who helped link such communities, not into a monolithic whole but into a web of acquaintances, contacts, and sources of information and support. Such individuals or groups provided a variety of services. They delivered messages between Catholics. They provided Catholics with the books, images, rosaries, and other items they wanted for their devotions. They acted as shields, protecting Catholics from prosecution or aiding those already in jail. They supported the English priesthood. The best-known of these individuals were Catholic peers and gentry residing in London. But, as mentioned above, their story has been well told. Less well known are the contributions of Catholic merchants, tradespeople, and foreign residents.

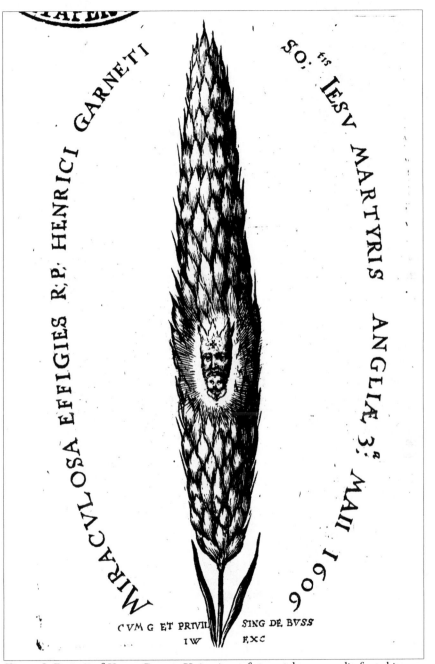

Figure 2: Portrait of Henry Garnet, SJ, in piece of straw taken as a relic from his execution. From Public Record Office, Kew, SP 12/216/218b. Reproduced with the permission of The National Archives, London.

MERCHANTS AND TRADESPEOPLE

Merchants and tradespeople provided a valuable service by tying together diverse communities of London's Catholics. Such people conducted types of business in which many deliveries were made and persons of many sorts were expected to come and go. Catholic priests and laypersons could arrive without arousing neighbors' suspicions. Messages could be delivered or picked up. Catholic books and rosaries could be sold in a shop—such as a stationery or grocery—where someone walking out with a wrapped parcel would not attract much notice.[57] Catholic merchants and tradespeople knew their clientele. Catholic items would only be offered and sold to those whom the seller knew to be Catholic.[58]

More dangerous was the selling of Catholic items on the streets. Poor vendors without shops carried their wares on their persons. If stopped and searched by the authorities, their guilt would be obvious, such as Darby Bantre's was in 1639. When he was apprehended at Euston for begging, authorities searched his knapsack and found his stock: "31 strings of rosary beads with pictures and crosses at them" and five copies of the *Office of the Blessed Virgin Mary*.[59]

Merchants or tradespeople were expected to have trading contacts on the continent, often with Catholic countries, and even with Rome.[60] Catholic books, rosaries, images, etc., could be smuggled in with a merchant's regular shipment of goods or with a tradesman's regular supply of raw materials. For example, James Duffield, a tailor from St. Dunstan's in the West, London, visited Antwerp in the early 1590s. He bought approximately forty Catholic missals, breviaries, and primers, as well as "certain pictures containing the persecution here in England of the saints (as he termeth them)." He returned to England with the books and his images of the English martyrs and sold them to diverse Catholics.[61] The Protestant authorities apprehended Duffield, but Duffield claimed he could not remember all those to whom he had already sold his imports. Merchants could even smuggle people in and out of the country. John Bucke, who claimed to be a London merchant, was captured while attempting to smuggle Jesuits into England from Calais in 1606.[62]

Although some Catholic merchants and tradespeople engaged in the risky business of smuggling Catholic goods into England, perhaps more were willing to distribute goods that had already escaped the notice of customs officials. Once a single shipment of Catholic items was inside the country, many merchants and tradespeople could disperse the items. The Court of High Commission fined many merchants large sums for trading in such items. In February 1633/4, for example, the court fined the stationer William Brooks of St. James, Clerkenwell £30 for dispersing Catholic books. Similarly, Thomas

Blomfield the younger was ordered to pay £23. William Pamplin, a merchant of London, received an even larger fine, 100 marks, for the same offense.[63]

When the Protestant government discovered this black-market trade in prohibited items, it attempted to dissuade London Catholics from taking part. Jean-Baptiste Van Male, the agent of the Archduke of Austria to the English Court, recounted such a warning in 1617. He described an enormous public bonfire in St. Paul's churchyard for "an extraordinary quantity of Catholic books such as Breviaries, Offices of Our Lady, and similar other [books] of devotion which had been discovered at the house of a certain London printer."[64]

One of the more complete pictures we have of a merchant or trades-man involved in Catholic traffic of goods and people into and out of London is that of a London grocer, James Tailor, of Fleet Street. His Fleet Street address placed him near the center of Catholic activity in London. His occupation as grocer placed him in legitimate contact with many suppliers and customers who would have been constantly arriving and departing from his store. Many of those walking through Tailor's doors, however, were not there to purchase groceries.

Instead, Tailor served as a first contact for many lay Catholics and priests traveling to London during the 1580s and 1590s. He allowed recently arrived Catholics to stay at his home, and he frequently traveled around the city in the company of these new arrivals, meeting with other Catholics and attending Catholic services. In 1586, for example, Justice Richard Young exam-ined the Cornish Catholic Gervaise Pierrepont. Pierrepont admitted that he had been traveling around London with Tailor and two other London Catholics. Young suspected Pierrepont of attending Mass with Tailor and the others, but Pierrepont would not admit to it.[65]

Tailor arranged for priests to say Mass in his home. In 1586, for exam-ple, the priest John Hambly was arrested for leading a Catholic procession through Holborn, celebrating the Mass at Easter at Gray's Inn, and reconciling people to the Roman Church, as described above.[66] Hambly admitted that approximately fourteen days after the above events, he said another Mass at the home of a Fleet Street grocer near the great conduit. Although he does not name Tailor, this description of the location near the conduit matches that of Tailor's home.[67]

Although a grocer, Tailor was acquainted with some of London's most powerful and well-known Catholics such Sir Thomas Fitzherbert whom Tailor visited in 1592. In 1608, his "man and kinsman" apparently visited the Spanish ambassador's house regarding a shipment of 2,500 Catholic books.[68] From this, we may infer that Tailor helped distribute Catholic books in London, in addi-tion to his better-known activities.

This grocer even conveyed messages between high ranking Catholics in England and abroad. In 1585, Henry III of France appointed a new Catholic ambassador to England. English Catholics arranged for this new ambassador, who was sympathetic to their cause, to transport letters in and out of England in the ambassador's diplomatic pouch. Protestant authorities theoretically could not touch the correspondence of a diplomat. Once in London, the ambassador was to give the letters to an Italian, "to be delivered to James Tailor, a grocer in Fleet Street, and by him as shall be directed. . . . "[69] Seven years later, in 1592, Protestant authorities had been unable to stem the flow of information through Tailor. London Catholics still recognized the grocer as one of the primary handlers of Catholic letters into and out of the city.[70]

In addition to these acquaintances of high rank, Tailor also trafficked with other merchants and tradespeople, such as Christopher Askwith, jerkin-maker, and other grocers.[71] There are indications that Catholicism was relatively strong among the grocers in London and that many Catholic grocers met together as Catholics, worked and socialized together, and even intermarried.[72] We know that Tailor, for example, enjoyed the acquaintance of a Mrs. Deacon, the daughter of London grocer Barnerd Field. Mrs. Deacon distributed Catholic books around London and visited the priests and Catholic prisoners in the Marshalsea. A former servant of Mrs. Deacon's, Henry Remington, informed upon Mrs. Deacon and described her visits to Catholic homes in London, including to "one Tailor's house, a grocer on against the Conduit and in Fleet Street."[73]

By piecing together the bits and pieces of Tailor's life, we can see the spider web of contacts and activities that a merchant or tradesperson could use to help create unity among London's Catholics. Tailor lived and worked in the heart of the "Catholic geography" of London in Fleet Street. He met with London Catholics, English Catholics, and with foreign Catholics, such as the Italian, French, and Spanish Catholics who lived and worked in London. He was acquainted with Catholics of a variety of ranks, from members of the gentry to other grocers and their families, as well as artisans. His activities reveal that he built communal ties among Catholics by organizing worship, introducing Catholics to one another, delivering messages and Catholic items, and opening his home to Catholics in need. Although Protestant authorities searched his home, it does not appear that they ever succeeded in convicting Tailor of violating any penal law.[74] Certainly the nature of the man contributed to his success and longevity in this dangerous business, but so did the very nature of his trade. The impact of the Catholic merchants and tradespeople, however difficult to detect, in fostering Catholic communities in London should not be underestimated.[75]

FOREIGN AID

As James Tailor's links with the French ambassador and the unnamed Italian messenger disclose, foreign Catholics in London were integrally bound up in English Catholic efforts to promote their common faith, identity, and community. Foreign Catholics in London conveyed messages between Catholics in England and the continent. They held Catholic rituals and provided the Catholic sacraments in their own chapels in London, which English Catholics often frequented. Foreign Catholics transported books, images, rosaries, and other sacramental items from the continent into England for English Catholic usage. Moreover, foreign Catholics interceded with the English government on behalf of English Catholics to protect them from the penal laws. Foreign Catholics in London also provided money to help support English Catholics, particularly priests, both in London and on the continent.

Catholic foreigners in London facilitated a continual flow of information between English and continental Catholics.[76] At times, such messages between foreign and English Catholics of high status discussed a Spanish-, French-, or Roman-led invasion of England to restore Catholicism, but not always. For example, diplomats and foreigners residing in London spread news of the creation of new English martyrs at the various London execution sites, as described earlier.[77] London's Catholics could also keep abreast of English Catholic friends and relatives overseas. English priests could maintain contact with their superiors in Rome or Spain by sending and receiving messages in diplomatic pouches, as a priest Conyard did in 1640 when he visited the Spanish, Venetian, and French ambassadors to send messages to Rome.[78] Even Catholic prisoners in London jails used foreigners to send and receive information.[79]

Foreign embassies rendered the most aid to London's Catholics. Diplomatic liberties allowed Catholic embassies to openly and legally maintain their own chapels and cadres of priests who celebrated Mass frequently. Although such activities were legal, the attendance of English subjects at such services was prohibited.[80] This did not stop London Catholics from frequenting the embassies' Masses.

English Catholics began attending Mass at foreign embassies as early as 1562. In June of that year, Elizabeth complained to Don Alvaro de la Cuadra, bishop of Aquila and Spanish ambassador to England, that many English and Irish Catholics had openly received the Eucharist at the Spanish embassy.[81] Despite Elizabeth's objections and de la Cuadra's denials, the Spanish embassy continued to receive English Catholics. Occasionally, the ambassador, himself a priest, celebrated the Mass. Elizabeth eventually demanded that de la Cuadra turn over the keys to Durham house, his London residence. She wanted the keys to all the doors that opened onto either the street or the river, where English Catholics would enter. She claimed that "conspiracies against her life were concocted there and that every Papist in London resorted thither to hear Mass; and that this was so well known."[82]

English Catholics continued to attend embassy services throughout the late sixteenth and early seventeenth centuries.[83] Sir Richard Grosvenor, in his election address of 1624, complained about London Catholics that:

> They have assumed to themselves a toleration of their religion without authority and in the chief city of this kingdom do by multitudes frequent the private houses of ambassadors where they blush not to be seen daily going in and coming forth from Mass as frequently as others go to church and fear not the penalties of law.[84]

Although the Spanish embassy probably provided the most frequent opportunities for London Catholics to hear Mass, other embassies—such as the French, Flemish, and Venetian embassies—were aiding English Catholics in this manner. Parliament grew increasingly concerned at its inability to halt such practices. The government spied on the embassies, authorized raids, and seized English subjects as they left.[85]

The popularity of the embassy Masses is exemplified by reports of a 1623 Mass at the French ambassador's house that was attended by so many London Catholics that the floor collapsed and approximately ninety-five people were killed.[86] An English Jesuit, Drury, was preaching in a large garret on the third floor of the French ambassador's house in Blackfriars. London Catholics entered discreetly through a passage outside the actual gates of the residence. An eyewitness described how approximately 400 London Catholics came to listen to Drury. Those of higher rank sat on chairs and stools. The rest stood, although many of the women sat on the floor.

About midway through Drury's sermon, the main support of the garret floor broke. The beam, portions of the floor, and many of the people sitting and standing crashed downward about twenty feet, through the second floor, until they lay upon the first floor. Some arose unhurt. Others were cut, broken, and bruised. Still others, including the priest, Drury, either died upon the French ambassador's floor or days later from their injuries.

English and foreign Catholics worked together to protect the English Catholic dead. They carried away approximately one-third of the victims' bodies that night, before the Protestant coroner arrived for the inquest. Presumably they wanted to ensure Catholic burials for the victims and to hide the victims' identities from the authorities. Of the remaining corpses, some—usually those of the wealthier Catholics—were claimed and buried, usually with the rites of the Church of England.[87] Others, possibly those of the poorer Catholics, were in danger of desecration. George Montaigne, bishop of

London, directed that the victims, as excommunicates, be stripped of their clothing and "buried on the refuse pile." To avoid this, the French ambassador had two pits dug in his back courtyard and the remaining corpses buried hastily.[88] The graves were marked with black crosses, but the Privy Council ordered them removed. Someone printed a sympathetic description of the disastrous events, but it was pulled from circulation.[89]

Embassy services such as the one at the French ambassador's house joined a multinational Catholic community. The host country welcomed not only its own Catholics and the London Catholics but any Catholics who chose to attend. Protestant raids upon the embassies found Spanish, Flemish, Italian, French, and Scots Catholics worshipping side by side.[90] Continental Catholics residing in London thus provided a visible continuity of traditional Catholic community, identity, and ritual that English Catholics could witness and in which they could occasionally participate.

The priests at the embassies publicly celebrated holy days and feast days of the Catholic calendar. The most popular feast was, of course, Easter, but the embassies also provided familiar ritual activities on days such as Candlemas, Shrove Tuesday, and Christmas.[91] These festivities often involved more than the Mass. English Catholics could also enjoy pious rituals such as processions, the wearing of ashes, and the distribution of sacramental items such as candles or palms. In 1614, for example, the Spanish ambassador Diego Sarmiento de Acuña reported to Philip III of Spain that King James had criticized him for celebrating Palm Sunday at the Spanish embassy with "processions, sermons, and other great solemnities as if I were in Seville, while a great number of his [James's] subjects were in attendance."[92]

Embassy priests also provided other sacraments, such as confession/penance, marriage, and baptism.[93] In 1614, for example, the Earl of Northampton lay on his deathbed in London and wished to be reconciled to the Catholic Church and to receive the last rites and make his last confession. The Spanish ambassador's secretary, the priest Agustin Perez, obliged. The earl evidently held onto life a little longer, because Perez heard three confessions from him. Perez told the earl that he must make some sort of public declaration of his Catholic faith, and the earl did so in his will, declaring that he died "an obedient son of the Roman Catholic Church."[94]

In addition to providing Mass and the other sacraments, foreign embassies of London provided many more services to aid English Catholics to maintain their Catholic identity and build communal ties. For example, they helped import Catholic books, images, and relics for distribution to English Catholics. Shipments bound for an embassy were unlikely to be checked by customs because of diplomatic privilege. If such shipments were checked, the ambassador could usually claim diplomatic privilege to get the shipment released into his custody.[95] In 1623, for example, the Commissioners of Passage at Dover apprehended three men who refused to take the Oath of Allegiance and who "have brought over prohibited books, pictures, and relics." Evidently, the men, all Englishmen, served the Spanish ambassador in London. The Commissioners of Passage were instructed to forward all the books, relics, and pictures to the king so that he could see what was being shipped into his country. If the Spanish ambassador sued for the items, however, they were to be returned to the three Englishmen. Moreover, the Commissioners were to release the three men if they posted bond, rather than imprison them for refusing the Oath of Allegiance.[96]

Even if an ambassador did not personally arrange the shipment of such items, members of his household could use his diplomatic clout as a shield to hide their own activities. In the summer of 1609, a Dutch priest residing in the house of the Venetian ambassador Correr helped English Catholics smuggle a large quantity of books, about twenty-five different titles, into London. The priest hid the books in the porter's lodge and the cellar of the ambassador's house.[97] Although several of the titles dealt with political issues involving Catholics, most of the books dealt with issues of personal piety and ritual activity. After discovering the Dutch priest's subterfuge, Protestant authorities inventoried many copies of such books as *The Rosary of St. Mary the Virgin, Mary's Psalter, The History of Our Lady of Loreto, The English Martyrlogue, The Rules of Good Life*, and the Bible.[98]

In addition to these types of printed works, Catholic embassies also publicized papal bulls and indulgences available to English Catholics. England's penal laws prohibited the bringing in or possession of such documents, but the embassies were exempt from such restrictions.[99] They spread the communications from Rome to their English co-religionists. In 1605, for example, the Spanish ambassador was the first to publish an indulgence issued by the pope. The indulgence was one that could be earned easily by English Catholics who only needed to "pray the next week after notice for a general good to Christendom."[100] Knowledge of positive pious action that they might take to help save their souls was important consolation to English Catholics, and London's foreign embassies provided access to such knowledge.

Moreover, foreign ambassadors would often protect English priests and laypeople from prosecution under the penal laws by claiming them as members of their diplomatic households. In this manner, English Catholics might avoid prison or escape banishment. In 1624, for example, the French ambassador, the Comte de Tilliers, spoke up on behalf of an English priest, John Chamberlaine, who had long been living at the ambassador's house. In spite of the English penal laws prohibiting English priests trained on the continent from residing in the country, Tilliers requested a warrant to allow Chamberlaine "to abide in any of his Majesty's dominions."[101]

With the aid of the embassies, English Catholics could return to England from the continent with relative freedom. In 1617, for example, authorities apprehended John Richardson of Malpas, Cheshire, in Dover as he attempted to enter England. He claimed the right to enter the country because he "belong[ed] to the Spanish Ambassador's son." He recounted that he had become a Catholic, left his father, arrived in London, and entered the service of Don Pedro, the ambassador's son. When Don Pedro left for Flanders, Richardson accompanied him. Now, Richardson maintained, he was returning to England on Don Pedro's business and should be allowed entrance.[102]

Ambassadors could also facilitate travel out of England. For example, in 1624, the Spanish ambassador claimed five or six English Catholic gentlemen's sons as his servants. In this manner, he took them to the continent where he presumably intended to educate and rear them in the Catholic tradition.[103]

Even if an English Catholic was not a member of an ambassador's household, an ambassador might still successfully intercede for him to prevent imprisonment or fines.[104] This proved to be especially true for English priests. If a priest was captured in England or while trying to enter England, he typically would be jailed. Subsequently, an ambassador or member of his household might intervene and arrange to have the priest released into his custody and perhaps sent back to the continent.[105] In July 1615, Ana Maria Camudio, wife of the Archduke's ambassador in London, requested the release of ten priests so that they might return to the continent. She promised that the priests' superiors would not attempt to send them back into England again.[106] James released a group of priests to the Archduke's ambassador, Ferdinand de Boisschot, "to be conveyed out of England" in November of that year.[107] Three years later, the Spanish ambassador, the Condé de Gondomar, made a similar request to insure the release of seventy-four priests, most of them incarcerated in London jails. James delivered them to Gondomar's custody with the stipulation that the priests leave the country.[108]

Fear of transgressing certain "gray areas" probably deterred Protestant efforts to enforce English penal laws within an embassy's jurisdiction. If Protestant authorities infringed upon diplomatic privileges, they could find themselves inside a jail cell. In 1626, for example, Secretary Conway issued three pursuivants, Richard Wainwright, John Griffin, and John Gray, a warrant to search for:

> Fr. Muskett, Fr. Smith, and Fr. Wordington, Jesuits, seminary priests or persons dangerous to the state; and also to seize all seditious books, papers,

Massing stuff, and other relics found in any place where they may be concealed, and to bring both persons and all such stuff before Lord Conway.[109]

Two months later the three pursuivants themselves were jailed in the
Gatehouse. They evidently took their instructions to search "in any place" quite
literally and raided the French ambassador's house, even arranging to have one
of the ambassador's servants imprisoned by local magistrates. The French
ambassador complained to the Privy Council, charging the men with "infring-
ing [the] privileges of an ambassador." The Privy Council agreed and confined
the pursuivants to the Gatehouse at King Charles's discretion. The magistrates
who were responsible for imprisoning the ambassador's servant were "called
before the Board to receive punishment."[110]

Moreover, ambassadors from Catholic countries worked vigorously to
assure a greater measure of toleration for all English Catholics. During the various negotiations for Charles's marriage, this proved especially true. In 1623,
during talks to arrange a Spanish match, the Spanish ambassador, the Marquis
Inijosa, requested and obtained a short-term halt in recusancy fines. He also
asked for concessions for English priests.[111] During the negotiations for a marriage between Charles and Henrietta Maria in 1624, the French ambassador
asked for even greater toleration for all English Catholics. He requested

> that recusants be freed from the payment of the £20 per month, and all
> other payments from Trinity term; that the sums levied on them since be
> returned, and their lands and goods made free as though the commissions
> had never been issued; that they also be discharged from all proceedings
> in Ecclesiastical Courts, by Judges, Justices of the Peace, etc.[112]

King James, while not granting all that the ambassador requested, did order a
stay of prosecution against all recusants before the ecclesiastical courts at
Canterbury and York. Further, he asked the two archbishops to instruct lesser
courts to stop their proceedings against Catholics as well and to halt the collection of the fine for nonattendance at Protestant church services.[113]

London's embassies also provided financial support for English
Catholics. They supplied money to maintain priests and educate young English
Catholics. They relieved Catholic prisoners inside London's jails.[114] They also
provided English Catholics with food and safe beds inside their embassies. In
1633, for example, the English priest Thomas Reynolds resided in the
Gatehouse prison. He protested his incarceration, claiming that Charles had
given him a reprieve earlier. He had been a free man, Reynolds complained,
receiving food and lodging from the French ambassador until a pursuivant
unjustly captured him again.[115]

Although the ambassadors enjoyed special influence with the English monarch on issues involving English Catholics, they were not the only foreigners to aid London Catholics. Foreign laypersons residing in London could also profoundly influence the quality of English Catholic life. An example of such influence was that of Doña Luisa de Carvajal. Carvajal lived in London for eight years, primarily at Ely House, one of the Spanish ambassador's residences. Protestant authorities arrested her twice, but the ambassador, Gondomar, secured her release each time.[116]

Like the grocer James Tailor, the foreigner Carvajal provided an important link between various communities of London Catholics. After Carvajal's arrival in England, probably in 1605, she corresponded with, met with, and concealed English priests from the authorities so that they could continue their work among English Catholics. Moreover, she provided a link between these priests, the foreign Catholic community, and London's Catholic prison communities through her continual visits to and maintenance of imprisoned priests and laypersons in London's many jails. In 1611, for example, she and several of her ladies visited two condemned priests at Newgate the night before their executions.[117] She dined with the priests and conversed with them at some length. We know of her visit because James caught wind of it and considered it a "disorder not to be suffered." He ordered a thorough investigation to discover how the ladies had been allowed such liberty.[118]

Carvajal's purpose in visiting prisoners appears to be twofold. First, she comforted her co-religionists whom she perceived as being persecuted for the faith. She provided food and money to help maintain them. She would engage the prisoners in conversation and dine with them.[119] Additionally, however, Carvajal appeared to be concerned with ensuring her own soul's salvation. She visited priests—such as the priests in Newgate—the night before their executions. She made a point of sharing the priests' last meal, their "last supper." When the soon-to-be-executed Christ enjoyed his final meal with his apostles, he created, according to the Catholic faith, the sacrament of the Mass with all its accompanying salvific power. The Mass, as Catholics understood it, was a recreation of this last meal of a condemned man who sacrificed his mortal body to save the souls of others.

How might Carvajal have seen these two priests' last meal? Obviously these priests were not Christ, but many Catholics viewed their own sufferings for the faith as similar to those of Christ.[120] These English priests were condemned as Christ was, and they were about to become martyrs. As such, they would have special intercessory abilities before God's throne. Carvajal placed herself before these priests at a critical juncture in this process, perhaps hoping to tap into any salvific power achieved through the priests' sacrifice of their own bodies on the gallows—the altar, so to speak—at the site of execution.

Carvajal's interests extended beyond the issue of her own salvation. Carvajal devoted herself to furthering piety among English Catholics and ensuring a continuous supply of English clergy to meet the country's pastoral needs. In 1604 she donated 12,000 ducats to create a foundation for an English Jesuit novitiate which was eventually established in 1607 in Louvain.[121] Moreover, she began a monastery of professed English nuns in England during the reign of James I. She maintained a small residence just outside of London at Spitalfields. It was there that she established her order. Nuns and novices wore habits and veils. Bells were rung.[122] The authorities discovered the monastery. They "stormed the house" and arrested Carvajal on October 28, 1613. The Spanish ambassador de Acuña, along with the ambassador from Flanders, de Boisschot, attempted to secure her release as a member of the Spanish embassy's household. She had, de Acuña argued, always kept a chamber at the Spanish ambassador's home since her arrival in London. She had only been at Spitalfields, he maintained, to recuperate from illness. The ambassadors failed to get Carvajal released. They did, however, manage to get her papers and other incriminating items out of the monastery in Spitalfields safely. The English government kept Carvajal imprisoned for three days, exiled her, and she died in Flanders just a few months later in 1614. Philip III of Spain ordered his ambassador to secure the release of the nuns arrested with Carvajal. Philip told de Acuña to claim diplomatic privilege since the women were "persons of her [Carvajal's] household."[123]

Carvajal also provides a connection to the community of London Catholic relic takers. She evidently believed strongly in the potency of martyrdom. She was one of the Catholics in London collecting relics after the executions. Carvajal was maintaining future martyrs while they were in prison and preserving their physical bodies after their deaths. After Carvajal's exile and death in 1614, Philip III directed his ambassador de Acuña to send Carvajal's possessions back to Spain under the protection of the Count de la Oliva, Rodrigo Calderón. These possessions included the papers and records of the nunnery at Spitalfields. Moreover, Philip specifically requested that "the bodies of the martyrs which the aforesaid Doña Luisa had retained" be returned to Spain. Both Carvajal and the Spanish monarch believed in the sacrality and intercessory ability of the physical remains of those who were especially blessed in heaven and had the ear of God.

Carvajal's combined efforts on behalf of English Catholics reflect the influence London's population of foreign residents could exert upon the ritual life, identity, and community of London's Catholics. Carvajal attempted to ensure the presence of an English priesthood by sheltering and maintaining priests in London and by providing for the education of more priests through her endowment of a Jesuit novitiate. She enabled English Catholic women to adopt a traditional religious lifestyle in the nunnery she created in Spitalfields. She contributed to the prisons' role as a center of Catholic community and identity through her financial support of and visits to incarcerated priests. She enhanced the status of the English martyrs through her taking of and preservation of the relics from their executions. Through her movements among all these groups, she ensured a measure of communication between these varied Catholic communities.

The efforts of the foreign ambassadors, their households, and nondiplomatic foreigners such as Carvajal helped provide London's Catholics with places to gather as Catholics for worship and community. They created opportunities for London's Catholics to receive the sacraments, books, and sacramental items they required to aid their piety and contribute to their sense of identity as Catholics. Foreigners protected London's Catholics from prosecution. They held together portions of English Catholic communities by conveying messages between English Catholic family and friends. And lastly, they upheld the example of continuing communities of traditional Catholics in which London Catholics could occasionally participate.

All of this is to emphasize that London's Catholics possessed a variety of options through which they could enhance their sense of Catholic identity and community. As chapters 2 through 4 addressed, much of English Catholic identity and community in this period revolved around opportunity, choice, and flexibility in both worship and lifestyle. Perhaps nowhere were choices more numerous than in London.

Many options existed for Catholics of all walks of life to participate in diverse Catholic communities in London. Catholics here could partake of the well-known "manor-house" Catholicism of the wealthy London Catholic families in their mansions and country homes on the outskirts of London. Some Catholics chose to surround themselves with other Catholic families, living in the pocket Catholic communities of Holborn and Fleet Street or around the prisons. Or they circulated through the Catholic underworld of the numerous prisons populated by Catholics from around the country. London's Catholics congregated with many of their own in private institutions such as the Inns of Court. Or they frequented the foreign embassies, seeking out the sacraments and the fellowship of Catholics of many nationalities.

To enhance their sense of Catholic identity—their self-perception of sameness, likeness, or oneness with other Catholics—London Catholics possessed a variety of choices as well. They could participate in the sacraments offered in many locations throughout London. They could read one of the many Catholic books imported into and distributed throughout London. They could acquire one of the many sacramental items created in or smuggled into

London by merchants, tradespeople, or foreign diplomats. Through their covert processions through the city, their presence at the many executions, and their relic taking, London Catholics could engage in devotions made common by the ancient Christians of the first centuries, thus maintaining a sense of oneness with one another and with the traditions of the church, as will be discussed in more detail in chapter 8.

Threaded through this web of choices was always the element of communication among these various groups of London Catholics. This is not to claim that some overarching network linked together all of London's Catholics. To the contrary, communication was haphazard at best. Yet the many small networks of London's Catholics provided opportunities for interaction and communication perhaps greater than anywhere else in the country. The prisons served as information centers for London's resident Catholics as well as for Catholics arriving in England or traveling about the country. Diplomats served as couriers, delivering messages between families, friends, and priests in England and on the continent. Merchants and tradespeople trafficked in information and Catholic goods, connecting diverse groups of Catholics throughout the city, the country, and the continent.

When the priests Robert Southwell, Henry Garnet, Robert Persons, and Thomas Cottam arrived in England from the continent, they set an immediate course for London. When the priest Thomas Bluet received a furlough from his jail in Framingham, he headed to London. When Luisa de Carvajal set up her nunnery in England, she set it up on the outskirts of London. Why? Was London the center of all Catholic activity in England? Certainly not. Many other areas provided Catholics with much more freedom to practice their faith, as will be seen in the next two chapters. But Catholic London provided access to choices and opportunities for Catholic worship, identity, and community not always readily available elsewhere.

CHAPTER 6

Katholik Kernow
Catholics of Cornwall

We speak your language now . . .
But we sing it to our own tune.
An ancient song
Lilting before you came.[1]

CORNWALL OWNS THE DISTINCTION—ONE WHICH THE CORNISH ASSUREDLY have never relished—of being the first Celtic country conquered and annexed by England. Cornwall lies on a peninsula on the southwest coast of England stretching away from the rest of the island toward Ireland and Brittany. Due to geography and settlement patterns, the Cornish in the late Tudor and early Stuart periods were somewhat isolated from one another as well as from the rest of England. During this time, the Cornish lived in small hamlets scattered throughout the county rather than in the larger, nucleated villages which were becoming more common throughout the rest of England.[2] Only three roads linked Cornwall to its only bordering county, Devon. All were in poor condition, unsuitable for wheeled traffic.[3] The cartographer John Norden, in his *Description of Cornwall* from 1584, described the county as

> full of hills, Rocks, and craggy mountains. . . . The rocks are high, huge, ragged, and craggy, not only upon the sea coast, the Rocks whereof are very high, steep, and hard, and are as a defensive wall against the continual furious assaults of the prevailing Ocean on all sides. . . . But also the Inland mountains are so crowned with mighty rocks as he that passeth through the country beholding some of these rocks afar off, may suppose them to be great Cities planted on the hills.[4]

Because of Cornwall's relative detachment from the rest of England, the Protestant government and church faced a different set of challenges in Cornwall than those they encountered elsewhere when they attempted to reform religion. Cornwall's isolation allowed the Cornish to nurture their own language, culture, and even separate religious traditions both before and after reform. It is the evolution of these separate religious traditions and their impact on Cornish religious identity and community that this chapter explores.

In general, previous histories of the Cornish Catholics have overlooked any distinctive aspects of Cornish piety, religious identity, and community. Historians of Cornwall such as A. L. Rowse and Anne Duffin either openly dismiss the importance of such issues or simply choose not to address them.[5] They focus primarily on the socio-demographic backgrounds and political activities of the wealthier Catholics, such as the Arundels and the Tregians, and their persecution under the penal laws.[6] While identifying the leaders among the Cornish Catholics and recording their deeds serves a valuable purpose, it in no way provides a complete picture of Cornish-Catholic experience in this period. I argue that Cornwall's distinctive history and identity impeded the success of both Protestant and Catholic religious reforms and allowed Cornish experiences of religious ritual, identity, and community to evolve in different directions than other English Catholics, such as those in London.

Cornish perceptions of religious identity and community tended to be more independent and insular than those in other areas of England. In the late sixteenth and early seventeenth centuries, the Cornish identified most closely with traditions of Celtic Christianity—a Christianity shaped largely by the efforts of Irish-inspired peripatetic priests and influenced strongly by traditions now associated with the Eastern Orthodox Church—rooted in the shire as early as the fifth century. Three characteristics of such religious identity were 1) loyalty to a community of Cornish saints usually not approved by Rome, 2) a lack of attachment to the institutional Roman Church, and 3) a remarkably strong belief in ideals of Catholic immanence. Regarding religious community, Cornish Catholics enjoyed links with Catholics throughout England and on the continent, however they privileged the religious interests and needs of their county and its inhabitants over larger issues impacting English Catholics as a whole.

CORNISH INDEPENDENCE

As hinted by their geographic isolation, the Cornish developed their own identity, language, and culture to which they remained fiercely loyal. The Cornish, for example, attempted to maintain their own language despite pressure to learn the English tongue. The anglicized Cornish gentleman Richard Carew, in his 1602 *Survey of Cornwall*, glossed over Cornish resistance to learning

English by claiming that much of the Cornish population knew English although if asked would state "*Meea navidna cowzasawzneck*," or "I can speak no Saxonage." In reality, what these Cornishmen insisted with this phrase was "I *will* not speak" English.[7] The Cornish consciously differentiated themselves from their English neighbors by refusing to speak and write the English language. Moreover, by referring to English as "Saxonage," the Cornish perhaps emphasized the alien status of the English as descendents of the Saxon invaders of the British Isles, in contrast to the Cornish who claimed descent from the native inhabitants.

Cornish politics developed differently from other counties. Cornwall developed a large, active gentry class which, although interested and involved in national affairs, maintained a sense of independence and individualism.[8] Despite the crown's large interests in the county, no member of the royal family resided in Cornwall. Likewise, although various noble families—such as the Warwicks and Spencers—possessed landed interests in the county, none of these nobles resided there. Perhaps the crown's strength made it difficult for nobles to build their own bases of influence in Cornwall. In any case, with little competition, local gentry interests flourished.[9]

The level of Cornish isolation from the interests and affairs of England has been much debated by scholars.[10] Although it is not the purpose of this study to enter this debate, a few examples from the early Tudor period—the Cornish Revolt in 1497 and the Prayer Book Rebellion of 1549—suffice to emphasize Cornish willingness to defy crown demands to protect local interests. In the protest against Henry VII's war with the Scots in 1497, the Cornish revolted against heavy taxation to support a war that did not interest or affect them.[11] In 1549, during the reign of Henry VII's grandson, Edward VI, the Cornish rebelled against the imposition of a new Protestant prayer book and English church service that did not meet their needs. In the prologue of a petition sent from Cornwall to London, the Cornish insisted:

> We will not receive the new service book because it is like a Christmas game, but we will have our old service of Matins, Mass, Evensong, and Procession as it was before. And we, the Cornish, whereof certain of us understand no English, do utterly refuse the new service.[12]

The Cornish also insisted upon retaining their traditional sacraments and their access to sacramental items. They demanded "the sacrament to be hung over the altar and worshipped as it was wont to be, communion in one kind and then only at Easter, holy bread and holy water made every Sunday, and palms and ashes at proper times."[13] In both these revolts, the crown eventually succeeded in imposing its will upon the Cornish. Yet the Cornish defense of their county and traditional religious interests indicates a willingness to resist calls to act in a "national" interest.[14]

This is not to imply that the Cornish were uninterested in, uninformed about, or uninvolved in larger issues. Anne Duffin's study, *Faction and Faith: Politics and Religion of the Cornish Gentry before the Civil War*, perhaps characterizes Cornish integration into a wider national stage most accurately as she claims:

> . . . while many [Cornish] interests had a specifically Cornish focus, they were rarely exclusively so. The principal issues which effected and concerned Cornish gentlemen in this period . . . all had a national impact. The local response to those issues over the period often involved non-Cornishmen, in the Privy Council, in Parliament, and at Court. Consequently, outsiders were drawn into local affairs, and Cornish gentlemen found ways of dealing with local problems in a wider, national context.[15]

Despite this gradual integration of the Cornish into a larger political arena, most Cornishmen still differentiated between what was Cornish and what was English, and they struggled to perpetuate the former. Perhaps nowhere was this more clear than in the area of religion. Cornwall's loyalty to its ancient Celtic heritage led the Cornish to identify closely with Celtic-Catholic traditions rather than the Roman-Catholic traditions familiar to most of England's Catholics. This allowed a distinctive, traditional Celtic-Cornish brand of religious identity and community to evolve both inside and outside the nominal boundaries of the Protestant church.

As with many of the more remote counties, it is particularly difficult to ascertain accurately the number of Catholics in Cornwall. As discussed in chapter 1, any estimates are based largely on recusant rolls and visitation records. As such, head counts often more accurately reflect the waxing or waning zeal of the authorities in prosecuting Catholics than they do the actual number of Catholics in a shire. In 1578, there were more recusants—sixty heads of household—recorded in Cornwall than in any other southwestern county in England during the reign of Elizabeth—in fact, as many as in the neighboring counties of Devon, Dorset, and Somerset together.[16] Of course, in addition to these known recusant heads of household, there were a substantial number of family members, servants, church papists, and dissimulators.[17] In 1625, the deputy lieutenants of Cornwall estimated that there were two hundred recusants in Cornwall.[18] According to the 1641 subsidy rolls, there were sixty-eight recusant Cornish heads of household.[19] John Bossy estimates that by 1641, between 6 and 10% of Cornish households were Catholic.[20]

For a variety of reasons, the Church of England found it difficult to engender loyalty to its prescribed doctrines and rituals among the Cornish.[21] One such reason was the lack of Anglican clerics, a problem facing many of the more remote shires in England.[22] Another was a long-standing Cornish desire to maintain a separate identity for their church, which they did organizationally, architecturally, and ritually from the late medieval period.[23] For example, Cornwall and Devon together formed the diocese of Exeter, under the jurisdiction of the bishop of Exeter. Cornwall existed as a separate archdeaconry within the diocese. As Duffin argues, the Cornish church, for many practical purposes, was isolated from the watchful eye of its bishop and the centralizing efforts of the diocese.[24] Due to the difficulty of the terrain and the paucity of roads into Cornwall, communication with and administrative oversight in Cornwall was difficult.[25] As a result, the archdeacon held his ecclesiastical court, handled Cornish administration, and managed the Cornish clergy in relative independence of the bishop of Exeter.[26]

The decentralized and occasionally confusing chain of command in the Cornish church resulted in a church that was largely controlled by the laity rather than by Protestant clerics.[27] Through this control, laypersons—many of whom tended to be traditional in belief—determined the character of the church and were responsible for the enforcement of the Church of England's will. Two scenarios typically resulted. In some parishes, traditional sacraments and rituals were allowed to continue openly in churches that were nominally Protestant. In other parishes, Cornish Catholics separated themselves as recusants from their parish churches but were not harshly prosecuted under the penal laws.

The result is a Cornish church and laity that defy the usual labels of Catholic, Protestant, church papist, or recusant. It is unclear whether many Cornish parishioners identified themselves as Protestants or Catholics. Many Cornish likely considered themselves Celtic-Cornish Christians and would have resisted being subsumed into either Roman Catholic or Anglican hierarchies as long as they were able to worship in a familiar manner in their local parishes. And on the whole in Cornwall this worship was characterized by elements associated with traditional rather than reformed religion. Because of the difficulty of applying labels of Catholic or Protestant to the Cornish, whenever possible I will instead distinguish between those Cornish who favored traditional forms of religion and those who preferred reformed religion.

The continuation of traditional religion in other shires has been called Catholic survivalism.[28] But in Cornwall such practices often continued *within* the institutional church structure well into the seventeenth century, long after they had been extinguished in other shires. With traditional practices continuing in nominally Protestant parishes, both conformity and church papism were perhaps easier here than elsewhere. In some of these parishes, clerics loyal to traditional ways continued to occupy Cornish parish posts.[29] As described above, as long as traditionally inclined laity exercised such strong influence in parish administration—controlling or influencing access to clerical posts— such practices continued.

Parishioners often maintained a traditional calendar of saints' days in their nominally Protestant parishes.[30] In 1602, Richard Carew affirmed that many Protestant ministers in Cornwall labored assiduously to convince the Cornish that their saints' feasts were useless and superstitious. But, he observed:

> Let it breed none offense for me to report a conference that I had not long since with a near friend. . . . 'I do reverence (said he) the calling and judg- ment of the ministers especially when most of them concur in one opin- ion, and that the matter controversed holdeth some affinity with their pro- fession. Howbeit, I doubt lest in their exclaiming or declaiming against church ales and saints' feasts, their ringleaders did only regard the rind and not pierce into the pith.' [31]

As Nicholas Orme has observed, even when familiar saints were no longer ven- erated in a parish church, the Cornish commemorated the feast days in their homes, "entertaining friends from nearby parishes who later returned the favor."[32] In other words, some Cornish churchgoers felt free to disregard Protestant teachings and continued to revere their traditional saints and observe their rituals and observe feast days, a practice which continues in the present day.[33]

The continued reverence of St. Meriasek[34] following reform provides a good example of Cornish efforts to preserve pre-reform traditions associated with local saints. The Cornish hagiographer Nicholas Roscarrock described the parish of Camborne's particularly fervent devotion to Meriasek. The parish commemorated three feast days in his honor. The parish also preserved a holy well named for the saint. Pilgrims visited the well believing the waters to be holy and curative.[35] The Cornish also continued to remember St. Meriasek through the performance of a late medieval didactic miracle play entitled *Beunans Meriasek*, written in the Cornish vernacular (c. 1500) and which detailed the life of the saint as it simultaneously educated about Christian beliefs.[36]

Despite the continuation of many traditional practices within some Protestant churches and in the community, some Cornish—who with relative confidence may be termed Catholic—chose to absent themselves from Protestant services. Perhaps they obeyed Rome's mandate to eschew any accommodation with the Protestants, or perhaps they lived in parishes in which a Protestant-inclined laity controlled their churches.

These openly Cornish Catholics do not appear to have been harshly persecuted. While a certain degree of division existed between Catholics and Protestants, the Cornish often preferred to stand together against outside influences. This inclination is illustrated in a letter from the deputy lieutenants of Cornwall to the Earl of Pembroke in 1625. The government, fearing a Catholic invasion from the continent, ordered all recusants found and disarmed for fear they would aid the enemy. The deputy lieutenants informed the Earl that they were fully aware of the "dangerous contagion that may grow in this kingdom by those kind of Jesuited Papists more to be feared than Pestilence." The *Cornish* Catholics, the deputy lieutenants assured the Earl, were of a different temperament. The deputy lieutenants recognized that while the papistical threat was real in the rest of England, they had cause to praise God that the Cornish Catholics were not of the malicious sort who would act as a fifth column for an invading force of foreigners. Any Cornish Catholics who might have been "Jesuitical Papists" inclined to helping the invaders luckily were "not to be feared for their power." Despite estimating that there were 200 recusants in Cornwall, that their numbers were increasing, and that these Catholics were becoming more active, the deputy lieutenants attempted to protect the Cornish Catholics from any further action by the government. They declared that they had disarmed the one Cornish Catholic, John Trevillian of St. Clether, who they found armed, taking his "drum, musket, and corselet."[37] Perhaps there were perceived to be few radical Catholics in Cornwall as a result of the blurring of boundaries between traditional and reformed religion in Cornish churches. Cornish Catholics did not need to rebel to regain traditional forms of worship. They often already enjoyed them. Regardless of the exact causes, the nominally Protestant Cornish authorities were often willing to leave their Catholic neighbors alone.

In this relatively remote environment in which a traditionally inclined laity could control some parish churches and where Catholic-Protestant enmity was low, what options were open to the Cornish who favored traditional religion to define their identity and community? To answer such questions, we must turn to what is most distinctive about Cornwall's religious past—its Celtic heritage. Then we can explore how Cornish Christians of the late sixteenth and early seventeenth centuries interpreted this heritage within the environment described above to create their own particular Celtic-Cornish religious identity and community.

CORNWALL'S CELTIC PAST: "AN ANCIENT SONG, LILTING BEFORE YOU CAME"

Although Roman Christianity was the first form of Christianity introduced in Cornwall, it was by no means the last or the most influential form. Celtic

Christianity—with its resemblance to Eastern Orthodox traditions rather than Roman Christian ones—would serve as the lasting foundation for Cornish Christianity. The Romans brought Christianity to Cornwall in the first centuries A.D. After the withdrawal of the Romans from Cornwall in approximately 426 A.D., however, most of the Cornish reverted to paganism until the first waves of Irish and Welsh missionaries and hermits arrived to re-Christianize Cornwall several decades later. The Roman brand of Christianity was re-introduced into southeastern England in the sixth century by St. Augustine of Canterbury, but Cornwall—off in the southwest—continued to be predominately influenced by the Irish, or Celtic, form of Christianity.[38] For example, loyalty to Celtic-Christian traditions and locally revered Celtic-Christian saints responsible for the county's re-conversion remained strong in the centuries prior to Henry VIII's reforms as revealed by twelfth-century and fourteenth-century copies of the Exeter Martyrology. The calendar of saints feasts overflows with days dedicated to the local saints who shaped Celtic beliefs and rituals.[39]

In the late sixteenth and early seventeenth centuries, those among the Cornish who favored traditional religion constructed their identity and sense of community around these Celtic-Christian traditions. Crucial to the creation of this Celtic-Christian identity was Nicholas Roscarrock, the early seventeenth-century Cornish hagiographer and author of *Lives of the English Saints*, the only extant sixteenth- or seventeenth-century compilation of the lives of the saints of Cornwall and Devon.[40] Despite the title, Roscarrock primarily chronicled the lives of saints with a connection to Cornwall. That these are the saints he considers English (in Roscarrock's mind, British) and that he felt the need to treat these saints separately from those revered by the rest of England and the Roman Church is indicative of the pride and independence that were so much a part of the identity and sense of community among the Cornish of this period.

Roscarrock was born into a lesser gentry family in the parish of St. Endelient on the north coast of Cornwall.[41] Nicholas and his younger brother, Trevennor, were staunchly loyal to the Catholic faith, losing much of their lands and income to recusancy fines. Nicholas spent a total of fourteen years in prison where he met many other influential Catholics.[42] When finally free, Roscarrock traveled northward to Cumberland in 1607 to live under the protection of Lord William Howard, with whom he had been imprisoned in the Tower.[43] It was while he lived with Howard that Roscarrock wrote *Lives of the English Saints*.

Treatment of Roscarrock's *Lives of the English Saints* by previous historians has concentrated upon the work more as an interesting historical or antiquarian study than as a source of evidence of Cornish piety.[44] Roscarrock, however, understood himself as both historian and hagiographer.[45] Although it doubtless would have been frowned upon by the Council of Trent, Roscarrock encouraged his readers to pray to these locally revered Celtic saints as effective intercessors of whom the church approved.

But was there a demand for Roscarrock's brand of Celtic-Cornish hagiography among those who favored traditional religion? Apparently so. A letter written by a William Webbe, likely from the 1640s or 1650s, is addressed presumably to the chaplain at Naworth where Roscarrock spent his last years.[46] Webbe, living hundreds of miles south in Cornwall, had heard of Roscarrock's work. He and others, he claimed, wanted to know more about "their" saints:

> Most worthy Sir:
>
> Mr. Trewenna Roscarrock[47] found in the library of Oxford a story of a certain Christian and his wife who came out of Ireland with their children to fly the persecution, and lived in Cornwall:[48] and after some time both he and his wife with the children suffered martyrdom in Cornwall, and in their honor were fair churches dedicated. Some of the names of these saints (as we suppose) were these as follow: S. Essye, S. Milior, S. Que, S. Einendor, S. Eue, S. Maubon, S. Breage, S. Earvin, S. Merrine, etc. . . .
>
> Now some worthy Catholics of Cornwall being desirous to understand the full story, to the end they may better honor the Saints of their county besought me to write unto the North about this, and get out of Mr. Nicholas Roscarrock's writings this story, they knowing that he was wont to compile together such monuments for further memory. . . . I did so and was assured that Sir William Howard, Lord William's son, had Mr. Nicholas Roscarrock's written books and papers. . . . Wherefore Worthy Sir I shall humbly entreat you for God's sake, and for the honor of these glorious saints [and] martyrs to deal . . . Sir William Howard to [obta]ine a copy of this story for all our comforts and we [shall be al]ways obliged to pray for you and Sir William [both in] this world and in the next.[49]

Celtic-Cornish Christians, at this late date, still showed loyalty to saints they considered their own and which they linked to the earliest days of Celtic Christianity in their county.[50]

Moreover, in the same period as Roscarrock was writing, other Cornish who favored traditional religion were preserving the ancient calendars of the Celtic-Cornish Church which honored Celtic saints. In the early seventeenth century, for example, Edward Ellis preserved the *Calendar of the Augustinian Priory at Launceston* (c. 14–15c.). We know of Ellis's efforts thanks to a small notation he wrote in the calendar in 1605.[51] Such liturgical calendars and the litanies contained therein included Celtic-Cornish saints' feasts dedicated to Piran, Petroc, Nonna, Nectan, Neot, Columba the virgin, and others.[52]

In writing about the lives of the Celtic saints, Roscarrock was not trying to create a new cult or resurrect a long dead cult of the saints in Cornwall. Instead, he was reflecting the atmosphere of reverence for such saints which still existed in the early seventeenth century among the Cornish who favored traditional religion, whether nominally Protestant or Catholic.[53] Whether consciously or unconsciously, Roscarrock also adapted the legends to the needs of his contemporaries. The Cornish could then interpret and use the stories of these early Celtic-Christian saints to develop their sense of religious identity and community.

LIVES OF THE CORNISH SAINTS

A peripatetic priesthood had always existed in Cornwall, so the first arrival of the wandering missionary priests during Elizabeth's reign likely did not seem much of a change.[54] Roscarrock repeated the traditional Cornish understanding that the Celtic missionary effort was begun in the fifth century by St. Brechanus, a prince of Wales, and his twelve sons and twelve daughters. All twenty-four children wandered the countryside in Cornwall and Devon, led the lives of hermits, and were later named martyrs or confessors by the Cornish (rather than by Rome). Missionaries also arrived from Ireland near the year 460, including St. Piran, a disciple of St. Patrick's, who would later become the patron saint of Cornwall and of its tin miners.[55] Many Cornish churches of the late sixteenth and early seventeenth centuries were successors to the oratories established by these early Celtic-Cornish missionaries and continued to bear their names.[56]

By the seventeenth century, many qualities differentiated the Celtic brand of Christianity in Cornwall from the Roman type. Two distinctions are most important to this analysis. First, Cornish adherents of traditional religion assigned little importance to Rome as the center of religious authority. While they did not ignore Rome's authority, they did not allow it to determine the character of Cornish religious belief or practice. Second, the Cornish evinced a particularly strong belief in the immanentist character of traditional religion: a belief in the sacred found in nature, whether inhering in physical locations, individuals, or objects. Cornwall itself was a sacred land.

As evidenced throughout *Lives of the English Saints*, Celtic Christians did not view Rome as the center of their faith. Cornwall was this center. Roscarrock describes a tightly knit Cornish religious community of saints, confessors, abbots, and ascetics who lived, in general, without an overarching Celtic institutional ecclesiastical community. Instead, Cornish saints were tied to one another by blood and to the Cornish land they lived upon.

The close blood ties connecting Cornish saints are evident in Roscarrock's *Lives of the English Saints*. Along with chronicling each saint's deeds, Roscarrock repeatedly traced a saint's lineage back to St. Brechanus and his twenty-four children. Even if Roscarrock could not corroborate blood ties between a saint and Brechanus, he sought an alternative connection between them. Roscarrock described, for example, St. Cletherus who sired twenty sons, all of whom he delivered to St. Brechanus for religious training.[57]

This recognition (or creation) of familial and associational ties between Cornish saints served valuable functions for Cornish who favored traditional religion. First, in a sense, this hagiographically constructed family of Celtic saints provided a visible community of which believers could feel a part. This familiar family of saints lived and worked miracles on Cornish cliffs, hills, and moors, probably spoke Cornish, and respected Cornish customs. The saints encouraged imitation among those who practiced traditional forms of religion and who enjoyed similarly strong family ties, linguistic background, and cultural norms.

Secondly, the blood connections among Celtic saints helped ground the traditional Celtic-Cornish faith firmly in the county itself rather than in Canterbury or Rome. Throughout sixteenth and seventeenth-century hagiography and art, this family of Cornish saints was portrayed as being focused on Cornwall and its people as the center of the faith. The Cornish claimed their own land as a holy land capable of producing a bounty of Christ-like saints, ascetic eremites, and miracle workers. Such religious self-sufficiency in establishing and perpetuating Celtic Christianity would likely have been attractive to the somewhat independent-minded Cornish. Moreover, such a Celtic-Cornish model portrays Cornwall as the epicenter of a faith which then radiated outward to the world. This countered the Roman model—a faith centered elsewhere in the world that needed to be brought in from outside and imposed upon Cornwall.[58]

Perhaps the legends of Cornwall's patron, St. Piran, and the ascetic St. Neot most clearly demonstrate Cornish authors' desire to depict their own land as a center of Christian faith and their saints as heirs to the traditions of the first centuries of Christianity. Cornish devotion to St. Piran remained strong into the late sixteenth century despite Elizabeth's Act of Uniformity. Nicholas Roscarrock recalled that Piran's relics "were wont to be carried up and down in the country upon occasion" and that as a child he himself had seen the relics carried during Mary I's reign. Roscarrock also reported that, according to their register of relics, Waltham Abbey kept a bone of St. Piran's.[59] Reflecting the lack of a clearly recognized distinction between Catholic and Protestant rituals in Cornish parishes, Piran's relics continued to be carried about, especially for Rogationtide processions, at least as late as 1588.[60]

The seventeenth-century version of St. Piran's life reveals a strong desire to draw connections between St. Piran and Christ and to show that holy miracles were possible in Cornwall as well as in the Holy Land. Various written lives of St. Piran report that he was born nobly in Ireland in the late fourth or early fifth century. Piran traveled to Rome and the Italian peninsula on pilgrimage where he met St. Patrick. Piran returned to Ireland and then journeyed to Britain, where he lived the Christ-like life of a peripatetic priest, wandering the countryside, converting people, and performing miracles.

In Roscarrock's portrayal, Piran's miracles bore an amazingly close resemblance to those of Christ's. Piran raised people from the dead, just as Christ raised Lazarus. Piran walked "on the water dryfooted," just as Christ walked on water before his disciples. Piran relieved "multitudes with a little." Recalling Christ's feeding of a crowd of thousands with but a few loaves and fish, Piran fed ten kings and ten armies for ten days with only three cows. Finally, Roscarrock reported that Piran turned water into wine, mimicking Christ's miracle at the wedding at Cana.[61]

Accounts of Piran's condemnation also drew many parallels between Christ's life and death and that of Piran. When a group of powerful men grew envious and fearful of Piran's influence among the people, they condemned him to death, just as a group of powerful Jewish citizens called for Jesus's imprisonment and death when their own influence was threatened. Piran was to be thrown into the sea. Piran's accusers brought him to a high cliff on a stormy day, chained him to a millstone, and pushed him over the edge. As Piran plummeted downward, a miraculous change in the weather occurred, just as at Christ's crucifixion. At Christ's death, the weather suddenly turned violent, and thunder roared. At the moment before Piran's death, the gale winds ceased, white-capped waves calmed, and the sun broke through coal-black clouds. The man who moments before was certain to drown survived. According to the legend, the instant the crowd witnessed the changes in the weather and Piran's survival, hundreds converted to Christianity, just as many witnesses to Christ's crucifixion at last believed that "Truly, this was the son of God."[62] Piran reportedly floated for several days upon the sea before landing on the Cornish beach that continues to bear his name: Perranporth (Perran's entrance).

Piran, an Irishman living hundreds of years after Christ and thousands of miles away from the Holy Land, was portrayed as having the ability to replicate Christ-like miracles and events within Cornwall. As discussed in chapter 4 on the sacrament of the altar, English Catholics felt a strong desire to build connections to Christ. Here we see a seventeenth-century Cornish hagiographer constructing ties between Celtic-Cornish piety and Christ by attributing Christ-like qualities to one of the best-known Cornish saints.[63]

The legend of the anchorite St. Neot reveals a similar tendency of the Cornish to focus upon Cornwall as a holy land capable of producing holy men comparable to those of biblical times. The legend of St. Neot in Cornwall was not even recorded until the sixteenth century.[64] The telling of his story, therefore, reflects the contemporary needs of the hagiographer and his audience more so than do the legends of other Cornish saints.

Instead of replicating Christ-like miracles, sixteenth and seventeenth-century evidence reveals that St. Neot was more comparable to the ascetic Desert Fathers and Mothers such as St. Anthony who wandered into the Egyptian desert to fast and pray. Such ascetics were popular Christian exemplars and foci of devotion in the first centuries of Christianity.[65] Living in the late ninth century, Neot reportedly entered religion at Glastonbury Abbey and became a Benedictine monk and later an abbot.[66] Renowned for his fasting, prayer, learning, and healing abilities, but uncomfortable with such esteem, Neot "withdrew himself into a desert at Hamstoke in Cornwall ten miles from the monastery at St. Petrocstowe now Bodmin where he lived austerely, which desert was after called of him Neotstowe (St. Neot)," according to Roscarrock.[67]

Roscarrock's choice of the term "desert" to describe Neot's place of retreat is telling of his likely desire to draw a link between the early Christian Desert Fathers and the Celtic ascetics. Cornwall possessed no "deserts" in the traditional sense. Neot really withdrew to Bodmin Moor and lived in a cell in the woods. In this remote location, Neot lived a life of fasting and devotion comparable to that of St. Anthony. Roscarrock therefore implies that the experiences of some of early Christianity's most holy individuals were duplicable in Cornwall by Cornish Christians.[68]

Devotion to Neot, as to Piran, remained strong in Cornwall in the sixteenth and seventeenth centuries. The sixteenth-century painted glass windows of the church of St. Neot's reflect this devotion. The third, seventh, and tenth windows all portray St. Neot in various roles: as monk, pilgrim, and hermit.[69] Significantly, these windows were not destroyed during the Protestant iconoclastic fervor that occasionally spread throughout much of England between the reigns of Henry VIII and Elizabeth I.[70] Perhaps the families who had so recently paid for the windows were powerful enough to prevent their destruction. Perhaps the majority of the parish of St. Neot remained faithful to their traditional patron and their traditional faith—further evidence of the difficulty of labeling Cornish Christians as either Catholic or Protestant based on their parish attendance or membership. Whatever the reasons, the parish of St. Neot preserved the windows and maintained St. Neot's holy well and cell which still stood in 1852.[71]

Describing Celtic saints of Cornwall such as Neot and Piran as undergoing similar experiences to Christ's or as enacting the same devotions as the early Christian ascetics reflected the tendency of the Cornish to view their own land and people as the center of faith and religious life. This is not to argue that Cornish who favored traditional religion saw themselves as independent from either Rome's or Canterbury's oversight. Instead, perhaps in religion as in politics, the Cornish favored their own autonomy while remaining faithful to a larger authority.

Hagiography, for example, depicts Celtic saints as recognizing Rome's importance but maintaining few connections to Rome or ecclesiastical authority. This is in marked contrast to those canonized English Christians who promoted Roman Christianity—such as Augustine of Canterbury and Wilfrid—whose reverence for and participation in the Roman hierarchy contributed greatly to their reputations for sanctity.[72] The legends of Piran, Neot, and other Celtic saints reveal few sustained ties with Rome. For example, while Piran seemingly recognized Rome's importance—enough to justify a pilgrimage to that city—Rome played little role in Piran's later religious life in Cornwall. Piran evidently wrote no letters to Rome asking for aid or decisions. He made no effort to set up an officially sanctioned mission in Cornwall. Instead, Piran appears to act independently and sufficiently to perpetuate the Christian faith.[73]

The legend of Neot reveals a similar glossing over of connections to Roman authority. Roscarrock reported that seven years after Neot's withdrawal into the desert:

> [H]e went from thence to Rome where he was well received by Pope Martin the Second, and returning from him with his benediction built the Monastery of St. Petroc's in Cornwall . . . where there was a well which miraculously relieved him with fish; he wrought many miracles, and namely one at a well in which he used to say the holy Psalter.[74]

Despite devoting many pages to telling the story of St. Neot, Roscarrock describes Neot's connection to Rome in just a few lines. The author seems to feel it is important to show Neot's recognition of Rome's and the Pope's authority. Roscarrock, however, spends much more time developing stories of Neot's healing, miracles and ascetic practices, all of which occurred at holy sites in or near Cornwall.[75]

Overall, Cornish hagiography—whether written by Roscarrock or by other anonymous authors—stressed the insularity and relative self-sufficiency of Cornish Christianity. Cornish saints were a tight-knit group bound together by blood ties or close communal ties. While briefly recognizing the importance of Rome to the early Celtic-Cornish church, the hagiographers emphasize the importance of Cornish saints working, performing miracles, and dying on Cornish land. These saints were so holy that they mimicked the miracles of Christ. They were so devout that they adopted the lifestyles of the holiest of

Christ's early followers. It is almost as if to say that anything important enough to occur throughout Christendom could likewise occur in Cornwall—if not the Holy Land, then a "holy-enough" land.

CELTIC-CORNISH IMMANENCE: PLACES, PEOPLE, AND THINGS

For early seventeenth-century Cornish who favored traditional religion in this holy-enough land, their faith remained a religion of Catholic immanence but with a Celtic flair. Traditional Celtic-Christian identity and community were characterized by a powerful belief in the immanence of God in nature and in a somatic experiencing of the sacred. This belief in remote, natural locales as opportunities for worshipping and experiencing close connections to God contrasts with many English Catholic efforts discussed in chapter 2 on religious spaces and chapter 5 on London Catholics. In these previous chapters, Catholics congregated in private homes or in institutions such as prisons, the Inns of Court, or foreign embassies. The closest connection that can be drawn between other Catholics' use of religious space and Cornish-Christian use was that suggested by Robert Southwell in chapter 2. Southwell encouraged Catholics to dedicate natural spaces such as paths, orchards, fields, and woods for use as pious spaces by dedicating them to a particular saint. In this way, a Catholic walking through such locations could call to mind the saint and use the natural spaces to meditate upon pious issues. But is this exactly what Celtic-Cornish Christians were doing?

Places

The Lady's Offering

A web of woven wool, fringed all around,
Ruddy and rich in hue, like Syrian wine;
With golden leaves inlaid on that dark ground,
That seemed just shed from some o'ershadowing vine:
Such was the lady's offering at Morwenna's shrine...

We offered it to Him:—scorn not the phrase
Ye proud and stately magnates of the land;
Grudge not the poor their pence, nor God his praise,
Though as our simple fathers stood, we stand,
And render thus our gifts with meek and votive hand.[76]

Cornish hagiography depicts natural spaces in a different light than Southwell. Southwell presumed that many of his readers lacked access to traditional religious spaces. They were to use natural spaces as *reminders* of a saint or tenet of belief that was itself unrelated to the actual physical site.

Cornwall, however, experienced little iconoclasm during reforming efforts and thus maintained many of its traditional holy sites. Moreover, many of these sites were natural spaces which were not just reminders of what was holy but which *in and of themselves* were holy.[77] Celtic saints had lived, worked, and died on these sites. The saints were immanently present at such spots. Woods, streams, and wells were all locations where Cornish who favored traditional religion could open a two-way channel of communication with the divine. Thus, the Cornish use of the ordinary as the locus of the sacred did not require the Cornish to adopt the ideas of English Catholic authors like Alabaster and Southwell. Natural locations such as orchards, paths, or rocks were *already* holy places in the Celtic-Cornish tradition.

An early-seventeenth-century manuscript detailing the life of St. Keyna the Virgin succeeds particularly well in portraying this belief in the presence and activity of God in the natural world. Significantly, it also displays a marked lack of reliance upon any centralized ecclesiastical institution or administration, similar to what we saw in the lives of Piran and Neot. Keyna was one of the twelve daughters of St. Brechanus. The hagiographer reported:

> The virgin when she was of years fit for marriage and desired to wife of many, despised carnal bed, and conservated herself to our Lord by vow of perpetual charity [chastity?]: whereupon in their tongue she is called Keynwire, that is Keyn the Virgin. Afterward she leaving her country the more freely to serve God remote from the world she passed over the Severne and came into a wood that was so infested with serpents that man nor beast before her durst not enter into it for fear of death. But she armed with great faith entered boldly into that wood, and with her prayers slew all those serpents, and vipers, and turned them into stones. . . . After that she had long conversed there in great perfection and by her example had drawn many to the love of God, she returned into her country; where on a certain little hill she served God with all devotion, still clad in hair, and lying on the ground.[78]

At the end of her life, an angel appeared to Keyna and revealed that her death was near. She returned to her family to die. After her death, her body reportedly exuded a sweet fragrance.

The story of the life of Keyna reveals many qualities characteristic of both Roman and Celtic hagiography. Her holiness was foretold before her birth. She remained a virgin. She exhibited great faith and performed miracles. She converted many through her holiness. Her corpse emitted sweet odors.

But other details of her life exemplify the importance of nature in the Cornish-Christian faith. She performed miracles in the woods, turning snakes into stones. She isolated herself on a hilltop where an angel visited her. She clothed herself sparely and slept upon the earth.

Also absent in the hagiographer's story is any evidence of links between Keyna and any larger ecclesiastical authority, whether centered in Rome, Cornwall, or elsewhere in England, which is unusual, particularly for a woman of this time. From whom did she learn her faith? She vowed perpetual chastity, but to whom did she make this vow? In what form did she make this vow? If she made it independently, what allowed her to think she might do so? No priest or other churchman instructed her or guided her prayers. Others traveled to see her and conversed with her freely, thus she was able to perpetuate her faith as she interpreted it. When she returned to her land, she continued living a life of solitary austerity, living alone on a hill, sleeping on the ground, dressed in haircloth. At the time of her death, an angel of the lord visited her. God spoke directly to Keyna. There were no intercessors or mediators between Keyna and God as the Roman Church advocated. There was no priest, no church. There was only God, faith, and the natural environment—the woods, hills, and moors—in which to practice that faith.

Sixteenth- and seventeenth-century Cornish Christians continued to identify with the simplicity of Keyna's faith and her ties to the land and nature of Cornwall. They believed in the miracle-working powers of St. Keyne's Well. Richard Carew described the well in his 1602 *Survey of Cornwall*, and included an anonymous poem which, despite its irreverent treatment of Catholic belief in the immanent powers of the well, described the natural rusticity of the "sacred stream." "In name and shape and quality, this well is very quaint," the poet wrote,

> The shape, for trees of diverse kind,
>   Withy, oak, elm and ash
> Make with their roots an arches roof,
>   Whose floor this spring doth wash.[79]

As this poem indicates, many of the natural spaces associated with early Celtic saints continued to exist in the late sixteenth and early seventeenth centuries. These sites bolstered Celtic-Cornish identity and community among those inclined to traditional religion, some of whom continued to preserve and use these traditional sacred places, even constructing shrines or protective buildings around some sites. Cornwall was peppered with patches of "holy land." The ground, the hills, the water could all work miracles and bring the faithful into closer contact with the divine.

Celtic crosses dotted the Cornish countryside, serving as constant reminders of the sacrality of the land and of the traditional Celtic-Christian identity of the people. The distinctive shape of the crosses testified to the distinctive nature of the Christianity practiced by the inhabitants' Cornish ancestors. Despite a few incidents of iconoclasm, most of the crosses remained intact during the late Tudor/early Stuart years, protected by nearby inhabitants. The crosses were so well known and ingrained in the lives of the Cornish that plans

Figure 3: Standing Celtic cross photographed in field near Ponsanooth, Cornwall.

of manor houses included the locations of the crosses. People gave directions using the crosses as guides.[80] (See Figure 3.)

Pelynt: The Well in the Valley

In the holy well tucked into the green hill
The yellow wings of moths, dead souls
Of the dead, lie on the still pool

A bent pin perhaps will bring your wish: but
Is this still a centre of mysteries, or
A holy place, of the mother of David?. . . [81]

Holy wells were also so much a part of community consciousness that they continued to show up on maps.[82] Wells worked to cement religious identity and community among traditionalists despite the derision of some reformers. Many survive today along with reports of miracles worked.[83]

Traditional Celtic Christians continued to have faith in the spiritual and physical aid that the saints could provide at these natural sites.[84] According to legend, many of the wells originally sprang up due to the prayers of a Cornish saint, martyr, or hermit who needed divine assistance. Celtic-Cornish saints also worked miracles and baptized converts at the wells.[85] The Cornish who favored the traditional faith often made pilgrimages to holy wells.[86] As the poem "Pelynt, The Well in the Valley" suggests, they would drop pebbles, pins, or even small crosses into the wells as they offered their prayers. In Catholic immanentist tradition, they believed that by leaving material items in the well, they would themselves remain physically present at the well even after they left, thus continuing to tie themselves to the saint's intercessory powers.[87]

Cornish who favored reformed religion often ridiculed traditional belief in these wells but, in contrast to elsewhere in England, made little effort to destroy the wells or stop Catholics from visiting them. [88] Carew reported in 1602 that Catholics, whom he termed "idle-headed seekers," would repair to Nant's Well, near Lanherne, on Palm Sunday bearing a palm cross (a sacramental item) in one hand and an offering in the other. They would throw the palm crosses into the well. According to Carew, "superstitious" Catholics used the well to discover whether they would outlive the year. If the palm floated, its bearer would live. If the palm sank, a death was imminent.[89] It seems unlikely that Carew provided a complete picture of traditional religious experience at the well.

The Cornish continued to revere other types of sacred natural spaces associated with particular Cornish saints, such as paths, hermits' cells, rocks, and gardens. Sixteenth- and seventeenth-century Cornish who favored traditional religion maintained many of the sites associated with St. Leven.[90] Leven, the founder of a hermitage in Cornwall near Bodellen, was identified with a hut, a garden, a path, a grouping of rocks, and a solitary stone. The walls of St. Leven's hermit's hut were allegedly still visible in 1740. Also still recognizable was a triangular garden named Johanna's Garden, after a woman who criticized St. Leven for fishing on a Sunday to catch his meal. Additionally, a small path where St. Leven reportedly walked, called St. Leven's Path, led down to a group of rocks where the saint would sit, called St. Leven's Rocks. Finally, still resting on the south side of the parish church is a large stone called St. Leven's Stone upon which St. Leven is supposed to have liked to sit. The stone is cracked through the center, supposedly from a blow of St. Leven's staff. The stone has not been removed nor was it used for the construction of the church.[91]

The continued association of all these sites with this Cornish saint reinforced identification with the cultural memory of traditional Celtic-Christian practices despite reformers' efforts to erase or ridicule such associations. The Cornish could walk along the paths and sit in the exact places where holy men and women walked and rested. They could pray to their saints in gardens where the saints themselves held counsel during their lives. Such continued intimate contact with the sacred places and intercessors of their traditional religion was difficult for Protestantism to dislodge, especially considering the weak hold the Protestant clergy had over the Cornish church.

People

As discussed in chapters 2 and 4, another "natural location" which could be dedicated to faith and worship was a believer's own body. Just like Catholics throughout England, the Cornish recognized Christ's body, the saints' bodies, and their own bodies as sacred sites in a myriad of ways, illustrating a particular desire to experience the faith somatically. Many of the best-known Cornish priests—such as the martyr John Cornelius—practiced rigorous fasting and self-mortification, and some among the Cornish laity also disciplined their bodies. [92]

While the desire to dedicate one's own body for religious use was most commonly expressed through activities such as crossing oneself, fasting, or by wearing a hair shirt, an exceptional case out of Cornwall deserves closer attention as it illustrates how Cornish Catholics were creatively using or perceiving their own bodies in intriguing pious ways. In what may have been an effort to practice a religious asceticism comparable to that of Caroline Walker Bynum's fasting women of the Middle Ages,[93] the Cornishwoman Anne Jeffries engaged in her own brand of fasting in the 1640s. According to accounts written by Protestant observers, the nineteen-year-old Jeffries was knitting in a garden in 1645 *when six fairies appeared to her clothed all in green.* She fell into a fit and was found by the Pitt family, for whom she worked, and was put to bed.

Afterwards she effected remarkable cures and was reportedly fed for months on nothing but "fairy bread."

This interpretation of events, as was perhaps intended by Jeffries's Protestant chroniclers, reads like a tale of country folklore, filled with super-stition.[94] Perhaps one reason for the misinterpretation of her actions was her fear of imprisonment, which caused her to be less than forthcoming about her experiences. Jeffries cooperated with Protestant civil and religious authority but did not appear to respect it or revere that for which it stood. When exam-ined by Protestant magistrates, she answered their questions but told them they would not be in their offices long. When questioned by Protestant the-ologians, she told them openly that none of them were able to hurt her.[95]

According to a member of the Pitt family, time and again, both magis-trates and ministers came to her home to examine her or hauled Jeffries in front of committees of theologians for questioning. Each time, she "gave a good account of her religion and hath the scriptures very perfectly though quite unlearned." Her neighbors considered her devout.[96] Fifty years later, Anne Jeffries was still alive and contacted about her experiences with the fairies. She refused to speak "for she said she had been questioned before jus-tices, and at the sessions, and in prison, and also before the judges at the assizes, and she doth believe that if she should discover such things now she would be questioned again for it."[97] Moreover, she feared the attention of com-mon people. She believed that if she divulged the details of her experiences "you would make books or ballads of it, and I would not have my name spread about the country in books or ballads if I might have £500 for doing it."[98] One wonders exactly how much of her story Jeffries told the first time around and how many of the blanks were filled in by curious onlookers.

A closer examination of events reveals Jeffries's probable Catholic lean-ings and her conscious or unconscious resurrection of a long-familiar form of female Catholic piety. While confined to the mayor of Bodmin's house in 1647, she reportedly prayed frequently and encouraged people to "keep the old form of prayer." She presumably meant the traditional or Catholic form, perhaps even in the Cornish vernacular. Jeffries appears to have enjoyed a one-on-one relationship with God, just as English Catholic authors such as Garnet, Crowther, Vincent, and Southwell were encouraging. Jeffries believed that God empowered her to heal.[99] Jeffries performed her first cure for her employ-er, Mrs. Pitt, shortly after her initial vision.[100] Jeffries went on to heal many people of almost any type of illness, and she was especially renowned for heal-ing the "falling sickness" and broken bones. The ill journeyed to Cornwall from as far away as London to be cured.[101]

Jeffries appears to have viewed herself as a channel for God, perhaps almost as a mediator.[102] Although she did not flaunt it, she obviously continued either to have visions from God or intelligence from him since she knew about injuries or illnesses without being told about them. When asked how she knew and how she cured, Jeffries said, "by the blessing of God." It was only onlookers, such as the Pitts, who claimed she cured by the aid of fairies, rather than by God. Jeffries accepted no payment for her cures and employed no medicines.[103]

Jeffries also trusted in God to provide for her physical needs, just as earlier Celtic saints such as St. Neot had trusted in God to sustain them.[104] While engaged in healing, Jeffries stopped eating for periods of as long as six months. Observers corroborate that she was given no food and yet was somehow sustained. John Tregeagle, a Justice of the Peace and steward to John, Earl of Radnor, examined members of the Pitt family, asking them if they had been bringing her food when it was claimed she was surviving without eating. They denied doing so. Tregeagle then issued a warrant for Jeffries's arrest and ordered that Jeffries be kept "without victuals." Jeffries did not starve.[105]

Although onlookers' reports state that she was fed upon "fairy bread," Jeffries apparently did not use this term herself. Instead, her experiences resemble those of medieval Catholic women who sustained themselves on nothing but Eucharistic bread. Moses Pitt, the son of Jeffries's employers, recalled:

> One time (I remember it perfectly well) I had a mind to speak with her, and not knowing where better to find her than in her chamber, I went thither, and fell a-knocking very earnestly at her chamber door with my foot, and calling to her earnestly, "Anne! Anne! Open the door and let me in." She answered me, "Have a little patience, and I will let you in immediately:" Upon which I looked through the keyhole of the door and saw her eating and when she was done eating she stood by the bedside as long as thanks might be given, and then she made a courtesy and opened the chamber door, and gave me a piece of the bread, which I did eat, and I think it was the most delicious bread that ever I did eat, either before or since.[106]

Where did the fasting Jeffries, a servant, procure such bread, bread so special that fifty years later Pitt recalled it as the best he had ever tasted? She refused to comment on her experiences, so we have only Pitt's interpretation to consider. Was what Pitt termed "fairy food" analogous in some way to the sacrament of the Eucharist which was believed the most delicious bread possible and capable of independently sustaining a believer? In her one-on-one relationship with God, did she perceive it was God feeding her with divine bread— the body of Christ himself? Possibly. In a potential further association of her asceticism with the physical body of Christ, Jeffries ended her fast on

Christmas day, the day commemorating Christ's physical entrance into the material world. As the Jeffries example—although exceptional—suggests, Cornish Christians disposed to traditional immanentist beliefs could still use the space of their bodies in traditional ways as channels to the divine.

Things

Just as Cornish Christians used their natural surroundings and their bodies as opportunities to connect with the divine and tap into a sense of Celtic-Christian identity and community, so too did they use religious objects. Cornish Christians apparently possessed a particularly strong attachment to sacramental objects and a belief in their efficacy. During the Prayer Book Rebellion in 1549 discussed earlier, the Cornish demanded access to such items as holy water, palms, and ashes. Their loyalty to these items remained powerful throughout the late Tudor/early Stuart period. Authorities frequently found sacramental items in the possession of the Cornish.[107] Cornish priests frequently distributed such items, which, as discussed in chapter 3, were small, portable, and easy to conceal. Many sacramental items could be made in an almost unlimited supply in almost any location through special prayers and blessings. Some sacramental objects, however, such as *agni dei*, were different. The small waxen discs—made from blessed paschal candles in Rome and specially stamped with an image of the lamb of God—could only be produced on the continent. As a result, they were especially prized. Cornish priests appear to have favored this sacramental object, risking searches by Protestant port authorities to bring them in. The Cornish martyr Cuthbert Mayne, for example, was arrested with an *agnus dei* hung about his own neck, and was indicted for distributing *agni dei* to at least eleven lay Cornish Catholics. During James's reign, the Cornishman Thomas Laithwaite, alias Scott, was apprehended in Plymouth for refusing the Oath of Supremacy and when searched was discovered attempting to bring in *agni dei*.[108]

Cornish-Catholic laypersons also traveled to the continent and returned with sacramentals to distribute, as did John Jenkyn, a native of Penzance. During James I's reign, Jenkyn journeyed to Seville where he resided as a lay brother with the Jesuits for many years. Authorities at Plymouth captured him as he attempted to return home in the autumn of 1633. Searchers found upon Jenkyn "diverse crucifixes, pictures, and other superstitious things, with two or three popish books."[109]

Rosaries were popular among Cornish Catholics. Lay devotion to Mary had been strong in Cornwall in the centuries prior to Elizabeth's Act of Uniformity and continued to be strong afterwards.[110] The primary lay devotion to access the intercessory powers of the Virgin was, as discussed in chapter 3, the rosary—one of the most readily available and popular sacramental objects.

Lay Cornish Catholics bequeathed their rosaries.[111] Cornish craftsmen made homemade rosaries, such as the artisan who fabricated a rosary for Cuthbert Mayne from metal hoops and brightly colored stones.[112] Protestant searchers and spies discovered beads in the possession of suspected Cornish Catholics.[113]

Perhaps the most interesting extant rosary associated with a Cornish Catholic is the Langdale Rosary, which simultaneously emphasizes the continued devotion of Cornish Catholics to sacramental items, to Mary, and to Cornish saints. It also demonstrates the community-building potential of rosary worship. The rosary, currently on display at the Victoria and Albert Museum in London,[114] was crafted of gold c.1500. It contains six large *Pater noster* beads, fifty smaller *Ave Maria* beads, and a pendant and measures approximately 40.5 cm in length. The artist engraved both sides of each bead either with an image of Christ or of a saint, identifying each saint with an inscription upon the bead's edge.

In an interesting example of how a sacramental item could build communal ties between a Cornish and a non-Cornish Catholic, Nicholas Roscarrock and his patron Lord William Howard appear to have shared the rosary. Two beads were either added or replaced which link the rosary to the devotions of both men, who were imprisoned together in London and who subsequently lived at Naworth from approximately 1610 to 1625. One of the new beads, associated with Roscarrock's Cornish-Catholic devotion, depicts his patron saint, St. Endelient, and images of her holy well and a cow, a symbol associated with the saint. Endelient, the third child of St. Brechanus, lived an ascetic life in Cornwall at Trentenny where Roscarrock was baptized and confirmed.[115] The second new bead depicts two saints named William, presumably patron saints of Howard. The rich rosary belonged to Howard and was passed to his descendants, but the inclusion of Roscarrock's patron saint either indicates Howard's adoption of Roscarrock's patron—an unlikely scenario—or their shared use of the rosary. It is probable that the two Catholics who suffered together in prison for their faith and who studied the history of that faith together at Naworth also enjoyed sharing their devotions. One of the benefits of sacramental items, recall, is their ability to be used by more than one person.

CORNISH-CATHOLIC PARTICIPATION IN A LARGER CATHOLIC COMMUNITY

As Roscarrock's relationship with Howard illustrates, some of the Cornish who overtly favored traditional religion or became Catholic recusants enjoyed contacts with Catholics from other English shires or from abroad. What remains to be explored is the nature of this contact and the ways in which Cornish who maintained such relationships with non-Cornish integrated these ties into perceptions of their own religious identity and community.

Although located in a remote corner of England, and although loyal to their county, kin, language, and culture, the Cornish enjoyed a measure of contact with larger movements and institutions within English and continental Catholicism. For example, Cornishmen attended Oxford University, an institution known for its tolerance of Catholic practices in certain colleges. One college notorious for such toleration was Exeter, known familiarly as the "West Country College" because of the high proportion of students enrolled from the western counties, such as Cornwall.[116] Between 1595 and 1665, 91% of Cornishmen enrolling at university attended Oxford. Of those attending Oxford, 58% of Cornishmen attended Exeter College.[117]

Exeter students could enjoy the benefits of a community of Catholics—fellowship of other Catholics, maintenance of Catholic rituals, and more frequent access to Catholic priests and sacraments—while at Oxford, if not in the actual college then in the town of Oxford. There are no reliable figures indicating how many Cornishmen loyal to traditional religion attended Exeter, but anecdotal evidence reveals that quite a few were there. Nicholas and Trevennor Roscarrock both attended Exeter. Cornish priests John Neal, John Cornelius, Francis Munday, and Christopher Small attended this college. Nicholas Bawden, a Cornish Catholic who converted the priest John Hambly (who led an Easter Day procession of Catholics through London) also attended Exeter. Some of those English Catholics who helped William Allen set up the first English College on the continent were Cornishmen from Exeter College.[118]

Cornishmen who can with confidence be termed Catholics also entered the Inns of Court in London, another institution harboring Catholics from all parts of England. Between 1595 and 1665, 260 Cornishmen entered the Inns of Court to pursue degrees in the legal profession.[119] As with Oxford, we have no figures estimating the number of Cornish Catholics attending the Inns. However we do have anecdotal evidence, such as that of the Cornish Catholics who engaged the Cornish priest John Hambly to live for over a year at Gray's Inn and perform the sacraments, a situation discussed in chapter 5 and in more detail below.[120]

Cornish Catholics were in contact with Catholics from all parts of England and involved themselves in isle-wide efforts to aid Catholics. The Cornishman William Wigges, a resident of Cornwall when not imprisoned in London, illustrates how this might be accomplished under the noses of the Protestant authorities. We first hear of Wigges at the Launceston assizes in 1577 in relation to the arrest of Cuthbert Mayne and Mayne's distribution of sacramental items to Cornish laypersons. The authorities indicted Wigges for not disclosing the *agnus dei* which Mayne offered him, for "extolling Romish authority," and for coming close to violating *praemunire*.[121] By 1607, it appears that Wigges had progressed from a recipient to a distributor of Catholic items. Authorities halted a large shipment of Catholic books intended for distribution primarily through London prisons. The books sent to Newgate and intended for Wigges included 100 bound and a small quantity of unbound copies of *Resolutions*, ten *Memorials*, and a special gilt *Memorial* for distribution to a Mrs. Poncefoote by Wigges.[122]

Wigges's efforts to further the Catholic cause despite his incarceration draw our attention to the strong insular relationships constructed among some Cornish Catholics congregating in London prisons. As discussed in chapters 2 and 5, prisons offered many opportunities for Catholics to meet and access both priests and sacraments. Within the prisons, the Cornish constituted a somewhat clannish group. Although the Cornish associated with those from other shires, they are most often seen congregating with one another.[123] For example, in the mid-1590s, when the Cornish recusant Francis Tregian languished in the Fleet in London, his wife and other family members set up households nearby. A Protestant spy, Benjamin Beard, gained Mrs. Tregian's confidence and thus passed on intelligence of the Cornish Catholics to the authorities.[124] Tregian and his family used the prisons as places to meet predominately with other Cornish priests and laymen, such as Roscarrock and Wigges.[125]

In addition to their efforts within England, Cornish Catholics also involved themselves with English Catholic efforts on the continent. Several Cornishmen from Exeter College at Oxford aided William Allen in setting up the English College at Douai in 1568. Additionally, the English Colleges on the continent trained some Cornish-speaking priests, such as Richard Pentry who attended the English College at Seville c.1600.[126] In the earliest years, according to Rowse, the Cornish appear to have been over-represented at the English Colleges but their attendance proportionally diminished thereafter.[127]

While Cornish seminarians may have participated in larger efforts upon the continent, many subsequently tailored their newly gained knowledge and skills to fit particularly Cornish needs once they returned to England.[128] Although it is not clear exactly how many Cornish seminary priests returned to work in Cornwall, some such as Cuthbert Mayne, John Hambly, and Francis Victor did minister primarily to the needs of Cornish Catholics.[129] Some Catholic priests in Cornwall even used and taught the *Pater noster*, *Credo*, and Ten Commandments in the Cornish language.[130] This was an important issue for Cornish Catholics. When the Church of England insisted that the Cornish adopt English prayers and use English in church services, it sparked such resistance as the Prayer Book Rebellion of 1549 mentioned earlier.

Pastoral literature published upon the continent was also accommodated to Cornish needs. Some of the books smuggled into England to succor

English Catholics were translated in whole or in part into Cornish. It is unclear how many titles were translated, but a 1632 translation of Robert Person's *Book of Christian Exercise* stands as evidence that such translations were occurring. This predominately Welsh text contained Cornish versions of Catholic prayers such as the *Pater noster* and *Credo*.[131]

Despite involvement in such larger English and continental efforts to aid the English Catholic cause, most Cornish priests appear to have favored local, grassroots efforts to strengthen the faith. After ordination, such priests often returned to their native county to minister to Catholics, bringing with them books, vestments, and sacramental items to distribute among the laity. Cuthbert Mayne, for example, first went to London after attending seminary but wanted to return to "his own country" of Cornwall to work on the mission. He asked friends at home to procure him a safe place to stay, and they arranged for him to use the Cornish home of Francis Tregian as a base of operations.[132] Protestant authorities in Cornwall knew of such Cornish priests but frequently received little cooperation in apprehending them.[133] As a result, such activities continued in Cornwall well into the mid-seventeenth century.[134]

The interconnectedness of all of the efforts of Cornish Catholics—in Cornwall, at Oxford, the Inns of Court, the seminaries on the continent, and the prisons—are well exemplified by the experiences of the Cornish seminary priest John Hambly. This is the same John Hambly discussed in chapter 5 who conducted a Catholic procession through Holborn before celebrating Easter at the Inns of Court. Protestant authorities captured Hambly, alias Tregwethan, in the west country in 1586. He was convicted for being an active seminary priest, celebrating Masses, and reconciling people to the Catholic faith.[135] Probably in the hope of saving his life, Hambly confessed his Catholic activities since childhood, often in minute detail.

Hambly hailed from the parish of St. Mabyn's in Cornwall where he was born into a family of yeoman rank. As a boy, he attended various schools in Cornwall where he learned Latin. Hambly confessed that in approximately 1582 another Cornish Catholic, a former student of Exeter College at Oxford, Nicholas Bawden, lent him Catholic books, one of which was entitled *The Reasons of Refusal*. Hambly admitted that he read the book and discussed it afterwards with the older Bawden. "By reasons of these books, himself having a mind withal to the Romish religion," Hambly confessed that around Christmas-time, he "began to forbear tending to the [Protestant] church" and that he had not been back since. The influence of Exeter's strong Catholic leanings bore fruit with the Catholics back home in Cornwall.

Instead, Hambly journeyed to London. He quickly became involved with a group of Cornish Catholics established in Holborn, including Cornish priests, some of whom he had met previously at Bawden's house in Cornwall.

At least one of these Cornish priests had attended the Inns of Court prior to traveling to the continent to be trained for the priesthood. One of these priests reconciled Hambly to the Catholic faith. Hambly began attending Masses which were often celebrated by Cornish priests with other Cornish Catholics in various homes.[136]

Although in London for just a short time, Hambly also tapped into the network of priests imprisoned in London so he could hear Mass and receive the sacraments. Hambly told the authorities that he used to "resort much" to priests in the Marshalsea, including the Cornish priest John Tippett, from St. Wenn, Cornwall. He heard several Masses there at which diverse Cornish Catholics were present, including Nicholas Bawden.

Hambly decided to enter the priesthood, and he traveled to the English seminary at Rheims where he studied from approximately 1583 to 1585. Hambly returned to London for twelve months in 1585. For the majority of his stay, Hambly lived in a chamber at Gray's Inn at the Inns of Court, where he admitted to celebrating Masses for gentlemen of the Inns of Court, many of them Cornish, and reconciling some to Catholicism, as discussed in chapter 5.[137]

In 1586, Hambly returned to the west country. A fellow Cornishman, Nicholas Bluet, arranged for him to live with the Mundys, the family of the former prior of Bodmin, Cornwall, who now resided at Beaminster, Dorset.[138] There he was in contact with various Cornish priests. He traveled about the countryside, celebrating Mass, reconciling, and providing the sacraments. It was while traveling to perform a Catholic marriage that the authorities apprehended Hambly. Incarcerated for almost a year, Hambly died in 1587 in prison at Salisbury.[139]

Overall, Hambly's experiences from his childhood to his imprisonment in 1586 reveal the interweaving of Cornish Catholic interests with those of other English Catholics at home and abroad. Hambly grew up in Cornwall and first turned to Catholicism in his home county under the influence of the Cornishman Bawden. Hambly admitted, however, that he was strongly persuaded by the books brought to him by Bawden and by discussions he engaged in with Bawden about the reading material. Although Bawden was Cornish, he filtered in Catholic influences from the continent and from Oxford University. During Hambly's short stay in London before his departure for Rheims, he kept company primarily with Cornish Catholics, including priests. Yet these Catholics exposed him to the influences of the Inns of Court, London's prison networks of Catholics from throughout England, and the continental seminaries, which he would soon attend. Finally, upon his return from the continent, he resumed his connections with Cornish Catholics in London. Cornish priests brought Hambly into contact with Catholic gentlemen—some Cornish, some not—at the Inns of Court with whom he would live for approximately one year.

With the help of a Cornish layman, Hambly returned to the western counties, near to his home. Although predominately identifying with and forming communal ties to Cornish Catholics throughout his journeys and training and apparently desiring primarily to serve them, Hambly's life also reveals the English and continental influences that simultaneously shaped his Catholicism and the Cornish whom he served.

As Hambly's example illustrates, those who identified themselves as Cornish Catholics were interested in, informed about, and involved in larger issues and movements effecting England's Catholics, but they concerned themselves largely with issues of Cornish religious identity and community within this wider communal context. For example, efforts such as the mission and the distribution of sacramental items and pastoral literature may have been pursued locally in Cornwall by Cornish priests and laypersons, but such efforts would not have been possible without the influence and resources of larger communities of English Catholics on the isle and on the continent. Participation in these larger efforts placed Cornish Catholics in contact with non-Cornish Catholics. They involved travel to locations outside Cornwall. But the fruits of these experiences were applied to the local religious challenges of Cornish Catholics.

Cornwall continued to be the focus of Cornish-Catholic community and identity but not exclusively so. This is reminiscent of Anne Duffin's conclusions about Cornish political loyalties to the crown, discussed above, in which the Cornish favored their own autonomy and interests while simultaneously remaining loyal to their sovereign. This also echoes the argument made above that Celtic-Cornish Christians—both those who separated from the Church of England to become recusants and those nominal Protestants who continued to favor and practice traditional Celtic-Christian religion—believed in their own shire and people as sufficiently holy to sustain their faith despite recognizing and honoring ties to Rome. Traditional Celtic-Cornish Christians identified themselves first and foremost as religious heirs to local, Celtic-Christian traditions dating from the fifth century. Their song was an ancient one, lilting from before the arrival of the English in Cornwall with their Roman brand of Christianity. But this did not stop the Cornish from participating in this wider community of Catholics both in England and abroad and using their involvement to further their own traditional Celtic-Cornish religious identity and community.

Perhaps the difficulty of applying the usual labels of Catholic and Protestant to the Cornish—considering their loyalty to their Celtic-Christian past and their conscious self-differentiation from the Church of England, the Roman Church, and other English Catholics—can best be seen by visiting

Truro Cathedral today. Truro Cathedral is an Anglican cathedral and the seat of the diocese of Cornwall. Reflections of locally based, traditional, Celtic, immanentist religious devotion continue to pervade the church. For example, the stained glass windows and tapestries of the cathedral depict many of the Cornish saints revered in the sixteenth and seventeenth centuries, including St. Petroc, St. Burien, and St. Piran, those saints chronicled in Cornish-Catholic hagiography such as Roscarrock's. The diocesan banner states its intention of representing the ancient Celtic Church and pictures the diagonal cross of the best known Celtic saint, St. Patrick, and the arms of the two major medieval religious houses of Cornwall: Bodmin and St. German's, both of which were dissolved during Protestant reform. Above the display case in which the banner rests is a Celtic cross, reminiscent of those that covered the countryside in the sixteenth and seventeenth centuries and which can still be found today. Celtic crosses decorate many other areas of the church as well. And the Lord's Prayer in Cornish hangs upon the wall of the church, illuminated with a large Celtic cross as its only decoration.

Artwork in various chapels supports the contention of the traditional Celtic-Cornish belief in their own land as a relatively independent, religiously self-sufficient, holy-enough land peopled by holy individuals comparable to those from the earliest years of Christianity. Christ's presence could be felt over the Cornish landscape and in the day-to-day lives of the Cornish faithful. For example, a reredos in the St. Margaret Chapel is comprised of a quartet of paintings of Christ's crucifixion. The background, however, is Mt. Goatfell, the Isle of Arran's highest peak. Similarly, a reredos behind the altar in the Chapel of Unity and Peace depicts Christ crucified among scenes of daily life in Cornwall, among miners and fishermen, not at Golgotha.

Along the walls are displayed pieces of statuary and furniture that recall Cornish dedication to pre-reform Christianity. A fourteenth-century statue of St. Nicholas, a gift from Brittany (a region which shares Cornish ties to Celtic forms of Christianity), rests along the wall. A wooden chair displaying a carving of St. Michael's Mount, the popular Cornish-Catholic monastery and pilgrimage site, sits nearby, with the top of each chair post engraved with different patterns of Celtic crosses.

But the most telling illustration of Cornish attitudes toward their Celtic-Christian past is the painting "Cornubia—Land of the Saints," which depicts an aerial view of the entire county of Cornwall as the sun sets in the west. The Celtic saints hover in the clouds, connected by a shaft of light to the cathedral. According to the description accompanying the painting:

> . . . as the natural sunlight recedes and darkness steals over the land, the Celtic Saints arrive with a new, spiritual light; the Enlightenment of the

Christian gospel. They carry staffs in the shape of 'T's symbolizing the sacrament of the Cross. The Dove above the leading cross symbolizes the Holy Spirit.

In this work, every church in Cornwall is marked by a Celtic cross, about which the description comments:

> Many churches stand on the same spot where early missionaries first established Celtic communities. Many still have their original wells, some of the remnants of the Saint's hermitage. To visit one of these ancient sites is to tread upon the very 'land of the Saints' where the first seeds of Cornish Christianity took root, living and growing until the present day in the heart of every Christian.[140]

Despite outside influences, the Cornish developed their own brand of faith, sung to their own Celtic tune, based upon some of the earliest traditions of Christianity on the peninsula.

CHAPTER 7

"Border of Wickedness?"

Catholics in the Northern Shires

I N BAMPTON, WESTMORELAND, A GROUP OF CATHOLICS ISSUED A PUBLIC
challenge to Protestant ritual and authority. In 1615, at Christmas, a
group of tenants and servants of Lord William Howard of Naworth
entered their Protestant parish church, disrupting services.[1] A Protestant
reporter described with derision the raucous scene as the group "did erect a
Christenmas lord" in the middle of the service.[2] Some of "these Christenmas
misrule men" drank toasts to the Protestant minister while he was in the midst
of reciting prayers. Others climbed into the pulpit and asked the parishioners
for a special offering to help pay for their celebration. Revelers rolled pies and
puddings down the church aisles. Some carried flags and banners. Some came
in costume while still others discharged their guns inside the church. Certain
of the carousers even brought their dogs into the church, turning them on the
parishioners and pretending that they were herding sheep. The Protestant
cleric tolerated the misrule, and there is no indication that Protestant parishioners challenged the revelers.[3]

Incidents of Catholics disrupting Protestant Prayer Book services are
common throughout England in the century after the 1559 Act of Uniformity.
Catholics typically heckled Anglican ministers in the pulpit, refused to participate in Protestant ritual, or prayed from Catholic prayer books or with rosaries
during Protestant services.[4] The events in Westmoreland, however, reveal
something distinctive about the resistance taking place in the north. Rather
than simply protesting the Protestant takeover of the church by interrupting
Protestant church activities, the Westmoreland revelers simultaneously
attempted to wrest control of the church from Protestant hands. The church

was again "theirs" even if only for a short time, and the Protestant parishioners likely recognized this.[5]

The Westmoreland disruption is emblematic of Catholic challenges to Protestant authority that took place throughout the north in this period. Stopping just short of what would bring prosecution, many northern Catholics shaped their rituals and communal activities—which often included violent challenges to Protestant authority—to meet their needs. For the most part, they succeeded.

But the Westmoreland incident also raises important questions. Why did northern Catholics adopt such an aggressive approach as part of adapting their sense of Catholic ritual, identity, and community to changing circumstances? How were such distinctive challenges to Protestant authority possible in the northern shires? Although historians such as Bossy, Haigh, and Aveling have recognized the large proportion of Catholics in the northern population and the particularly lax enforcement of the penal laws in the north, these two factors alone are not enough to account for a distinctive evolution of northern Catholic rituals, identity, and community. I argue that demographics, law enforcement, and geography—northern Catholics' proximity to the Anglo-Scots border—all combined to allow northern Catholics opportunities for religious expression not available in other areas of England. English and Scots Catholics flowed back and forth across this border with few restrictions. This two-way traffic of clergy and laypersons often—but not always—constituted part of a larger network of Catholics working between Scotland, the northern shires, and London. The result of this continuous exchange was a perception of Catholic identity and community in the northern shires that was neither definitively English nor Scottish but a blending of both.[6] Moreover, although northern Catholics' primary loyalty would remain to their region, such access to the resources of larger Catholic networks likely resulted in a northern consciousness of and loyalty to a Catholic identity and community beyond their own shires.

A CONVENIENT PARTNERSHIP

The northern counties—Cumberland, Westmoreland, Northumberland, Durham, Yorkshire, and Lancashire—have long been recognized as more religiously conservative than most shires in England following Elizabethan reform.[7] The northern shires as a whole sheltered more Catholics than any other area of England. John Bossy estimated that in the mid-seventeenth century more than 20% of the households in Durham and Lancashire and between 11 to 20% of those in Yorkshire and Northumberland were recusant households.[8] As the governor of Berwick complained to Lord Burghley, Lord High Treasurer and chief minister to Elizabeth, in 1587, "from Yorkshire hither, the most part of Richmondshire, the Bishopric [of Durham], the Middle and East March, are almost all become Papists; for where in this East March at my going hence I knew not three Papists, I find not now three Protestants. . . ."[9] Moreover, although always proportionately large, the number of Catholics was increasing after 1604, and people of all ranks—aristocratic, gentry, and non-gentry—appear to have remained loyal to Catholicism well into the reign of Charles I. [10]

Although the enforcement of the penal laws against these Catholics varied in severity according to the domestic and foreign political situations, generally the enforcement in the northern shires remained lax.[11] Many of the more zealous Protestant clerics in the north repeatedly complained, as did Tobie Matthew, Bishop of Durham and future Archbishop of York, in 1597 when he disparaged what he thought were the mediocre efforts of the government and his ecclesiastical colleagues in the north to combat papistry. Laws and statutes were not evenly and firmly applied. Fines were minimal, and even these were rarely collected, particularly in the cases of recusant wives of outwardly conforming male heads of household. The power to search homes of suspected Catholics and seize any Catholic belongings was granted too infrequently. There were too few jails to house offenders, and those that existed were poorly governed.[12] Making a biblical reference, Matthew called the region a "border of wickedness" where "every cunning Papist takes advantage of the defect to our disgrace."[13] But as Michael Questier has observed:

> It has often been argued that the reason for this messy state of affairs was because the authorities were too inefficient to compel all Catholics to obey the Act of Uniformity. Yet this supposed "failure" was not always the result of corrupt, bribed and overawed churchwardens or hopeless Dogberries. (Sometimes churchwardens were not overawed, constables were not hopeless and the State was quite sophisticated when dealing with Catholic recusants.) Recusancy was, in fact, like conformity, a negotiable quantity . . .[14]

Occasionally, it appears that a "don't-ask, don't-tell" attitude was informally negotiated between northern Catholics and Protestant authorities. Many Protestants feared a repeat of the Northern Rising of 1569.[15] As long as the Catholics of the north remained quiet, many Protestants were content with a veneer of conformity. For example, the Archbishop of York, Matthew Hutton, acting head of the Council of the North (the administrative body with authority to prosecute Catholics) in 1595 was "willing to tolerate recusants and Catholics who went quietly about their daily affairs."[16]

After his ascension in 1603, James I refused to prosecute many of the powerful northern Catholic lords and often looked to such lords to protect the peace in the border shires.[17] For example, although some of the more zealous northern Protestants attempted to prosecute Lord William Howard for recusancy, James would not permit it nor would Charles I.[18] Howard was a staunch Catholic and the greatest magnate on the border at this time, controlling lands in Westmoreland, Cumberland, Northumberland, Durham, and Yorkshire. If Howard were successfully prosecuted, the crown would gain two-thirds of his land as fines under the penal statutes, and James certainly needed the money. Yet James and Charles continued to protect him. Why? Howard exercised social, economic, and even political and judicial power in the north. James looked to Howard to keep peace in the region, which despite the elimination of the border in 1603, continued to be unstable.[19] At the same time as the hotter sort of Protestants complained of Howard's recusancy and thwarting of the law, English commissioners wrote that Howard was "a great furtherer of justice and a persecutor of the wicked cankers of our country."[20] In sum, a convenient partnership arose between northern Catholics in general, powerful Catholic lords, and Protestant authorities.[21]

This pattern of *de facto* toleration is in contrast to the experiences of many of the London Catholics discussed earlier. In London, powerful Catholics did not control the political and judicial systems as they did in the northern shires. For example, they typically could not *prevent* the arrest or trial of a Catholic associate as the northern Catholic lords could and did. Instead, London Catholics of high rank or great wealth were often able to assist Catholics in trouble with the law by intervening politically or diplomatically *after* a Catholic had completed his journey through the judicial process.

Northern Catholics also appear to have butted heads with Protestant authority more frequently than did Catholics in Cornwall. Because of the relative isolation of Cornish parishes from the bishop of Exeter and the pro-Catholic laity's large degree of control over parishes that was discussed in chapter 6, we do not see a powerful Protestant churchman such as a Tobie Matthew or a William Morton, archdeacon of Durham, attempting a crackdown on Cornwall's Catholic population as sometimes occurred in the northern shires. Moreover, as was also explained in chapter 6, there were few powerful nobles resident in Cornwall. Concomitantly, there were fewer opportunities for a Cornish Catholic to build a strong power base from which to negotiate with or challenge the Protestant authorities as there were in the northern shires. Luckily for the Cornish, there appears to have been less need for such a challenge.

Also contributing to Catholic strength in the north was the absence of a strong Protestant clerical presence in that area. Although the occasional powerful Protestant churchman—such as Matthew—might hold a leadership position in the north, there was a shortage of dedicated Protestant ministers of low and middle rank.[22] In 1582, for example, the two overseers of the Salford Jail in Lancashire had to beg the Privy Council in London to send Protestant preachers to try to convert their Catholic prisoners. The overseers, Edmund Trafforde and Robert Worsley, wrote the Council in February 1582 that they had no hope of conformity from any of the incarcerated Catholics "by reason of the want of a preacher for that purpose." In April, the overseers became more persistent in their request, writing that the priests and laypersons "do still continue in their obstinate opinions, neither do we see any likelihood of conformity in any of them by reason of the want of a preacher for that purpose, whereof in our last certificate [i.e., report] to your honors we then did and yet do most humbly crave to consider of." In May, the overseers wrote again, praying the Councilors "in whom our greatest hope consisteth for the accomplishment of [the conformity of the prisoners] to remember us touching a preacher to be appointed for that purpose. . . ." In the overseers' last letter to the Council in mid-October, a preacher had still not been sent.[23]

Years after the elimination of the border in 1603, conditions in the north were little improved. As Morton observed in 1617, "surely there is a great defect of teachers and many of them of the worst sort, yet to speak truly, [Northumberland] is better of late supplied than formerly it hath been, for now there be some twelve or thereabouts of preaching ministers in the whole county."[24]

Moreover, here as in Cornwall and many remote counties, many nominally Protestant clerics outwardly subscribed to the Church of England's authority and service while maintaining Catholic rituals and practices in their own churches.[25] In Cornwall, this was often possible because of the traditional Celtic-Cornish laity's control over church appointments. In the northern shires, however, dissimulating Catholic priests had to be more subtle as they practiced under the supervision of more zealous Protestant churchmen such as Matthew and their own Protestant parishioners. Some priests were turned in and investigated. For example, George Dobson, the vicar of Whalley in Lancashire was first denounced as a popish priest in 1561. In 1575, however, he was still in office and would be for five more years despite complaints such as the following:

> he doth teach in the church the seven sacraments and persuadeth his parishioners that they shall come and receive, but in any case but to take it but as common bread and wine as they may take it at home or elsewhere, for that it is so far differing from the word of God; and that this Church of England is a defiled and spotted church and that no man may come to it lawfully in time of divine service except that he at his coming in his heart exempt himself from this service and all that is partaker of it, and make his prayer by himself according to the doctrine of the Pope of Rome. . . . he

> hath been accustomed at every Easter to give to certain of his parishioners
> as he termeth them 'consecrated hosts,' saying in them was salvation, but
> in the other there was nothing worthy of acceptance.[26]

Dobson denied the charges and held his benefice until his resignation in 1580.

Even when Protestant ministers adhered firmly to Protestant doctrine and liturgy in their parishes, they sometimes joined the pro-Catholic political and judicial officials in their leniency toward northern Catholics. In 1632, for example, Dorothy Lawson—who had kept a Catholic household, aided seminary priests, Jesuits, and the poor regardless of religious affiliation, and hosted Mass and all manner of Catholic feasts and rituals for her neighbors—died. The pomp and ceremonies surrounding her funeral cortege are reminiscent of pre-reform grandeur. Visitors enjoyed a banquet. The poor received meat and alms. In the evening, boats full of mourners accompanied Lawson's body down the Tyne River toward Newcastle while more people lined the shores. Catholics of Newcastle lined the streets with tapers shining "as light as if it had been noon." The magistrates and alderman of Newcastle waited on the landing and covered Lawson's coffin with "a fine black velvet cloth and a white satin cross, and carried it to the church door." The mourners, clearly Catholics by their ceremonies, hoped at this point that the small assembly of Protestants, including the ministers present, would ignore what they were seeing and conduct the Protestant rites so that Lawson could at least be buried in holy ground. Instead, according to an eyewitness, the Protestant vicar, assuming that at least one of Lawson's mourners must be a Catholic priest, ignored the penal laws and invited any Catholic priest present to come and perform Lawson's funeral. An unnamed priest stepped forward and buried Lawson with the rites of the Roman Church as Lawson was laid to rest in a Protestant church with Protestant ministers looking on.[27]

Between the Catholics who pretended to follow Protestant law, the pro-Catholic authorities unwilling to prosecute other Catholics, and the Protestant authorities interested mainly in the appearance of conformity or who chose to turn a blind eye, the northern shires produced an environment conducive to the practice of Catholic behaviors. Understandings and experiences of belief and ritual, of course, changed, and Catholic self-perceptions of identity and community assumed forms that were related to but still distinct from those seen already among the Catholics of London and those of Cornwall. But overall, to use Questier's term, Catholicism in the north was a "negotiable quantity," and the northern Catholics negotiated well.

NEW EXPERIENCES IN THE NORTH

Opportunities wider than the borderlands were opening in the north—the opportunity for Catholics to mold their religion to fit their new circumstances and the opportunity to dictate some of the terms under which this would be accomplished. By highlighting the many opportunities available for Catholic ritual in the north, my intent is not to reveal any new factual information about what Catholics were doing but rather to nuance the interpretation of Catholic religious practice away from a more traditional view of Catholics habitually continuing in the old ways to one of Catholics consciously adapting religious ritual and belief to accommodate their changed circumstances and meet their own religious needs. The large quantity of information on northern Catholic practice makes this possible. Such Catholics continued to uphold traditional beliefs, perform Catholic rituals, and occupy sacred spaces. But Catholics adapted these beliefs, actions, and spaces, and their experiencing of them was different than in other shires. Changes in pilgrimages and burials help illustrate this evolution in ritual and behavior.

Many Catholic beliefs and behaviors remained openly acceptable despite prohibitions, as discussed above.[28] Catholics retained the sacraments whenever possible, but Masses, baptisms, marriages, and burials were often conducted separately or secretly, not in Protestant churches.[29] Catholic testators occasionally continued to leave money in their wills for pious works, to monastic orders, and to priests to celebrate Mass for their souls or the souls of loved ones.[30] They sustained a belief in the value of good works.[31] Many northern Catholics did not allow the physical absence of a priest to deter them from enjoying their Catholic rituals.[32] They prayed their traditional Catholic prayers and used images and sacramental objects, such as rosary beads, candles, and holy water.[33] Catholics in the north recognized and celebrated traditional feast days.[34] They continued to catechize the young.[35]

Contrary to previous interpretations of such behavior as the retention of Catholic practices from superstitious habit rather than conscious choice,[36] northern Catholics made deliberate decisions to maintain Catholic rituals and beliefs. They frequently altered these behaviors within the give-and-take relationship developing between Protestant authorities and Catholics in the north. John Coppage, a priest incarcerated in Salford Jail, for example, was formerly a fellow at Manchester College. Unable to enjoy the communal life in which he had formerly participated, Coppage organized the other priests in Salford Jail into a "college" in 1584. Presumably, members of the college congregated to enjoy a common devotional life within the prison. Prisoners in other jails, such as York Castle, did the same, "engaging in corporate religious exercises and penances."[37] As such examples demonstrate, northern Catholics could choose to live a Catholic communal life of devotion and penance. Yet this was not the unthinking continuation of communal forms popular before 1559. Conscious decisions had to be made about how to adapt traditional forms of community to post-reform circumstances.

With the diminished role played by churches in Catholic life, alternative locations such as shrines, pilgrimage sites, and holy wells assumed a more important role as sacred places where Catholics of the north could assemble. This situation contrasts with that of London, where many Catholics possessed alternative locations where they could congregate, such as the many London prisons, the Inns of Court, or the foreign embassies. While some London Catholics did make pilgrimages, it was not for lack of religious space.

Moreover, northern Catholics' preference for shrines, pilgrimage sites, and holy wells appears similar to traditional Celtic-Cornish Christians' devotion to such sacred places—but with important distinctions. There were fewer Protestant iconoclasts in Cornwall, and thus more shrines were left standing there. In contrast, many northern Catholics found themselves visiting the ruins of shrines, and this activity undoubtedly influenced the religious experience of pilgrimage, as will be discussed below. Additionally, many of the Cornish favored the holy sites of traditional native Celtic saints, whereas there appears to have been no such predisposition on the part of northern Catholics, despite their own Celtic roots. Furthermore, there is little evidence of the Cornish going on pilgrimage outside their own shire, while northern Catholics often left their home shires to travel throughout the north and even into Wales or Scotland.

Pilgrimages served to unite and rally Catholics of the north. Two particularly popular pilgrimage sites for northern Catholics were St. Winifred's Well, just across the Welsh border in the town of Holywell, and Holy Island, off the Northumberland coast near the Scots border.[38] Large numbers of northern pilgrims continued to congregate at such sites as late as 1640 and during the Commonwealth.[39]

These visits were not merely the duplication of pre-reform assemblies made at traditional, late medieval pilgrimage sites. For example, during the dissolution of the chantries under Edward VI, Protestants tore down the chantry at Fernyhalgh near Preston, Lancashire. Although the building was gone, Catholics revered the site as holy and began to assemble at the chantry's Lady Well for prayers, and they attributed miraculous powers to the water from the well. This practice began during the reign of Elizabeth and continued under the early Stuart kings.[40] Although the chantry was traditionally a site for Catholics to congregate, now Catholics used this site to congregate in a new way: out of doors among the ruins and for prayers usually conducted without a priest.

Northern Catholics also carved out other new communal religious spaces, such as burial grounds. Open recusants might be denied burial in the hallowed ground of their now-Protestant parish churches, so some Catholics created new places in which they could be properly interred. Although we saw the creation of an impromptu Catholic burial ground for London Catholics in 1623 in the courtyard of the French ambassador's house after many attendees of a Mass died when an upper floor collapsed, this differs significantly from northern Catholic efforts to create their own burial grounds. The London burials were a one-time, emergency undertaking to prevent the desecration of the corpses by Protestants. In comparison, some northern burial grounds were established as permanent cemeteries.

One of the best documented of the new northern Catholic burial grounds was established in Lancashire. Known as Harkirke or the New Churchyard of Little Crosby, it was created after Jane Harvie, a neighborhood Catholic, was denied burial in the parish churchyard at Sefton in 1610.[41] Harvie's daughter, Margery Coppall, a sixty-eight-year-old weaver from Thornton, reported that the corpse-bearers interred Harvie outside the churchyard along the road near a cross, the closest they could come to burying her in hallowed ground. Soon afterwards, some swine "rooted the earth upon the grave" and devoured part of Harvie's corpse.[42] A prominent Catholic, William Blundell of Little Crosby, hearing of these events, began allowing a portion of his land to be used for Catholic burials. Between 1611 and 1631, neighborhood Catholics buried approximately eighty laypersons and priests there.[43] Again, Catholics were making conscious decisions to alter traditional behaviors to fulfill their religious needs.

Overall, in changing their religious behaviors by forming communal penitential groups in prisons, by making pilgrimages to ruined chantries, and by finding new places for burials, Catholics enjoyed different religious experiences than they had prior to reform. This is not to say that these practices were in any way unorthodox. The Roman Church had always been somewhat flexible in cases of emergency, and England's case certainly qualified. Northern Catholics were still practicing within the Roman faith, although not necessarily with the same sets of rituals, understandings, and experiences that they had prior to the Act of Uniformity.

PROTECTING WHAT WAS THEIRS: DISTINCTIVE ATTEMPTS TO THWART PROTESTANT AUTHORITY

While these northern Catholics quietly altered their Catholic traditions hoping not to draw attention to themselves, other northern Catholics issued public, direct challenges to Protestant ecclesiastical authority. For example, as in the case of the Westmoreland revelers, they often hindered Protestant ministers from conducting Prayer Book services. This was common in many shires, but Northern Catholics were taking their challenges a step further.

In the north, Catholics not only stopped Protestant services, but they attempted to re-institute their own Catholic rituals and even attempted to take some measure of official control of what they still perceived to be *their* churches. In Cawthorne, Yorkshire, in 1596, for example, the gentleman Charles Barnaby complained against William Skarer, William Ausborough, and other members of the parish for organizing, participating in, being present at, or consenting to rushbearings at the church. In May, June, and July of that year, members of the parish "made bowers, and garlands, and other forms of things covered with flowers" or procured them and/or carried them into the church upon the Sabbath day. As the parishioners set up the greenery, participating in a traditional Catholic ritual, they forced the Protestant minister to delay the service until they had finished.[44]

At the rushbearings, the Catholic-inclined parishioners attempted to mold the church services to their satisfaction. If this were merely an attempt to resurrect the traditions of a festive culture, the participants could have decorated some area other than the church and done so on a day other than the sabbath. Barnaby does not report that the rushbearers mocked the Prayer Book service or attempted to draw other parish members out of the church and away from Protestant services. Instead, they performed a ritual activity within their regular church service which was traditionally Catholic, driven by lay participation, and was an addition to the Protestant service rather than a replacement for it. The inclusion of the rushbearing implicitly criticized the Protestant service as being somehow inadequate to meet parish needs, but the criticism was made within the boundaries of the church, not from outside. The rushbearers still viewed their church as their own and as malleable to their religious needs to a certain extent. Rather than becoming recusants or church papists and rejecting their church services, these northern Catholics were still participants and active voices in their Protestant parish churches.[45]

Some northerners even attempted to gain control of their churches through legitimate means in the event that Protestant ministers were not willing to accommodate their needs. In 1624, Gilbert Stapleton of Carleton stole the key to the chapel of Carleton. He ensured, thereby, that the minister and the curate would not be able to hold services there. After five weeks, Stapleton gave up the key, but not to the minister or curate. Instead, he turned over the key to the clerk "to the end that the inhabitants and parishioners there might have prayers at the usual times (if they pleased)."[46] The chapel, according to Stapleton's viewpoint, existed to serve the needs of the parishioners. If it was not meeting these needs, the parishioners had every right to challenge the clergy and encourage changes in the personnel and service of the chapel to meet the laity's religious requirements.

Parishioners in Boroughbridge, Yorkshire, attempted to force out their vicar, Thomas Hunsley, and their clerk and replace these church officers with two laymen, one of whom may have been a Catholic priest. Hunsley brought suit against Thomas Smithson, William Nicholls, and John Thomson after events transpiring on Trinity Sunday, June 4, 1597. The community had put on a running match that Sunday, and all the parishioners save two missed Hunsley's evening prayer service, presumably because they were attending the match. Smithson, Nicholls, Thomson, and other parishioners arrived at the church after the evening service. They were only late because of the match and asked the clerk to ring the bell for services again. Moreover, they asked Thomson, an unlicensed schoolmaster, to repeat the reading of divine service rather than having Vicar Hunsley do so. Thomson had been brought into the area by Francis Barrocke of Aldborough, "an obstinate recusant." Unlicensed schoolmasters maintained under such circumstances were widely known to be Catholics and often were priests.[47]

The clerk refused to ring the bell and told the tardy parishioners that "it could not stand with any good order that it [the evening prayer service] be done again especially by the said John Thomson being a layman not licensed thereunto." Smithson, Nicholls, and other laypersons of the town took matters into their own hands and took the chapel key from the clerk. They unilaterally discharged him from his office and named Smithson their new parish clerk. Smithson and the other parishioners then appointed the possible-Catholic Thomson to "read prayers [and] say divine service in the said chapel of Boroughbridge," and Thomson agreed.[48]

Significantly, Vicar Hunsley, who made the complaint, never mentioned any of the parishioners being drunk or disorderly. This was not an action brought about in the heat of the moment by alcohol and revelry after a sporting match. Smithson, Nicholls, Thomson, and the other parishioners assumed control of their own church because the vicar and clerk refused to meet the laity's religious needs.

Moreover, the parishioners attempted to legitimate their takeover of their church. After Trinity Sunday, they applied to the "commissary or archdeacon of Richmond" to have Smithson approved as their new clerk and Thomson approved to read the services. Hunsley brought suit against the above-named individuals to protest this action.

A battle ensued for control of the chapel and services, with both Hunsley and the likely-Catholic Thomson vying to outmaneuver one another. For example, on the fourth Sunday of St. John the Baptist, both men apparently showed up to conduct divine service at the same time. Thomson, however, got the upper hand. He rang the bells to call the parishioners to services. He then refused to give Hunsley any of the service books. He reportedly told Hunsley that he would keep the books and that "a good reader was better than a bad preacher." The following Sunday, Thomson withheld the books again and held his own prayer service in the chapel instead.

This conflict centered around the differing perceptions of the role of the chapel and clergy in the community and the persistence of both the Vicar Hunsley and the parishioners of the chapel of Boroughbridge in making sure these roles were fulfilled. Hunsley was an administrator and a rule follower. He sought to uphold the proper order of the institutional church and his own place within this structure above all else. When the parishioners failed to attend his evening service, he complained that this was "to the manifest violation and breach of the laws and statutes of the realm, the great offense to god, and to the most pernicious example to others." He did not mention the good of the souls of the parishioners themselves. When Hunsley cited the schoolmaster Thomson as being unlicensed to teach or to minister, he did so only after having already proven that he was lawfully licensed and the lawful possessor of his office. Hunsley disputed the ability of the parishioners to dismiss the clerk and appoint Smithson their new clerk without "the election, consent, or approbation" of their vicar. Likewise, he denied their ability to appoint the schoolmaster Thomson to read prayers without the vicar's consent.

Furthermore, Hunsley asserted the precedence of the proper chain of command within the church. The archdeacon of Richmond, to whom Smithson and the others had appealed for approval of Smithson and Thomson in their new offices, did not have authority to decide such matters, Hunsley argued. Normally Boroughbridge would be administered by the diocese of Chester and was thereby under the authority of the archdeacon of Richmond. The chapel in question, however, was attached to the parish church of Aldborough which was under the jurisdiction of the dean and chapter of the Cathedral Church of York, Hunsley argued.[49] The parishioners' petitions for control of the church should therefore be denied. He and the original clerk should be upheld in their offices to maintain proper order.[50]

The Boroughbridge parishioners, on the other hand, sought to meet their religious needs when they requested a repeat of evening services that Trinity Sunday and when they chose new men to conduct their services. They did not have to congregate at their chapel after the running match was over. They would have heard the original clerk ringing the bell for evening service. They would have known they had missed the prayers. They could have simply returned home. Yet they arrived at the chapel late wanting their service anyway. When the clergy in charge of the chapel refused to meet their requests, they assumed control of what they considered their chapel. They acted to ensure their pious needs were met. The proper order so earnestly upheld by Hunsley was of secondary concern to the parishioners. They valued it enough to petition to have Smithson and Thomson recognized by the diocese, but not enough to honor Hunsley's and the original clerk's right to their offices. And it evidently was not that important to the parish laity to be served by licensed clergymen, since they deposed their lawful cleric and his properly elected clerk, and replaced them with two laymen (although we cannot be sure what Thomson's clerical status was since he fits one of the predominant profiles of a Catholic cleric).

The Boroughbridge parishioners' efforts are significant for two reasons. First, the parishioners considered it well within their rights and abilities to organize their church as they saw fit to ensure their religious needs were met.[51] Second, they appointed Thomson, a man brought into the parish by a recusant to teach, which very likely means the parishioners appointed a Catholic to conduct their prayer services. If Thomson was Catholic, which is probable, the other Boroughbridge parishioners would have known.

By popularly electing a Catholic to read prayers in a nominally Protestant church, these northerners differentiated themselves from their co-religionists in other areas such as London or Cornwall. Many shires could claim a number of residents who were sympathetic to Catholicism. Usually, these sympathies were revealed in recusancy or church papism. In this example, however, Catholic sympathizers did not refuse to attend church or grudgingly agree to be present at the church in body but not in spirit. Instead, they took control of their church and made it into what they needed and wanted it to be. Even in Cornwall where the laity often exercised much control over church appointments, their authority was exercised legitimately through the decentralized organization of the archdeaconry of Cornwall. These Catholics of the north, however, were challenging church authority in an effort to gain a larger voice in their parish.

The Catholics of the north also differed from Catholics residing in other English shires in their willingness to use violence to protect their fellow Catholics, their goods, and their rituals. This violence might be both religiously and politically motivated and organized, as in the Northern Rising of 1569. Most often, however, it was spontaneous and small scale, as it was in Cumbria in the 1580s when Catholics beat Thomas Lancaster for arresting their fellow Catholic, Christopher Robinson.[52] Or as in 1602 in Lancashire when recusants reportedly beat many pursuivants—hunters of priests and lay Catholics—compelling them to promise never to bother recusants in the future. Allegedly, these Catholics forced one pursuivant to eat his warrant.[53]

The spontaneous willingness of northern Catholics to draw the blood of Protestant authorities to protect other Catholics is revealed in a particularly well documented case from 1624. In that year, the pursuivant Roger Blanchard served as a messenger from Charles I's Chamber and was appointed to work with the Ecclesiastical Commission at York to locate and apprehend priests and recusants. Having heard rumors that Catholics, particularly the priest Peter Harrison, frequented the home of Francis Goodricke and his wife at Kirby Hill, Blanchard obtained a warrant to search the premises. Blanchard took two men—his brother, Pickering Blanchard, and Pickering's man, Crosby—with him to the Goodrickes' home. They found their entrance blocked. Blanchard and his men circled to the back and found a way into the home from behind a stack of broom or gorse that the Goodrickes kept for fuel. Inside they discovered the priest Harrison. Blanchard promptly arrested Harrison and ordered him to appear before the Ecclesiastical Commission.

Trouble began after Harrison became evasive in answering Blanchard's questions, and Blanchard decided to present Harrison before Sir Timothy Hutton, a justice of the peace. Traveling on foot on a lane outside Kirby Hill, the group passed James Barton and another man, both upon horseback. Harrison called out, "Mr. Barton! The pursuivant is carrying me to Richmond for a seminary priest." The court maintained that Barton knew Harrison was a seminary priest and that, moreover, Barton was known to favor and maintain recusants.

Barton quickly came to Harrison's aid, dismounting and asking to see Blanchard's commission. Blanchard maintained that he attempted to remove his papers from his pocket with one hand while holding Harrison with the other. While Blanchard was thus distracted, Barton reportedly seized Blanchard's sword and used it to slice the pursuivant's hand so that the priest could wrench himself free. At this point, the entire group was making so much noise that it attracted the attention of neighbors and others passing by. When these onlookers understood that Blanchard and his companions had arrested Harrison as a priest and were taking him away, they converged upon the three pursuivants with "staves, swords, and pitchforks." Harrison escaped during the melee, and the pursuivant's assistants fled unharmed but "affrighted and put in fear of their lives."[54] Northern Catholics spontaneously engaged in violence to protect one of their own.

Northern Catholics also fought violently to protect property that the government wished to seize under the penal laws against recusancy. In 1607, for example, John Thornborough, bishop of Bristol, wrote from York to Sir Julius Caesar about the Catholics' "daily riotous rescues" of goods which had been lawfully seized from recusants "as if authority durst not or could not punish them." In particular, the bishop railed against Sir William Blakestone of Durham, from whom the authorities had seized £800 in goods. Blakestone "violently rescued" his goods. Evidently other Catholics, witnessing

Blakestone's successful liberation of his property, followed suit. Most recently, the bishop reported, came reports of "a rescue performed with bow, gun, horsemen, staves, by men well mounted with vizards on their faces."[55]

In addition to protecting individuals or goods, northern Catholics defended their perceived right to engage in religious ritual. In 1620, for example, northern Catholics violently protested to protect pilgrimages to St. Winifred's Well. Lewis Bayley, bishop of Bangor (1616–31) and puritan sympathizer, visited the well that year. The well was reputed to be the place of Winifred's martyrdom and was one of the oldest Catholic pilgrimage sites on the isle. Northern Catholics continued to frequent the spot well into the mid-seventeenth century despite prohibitions. Calling such practice superstitious, Bishop Bayley wished to put a stop to it, and he personally visited the well in order to arrest Catholic priests and pilgrims. Learning of his intent, Catholic laypeople seized Bayley, tossing him into a ditch.[56] Three years later, in 1623, English Catholics again asserted their right to religious ritual at this site. Near midsummer, the most popular time for pilgrimage, Catholics took over a nearby church and held Mass.[57] Rather than protesting with words, non-attendance at church, or in their own consciences—actions typically taken or encouraged by English Catholics—these examples reveal northern Catholics stepping forward to protect physically what was "theirs" and to take what they perceived as their right.

This is what likely occurred in Bampton, Westmoreland, at Christmas 1615 when the Catholic "Christenmas misrule men" took over the parish church. Such rowdy celebrations at Christmas were not new and in the past had been used to reinforce community ties. In pre-reform years, the laity commemorated many holy days with mock takeovers of the church or town, the elections of boy bishops to preside over services, and other attempts to "turn the world upside down." With such activities, laypersons drew together temporarily to challenge traditional leadership. These assertions of control for a day or two allowed the laity to blow off steam. While the laity mocked church authority and practice in the short term, community-wide tensions eased in the long term, binding the community more closely.[58]

But this seventeenth-century demonstration in Westmoreland was different. It possessed the added element of uniting the Catholic-inclined members of the church into a community set against the Protestants in this attempt to take over the church. Instead of reconciling differences in the long term, these "Christenmas misrule men" reinforced differences within the congregation and encouraged others to join their separate "community." Bampton's Christmas revelers indulged in many pre-reform lay rituals familiar to all parishioners: the election of a lord to preside over the misrule, the usurpation of the church and pulpit, the use of costumes, the playing of games, solicitations for money to fund the entertainment, and the presence of banners and special celebratory foods to commemorate the day. But the solicitation of money might also have been interpreted as a call to declare allegiance to one side or another. To have financially supported the interruption of Protestant services by the unruly Catholics would have publicly marked parishioners as Catholic sympathizers.

Moreover, the playing of certain games, particularly those played with animals inside the church, might have been intended to show disrespect for Protestant presence in the church, further uniting Catholic elements in the congregation to one another and in opposition to the Protestants. In pre-reform years, parishioners often played games within the church walls as part of feast day celebrations and misrule. The Bampton revelers, however, used dogs "as they would to fear sheep"—in other words, as they would use to terrify or alarm sheep during the herding process to get the sheep to go where and do what the shepherds wanted.[59] One wonders how those in control of the dogs used the animals to "cut" certain parishioners apart from the rest of the congregation. How were groups of individuals herded together or separated from the rest? And did parishioners feel a certain element of terror or alarm as dogs snapped at their heels or barked? Such a "game" could easily have been used to define two competing religious communities rather than uniting parishioners through misrule. As we have seen, such aggressive tactics were not uncommon in the north.

THE IMPORTANCE OF THE BORDER

And there *was* something distinctive about this aggressiveness among northern Catholics, as suggested by letters written by the English Catholic Sir Thomas Stuckley to King Philip II of Spain. In July 1572, Stuckley wrote to broker an offer from the northern Catholic Lord Dacre to help Spain invade England.[60] Lord Dacre requested financial assistance for:

> the hire of 6,000 soldiers, 1,000 being foreign arquebusiers, in 6 months to wrest the kingdom [of England] from the pretended [Queen], or at least to wrest from her, despite all her forces, the six following provinces, to wit Cumberland, Westmoreland, Northumberland, Durham, Yorkshire, and Lancashire, and make them a safe refuge, and, as it were, a realm free and independent, whither all Catholics in England may repair, and ever abide at your majesty's obedience and service. . . .[61]

Presumably not receiving the desired response to this first offer, Stuckley wrote again with an alternative, scaled-down version of Dacre's plan.

On a former occasion, I wrote that, if the scheme should appear too big, my Lord Dacre likewise offers, for the pay of 600 horse, with them to compel the enemy to spend six times as much and keep them always too busy to think of ought else, inasmuch as my Lord Dacre has all the border country and even the outlaws thereof to the number of 3,000 horse, more at his service than at any other's, and besides he would have the assistance of those of the Queen of Scotland's faction that are in the neighborhood.[62]

Stuckley's two letters hint at unique characteristics of Catholic community and identity in the northern shires. First, in the event that Spain failed to conquer all of England, Stuckley singled out six shires—all in the north—that might be taken and set up as a Catholic realm. Although Stuckley recognized that there were large pockets of Catholics in other parts of England, he did not consider it feasible to carve out a separate Catholic territory in these areas.

In his second letter, Stuckley revealed some of his reasons for favoring the northern counties: the powerful northern lords, their ties to outlaws, and ties to Scots Catholicism through the figure of the imprisoned Mary Queen of Scots. Catholic lords such as Dacre, who "has all the border country," were a powerful presence in these counties, frequently circumventing the penal laws to maintain Catholic practices and protect Catholic clergy and laity on both sides of the border. Moreover, Stuckley's allusion to Dacre's control of "even the outlaws" suggests some type of cooperation between Catholics and criminals—both liminal, disorderly elements in the eyes of Protestant authorities—in the north.

Border Instability

While the border between England and Scotland could easily be located on any map, those inhabiting the border regions did not consider it much of a barrier. They crossed it all the time with little thought to restrictions. The border remained restless throughout Elizabeth's reign. Even after 1603 when James ruled as king of both countries and technically eliminated the border, the area continued to be unstable. Although one king ruled both countries, the governments of England and Scotland were kept separate until the Union in 1706, and the border region was populated by residents of mixed loyalty throughout the period of this study.[63]

The governments of England and Scotland were well aware of the problem. In 1597, Lord Burghley's secretary endorsed a report of the many secret passages into Scotland along the Middle March from its eastern border to its western border, and the East and West Marches experienced similar difficulties. The report lists the points of crossing, such as that at Gribbhead, "a passage and highway for the thief, joining on the west end of Cheviot and one mile distant from Hexpeth." The next crossing lies only one mile away at Hexpeth itself. In fact, almost all of the reported sites where people might sneak across the border are separated by only one-half to three miles. Anyone seeking to cross the border need not travel too far out of his way.[64]

To a large extent, rugged geography frustrated Protestant officials, as it did in Cornwall.[65] The mountains, forests, and desolate moors of the region offered many hiding places for anyone seeking to evade notice, including Catholics. As the pursuivant Anthony Atkinson complained to Robert Cecil in 1593:

> And whenever any search is made in Yorkshire, Durham, Northumberland, Cumberland, Westmoreland, and Lancashire for any papist priest, then either they are conveyed into caves in the ground or secret places not possible to find them. . . . Recusants give warning when any search is pretended and so make them flee into the mountains in the Peek country, where the papists have harbors in the stony rocks and then are relieved by shepherds, so that the country is a sanctuary for all wicked men, and is more used of late than ever was. . . .[66]

Moreover, the troops assigned to guard the borders were frequently poorly led and few in number.[67]

Outlawry became a fact of life, and for the first 35 to 40 years after the Act of Uniformity, the entire border remained open to the passage of many English and Scots who thumbed their noses at any attempt to curtail their travel and activities. As Thomas Musgrave reported to Burghley near the end of 1583, "Thus your lordship may see the view of our lawless people, who are grown to such strength as almost none dare offend them. They are a people that will be Scottish when they will, and English at their pleasure."[68]

Musgrave astutely noted that the creation of a border between two countries could not define or ensure the loyalty of the inhabitants of either side. Many centuries spent redrawing the border had left a patchwork of border settlements of questionable national loyalty that expended little effort to maintain the border's integrity. Catholics, as Atkinson indicated above, were just as likely to take advantage of the permeable Anglo-Scots border as were outlaws.[69] Of course, in the eyes of the Protestant authorities, thieves, petty criminals, disorderly people (such as vagrants and bastards), and Catholics were all considered "outlaws." Officials frequently lumped these groups together as causing similar types of disorder. Atkinson, for example, described Richard Tailler of Cartmel as a conveyor of priests and bad persons from England to the Isle of Man or into Scotland when Protestant authorities made any search for such individuals in the northern counties.[70] Atkinson did not differentiate between Tailler's use of his boat to transport men of God and to transport potential thieves or murderers. These liminal members of society used the same pipeline to travel to the same areas to avoid arrest. Similarly, in 1616, Sir Henry Anderson bitterly noted the simultaneous increase in northern papists and in thefts and murders in Northumberland. Anderson did not assert that the papists were responsible for the increase in crime, but his relatively seamless transition from discussing one to the other reveals the linking of the two in his mind. As he concludes, ". . . the greater part of the people are become professed papists, thieves, or atheists, and so live without fear of God or regard for any wholesome laws."[71]

WHY AND HOW CATHOLICS FLOWED BACK AND FORTH ACROSS THE BORDER

Border Catholics aided seminary priests, Jesuits, and laypersons of either nationality, receiving them into their homes, hiding them from Protestant authorities, and conveying Catholic individuals, letters, and news back and forth across the border.[72] Sir William Bowes, Elizabeth's ambassador to Scotland, wrote to Lord Burghley in November 1595 about the "complottes and combinations" of those English "of false and disloyal religion" with the Scots across the border.[73] The borderland was the home and the "country" of the region's residents regardless of any arbitrary line drawn through it, and border residents worked to help both the English and the Scots Catholics in this two-way traffic of people and information.

Why Was This Possible?

The words and experiences of the Herefordshire-born priest John Ingram hint at the links between Catholics of the two countries. Ingram, who was ordained at the English College in Rome, served both in England's northern counties and Scotland. He wrote several verses prior to his execution in 1594. He addressed some to the Scots Catholics, and in one he remembered, "Scotland loved me, Scotland succoured me in my need." Scots Catholics even offered 1,000 crowns to secure Ingram's release from an English prison, but Ingram, prepared to die for his faith, refused their offer.[74]

But why and how were Catholics of the north willing and able to work with Scots Catholics? The "why," put simplistically, is that many Scots and English Catholics viewed their religious and political interests as linked, although they had operated with separate organizational structures within the Roman Church for centuries. When formulating policy to bolster Catholicism in the British Isles, Rome did not lump England and Scotland together. Rome appointed separate officials and issued separate policies for each country. In day-to-day operations, however, Rome clearly recognized that the Anglo-Scots border did not separate English and Scots Catholics. In 1626, for example,

John Francis, the archbishop of Patras and legate from Pope Urban VIII, issued a license to the priest John Trumbull (Tromble) to administer the sacraments of baptism, penance, the Eucharist, extreme unction, and matrimony throughout Scotland and Ireland. Furthermore, Francis authorized Trumbull, if he could obtain a similar license from the Bishop of Chalcedon—the bishop with authority over England—to administer the same sacraments throughout England.[75] Francis clearly understood that the institutional Catholic Church in Rome had subdivided the British Isles for administrative purposes, largely along national lines, with different bishops and archbishops possessing authority in different areas. Equally apparent, however, is that the priest Trumbull would be traveling and ministering throughout the British Isles with little regard for borders. The needs and interests of the areas were so similar that Trumbull could be an effective clergyman wherever he went.

Many Scots and English apparently felt that way as early as 1582. Cardinal William Allen wrote to the Cardinal of Como in February of that year describing the religious affinities between Catholics of the two nations:

> The [Scots] nobles of highest rank, as well as many other persons, gladly receive our English priests, nominally as fugitives from England . . . but in reality from a desire to be present at Mass and hear their sermons as the difference between the two languages is very slight. . . . Scotchmen are generally agreed that the Scottish priests cannot at present reside in the country either so safely or with so much advantage as English priests who . . . are received everywhere in the character of exiles. The Queen of Scots has always been afraid that, because of ancient animosity between the two nations, English priests could not labor with advantage in Scotland. But we have not found this to be the case.[76]

English and Scots Catholics aided one another for religio-political reasons as well, often in an effort to put an open Catholic on either the English or Scots throne or to persuade the reigning monarch to tolerate Catholicism within his or her realm. In this sense, the interests of the northern Catholics can be viewed as linked to those of London Catholics, as will be discussed in more detail below. In 1592, for example, an English priest named Holland resided in Scotland and reportedly received letters from powerful English Catholics bemoaning their lack of success in persuading Spain to intervene on the isle on behalf of English and Scots Catholics. The letter writers pushed Holland to use his influence in Scotland, presumably upon powerful Scots Catholics, to put pressure upon the Spanish king to act. Then Holland was to return to England for further instructions.[77] Furthermore, in 1599, Henry Constable and Laird Bonyton fulfilled a papal commission to James VI. Calling James the "heir of a martyr[78] called by God to punish a heretic Queen," Pope Clement VIII offered

James £20,000 provided by English Catholics and the service of 20,000 Englishmen in return for James's aid against the Protestant Elizabeth.[79] An Englishman and a Scotsman served Rome side by side in an attempt to resolve what England, Scotland, and Rome viewed as a mutual problem on the island.

This contrasts with Cornish Catholic involvement in such religio-political intrigues. Cornish Catholics, as discussed in chapter 6, participated in many of the larger efforts to aid English Catholics, such as the English mission and the transport and distribution of sacramental items and books. Catholics in Cornwall, however, tended to involve themselves in such larger efforts only in so far as to enable themselves to aid the devotions of other Catholics within Cornwall. We rarely see such international intrigues among Catholics in Cornwall as are described among the northern Catholics and those of London. Similarly, we rarely see such close ties to Rome among Catholics in Cornwall.

How Was This Possible?

The growing market economy between England and Scotland, particularly after 1603, helped Catholics breach the border.[80] Both before and after the elimination of the border, traders played a key role in maintaining contact between English and Scots Catholics. Traders frequently aided Catholics, spread the news of Catholic activities, and passed on messages from one Catholic to another. For example, in the 1580s, a Protestant spy named Ballard (alias Fortescue) reported that he had met a Scots trader who had crossed over the river Tweed into England to sell hawks. Ballard pretended that he had fled to the north of England because of religion. Believing Ballard to be a fellow Catholic, the trader began to pass on bits of Catholic news from Scotland, including information that a messenger had recently landed in Leith to offer French aid to James VI who was mourning the death of his mother, Mary Queen of Scots.[81]

Even when England and Scotland were at odds politically, the border locals kept up this trade, thereby keeping the pipeline for Catholic communication open.[82] In 1640, Edward, Viscount Conway, complained to Archbishop Laud that the Scots "suffer not any Englishman to enter their country without apprehending him and having taken away his letters, send him back, but diverse Englis(h)men of the Borders go constantly to market without interruption."[83] Once again, regardless of the political border between the two countries, the residents of the border shires conceived of their own brand of allegiance, loyalty, and trust.

Just as helpful to the English Catholics as these legal traders, however, were the illegal traders: the thieves, bandits, and even murderers of the border. As described earlier, outlawry was widespread throughout this period. Outlaws frequently transported illegal goods, were familiar with the passages over the border described earlier, and were experienced at avoiding the authorities.[84] Sir Robert Carey, Warden of the Middle March, described his futile attempts to capture such border outlaws at the end of the sixteenth century:

> The chief outlaws at our coming fled their houses where they dwelt and betook themselves to a large and great forest (with all their goods) which was called the Tarras [Tarras Moss]. It was of that strength and so surrounded with bogs and marsh grounds, and thick bushes and shrubs, as they feared not the force or power of England nor Scotland so long as they were there. . . . Those gentlemen of the country, that came not with me, . . . they knew (or thought at least) that my force was not sufficient to withstand the fury of the outlaws.[85]

Such outlaws became involved in transporting Catholics and their messages across the border thanks to the financial and legal support that many northern Catholic lords provided various outlaw groups, as Sir Thomas Stuckley alluded to in his letter to Philip II. The Protestants believed the lords and outlaws were cooperating to aid Catholics in 1586, when Lord Henry Scrope, Warden of the West March, reported to Walsingham that

> They [Catholics, priests, and Jesuits] are received and quietly kept at Cardington, Mr. Ratcliffe's house, himself being absent from the same. They frequent the houses of Stephen Phennycke [Fenwick] at Longshare, Mr Ralph Gray, Medfordes of Riall, and Carres of Foard. The chief conveyors of these and the like in and out of Scotland are Edward Collingwood, an outlaw, often using one Brown's house in Foard, Robert Carr of Swarland, an outlaw also, and one Carr of Lynton, a Scotsman that most commonly cometh into England to fetch any person that is to be conveyed into that realm.[86]

The interests of all three groups—Catholics, lords, and outlaws—were inextricably linked. Many of the northern lords, such as Howard of Naworth, lord of the Westmoreland revelers, were Catholics or sympathizers. These lords provided financial and legal support for northern Catholics of lesser rank. Simultaneously the lords received, maintained, and even controlled many of the outlaw groups who worked the border. Border outlaws then, among their other activities, transported Catholics (who were themselves outlaws) and Catholic news and messages in and out of Scotland for the lords. This three-way cooperation continued even after the elimination of the border in 1603.[87] On the Scots side of the border, Scots Catholic outlaws and lords enjoyed a similar relationship.

In addition to facilitating passage across the border and maintaining Catholics in their households, these northern lords aided the cause of northern Catholicism in many other ways. Some distributed Catholic books to their followers and openly encouraged them to remain loyal Catholics. Roger Widdrington, for example, frequently invited tenants and freeholders to skip Protestant services and meet together at alternative locations.[88] Widdrington possibly provided a priest at such occasions. Others, such as Howard of Naworth, received the chief recusants of the north into their homes and organized secret meetings of powerful Catholics in out-of-the-way locations. Such efforts provided some central congregation points for the Catholic leaders.[89] The Catholic lords, as powerful patrons of Catholics of lower ranks, legally protected their unruly tenants and servants who sought to challenge Protestant dominance in the local parishes, just as Howard protected the "Christenmas misrule men" of Bampton, Westmoreland. Northern Catholic lords also regularly provided large amounts of money to fund the English seminaries on the continent.[90] The influence of such men could thereby be felt beyond northern borders. The high proportion of Catholics in the north and the "don't-ask, don't-tell" atmosphere of toleration thus combined with the inherent instability of the border region to foster an environment in which northern Catholics of varying ranks could constructively work to fulfill their religious needs in ways that Catholics in other areas could not, or at least not to as great a degree.

NORTHERN CATHOLIC IDENTITY AND COMMUNITY

This permeability of the Anglo-Scots border to Catholic individuals and ideas is important because it allowed Scots Catholics and northern English Catholics to interact with and influence one another. Furthermore, northern Catholics could enjoy the benefits of living along the travel routes of Catholics journeying between Scotland and London, such as greater access to priests, books, and Catholic news from other areas. The result is a northern Catholic identity and sense of community that was Anglo-Scottish in character. The northern Catholics appear to have been regionally focused while simultaneously enjoying ties to larger Catholic communities in England and on the continent.

Many Catholics in Scotland did manage to practice the old religion. This occurred despite the official Protestant position against Catholicism embodied in Scotland's Confession of Faith of 1580:

we abhor and detest all contrary religion and doctrine, but chiefly all kind of papistry in general . . . but in special we detest and refuse the usurped authority of the Roman antichrist . . . his devilish Mass, his blasphemous priesthood, his profane sacrifice for the sins of the dead and quick, his canonization of men, calling upon angels or saints departed, worshipping of

imagery, reliefs, and crosses, dedicating of kirks, altars, days, vows to crea-
tures, his purgatory, prayers of the dead . . . his possessions and blasphemous litanies and multitude of advocates or mediators . . . merits, pardons,
peregrinations, and stations, his holy water, baptizing of bells, conjuring of
spirits, crossing . . . anointing, conjuring . . . his erroneous and bloody
decrees made at Trent . . . and finally we detest all his vain allegiances,
rites, signs, and traditions brought in the kirk without or against the word
of God and doctrine of this true Reformed Kirk.[91]

Regardless of the Confession of Faith and occasional spurts of persecution, Scots Catholics enjoyed more freedom of worship because of King
James VI's willingness to overlook religious transgressions before he ascended
to the English throne and was threatened by the Gunpowder Plot in 1605.[92]
Despite passing laws intended to suppress Catholicism in Scotland, James
openly acknowledged his own laxity in enforcing them. His actions rarely fulfilled the promises he made to Elizabeth to curb the Jesuits and seminary
priests and to restrain the practice of Catholicism in general.[93] Moreover, local
Scots ministers sometimes claimed not to know of laws against Catholics and
their duty to enforce them. Whether their ignorance stemmed from poor
advertising of the laws or the ministers' unwillingness to act against their
Catholic neighbors is unclear.[94] On the whole, Catholics enjoyed more freedom to worship and congregate in Scotland than they did in England.[95]
Northern Catholics crossing the border took advantage of such opportunities,
as will be discussed below.

James's accession to the English throne and subsequent elimination of
the border in 1603 had little practical effect on the tolerance shown to either
English or Scots Catholics.[96] In 1605, however, his policy toward Catholics did
undergo a significant change. Prior to that year, he had shown leniency to and
even protection of Catholics and their rituals. After Catholics were strongly
implicated in the Gunpowder Plot, the botched attempt of 1605 to bomb the
English Parliament, James began to take a harder line with both English and
Scots Catholics. [97]

Contact among the northern Catholics and Scots Catholics produced a
very different type of Catholic identity and set of communal relations in the
northern shires: identity and community that were regionally Anglo-Scottish in
character. As discussed earlier, many priests served both sides of the Anglo-
Scots border, taking advantage of the numerous border passages.[98]
Additionally, many of the English priests participating in this type of interchange—such as Richard Kirkman of Yorkshire, John Boste of Westmoreland
and Lawrence Richardson of Lancashire—were native northerners.[99] They
would have been familiar with Catholic society on both sides of the border
prior to their attempts to minister in the area.

As the experiences of the Yorkshire priest, David (Davy) Ingleby reveal, a northern Catholic could participate in and assume a variety of roles while working within networks of both English and Scots Catholics. Ingleby attended seminary abroad and returned to his native northeast coast of England in the early 1580s. He spent the next two years serving the Catholics of York. By 1586, Ingleby was certainly traveling between York and Dumfries, Scotland, perhaps involved in the politics of the Catholic earls of Scotland while fulfilling his clerical duties to English and Scots Catholics. Reportedly, the Carr (Kerr) family—powerful on both sides of the border—facilitated Ingleby's passage across the border.[100] Ingleby was allegedly linked with powerful Scots Catholics such as Lords Maxwell and Harris.

When reportedly visiting Dumfries, the probability is high that Ingleby was visiting New Abbey, a bastion of Catholicism near Dumfries frequented by both northern English and Scots Catholics. Having experienced no dissolution of the monasteries as England had, many of Scotland's Catholic religious houses still operated.[101] New Abbey still celebrated Mass. The abbot allegedly encouraged area residents to maintain Catholic practices, and with priests and sacraments known to be readily available, Catholics on both sides of the border, such as Ingleby, congregated at the abbey.[102] In 1599, John Colville warned Cecil about New Abbey. Henry Constable and Laird Bonyton, on commission from the Pope to James VI, reportedly "desired the Abbey of New Abbey on the West Border to be a retreat to such as for their conscience shall flee out of England, which the King promises to do connivently."[103] Sir William Bowes, Elizabeth's ambassador to Scotland, referred to the abbot of New Abbey as "a notorious lewd instrument in these treasons for religion." He reported to Sir Robert Cecil in 1599 that the Scots Catholics were "trafficking both with some papists of ours and those of Ireland by the special employment" of the abbot.[104] Dumfries served as the point of origin and drop off for messages between Catholics from all three countries.[105]

Northern Catholics thus participated in larger networks of Catholics operating between Scotland and England, passing through the northern counties, perhaps all the way to London. As discussed in chapter 1, Patrick McGrath and Joy Rowe have argued that northern Catholics preferred to organize themselves into small networks. For example, in the 1580s, the secular priest Thomas Bell set up networks of safe houses in Lancashire and Yorkshire and marshaled an "underground railway" to convey priests throughout these remote areas.[106]

Yet despite this preference for localized association, it appears that these smaller networks often fit into larger networks of Catholics operating between Scotland and London. While Bell intended his safe houses and routes to be used for the Catholics *in* the north, they were also useful for individuals traveling *through* the north. English Catholics often traveled northwards—sometimes to convey messages, sometimes to escape Protestant authorities, sometimes to visit other Catholics.[107] Protestant authorities of Carlisle in 1591 captured a Catholic, James Clayton, making just such a journey. Clayton had been in London and was acquainted with the famous Cornish recusant Francis Tregian, lodged at the Fleet prison. He journeyed north toward Scotland, planning to find passage to France because he was "a papist and a recusant." On his way northwards, Clayton met another Catholic, Adam Elwood, at St. Albans. Elwood instructed Clayton to find Cuthbert Rumney in Carlisle who would take Clayton to Christopher Elwood, his father. Christopher Elwood would guide Clayton into Scotland.[108]

Likewise, Scots Catholics and northern Catholics frequently traveled from the border regions to London, such as in 1600 when the Scots Capuchin friar Campbell visited and preached at the Marshalsea,[109] or as in 1592 when James Jackson and his companion, Firbeck, both of the bishopric of Durham, visited James Young in London. Young, also a Durham native, had been ordained in Rome in 1591, had worked at the English College in Valladolid, and had recently arrived in England to work on the mission. He was to have landed in Scotland to minister to Catholics, but had been forced to disembark at the Thames. Jackson and Firbeck—both of whom had traveled from the north to London—attempted to convince Young to continue northward to work in Durham.[110]

The importance of northern participation in these larger networks—in addition to their own smaller, localized networks—is multifold. Most importantly, Catholic priests traveling this route were a valuable source of the sacraments for area Catholics who might not have a priest regularly ministering in their neighborhood.[111] For example, while in London, James Young would also dine with two other priests, Thomas Bell and John Mush, both of whom would trek northward from London to provide such services.[112]

Moreover, northern Catholics likely considered themselves participants in a larger Catholic community that extended beyond the borders of their own locales. Like London's Catholics, many northern Catholics would have been informed about larger scale Catholic interests involving the rest of England and even the continent. Catholics trekking northward and southward through the northern shires stopped in the local safe houses, passing along valuable news of Catholics in London, Scotland, and other northern shires.[113] They could circulate Catholic books and perhaps spread sacramental objects among the region's Catholics.[114] When compared to London's Catholics, however, the Catholics of the northern shires were likely less well informed and less well provided for in terms of such priests, sacraments, and books.

Northern Catholics appear to occupy a middle ground between the more centrally organized London Catholics, many of whom had multinational interests and participated in multiple Catholic communities, and the relatively independent-minded and isolationist traditional Celtic Christians of Cornwall who preferred their Cornish holy land, beliefs, and rituals. Although they regarded London as an important source of information and resources, it is unlikely that the northern Catholics regarded London as the center of their Catholic identity or sense of community. As discussed above, regional loyalties and smaller local networks tended to be the focus of northern Catholics. Catholics of the northern shires may have been hooked into larger networks of English and continental Catholics in which both London and northern Catholics took part, but this participation did not define the northern Catholics, nor were northern Catholics second-class Catholics when compared to the Londoners.

Northern Catholics and traditional Celtic-Cornish Christians both appear to have regarded support of local or regional Catholic interests as their first priority. This loyalty did not restrict these Catholics from participating in larger efforts to aid English Catholics. An important distinction, however, between northern Catholics and their Cornish counterparts, is that the day-to-day operations of large-scale English and continental networks ran through the northern shires. Ordinary Catholics in the north, not just seminarians or Jesuits, were often aiding a larger Catholic cause by sheltering Catholic travelers, transporting goods, or ferrying Catholics across the border. In Cornwall, participation in larger English and continental Catholic efforts was limited. Few Catholics traveled through Cornwall en route to other destinations. Catholics generally had to leave the shire to take part in such activities. It is likely that the Catholics of the north, more so than the Celtic Christians in the isolated southwestern shire of Cornwall, consciously identified with Catholics beyond their own local borders.

CONCLUSION

As Sir Thomas Stuckley recognized, the six northern counties collectively were unique. Not only did a proportionately large number of Catholics reside in these counties, but the opportunities to practice the Catholic faith differed from those in other areas. This is not to argue that northern Catholic experience was uniform across the shires. Instead, the particular geographic, social, and cultural environment of the northern shires—their distance from London, their situation along the Anglo-Scots border, the presence of the powerful northern lords, and the influence of the border outlaws—all combined to provide northern Catholics with novel sets of opportunities and expectations to mold the practice of their faith as they saw fit. Moreover, in Stuckley's opinion, the nature of Catholic identity and community in these shires made them the shires most likely to separate from England to form an independent Catholic realm. In large part, this was due to higher expectations among northern Catholics of all ranks to be able to practice their religion and their willingness to defend aggressively their perceived right to do so.

Northern Catholics' expectations were raised by the factors alluded to in Stuckley's letter: powerful northern lords, their relationships with border outlaws, and even their connections with Scots Catholics. All three of these phenomena *worked independently* in the northern shires to facilitate passage of Catholic priests and laypersons across the border, to spread Catholic news and ideas throughout the region, and to help foster a regional Anglo-Scottish religious identity among resident Catholics that transcended the political border between England and Scotland. Although northern Catholics appear to have privileged this regional Catholic identity and community above all others, this did not hinder their recognition of and active participation in larger English and continental Catholic communities and their widespread efforts on behalf of the isle's Catholics.

Additionally, all three of these phenomena *could work together* in some areas of the north. When they did so, Catholic identity was particularly strong and Catholic expectations of religious tolerance were particularly high. The activities of the Widdrington family exemplify how one powerful northern family could utilize its own power base while simultaneously drawing upon the resources of the border outlaws and Scots Catholics to aid northern Catholics (although hardly in the way Thomas Stuckley had proposed).

In 1600, Sir Robert Carey, then Warden of the Middle March, described Roger Widdrington as "an honest and discreet fellow and such a borderer as he hath not his fellow." According to Carey, if the government wanted to know anything about the border, Widdrington was their man. Moreover, Widdrington had turned in 20 English and Scots thieves, thereby proving his loyalty. Richard Lowther wrote to Sir John Stanhope that Widdrington was the "only borderer to wholly depend on," and that he should be preferred.

The true nature of Widdrington's power, however, proved to be akin to that which Stuckley attributed to Lord Dacre. Carey remarked that Widdrington "has such 'moyen' of the border that almost no attempt can be made but that he gets notice beforehand." Carey employed both Roger and his brother, Henry, as his assistants.[115] In 1617, Sir Ralph Winwood, the king's secretary, received news that powerful Catholic families such as the Widdringtons were still aiding the thieves and, hence, other Catholics. The report described the organization thus:

> The gentlemen have all of them thieves and thieves' masters towards them who depend upon the best men of the shire, according as in blood, living, or dependency, he is tied. The great ones to whom they belong support the middle sort, and they the worst thieves that are under them, and so what the great ones will have done, the middle sort receive from them, and the inferior sort must act, be it whatsoever. [116]

One of these "inferior sort" broke ranks in that same year and provided a list of thieves "maintained specially by some great ones of the Popish faction," the Widdrington family. Richard Foster claimed he regretted his "former evil courses," having been a "witness and an actor in this business" and begged pardon for his previous actions. Foster feared retaliation from his former associates.

> . . . they do most cruelly seek my life and overthrow as they do the lives and overthrow of all such as do hate their villainies and seek their reformation, for look how long a man will go on in an evil course they will do anything for him but no sooner he gives over the same but they will pursue him to the death.

In return for the government's protection, Foster provided the names of approximately twenty-five prominent outlaws operating in Northumberland under the protection of the Widdringtons. According to Foster, ". . . nothing is done by them but the said Roger Widdrington is acqua(inted) with which he will take notice thereof, for the most part they are all of his profession and popishly affected."[117] Two years earlier, the rector at Elsdon in Redesdale provided corroborating evidence, accusing Widdrington of drawing border thieves and outlaws to Catholicism and placing them under his protection. The rector, like Foster, named names.[118]

Despite such damning testimony, such powerful families proved almost impossible to remove from their seats of influence in the north. Twenty-five years later, the Widdringtons still exercised substantial control of their portion of the border, especially since the elimination of the border and the March Wardens had halted a great deal of the former surveillance. In 1625, the Privy Council requested that the Earl of Suffolk remove Roger Widdrington as governor of his estate near the Scots border. Widdrington, the council argued, was using Suffolk's estate as a base from which to encourage Catholicism in the area.[119] Despite this knowledge, a King's Commission appointed Widdrington to deal with malefactors along the border in 1635 when tensions with Scots Covenanters began to rise. Widdrington gave tours of border defenses and to government representatives, one of whom, Sir Jacob Astley, commented that the border men

were all short and broad-shouldered men with broadswords and blue caps
all upon little nags. They are fit for time of war to burn and spoil, and there
is good use to be made of them. Mr. Roger Widdrington holds them all at
his command and is entirely for his Majesty's service.[120]

The arguably pro-Catholic Charles was certainly a better choice for the
Widdringtons to support than the Scots Presbyterians. Yet the point cannot be
ignored that such men as Astley described, in addition to being useful during
wartime, could also burn and spoil for Widdrington during peacetime.
Although in 1635 Widdrington served King Charles's interests against the Scots
Protestants, he had been using the same men against the English Protestants
for decades, and his power to do so had not been diminished.

The Widdringtons help illustrate the distinctive nature of northern
Catholicism. The group they helped maintain was composed of Catholics of all
levels of northern society. This group trafficked Catholic persons, goods, and
news back and forth across the border. Due to this interchange of people,
beliefs, and ideas, Catholic identity and Catholic sense of community in the
northern shires were neither definitively English Catholic nor Scots Catholic
but a blending of both. Various local and regional networks helped force the
border open for Catholicism, and northern Catholics were willing to protect
aggressively—as in the case of the Westmoreland "Christenmas misrule
men"—or perhaps even violently—as Stuckley suggested to the Pope—their
religious rituals, their identity, and their community.

CHAPTER 8

From the Old Comes the New
Catholic Identities and Alternative
Forms of Community

Y ORKSHIRE'S MAGISTRATES AND MINISTERS ATTEMPTED TO CONVINCE
the future martyr Margaret Clitheroe to attend Protestant services at
least once. She refused. "Answer me," a minister demanded, "What
is the church?" Clitheroe replied:

> It is that wherein the true word of god is preached which Christ langhs[1]
> and left to his Apostles and they to their successors: ministering the seven
> sacraments which the same church hath always observed, doctors
> preached, and martyrs and confessors witnessed. This is the church which
> I believe to be true.[2]

Clitheroe identified a church of continuity. She looked back to the church's
ancient past to define her faith. She professed her belief in an unbroken chain
of authority descending from Christ to his apostles to their consecrated representatives. She claimed a continuity of doctrine, sacrament, ritual, and belief
that the church had always upheld and that true believers had always professed. English Catholics such as Clitheroe faced a significant challenge in
identifying with this ideal of religious continuity when they were seemingly cut
off from Rome and so many of its traditions.

As important to English Catholics as this archetype of religious continuity was the related goal of religious unity. English Catholic clerics encouraged unity among English Catholics, arguing that through union came strength
and power to propagate the Catholic faith in times of adversity. William
Stanney attributed the successes of the early church to its unity.

> For what was it that gave such strength and power unto the Christians of
> the primitive church to overcome in such sort and plant the faith of Christ
> throughout the whole world, but concord, peace, and unity whereby they
> were united together that, 'The whole multitude of the believers were but
> one heart and one soul.' (Acts 4).

For the ancient church, unity meant power. Unity meant triumph over competing religions.

Arthur Crowther and Thomas Vincent agreed and counseled that unity
could be a valuable tool for English Catholics in the seventeenth century.

> Where many are united together, if one falls he may be raised up by his
> fellow; and if one be assaulted, two may be able to repulse the adversary
> . . . And one man alone is as a small, single, slender thread; feeble, frail,
> and easily pash'd to pieces; but being twisted and tied to many others by
> the strong bands of spiritual friendship, he becomes formidable. . . .[3]

If Catholics remained independent of one another, Crowther and Vincent suggested, they would become easy prey for Protestant aggressors. Tied together
with other Catholics, however, the English might be able to "repulse the adver-
sary." But what was this unity of which these clerics spoke so enthusiastically,
and how was it achieved?

This search for English Catholic continuity and unity is, in actuality, the
striving for a sense of religious identity and community that has been the focus
of this study. As defined in the Introduction, identity refers to perceptions of
sameness, likeness, or oneness with other Catholics. A sense of continuity with
Catholics past and present was the primary vehicle through which English
Catholics could continue to identify themselves with their church. Community,
on the other hand, deals with the relationships constructed by English
Catholics who shared a similar religious identity. English Catholics might identify with their co-religionists throughout England and on the continent in a
broad sense, but they did not necessarily share communal relationships with all
these Catholics. The two concepts of identity and community are related yet
distinct, and as such they will at first be treated separately.

This concluding chapter will examine how Catholics perceived themselves *as Catholics*, their relationships to other Catholics, and their relationship
to the institutional Roman Church. English Catholics primarily identified
themselves as heirs of the martyrs of the primitive church. They built continuous links between themselves and the first Christians. In doing so, they built
ties of sameness, likeness, and oneness with believers throughout the globe and
throughout the centuries. These were ties of identity but not necessarily of
community.

Catholics did not join into one monolithic community in England. As demonstrated in chapters 5 through 7, many types of communities were possible: communities based on Celtic-Christian traditions, merchant communities, communities fostered by powerful lords aided by outlaws, or communities centered in prisons or foreign embassies. These communities could enjoy ties to one another, and one Catholic could participate in multiple communities.

Such communities are relatively easy to discuss. They are defined in large part by location or physical proximity to other Catholics. Participation in such communities can be demonstrated by Catholics' resort to such places or interactions with one another.

Not all communities, however, are based on such contact, and this chapter will attempt to pinpoint some of these alternative communities. Some English Catholics participated in communities built upon the common experience of rituals and beliefs—upon the bonds of spiritual friendship promoted by Crowther and Vincent or what Henry Garnet promoted as "a concord, a union, a conjunction of minds."[4] They created communities based upon one-on-one connections with God and upon *ritual and imaginative separation* from Protestants. While such communities can be difficult to define and quantify, they did exist and were no less real or important to believers than the Catholic communities defined by physical proximity.

Finally, this chapter attempts to weave the threads of English Catholic identity and community together, showing the interrelationship of both concepts, by examining English Catholic relations with Rome. Such an inquiry will shed light on how English Catholics mediated between their sense of identification with the ancient church and their willingness to be bound by the contemporary hierarchy and institutional community within that church. In sum, I argue that while devotion to Rome became stronger in the first decades following the Act of Uniformity, English Catholics eventually began to think about accommodation with English Protestants.[5] When the papacy rejected accommodation, many English Catholics, including priests, began to distinguish between spiritual and temporal unity with their Church. In their own minds, believers remained heirs to the primitive church and wedded to the sacraments, traditions, rituals, and beliefs of their faith. They refused, however, to conduct their relationships with one another and the Church along the lines defined by Rome. In other words, many English Catholics maintained a strong sense of Catholic identity while redefining their sense of community.

ENGLISH CATHOLIC IDENTITY: HOW ENGLISH CATHOLICS PERCEIVED THEMSELVES

English Catholics identified themselves as heirs to traditions of Christianity formed in the first three centuries after Christ when the practice of

Christianity was illegal.[6] Early Christians were persecuted, even martyred, for their beliefs. At a time when many English Catholics felt separated from a visible Catholic Church and bereft of its rituals and institutional forms, they could still connect to the church's past by fulfilling such traditional roles. Through their handling of adversity, they could still make important contributions to their faith.[7]

It is impossible to quantify exactly how many English Catholics drew parallels between English Catholic sacrifices and the experiences of the early Christians as their primary means to identify with the Catholic Church. The preponderance of available evidence, however, does show this as the fundamental form of identification. Certainly English Catholics continued to share bonds of identity based upon the common belief in doctrine and common methods of catechesis. There is little evidence, however, that such commonalities led to strong feelings of Catholic identity to the degree produced by English Catholic associations with early Christians.

English Catholics revered and claimed membership in the "true, ancient" Catholic Church.[8] They continued to esteem the earliest church saints, particularly those of English or Celtic origin.[9] They trusted the knowledge of the apostles and church doctors such as Jerome and Augustine. As seen in previous chapters on religious space, the rosary, and Mass, English Catholic authors continually referenced writers and doctors of the early centuries of Christianity to justify their recommendations, thus building pedigrees for their new interpretations of church belief and ritual. Writers might reinterpret the efficacy of the rosary or the Mass but they would cite the works of the earliest church doctors as justification for doing so. Imported martyrologies and hagiographies might emphasize English, Scottish, and Irish martyrs and saints, but authors would justify their choices by consulting the writings of apostles and early church fathers.[10]

But English Catholics did more than revere the ancient church; they constructed a new identity for themselves based upon parallels drawn between their present experiences and those of Christians of the earlier centuries. Prior to the Emperor Constantine's legalization of Christianity with the Edict of Milan in 313, the earliest Christians were a religious minority and seldom enjoyed legal protection. Many early Christians were imprisoned, tortured, and executed.

Closer to home, the ancient Christians of Britain knew persecution as well. Following the withdrawal of Roman forces from Britain in around 426, Christians became an unprotected minority as earlier pagan religions reasserted themselves. These early British Christians had battled heresy and called upon foreign aid just as English Catholics were doing in the late sixteenth and early seventeenth centuries.[11]

English Catholic lifestyles often mimicked those of earlier Christians, and believers recognized the similarities. English Catholics united themselves in small groups for worship. They often practiced their devotions in private homes or in secluded places out of doors, just as primitive Christians had done in the first centuries A.D.[12] Ancient Christians constructed hiding holes to avoid arrest, just as some English Catholics built secret rooms or closets for priests and laypersons to hide in when evading the Protestant authorities.[13] Some English Catholic authors encouraged the prayers used by Christians of the first centuries.[14] And many English Catholics continued the ancient tradition of traveling together as pilgrims to holy sites.[15]

Authors of English Catholic pastoral literature told readers that contemporary conflicts between Catholics and Protestants were a continuation of age-old conflicts over issues of proper worship. The introduction to a late sixteenth- or early seventeenth-century *Lives of Saints*, for example, criticized English Protestant attempts to curb worship of the saints:

> They [heretics] seek by all means possible to dishonor them [saints] by plucking down churches dedicated to god in their name, by abolishing their feasts, by prohibiting Invocation, adoration, all manner of worshipping and therefore consequently imitation of them as idolatry and flat superstition.

But such efforts, this hagiographer remarked, were "first broached by the heretics Eustachius, Eunomius, Vigilantius, and Wycliff."[16] According to this view, Luther and Calvin were merely continuing old heretical efforts that the Roman Church succeeded in quashing in the past. English Catholics, therefore, should perceive that their present situation was neither unique nor insurmountable. Just as earlier Britons succeeded in overcoming heresies such as Pelagianism, so would contemporary Catholics overcome Protestantism. English Catholics should maintain the traditional practices, assured of their legitimacy and effectiveness, until this current spate of disputation and persecution ended. In the meantime, English Catholic authors suggested, Catholics could feel confident that they remained valuable members of a universal Catholic Church, just as persecuted Catholics had in earlier times.[17]

IDENTIFYING WITH PERSECUTION AND MARTYRDOM

They, for thy sake, with stout contempt have borne
The causeless rage of men and torments fierce
And cruel hooks, which have their bodies torn
But had no power their souls to pierce. . . .

Thou conquering in thy Martyrs' pains
Confessors savest in threatening times
So vanquish sin, which in us reigns
Forgiving our ungrateful crimes.[18]

The parallel that English Catholics drew most frequently between themselves and ancient Christians was that of enduring persecution for Christ's church and in his memory. But why was it so necessary for English Catholics to view their identity primarily through this filter of the past experiences of the church? How did English Catholics enact and interpret persecution and martyrdom, and how did it form a core of their new religious identity?[19]

In general, English Catholics had lost much of their pre-reform identity as members of the Roman Church. English Catholics prior to Protestant reform largely identified themselves as part of an institution. They were church members. They were parish members. They might be guild members, confraternity members, monks, or nuns. They paid tithes. They sought the guidance of representatives of the institutional church in matters of faith, matters of conscience, and even legal matters. The institutional church taught them what to believe through catechesis. The church *as institution* largely defined their identity as Catholics.

Following Protestant reform, however, there was no longer an institutional church present by which most English Catholics could identify themselves and differentiate themselves from the Protestants. In the absence of the institution, English Catholics faced the challenge of maintaining an identity— a sameness, a oneness, a continuity—with their church and with their faith. This was done by building new connections to the *universal* Catholic Church by identifying themselves as the heirs of ancient traditions, particularly those of persecution and martyrdom.[20]

English authors encouraged such comparisons by quoting the Bible and authoritative sources within the church. William Stanney did so when he quoted the gospel of *Matthew* and bolstered it with commentary from St. Basil:

> [Christ said to his apostles] Behold I send you as lambs amongst the midst of wolves. . . . They will deliver you unto counsels, and they will whip you in their synagogues and you shall be led before Kings and Presidents for my sake. . . . (But as St. Basil sayeth) 'With humble meekness of heart and mind [they] did subject themselves to the yoke of obedience, and with all alacrity of heart, went forward into all dangers, reproaches, ignominies, Crosses, and diverse kinds of death, and did with such willingness and joy suffer all things, that they did wonderfully rejoice, when they were thought worthy to suffer reproaches for his sake.'[21]

English authors suggested prayers to help Catholics understand their sufferings in the light of the persecution of Christ and the early martyrs. A seventeenth-century prayer book providing prayers for all occasions suggested the following prayer for the feast of the proto-martyr St. Stephen:

> Grant us, o God, we beseech thee, to imitate the holy Martyr St. Stephen whom this day we have in commemoration, that by his example we may learn patiently to suffer persecution and both to love our enemies and to pray for our persecutors; even as he prayed for his enemies and persecutors to our Lord Jesus Christ.[22]

Some English Catholics did seem to welcome persecution, as did a Londoner named Wallis[23] in 1594. As pursuivants searched the house on Golden Lane in which Wallis was staying, they questioned him about his religious beliefs. Wallis was quite forthcoming:

> One of the Wallises said he loved a Mass and had loved Mass as well in Queen Mary's as in her Majesty's time; and upon being asked if he were a seminary or a Jesuit, [Wallis] replied, 'Oh Lord! No, I am not learned, and would to God I were worthy to carry their shoes.' . . . He also said he was glad that they made search, as he should now suffer some persecution for his religion.[24]

Similarly, in 1591 in Winchester, a group of Catholic women begged to share in the punishment meted out upon the Catholic men with whom they had been arrested. Protestant authorities arrested Roger Dicconson and Ralph Milner along with eight or nine unnamed young women. At the trial, the judges sentenced Dicconson and Milner to death but refused to sentence the women. The women allegedly became quite vocal with the judges, exclaiming that all of those arrested, both men and women, were guilty of the same crime. All had heard Mass, confessed, helped a priest, and "serv[ed] their Savior after the rite of the Catholic Church." Both the men and the women, therefore, should "drink all of the same cup," the women argued.[25]

But why would English Catholics welcome persecution and even seek it out? In one sense, Catholics were linking themselves to an unbroken tradition of witnessing to the faith through suffering. Other goals could be achieved as well. As discussed in chapters 2 through 4, some English Catholics were searching for alternatives to traditional forms of Catholic worship. They feared for their souls in the absence of priests and the sacraments. Suffering and martyrdom were two of the most traditional and effective means to preserve the soul.[26]

Others sought a closer relationship and identification with Christ. For example, when the women in Winchester asked to "drink all of the same cup" and suffer the same punishment as the Catholic men, the women were asking to share in Christ's suffering. As he prayed in the garden at Gethsemane the night of his arrest, Christ asked God whether the cup of suffering might not pass from his lips, if there was not some other way to accomplish what he must do.[27] Christ came to understand he had to accept the bitter cup as the only path to redemption. By refusing to let the cup pass from their lips, the Winchester women asked to share in Christ's suffering and in the consequent redemption. Simultaneously, they forged a common identity between their own persecution and Christ's—the church's earliest example of persecution and martyrdom. In its extreme forms, such desire to identify with Christ led imprisoned and condemned Catholics to attempt various forms of *imitatio Christi*, to equate their sufferings and deaths with Christ's.[28]

Some Catholics viewed themselves as akin to the ancient apostles, and other English Catholics viewed them in the same light.[29] Imprisoned Catholic priest John Ingram, for example, compared himself to St. Paul. Just as Paul used his time in jail to compose letters of comfort to other Christians, so Ingram wrote letters to console his fellow Catholics.[30] In his autobiography, the Catholic poet William Alabaster identified himself with the apostle Paul as well, trying to find comfort and joy in all his difficulties and to practice the prayers and meditations favored by Paul.[31] And when the layman John Hamerton of Hellifield Pele in Yorkshire described the execution of a group of English Catholics, he claimed they died "like apostles and martyrs."[32]

Some Catholics interpreted the missionary priests' activities as mimicking those of the early apostles. When priests preached in barns and held services in private homes or public places, they spread the word of God as Christ's first disciples did. When priests catechized children, heard confession, celebrated the Mass, and disputed with Protestants, they were viewed as "performing all the other functions of Apostles."[33]

English Catholic women interpreted their challenges as opportunities to identify with Mary and Mary Magdalene. Unlike the women of Winchester who sought to identify with Christ by accepting the same cup as he did, approximately 300 women of York consciously imitated the two "Maries." Mary and Mary Magdalene accompanied Christ to Golgotha and stayed at the cross until he died. In 1594, the York women followed the seminary priest John Boste to the execution site to witness his death. They claimed they were going to "accompany that gentleman, that servant of God, to his death as the Maries did Christ."[34] They used the creation of a martyr as an opportunity to create meaning for themselves out of persecution by identifying with the experiences of the very first Christians despite differences of time and space.

Furthermore, imprisoned laypersons and priests equated their circumstances with those of the ancient martyrs. The priest Edward Jones, arrested at a grocer's house in Fleet Street (possibly James Tailor's), was martyred in 1590.[35] After being sentenced to death, the judge asked Jones if he could provide a good reason why he should not be executed. Jones replied:

> In the primitive church when there were more pagans than Christians rather than they would deny their faith, (they) yielded themselves to any kind of death, and Mauritius, serving under a heathen prince, being commanded with his soldiers to worship an idol, threw down his weapons and so did his soldiers, submitting themselves to any kind of torture rather than to deny their God. Even so I rather submit myself to any death whatsoever before I will forsake the Catholic faith.[36]

Those reporting the sufferings of English Catholics also equated them with those of the primitive martyrs.[37] English Catholics were forfeiting their property, being imprisoned, and sacrificing their lives simply for remaining loyal to their faith, just as ancient martyrs had. Chroniclers told the stories of the new martyrs using the same language and literary forms as are found in stories of the ancient martyrs. For instance, the new martyrs were described as showing no fear before the heretical magistrates. They smiled and were happy in spite of their predicaments, comforted by the knowledge of their faith. They practiced great abstinence and piety, engaging in constant prayer. They were pleased to suffer death for their faith.[38] Priests who spoke to the crowds prior to their executions were described as having used words "similar to those of the martyrs of the primitive church."[39] People who witnessed or heard about executions described those who died as martyrs.[40]

The identification of ancient martyrs with contemporary ones went beyond a comparison of their deeds and personal sacrifices. English Catholics revered the bodies and personal effects of contemporary martyrs with the same reverence granted the relics of ancient martyrs. They collected relics, often assuming great risks to acquire a choice bit of a martyr's body. They housed these new relics in reliquaries. They created images of the martyrs or of their relics, such as the portraits that were circulated of Henry Garnet's head, crowned with martyrdom, revealed in a stalk of wheat.[41] One nominally Protestant priest even kept a martyr's relic in the altar of his now-Protestant church, perhaps to give efficacy to what he viewed as the spiritually bereft services of the Church of England.[42] Relics were passed down through generations in the same family, and many, such as Cuthbert Mayne's skull and Edmund Arrowsmith's hand, still exist.[43]

Hagiographers endowed the bodies of English martyrs with the same attributes used to describe the church's holiest saints. There were bodies that refused to decompose, bodies that failed to show signs of the torment they had undergone at the hands of the executioners, and bodies that gave off sweet fragrances weeks after execution.[44] For English Catholics, these new martyrs became as important to church history and tradition as the past martyrs.

As Margaret Clitheroe indicated, an important aspect of Catholic identity involves the maintenance of an unbroken chain with the past. The doctrine of apostolic succession—which Clitheroe referred to when she defined the church as the true word of god preached by Christ, left to his Apostles, and transferred to successors through clerical ordination—claimed an unbroken chain of authority within the Roman Church. Despite a large degree of institutional separation from the Roman Church, English Catholics strove to maintain a similar unbroken chain with the past.[45] While innovation was necessary, it was imperative to ground it upon the traditional teachings of the church. This is one reason why authors of English Catholic pastoral literature backed up their new interpretations of the Mass and the rosary with references to early church writings. This is also why laypeople and priests viewed themselves and one another as ancient martyrs, apostles, Mary, and as Christ-like. To maintain their Catholic identity, there must be no perceived break in the history, the belief, the ritual, the tradition of the Catholic Church.[46] The goal was not to look to the future but to reach into the past for solutions to the current crisis.

BUILDING NEW CATHOLIC COMMUNITIES

As discussed above, the issues of identity and community among English Catholics are equally important, yet they are distinct. Identity constructs a perception of sameness or likeness among Catholics. Community then ties those of similar identity to one another in relationships of varying types and degrees.

A community is a set of relations unifying a body of individuals with common interest living within a larger society. As Michael Hunt has observed, communities are fluid, endlessly dying and being reborn, or assuming new forms.[47] As mentioned above, prior to Protestant reform, the institutional church—whether regarded as based in Rome or in the two English provinces of Canterbury and York—served to define English religious identity. It also unified the English into visible religious communities by constructing devotional, administrative, and social ties between Christians and to Rome. When Protestants assumed control over Catholic cathedrals, monasteries, parishes, deaneries, bishoprics, ecclesiastical courts, public festivals, and the other visible trappings of the *institution* of the church, it was understandable for many Catholics to have perceived these changes as a loss of Catholic community as well as identity.[48]

Some English Catholics, however, were altering their ideas about what constituted an acceptable form of religious community. Many grudgingly recognized that their community could not survive as they had known it. As discussed in chapter 1, the execution of Mary Queen of Scots and the failed Spanish attempts to conquer England in the late 1580s and 1590s brought a harsh truth home to many English Catholics. Their hopes of returning England to the Roman Church were slim.

Consequently, an ever-increasing number of English Catholics reluctantly accepted their status as members of a non-official religion in England and simultaneously sought accommodation with the government and with Rome's expectations. Catholic opinion was not unified on the issue of accommodation, and Catholic efforts tended to be piecemeal. An important turning point occurred with the accession of James VI of Scotland to the English throne in 1603. Believing in James's sympathy to their cause, a group of Catholics presented their new king with two petitions asking for toleration.[49] In these supplications, English Catholics specifically relinquished the possibility of re-creating or seeking toleration of an *institutional* Catholic Church within England. In 1603, *The Catholics' Supplication unto the King's Majesty for toleration of Catholic religion in England* asked James for the freedom to practice Catholicism "if not in public churches, at least in private houses, if not with approbation, yet with toleration, without molestation."[50] The following year's petition for toleration was even more direct in electing not to seek the re-establishment of a public, institutional Catholic Church.

> We do not presume to beg the allowance of some few churches for the exercise of our religion, nor yet the allotting of any ecclesiastical living towards the maintaining of the pastors of our souls . . . but the only degree of favor that we seek at your majesty's hands in this case, is that out of your princely compassion, you would be pleased to reverse the penal laws enacted by our late sovereign against Catholic believers and to license the practice of our religion in private houses, without molestation to priest or lay person for the same.[51]

The Catholics who presented these petitions were not publicly renouncing the pope or the Roman Church, an issue that will be discussed below. Instead, they sought to protect what they perceived to be the minimum requirements for the continuation of the Catholic faith: the presence of the clergy, a place to congregate, the right to rituals, and the ability of the laity to practice Catholicism without fear.

Additionally, the Catholic clergy in England recognized their inability to re-establish the traditional institutional church according to the Roman or provincial model. But the absence of the usual hierarchies and administration did not necessarily inhibit the clergy from organizing themselves to better aid English Catholics. In 1623, for example, Dr. William Bishop, the newly appointed bishop of Chalcedon with authority over England, discussed the difficulties of trying to reestablish the hierarchical order of the Roman Church in England.[52] The pope had ordered Bishop to organize his territory into deaneries and chapters, just as was done in Catholic countries on the continent. With a heavy dose of realism, Bishop commented that

> Neither is it material that I have no cathedral church to give them residence in, nor revenues to maintain them: of both which, God be thanked, they can provide for themselves: for it is not the place or maintenance that makes men fit for that calling, but the qualities and gifts which be in the men, which will in time, we hope, draw the rest after them. The ancient bishops in the primitive church, during the time of persecution, had, no doubt, such worthy men about them, as might well have been named a dean and chapter: but it sufficed them to have the matter itself, though not under those terms. . . .[53]

Again, an English Catholic drew a parallel between the experiences of English Catholics and those of primitive Christians under persecution. Again, as we saw so many times in chapters 2 through 4, English Catholics focused on the *functions* of their religion rather than strict adherence to institutional forms.

But what sense of Catholic community could English Catholics expect to have if there were no churches and no benefices, no cathedrals and no clearly defined chain of church hierarchy? Would Catholics unite in private little groups as they worshipped in one another's houses? Would Lancashire's Catholics feel isolated from Lincolnshire's Catholics without the administrative bonds of the old Catholic archbishopric of York? How would Catholics across England communicate with one another, coordinate their actions and doctrines, monetarily fund a church, or set up a parochial structure?

Or perhaps these are not the correct questions to be asking. Instead of rebuilding religious communities based upon the institutional relationships of the late medieval church, English Catholics would rebuild communities based upon common spiritual bonds and upon ritual separation from the Protestants.[54] Most English Catholics were willing to co-mingle with the Protestants in social circles, business dealings, neighborhood life, and government affairs. Many were even willing to attend Protestant Prayer Book services, albeit to avoid the recusancy fines. When it came to religion, however, Catholics would separate themselves from the Protestants by maintaining spiritual beliefs and rituals designed to draw boundaries between their religious communities and those of the Protestants.

As argued earlier, while engaging in spiritual activities, English Catholics focused on building direct, personal relationships with the divine.[55] With clergy frequently unavailable to act as mediators, Catholics had to turn directly to God or ask for intercession from Mary and the saints.[56] English Catholics were not denying the necessity of priests. They simply used what they had available. It was, in fact, priests who often encouraged English Catholics to construct these direct relations with the divine.[57]

Along this same line, some Catholics throughout England created religious communities based on what they had available to unify themselves around a common interest and to ritually separate themselves from the Protestants. It was a conjunction of mind, spirit, activity, and faith. They constructed many different types of Catholic communities: communities of prayer, communities of the book, and communities of the living and the dead to name a few. A Catholic might belong to one of these communities or to many, depending on her beliefs and the rituals she chose to practice. Some of these communities overlapped. A Catholic might live near to others in his community and meet with them for Catholic worship and fellowship. Or he might read and adopt the practices of the same book that other Catholics throughout England were reading and adopting. He might be aware of his membership in such a particular community of believers, or he might not. But he knew he was one in faith with fellow English Catholics.[58]

Even when individuals acted solitarily, they understood their private actions in the context of wider Catholic traditions practiced by Catholics throughout Christendom. They participated in traditional rituals that they knew other Catholics in their own country and in other parts of the world were continuing. But English Catholics understood their participation in such activities differently than did Catholics practicing in Catholic countries. By imbuing their actions with religious significance, Catholics drew themselves together, marking themselves off from others who did not participate. They could count themselves part of communities of faith and action—communities of concord, of union, of conjunction of minds. This suggests a very broad view of Catholic community but one no less real to the participants.

COMMUNITIES OF PRAYER

Many English Catholics defined the boundaries of their communities by ritually separating themselves from Protestants. In extreme cases, this could involve living in separate areas from Protestants, refusing to socialize, intermarry, or conduct business with Protestants, and, of course, eschewing Protestant churches and their services. But, as discussed in chapter 1, such whole-scale separation from English Protestants was rare, and it is unrealistic to expect English Catholics to have distanced themselves from neighbors, family members, business associates, government, and community.

In many cases, therefore, English Catholics engaged in *ritual* activities, such as prayer, that united them as Catholics and distinguished them from their Protestant neighbors, thus creating Catholic communities based upon prayer. English authors who advocated such communities of prayer justified them by quoting the gospel and reminding readers of the practices of primitive Christians, who because of persecution could not worship publicly. Richard Broughton, in his 1617 compilation of prayers of the primitive church, *A new manual of old Christian Catholick meditations & praiers faithfully collected and translated*, turned to the gospel of Matthew and the commentary of St. Clement of Rome to justify separating from the Protestants.

> If because of misbelievers, we cannot go to the Church, but the wicked occupy the place, thou must flee from that place because it is profaned by them. For as the priests do sanctify holy things, so do the impious defile them. If the true believers can not assemble together neither at home nor in the Church, let everyone by themselves sing, read, pray or two or three gathered together. "For where there be two or three gathered together in my name, there am I in the midst of them." (*Matthew 16*)[59]

In a positive context, such separation from heretics also implied unity in their own church: Christ's church.

Some Catholics agreed that it was best not to attend Protestant church or services, preferring to recite their Catholic prayers at home.[60] Many other Catholics—the so-called "church papists" who sat through Protestant services to avoid recusancy fines but who privately remained Catholics—used Catholic prayers to separate themselves from Protestants as they sat through Prayer Book services. Some would bring their Catholic prayer books with them and read prayers of their own faith. Others would recite the prayers of the rosary, fingering the beads in their pockets. Still others would pray the only Catholic devotions they knew, such as the *Pater noster* or *Ave Maria*. Even the language of the prayers could serve to separate Catholics from the Protestants at the service. While the minister of the Church of England conducted his service in English, many church papists likely prayed in Latin.

While such prayers ritually separated Catholics from their Protestant neighbors, they also served to unite English Catholics with one another and, more broadly, to Catholics throughout Christendom. They tied together those who recited the prayers with bonds of common faith, common activity, and a common reaching out with prayers for one another and the universal Catholic Church. English Catholics could actively join in the offering of sacraments and prayers spiritually even if they could not be physically present in a church or before a priest. The martyred Jesuit Robert Southwell recommended just such a community of prayer when he advised English Catholics who could not attend Mass to present themselves before God at a certain hour and join themselves "in desire with the Sacrifice of the Eucharist being offered in all parts of the globe."[61] As we have seen in chapter 4, such spiritual participation in the Mass could garner similar benefits as physical presence at or corporal reception of the Eucharist.

Similarly, the prayers of Catholics from around the world were working on behalf of the English Catholics. As the Benedictine Anthony Batt pointed out, all those who were members of the Catholic Church were partakers of the prayers of the entire church, wherever they might be, even if they could not be present at traditional Catholic services.[62] Catholics dispersed around the world who prayed for their church as a whole also prayed for each member of the church, including each English Catholic. Just "as one prays for all, so do all pray for one."[63]

Catholics could procure additional benefits of prayer by joining worldwide lay orders or confraternities dedicated to prayer—organized communities of prayer. One such was the Society of the Rosary. The good works of all society members—fasting, almsgiving, etc.—benefited each member.[64] Similarly, the priest William Stanney advocated membership in the Third Order of St. Francis, promising that brothers and sisters of this lay penitential community would spiritually receive the benefits of the Mass as if they had been present if they would join themselves in desire and prayer with the sacrifice.[65]

Many types of prayer-based communities were possible, and certain types were occasionally visible, particularly in Catholic wills and at executions. One such community was that united by prayers for the dead. Protestants discouraged prayers for the souls of the dead. Such prayers, they argued, were useless, having no power to change the fate of one's soul. Some English Catholics, however, continued to hold the traditional Catholic belief that prayers said for the soul of the deceased could ease the soul's pains in Purgatory and help the soul earn its way to heaven. Despite prohibitions, some English Catholics left wills specifically asking for prayers for their own souls and the souls of family members. Such testators often made their bequests contingent upon the recipient praying for the testator's soul.[66] By encouraging such prayers, Catholic testators fostered a community of prayer, comprising those who prayed together as well as the souls of the dead themselves. These Catholics, both alive and deceased, were bound in a common belief, ritual, and purpose.

Similarly, those about to be executed would ask the Catholics in the crowd for their prayers or to pray with them at that moment, consequently building communities based upon prayer. Henry Garnet did this in 1606. The government executed Garnet at St. Paul's churchyard on May 3rd—in the Catholic calendar, the Day of Invention of the Holy Cross. Garnet explained the significance of the day to the crowd, directed their prayers, and reinforced

possible comparisons of his death with Christ's by his choice of words and bodily actions. After climbing the gallows, Garnet addressed the crowd:

> Upon this day is recorded the Invention of the Cross of Christ, and upon
> this day I thank God I have found my cross, by which I hope to end all the
> crosses of my life and to rest in the next by the grace and merits of my
> Blessed Saviour.[67]

He emphasized the reasons for Christ's execution: Christ's steadfast proclama-
tion of God's truth. Garnet drew implicit parallels with his own execution in his
upholding of the true faith.

Garnet then received permission to pray. He made the sign of the cross,
thus sanctifying his words, identifying himself as a Catholic to the crowd, and
using his body to remind the crowd of Christ's cross and Garnet's own.[68] He
then asked all good Catholics to pray for him. The Catholics were probably dispersed individually or in small groups throughout the crowd. They enjoyed
some degree of physical proximity but not much. They likely did not consider
themselves an organized, self-conscious group. While this union was spontaneous, it was not necessarily less effective for the lack of prior planning.

By requesting their prayers, Garnet encouraged a spiritual union of the
Catholics in the crowd. They would be engaged in a similar activity and united
for the same purpose. Moreover, they would be *aware* that all the other
Catholics in the crowd, whether known or unknown to one another, were acting as one to pray for Garnet. Garnet created a sense of community—a group
of people unified in a common interest within a larger society—based upon
prayer.

Finally, the priest/authors who composed the many spiritual guides
used in previous chapters of this study also sought to create communities based
on prayer. They intended for individuals—alone or in small groups—to use the
prayers provided in these guides. But if many Catholics used these prayers, the
authors were creating a body of believers unified in common belief and action.
Evidence of the extensive trade in Catholic books discussed in chapter 1 indicates that large numbers of English Catholics were exposed to such works.
Moreover, these authors invited readers or listeners to enlarge the communities of prayer by sharing the prayers with others. Other authors encouraged
readers and listeners to join themselves spiritually with other Catholics, both
in England and abroad, who were also using the prayers.[69]

Prayer served multiple purposes. It helped construct ritual boundaries
between Catholics and Protestants. Either one said the ritual prayers and was
Catholic or one did not. But more important than separating people, prayers
also united people. It created "a concord, a union, a conjunction of minds."

Catholics formed communities of prayer based on their shared ritual, thought, aspiration, and experience.

COMMUNITIES OF THE BOOK

While the authors of spiritual guides may have created communities based on prayer, they simultaneously created Catholic communities based upon books. A group of people possessing a common book, instructed by the information contained therein, and acting and believing based upon the information in the work create a type of community.[70] Not all members of a book's audience need experience the book in the exact same way in order to create a book-based community. Moreover, a Catholic did not need to possess a book himself or be able to read in order to be a member of a book-based community. He could be a listener, exposed to the practices or ideas contained in the book and interacting with those practices or ideas in his own life, as occurred in the Wiseman household when visiting Jesuit priest John Gerard described how he began the practice of "reading ascetical books, which we did even at table" to the entire family (which would have included servants and close friends, as well as blood relatives).[71] Another excellent example of such a phenomenon which merits further inquiry would be the secret and/or informal schools for Catholic children organized by families or in communities. Children would communally learn from the schoolmasters and their texts.[72]

English Catholics possessed many different types of books in common, including breviaries, catechisms, psalters, primers, manuals, the Office of the Blessed Virgin Mary, martyrologies, and hagiographies, in addition to spiritual works such as Thomas á Kempis's *Imitation of Christ* and the pastoral works discussed throughout this study. For example, records of Protestant search efforts reveal that many Catholics kept breviaries. In one search of prison cells of various Catholic prisoners in 1614, eleven out of thirteen prisoners reported as possessing books possessed a breviary.[73]

And a particular group of Catholics could possess many different books among its various members. The books could be lent to one another or lent to other Catholics outside the immediate group, thereby widening the membership in book-based communities. In the 1584 search of a Mistress Hampden's house in Stoke, Buckinghamshire, the pursuivant Paul Wentworth discovered just such a collection of books among the occupants of the home. Searching bedchambers and other rooms, Wentworth found Jesus psalters, an Office of the Blessed Virgin Mary, a Rheims Bible, a Mass book, a book of Masses dedicated to particular saints, Vaux's *Catechism*, a manual of prayers, a "service book," and many others. Books were even being delivered during the search. A man rode up to the Hampden home, and, seeing that the authorities were searching the house, fled. When the searchers caught up with him, they discovered a Catholic service book the man admitted he was delivering to one of the occupants of the house. The rider also carried his own copy of the Office of the Blessed Virgin.[74]

Books evidently played a large, perhaps even a defining role, in this small Catholic community. Moreover, the inventory of books was changing, with new books being brought in, and some perhaps going out. The Catholic community inside Hampden's house was not insular, apparently enjoying ties to other Catholics to whom books played an important role as well.

Because books were often written or compiled by priests or theologians, the influence of the institutional church in Rome might be strongest in book-based communities. Although many books extant in England were written by English priests and printed on presses within England, many other books were written, printed, and shipped from Catholic countries on the continent. Such books typically encouraged stronger loyalty to Rome and stricter adherence to its traditions, such as weekly attendance at Mass and confession to a priest. Books such as breviaries were often compiled based on instructions from the papacy, thus allowing the Roman Church some measure of indirect influence over the practices of English Catholics.[75]

Laurence Vaux's *A catechisme or A Christian doctrine, necessarie for children & the ignorant people*, otherwise known as Vaux's *Catechism*, provides a good example of how a Roman-influenced, post-reform book written by a continentally based English Catholic might unite both literate and non-literate Catholics into a book-based community.[76] Vaux's *Catechism*, first published in 1567, set the standard for Catholic behavior in England. Printers issued the catechism nine times between 1567 and 1620.[77] To accommodate the non-literate English Catholics for whom his catechism, based on its title "for ignorant people," was particularly intended, some later editions of the text included a pictorial catechism. As would be expected from an English priest living on the continent, the *Catechism* mandated strict adherence to traditional forms of the sacraments with no accommodation to the Protestants or to Catholic difficulties in accessing priests.[78]

Many English Catholics possessed copies of Vaux's *Catechism*, and it remained popular in James's and Charles's reigns.[79] In 1623/4, for example, the authorities seized approximately 152 books wrapped in canvas from a man who dropped his load and fled. Vaux's *Catechism* comprised approximately 16% of the load, and there were more of these catechisms than any other title, save one, of which there were equal number.[80]

By providing a uniform standard of instruction of the basic tenets of Catholic belief, Vaux helped to create a book-based community. The book would have built a certain foundation of belief or knowledge common to those exposed to it. This is not to suggest that all who had access to Vaux's teachings accepted them uniformly. Just as occurred prior to English reforms, English Catholics would accept or reject certain tenets or recommended activities based on their own needs. So while English readers might accept Vaux's basic instruction on the Ten Commandments, the real presence of Christ in the Eucharist, or the *Pater noster*, they might accept or reject Vaux's mandates to attend Mass once a week or to avoid the Church of England's services depending on their particular circumstances, abilities, and beliefs.

Finally, the act of distributing books could help join communities of Catholics. English laypersons and clerics formed networks to print, transport, and pass out or sell books.[81] In 1584, the authorities complained about London Catholics, who reportedly did "conceal many popish, pernicious, heretical, and forbidden books, bringing them forth and dispersing them to their allies. . . ."[82] Decades later, in 1605, a letter to Lord Salisbury informed him of another such community. An Englishman, "in outward appearance a Protestant yet in religion a papist," kept a library of Catholic books in his home. This Catholic reportedly bought, sold, and "scatter[ed books]" in his Majesty's dominions by the hands of seminaries and other disobedient persons."[83] Moreover, the book trade taking place in London's jails which was discussed in chapter 5 helped tie together communities of Catholics centered in the prisons.

Like prayer, books united Catholics into communities. In sum, books exposed large numbers of Catholics to similar rituals, ideas, interests, or activities. Catholics constructed ties with one another as they lent and borrowed books. Catholics had to build bonds of trust, communication, and common interest as they distributed books. Moreover, clergy and laity could work together in this shared cause. Participants in such book-based communities had to visit one another's homes and businesses. They had to travel across cities, shires, or the isle to visit Catholics in different areas. In this process, books provided a starting point from which more communal ties might be built. Fellowship was enjoyed. Information was exchanged. Services and sacraments were celebrated if a priest were among those delivering or receiving books.

Although Catholics were not joined into communities such as those described in earlier chapters, they were linked by the bonds of spiritual friendship and of concord, union, and conjunction of minds encouraged by pastoral authors. This particular type of community was rather nebulous, the size and strength of which cannot be quantified. Yet such ties were important to some English Catholics who sought communal relationships with one another as evidenced by the webs of book possession, borrowing, and trading demonstrated above.

COMMUNITIES OF THE LIVING AND THE DEAD

Another type of Catholic community that blended many of the communal types discussed thus far was the Catholic belief in a community of the living and the dead. Catholics devoutly believed that prayers, Masses, and good works undertaken by the living could affect the health of the souls of the deceased. Moreover, spirits of the dead could communicate with the living, usually for important purposes. For Catholics, the souls of the living and the souls of the dead were bound together into a single community of belief, prayer, ritual, and sacrament.

In contrast, Protestants did not believe in an interactive community of the living and the dead.[84] Prayers and rituals performed on behalf of deceased persons had no effect on the health of souls. The souls of the dead did not communicate with the living.[85] Protestants derided any prayer or ritual that implied otherwise as superstitious and popish.[86]

English Catholics continued to believe in and maintain their union of the living and the dead and often did so in new ways. The Catholic Church traditionally united the community of the living with the dead by its use of common burial grounds, special Masses and prayers, and ritualized activities often involving the bodies of the dead. All of these basic elements theoretically were available to English Catholics, but Protestant prohibitions encouraged Catholics to combine the elements in new ways to achieve the sense of community they desired.

As discussed in the earlier chapter on northern Catholics, some Catholics joined together to create their own burial grounds, such as the cemetery of Harkirke (or New Churchyard) in Little Crosby, Lancashire. Catholics traditionally buried the faithful in hallowed ground within and around parish churches. In this way, living members of the church kept dead relatives and friends physically near to themselves as well as to the physical presence of God upon the altar in the form of the Eucharist. Physical proximity reinforced communal ties between the living and the dead. It was also easier to remember to pray for the souls of the deceased when one passed their memorials, headstones, and graves at least once a week. After Protestants took control of the churches, they continued to bury parishioners in the churchyards but with Protestant rites. Many Protestant ministers refused to bury Catholics in the churchyards. Likewise, many Catholics refused burial there if it meant being interred with Protestant prayers.[87]

Catholics attempted to replicate the communal and spiritual functions of the old parish cemeteries by creating new burial grounds. Enclosed plots of land dedicated as cemeteries continued a close physical proximity between Catholics, both living and dead. Catholic priests blessed the ground. Catholics used traditional Catholic prayers and rituals to bury their dead. There were even headstones to mark some of the graves.[88] Some of these new cemeteries even sported their own altar stones.[89] A priest could say Mass for the souls of the dead right in the middle of the burial ground, perhaps insuring an even closer proximity to the body of Christ in the form of bread and wine than the deceased would have had in a parish churchyard.

Since traditional Catholic burial services were forbidden and Protestant ones were often viewed as inadequate, Catholics had to conduct funeral services surreptitiously, often at night.[90] If the deceased were fortunate, a Catholic priest would be present to conduct the service.[91] Sometimes a priest who had conformed to the Church of England but who remained a Catholic at heart would conduct a secret service.[92] In the absence of proper clergy, lay Catholics might meet—perhaps in a churchyard in the small hours of the morning—and recite prayers or psalms for the dead.[93] It was important to Catholics to use many of the traditional rituals and symbols at these funerals to improve the health of the soul of the deceased person. At the Catholic funeral of Alice Wellington of Allensmore in March 1605, for example, one attendee, Phillip Giles, carried a cross while another attendee, Richard Smith, carried and presumably rang a bell.[94]

In the absence of a Catholic funeral service, Catholics affirmed connections between the community of the living and the dead in a variety of ways. Some Catholics tried to slip Catholic elements into the Protestant service. One of the easiest ways to accomplish this was to hide Catholic symbols upon the corpse prior to the funeral, as discussed in chapter 4. Doing so after the funeral worked too. At some unknown time after the interment of Sir William Courtenay of Powderham Castle, someone threw a small Maltese cross made of brass into the lower part of the family tomb. The inscription on the cross requested the intercession of the Virgin and all the saints for Courtenay's soul.[95] Someone discovered the cross a century later when the tomb was reopened to bury another family member.

Another interesting case highlighting English Catholic creativity in such circumstances is that of Anne Foster. When Foster, an associate of Margaret Clitheroe's, died in prison in York, her hands clutched a written profession of her Catholic faith. She insisted upon a Catholic burial and adamantly refused any Protestant ceremony. An indignant Protestant minister arranged for her corpse to be left out on a bridge to rot. Foster's husband, John, the city coroner, pulled a few strings and arranged for his wife's body to be released into his custody to "bury her where he would, without any other solemnity than to put her in the grave." In other words, there was to be no Mass, Catholic priest, prayer, or ceremony. John Foster abided by the arrangement but simultaneously managed to fulfill his wife's last request to the best of his ability. Knowing his wife's reverence for the English Catholic martyrs, John Foster opened up the grave of one of those martyrs, the Earl of Northumberland, and placed his wife's body on top of the martyr's. [96] Although he could not provide a proper Catholic burial, he hoped to gain for her as much saving grace as possible by laying her body to rest over martyrs' relics, thereby gaining the martyr's intercession for his wife's soul and tying her to the community of the living and the dead.

Most often, however, individual Catholics would pray for the souls of their loved ones and acquaintances, uniting Catholics into a community of the living and the dead as well as into communities of prayer. [97] English Catholics were concerned over the continued spiritual wellbeing of the deceased members of their community. Prayers were not just recited at burials or funeral services but continued to be offered—often for years afterward—for the benefit of the souls of the deceased.

The influence of books in maintaining the community of the living and the dead was likely strong. In Catholic countries, the family and friends of a deceased person might arrange to have Masses celebrated or special prayers said in churches or monasteries to benefit a deceased person's soul. Most English Catholics no longer had these options.[98] Instead, they prayed for the dead themselves, often using prayer books as guides. Books offered English Catholics a tool they could employ to help their friends and loved ones, thereby cementing relationships between the living and the dead (while simultaneously fostering book-based and prayer-based communities).

This brief examination of the variety of Catholic communities possible in this period only begins to touch on the opportunities available to rebuild communal religious ties. Other communities remaining to be explored—but which cannot be investigated here for reasons of space—include communities of time. Catholics' common adherence to old calendars of feast days created communities of sacred time, based upon a common understanding of and participation in the special holiness of given days, regardless of whether individuals celebrated with other Catholics. Moreover, just as English Catholics' ritual use of time could unite them into communities, so could the ritual use of their own bodies. When experienced in common, ritualized activities centered around the body—around what the body does or what the body looks like—can create a sense of community. Ritual actions, such as processions or pilgrimages, or special dress, for example, can create shared experiences that unify actors into a community, however temporary. These suggestions are just the tip of the iceberg. More possibilities remain to be explored.

CONJUNCTIONS OF IDENTITY AND COMMUNITY: HOW ENGLISH
CATHOLICS PERCEIVED THEIR RELATIONSHIP TO ROME

But was the construction of these new types of communal ties and the absence
of institutional church structures indicative of a decline in loyalty to the Roman
Church? English Catholics obviously identified strongly with certain aspects of
the church—traditions of the ancient martyrs, church doctrine, and catechesis—as demonstrated above. They tried to tie themselves communally to
Catholics throughout Christendom through their experiencing of sacraments,
prayers, and rituals. It is time to weave together these various threads of identity and community that have heretofore been treated separately to attempt to
answer the problematic question of how English Catholics envisioned their
relationship with Rome.

English loyalty to Rome had never been absolute. J. J. Scarisbrick
observes that "Papal authority in England . . . did not matter very much in daily
life."[99] Ralph Brentano posits that even prior to reforms, English-born churchmen and the English laity had little use for many of Rome's administrative policies and financial exactions.[100] Rome was too far away to enforce its policies
effectively, and the English Church evolved in its own direction.

If Rome could not engender loyalty in pre-reform years, what success
could it have after Protestant reform when the majority of Rome's administrative structure disappeared? Formulating an answer is complicated. It calls to
mind the question with which this chapter and this book opened: What is the
church? Is it an institutional organization such as that based in Rome? Is it a
foundation of beliefs and rituals defined by Rome? Or is it defined by the people who hold those beliefs and practice those rituals? Does a rejection of Rome
imply a rejection of identity and community with the Catholic Church? And
who gets to decide these issues for the English Catholics? Rome? English
Catholics themselves? Historians?

I argue that while English Catholic loyalty to Rome remained relatively strong until the mid-1580s and early 1590s, such loyalty decreased afterward. Devotion to the beliefs and rituals of the Catholic faith centered in
England and held in common with Catholics throughout Christendom, however, remained strong and continued evolving in new directions. The Oath of
Allegiance controversy, which reached its peak in the 1610s, will be used to
highlight the issues involved in ongoing Catholic negotiations of identity and
community with Rome.

In the first decades after Elizabeth's Act of Uniformity, many Catholics
clung to hope that Rome would help restore their religion. There was a viable
Catholic candidate—Mary Queen of Scots—to occupy the English throne.
Likewise, some Catholics believed that either the pope or one of the Catholic

monarchs on the continent, such as Philip II of Spain, would invade England, place a Catholic monarch on the throne, and reconvert the island. During these years, some wealthy Catholics, particularly those of the northern shires—such as the Dacres discussed in chapter 7—contacted Rome and Spain promising men and money to aid such an endeavor.

When hope of Rome's aid waxed high, loyalty to Rome remained relatively strong. English priests naturally assured Rome of the laity's continued devotion, often claiming miraculous success at reconciling the English to Rome.[101] Priests and lay Catholics valued communications from Rome highly, particularly papal bulls, and took great risks to publish decrees, messages, and indulgences.[102] Moreover, during these years, if a Catholic wanted to become a church papist—attend Protestant services to avoid recusancy fines—he turned to the pope for permission first, seeking a dispensation.[103]

In these early decades, priests and laypersons were more likely to proclaim loyalty to the pope and criticize the English monarch.[104] Many English Catholics identified their faith with the person or authority of the pope and considered him the incontrovertible head of a united Catholic community. In the late 1560s, for example, priests circulated an oath in Lancashire and Cheshire asking Catholics to declare the pope to be the supreme head of the church. The oath taker promised to follow instructions from Rome and to abstain from Protestant services. Both men and women, as well as entire families, took the oath.[105]

Jailed Catholics often used their notoriety to advertise their loyalty to Rome. For example, in 1570, John Felton, the first English Catholic martyr created under Elizabeth's rule, exited Newgate prison bound for the execution site. In front of the gathered crowd, he loudly proclaimed his fidelity to the church in Rome. He was going to die, he said, "for the Catholic faith and because he acknowledged the primacy of the Sovereign Pontiff and denied the pretended queen to be the supreme head of the church."[106]

Such messages could exert lasting influence on other English Catholics. In 1582, the authorities questioned John Hamerton of Hellifield Pele, Yorkshire. Hamerton admitted his Catholic beliefs, asserted that Felton had been unjustly executed, and declared that "the Pope is head of the Church, next under God. . . ."[107]

Priests in the 1580s and early 1590s were more likely to promote loyalty to an international Catholic community headed by the pope and to declare that no compromise or contact with the Church of England was allowable. Vaux's *Catechism* instructed English Catholics that no Catholic stood in hope of salvation who attended Protestant services, partook of Protestant communion, or presented children for baptism in the Protestant church.[108] The Cornish martyr Cuthbert Mayne went further, advising English Catholics to assist any foreign forces who might invade the island to restore the faith.[109]

INCREASING FRUSTRATION WITH ROME

But as time passed, identification with Rome began to wane along with the sense of primary loyalty to the pope as the unquestioned source of authority and acceptable practice. Some English Catholics did remain fiercely loyal to Rome. In 1615, for example, twenty-two-year-old John Owen arrived in Dover from the continent where he had been studying at the English College at Douai. The authorities asked him to take the Oath of Allegiance. Owen refused. Owen affirmed his belief in the certainty of the pope's authority, and "he remarked that should the pope declare the king to be excommunicate, he would slay him if he could."[110] In light of the French monarch Henri IV's recent assassination by a zealous Jesuit, England took such threats seriously.

But fidelity such as Owen's was the exception rather than the rule after the 1590s—after the execution of Mary Queen of Scots and the long-term failure of continental powers to restore Catholicism in England. By 1600, many Catholics began to accept their status as members of a minority religion in a Protestant-ruled country. Contrary to Rome's aspirations, they began negotiations with their monarch for toleration rather than re-conversion.

In addition, as re-conversion hopes faded, many English Catholics became increasingly frustrated with Rome.[111] These Catholics found it unrealistic to follow the dictates of conservative priests who instructed believers not to attend Protestant services or partake of Protestant sacraments if they wanted to remain members of the Catholic Church and gain salvation. As early as 1581, after the passage of the penal statute that assessed Catholics a £20 monthly fine for non-attendance at Protestant services, lay Catholics began asking for the relaxation of Rome's standards. Their families would be ruined, they claimed. Could not the Roman Church allow them to be present at Church of England services as long as they privately renounced the Protestant church and its beliefs and rituals?[112]

Rome refused any such accommodation and would continue to do so for religious and political reasons. Theologians such as the Jesuit Francis Toletus declared that attendance at Protestant services showed "favor and confirmation of heresy." Even if a Catholic protested in his mind against his coerced attendance, he was still committing a sin, according to Toletus.[113] Politically, Rome refused to compromise because it might weaken any future claims to authority over the monarch and church in England.

English priests walked a fine line between enforcing papal policy and meeting the pastoral needs of English Catholics. In 1592, for example, Cardinal William Allen, the designated protector of England, wrote an open letter to Catholics in England assuring them of Rome's understanding and support. Allen had pleaded the Catholic cause directly to Pope Clement VIII. The pope told Allen in no uncertain terms that "to participate with the Protestants either by praying with them or coming to their churches or service or such like was by no means lawful or dispensable." In his letter, Allen instructed English priests to make certain that they did not teach English Catholics that it was lawful for them to attend Protestant services or communicate with the Protestants. Such would be "contrary to the practice of the church and the holy doctors in all ages who never communicated or allowed any Catholic person to pray together" with heretics. Instead, Allen asked English priests to show compassion and mercy:

> towards such of the laity especially as from mean fear or saving a family, wife and children from ruin, are so far fallen as to come sometimes to their [Protestant] churches or be present at the time of their services: for though it be not lawful to do so, not in itself any way excusable, yet since necessity of that kind of men maketh the offense less and more compassionable, yea more easily by you to be absolved. And therefore be not hard, nor rough, nor rigorous . . . in receiving again and absolving them when they confess their infirmities and be sorry for the same and yield some reasonable hope that they will hereafter stand more strongly. . . . mercy you must use though they fall more than once and though perchance you have some probable fear that they will of like infirmity fall again. . . . no more severity is to be required of the penitent than in any other sins that be subject to the sacrament of penance. . . .[114]

In effect, Allen advised priests to accept the sin and forgive the sinner. Roman policy was maintained, and English Catholic needs were somewhat met.[115]

But English Catholics needed more. They wanted to be good Catholics and good subjects of their monarch. By willfully sinning against their church and circumventing their sovereign's laws, they likely felt like neither, even though they typically got away with it. Some compromises had to be made, but who would make them? Rome would not change its dictates. Perhaps the English sovereign might soften the crown's stance. From a traditional standpoint, English Catholics faced a series of difficult—and to some degree, unsatisfying—choices. Could English Catholics redress this situation by revising their way of thinking about their Catholic identity, religious community, and their country and at least satisfy themselves that they were neither damned nor traitorous? For many Catholics, the answer would be yes.[116]

Pastoral clerics and laypersons took matters into their own hands. They began drawing lines between what they owed to God and what they owed to their sovereign. They began negotiating with their monarch for toleration, directly contradicting Rome's policies toward England.

Perhaps the largest obstacle to rapprochement between the English government and the Catholics was the question of loyalty. In a real-world test case of what philosophers were arguing theoretically, English Catholics began to distinguish between the loyalty they owed to God, the loyalty they owed to the pope, and the loyalty they owed to their monarch. Such Catholics searched for a way to prove that loyalty to both their faith and sovereign were not mutually exclusive. A few months before Elizabeth's death, for example, thirteen incarcerated priests issued "A Protestation of Allegiance." In it, the priests recognized the monarch's fears over Catholic insurrection or disloyalty in the face of a Catholic-led invasion. Catholics, they wrote, "by reason of their union with the see apostolic in faith and religion, were easily supposed to favor these conspiracies and invasions." To correct such negative supposition, the priests advertised that

> . . . in these cases of conspiracies, of practicing her majesty's death, of invasions, and of whatsoever forcible attempts which hereafter may be made by any foreign prelate, prince, or potentate whatsoever, either jointly or severally, for the disturbance or subversion of her Majesty's person, estate, realms, or dominions, under color, show, pretense, or indictment of restoring Catholic religion in England or Ireland, we will defend her majesty's person, estate, realms and dominions. . . . And moreover, we will not only ourselves detect and reveal any conspiracies or plots which we shall understand to be undertaken by any prelate, prince, or potentate against her majesty's person or dominions (and resist them) . . . but also will earnestly persuade, as much as in us lieth, all Catholics to do the same.[117]

They swore to uphold this oath even if the pope excommunicated the monarch or threatened to excommunicate any Catholic who refused to support a Catholic-led invasion against a Protestant monarch. The priests promised to obey their monarch in all civil or temporal matters, obey the laws and magistrates of England, and pray to God for the monarch's peaceful, prosperous reign and the eternal health of the monarch's soul.[118]

The priests also carefully defined the loyalty they would continue to show Rome. They promised to shed their blood in defense of their sovereign and England but also proclaimed their willingness to die rather than deny the spiritual authority of the Catholic Church:

> And therefore we acknowledge and confess the bishop of Rome to be the successor of St. Peter in that see, and to have as ample, and no more, authority or jurisdiction over us and other Christians, than had that apostle by the gift and commission of Christ our Savior; and that we will obey

him so far forth, as we are bound by the laws of God to do; which we doubt
not but will stand well with the performance of our duty to our temporal
prince. . . . For as we are most ready to spend our blood in the defense of
her majesty and our country, so we will rather lose our lives than infringe
the lawful authority of Christ's Catholic Church.[119]

These priests chose their words and phrasing carefully. They used the
title "bishop of Rome" rather than "pope." They limited the bishop of Rome's
power to successorship of Peter over the see of Rome only. They restricted his
authority to the commission with which Christ originally endowed Peter.
Seemingly, these priests would deny many of the powers and authority claimed
by the papacy in the many centuries following the death of St. Peter. Most
importantly to an English monarch, they would deny the pope's claimed
authority to remove monarchs from their thrones.[120] This would mean that, in
the case of a papally sponsored invasion of England to remove a Protestant
sovereign, English Catholics would not owe primary loyalty to the pope. They
could defend their English monarch to whom they owed ultimate loyalty in all
temporal matters. Elizabeth died before she could accept or reject this appeal.

Catholics' best hope for increased toleration came with the accession of
James I in 1603. As mentioned above, Catholics petitioned James twice—once
in 1603 and again in 1604—for greater toleration of the private practice of
Catholicism. They did not ask for churches or financing. They did not ask for
a restoration of Roman administration or courts. They simply requested the
right to have clergy and to gather privately to practice their rituals and sacraments unmolested by the Protestant authorities. James appeared sympathetic.
They also professed their willingness to fight and die in defense of their
monarch, whether the threat stemmed from domestic insurrection or foreign
invasion.[121] They negotiated to preserve the sacraments and rituals of
Catholicism while limiting their ties to the institutional church in Rome.

The Gunpowder Plot in 1605 put an end to those aspirations. James
appeared increasingly tolerant of the private practice of Catholicism until this
Catholic-backed conspiracy to blow up Parliament. James's fear of domestic
insurrection led him to increase the stringency with which the penal laws were
enforced. His fears impelled him to require more Catholics to take the Oath of
Allegiance. Refusal to take the oath could result in a charge of treason or, more
commonly, heavy fines. As discussed in chapter 1, James hoped, in part, to
weaken the English Catholic cause by dividing Catholics based on acceptance
or rejection of the oath.

Without Rome's approval, English Catholics had begun a struggle for
accommodation. Proving loyalty to the monarch was of utmost importance to
most laypersons and many pastoral clerics. The vast majority of Catholics never
encouraged or participated in plots to overthrow their sovereign, and they

abhorred the thought of foreigners invading their land. Most were willing to pledge their lands, goods, and lives to the service of the monarch.[122] Would Rome accept this compromise? Did the English care?

OATH OF ALLEGIANCE CONTROVERSY

The controversy over the Oath of Allegiance during James's reign illuminates many of the issues facing English Catholics as they re-conceptualized their relationship with Rome. The Oath of Allegiance, in essence, required English Catholics to swear primary loyalty to the monarch. An individual taking the oath was required to swear:

> I, A.B., do truly and sincerely acknowledge . . . that our sovereign Lord King James is lawful and rightful king of this realm . . . and that the pope, neither of himself nor by any authority of the Church or See of Rome . . . hath any power or authority to depose the king . . . or to authorize any foreign prince to invade or annoy him in his countries, or to discharge any of his subjects of their allegiance and obedience to his Majesty, or to give license or leave to any of them to bear arms, raise tumult, or to offer any violence or hurt to his Majesty's royal person, state, or government. . . . Also I do swear . . . that notwithstanding any declaration . . . of excommunication . . . by the pope . . . against the said king . . . or any absolution of the said subjects from their obedience, I will bear faith and true allegiance to his Majesty . . . and will defend to the uttermost of my power against all conspiracies . . . which shall be made against his . . . person . . . And I do further swear that I do from my heart abhor . . . as impious and heretical this damnable doctrine and position that princes which be excommunicated . . . may be deposed or murdered by their subjects . . . And I do believe . . . that neither the pope nor any person whatsoever hath power to absolve me from this oath . . .[123]

The Oath was not new, and the exact wording of the Oath changed over time. What was new was James's increasing insistence that more and more lay Catholics take the oath and his more rigorous enforcement of the penalties against those Catholics who refused.

Rome ordered English Catholics to refuse the Oath of Allegiance.[124] Some English clerics supported Pope Paul V's decision and discouraged English Catholics from taking the oath. As the priest William Herbert, a prisoner in Newgate in 1615, contended, "whatsoever the Catholic Roman Church shall determine, [I] holdeth it a point of faith, and everyone is bound to lose his life in the maintaining thereof."[125] And a few years earlier, in 1609, the priest Oswald Needham:

> Being demanded if he will take the Oath of Allegiance to his majesty, made lately in Parliament, he refuseth so to do. Being asked some reason for this refusal, he saith that, although he thinketh nothing contained therein to be unfit for him to swear, yet in regard the pope hath commanded the contrary, he ought not therefore to take the same.[126]

Oswald weighed his own opinion against the pope's and privileged the pope's. Herbert and Needham were priests. As such, they observed the hierarchy of authority in the church that bound them ultimately to the pope as Christ's representative on earth.[127]

Many among the English laity held different priorities. They had families to preserve and social, economic, and political positions to protect. They agreed with Needham that there seemed nothing objectionable in much of the Oath of Allegiance. Why not compromise? Why could they not swear the portions of the oath affirming the monarch's temporal authority and which did not threaten the pope's spiritual authority?

Eight priests imprisoned in Newgate in 1610 asked such questions in a supplication to Pope Paul V. They asked the pope to explain his prohibition of the oath, arguing that the pope had never specified to which points he objected. The pope only stated that there were "many things" in it to which Catholics could not swear in good conscience. The priests described the sufferings of the English Catholics to Paul V: their imprisonment in crowded jails, the executions upon the scaffold. They implored the pontiff for help. Rome did not answer "lest explanations might overthrow its claims to temporal jurisdiction" in England.[128] Rome's refusal to clarify its objections were increasingly frustrating as James indicated that he might be willing to accept a compromise on certain portions of the oath.[129]

English Catholics were angry. The northern priest John Mush openly criticized Paul V's handling of the Oath of Allegiance.

> The Jesuits report that Paul hath prohibited all here to give the king any oath of temporal allegiance, unless it be first approved at Rome. This scandalizeth many, that he should so little regard our afflictions; for they looked rather his holiness should have sent them a lawful Oath of Allegiance, which everyone might have had in readiness at all assays, and whereby there might have been conformity amongst us, than to forbid a lawful thing, we being in so great extremities . . . The axe is over our heads. . . .

Mush remarked that certainly there must be some miscommunication, "for it is not likely [Pope Paul V] would forbid a thing wherein few or none think themselves bound to obey him. . . ."[130]

Many Catholics elected to deny Rome publicly by taking the Oath of Allegiance while remaining loyal to the Catholic faith privately.[131] In 1611, the priest John Nelson, assistant to Archpriest George Birkhead, wrote to Dr. Thomas More, Birkhead's agent in Rome, that:

> . . . men in England stick not to say that none of them would lose lands or liberty for [obeying the pope's mandate not to take the oath] if the case were theirs; and many say that they see not why they should lose their lands and goods for an oath which no man will take pen in hand, at home or abroad, to defend.

And Nelson evinced sympathy with those Catholics who took the oath and any priests who might support them. If anyone in Rome criticized such allowance of the oath, Nelson fumed, ". . . you may well and truly check them with this— bid them show you where any, either lay or ecclesiastics, have suffered so much for it as they [English secular priests] and their friends." In other words, what judgmental Catholic cleric in Rome had lost anything in the English struggle? Why were Rome's opinions so right and English ones so wrong?[132]

As Nelson's letter indicates, some English priests disagreed with Rome's mandate to refuse the Oath of Allegiance, and these priests advised English Catholics that it was permissible to take the oath under certain conditions. Like the laity, these priests struggled to separate the temporal obligations of a subject of the English monarch from the spiritual duty a Catholic owed the church.[133] Controversial books written by English priests, such as Richard Sheldon's *General Reasons proving the Lawfulness of the Oath of Allegiance* (London, 1611), circulated among English Catholics and provided them with the justifications they needed to take the oath, protect their families, and remain loyal Catholics.[134]

Even English clerics might take the Oath of Allegiance when pressed. For example, two priests named Braddell and Myllington took the oath after they were unable to leave England following their banishment as seminary priests. Braddell did not have enough money to leave the country. When the authorities jailed him in Lancaster, he took the oath to avoid punishment. He then wrote to the earl of Salisbury asking for sufficient funds to leave the country. He conformed in time of necessity but clearly still considered himself Catholic. Similarly, Myllington tried to go into exile but a storm blew his ship back to England. Since the grace period for priests to leave England had passed by this time, he took the oath before a judge.[135]

Why were priests willing to reject a direct order of the pope in their writings and actions? Perhaps it was because many seminary priests and Jesuits witnessed the financial ruin of many Catholic families. They sympathized with the state of fear in which many Catholics lived during these years. Perhaps it was also because, like Needham, many saw nothing in the oath that detracted from the loyalty that Catholics owed their pontiff. If this were true, why should English Catholics suffer for refusing to take the oath? Additionally, many priests became as frustrated as the laity with Rome's unwillingness to accommodate their needs by compromising on any part of the oath.

English clerical leadership vacillated on the issue of the oath, and a rift grew between English clerics who supported Rome's prohibition of the Oath of Allegiance and those who maintained that English Catholics might lawfully swear the oath.[136] In 1607, the highest-ranking priest in England, Archpriest George Blackwell, announced to English clergy that it was lawful for them to take the oath.[137] The numerous clerics who supported this stance became known as the Clinkers, since many of them, including Blackwell, were imprisoned in the Clink in London.

But what exactly were the Clinkers—or any priest supporting the taking of the oath—advocating? In reality, they offered a variety of options. No organized policy existed among those encouraging the taking of the oath. Some clerics, such as the Jesuit Nicholas Smith, advised the laity that they might take the oath without any reservations because none of it was against the faith.[138] Other clerics advised that it was lawful to take the oath with certain mental qualifications or reservations. Such priests conceded that Rome forbade the oath, but they maintained that a Catholic could take the oath if he mentally swore only the parts of the oath that dealt with temporal allegiance to the king. Such priests did not forswear their allegiance to Rome, they opined. They simply disagreed with the papacy over the difficult issue of the oath.

Pope Paul V deposed Blackwell as archpriest in 1608 and replaced him with George Birkhead.[139] Birkhead announced that priests who did not conform to the pope's prohibition of the oath within two months would by order of the pope be deprived of their "faculties and privileges granted by the holy see." In other words, they would be stripped of their priestly authority.[140] The Clinkers ignored Birkhead's threat and continued to practice as priests, administering the sacraments and holding "themselves innocent and free of the loss of their faculties."[141] Sitting in England, Birkhead knew he sat on a powder keg, caught between the will of the pope and the determination of many of the pastors working with and trusted by English Catholics.[142]

Even priests who supported the pope's prohibition against the oath implored the pope to soften his stance and allow some equivocation in the taking of the oath. Birkhead asked More to consult the pope regarding the taking of the oath with mental reservations.

> It were a great help to me, if I could express his holiness's will, in such cases as these; for then we should not be left in the suds as we are. . . . I

understand that [Laurence] Blanchetti [cardinal priest of the title St. Laurence in Pane et Perna] hath said that such qualifications would never be approved [by Rome], but yet perhaps such they might be winked at. If our superiors may be drawn to wink at such doings, then would I fain know how far we might proceed without offence of God and the holy see.[143]

As archpriest, Birkhead was now the pope's highest-ranking priest within England, and even he was confused as to Rome's working stance on the oath. He supported the pope's *official* prohibition of the oath, yet his frustration over the day-to-day implementation of that prohibition is obvious. English priests were "left in the suds" trying to encourage refusal of an oath that much of the laity saw nothing wrong with. Birkhead searched for some way to reconcile the pope's demands with the immediate needs of the English laity, even to the point of overlooking noncompliance to the pope's official mandate if the pope would only approve it. The pope would not. In less than a month, Birkhead received his answer from Rome. "(His holiness) commandeth me to reject all such interpretations and to instruct Catholics that they must absolutely refuse the oath and adhere to the breve which he hath published." Birkhead agreed to enforce the pope's will.[144]

The controversy arising between the Clinkers and the supporters of Rome's prohibition of the oath reveals the problematic nature of English Catholics' identification and sense of belonging to a united church under Rome's authority. Rome refused to allow any compromise over the taking of the oath. In general, clerics and laity who resisted the pope's mandates did so without renouncing their spiritual identification with Rome or denying their community with Rome. They simply redefined the nature of the communal relationship.

In light of Rome's refusal to compromise, some laypersons joined English clerics in taking matters into their own hands, much as they had in 1603 and 1604 by petitioning the monarch for toleration. Some laypersons worked with clerics to devise a way of taking the oath without offending God or king. Whether this was allowable by Rome was hotly debated. In 1610, John Mush described the philosophical somersaults English Catholics performed:

About Michelmas, 1610, there was terrible ado about the oath everywhere, but this persecution, as it ever hath been, was more hot in Yorkshire and the north than elsewhere. . . . In truth, Catholics were never in like terror or fright as then, neither men nor women knowing which way to turn them, or how to avoid utter ruin of themselves and posterity. In this woeful confusion and desperation, diverse of the best Catholics in Yorkshire, desirous by any lawful means to save themselves both from temporal subversion and spiritual damage of soul, devised ways how they might both

satisfy the king in taking an oath of temporal allegiance, and not offend
God by any unlawful oath; which they thought might be done, if first,
before taking the king's oath, they made this protestation. 'I will take this
oath so far forth as it concerneth my temporal duty or obedience to the
king' after which they thought they might kneel down and take the oath
verbatim.[145]

These laypersons were not trying to subvert clerical authority. They
consulted Jesuits and seminary priests about the acceptability of such a mental
reservation prior to swearing the oath. And yet again there was disagreement.
Some clerics told laypersons that they might swear in this fashion without sin.
Other clerics declared that a Catholic could not lawfully take the oath in this
manner.[146] In this latter case, laypersons asked clerics, "What remedy then?"
Mush answered, "God knoweth."

So the Yorkshire Catholics devised another alternative to the above
mental reservation. Mush reported that Catholics asked him:

> What if, when the magistrate doth tender us the oath, we pray him that we
> may hear it read, or that we may privately read it ourselves, without mak-
> ing any sign or show or swearing, or reverence at all; and after we have
> heard it read say 'This oath containeth many difficult points which we do
> not understand . . . but to so much of it only as doth truly concern our tem-
> poral allegiance to the king, we will and do swear sincerely and willingly'
> and without more ado, kneel down and lay our hand upon the book?[147]

Mush told the Yorkshire group that this style of taking the oath would be lawful, but other clerics likely disagreed. In the end, individual Catholics decided
for themselves what to believe.

Other English clerics and laypersons accepted Rome's prohibition
against taking the Oath of Allegiance but wanted the pope to issue a separate
mandate ordering all English Catholics to swear temporal allegiance to the
English monarch. Archpriest Birkhead sought to define the nature of such allegiance in a letter to his agent in Rome wherein he asked the agent to petition
the pope:

> . . . that it would please him of his fatherly compassion, upon the increased
> miseries of our country, to make and direct a breve unto you to publish
> wherein he would expressly and most strictly command all Catholics of the
> realm, both laics and ecclesiastics, under censure of excommunication *ipso
> facto* to be incurred, neither to confederate, plot, consent to, or execute
> any violence, hurt, or prejudice against his Majesty's person; but that they
> should carry themselves in all temporal and civil affairs [with] fidelity and

allegiance as it becometh good and obedient subjects to their lawful and undoubted sovereign, etc. If such a breve would be procured from his holiness, there is great hope, and not ungrounded, conceived of much ease and mitigation of pressures to follow to the body of Catholics thereby.[148]

A separate oath might assuage James's fears over Catholic loyalty. If the new oath were written and mandated from Rome, it might calm Rome's fears over losing its authority in England.

Other clerics or laypersons tried to rewrite the Oath of Allegiance themselves, putting it into a form that they hoped both James and the pope might accept. One such rewrite, submitted to James by clerics and laypersons in 1606, declared James as, after God, the head of "the civil body without dependence on any other earthly power or jurisdiction." In a form reminiscent of the 1603 and 1604 petitions, "We, the secular and regular priests and other Catholics of England" promised to protect and defend the monarch and his realm from any foreign or domestic insurrection.

Other rewrites took the form of individual (rather than collective) oaths in which the oath-taker swore allegiance to the sovereign, promising to defend the king against all conspiracies. One such individual oath included the statement, "And I do also think and verily believe that princes which be excommunicate ought not to be murdered by their subjects nor any other."[149] The martyred priest Thomas Garnet refused to take James's version of the oath because the "Supreme Pastor of the Church and Representative of Christ on the earth" prohibited it. Instead, he composed his own personal oath to his monarch, professing all obedience to James in temporal matters "by the law of nature and the divine law of the true Church of Christ.[150]

As the Oath of Allegiance controversy reveals, English Catholics were the group that had to compromise. Despite pleas from English Catholics, Rome refused to change its stance on the oath. The English monarch, James I, indicated he would have been willing to accommodate the English Catholics if Rome had evinced some willingness to back down on certain issues. Of course, this was easy enough for James to say when he did not actually have to compromise. This left English Catholics, both laypersons and clerics, to forge their own bonds of identity and community with Rome and with their sovereign: ties they could live with that would allow them to perceive themselves as good Catholics and good subjects. It was their own opinions of themselves that mattered in the long run. Rome might disapprove of their actions and the sovereign may not have been entirely satisfied, but English Catholics could go to bed at night believing they simultaneously walked in a state of salvation, loyally served their king, and protected their families and livelihoods.[151]

What emerges is a portrait of English Catholics who wanted to identify with and enjoy a sense of religious community with a universal body of believers, loyal to the Catholic faith. They identified with the sacrifices of the ancient martyrs, thus constructing ties to this universal church. They wanted to fulfill all spiritual obligations they owed to God to ensure the health of their souls. In large measure, English Catholics interpreted their spiritual obligations as the maintenance of the sacraments, rituals, traditions, and beliefs of the Catholic Church. These were rituals and beliefs in which English Catholics joined with their co-religionists throughout Christendom in celebrating, thus creating communities based upon prayer, ritual, and doctrine. If Rome facilitated English Catholics' ability to uphold this identity and these obligations and communities, English Catholics followed Rome. But many English Catholics after 1590 perceived that Rome actually made it more difficult for most Catholics to fulfill their duty to God and identify and maintain communal ties with the universal body of believers. English Catholics, therefore, sought alternatives, either through accommodation with their monarch or through consultation among themselves and their pastoral clergy, that would allow them to maintain their Catholic identity, build Catholic communities, and practice the sacraments, rituals, traditions, and beliefs of their faith unmolested.

Conclusion

LL OF WHICH BRINGS US BACK TO the question with which this study began: What was "the church" to ordinary English Catholics attempting to continue as Catholics in Protestant England? There is no one answer to which all English Catholics subscribed. One monolithic union of Catholics did not exist in England. As the entirety of this study has aimed to prove, many religious communities could exist among English Catholics: in isolation or overlapping, large and small, sharing different conceptions of sacraments, rituals, and beliefs. But unity amidst diversity had served the Catholic Church well for centuries and would continue to do so now.

But laypersons such as Margaret Clitheroe and authors such as Arthur Crowther, Thomas Vincent, William Stanney, and Henry Garnet provide us with clues to how ordinary English Catholics conceived of their "church." They discuss issues of religious continuity and the "strong bands of spiritual friendship." In the absence of the institutional structure and administrative ties that had largely defined the pre-reform English Church, these continuities and bonds still existed, and they took many forms.

English Catholics rebuilt their connections to the church by redefining religious ritual, identity, and community. Many created new holy places to congregate and worship. Some reinterpreted their relationship to sacraments such as the Mass. Others continued traditional rituals, such as the rosary, but adapted their understandings about their ritual actions and their efficacy. They made such changes in their beliefs, actions, and experiences not to challenge Rome or separate themselves further from the Roman Church but to maneuver themselves closer to it. Moreover, by identifying their struggles with primitive

Christians' struggles as a minority religion, English Catholics believed themselves part of the church's continuing battle against its enemies. Just as the church prevailed in the past, so would English Catholics, by adapting to preserve their faith, and by continuing to participate in the sacraments, rituals, traditions, and beliefs of the church in whatever ways they could.

Finally, English Catholics bound themselves into many types of communities. These communities were based on diverse sets of connections: upon spiritual ties rather than institutional ones: upon prayers rather than parishes, upon books rather than bishops, upon a concord, a union, a conjunction of minds. Other forms of communities were based upon the mutual support of Catholics who were in physical proximity to or contact with one another, such as the communities that developed in prisons, the foreign embassies, or among the lords and outlaws on the border with Scotland. And such English Catholics still identified themselves as part of a universal, ancient Catholic Church, led from Rome, even if they did not always elect to follow Rome's lead.

This sense of English Catholics twisting and tying themselves to others "by the strong bands of spiritual friendship" nourished by reconceptualizations of ritual, identity, and community can perhaps best be seen by examining the actions of a group of Yorkshire Catholics in 1612. In that year, Protestant authorities caught seventeen Catholics from Thornton le Beans and Dishforth meeting by one of the old standing crosses that dotted the Yorkshire countryside. They met at the cross to say prayers for the dead.[1] They used the traditional prayers of the church in a nontraditional setting, and yet in reality, the setting *was* a Catholic one. Catholics had erected such crosses centuries earlier, but most English Catholics had not used the crosses for such purposes in many years. Congregating around these monuments, the Yorkshire Catholics united with one another and linked themselves to pre-reform English traditions.

This group of Yorkshire Catholics standing outside, exposed to the elements, gathered around an old stone cross to pray for the souls of their deceased loved ones exemplifies how many English Catholics may have perceived their connections to one another. In the absence of church buildings, these Catholics found a new location at which to congregate. In the absence of priests and the parish institutional structure, these Catholics found a way to tie themselves into a pious community comprising both the living and the dead. These were not fellow parishioners in the traditional sense. They were not gathered upon hallowed ground inside or outside their church. Most of the recognizable symbols, material objects, rituals, and gestural actions of the Catholic Church were missing. And yet despite all these "absences," these Catholics formed a community—a unified body of individuals joined together, however temporarily, within a larger society. What unified them into this community was their shared experience of ritualized activity in what they demarcated as sacred space. Standing around a stone cross erected by earlier English Catholics, they offered prayers together for common benefit of Catholic souls. It was a community of prayer, a community of ritualized activity, a community of the living and the dead, a Catholic community of concord, of union, of conjunction of minds.

In sum, many English Catholics—such as those standing around the Yorkshire cross—did not understand their participation in "the church" as allegiance to Rome or to the Pope as head of the church. They did not define "the church" as a return to the public, state-sponsored ritual and material culture of late medieval English Christianity, filled with a plethora of priests and a cornucopia of feast days and ceremonies. Nor were ordinary Catholics overly concerned to ensure "the church" adopted the new standards of belief and practice set down by the Council of Trent. Instead, they defined their "church" not as an administrative or hierarchical institution but as loyalty to and common participation in the sacraments, beliefs, and rituals of Catholicism—the same sacraments, beliefs, and rituals that English Catholics were re-conceptualizing in a myriad of ways. This "church" was a union of believers typically seeking to maintain the functions of spirituality rather than strict adherence to institutional forms in order to ensure their salvation.

In sixteenth and seventeenth century England, the popular religious climate was one of experimentation, diversity, and intolerance whether one labeled oneself Protestant or Catholic. Certainly, there were extremists on both sides, from the "hotter" sort of Protestants pushing for an overhaul of dress, manners, lifestyle, and entertainment, to the "Jesuited Papists" plotting Elizabeth's overthrow or the blowing up of Parliament. Yet these extremes are hardly reflective of the priorities and experiences of the vast majority of Christians in England during the years of reform. Protestantism did not emerge fully formed from the heads or pens of Henry VIII, Elizabeth I, and their advisors. Likewise Catholicism did not remain mired in its late medieval form or in the impossible-to-implement (at least for England) Decrees of the Council of Trent.[2] Both faiths evolved. Believers of both faiths debated one another and amongst themselves. They experimented, wandering down different paths, turning around, and trying new routes. And although many of these debates and wanderings involved theologians and intellectuals at home and on the continent, this process also involved ordinary engaged laypeople and the clerics who worked with them pastorally on a daily basis. It was an ongoing interaction—a give and take—between the institutions and ideas of religion and the needs of believers. And although England was undoubtedly a Protestant nation by the seventeenth century, Catholics had not all been subsumed into a ritualistic parish Anglicanism. Catholicism had not withered and lost its vitality. It had simply and complexly metamorphosed in ways we are just beginning to question.

Such diversity and intolerance in early modern England closely resembles negotiations within and among religions today and emphasizes the impact individual believers exercise on the popular experience of religion. From longstanding controversies and debates among Christian denominations (such as the Methodists vs. the Baptists) and within Islam (such as the division between Sunnis and Shi'ites), there is often little agreement or tolerance for those of differing beliefs within what is ostensibly the same religion. Yet such individuals continue to live and even worship side by side, much as Catholics and Protestants did in sixteenth and seventeenth century England. In addition, contentious issues such as birth control and homosexuality have troubled individual consciences and divided parishes. Yet despite the fact that such controversial practices are often officially condemned, many individuals who use birth control or are active homosexuals continue practicing within such faiths. They consider themselves members in good standing at their churches regardless of their various accommodations or adaptations to institutionally established rules. When such activities occur openly, many of their co-religionists publicly support these "rule breakers." Day-to-day experiences of religion are often different than those intended by the powers that be, just as they were for English Catholics.

I have also highlighted the day-to-day experiences of English Catholics as a reflection of the debates between secular and spiritual authority that grew heated and deadly in the Reformation period. It should never be forgotten that rulers and subjects in England and on the continent generally considered religious loyalty and political allegiance to be indivisible during the age of reform. The monarch took responsibility for the care of souls, and subjects believed individual salvation to be tied to the actions of their sovereigns and communities. It was inconceivable to most individuals that they could be loyal subjects and not adhere to the sovereign's faith. European intellectuals such as Jean Bodin and Francis Bacon were just beginning to experiment with separating the two concepts, compartmentalizing politics and religion.[3] I have discussed English Catholics as a real-world test case of what philosophers were arguing theoretically as ordinary English Catholics began to distinguish between the loyalty they owed to God, the loyalty they owed to the Pope, and the loyalty they owed to their monarch. Such negotiations at the popular level exist as early stages in the eventual creation of modern national identities, as religion took a back seat to emerging primary loyalties to nation and sovereign. Typically, this has been analyzed as a Protestant phenomenon, but here we can see Catholic participation in the same debates.

And such issues hit a little closer to home today than we may be comfortable with. Many of the issues of spiritual and secular authority being worked out by English Catholics and Protestants resemble those taking place worldwide between religions and governments in the twentieth and twenty-first centuries.[4] For example, although today we may chuckle at early modern English Protestant fears of Catholics rising up as a fifth column to aid a Catholic invasion from Spain, one has only to look at popular American fears of American Muslims rising up to aid Islamic terrorist efforts in the U.S. to understand how the Protestant point of view could have developed and spread in late Tudor England. And although today's debates may not overtly bring up religious or theological arguments in defense of policy decisions, the subtext still exists. World leaders and journalists cloak the terms of contemporary controversies in rational, secular language that makes us feel comfortable in our modernity, yet such language cannot fully conceal underlying tensions such as "Jew versus Muslim" or "Muslim versus Christian" in their totality. But even Elizabeth I did this in sixteenth-century England. Even Elizabeth—the sovereign who did not wish to make windows into men's souls—imprisoned and executed Catholics in the name of national security rather than in the name of the Protestant faith.[5]

The fact remains that religious intolerance and persecution remain commonplace throughout the world, on every continent, no matter how secular or theological the justification or terms of the debate. Books are burned, martyrs are made, holy wars are declared, acts of religiously motivated terrorism proliferate. The goal of religious pluralism sought in early modern England has yet to be achieved, even in the British Isles themselves. The issues of this study—and the ways in which individual believers, church leaders, and secular leaders choose to address them and work together to accommodate one another—are as relevant today as they were four centuries ago.

Notes

NOTES TO INTRODUCTION

1   York Minster Library, Add MS 151, 58r.

2   Defined as prior to the first English Reformation initiated by Henry VIII's Act of Supremacy in 1534. It is now generally accepted that pre-reform English Christians were neither champing at the bit for reform of a decaying church nor universally and uniformly participating in an idyllic religious culture fiercely devoted to the Pope and the doctrinal teachings of Rome. For a detailed examination of this culture, see Eamon Duffy, *The Stripping of the Altars, Traditional Religion in England 1400–1580* (New Haven: Yale University Press, 1992) who describes the varied experiences of the majority of pre-reform Christians who were loyal to and involved with their faith.

3   Duffy, *Stripping*, 3.

4   See Virginia Reinburg, "Liturgy and the Laity in Late Medieval and Reformation France," *The Sixteenth Century Journal* 23, no. 3 (1992): 526–546.

5   No longer recognized as sacraments were confirmation, penance, extreme unction, holy ordination, and marriage.

6   The Catholic clerics with the most influence over lay Catholics were priests directly ministering to the laity within England. The secular priest John Sergeant, for example, criticized English Catholics' propensity to be guided by no one but their immediate priests, writing that "because they have been too long without the curb of Episcopal authority . . . there is no church discipline or other superiority over them further than that priest whom they please to take for their ghostly father and whom generally they look upon as a kind of honorable servant alterable at pleasure." This document is unsigned but John Bossy, *The English Catholic Community, 1570–1850* (London: Darton, Longman & Todd, 1975) 256, attributes it to Sergeant. Quoted in Colleen Marie Seguin, *Addicted unto*

Piety: Catholic Women in England, 1590–1690 (PhD Dissertation, Duke University, 19▨7) 48.

7   After the Council of Trent (1545–63). The Council of Trent, through its decrees, attempted to reform and streamline Catholic belief and ritual and tighten clerical authority over the laity. See *Decrees of the Ecumenical Councils*, vol. 2, *Trent to Vatican II*, ed. Norman P. Tanner, original text established by G. Albergio, J.A. Dossetti, P.-P. Joannou, C. Leonardi, and P. Prodi, in consultation with H. Jedin (London: Sheed and Ward, Ltd., and Washington, D.C.: Georgetown University Press, 1990).

8   Duffy, *Stripping*; Christopher Haigh, *English Reformations: Religion, Politics, and Society under the Tudors* (Oxford: Clarendon Press, 1993), *Reformation and Resistance in Tudor Lancashire* (Cambridge: Cambridge University Press, 1975) and "The Continuity of Catholicism in the English Reformation." *Past and Present* (GB) 93 (1981): 37–69; See also J. J. Scarisbrick, *The Reformation and the English People* (Oxford: Basil Blackwell Ltd., 1984); Peter Marshall, *The Catholic Priesthood and the English Reformation* (Oxford: Clarendon Press, 1994).

9   See Haigh, *Reformations*; Bossy, *ECC*; See also J. C. H. Aveling, *The Handle and the Axe: The Catholic Recusants in England from Reformation to Emancipation* (London: Blond & Briggs, 1976).

10   J. C. H. Aveling, *Northern Catholics: Recusancy in the North Riding, 1558–1791* (London: Dublin Chapman, 1966); S. J. Watts, *From Border to Middleshire: Northumberland, 1586–1625* (Bristol: Leicester University Press, 1975); A. L. Rowse, *Tudor Cornwall: Portrait of a Society* (New York: Charles Scribner's Sons, 1969). Other fine county studies include Haigh, *Lancashire*, and Roger B. Manning, *Religion and Society in Elizabethan Sussex: A Study of the Enforcement of the Religious Settlement, 1558–1603* (Bristol: Leicester University Press, 1969).

11   See Patricia Crawford, *Women and Religion in England, 1500–1720* (London: Routledge, 1993) and more recently, Sara Heller Mendelson and Patricia Crawford, *Women in Early Modern England, 1550–1720* (Oxford: Clarendon Press, 1998). Crawford, however, does not focus her analysis exclusively on Catholic women. See also Roland Connelly, *The Women of the Catholic Resistance: In England, 1540–1680* (Edinburgh: The Pentland Press Limited, 1997); Seguin, *Addicted*; Dorothy Latz, *Glow-worm Light: Writings of Seventeenth-Century English Recusant Women from Original Manuscripts*, Salzburg Studies in English Literature (Salzburg: Aus Institut fur Anglistik und Amerikanistik, Universitat Salzburg, 1989).

12   Haigh, "Continuity," 61–3. Haigh looks primarily at efforts of priests to maintain late medieval traditions, what Haigh refers to as "survivalism" of older Catholic traditions. When Catholics lost access to the priests and sacraments, Catholics "slipped into conformity" with the Protestants. Bossy, *ECC*, 108–110, looks as well at traditional performance of collective religious and sacramental acts to

chronicle what he saw among both the laity and clergy as the "death of the church."

13   The flexibility of the Roman Church's efforts to convert pagan England in the sixth and seventh centuries through St Augustine of Canterbury and his successors provides an excellent example.

14   For example, see Peter Holmes, *Resistance and Compromise: The Political Thought of the Elizabethan Catholics* (Cambridge: Cambridge University Press, 1982); Lucy E. C. Wooding, *Rethinking Catholicism in Reformation England* (Oxford: Clarendon Press, 2000); Alexandra Walsham, *Church Papists: Catholicism, Conformity and Confessional Polemic in Early Modern England* (Woodbridge, Suffolk: The Royal Historical Society, The Boydell Press, 1999) chaps. 2–3

15   This is in contrast to Wooding's conclusion that "The [English Catholic intellectual] writers [of the Elizabethan years] . . . were perhaps more representative of common feeling, and to understand their motivations and convictions is to draw closer to the more mundane experience of the Reformation." Wooding, *Rethinking*, 269.

16   Alexandra Walsham, "'Yielding to the Extremity of the Time'": Conformity, Orthodoxy and the Post-Reformation Catholic Community," in *Conformity and Orthodoxy in the English Church, c. 1560–1660*, eds. Peter Lake and Michael Questier (Woodbridge: The Boydell Press, 2000) 213–4, 216; Walsham, *Church Papists*, xi, 6; Walsham, *Providence in Early Modern England* (Oxford: Oxford University Press, 2001) introduction.

17   Questier argues that recusancy (or the refusal to attend Protestant services) was not a Catholic choice filled with "ideological vigor" while nominal conformity was "vacuous" or "watered down." In "Conformity, Catholicism, and the Law," in *Conformity and Orthodoxy*, 256–8, for example, Questier examines Catholics who manipulated "grey areas" in the law demanding conformity and moved between recusancy and church papistry in similar sorts of ways as Protestants were subtly negotiating Protestant ideas of conformity. (240–1, 256, 258, 260); See also Questier, *Conversion, Politics, and Religion in England, 1580–1625* (Cambridge: Cambridge University Press, 1996); Anthony Milton, *Catholic and Reformed: The Roman and Protestant Churches in English Protestant Thought, 1600–1640* (Cambridge: Cambridge University Press, 1995) 542; Tessa Watt, *Cheap Print and Popular Piety, 1550–1640* (Cambridge: Cambridge University Press, 1991).

18   While Jones, for example, investigates how ordinary English had to adapt in matters of religion and possessed choices, his overarching question remains "how a nation of habitual Catholics turned into Protestants." Norman Jones, *The English Reformation: Religion and Cultural Adaptation* (Oxford: Blackwell Publishers Ltd., 2002) 2, 135–7, 198. Jones investigates the process of "exploration and redefinition" going on during Elizabeth's reign when ordinary individuals tried to

"find their way through life in a culture whose habits, damaged and distorted, had to be reformulated," but only investigates it in the Protestant context.

19 Walsham describes her study's "emphasis on the continuities within the Elizabethan Settlement which eased the passage of society into the Protestant era." Walsham, *Church Papists*, xvi, 3, 70.

20 Church papists' participation in the Anglican Church, for example, may have helped preserve traditional ritual and belief within Protestantism. Walsham, *Church Papists*, chap. 4. For the active role of Protestant laity in such debates, see Judith Maltby, *Prayer Book and People in Elizabethan and Early Stuart England* (Cambridge: Cambridge University Press, 1998); Doreen Rosman, *From Catholic to Protestant: Religion and the People in Tudor England* (London: UCL Press, 1996) 54, 69, 84–5. Walsham discusses literature regarding recusancy and church papism as "an attempt to establish a more stringent definition of what it meant to be a Catholic in the context of post-Reformation England. It was an assertion of clerical control in a set of circumstances in which traditional structures of authority and communication had all but dissolved and in which lay people had begun to devise their own sort of compromise with the late Tudor State. It symptomised a wider struggle to forge a fierce and resilient confessional identity in the face of de facto religious pluralism and to foster a spirituality which went far beyond merely formal adherence to a set of beliefs." Walsham, "Yielding," 213–4, 216, and *Church Papists*, chaps. 2–3.

21 As Ann Ramsey has argued for France in *Liturgy, Politics, and Salvation: The Catholic League in Paris and the Nature of Catholic Reform, 1540–1630* (Rochester: University of Rochester Press, 1999) 1, while Protestant reforms were one of the most important cultural shifts in sixteenth and century Europe, "Only recently has a general recognition emerged that the story of the transition from late-medieval to early modern forms of worship cannot be told without considering the Catholic variants of this larger process of cultural change."

22 Walsham, *Church Papists*, xii.

23 Joyce Appleby, Lynn Hunt, and Margaret Jacob, *Telling the Truth about History* (New York: W. W. Norton, 1995) 250.

24 As Pierre Bourdieu suggests, we must understand the contexts in which religious practice originates in order to understand its functions and how the means used to attain a desired end were developed. Pierre Bourdieu, *Outline of a Theory of Practice*, trans. Richard Nice (Cambridge: Cambridge University Press, 1977) 114–5.

25 Roger Chartier and others have encouraged the need to examine the plural uses and the diverse interpretations and relations individuals establish with particular objects and texts. See Chartier, *Forms and Meanings: Texts, Performance, and Audiences from Codex to Computer* (Philadelphia: University of Pennsylvania Press, 1995) esp. chap. 4; and Chartier, "Culture as Appropriation: Popular Cultural Uses in Early Modern France," in *Understanding popular culture: Europe from the Middle Ages to the nineteenth century*, ed. Steven L. Kaplan

(Berlin: Mouton, 1984). See also Michel de Certeau, *The Practice of Everyday Life*, trans. Stephen Rendall (Berkeley: University of California Press, 1984); Peter Burke, *Popular Culture in Early Modern Europe* (New York: New York University Press, 1978) and *The Historical Anthropology of Early Modern Italy: Essays on Perception and Communication* (Cambridge: Cambridge University Press, 1987).

26   Natalie Zemon Davis, *Society and Culture in Early Modern France: Eight Essays by Natalie Zemon Davis* (Stanford: Stanford University Press, 1975) xvi–xvii. See also Michel Vovelle, *Ideologies and Mentalities* (Chicago: University of Chicago Press, 1990) espec. chaps. 1, 2 and 5.

27   Interestingly, Bossy, *ECC*, 51, points out that the mission in England had to accommodate itself *organizationally* to the special circumstances within England. Parochial divisions and jurisdictions no longer functioned in the absence of an institutional Catholic Church. As a result, Catholics were no longer tied to one parish priest or physical location of worship, and this proved to be an advantage, blending well with the peripatetic, irregular efforts of the missionaries. This marks a great departure from the Council of Trent's attempts to tie continental Catholics closely to their local parish and clergyman. Additionally, he notes priests' efforts at disguise and dissimulation and their ability to "accommodate themselves to a wide variety of external situations" which allowed them to work in a Protestant environment (251). So while Bossy recognizes the priests' flexibility and accommodation in external habits and organization, he does not investigate in depth new directions in pastoral care within the new environment.

28   Peter L. Berger and Thomas Luckmann, *The Social Construction of Reality: A Treatise in the Sociology of Knowledge* (Garden City, NY: Anchor Books, 1967) esp. 15–9 and parts II & III.

29   Hans Medick and Alf Lüdtke examine similar sets of issues in *The History of Everyday Life: Reconstructing Historical Experiences and Ways of Life*, trans. William Templer (Princeton: Princeton University Press, 1995), chaps. 1, 2.

30   For example, see Carlo Ginzburg, *The Cheese and the Worms: The Cosmos of a Sixteenth-Century Miller*, trans. John and Anne Tedeschi (New York: Penguin, 1982), introduction; Davis, *Society and Culture*, particularly chap. 4; Robert W. Scribner, *Popular Culture and Popular Movements in Reformation Germany* (London: Hambledon Press, 1987); John C. Olin, *Catholic Reform from Cardinal Ximenes to the Council of Trent 1495–1563: An Essay with Illustrative Documents and a Brief Study of St. Ignatius Loyola* (New York: Fordham University Press, 1990); John W. O'Malley, *The First Jesuits* (Cambridge: Harvard University Press, 1993); R. A. Markus, *The End of Ancient Christianity* (Cambridge: Cambridge University Press, 1990); Jonathan D. Spence, *The Memory Palace of Matteo Ricci* (New York: Penguin Books, 1985); Catherine Bell, *Ritual Theory, Ritual Practice* (Oxford: Oxford University Press, 1992).

31   In using the term pastoral clergy to refer to lower-level, non-administrative clergy whose primary duties revolved around the care of laypersons, I do not seek to

deny that administrative clerics exercised pastoral duties. Instead, I attempt to differentiate the primary concerns and duties of each group.

32   Theodor Klauser, *A Short History of the Western Liturgy: An Account and Some Reflections*, trans. John Halliburton (Oxford: Oxford University Press, 1969) espec. chap. 2.

33   See Olin, *Catholic Reform*. And as John W. O'Malley, points out in *The First Jesuits*, Jesuits, in particular, would have felt the necessity of providing alternatives to traditional worship to meet the special needs of the English Catholics struggling against the flow of Protestant reform in England. The Jesuits viewed the Reformation as a pastoral problem, not a doctrinal one.

34   See Berger and Luckmann, *Social Construction*, 60.

35   *Matthew* 16: 18–20, used by Pope Leo I to modify the pre-existing doctrine of apostolic succession to establish the Petrine Doctrine justifying the popes, as successors to Peter as Bishop of Rome, as the "first" priests, having authority over remaining clerics.

36   Concepts such as mediation, intercession, and the efficacy of the sacramental system will be discussed in subsequent chapters as particular issues arise.

37   *Decrees*, 732–3, 742.

38   For example, see Clifford Geertz, *The Interpretation of Cultures: Selected Essays* (New York: Basic Books, 1973); Victor Turner, *The Ritual Process: Structure and Anti-Structure* (Ithaca: Cornell University Press, 1969) 127.

39   Philip Selznick, *The Moral Commonwealth: Social Theory and the Promise of Community* (Berkeley: University of California Press, 1992) 369.

40   Michel de Certeau, *The Mystic Fable*, trans Michael B. Smith (Chicago: University of Chicago Press, 1992) 97–8.

41   As Berger and Luckmann argue, institutions tend to exist with members holding certain relevancies in common at the same time as they diverge over other issues. *Social Construction*, 63–4.

42   BL, Sloane MS 4035, ff. 9v–10.

43   Judith Maltby agrees, noting that "Elizabeth's reign can rightly be seen as the crucial period of consolidation" of reform. Maltby, *Prayer Book*, 17. Duffy, *Stripping*; Miri Rubin, *Corpus Christi: The Eucharist in Late Medieval Culture* (Cambridge: Cambridge University Press, 1991); Robert Scribner, *For the Sake of Simple Folk: Popular Propaganda for the German Reformation* (Oxford: Clarendon Press, 1994) and "The Reformation, Popular Magic, and the 'Disenchantment of the World.'" *Journal of Interdisciplinary History* 23, no. 3 (1993): 475–494; William A. Christian, Jr., *Local Religion in Sixteenth Century Spain*, reprint ed. (Princeton: Princeton University Press, 1989); Ramsey, *Liturgy*; Susan Karant-Nunn, *The Reformation of Ritual: An Interpretation of Early Modern Germany* (London: Routledge, 1997).

44   Religion and politics were beginning to be distinguished from one another in this period, as will be discussed in chapter 8. Popular understanding was that loyalty

to one's sovereign and the sovereign's religion were inseparable and constituted a large measure of one's national identity. Rosman, *From Catholic*, 92.

NOTES TO CHAPTER 1

1. BL, Sloane MS 4035, ff. 9v–10.

2. With slight modifications—1 Elizabeth c. 2.

3. For examples, see J. C. H. Aveling, *Northern Catholics: The Catholic Recusants of the North Riding of Yorkshire, 1558–1790* (London: Dublin Chapman, 1966) 22–3, 48–9; Christopher Haigh, "The Continuity of Catholicism in the English Reformation," *Past and Present* (GB) 93 (1981): 41, 45, 61, 68; D. Mathew, *Some Elizabethan Documents* (Bull: Board of Celtic Studies, 1931) vi, 77–8; F.B. Raines, ed., *The State, Civil and Ecclesiastical, of the County of Lancaster*, in Chetham Miscellanies, vol. 5 (Manchester: Chetham Society, old ser., XCVI, 1875) 2, 4–7; Christine Kelly, *Blessed Thomas Belson, His Life and Times, 1563–1589* (Gerrards Cross: Colin Smythe, 1987) 18; Michael Questier, "English Clerical Converts to Protestantism 1580–1596," *Recusant History* 20, no. 4 (October 1991): 458.

4. Raines, *The State*, 2, 4–7.

5. E. E. Reynolds, *Campion and Parsons, The Jesuit Mission of 1580–1* (London: Sheed and Ward, 1980) 17.

6. Marian priests were those ordained during the reign of the Catholic Mary Tudor. The word "mission" will continue to be used in this sense throughout this paper, without regard to the purpose or goals of such activities.

7. The English College at Douai became the mother institution of many English educational institutions across the continent, including English Colleges at Rome, Valladolid, Madrid, and Seville, whose sole purpose was to train the English as priests.

8. Michael Hodgetts, "*Loca Secretiora* in 1581," *Recusant History* 19, no. 4 (1989): 393.

9. Bossy, *ECC*, 217.

10. SP Dom 14/163/74.

11. 13 Eliz I, c. 1 & 2, building upon 35 Henry VIII, c. 2. See also Reynolds, *Campion and Parsons*, 26.

12. Persecution of Catholics and radical Protestants was worse in England than virtually anywhere else during the age of reform. John Coffey, *Persecution and Toleration in Protestant England, 1558–1689* (Harlow, England: Longmans, 2000) 103. Coffey's introduction (3–20) provides a good overall introduction to competing issues and concerns in the struggle for religious uniformity during the Elizabethan and early Stuart years and the post-1640 transition to acceptable religious pluralism.

13   23 Eliz. I, c. 1 discussed in S. J. Watts, *From Border to Middle Shire: Northumberland, 1586–1625* (Bristol: Leicester University Press, 1975) 76. See also Perez Zagorin, *Ways of Lying: Dissimulation, Persecution, and Conformity in Early Modern Europe* (Cambridge, MA: Harvard University Press, 1990) 131.

14   Robert Persons, *Letters and Memorials of Father Robert Persons, SJ, Volume I (to 1588)*, ed. L. Hicks (London: Catholic Record Society, XXXIX, 1942) 86.

15   William Hunt, *The Puritan Moment: The Coming of Revolution in an English County* (Cambridge: Harvard University Press, 1983) 147.

16   27 Eliz I, c. 2.

17   29 Eliz I, c. 6 in Watts, *From Border*, 77.

18   See J. Stanley Leatherbarrow, *The Lancashire Elizabethan Recusants* (Manchester: Chetham Society, new series, CX, 1947) 97–8. Fears of Catholics becoming a "fifth column" to aid a foreign invasion surfaced many times in these decades, for example in 1602 with Spain's landing in Ireland. *CSP Dom* 12/285/52.

19   William Weston, *The Autobiography of an Elizabethan*, trans. Philip Caraman (London: Longmans, Green and Co., 1955) 32.

20   John Gerard as quoted by Christopher Devlin, *The Life of Robert Southwell, Poet and Martyr* (London: Longmans, Green and Co., 1956) 236.

21   Reynolds, *Campion and Parsons*, 208–9.

22   35 Eliz I, c.2.

23   In contrast, the puritans also hoped that James would support their reforms. As he journeyed southward from Scotland to claim the English throne, puritans presented James with the Millenary Petition outlining their platform. See Hunt, *The Puritan Moment*, 105.

24   3 and 4 James I, c. 4, 5; *Statutes of the Realm* IV, ii, 1071; *Statutes at Large*, vol. ii, 542, cited in T.E. Bridgett, *Our Lady's Dowry: How England Gained that Title* (London: Burns & Oates Ltd, n.d.) 451; J.M. Blom, *The Post-Tridentine English Primer* (London: Catholic Record Society, 1982) 35.

25   7 James I, c. 6.

26   *CSP Dom* 14/151/61, 62, 63, 76; 14/155/21.

27   *CSP Dom* 14/163/32, 33, 34; 14/164/47. Also see *CSP Dom* 14/163/74.

28   *CSP Dom* 14/168/22, 64; 14/177/23, 25, 27, 28.

29   Watts, *From Border*, 84; *CSP Dom* 16/5/41.

30   For an example, see BL, Additional MS 33207, ff. 31–4. For a discussion of various aspects of this problem, see Reynolds, *Campion and Parsons*, 3; also Kelly, *Blessed Thomas Belson*, 64–5; A.D. Wright, "Catholic History, North and South, Revisited," *Northern History* 25 (1989): 133.

31   Aveling, *Northern Catholics*, 77–8, 98; Alfred John Kempe, ed., *The Loseley Manuscripts* (London: John Murray, 1836) document #102.

32   Aveling, *Northern Catholics,* 13.

33   Kelly, *Blessed Thomas Belson,* 35.

34   Devlin, *Life of Robert Southwell,* 183.

35   BL, Lansdowne MS 61, f. 47, in Kelly, *Blessed Thomas Belson,* 103, 145.

36   For an excellent discussion of the various elements in play in inadequate enforcement of recusancy laws in Yorkshire, see Aveling, *Northern Catholics,* particularly 92, 95, 104–5, 114, 140.

37   Alexandra Walsham, *Church Papists: Catholicism, Conformity and Confessional Polemic in Early Modern England* (Woodbridge, Suffolk: The Royal Historical Society, The Boydell Press, 1993) 1. See also J. A. Hilton, "The Cumbrian Catholics," *Northern History* 16 (1980): 45.

38   Bossy, *ECC,* Appendix B and 191–2.

39   See, for example, Watts, *From Border,* 75; Haigh, *Lanc,* 269; P.R. Newman, "Roman Catholics in Pre-Civil War England," *Recusant History* 15 (1979): 148–9, cited in Walsham, *Church Papists,* 97; BL, Additional MS 32092, ff. 218r–219v.

40   As John W. O'Malley has pointed out at the macro-level in *Trent and All That: Renaming Catholicism in the Early Modern Era* (Cambridge, MA: Harvard University Press, 2000), the present vocabulary used to discuss issues of Catholic "reform" and "reformation" needs a greater degree of analytical sophistication. And as Walsham has argued regarding England's labels of Catholic vs. Protestant, the presence of a body of active Catholics within the Church of England was a "lasting feature of a complex contemporary religious scene, rather than a bewildered biconfessionalism that disappeared with Dicken's decades of 'survivalism' in the 1570s." Walsham, *Church Papists,* 95 and chap. 1; also Judith Maltby, *Prayer Book and People in Elizabethan and Early Stuart England* (Cambridge: Cambridge University Press, 1998) 2. More recently, Lucy E.C. Wooding, in *Rethinking Catholicism in Reformation England* (Oxford: Clarendon Press, 2000) introduction, discusses in detail the difficulties of modern historians discussing English reform in terms of "Catholic" vs. "Protestant" orthodoxy. See also J.A. Hilton, "The Cumbrian Catholics," *Northern History* 16 (1980) 95.

41   Anne Duffin, *Faction and Faith: Politics and Religion of the Cornish Gentry before the Civil War* (Exeter: University of Exeter Press, 1996) 212. For a detailed discussion of the often unconscious balancing act between conflicting roles in creating identity, see Denise Riley. *"Am I That Name?" Feminism and the Category of "Women" in History* (Minneapolis: University of Minneapolis, 1988).

42   ChRO, DMW 6/118.

43   See also Michael Questier and Simon Healy, "'What's in a Name?' A Papist's Perception of Puritanism and Conformity in the Early Seventeenth Century," in *Catholicism and Anti-Catholicism in Early Modern English Texts,* Arthur F Marotti, ed. (New York: St. Martin's Press, 1999) 137–153; Roland Connelly, *The Women of the Catholic Resistance: In England, 1540–1680* (Edinburgh: The

Pentland Press Limited, 1997) 158; Colleen Marie Seguin, *Addicted unto Piety: Catholic Women in England, 1590–1690* (PhD Dissertation, Duke University, 1997) 55, 113–4, 118, 155, and chap. 4, for similar instances of personal writings of lay English Catholics negotiating issues of importance to English Catholic men, women, and couples.

44   BL Lansdowne MS 776, f. 13, quoted in Questier and Healy "'What's in a Name?'" 137–153.

45   John Nelson to Dr. More, Archpriest George Birkhead's agent in Rome, 8 June 1611, in M. A. Tierney, *Dodd's Church History of England from the Commencement of the Sixteenth Century to the Revolution in 1688*, 5 vols. (London: Charles Dolman, 1839) iv, clxxiii–v.

46   CRO, EDV 1/13, ff. 113v–114, cited in Haigh, *Lanc*, 277, 330–1. See also the example of Richard Eldershawe of Andlyn, Cheshire, cited in Walsham, *Church Papists*, 74; Clare Talbot, ed., *Miscellanea Recusant Records* (London: Catholic Record Society, LIII, 1961) 73, 76, 85; *VCH Staffordshire*, ed. M.W. Greenslade (Oxford: Oxford University Press, 1970) iii, 99–100; as well as Haigh, *Lanc*, 215–6; Haigh, "Continuity," 68.

47   Michael Questier suggests that periodic Catholic conformity teamed with periods of recusancy indicates "more of a relationship between recusancy and conformity" than standard historiography has explored. See Questier, "Conformity, Catholicism and the Law," in *Conformity and Orthodoxy*, 240–1, 248.

48   Haigh, *Lanc*, 249; See also Laurence Vaux, *A catechisme or A Christian doctrine, necessarie for children & ignorant people* (Rotho Magi: Henricum Mareschalum bibliopolum, 1580) xxxiii–iv; Walsham, *Church Papists*, 44, who cites Henry Garnet, *An Apology against the defense of schisme . . .* (n.p.d., 1593) 95; St. Peter Canisius, *Certayne Necessarie Principles of Religion . . .* , trans. T.I. (Douai: 1578–9) sig. B1v; and (Edmund) Thomas Hill, *A Quarton of Reasons of Catholike Religion, with as many briefe reasons of refusall* (Antwerp, 1600) 184.

49   For example, see Gregory Martin, *A Treatise of Schisme, Shewing that al Catholikes ought in any wise to abstain altogether from heretical Conventicles, to witt, their prayers, sermons etc* (Douai: Joannem Foulerum, 1578).

50   See Albert J. Loomie, *The Spanish Elizabethans: The English Exiles at the Court of Philip II* (New York: Fordham University Press, 1963); Wooding, *Rethinking*, 225, 257–8, for more details; see also T. F. Knox, ed., *The First and Second Diaries of the English College at Douai* (London: David Nutt, 1878) introduction.

51   John Bossy, *ECC*, 108–9, 182–194 and "The Character of Elizabethan Catholicism," *Past & Present* 21 (1962): 40–9.

52   These authors' search for Catholics is limited to refusal to attend Prayer Book services. See Watts, *From Border*, 82; Hilton, "The Cumbrian Catholics," 41; Hunt, *The Puritan Moment*, 148; Peter Clark, *English Provincial Society from the Reformation to the Revolution: Religion, Politics, and Society in Kent, 1500–1640* (Hassocks: Harvester Press, 1977) 152, 179; K. L. Wark, *Elizabethan Recusancy in Cheshire* (Manchester: Chetham Society, third series, XIX, 1971) vii, 130.

53 Haigh, *Lanc*, 276; "The fall of the church or the rise of a sect? Post-Reformation Catholicism in England," *Historical Journal* 21 (1978): 181–6; "From monopoly to minority: Catholicism in early modern England," *Transactions of the Royal Historical Society*, fifth series, 31 (1981): 129–47; "The continuity of Catholicism in the English Reformation," *Past & Present* 93 (1981): 37–69. Reprinted in Christopher Haigh, ed., *The English Reformation Revised* (Cambridge: Cambridge University Press, 1987) 176–208; Walsham, *Church Papists*, 49, 95, and "'Yielding to the Extremity of the Time': Conformity, Orthodoxy and the Post-Reformation Catholic Community," in *Conformity and Orthodoxy*, 212; Michael Questier, "Conformity, Catholicism and the Law," *Conformity and Orthodoxy*, 238–41, 256–7. See also Wooding, *Rethinking*, 3; Caroline Hibbard, "Early Stuart Catholicism: Revisions and Rerevisions," *Journal of Modern History* 52 (1980): 1–34; Newman, "Roman Catholicism," 148–52; Patrick McGrath, "Elizabethan Catholicism, a reconsideration," *Journal of Ecclesiastical History* 35 (1984): 414–28.

54 Roger B. Manning, *Religion and Society in Elizabethan Sussex: A Study of the Enforcement of the Religious Settlement, 1558–1603* (Bristol: Leicester University Press, 1969) 241–2.

55 Walsham, "Yielding," *Conformity and Orthodoxy*, 23.

56 See Ann W. Ramsey, *Liturgy, Politics, and Salvation: The Catholic League in Paris and the Nature of Catholic Reform, 1540–1630* (Rochester: University of Rochester Press, 1999) 3–4; Carlos Eire, *War Against the Idols: The Reformation of Worship from Erasmus to Calvin* (Cambridge: Cambridge University Press, 1986) introduction, 24–6, 312–7; Natalie Zemon Davis, "The Sacred and the Body Social in Sixteenth-Century Lyon," *Past and Present* 90 (February 1981).

57 Robert W. Scribner, "The Reformation, Popular Magic, and the 'Disenchantment of the World,'" *Journal of Interdisciplinary History* 23, no. 3 (1993): 478–9.

58 *Decrees of the Ecumenical Councils*, vol. 2, *Trent to Vatican II*, ed. Norman P. Tanner, original text established by G. Albergio, J. A. Dossetti, P.-P. Joannou, C. Leonardi, and P. Prodi, in consultation with H. Jedin (London: Sheed and Ward, Ltd., and Washington, DC: Georgetown University Press, 1990) 693-Session 13; For an explanation of the Catholic Church's doctrine of transubstantiation describing what is believed to occur at the moment the priest consecrates the bread and wine, see Thomas Aquinas, *Summa Theologiae* III, questions 75–77. See also Caroline Walker Bynum, *Holy Feast and Holy Fast: The Religious Significance of Food to Medieval Women* (Berkeley: University of California Press, 1988) and "Women mystics and eucharistic devotion in the thirteenth century," *Women's Studies* 11 (1984): 179–214. Many late medieval women and men claimed to be able to see the bread and wine change into Christ, either as the Christ child, the crucified Christ, or as lumps of flesh and blood.

59 Robert Scribner, "Reformation and Desacralisation: from Sacramental World to Moralized Universe," in R. Po-chia Hsia and R. W. Scribner, eds., *Problems in the Historical Anthropology of Early Modern Europe* (Weisbaden: Harrassowitz

Verlag, 1997) 75–92; See Diarmaid MacCulloch, *Thomas Cranmer: A Life* (New Haven: Yale University Press, 1996) espec. 412–7, 505–8, 527–9, 614–22, for a discussion of doctrinal issues involved within the Church of England and a comparison with continental debates.

60   See chapter 4, fn. 3 for further exposition.

61   For an explanation of the Church of England's belief in the presence of God in the natural world and as accessed through the scriptures, see Hunt, *The Puritan Moment,* 117–8; Alexandra Walsham, *Providence in Early Modern England* (Oxford: Oxford University Press, 2001), intro, chaps. 1, 5.

62   According to the papal bull *Unigenitus,* saints allegedly possessed "superfluous merits," or an excess of grace which they might share with those who prayed to them.

63   *Matthew* 16: 18–20, used by Pope Leo I to establish the Petrine Doctrine justifying the popes, as successors to Peter as Bishop of Rome, as the "first" priests, having authority over remaining clerics.

64   *Decrees,* 732–3, 742.

65   J. H. Pollen, ed., *Unpublished Documents Relating to the English Martyrs, vol. 1, 1584–1603* (London: Catholic Record Society, V, 1908) 313–4.

66   Returns from the Ecclesiastical Commission in York taken before the Lord Mayor and aldermen, 20 Nov 1576, cited in John Morris, ed., *The Troubles of Our Catholic Forefathers Related by Themselves,* 3 vols. (London: Burns & Oates, 1877) iii, 248–50. For a similar account during the reign of Mary, see Claire Cross, "Lay literacy and clerical misconduct in a York parish during the reign of Mary Tudor," *York Historian* 3 (1980): 10, 12, 14 cited in Maltby, *Prayer Book,* 5. Alexandra Walsham agrees that ordinary laypersons understood the issues and participated in the doctrinal controversies of the Reformation to a greater extent than previously expected. Walsham, *Providence,* 32.

67   John Gerard, *The Autobiography of a Hunted Priest,* trans. Philip Caraman (Garden City, NY: Image Books, 1955).

68   See BIY, RVII, HCAB 6, ff. 89, 92v, 110; HCAB 9, f. 175; RVI, a7, ff. 37, 47, 57, 58; Leeds City Library Manuscript Collection, RD/AC/1/4 no. 41; *History of the Chantries within the County Palatinate of Lancashire,* ii, 206, cited in Haigh, *Lanc,* 258.

69   Peter Ackroyd, *The Life of Thomas More* (New York: Nan A. Talese/Doubleday, 1998) quoted by Andrew Sullivan, "Public Man, Public Faith," *New York Times Review of Books,* October 25, 1998: 8.

70   SP Dom 14/22/61.

71   SP Dom 14/21/48. See also BL, Harleian 6211, f. 87r, stanza 67; Harleian 4149, ff. 11v, 14r–17; York Minster Library, Add MS 151, ff. 2, 4, 27–27v. For more on the medicalization of the health of the soul, see Barbara Duden, *The Woman Beneath the Skin: A Doctor's Patients in Eighteenth-Century Germany,* trans. Thomas Dunlap (Cambridge: Harvard University Press, 1991).

72   John A. Hardon, SJ, *Modern Catholic Dictionary* (Garden City, NY: Doubleday and Co., 1980) 236, 488. For a discussion of reformed Catholic and Protestant intellectual debates on salvation, see Wooding, *Rethinking*, ch. 3.

73   See *New Catholic Encyclopedia* (New York: McGraw Hill Book Co., 1967) vi, 666, 672, and particularly xii, 995–7, for a full discussion of the historical development of the doctrine of salvation within the Catholic Church. The necessity of participation in the Catholic Church for reception of saving grace is largely based on Paul's epistles to the Ephesians and Corinthians wherein he claims whoever is separated from this living Mystical Body of Christ which is the church cannot have divine life in him. *Eph* 1.22; 4.4; 5.23; 1 *Cor* 12.27; Thomas Aquinas, *Summa Theologiae*, 1a, 2ae, 110.1–3.

74   The seven sacraments of the Catholic Church are: baptism, confirmation, Eucharist, penance, extreme unction, holy ordination, and marriage. The 1281 Council of Lambeth formulated basic instructions for the English laity on issues of faith. The catechetical form of these instructions, the *Ignorantia Sacerdotum*, formed the foundation of lay belief until Henry VIII's reformation in 1534. See Duffy, *Stripping*, 53–4, 70–3, 75, 81, 86. The Council of Trent, in its attempt to control access to the divine more rigorously, made clear in session 4 (1546) that salvation "is to be sought within the institution and the practices of the church." The most popular English post-Tridentine catechism was Laurence Vaux's *A catechisme or A Christian doctrine, necessarie for children & the ignorant people*, first published in 1568 and reprinted eight times between that date and 1620. The church was considered holy, Vaux instructed, because "in it we are sanctified and made holy in receiving the benefits of God."(12) Vaux taught that "grace, mercy, and sanctification is given to us in the sacraments,"(4) and that the Holy Spirit "sanctifieth us by the Holy Sacraments."(10–11). Holy sacraments were the means to forgiveness of sins, according to Vaux (15). While Vaux never explicitly says that the sacraments are the *only* means to receive grace and sanctification, he never offers any other vehicles that would earn the believer these same benefits.

75   Donald Attwater, ed., *A Catholic Dictionary*, second ed., revised (New York: MacMillan Co., 1949) 441; *New Catholic Encyclopedia*, 658.

76   *Lancashire and Cheshire Wills*, ii, 158; iv, 85–6; v, 33–6, cited in Haigh, *Lanc*, 220–1. Indulgences were granted by Rome "for the remission or payment in whole (plenary indulgence) or in part (partial indulgence), valid before God, of the debt of temporal punishment after the guilt of sin has been forgiven." *New Catholic Encyclopedia*, v. 7, 482–3.

77   SP-Rome, 1572–78, vol. 38, 92, 409.

78   SP Dom 12/256/71.

79   SP Dom 12/206/53.

80   Southwell quoted in Devlin, *Life of Robert Southwell*, 139.

81   As Ramsey, *Liturgy*, chap. 3, explains, "The primary goal of the Tridentine decrees was to provide a new doctrinal clarity about the nature of the sacred and about proper access to it." (44) The Council decreed that the sacraments were to provide the primary channel of access to the sacred. Concomitantly, the priesthood, as the purveyors of the sacraments, would provide supervised access to the sacred. All other avenues to the sacred that remained, such as Mary, the saints, and sacramental items, were carefully controlled and defined by the Council through a careful negotiation between church tradition and doctrine. Such attempts to control access to the sacred, Ramsey postulates, may have contributed to long-term secularization as believers' traditional ability to shape liturgy, religious action, and a personal identification with the sacred was curtailed thus making religion less responsive to believers' needs. (197, 218)

82   For example, see Haigh, "Continuity," 57–9, where Haigh asserts that 51% of the priests who were arrested by Protestant authorities appear to have worked in London and the surrounding Thames valley, although the region was home to only 19% of English Catholics. "Only 18% of the priests worked in the six Northern counties, but 38% of known recusants were in the North." Also 62–3, 67. See also Haigh, *English Reformations*, Chapter 15; Haigh, "Revisionism, the Reformation and the History of English Catholicism," *Journal of Ecclesiastical History* 36 (1985): 394–408; Bossy, *ECC*, 206, 216, 224, 251, 282; Bossy, "Character," 39–59; Hilton, "The Cumbrian Catholics," 41, 58. These characterizations are questioned by McGrath, "Elizabethan Catholicism," 420, 422–28; Walsham, *Church Papists*, 92, and "Yielding," 215, Wright, "Catholic History," 120–34.

83   See Haigh, "Continuity," 52, 58, 60–1; Hilton, The Cumbrian Catholics," 41; Bossy, *ECC*, 4–5, 11–24, 182–4.

84   Weston, *William Weston*, 93.

85   Patrick McGrath and Joy Rowe, "The Elizabethan Priests: Their Harborers and Helpers," *Recusant History* 19, no. 3 (1989): 215, 228–9.

86   For examples, see Gerard, *The Autobiography*, 57, 116, 216.

87   Gerard, *The Autobiography*, 185.

88   Gerard, *The Autobiography*, 44, 193–8.

89   Gerard, *The Autobiography*, 176–8.

90   Wilfrid R. Prest, *The Inns of Court under Elizabeth I and the Early Stuarts 1590–1640* (London: Longman Group Ltd., 1972) 177.

91   Quoted in Kelly, *Blessed Thomas Belson*, 44.

92   From William Warford's "Relation of Martyrs" in Stonyhurst MSS, Grene's Collectanae, quoted in Kelly, *Blessed Thomas Belson*, 74.

93   Morris, *The Troubles*, iii, 18, quoted in McGrath and Rowe, "The Elizabethan Priests," 213. See also Scarisbrick, *The Reformation*, 155–9.

94   Michael Hodgetts, "Topographical Index," *Recusant History* 16: 181, quoted in McGrath and Rowe, "The Elizabethan Priests," 213.

95   McGrath and Rowe, "The Elizabethan Priests," 226–7.

96   For evidence on these pockets in Newcastle and Durham, see Wright, "Catholic History," 132; also Aveling, "Catholic Households," 85.

97   Nancy Pollard Brown, "Paperchase: The Dissemination of Catholic Texts in Elizabethan England," in *English Manuscript Studies, 1100–1700*, vol. I, eds. Peter Beal and Jeremy Griffiths (Oxford: Basil Blackwell, 1989) 121; *A Tudor Journal: The Diary of a Priest in The Tower 1580–1585*, ed. Brian A. Harrison (London: St. Pauls Publishing, 2000) 45, 61; Connelly, *Women*, 41.

98   For an illustration, see Aveling, "Catholic Households," 86. His statistics for Yorkshire between 1568 (the year Douai opened) and 1603 (the end of Elizabeth's reign) reveal that 25% of Jesuit priests were culled from below the gentry class, while 65% of the far more numerous seminary priests possessed non-gentry backgrounds.

99   Wright, "Catholic History," 127.

100   Devlin, *Life of Robert Southwell*, 183; Wright, "Catholic History," 131.

101   Weston, *William Weston*, 62.

102   Weston, *William Weston*, 52.

103   Reynolds, *Campion and Parsons*, 84, 93.

104   Letter from Edmund Campion traveling the countryside in 1580 quoted in Reynolds, *Campion and Parsons*, 85.

105   Walter Mildmay speaking before Star Chamber during the trial of the priests Laurence Vaux, Thomas Tresham, and others, quoted in Anthony G. Petti, ed., *Recusant Documents from the Ellesmere Manuscripts 1577–1715* (London: Catholic Record Society, LX, 1968) 11; For further examples, see Letter of Robert Southwell, 28 December 1588, in Devlin, *Life of Robert Southwell*, 179, as well as 181, 208; Gerard, *The Autobiography*, 63.

106   Aveling, *Northern Catholics*, 93.

107   SP Dom 12/155/8 in Pollen, *Unpublished Documents*, 31–4.

108   Richard Challoner, *Memoirs of Missionary Priests and Other Catholics of Both Sexes that have Suffered Death in England on Religious Accounts from the Year 1577–1684*, vol. 1 (Edinburgh: Thomas C. Jack, Grange Publishing Works, 1878) 74.

109   Hilton, "The Cumbrian Catholics," 44–5.

110   John Radford, *A Directorie Teaching the Way to the Truth in a Briefe and Plaine Discovrse against the heresies of this time* (Printed with License, 1605) A3. See also Kelly, *Blessed Thomas Belson*, x; Reynolds, *Campion and Parsons*, 1; Haigh, "Continuity," 39.

111   Persons, *Letters*, 98.

112   Peter Holmes, *Resistance and Compromise: The Political Thought of the Elizabethan Catholics* (Cambridge: Cambridge University Press, 1982) 57, 62. See also Questier, *Conversion*, chap. 7.

113   Gerard, *The Autobiography*, 58.

114   Haigh, *Lanc*, 249: "By 1563, both the Inquisition in Rome and a committee of the Council of Trent had ruled that in no circumstances was it lawful for English Catholics to be present at the services and sermons of heretics." See Walsham's analysis of this literature in *Church Papists*, chaps. 2–3.

115   Laurence Vaux, *A catechisme or A Christian doctrine, necessarie for children & ignorant people* (orig. 1599), ed. D. M. Rogers (Menston, Yorkshire: Scolar Press, 1969) xxxiii–iv.

116   Vaux, *A catechisme*, 38, 44, 52–3, 81–2.

117   SP Dom 12/118/46. See also Radford, *A Directorie*, 496; Martin, *A Treatise of Schisme*, sigs G3rf, G6v; Garnet, *An Apology*, 189.

118   A. L. Rowse, *Tudor Cornwall: Portrait of a Society* (New York: Charles Scribner's Sons, 1969) 364.

119   For example, John Bucke, in *Instructions for the use of the beades* (orig. 1589) (Menston, Yorkshire: Scolar Press, 1971) 28–9, instructs readers to "suffer all pains, afflictions and adversities which fall upon us for sins or for his sake that endured so much for us. And here learn to detest all false Judgment and corruption of conscience for any fear or reward, lest thou become another Pilate by condemning Christ in his members as he did Christ in his own person." Denying the Catholic faith was deemed synonymous with denying Christ. Even occasional conformity might be too dangerous.

120   Walsham suggests that missionaries may have "modified, softened, and actively resisted" the Roman Church's hard-line stance on strict separation from the Protestants. See "Yielding," 236, and *Church Papists*, chap. 3. Wooding argues that English Catholics began "reconfiguring their own notions of orthodoxy" as early as the 1530s and 1540s as they attempted to convince Henry VIII that he was still "Catholic at heart." She states Catholics searched practically for "a middle ground" to deal with popular religious issues and dispel confusion. Wooding, however, argues that Catholics in the Elizabethan era ceased such activities as they emigrated to the continent and became more dependent on the papacy. Her study ends, however, before 1590. Wooding, *Rethinking*, 49, 271.

121   Holmes, *Resistance*, 117–9. Wooding, *Rethinking*, 139–40, describes earlier Marian priests as understanding that it was their job to reinvigorate the religiosity of the laity and that this might require radical approaches.

122   Holmes, *Resistance*, 100. See also Walsham, *Church Papists*, 65–6.

123   Holmes, *Resistance*, 124–5, 177–81. Caroline Hibbard, on the other hand, argues that certain English Catholic developments such as church papistry perhaps developed from lay freedom when left to make their own way in the absence of an omnipresent priesthood. Hibbard, "Early Stuart Catholicism," 16–8, 21.

124 Reynolds, *Campion and Parsons*, 24.

125 Haigh, "Continuity," 55, refers to the mission "not as an evangelical movement but a pastoral organization: its objective was not the conversion of heretics but the care of Catholics." Haigh, however, does not distinguish changing goals of priests' pastoral efforts over time or seek to identify any changes in the menu of pastoral comforts which priests might offer English Catholics.

126 Haigh admits that the mission was less of a spiritual crusade and more of a series of adjustments to the fact of disestablishment, but he only examines the survival of traditional, late medieval Catholic practices rather than examining the pious practices to see what adjustments might have occurred within the traditions themselves.

127 William Stanney, *A treatise of penance, with an explication of the rule, and maner of living, of the brethren and sisters, of the Third Order of St. Frauncis, comonli called the Order of Penance, ordained for those which desire to leade a holy life, and to doe penance in their owne houses*, Part I (Douai: John Heigham, 1617) epistle.

128 Stanney, *A treatise*, 228–9.

129 Stanney, *A treatise*, 259.

130 *New Catholic Encyclopedia*, xii, 996.

131 For example, see York Minster Library, Add MS 151, f. 18.

132 See Walsham, *Church Papists*, 26–7, who argues that priestly counsel through Catholic polemical works was "the protest of the Counter Reformation priesthood against an ascendant and increasingly autonomous laity and its seemingly studied evasion of sacerdotal supervision."

133 The Legatine Synod at Lambeth in 1556 decreed that when preachers were unavailable, printed works such as books of homilies should be used. Wooding, *Rethinking*, 153. Elizabethan priests, I argue, push this allowance further.

134 York Minster Library, Add MS 151, f. 8. Also Stanney, *A treatise*, 263.

135 For example, a bookseller, James Duckett, admitted that he dealt in Catholic books, providing them to various Catholics for their own comfort and for the comfort of their Catholic neighbors. He clearly assumed a book's audience went beyond the individual to whom he provided the book. Duckett was executed at Tyburn in 1601 for distributing Catholic books. See Challoner, *Memoirs* (1924 ed.), 261–3.

136 See Nancy Pollard Brown's reconstruction of a copying and distribution network (both manuscript and print) for English Catholic pastoral literature in Brown, "Paperchase," 120–143.

137 SP Dom 12/167/47, 12/172/105, 107, 111, 113, 114,

138 SP Dom 12/164/14.

139 i.e. Haigh, "Continuity," 67: "For the illiterate, the book based piety of the gentry household was impossible, and for the Catholic peasants of upland England

in particular, contact with a priest was too irregular and brief to sustain intensive devotion."

140 As Walsham argues, at least until 1600, the worlds of orality and literacy were "tightly interwoven" with print providing a complement and supplement to the spoken word rather than providing a separate sphere of fixed knowledge. *Providence*, 6, 32–5.

141 *CSP Dom* 12/248/37, 39; SP Dom 12/164/59, 60, 61.

142 Radford, *A Directorie*, A3. See also York Minster Library, Add MS 151, 32v–33v, 39–40, and Stanney, 310–1 for further examples of simplified didactic messages.

143 SP Dom 12/164/59, 60, 61.

144 For example, BIY, HCCP 1567/2.

145 For examples, see Thomas Worthington, *Rosarie of Our Lady* (Ingolstadii: Ederiana apud Andreas Angermarium, 1603) and later editions of Vaux's *A catechisme, or a Christian doctrine, necessarie for chyldren and the ignorant people*, which apparently included pictorial catechisms for those who could not read (A&R 749, 750). See also Lewis Richeome, *Holy pictures of the mysticall figures of the most holy sacrifice and sacrament of the Eucharist . . . translated into English for the benefit of those of that Nation as well Protestants as Catholikes*, trans. C.A. (n.p., 1619); SP Dom 12/172/102, where books with images are found in the possession of English Catholics. See Tessa Watt's analysis of the blending of written and pictorial traditions in *Cheap Print and Popular Piety, 1550–1640* (Cambridge: Cambridge University Press, 1991) chap. 4.

146 For example, see Richeome, *Holy pictures*, 4–5.

147 1605 Act of Parliament in Bridgett, *Our Lady's Dowry*, 451.

148 See also, ChRO, EDA 12/2/132r, 132v (2); *SP Dom* 12/230/34, 12/235/40, 14/7/89; Michael G. Brennan, "The Book of Hours of the Braddyll Family of Whalley Abbey (University of Leeds, Brotherton MS 15)," (Liverpool: Historic Society of Lancashire and Cheshire, CXLVI, 1997) 1–12; Brown, "Paperchase," 125–129.

149 SP Dom 16/22/111; Brown, "Paperchase," 121–3, 139.

150 Henry Garnet to Claudio Aquaviva, 16 April 1596, Stonyhurst MS Anglia 2, 16, quoted in Brown, "Paperchase," 140.

151 Blom, *Post-Tridentine*, 43–4.

152 Devlin, *Life of Robert Southwell*, 262.

153 Reynolds, *Campion and Parsons*, 88–91, 99;

154 P. R. Harris, "The Reports of William Udall, Informer, 1605–1612, pt. 1," *Recusant History* 8, no. 4 (Jan 1966): 192. Also BL, Lansdowne MS 153, ff. 11–2, 25–6; SP Dom 14/35/31.

155 Haus Hof und Staats archiv, Vienna PC53 ff. 34–35v in Loomie, *Spain and the Jacobean Catholics, volume 2*, 74.

156 BL, Lansdowne MS 153, ff. 20–1, 70; SP Dom 12/156/15, 12/178/36.

157 Robert Persons to Claudio Aquaviva, 26 Sept 1581, quoted in William Forbes-Leith, *Narratives of Scottish Catholics under Mary Stuart and James VI, Now First Printed from the Original Manuscripts in the Secret Archives of the Vatican and Other Collections* (Edinburgh: William Patterson, 1885) 172–4. Also Fr. James Tyrie to Claudio Aquaviva, 18 Jan 1586, in Forbes-Leith, *Narratives*, 208–9.

158 BL, Lansdowne MS 153, ff. 6, 28–9, 30, 67, 70, 73–4; *Miscellanea VII* (London: Catholic Record Society, IX, 1911) 116–7; SP Dom 12/156/15, 12/158/18, 12/175/74, 14/44/53, 14/151/83.

159 SP Foreign, Flanders, Bundle 9, f. 290, quoted in Harris, *William Udall*, 203–4.

160 BL, Lansdowne MS 153, ff. 22, 68.

161 Earl of Leicester, ambassador to court at France, to Lord Mandeville, February 1640/1, contained in William Drogo Montague, *Court and Society from Elizabeth to Anne*, vol. 1 (London, 1864) 362–4, quoted in Blom, *Post-Tridentine*, 41–2.

162 An excellent example is Thomas Wright, *The Passions of the Mind in General*, ed. William Webster Newbold (New York: Garland Publications Inc., 1986) 3.

163 BIY HCCP 1637/4, 1634/16, Haigh, *Lanc*, 220, 292; ChRO, EDA 12/2/80, 81v, 131, 132–132v, 12/3/28–28v, EDV 1/126/158v, EDC 5, 1596; *Selections from the Household Books of Lord William Howard of Naworth Castle* (Durham: Surtees Society, LXVIII, 1878) 257, 292–3, 363; *CSP Dom* 12/272/36, 16/261/1, 12/271/71, 12/272/81, 12/275/83, 12/287/49; SP Dom 12/154/75, 12/167/47, 12/172/102, 105, 107, 111, 113, 114, 12/176/16, 12/192/54, 12/195/77, 14/7/89, 14/35/31, 14/80/83, 14/87/15, 14/118/102; Wark, *Elizabethan Recusancy*, 138, 160, 167; *Miscellanea VII*, 116–7; BL, Lansdowne MS 42, f. 174; Petti, *Recusant Documents*, 40.

164 BIY HCCP 1567/2; *CSP Dom* 12/248/36, 16/261/1; SP Dom 14/17/47, 14/118/102; Colin Clare, "Christopher Plantin's Trade Connections with England and Scotland," *The Library*, 5th series, 14 (1959): 28–45, quoted by Blom, *Post-Tridentine*, 39.

165 SP Dom 14/80/107.

166 BL, Lansdowne MS 153, ff. 30–1; SP Dom 12/172/8.

167 CRO, Arundel MS 21/15/1, 2, 16, 22; J.H. Pollen, contrib. "Bedingfeld Papers," in *Miscellanea IV* (London: Catholic Record Society, VII, 1909) 28–9, Brennan, "Book of Hours," 1–30.

168 SP Dom 12/238/126ii, iii.

169 SP Dom 12/248/36, 37; SP Dom 14/118/24ii.

170 For examples, see York Minster Library, Add MS 151 and *CSP Dom* 12/248/37.

171 SP Dom 12/158/9, 12/248/36, 14/111/91–2; BL, Lansdowne MS 153, f. 123.

172   Haigh, *Lanc*, 292; BL, Lansdowne MS 153, f. 23.

173   Chamberlain, *Letters*, 186; SP Dom 14/61/111.

174   Robert Southwell to Richard Verstegan in Richard Verstegan, *The Letters and Dispatches of Richard Verstegan (c. 1550–1640)*, ed. Anthony G. Petti (London: Catholic Record Society, LII, 1959) 7–8; SP Dom 14/7/89, 14/35/31; BL, Lansdowne MS 153, ff. 11, 12, 14, 18, 19.

NOTES TO CHAPTER 2

1   Portions of this chapter were previously published as an article entitled "Without Church, Cathedral, or Shrine: The Search for Religious Space among Catholics of England, 1559–1625," *The Sixteenth Century Journal* 33, no. 2 (2002): 381–400.

2   SP Dom 14/8/34.

3   See Margaret Aston, *England's Iconoclasts: vol. 1, Laws against Images* (Oxford: Clarendon Press, 1988). Doreen Rosman, *From Catholic to Protestant: Religion and the People in Tudor England* (London: UCL Press, 1996) 45, argues that such iconoclasm "did much to destroy the concept of sacred space." Alternatively, I propose that the concept of sacred space evolved in new directions.

4   For a more thorough discussion of Catholic immanence, see Chapter 1.

5   Benjamin J. Kaplan investigates similar issues in his study of clandestine churches and changing interpretations of the public and private nature of worship in "Fictions of Privacy: House Chapels and the Spatial Accommodation of Religious Dissent in Early Modern Europe," *American Historical Review* (October 2002): 1031–64.

6   For examples, see SP Dom 12/192/46, 12/216/153, 14/17/31, 14/19/35, 16/61/13; William Brereton, *Journal of Sir William Brereton 1635* (Durham: Surtees Society, CXXIV, 1915) 3; Haus Hof und Staats archiv, Vienna, PC 56, ff. 399–99v, translated in Albert Loomie, ed., *Spain and the Jacobean Catholics: vol. 2, 1613–1624* (London: Catholic Record Society, LXVIII, 1978) 140; Henry Foley, *Records of the English Province of the Society of Jesus*, 7 vols. (London: Burns & Oates, 1877) iv, 147; M. Quiller-Couch and L. Quiller-Couch, *Ancient and Holy Wells of Cornwall* (London: Chas. J. Clark, 1894) 36–41; David Shorney, *Protestant Non-Conformity & Roman Catholicism: a guide to sources in the Public Record Office* (London: PRO Publications, 1996) 74; E.B. Saxton, "A Speke Inventory of 1624" (Liverpool: Historical Society of Lancashire and Cheshire, XCVII, 1945) 109; Christopher Haigh, "The Continuity of Catholicism in the English Reformation," *Past and Present* (GB) 93 (1981): 61; Gilbert H. Doble, *The Saints of Cornwall*, 5 vols. (Chatham: Parrett & Neves Ltd., 1960–1970) ii, 16–17; J.C.H. Aveling, ed., "Recusant Papers of the Meynell Family," in E. E. Reynolds, ed., *Miscellanea VI* (London: Catholic Record Society, 1964) xxv.

7   There is a large body of work, much of it in the field of cultural anthropology, debating the nature and effect of ritual, as Robert W. Scribner discusses in "Historical Anthropology of Early Modern Europe" in R. Po-chia Hsia and R. W. Scribner, eds., *Problems in the Historical Anthropology of Early Modern Europe* (Weisbaden: Harrassowitz Verlag, 1997) 11–34. See also Edward Muir, *Ritual in Early Modern Europe* (Cambridge: Cambridge University Press, 1997) 6, 37; Catherine Bell, *Ritual Theory, Ritual Practice* (Oxford: Oxford University Press, 1992); David Kertzer, *Ritual, Politics, and Power* (New Haven: Yale University Press, 1988); Don Handelman, *Models and Mirrors: Towards an Anthropology of Public Events* (Cambridge: Cambridge University Press, 1990).

8   St. Clement, "Where and with whom we may pray," quoted in Richard Broughton, *A Manual of Praiers vsed by the Fathers of the Primitive Church, for the most part within the foure first hundred years of Christ, and all before the end of the sixt hundred yeare* (n.p., 1618) 25–6. Ironically, the Protestants used this same passage from *Matthew* to deny the Catholic priesthood's role as mediators between Christ and the faithful.

9   John Bossy, *The English Catholic Community, 1570–1850* (London: Darton, Longman & Todd, 1975) 125, has noted that historians tend to focus more upon a withdrawal of Catholics from Protestant sites and practices than they do upon the creation of new experiences. Bossy, however, never follows the logical consequences of this statement to explore in depth the multitude of experiences possible for Catholics in this era other than by looking at withdrawal.

10   For example, see *Quarter Sessions Roll* 32 Eliz (1590) in James Tait, ed., *Lancashire Quarter Sessions Records*, vol. 1 (Manchester: Chetham Society, new series, LXXVII, 1917) 12.

11   York Minster Library, Add MS 151, ff. 34v–35v.

12   York Minster Library, Add MS 151, ff. 34v–35v.

13   York Minster Library, Add MS 151, ff. 34v–35v.

14   SP Dom 14/8/34.

15   Foley, *Records*, iv, 141.

16   *Biography of Dorothy Lawson*, 30, quoted in Connelly, *Women*, 187.

17   See David Hillman and Carla Mazzio, eds., *The Body in Parts: Fantasies of Corporeality in Early Modern Europe* (London: Routledge, 1997) xiii. Hillman and Mazzio argue that "the spatially imagined body was perhaps the most common vehicle for the making of social and cosmic metaphors in early modern Europe."

18   York Minster Library, Add MS 151, f. 36r.

19   Connelly, *Women*, 209.

20   Stanney, *A treatise of penance*, 145–6, 259.

21   J. A. Twemlow, ed., *Liverpool Town Books, vol. 2, 1571–1603, Proceedings of Assemblies, Common Councils, Portmoot Courts, etc.* (Liverpool: University

Press of Liverpool, 1935) 243. For other uses of the sign of the cross, see *Selections from the Household Books of Lord William Howard of Naworth Castle* (Durham: Surtees Society, LXVIII, 1878) lxii; Richard Challoner, *Memoirs of Missionary Priests and Other Catholics of Both Sexes that Have Suffered Death in England on Religious Accounts from the Year 1577–1684*, vol. 1 (London: Burns, Oates & Washbourne, Ltd., 1924) 276.

22   Arthur Crowther and Thomas Vincent, *Jesus, Maria Joseph, or, The Devout Pilgrim, of the Ever Blessed Virgin Mary, in His Holy Exercises, Affections, and Elevations* (Amsterdam, 1657) 238–40. See also Richard Bristow, *A Briefe Treatise of diverse plaine and sure wayes to finde out the truthe in this doubtful and dangerous time of Heresie* . . . (Antwerp, 1574) 38–9.

23   Richard Challoner's account taken from Dr. Anthony Champney's *Annals of 1618* in Connelly, *Women*, 110.

24   See Julian Yates, "Parasitic Geographies: Manifesting Catholic Identity in Early Modern England," in *Catholicism and Anti-Catholicism in Early Modern English Texts*, ed. Arthur F. Marotti (New York: St. Martin's Press, 1999) 63–84, who contrasts Protestant and Catholic ideas regarding religious use of space.

25   Patrick McGrath and Joy Rowe, "The Imprisonment of Catholics for Religion under Elizabeth," *Recusant History* 20, no. 4 (October 1991): 415–35.

26   McGrath and Rowe, "The Imprisonment," 416–420; Christine Kelly, *Blessed Thomas Belson, His Life and Times 1563–1589* (Gerrards Cross: Colin Smythe, 1987) 23.

27   For a full discussion of the Catholic prison system, see E. E. Reynolds, *Campion and Parsons, The Jesuit Mission of 1580–1* (London: Sheed and Ward, 1980) 69, as well as Geoffrey de C. Parmiter, "The Imprisonment of Papists in Private Castles," *Recusant History* 19, no. 1 (May 1988): 17.

28   Geoffrey de C. Parmiter, "Sir Alexander Colepepper of Bedgebury," *Recusant History* 19, no. 4 (October 1989): 374.

29   As quoted by Christopher Devlin, *The Life of Robert Southwell, Poet and Martyr* (London: Longmans, Green and Co., 1956) 106.

30   For an example, see Devlin, *Life of Robert Southwell*, 106.

31   *CSP Dom* 12/274/5; Devlin, *Life of Robert Southwell*, 106.

32   William Weston, *William Weston: The Autobiography of an Elizabethan*, trans. Philip Caraman (London: Longmans, Green and Co., 1955) 165.

33   *CSP Dom* 16/26/89; "Notes by a Prisoner in Ousebridge Kidcote (York)," Stonyhurst MS, Angl. A, ff. 41–8, in John Morris, ed., *The Troubles of Our Catholic Forefathers Related by Themselves*, 3 vols. (London: Burns & Oates, 1877) iii, 270–1.

34   *CSP Dom* 12/273/23 ii, iii, vii, viii.

35   For examples, see Weston, *William Weston*, 163–4; Challoner, *Memoirs*, 92. See also Coffey, *Persecution*, 88–91.

36 Devlin, *Life of Robert Southwell*, 275.

37 Foley, *Records*, vi, 149.

38 Devlin, *Life of Robert Southwell*, 183.

39 Challoner, *Memoirs*, 80. See also Richard Vaughan, bishop of Chester, to Thomas Hesketh, 29 Jan 1598, quoted in Philip Caraman, ed., *The Other Face: Catholic Life Under Elizabeth I* (London: The Camelot Press Ltd., 1960) 216; Also, McGrath and Rowe, "The Imprisonment," 429; "Notes by a Prisoner in Ousebridge Kidcote (York)," ff. 41–8; *CSP Dom* 12/285/52.

40 Ellesmere MS 2124, f. 45v, printed in Anthony G. Petti, ed., *Recusant Documents from the Ellesmere Manuscripts 1577–1715* (London: Catholic Record Society, LX, 1968).

41 Ellesmere MS 2132, f. 59v.

42 Ellesmere MS 2139, ff. 70v–71.

43 English College Rome, Collectanea F, f. 90, printed in J. H. Pollen, ed., *Unpublished Documents Relating to the English Martyrs, vol. 1. 1584–1603* (London: Catholic Record Society, V, 1908) 345. For further examples, see Ellesmere MS 2128, f. 51; Ellesmere MS 2129, f. 53; Ellesmere MS 2130, f. 55v; Ellesmere MS 2131, f. 57; Ellesmere MS 2134, f. 63v; Ellesmere MS 2137, ff. 67–67v; Challoner, *Memoirs*, 61, 92.

44 McGrath and Rowe, "The Imprisonment," 425. See also *CSP Dom* 12/248/43.

45 *CSP Dom* 12/256/116.

46 SP Dom 12/248/36; *CSP Dom* 12/272/107.

47 Ellesmere MS 2134, f. 63.

48 Ellesmere MS 2126, f. 48.

49 Ellesmere MS 2123, f. 43.

50 Ellesmere MS 2128, f. 51; Ellesmere MS 2129, f. 53; Ellesmere MS 2130, f. 55v; Ellesmere MS 2131, f. 57; Ellesmere MS 2134, f. 63v; Ellesmere MS 2137, ff. 67–67v.

51 Oscott MS, Kirk's Collections, vol. 1, 33, printed in Pollen, *Unpublished Documents*, 182.

52 Weston, *William Weston*, 154.

53 *CSP Dom* 12/283/70. See also Devlin, *Life of Robert Southwell*, 91; Weston, *William Weston*, 176; Challoner, *Memoirs*, 69–71, for further examples.

54 SP Dom 14/91/20. See also, "The undated Petition of William Tirwhit from the Tower to Sir Francis Walsingham" in *A Tudor Journal: The Diary of a Priest in The Tower 1580–1585*, ed. Brian A. Harrison (London: St. Pauls Publishing, 2000) 162; McGrath and Rowe, "The Imprisonment," 422–3.

55 BL, Lansdowne MS 38, f. 87; *CSP Dom* 12/194/32, 12/268/3, 12/285/52.

56   For example, see SP Dom 14/80/78. See also Parmiter, "The Imprisonment of Papists," 31.

57   Richard Verstegan, *The letters and dispatches of Richard Verstegan*, ed. Anthony G. Petti (London: Catholic Record Society, LII, 1959) 250; SP Dom 12/151/5, 12/190/51, 62.

58   Weston, *William Weston*, 167. For a further example of English Catholics interpreting such visits to priests as pilgrimages, see John Mush's description of Margaret Clitheroe's activities in Arthur F. Marotti, "Alienating Catholics in Early Modern England: Recusant Women, Jesuits and Ideological Fantasies," in *Catholicism and Anti-Catholicism*, 6

59   *Acts of Privy Council*, vol. 25, 418–9; *Acts of Privy Council*, vol. 23, 235; SP Dom 12/203/38i–iv.

60   Fr Curry to Fr Robert Persons, Stonyhurst MS, Grene's Collectanae M, f. 193, quoted in Weston, *William Weston*, 176; SP Dom 14/80/78.

61   For examples of Mass in prisons, see BIY, R VI, A 14, f. 2v; Westminster Archives, iv, 293, 309, quoted in Pollen, *Unpublished Documents*, 208; *CSP Dom* 12/248/116, 12/285/59, 14/72/77; Stonyhurst MS, Angl. A, ff. 41–8, quoted in Morris, *Troubles*, iii, 270–1; McGrath and Rowe, "The Imprisonment," 421–5 (quoting *Salisbury* XI, 363); *A Tudor Journal*, 152; Devlin, *Life of Robert Southwell*, 106, 191; Weston, *William Weston*, 163–4; Challoner, *Memoirs*, 96, 252; K.R. Wark, *Elizabethan Recusancy in Cheshire* (Manchester: Chetham Society, third series, XIX, 1971) 169; Connelly, *Women*, 54.

62   Weston, *William Weston*, 117.

63   Challoner, *Memoirs*, 252.

64   Reynolds, *Campion and Parsons*, 69.

65   For examples of confessions in prisons, see Pollen, *Unpublished Documents*, 265, 287; Weston, *William Weston*, 201; *CSP Dom* 12/97/27; SP Dom 12/248/43.

66   Pollen, *Unpublished Documents*, 287.

67   For examples of marriages in prisons, see SP Dom 12/243/93, 12/256/71.

68   SP Dom 16/22/111; Morris, *Troubles*, iii, 38, 40, 322; Edwin H. Burton, *London Streets & Catholic Memories* (London: Burns, Oates & Washbourne Ltd., 1925) 33; Connelly, *Women*, 117; McGrath, "Apostate priests," 69; J. C. H. Aveling, "Catholic Households in Yorkshire, 1580–1603," *Northern History* 16 (1980): 89–90; Stanney, *A treatise*, 236–44.

69   Devlin, *Life of Robert Southwell*, 117; Weston, *William Weston*, 117, *CSP Dom* 12/286/57.

70   A.L. Rowse, *Tudor Cornwall: Portrait of a Society* (New York: Charles Scribner's Sons, 1969) 364–5.

71   See also, *CSP Dom* 12/248/116.

72   Thomas Dowlton, examination at Rye and later at Lambeth in June 1595, quoted in Appendix to Weston, *William Weston*, 243. For further evidence of reconciliation performed in the prisons, see Challoner, *Memoirs*, 261–3.

73   Weston, *William Weston*, 169.

74   SP Dom 14/80/84. For conversion of a yeoman warder at the Tower of London, see *A Tudor Journal*, 69.

75   McGrath and Rowe, "The Imprisonment," 417.

76   Michel de Certeau, *The Mystic Fable*, trans. Michael B. Smith (Chicago: University of Chicago Press, 1992) 97–8, argues that secrecy itself creates a "play between actors" and this, in essence, is a type of communal relationship. "The hidden organizes a social network."

77   For example, see Walsham's treatment of the apostatizing of the priest Thomas Bell in "'Yielding to the Extremity of the Time': Conformity, Orthodoxy and the Post-Reformation Catholic Community," in *Conformity and Orthodoxy in the English Church, c. 1560–1660*, eds. Peter Lake and Michael Questier (Woodbridge: The Boydell Press, 2000) 228–36.

78   Challoner, *Memoirs*, 38. See also example in York Minster Library, Add MS 151, f. 53v.

79   For examples, see SP Dom 12/150/72, 12/152/39; See also entries for 5 Feb 1581 and 31 Aug 1581 in *A Tudor Journal*, 41, 45.

80   See P. J. Holmes, ed., *Elizabethan Casuistry* (London: Catholic Record Society, LXVII, 1981) and Alexandra Walsham, *Church Papists: Catholicism, Conformity, and Confessional Polemic in Early Modern England* (Woodbridge, Suffolk: The Royal Historical Society, The Boydell Press, 1993) chaps. 2–3, for a comprehensive treatment of rhetorical training of the English priesthood at the English colleges on the continent.

81   Devlin, *Life of Robert Southwell*, 305–15.

82   English College Rome, Collectanea F, f. 90, in Pollen, *Unpublished Documents*, 354–5.

83   Gerard, *Autobiography*, 85 quoted in Connelly, *Women*, 110.

84   Challoner, *Memoirs*, 261–3.

85   For an example, see *CSP Dom* 12/279/53.

86   Challoner, *Memoirs*, 86–90.

87   Challoner, *Memoirs*, 90.

88   See chapter one for a full discussion of the mission.

89   SP Dom 12/238/168, 14/119/47.

90   Thomas H. Clancy, SJ, "Priestly Perseverance in the Old Society of Jesus: The Case of England," *Recusant History* 19, no. 3 (1989): 289, 292.

91   Sir Charles Somerset, *The Travel Diary (1611–1612) of an English Catholic*, ed.
      Michael Brennan (Leeds: Leeds Philanthropical and Literary Society Ltd., 1993)
      221.

92   For example, see the account of the future martyr Margaret Clitheroe's pilgrim-
      age to the execution site of English martyrs at Knavesmere, in John Mush, "A
      True Report of the Life and Martyrdom of Mrs. Margaret Clitherow," in Morris,
      Troubles, 395.

93   Challoner, *Memoirs*, 96. As Brad S. Gregory has pointed out, the sites of public
      executions could serve as "powerful arena[s] for evangelization," sparking inter-
      est in and perhaps conversion to the persecuted faith. *Salvation at Stake:
      Christian Martyrdom in Early Modern Europe* (Cambridge: Harvard University
      Press, 1999) 7.

94   Or Sandys.

95   George Oliver, *Collections Illustrating the History of the Catholic Religion in the
      Counties of Cornwall, Devon, Dorset, Somerset, Wiltshire, and Gloucester, in two
      parts, Historical and Biographical. With notices of the Dominican, Benedictine,
      & Franciscan Orders* (London: Charles Dolman, 1857) 101.

96   SP Dom 14/71/64, 65. See also SP Dom 14/69/67, 14/80/102; Oliver, *Collections*,
      101; and Joseph Mawson, "John Mawson, layman, martyr 1612, & Some Catholic
      Mawsons," in *Miscellanea XII* (London: Catholic Record Society, XXII, 1921) for
      further examples.

97   See also the analysis of the martyrdom of Margaret Clitheroe in Chapter 4.

98   Stonyhurst MS, Collectanea M, f. 160, in Pollen, *Unpublished Documents*,
      285–6.

99   For a similar example, see the description of Father Thomas Bullaker's trip to the
      gallows in 1642 in which he is accompanied by gentlewomen and "penitents" who
      disguised themselves and walked through deep dirt by the side of the hurdle,
      speaking with the priest and kissing his hands. Stonyhurst MS, Collectanea M,
      1642, discussed in Connelly, *Women*, 214.

100   SP Dom 12/53/78.

101   Reynolds, *Campion and Parsons*, 199–200.

102   Devlin, *Life of Robert Southwell*, 319.

103   For an example, see Robert Southwell's description of his service to the men con-
      demned in the Babington plot in Devlin, *Life of Robert Southwell*, 122, as well
      as the description of Thomas Bullaker's execution in Challoner, *Memoirs*, 454.

104   Don Jaime Nochera from an Irish manuscript in Historical Manuscripts
      Commission, LXV, 212–3, from the Franciscan Library at Killiny MS D4, f. 452,
      quoted in Timothy J. McCann, "Some Unpublished Accounts of the Martyrdom
      of Blessed Thomas Bullaker, OSF of Chichester in 1642," *Recusant History* 19,
      no. 2 (1988): 174. See also *CSP Rome*, ser. 38, vol. 2, 568, appendix 7; *CSP Dom*

14/71/65; Verstegan, *The letters*, 242; Rowse, *Tudor Cornwall*, 364–5; Morris, *Troubles*, iii, 221; Burton, *London Streets*, 52.

105 SP Dom 14/80/84. See fn. 93 of this chapter for an example of another priest, George Haydock, making this request in 1584. Either Ainsworth had been in prison and instructing condemned prisoners for approximately 30 years, or Ainsworth was just one in a line of priests making such a recommendation and promoting Catholic unity.

106 Perhaps fearing that his voice would be silenced upon the gallows before he could speak, the martyred English priest Ingram wrote verses prior to his execution, exhorting Catholics to cling to their faith.

> *I have lived in the religion of my sir[e]s, for it I am a prisoner*
>
> *Do you according to the example given you in my death.*

Stonyhurst MS, Angl, vii, no. 8, in Pollen, *Unpublished Documents*, 278. See also Challoner, *Memoirs*, 28.

107 The Christocentric symbolism and significance of this example and the next have been analyzed in more detail in Chapter 4. Weston, *William Weston*, 114.

108 Challoner, *Memoirs*, 43–6.

109 BL, Lansdowne MS 350, f. 9; Reynolds, *Campion and Parsons*, 205; See also Seccion de Estado, Archivo General de Simancas 2589/45, quoted in Albert Loomie, ed., *Spain and the Jacobean Catholics: vol. 1, 1603–1612* (London: Catholic Record Society, LXIV, 1973) 196.

110 For details and an alternative interpretation of this event, see Rowse, *Tudor Cornwall*, 364–5.

111 BL, Lansdowne MS 153, f. 68; SP Dom 14/21/5, 14/216/218 a–b; *CSP Dom* 12/287/51.

112 *CSP Dom* 12/192/57.

113 Quoted in J. M. Blom, *The Post-Tridentine English Primer* (London: Catholic Record Society, 1982) 89. See also "Verses in Praise of Campion & Others" in SP Dom 14/32/4.

114 Stonyhurst MS, Collectanae M, f. 160, in Pollen, *Unpublished Documents*, 286.

NOTES TO CHAPTER 3

1 Portions of this chapter were previously published as an article of the same name in *The Journal of Religious History* 27, no. 2 (2003): 161–176.

2 Helen Whelan, *Snow on the Hedges: A Life of Cuthbert Mayne* (Leominster, Herefordshire: Fowler Wright Books, 1984) 119, 130.

3 Crafted c. 1500 and used by the English Catholic Lord William Howard of Naworth in the first half of the seventeenth century and currently on display at the Victoria and Albert Museum in London, Ref. no. M. 30–1934.

4   Stephen Greenblatt, *Shakespearean Negotiations: The Circulation of Social Energy in Renaissance England* (Berkeley: University of California Press, 1988) 4–5, suggests scholars examine the ways in which meanings were shifted from medium to medium and "concentrated in manageable aesthetic form. . ."

5   English priests went to great lengths to conform to the Council of Trent's reforms at the same time as they reconceptualized the rosary and Mary to fulfill their pastoral roles. Their instructions educated rosarists about the histories of each type of prayer and explained how the prayer gained its efficacy. They wanted no misunderstanding or misapplication of the prayers for purposes for which the Church did not approve. See Anthony Batt, *A Poore mans mite. A letter of a religious man of the Order of St. Benedict unto a Sister of his, concerning the Rosarie or Psalter of our Blessed Ladie, Commonly called the Beads* (Douai: Widow of Mark Wyon, 1639) 9–11; Arthur Crowther and Thomas Vincent, *Jesus, Maria, Joseph, or, The Devout Pilgrim, of the Ever Blessed Virgin Mary, in His Holy Exercises, Affections, and Elevations* (hereinafter referred to as *JMJ*) (Amsterdam, 1657) 80–2; See also Eamon Duffy, *The Stripping of the Altars: Traditional Religion in England, 1400–1580* (New Haven: Yale University Press, 1992) 362; Keith Thomas, *Religion and the Decline of Magic* (New York: Charles Scribner's Sons, 1971) 41–3; Virginia Reinburg, "Liturgy and Laity in Late Medieval and Reformation France," *Sixteenth Century Journal* 23, no. 3 (1992): 526, 529.

6   Crowther and Vincent, *JMJ*, 295.

7   This may be followed by a *Gloria Patri*.

8   Henry Garnet, *The societie of the rosary* (n.p., 1596/7) 182–3. See also Thomas Worthington, *Rosarie of Our Lady* (Ingolstadii: Ederiana apud Andreas Angermarium, 1603) 8a.

9   The angelical salutation is another name for the *Ave Maria*.

10   Crowther and Vincent, *JMJ*, 189. Garnet, *The societie*, 169, also cites Christ's and Paul's use of prayers of this type.

11   Batt, *A Poore mannes mite*, 3, 14.

12   This would have been neither unusual nor undesirable within the Catholic Church. See Theodor Klauser, *A Short History of the Western Liturgy: An Account and Some Reflections*, trans. John Halliburton (Oxford: Oxford University Press, 1969) and John C. Olin, *Catholic Reform from Cardinal Ximenes to the Council of Trent, 1495–1563: An Essay with Illustrative Documents and a Brief Study of St. Ignatius Loyola* (New York: Fordham University Press, 1990).

13   For example, Thomas Stapleton, *Promptuarium Catholicum* (Louvain, 1589) Op. tom. iv, 838, who lists the five joyful mysteries as the Annunciation, Visitation, Nativity of Christ, Adoration of the Magi, and the Confession of Simeon and Anna. Alternatively, Father Arias, a Spanish Jesuit writing at the end of the sixteenth century as well, lists the five joyful mysteries as the Annunciation,

Incarnation, Visitation, Birth, and Presentation. T. E. Bridgett, *Our Lady's Dowry: How England Gained that Title* (London: Burns & Oates Ltd., n.d.) 214–5. Certain special types of prayers which focused on a more specific Marian or Christocentric devotion were also often attached to the beads, i.e. the Golden Rosary in Batt, *A Poore mans mite*, 14; the brief rosary "in memory of seven principal sorrows and eight joys of our Blessed Ladie" in Worthington, *Rosarie*, 5b; or the Rosary of the Holy Name of Jesus in Crowther and Vincent, *JMJ*, 463.

14   See chapters 1 and 4 for a more full explanation of the sacraments.

15   This distinction was made in the twelfth and thirteenth centuries. Sacramentals were defined in canon law (CIC c. 1144) as "things or actions that the Church is accustomed to use, in imitation of the Sacraments, in order to obtain through her intercession certain effects, especially spiritual ones." Vatican II ceased identifying objects as sacramentals, limiting the definition to the rituals performed upon the objects. See *New Catholic Encyclopedia*, vol. 12, 790–2.

16   Robert Scribner, "The Reformation, Popular Magic, and the 'Disenchantment of the World,'" *Journal of Interdisciplinary History* 23, no. 3 (1993): 478–9. By the later Middle Ages, Catholic priests blessed many objects for sacramental use, and their effectiveness was held to be "analogous to that of the sacraments" but not identical. Sacramental rituals include actions such as prayer, dipping, anointing, eating, confession, giving, and blessing. See Donald Attwater, ed., *A Catholic Dictionary*, 2nd ed., revised (New York: MacMillan Company, 1949) 441.

17   *New Catholic Encyclopedia*, vol. 12, 790–2. See also chapter 1's discussion of the nature of the power given to the priesthood and of apostolic succession.

18   Canon law (CIC c. 1144) declared that "through them [sacramentals] in their own way come graces, remission of sin and temporal punishment, etc." *New Catholic Encyclopedia*, vol. 12, 790–2.

19   The Jesuits, in particular, would have felt the necessity of providing alternatives to traditional worship to meet the special needs of the English Catholics struggling against the flow of Protestant reform in England. The Jesuits viewed the Reformation as a pastoral problem, not a doctrinal one. The declining spiritual morale of the laity allowed Protestant reform to take root, therefore Jesuits felt the need to address this condition and provide avenues to renew individual piety and devotion. See John W. O'Malley, *The First Jesuits* (Cambridge: Harvard University Press, 1993).

20   Scribner, "The Reformation," 480.

21   Thomas Wright, *The Passions of the Mind in General*, ed. William Webster Newbold (New York: Garland Publications, Inc., 1986) 200–1.

22   See chapter 1 for a discussion of the penal laws' prohibitions against such objects. See also BL, Cotton MS, Titus CVII, f. 60.

23   ChRO, EDA 12/2/82; EDA 12/3/4–4v; EDV 1/10/122v; EDV 1/10/155; EDV 1/13/163–4; SP Dom 12/167/47, 12/168/6, 12/198/12, 12/206/53, 12/248/31, 12/248/36, 12/256/71, 14/18/82, 14/81/54, 58, 14/89/24, 14/94/1, 16/12/58.

24   BL, Lansdowne MS 25, f. 167; *CSP Dom* 12/27/93, 16/12/58; John Morris, ed., *The Troubles of Our Catholic Forefathers Related by Themselves*, 3 vols. (London: Burns & Oates, 1877) iii, 221.

25   SP Dom 12/167/30. See also PRO Coram Rege Roll 26, 27 Eliz, Michaelmas, Crown side, rot. 3, printed in J. Hungerford Pollen, ed., *Unpublished Documents Relating to the English Martyrs: vol. 1, 1584–1603* (London: Catholic Record Society, V, 1908) 100.

26   *CSP Dom* 14/81/54; see also SP Dom 14/123/115 and 14/124/30.

27   ChRO, EDC 1/17/88v; EDV 1/4/13v; Christopher Haigh, *Reformation and Resistance in Tudor Lancashire* (Cambridge: Cambridge University Press, 1975) 219.

28   ChRO, EDV 1/12a/117.

29   Examinations of Francis Richardson and Thomas Marrow, *Miscellanea VII* (London: Catholic Record Society, IX, 1911) 116–7; SP Dom 12/167/4; *CSP Dom* 12/153/41, 12/179/4; SP Dom 14/123/115.

30   *CSP Dom* 12/27/9, 12/137/47, 12/156/15, 12/179/4.

31   CRO, AD 37/50/20; *PCC* 30, A.L. Rowse, *Tudor Cornwall: Portrait of a Society* (New York: Charles Scribner's Sons, 1969) 434.

32   HMC, 12th Report, *The MSS of the Earl Cowper*, Appendix, ii, 216 contained in J. M. Blom, *The Post-Tridentine English Primer* (London: Catholic Record Society, 1982) 40. For further examples, see William Forbes-Leith, *Memoirs of the Scottish Catholics during the Seventeenth and Eighteenth Centuries, selected from hitherto unedited manuscripts* (London: Longmans, Green, 1909) 161–2; Foley, *Records*, v, 764, quoted in Roland Connelly, *The Women of the Catholic Resistance: In England, 1540–1680* (Edinburgh: The Pentland Press Limited, 1997) 195. Also, those who wandered professionally possessed opportunities to distribute sacramentals. Minstrelsy was seen as a cover for recusants, says A. L. Beier in *Masterless Men: The vagrancy problem in England 1560–1640* (London: Methuen, 1985) 97. Beier reports that "an ecclesiastical inquiry in Durham diocese in the 1570s warned that popery and rebellion were spread by minstrels singing bawdy songs. The charge was not wholly absurd: in 1608 a man was presented at North Riding quarter sessions for harboring a fiddler suspected of recusancy, and a Derbyshire piper was ordered to stand trial in 1616 in Nottinghamshire for carrying beads, crucifixes and books." Beier lists his source as Walter Woodfill, *Musicians in English Society from Elizabeth to Charles I* (Princeton: Princeton University Press, 1953) 129–30; NRQS (North Riding Quarter Sessions Records), ed. J. C. Atkinson (1884–1892), i, 105; Notts. RO QSM IV.181.

33   SP Dom 16/22/111.

34   *CSP-Scotland, Mary Queen of Scots Papers*, 16/7.

35 Bridgett, *Our Lady's Dowry*, 493. See also William Eric Brown, *John Ogilvie: An account of his life & death with a translation of documents relating thereunto* (London: Burns, Oates & Washbourne, Ltd., 1925).

36 Worthington, *Rosarie*, 3b–4a.

37 Stonyhurst MS, Angl. A., ff. 41–48, in Morris, *Troubles*, iii, 270–1. For a related situation, see Stonyhurst MS, Collectanea M, f. 160, in Pollen, *Unpublished Documents*, 286.

38 SP Dom 12/152/39. See also SP Dom 16/22/111.

39 SP Dom 12/251/13.

40 John Bucke, *Instructions for the use of the beades* . . . (1589; reprint, Menston, Yorkshire: Scolar Press, 1971) insert. See Anne Winston-Allen's discussion of medieval pictorial instructions for rosary use in *Stories of the Rose: The Making of the Rosary in the Middle Ages* (University Park, PA: Pennsylvania State University Press, 1997) chap. 2.

41 Crowther and Vincent, *JMJ*, 307–8, provide a series of pithy verses to aid in remembering the mysteries of the rosary in the event the petitioner has no beads.

42 Garnet, *The societie*, 1–5. According to Winston-Allen, *Stories*, 28, the Society's popularity was largely related to its unrestrictive membership policy. Anyone could join, even women, of any rank.

43 Bridgett, *Our Lady's Dowry*, 490; Hilda Graef, *Mary: A History of Doctrine and Devotion*, 2 vols. (London: Sheed and Ward, 1987), ii, 18–9.

44 Bucke, *Instructions*, 84–5; Also Garnet, *The societie*, 182–3.

45 For examples, see BL, Lansdowne MS 153, ff. 67–8, 73–4; SP Dom 12/195/77; *The MSS of the Earl Cowper*, Appendix, ii, 216, in Blom, *Post-Tridentine*, 40; Linda Kay Hoff, *Hamlet's Choice: Hamlet—A Reformation Allegory*, Studies in Renaissance Literature, ii (Lewiston, NY/Queenston, Ont./Lampeter, Wales: The Edwin Mellon Press, 1988) 199.

46 For example, see *A chayne of twelve links. To wit XII Catholick conditions concerning certaine graces & indulgences, of Christes Catholick Church . . . Translated out of Italian into English by I.W. Whereunto are annexed, the indulgences graunted unto the Society of the Rosary . . . together with those that are geven to holy graynes, crosses & medales of the English pardon, & the pardon of Boromeus* (n.p., 1617), 99–. Also BL, Sloane MS 3785, ff. 16–16v; SP Dom 12/137/47 (1580), 16/22/111; *CSP Dom* 12/143/33.

47 Garnet, *The societie*, A3v–5v. See also Hoff, *Hamlet's Choice*, 197.

48 Typically known as the Confraternity of the Rosary on the continent, the entire organization boasted over a million members (living and deceased) immediately prior to the Reformation era. Winston-Allen, *Stories*, 2, and see chap. 3 for a detailed discussion of the controversy over the origins of the organization. See also Donna Spivey Ellington, *From Sacred Body to Angelic Soul: Understanding*

Mary in Late Medieval and Early Modern Europe (Washington D.C.: Catholic University of America, 2001) 215–7.

49   Winston-Allen, *Stories*, 120.

50   Previous popes such as Julius III and Pius V denied indulgences to any branches of the society not instituted by the General of the Dominicans. Garnet, *The societie*, 16–7. SP Dom 12/238/168 from 1591 mentions "an authority of the general of the Dominicans to institute a confratia of the Rosary" in England.

51   See Garnet, *The societie*; Arthur Crowther and Thomas Vincent, *JMJ*, as well as *The Dayly Exercise of the Devout Rosarists Containing several most pithy Practices of Devotion: profitable not only for such as are members of the sacred Rosary, but also for all pious Christians* (Amsterdam, 1657); Batt, *A Poore mans mite*; Bucke, *Instructions*; *A chayne of twelve links*.

52   *CSP Dom* 12/238/168.

53   Crowther and Vincent, *JMJ*, 112–129.

54   SP Dom 12/243/80; *CSP Dom* 12/243/80.

55   Garnet, *The societie*, 18–21.

56   Crowther and Vincent also modified entrance requirements into the Society. See Crowther and Vincent, *JMJ*, 109. For this reason, of course, it is impossible to estimate how many English Catholics joined the Society of the Rosary. There are the scattered descriptions of a certain layperson's actions adhering to the requirements of Society worship and various mentions of laypeople's desires to join the Society or actually procuring membership, such as Anne Dacres, countess of Arundel, did, but there is no way to quantify the popularity of the Society among the laity. See Morris, *Troubles*, iii, 40; Bridgett, *Our Lady's Dowry*, 494. But the prevalence of rosaries in the late Tudor and early Stuart years, coupled with the popularity of books touting the benefits of rosary worship and membership in the Society in shipments of Catholic books intercepted by Protestant authorities provide good clues that priests' messages were being broadly circulated. When the enforcement of laws against Catholics eased after 1700, many Catholics, especially those in the Northern counties, did avail themselves of the opportunity to be enrolled in writing in the Society of the Rosary. See "Rosary Confraternity Lists," contrib. Bede Jarrett, OP, in *Miscellanea IX* (London: Catholic Record Society, XIV, 1914) 205, 217, 222.

57   Garnet, *The societie*, 26. See also 18–9, 21, 24–5; Crowther and Vincent, *JMJ*, 111.

58   The papacy's cooperation in adapting its requirements for the reception of indulgences attached to the Society of the Rosary stands in marked contrast to its refusal to compromise on other adaptations English Catholics wanted to make in their worship. See in particular, chapters 4 and 8. Perhaps the papacy was willing to compromise in this instance because no issues of doctrine or authority were involved. Neither the nature of sacraments nor sacramentals was being reconceptualized. The actual performance of the rosary was not being altered. The

chain of authority within the Church was not being rerouted in England's emergency circumstances. The issue of making concessions on indulgences was one on which the papacy could compromise without endangering its claims in other areas.

59 Crowther and Vincent, *JMJ*, 102. For examples of concessions from Gregory XIII, Pius V, Sixtus V, and Paul V, see *A chayne*, 98, 101; See also Garnet, *The societie*, 30, 211–2; Crowther and Vincent, *JMJ*, 100–1, 625–31.

60 Crowther and Vincent, *JMJ*, 93.

61 *CSP Dom* 12/143/33: William Middelmore was nephew of "Mr. Middelmore of the Privy Chamber."

62 SP Dom 12/137/47 (1580). See also SP Dom 16/22/111.

63 Bridgett, *Our Lady's Dowry*, 49. Pope Paul V renewed the indulgences May 30, 1605. The preface is dated October 20, 1605. A detailed list of the indulgences renewed is available in *A chayne*, 99–. For another example, see BL, Sloane MS 3785, ff. 16–16v.

64 Crowther and Vincent, *JMJ*, 104–5.

65 Garnet, *The societie*, 211–2. Other, more questionable attempts to quantify the indulgences available placed the number of years as high as 120,000. Winston-Allen, *Stories*, 5.

66 André Vauchez, *The Laity in the Middle Ages: Religious Beliefs and Devotional Practices*, ed. Daniel E. Bornstein, trans. Margery J. Schneider (Notre Dame: University of Notre Dame Press, 1993) 111, 114, and Richard Kieckhefer, "Major Currents in Late Medieval Devotion" in *Christian Spirituality: High Middle Ages and Reformation*, ed. Jill Raitt (New York: Crossroad, 1989) 100, cited in Winston-Allen, *Stories*, 80. Late medieval writings advertising the Society stressed the increase in virtue associated with the organization's practices, and popular continental songs about the rosary failed to mention indulgences. *Stories*, 118–20, 141.

67 Crowther and Vincent, *JMJ*, 31, 84–5. David Warren Sabean, *Power in the Blood: Popular Culture and Village Discourse in Early Modern Germany* (Cambridge: Cambridge University Press, 1984) chap. 1, argues that if people are not integrated as individuals into their communities, they can still have a group consciousness unified by mediated experiences. Sabean uses the example of receiving communion as a group experience capable of joining individuals bonded by few other active unifying forces. English Catholics' needed somehow to experience the Eucharist, whether spiritually or corporally, in order to feel a bond to other Catholics, whether in their own communities, in England, or in the world.

68 Batt, *A Poore mans mite*, 36–7. Also see Sally Cunneen, *In Search of Mary: The Woman and the Symbol* (New York: Ballantine Books, 1996) 189, for discussion of prayers of the faithful sustaining the Virgin's protective power for all.

69 Garnet, *The societie*, 26, 53–4.

70   For example, see Crowther and Vincent, *JMJ*, 290–1; Garnet, *The societie*, 182–3:
      Ellington, *Sacred Body*, 226–34.

71   Garnet, *The societie*, A6r–v.

72   Hoff, *Hamlet's Choice*, 192.

73   Horace Keast, *Our Lady in England* (Helston: Society of Mary, 1984) 16.

74   Robert A. Orsi, "The Many Names of the Mother of God," in Melissa R. Katz and
      Robert A. Orsi, eds., *Divine Mirrors: The Virgin Mary in the Visual Arts* (Oxford:
      Oxford University Press, 2001) 4.

75   *Visitation Articles and Injunctions of the Period of the Reformation*, eds. W. H.
      Frere and W. M. Kennedy (London: Green & Co., 1908–10) ii, 103–30, 176–89,
      190–6, quoted in Duffy, *Stripping*, 450, 461–2, 467–8; Keast, *Our Lady*, 16,
      30–1; Cunneen, *In Search of Mary*, 205; Bridgett, *Our Lady's Dowry*, 433. See
      also Edwin H. Burton, *London Streets & Catholic Memories* (London: Burns,
      Oates & Washbourne, Ltd., 1925) 10–11; Donald Hole, *England's Nazareth: A
      History of the Holy Shrine of Our Lady of Walsingham* (Ipswich: Suffolk Press,
      n.d.); Thomas A. O'Meara, *Mary in Protestant and Catholic Theology* (New York:
      Sheed and Ward, 1966) esp. chaps. 2–3.

76   Orsi argues that efforts to remove icons and symbols "are efforts to foreclose the
      power of presence in things or to limit the access of particular communities or
      individuals to that power." Orsi, "Many Names," 5. See chapter 1 for explanation
      of how saints intercede on behalf of believers.

77   Garnet, A3v–5v. In an interesting contrast, Marina Warner notes a woodcut
      image from Augsburg showing God clutching arrows representing pestilence
      while Mary shelters believers from his anger. Warner, *Alone of All Her Sex* (New
      York: Vintage Books, 1976) 307.

78   Hilda Graef, *Devotion to the Blessed Virgin* (London: Burns & Oates, 1963) 30.

79   An exception exists in crusaders' occasional references to Mary as a protector in
      battle. See Melissa R. Katz, "Regarding Mary: Women's Lives Reflected in the
      Virgin's Image," in Katz and Orsi, eds., *Distant Mirrors*, 59. Following the split
      between Eastern and Western churches, the Eastern Church maintained its
      image of Mary as a strong warrior for the faith. This Greek influence periodical-
      ly infiltrated the Western Church in such works as the Benedictine nun
      Hroswitha of Gandersheim's edition of the Theophilus legend in which she por-
      trays Mary as Queen of Heaven, full of power, uniquely reconciling sinners by
      her intercession and consoling all Christians. From Migne, *Patrologia Latina*,
      137, 1101–10, quoted in Graef, *Mary: A History*, i, 204. The legend, dating from
      fifth century Greece, chronicles the struggles of Theophilus, who gave his soul to
      the devil in exchange for a post he coveted. Theophilus repents and asks Mary to
      obtain forgiveness for his sin. Mary "by her power" compels the devil to rescind
      the contract. The Eastern Church quoted the story throughout the Middle Ages
      to reveal Mary's power over hell. See also Graef, *Devotion*, 30. In late sixteenth-
      century Protestant England, however, Christopher Marlowe wrote the play *Dr.*

Faustus, in which an aging doctor is willing to sell his soul to the devil for 24 years of money, power, and sex. In this adaptation of the Theophilus legend, reflecting Protestantism's de-emphasis on Mary, Mary is not there to save the doctor from hell.

80   Cunneen, *In Search of Mary*, Plate 10. The Council of Ephesus (431) granted Mary the title *Theotokos*, or "god bearer."

81   Garnet, A5–5v. This contrasts with Nicholas Sanders, *A Treatise on the Images of Christ, and of his Saints* (Louvain, 1567) Sig. ° viii, quoted in Wooding, *Rethinking*, 249. For this exile writing from the continent, it is not Mary but the Church of Christ that is described as "like an army of men well set in array . . ."

82   In the modern era, the rosary has also emerged as a weapon in certain contexts. Robert A. Orsi describes such use by abortion-rights protestors who declare themselves "soldiers in Mary's army" and who brandish rosaries at women entering or leaving abortion clinics. See Orsi, "Many Names," 9.

83   Colleen Marie Seguin, *Addicted unto Piety: Catholic Women in England, 1590–1690* (PhD Dissertation, Duke University, 1997) 290, notes that Mary Ward, the Englishwoman who founded the Institute of the Blessed Virgin Mary which organized female missionaries in England, called her nuns—devotees of Mary—"soldiers of God."

84   Crowther and Vincent, *JMJ*, B3v:

85   Crowther and Vincent, *JMJ*, A2v. See also BL, Harleian MS 494, ff. 105–106v.

86   Crowther and Vincent, *JMJ*, A2v, B4–5.

87   Crowther and Vincent, *JMJ*, 63–6.

88   Orsi comments that Marian objects can forge "bonds of reciprocity, affection and responsibility, and they are used to achieve effects . . . They are conduits of power. Such objects cannot be understood apart from the phenomenology of presence; what makes them desirable and valued is the experience, in and through them, of presence." Orsi, "Many Names," 6.

      A present, protective Mary is evident in a votive painting of the Bedingfeld family commemorating their escape from the Civil War, probably dated from the Restoration (c. 1660). Mary is dressed as Queen of Heaven protecting the Bedingfeld family from the war, sheltering individuals beneath her robe. She shelters them from ships at sea and mounted men, probably soldiers. She is shielding them from the dangers of this world, not the next. See J. H. Pollen, contrib., "Bedingfeld Papers," in *Miscellanea IV* (London: Catholic Record Society, VII, 1909) *frontis.*

89   Garnet, *The societie*, 178–9.

90   Garnet, *The societie*, C1v–2v.

91   Garnet, *The societie*, 1–5.

92   BL, Sloane MS 3785, ff. 3–3v.

93   As Orsi contends, Mary's "presence changes things, alters experience, reconfig-
     ures relationships, necessitates new maps for familiar landscapes. . . ." Orsi,
     "Many Names," 15.

94   BL, Sloane MS 3785, ff. 2–3, 4–5.

95   BL, Sloane MS 3785, f. 13.

96   BL, Sloane MS 3785, f. 5v.

97   For a more radical interpretation of the nature of Mary's power in the process of
     salvation, see the Capuchin Lawrence of Brindisi's (d. 1619) conceptualization of
     Mary as a spiritual priest in *Salut. Angel.*, 3,5 in the 1927 edition of Brindisi's
     Works, quoted in Graef, *Mary: A History*, ii, 26.

98   The one volume of instructions for the rosary written by an English Catholic
     priest that I found which does not conform to the above changes in Marian
     themes and emphases is Thomas Worthington's *Rosarie of Our Lady*.
     Worthington continues to portray Mary using the largely continental models of
     passivity and modesty that will be discussed below. The particular circumstances
     under which Worthington wrote his prayers upon the beads and under which
     they were finally published aid in explaining why Worthington's interpretation of
     Mary differs so sharply from those of the other English priests discussed.
     Worthington, an English Catholic priest, wrote these prayers while imprisoned in
     the Tower of London for religion and while waiting to be executed. He never
     intended these prayers to be published and distributed for pastoral use among
     English Catholics, as the writers discussed above intended. Worthington had no
     books and no beads in prison and wrote his text to comfort himself alone. His
     prayers upon Christ's crucifixion provide clues that Worthington used the
     prayers, in part, to prepare himself for his own execution (See 15, 25, 44–5, 59).

99   The Cistercian order strongly advocated appeals to Mary for intercession with
     Christ. The Cistercians were active in England prior to Henry VIII's Dissolution
     of the Monasteries. It is not clear, however, that the Cistercians were encourag-
     ing rosary use as the primary channel to appeal to the Virgin and certainly not to
     a warrior-like Virgin.

100 See Jaroslav Pelikan, *Mary through the Centuries: Her Place in the History of
     Culture* (New Haven: Yale University Press, 1996) 85–94, 218–9.

101 In general, the Roman Church's glorification of Mary in this manner remained
     limited to the times and areas of the Mediterranean suffering immediate threat
     from the Ottoman empire. When Mary is associated with military victory, there
     is no mention of Mary as a warrior herself. See William Addis and Thomas
     Arnold, *A Catholic Dictionary* (London: Virtue and Co., Ltd., 1953) 540–1;
     Warner, *Alone*, 308–13.

102 Cunneen, *In Search of Mary*, 185.

103 Bridgett, *Our Lady's Dowry*, 483–4. Winston-Allen, *Stories*, 2, 145, states this
     phrase began to be added to the prayer in the sixteenth century but did not
     become standard on the continent until the seventeenth century.

104   John Strype, *Annals of the reformation and establishment of religion, and the var-*
      ious occurences in the Church of England, during Queen Elizabeth's happy reign
      . . . , 4 vols. (Oxford, 1824) ii, part I, 358, quoted in Bridgett, *Our Lady's Dowry*,
      484.

105   Lawrence Vaux, *A catechisme or a Christian doctrine, necessarie for children &*
      the ignorant people, quoted in Bridgett, *Our Lady's Dowry*, 484.

106   For such representations in the art of the period, see Katz, "Regarding Mary,"
      particularly 28–9, 45, 47–8, 55.

107   This image of Mary became popular in the twelfth and thirteenth centuries, but
      was on the decline after the Council of Trent. See Pelikan, *Mary*, 125; Ellington,
      Sacred Body, chap. 5.

108   Pelikan, *Mary*, 140–161; Cunneen, *In Search of Mary*, 186–7, 192, 309.

109   Pelikan, *Mary*, 130–1.

110   *Horae Eboracenses: The Book of Hours of the Blessed Virgin Mary with Other*
      Prayers According to the Use of the Church of York from the edition printed in
      1536 (Surtees Society, CXXXII, 1920), Appendix 1: "Steeple Ashton MS: Horae
      of the Early Fifteenth Century," 162; See also Pelikan, *Mary*, 133.

111   For a discussion of this representation, see Cunneen, *In Search of Mary*, 189;
      For another example, see Thomas à Kempis, *Meditations on Our Lady*, mid-fif-
      teenth century, trans. W.H.F.S. (Ditchling, Sussex: St. Dominic's Press, 1929)
      24–5, and Katz's discussion of this work in "Regarding Mary," 87–8.

112   For a discussion of the medieval shift from rosary as psalter to rosary as
      Christocentric exercise, the form of which was made official by the papacy in
      1569, see Winston-Allen, *Stories*, chapter 1.

113   See Katz, "Regarding Mary," 99, for a discussion of the language of the annunci-
      ation and Mary's assumption that portrays her as passive recipient of grace.

114   Crowther and Vincent, *JMJ*, 50–1.

115   For example, see images from Alberto da Castello, *Rosario della gloriosa vergine*
      Maria (Venice, 1524 ed.) which was issued in 18 editions, as well as Andrea
      Gianetti da Salò, *Rosario della sacratissina Vergine Maria, raccolto dall' opere del*
      R.P.F. Luigi di Granata (Venice, 1587) f. 73 v; and the painting *The Celebration*
      of the Rosary by Albrecht Dürer in Winston-Allen, *Stories*, 61–2, 71. By the
      1570s, on the continent, the coronation of the Virgin had been inserted as the
      final rosary meditation, replacing the Last Judgment. *Stories*, 145.

116   Cunneen, *In Search of Mary*, 207; Hoff, *Hamlet's Choice*, 179; Katz, "Regarding
      Mary," 39.

117   Ellington, *Sacred Body*, viii, 142–3, 181–7, 205–7, argues that post-Tridentine
      portrayals of Mary portray her as an exemplar for humility, obedience, and faith
      and increasingly focused on the soul rather than the body of Mary. This charac-
      terization dominated Mary's portrayal in post-Tridentine continental art and
      music as well. See Katz, "Regarding Mary," 64–85; Claire Fontijn-Harris, "The

Virgin's Voice: Representations of Mary in Seventeenth-Century Italian Song," in Katz and Orsi, eds., *Distant Mirrors*, 139–41.

118   Luca Pinelli, *The Virgin Marie's life, faithfully gathered out of auncient & holie fathers*, trans. Richard Gibbons (Douai, 1604) Introduction, 4–7 (pagination starts over at page 1 in the first chapter). Gibbons is representative of a number of English Catholics exiled on the continent who translated continental authors such as Pinelli. Most of these translators had never experienced first hand the challenges of practicing Catholicism in Protestant England. The books they chose to translate were meant for use in countries where all seven sacraments were readily available without any accommodations made to the realities of Catholic life under a Protestant government. For similar continental views of a humble Mary, see Gasparo Loarte, *Instructions and Advertisements How to Meditate upon the misteries of the Rosarie of the most holy Virgin Mary*, trans. Anonymous (1613; reprint, Menston, Yorkshire: Scolar Press, 1970) 33–7, 41–2, 45; St. Francis de Sales, *Oeuvres completes de Saint François de Sales, èvêque at prince de Genève*, 16 vols. (Paris: J. J. Blaise, 1821) x, 308, and other post-Tridentine continental writers translated and quoted by Ellington, *Sacred Body*, chap. 4; Popular literature such as Dante's *Purgatorio* emphasizes similar qualities of Mary's, such as in *Purgatorio*, X, quoted in Pelikan, *Mary*, 143.

119   Loarte, *Instructions*, 33–7. Underlining is my emphasis. See also Ellington's discussion of similar metaphors used by Robert Bellarmine and Lawrence of Brindisi in *Sacred Bodies*, 223–4.

120   For examples, see Loarte, *Instructions*, 8, 11, 14, 18, 27, 29, 36, 44, 62, 68.

121   Loarte, *Instructions*, 38, 43; St. Francis Borgia, "Pious Meditations upon the Beades: For detestation of Synne; obtayning of Christian Perfections; and dayly Memory of the Life and Passion of Christ our Saviour," in *The Practice of Christian Workes*, trans. John Wilson (1620; reprint, Menston, Yorkshire: Scolar Press, 1970) 67, 91, 148, 184 (misnumbered as 148 in this edition), 261 "Prayer to our Blessed Lady"; Winston-Allen, *Stories*, 119–20.

122   For example, Mary as Queen of Heaven is depicted as sitting upon the throne of wisdom. See Henry Adams, *Mont-Saint-Michel and Chartres* (Princeton, 1933) 264, cited by Cunneen, *In Search of Mary*, 180–1; Also Ellington, *Sacred Body*, 163

123   Loarte, *Instructions*, 14. A general continental shift toward the rosary as Christocentric exercise was formalized in 1569 with the papacy's issuance of an "official" rosary that was clearly Christocentric in focus. The goal was to encourage the rosarist to follow the model of Christ, become more virtuous, and thus achieve grace. Continental authors in general, but particularly the Jesuits, stressed these benefits of the rosary. Winston-Allen, *Stories*, 27, 147.

124   Loarte, *Instructions*, 16–20.

125   Loarte, *Instructions*, 7–10; Borgia, "Pious," 197; De Sales, *Oeuvres*, ii, 496–7, discussed in Ellington, *Sacred Body*, 221–2.

126   Orsi argues that Catholics' need for Mary appears to increase during times of "social, political, and economic transformations [that] disrupt the customary ways people have been connected to each other and to the social world." Such, I argue, is the case for England and its Catholics. Orsi, "Many Names," 8.

127   For discussions of the manipulability of Mary as symbol by both clergy and laity, see Warner, *Alone*; Orsi, "Many Names," 7–15. For a dissenting view, see Michael P. Carroll, *The Cult of the Virgin Mary: Psychological Origins* (Princeton: Princeton University Press, 1986).

128   Brown, *John Ogilvie*, 144; Bridgett, *Our Lady's Dowry*, 495; See also *Relatio incarcerationis et martyrii P. Ioannis Ogilbei natione Scoti e Societate Iesu presbyteri* (Doaui, 1615); BL, Lansdowne MS 350, f. 8.

129   See also Richard Challoner, *Memoirs of Missionary Priests and Other Catholics of Both Sexes that have Suffered Death in England on Religious Accounts from the Year 1577–1684: vol. 1* (London: Burns, Oates & Washbourne, Ltd., 1924) i, 37, 194, 341, 394, 423, 431, 464, 594; BL, Lansdowne MS 350, ff. 18–19.

130   Much historical, anthropological, and sociological work has been done on this subject. For examples, see Jonathan D. Spence, *The Memory Palace of Matteo Ricci* (New York: Penguin Books, 1985); R. A. Markus, *The End of Ancient Christianity* (Cambridge: Cambridge University Press, 1990); Klauser, *A Short History*, chapter 2.

131   SP Dom 12/156/15.

132   SP Dom 12/143/33, 12/146/102, 12/176/16, 12/179/4, 12/238/126ii, 14/16/34, 14/123/115, 16/250/19; *CSP Dom* 14/94/1; *Calendar of Scottish Papers* 13/1/299, 300; *CSP Rome*, vol. 38, 409.

133   Cheshire Record Office, EDC 1/18; BL, Cotton Titus MS C VII, f. 60; *CSP Dom* 12/27/9, 12/151/5, 12/237/126iii, 12/274/103, 14/7/89, 14/34/63; SP Dom 12/118/46, 47, 12/156/15, 12/164/14, 12/183/33ii, 12/192/54, 12/230/34, 16/22/111; From a sermon of John Jewel printed in John Oliver Williams Haweis, *Sketches of the Reformation and Elizabethan Age taken from the Contemporary Pulpit* (London: William Pickering, 1844) 40–41; Letter to Archbishop Sandys of York in Haweis, *Sketches*, 174; George Oliver, *Collections Illustrating the History of the Catholic Religion in the Counties of Cornwall, Devon, Dorset, Somerset, Wiltshire and Gloucester, in two parts, Historical and Biographical. With notices of the Dominican, Benedictine, & Franciscan Orders* (London: Charles Dolman, 1857) 4–5; Connelly, *Women*, 188.

134   William Brereton, *Journal of Sir William Brereton 1635* (Durham: Surtees Society, CXXIV, 1915) 1–3; BL, Lansdowne MS 153, f. 68; BL, Lansdowne MS 42, f. 174; BL, Lansdowne MS 350, f. 13; Morris, *Troubles*, iii, 52; *Selections from the Household Books of Lord William Howard of Naworth Castle* (Durham: Surtees Society, LXVIII, 1878) 462; SP Dom 12/155/27, 12/193/35, 12/198/12, 14/4/66, 14/21/5, 16/61/13.

135   *Acts of the High Commission Court within the Diocese of Durham* (Durham:
       Surtees Society, XXXIV, 1858) 77; *CSP Dom* 12/248/99; ChRO, EDV 1/13/102v;
       Stonyhurst MS, Angl. A, ff. 41–48, as quoted in Morris, iii, 270–1.

NOTES TO CHAPTER 4

1   "Returns from the Ecclesiastical Commission in York, 20 November 1576," con-
       tained in John Morris, *The Troubles of Our Catholic Forefathers Related by
       Themselves*, 3 vols. (London: Burns & Oates, 1877) iii, 248–50.

2   The English Protestant church taught that their Eucharist was not a recurring
       recreation of Christ's sacrifice performed by the priest at the altar. The Church
       of England may not have explicitly denied the real presence of Christ in the
       Eucharist, but Christ's body was not present upon the Protestant communion
       table in the same way as it was believed to be upon the Catholic altar to procure
       God's saving grace. For a detailed discussion of the debates surrounding
       Eucharistic theology within the Church of England and a comparison of such
       views with other Protestant theologies, see Diarmaid MacCulloch, *Thomas
       Cranmer: A Life* (New Haven: Yale University Press, 1996) espec. 412–7, 505–8,
       527–9, 614–22.

       It has been argued that Elizabeth's adoption of the 1552 Book of Common Prayer
       and her slight modifications to it allowed for a more "Catholic" understanding of
       the real presence of Christ in the bread and wine. See, for example, C. W.
       Dugmore, *Eucharistic Doctrine in England from Hooker to Waterland* (New
       York: Macmillan, 1942) 4–6, and Doreen Rosman, *From Catholic to Protestant:
       Religion and the People in Tudor England* (London: UCL Press, 1996) 34. In
       reality, her modifications did little more than confuse the issues by allowing both
       Protestant and Catholic elements in the service to stand side by side. By strad-
       dling the fence, she likely satisfied neither side. For example, see Michael Hunt,
       The Puritan Moment, The Coming of Revolution in an English County
       (Cambridge, MA: Harvard University Press, 1983) 90; Walsham, *Church Papists*,
       18; Wooding, *Rethinking*, 166–76; Norman L. Jones, *Faith by Statute: Parliament
       and the Settlement of Religion, 1559* (London: Royal Historical Society, 1982);
       Christopher Haigh, *English Reformations: Religion, Politics, and Society under
       the Tudors* (Oxford: Clarendon Press, 1993) 240–2. The above statements by
       Elizabethan laypersons, however, suggest that Elizabeth's "liturgical compro-
       mise" did not satisfy all Catholics, just as it failed to satisfy the hotter sort of
       Protestants who criticized the liturgy as being too papist.

3   Despite these similarities in functions of the Mass, there was no "single experi-
       ence of the Mass," for pre-reform Christians, as Eamon Duffy, *Stripping*, 116
       states. Perhaps the range of possible experiences of the Mass is one factor con-
       tributing to the acceptability of post-reform alternatives that this chapter dis-
       cusses.

4   This contrasts sharply with reforms on the continent. The Council of Trent's rec-
       ommendations for Catholic reform and worship confirmed the primacy of church

traditions emphasizing medieval theologians' writings on the immanentist aspects of the sacraments and the supremacy of clerical authority over the laity. See Ramsey, *Liturgy*, chapter 3.

5   Miri Rubin, *Corpus Christi: The Eucharist in Late Medieval Culture* (Cambridge: Cambridge University Press, 1991) 1–11, claims that the Eucharist was an idiom through which many experiences and requirements could be articulated through various interpretations of the rituals and symbols used. Rubin cites (7–8) Chartier's encouragement to move from the consideration of a historical artifact, such as Christ's body contained in the Eucharistic bread, to how people used and understood it. Different people, Chartier argued, would use symbols and rituals in different ways depending on what interests they already had invested. Rubin agrees and suggests that rather than trying to synthesize the different interpretations and uses into some sort of uniformity, historians should instead try to locate meaningful patterns within the diversity, which is what I try to do here by finding common threads within the options offered to and practiced by English Catholics to reclaim what they felt they had lost in the frequent absence of the Mass.

6   Baptism, confirmation, Eucharist, penance, extreme unction, holy ordination, and marriage

7   Wooding, *Rethinking*, 83, argues that loyalty to the Mass increased after Henrician reform as English Catholics defended the sacrament from Protestant attacks, but because of the influence of humanism, English Catholic intellectuals shifted their understandings about the Mass as they defended Catholic doctrine.

8   Although the terms "Mass" and "sacrament of the altar" are often used interchangeably by both clerics and laypersons alike, a distinction should be made between the Mass, a service which on rare occasions does not contain the celebration of the sacrament, and the Eucharistic celebration itself which is typically part of the Mass and during which the sacrament of the altar is recreated.

9   Pre-reform English Christians received this message in popular works such as *The Lay Folk's Mass Book*, ed. T. F. Simmons (Early English Text Society (EETS), 1871) 38, quoted in Duffy, *Stripping*, 91. Post-reform, see Antonio Possevino, *A Treatise of the Holy Sacrifice of the Altar, called the Masse*, trans. Thomas Butler (Louvain: Ioannem Foulerum, 1570) 45, who describes the sacrifice made at the altar as a sacrifice of the "flesh of the Son of God" and writes of the "offering of the death of our Savior, where he is himself present."

10   Duffy, *Stripping*, 117–8.

11   The Council of Florence (1431–43) decreed that the effect of the Eucharist was to increase grace to help preserve eternal life and to unite the worthy receiver with Christ. See Wolfgang Beinert and Francis Schussler Fiorenza, eds., *Handbook of Catholic Theology* (New York: Crossroads, 1995) 226–228.

12   *Horae Eboracenses: The Book of Hours of the Blessed Virgin Mary with Other Prayers According to Use of the Church of York from the edition printed in 1536*, ed. C. Wordsworth (Durham: Surtees Society, CXXXII, 1919) 86. See also Guy

de Roye, *The Doctrinal of Sapyence*, ed. William Caxton (1489) RSTC 21431, f. 63; John Fisher, *English Works*, ed. J. E. B. Mayer (EETS, 1876) 109 quoted in Duffy, *Stripping*, 108; E. S. Dewick, "On a manuscript Sarum primer" *Transactions of the St. Paul's Ecclesiological Society* 5 (1905): 170–5. See also *New Catholic Encyclopedia*, v. 5, 606–7.

[13]   *Horae Eboracenses*, 73.

[14]   Although Wooding argues for changing emphases in interpreting the sacrament in the Marian years, she states that "This idea of the gift of salvation being channeled through the Sacrament was one of the chief descriptions of the Mass used by Marian writers." *Rethinking*, 173.

[15]   Parishioners did not partake of the Eucharistic bread frequently, although the priest did so at every Mass. Theoretically, the priest's reception of the body of Christ was sufficient to aid the salvation of all those who heard and saw the Mass. People shared in the priest's sacrifice through their prayers and by their faith. See Duffy, *Stripping*, 93–101, 125. However, the term "communion" when referring to participation in the sacrament of the altar can refer to "any one of different forms of togetherness." See John A. Hardon, SJ, *Modern Catholic Dictionary* (Garden City, NY: Doubleday and Co., 1980) 116.

[16]   In the patristic period, Cyril (or John) of Jerusalem (c. 348) described the necessity of using all of one's senses to experience this sacrament and worship God through it. (*Catech.* 5. 21 f.) in J.G. Davies, ed., *A Dictionary of Liturgy and Worship* (London: SCM Press Ltd., 1972) 143.

[17]   Laypersons also flocked to see Christ's body in the host at Corpus Christi processions, during which time parishioners carried the Eucharistic bread/body of Christ around town in special reliquaries.

[18]   See *The Lay Folk's Mass Book* and *The Golden Legend or Lives of the Saints as Englished by William Caxton*, ed. F. S. Ellis (London: Temple Classics, 1900) VII, 225–62, as discussed by Duffy, *Stripping*, 118–9.

[19]   Duffy, *Stripping*, 102–3, 106, 108–9, 188–9.

[20]   *Horae Eboracenses*, 85.

[21]   Robert W. Scribner, "The Reformation, Popular Magic, and the 'Disenchantment of the World,'" *Journal of Interdisciplinary History* 23, no. 3 (1993): 478. Scribner writes that Catholic sacraments targeted the entire person "body, soul, and spirit—so that they were seen as offering consolation, succor, and nourishment for the body as well as the soul."

[22]   See Bynum, *Holy Feast*, particularly 77–8, 117–9, 127–9, for descriptions and interpretations of physical responses experienced by laypersons and religious persons ingesting the host.

[23]   Lewis Richeome, *Holy pictures of the Mystical Figures of the most holy Sacrifice and Sacrament of the Eucharist translated into English for the benefit of those of that Nation as well Protestants and Catholikes*, trans. C.A. (n.p., 1619) 20–1. See also St. Francis Borgia, *The Practice of Christian Workes* (orig. 1620), trans. John

Wilson (Menston, Yorkshire: Scolar Press, 1970) 166–9, who claims that just as the body needs material meat, the soul needs the Eucharist. Borgia quotes the sixth chapter of *John*, "For he who eateth my flesh abideth in me and I in him."

24   *Horae Eboracenses*, 73; Richeome, *Holy pictures*, 286; Thomas Wright, *The Passions of the Mind in General*, ed. William Webster Newbold (New York: Garland Publications Inc., 1986) 319–20.

25   Richeome, *Holy pictures*, 54–5.

26   English Catholic records reveal that laypeople understood and discussed many abstract concepts ranging from transubstantiation to Purgatory. See, for example, Jane Owen, *An Antidote to Purgatory* (orig. 1634) in D. M. Rogers, ed., *English Recusant Literature, 1558–1640* (Menston, Yorkshire: Scolar Press, 1973) vol. 166, cited in Seguin, *Addicted*, 57. Previous scholars point out that Catholics in remote areas could often continue many Catholic rituals connected with the Mass, although they have not shown through anecdoctal evidence that such access was regular and reliable enough in the long term to provide spiritual comfort to Catholics over the fate of their souls. Christopher Haigh, *Reformation and Resistance in Tudor Lancashire* (Cambridge: Cambridge University Press, 1975) 217, 219; J. C. H. Aveling, *Northern Catholics: The Catholic Recusants of the North Riding of Yorkshire, 1558–1790* (London: Dublin Chapman, 1966) 48–9; Christine Kelly, *Blessed Thomas Belson: His Life and Times, 1563–1589* (Gerrards Cross: Colin Smythe, 1987) 18.

27   Letter of Robert Southwell to Claudio Aquaviva, 21 December 1586, in Pollen, *Unpublished Documents*, 313–4.

28   Weston, *William Weston*, 65.

29   After 1590, the continental literature continued to be imported into England, but it co-existed with works written by English Catholics, written in England, and intended for an English audience, as will be discussed later.

30   See *Decrees of the Ecumenical Councils*, vol. 2, *Trent to Vatican II*, ed. Norman P. Tanner, original text established by G. Albergio, J. A. Dossetti, P.-P. Joannou, C. Leonardi, and P. Prodi, in consultation with H. Jedin (London: Sheed and Ward, Ltd., and Washington, DC: Georgetown University Press, 1990) 693, 742.

31   Vaux's *Catechism* was reprinted eight times between 1568 and 1620. See also Kelly, *Blessed*, 23, 130; Wooding, *Rethinking*, 227, argues that English exiles on the continent in the 1570s wrote to "compel obedience to a Catholic Church whose authority and doctrine was put beyond question" rather than to provide pastoral care. See also 212–7, 246.

32   Vaux, *Catechism*, 52–3, 81–2.

33   Vaux, *Catechism*, 82–3.

34   Vaux, *Catechism*, 28–9.

35   Vaux, *Catechism*, 28–9.

36   Vaux, *Catechism*, 111–4.

37   Borgia, *The Practice*, 123–7. Borgia made it clear that his recommendation was
      to hear Mass daily and not receive the Eucharist corporally this frequently.

38   Possevino, *A Treatise*, 43v, 44v.

39   Richeome, *Holy pictures*, 54–5.

40   Possevino, *A Treatise*, 46.

41   Richeome, *Holy pictures*, 53. "Secondly, a Sacrament profits only him, which
      receiveth it, being well disposed and prepared . . ." See also Possevino, *A Treatise*,
      44v.

42   Vaux, *Catechism*, G. See also Letter of Henry Garnet to Marco Tusinga, 21 July
      1599, in *CSP Dom* 12/271/105.

43   A willingness to subsume doctrinal and theological debates to the pastoral and
      even administrative necessities of a workable Catholic Church was not unique to
      English churchmen of this period. Scribner, *For the Sake of Simple Folk: Popular
      Propaganda for the German Reformation* (Oxford: Clarendon Press, 1994) chap-
      ter 8, suggests that literature intended for mass audiences, whether Catholic or
      Protestant, during this period often served to both evoke and ease tensions. As
      Elisabeth G. Gleason has shown in *Gasparo Contarini: Venice, Rome and Reform*
      (Berkeley: University of California Press, 1993), churchmen on the continent
      were also capable of viewing the needs of the institutional church, the state, the
      clergy, and the lay population as a system of interests to be balanced, regardless
      of strict doctrine or institutional dictates.

44   John Radford, *A Directorie Teaching the Way to the Truth in a Briefe and Plaine
      Discovrse against the heresies of this time* (n.p., 1605) A3.

45   Radford, *A Directorie*, 71. For a similar de-emphasis on the institutional forms of
      the sacraments and promotion of alternative channels to God's grace, see Wright,
      Passions, 319–20. In a related concept, Steven Ozment discusses the debates of
      medieval theologians such as Jean Gerson and Bonaventure regarding the differ-
      ence between *potentia Dei absoluta* and *potentia Dei ordinata* in Ozment's
      *Mysticism and Dissent: Religious Ideology and Social Protest in the Sixteenth
      Century* (New Haven: Yale University Press, 1973). *Potentia Dei absoluta*, or
      what God can do, is quite different from *potentia Dei ordinata*, or what God
      chooses to do on earth at any particular time. For English Catholics like Radford,
      when what God chose to do on earth through the institution of sacraments per-
      formed by priests no longer proved sufficient, Catholics must rely on the absolute
      power or capability of God to operate beyond what he had ordained thus far.

46   Radford, *A Directorie*, 71, 104–5.

47   Radford, *A Directorie*, 190. Continental authors contemporary to Radford dis-
      cussed similar principles, i.e. Possevino, *A Treatise*, 42v–43. Radford, however,
      pushed such theories to their limits.

48   For example, Alexander of Hales, *IV Sent*. d. 13, q. 8, 204–5 and Alan of Lille,
      Lib poen lib. 3, c. 24, 141 in Rubin, *Corpus Christi*, 67, 69. The Council of Trent
      promised that the spiritual communicants received "if not the entire, at least very

great benefits" from the sacrament of the altar, however, the authors wrote with the assumption that this spiritual desire to communicate preceded the actual sacrament. See Hardon, *Modern Catholic Dictionary*, 116.

49 Rubin, *Corpus Christi*, 50. See also Borgia, *The Practice*, 123–7.

50 Stanney, *A treatise of penance*, 266.

51 See also Wright, *Passions*, 234.

52 William Perin, *Spiritual Exercises and Goostly Meditations, and a neare way to come to perfection and lyfe contemplatiue, very profytable for Religyous, and generally for al other that desyre to come to the perfecte loue of God, and to the contempte of the world* (Caen: Peter le Chandelier, 1598). Perin originally adapted and translated Nicolaus van Ess's *Exercitia theologiae mysticae* in 1557. Writing in the final years of Mary's reign, he may have foreseen the difficulties English Catholics would have experienced if the Protestant Elizabeth became sovereign. The possible reasons to reprint Perin's work over 40 years later surely must include the nature of the messages contained in the exercises which would have succored English Catholics living without priests.

53 Perin, *Spiritual Exercises*, 9. My emphasis.

54 Perin, *Spiritual Exercises*, 14. Note how Perin never mentions a sacrifice, a meal, a priest, or a Mass in statements such as "Wherefore most merciful mediator Jesus, by whose only merciful means and the blessed merits of thy holy manhead all grace is given to wretched sinner of thy father celestial. . . ." The body of Christ remains important, but not the body as created in the Mass.

55 Perin, *Spiritual Exercises*, 16.

56 Perin, *Spiritual Exercises*, 10.

57 Klauser, *A Short History*, 135.

58 Robert V. Caro, SJ, "William Alabaster: Rhetor, Mediator, Devotional Poet-1," *Recusant History* 19, no. 1 (1988): 67. Also see Jones, *English Reformation*, 151–3, on Alabaster's career and influence, including evidence of Alabaster's influence on converts to Catholicism.

59 William Alabaster, sonnet 56, *ll.* 1–8, in Caro, "William Alabaster: Rhetor, Mediator, Devotional Poet-2," *Recusant History* 19, no. 2 (1988): 157.

60 Bynum, *Holy Feast*, 26, 85–6, 150–62, 178, 246–50, discusses nuptial or erotic relations with Christ.

61 Believers facing this issue frequently turned toward Mary as mediator between God and humankind. Perhaps the growing popularity of rosary worship among English Catholics discussed in chapter 3 might also be seen as an attempt to regain a sense of divine presence in the material world following the decline in access to the physical presence of Christ sacrificed on the altar.

62 Rubin, *Corpus Christi*, 302, 306, 315. Sometimes the round, white host was placed upon a cross, substituting for the mortal body of the crucified Christ. See

also the late medieval *Instructions for Parish Priests*, 9, ll. 290–301, quoted in Duffy, *Stripping*, 117. Also Duffy, *Stripping*, 108; Wooding, *Rethinking*, 149.

63   Klauser, *A Short History*, chapter 3.

64   John Bucke, *Instructions for the use of the beades* (orig. 1589) (Menston, Yorkshire: Scolar Press, 1971) 29–30. See also Henry Garnet, *The societie of the rosarie* (n.p., 1596) who in his meditations upon the Rosary of the Five Wounds graphically describes Christ's physical sufferings and asks "I humbly beseech thee that the memory of thy Passion may fill all my senses, and may so wholly ravish and possess me that I may see no other thing, know no other thing, than thee my Lord crucified and died for my sake." Arthur Crowther and Thomas Vincent, in *Jesus, Maria, Joseph, or the Devout Pilgrim . . .* (hereonafter referred to as *JMJ*) (Amsterdam, 1657) 642, also take their readers on a guided exhibition of Christ's bodily torments, for example, when Christ carried his own cross to Golgotha.

65   BL, Harleian MS 791, f. 43, "A Meditation on Our Savior's Passion," seventeenth century.

66   Not upon the Eucharistic bread or altar

67   BL, Harleian MS 791, f. 43v.

68   BL, Harleian MS 791, f. 43.

69   BL, Harleian MS 791, f. 43–43v.

70   Bucke, *Instructions*, 28–9. Christ advised anyone who would be his disciple to pick up his or her own cross and follow him. For example, *Mark* 8:34.

71   Many of these clerical authors were no doubt inspired by Loyola's *Spiritual Exercises* but modified the practice to meet the needs of England's Catholics. Loyola recommended directed, individualized contemplation of Christ in his *Spiritual Exercises*, however, the manner of training readers how to contemplate Christ's experiences differs from that of the authors of this English Catholic pastoral literature. First, English Catholics writing pastoral literature provided detailed instructions for meditation upon Christ, walking the reader step by step through each prayer and exercise. Loyola, on the other hand, specifically requested that the Jesuit directing the exercitant not provide too much guidance to his student. Second, Jesuits' promotion of Loyola's *Exercises* cannot be viewed as identical to English Catholics' promotion of contemplation of Christ's crucifixion discussed above because most exercitants never would have reached the stages of the *Spiritual Exercises* in which Christ was the subject. Loyola's *Spiritual Exercises* consists of a four-week program. If the exercitant cannot master the exercises of the previous weeks, he is never to be given the material of the following weeks. Indeed, most Catholics who undertook the *Spiritual Exercises* never progressed past week one and therefore never would have tackled the more advanced meditations upon Christ's life, death, and resurrection, nor did Loyola intend them to. Finally, when Loyola reached the subject of Christ's passion in week three, a quite advanced stage of the exercises, the style of meditation upon Christ's crucifixion proves to be quite different from what English priests recommended and what English laity experienced in their attempts to

connect to the suffering Christ. Loyola instructs the exercitant to banish all joyful or hopeful thoughts from his mind and to rouse himself to "sorrow, suffering,
and deep pain" as he contemplated Christ's tribulations. However, when the time
comes to meditate upon the passion, Loyola's only description of it and instructions are "At midnight, from the house of Pilate to the nailing to the cross, and in
the morning, from the raising of the Cross to his death. Then the repetitions and
applications of the senses." That is all the direction Loyola provides on how to
contemplate the crucifixion. See also John Olin, *Catholic Reform from Cardinal
Ximenes to the Council of Trent 1495–1563: An Essay with Illustrative
Documents and a Brief Study of St. Ignatius Loyola* (New York: Fordham
University Press, 1990) 138. Jesuits were to visualize events of Christ's life graphically, but their directions never suggested they attempt to become Christ himself.

72   Perin, *Spiritual Exercises*, 48.

73   Perin, *Spiritual Exercises*, 51.

74   Garnet, *The societie*, 113–4.

75   SP Dom 14/21/48. For another example, see a peasant's association of his own
       public beating through the streets with Christ's suffering in a letter of Robert
       Southwell to the Provincial of Naples, 3 Feb 1584, from the Archives SJ, Anglia
       I, f. 290 in J. H. Pollen, *Unpublished Documents Relating to the English Martyrs:
       vol. 1, 1584–1603* (London: Catholic Record Society, V, 1908) 305–6.

76   SP Dom 12/152/39.

77   J. C. H. Aveling, "Recusant Papers of the Meynell Family," in E. E. Reynolds,
       ed., *Miscellanea* (London: Catholic Record Society, LVI, 1964) xxii.

78   For refusing to enter a plea, in essence refusing to recognize the court's jurisdic-
       tion over her, Clitheroe was subjected to *peine forte et dure*.

79   York Minster Library, Add MS 151, *A Short Rule of good lyfe, including the
       apprehension of Margaret Clitheroe with sonnets in commendation of the book*,
       c. 1600, 55v. Robert Southwell wrote the *Short Rule*, but John Mush is credited
       with the account of Margaret Clitheroe.

80   York Minster Library, Add MS 151, 53v–57.

81   York Minster Library, Add MS 151, 57v–65v. In a similar equation of a martyr's
       death with Christ's, the English Catholic Richard Verstegan wrote to Roger
       Baynes in Rome in May 1595 to spread the news of the death of Father Walpole.
       Verstegan reported that Walpole had been sent "from the Tower to York and
       there executed, and Topcliffe released 'so that Barabbas is free, and Christ deliv-
       ered to be crucified.'" *CSP Dom* 12/252/15.

82   York Minster Library, Add MS 151, 63r.

83   CRS, v, 363, 367; Gerard, *Autobiography*, 53, in Connelly, *Women*, 90–1; and
       Adam Hamilton, *Chronicle of the English Augustinian Canonesses of St.
       Monica's at Louvain 1548 to 1625* (Edinburgh, London: Sands, 1904) 83, cited in
       Susan M. Cogan, *Patrons and Saints: Patronage, Kinship, and Catholics in Early*

Modern England (MA Thesis, Utah State University, Logan, UT, 2001) 49. Wiseman later received a pardon.

84   Richard Challoner, *Memoirs of Missionary Priests and Other Catholics of Both Sexes that have Suffered Death in England on Religious Accounts from the Year 1577–1684* (London: Burns, Oates and Washbourne, Ltd., 1924) 35–9.

85   Weston, *William Weston*, 114. Challoner, *Memoirs* (1924 ed.) recorded the words of the layman James Duckett prior to his execution at Tyburn in 1601 for distributing Catholic books. Duckett likened his own experience to Christ's crucifixion between two thieves as he said, "I take it for a great favor from Almighty God that I am placed amongst the thieves, as He Himself, my Lord and Master, was." See also Challoner, *Memoirs* (1924 ed.) 276, and the description of Henry Garnet's execution in Henry Foley, *Records of the English Province of the Society of Jesus*, 7 vols. (London: Burns & Oates, 1877) iv, 115, 118; A.L. Rowse, *Tudor Cornwall: Portrait of a Society* (New York: Charles Scribner's Sons, 1969) 364–5.

86   ChRO, EDV 1/17/123. OED states that "towel" is a blessed towel for the high altar, a cloth either of linen for use at communions or of silk for covering the altar. For further examples, see EDV 1/25/21–21v; William Palmes, SJ, *The Life of Mrs. Dorothy Lawson* (1646) 60, quoted in Connelly, *Women*, 190

87   ChRO, EDV 1/25/42.

88   PRO *Star Chamber* STAC 5 8/31 contained in Roy G. Dottie, "The Recusant Riots at Childwell in May 1600: A Reappraisal" (Liverpool: Historic Society of Lancashire and Cheshire, CXXXII, 1982) 9.

89   For examples, see CRO, AD 37/50/10,11,12,13,14.

90   CRO, AD 37/11. A similar association is implied by the seventeenth-century hidden burial of 5-year-old Abigail Rashleigh, near the altar at Mortlake church in Cornwall. In June 1805, an inscription was discovered *underneath* the pavement of the altar commemorating the burial there in 1616. See CRO, RS 1/504.

91   Crowther and Vincent, *JMJ*, 494.

92   Crowther and Vincent, *JMJ*, 533–4.

93   Crowther and Vincent, *JMJ*, 504–6.

94   Crowther and Vincent, *JMJ*, 504–6.

95   Crowther and Vincent, *JMJ*, 504–6. Emphasis is in the original.

96   Crowther and Vincent, *JMJ*, 506–7.

97   Crowther and Vincent, *JMJ*, 511: "I give myself to the Grace of your Mystery of the Incarnation: Grace which ties me unto you in a new manner: Grace which separates me from myself, unites and incorporates me into you; Grace which makes me yours in so noble, so intimate and so powerful a fashion, and renders me yours, as a parcel of yourself; Grace, of life and death both together; Grace of annihilating, and also of establishing."

98   The authors' use of the term "annihilation" is significant. As Benedictines, Crowther and Vincent would have been aware of the many discussions and

debates which emerged in the eleventh through the fifteenth centuries surrounding the exact nature of the transformation that occurred in the Eucharist at the time of consecration. Duns Scotus used the term "annihilation" to describe the transformation. Scotus argued that the substance of the bread being consecrated did not metamorphose into Christ's body. Instead, the bread's substance was annihilated completely, and Christ's body was substituted in its place. See Rubin, *Corpus Christi*, 30.

99   Crowther and Vincent, *JMJ*, 511–2. My emphasis on last sentence.

100   Crowther and Vincent, *JMJ*, 519–20.

101   Rubin, *Corpus Christi*, 233, 346, 357–8, 361, and Duffy, *Stripping*, chap. 3.

102   Rubin, *Corpus Christi*, 51–58, 62, 77.

103   Particularly in its thirteenth, twenty-second, and twenty-third sessions. Ramsey, *Liturgy*, chap. 3, espec. 45–51.

104   Rubin, *Corpus Christi*, chapters 3 and 4, especially 196, 233, 240–61, 263.

105   Steven E. Ozment, *Mysticism and Dissent*, 10. See also Ozment's *The Age of Reform, 1250–1550: An Intellectual and Religious History of Late Medieval and Reformation Europe* (New Haven: Yale University Press, 1980) section III.

106   For precedents, see Margery Kempe, *The Book of Margery Kempe, 1436*, trans. W. Butler-Bowden (New York: The Devin-Adair Company, 1944) 1–12, 102; St. Teresa of Avila, *The Way of Perfection*, trans. and ed. E. Allison Peers, from the critical edition by P. Silverio de Santa Teresa (New York: Image Books/Doubleday, 1964).

107   Sally Cunneen, *In Search of Mary: The Woman and the Symbol* (New York: Ballantine Books, 1996) 214–5.

108   See Jonathan Sumption, *Pilgrimage: An Image of Medieval Religion* (Totowa, NJ: Rowman and Littlefield, 1976) chap. 16, especially 300–1.

NOTES TO CHAPTER 5

1   John Bossy, *The English Catholic Community, 1570–1850* (London: Darton, Longman & Todd, 1975); Christopher Haigh, *English Reformations: Religion, Politics, and Society under the Tudors* (Oxford: Clarendon Press, 1993); Haigh, "The Continuity of Catholicism in the English Reformation," *Past and Present* (GB) 93 (1981): 37–69; Haigh, "From Monopoly to Minority: Catholicism in Early Modern England," *Transactions of the Royal Historical Society* 31 (1981): 129–147; Haigh, "Revisionism, the Reformation and the History of English Catholicism," *Journal of Ecclesiastical History* 36 (1985): 394–408. Also, A. L. Rowse, *Tudor Cornwall: Portrait of a Society* (New York: Charles Scribner's Sons, 1969) 361; SP Dom 12/178/74; CSP Dom 12/281/65. For information on the Wiseman family in particular, see CSP Dom 12/242/121, 12/243/95, 12/247/3, 12/248/31, 12/248/36, 12/248/37, 12/248/68, 12/249/13, 12/259/44, 12/272/36; Stonyhurst MS, Angl. A, ii, 41 quoted in M. A. Tierney, *Dodd's Church History*

of England from the Commencement of the Sixteenth Century to the Revolution in 1688, 5 vols. (London: Charles Dolman, 1839) vol. 3, ccviii; William Weston, *William Weston: The Autobiography of an Elizabethan*, trans. Philip Caraman (London: Longmans, Green and Co., 1955) 176.

2   Wilfrid R. Prest, *The Inns of Court under Elizabeth I and the Early Stuarts 1590–1640* (London: Longman Group Ltd., 1972) 176; Norman Jones, *The English Reformation: Religion and Cultural Adaptation* (Oxford: Blackwell Publishers Ltd., 2002) 21–2; *CSP Dom* 12/242/121. From the Catholic area of Holborn was an alley leading to a back gate of the Gray's Inn gardens. See William Newton, *London in the Olden Time* (London: Bell and Daldy, 1855) 99.

3   Jones, *English Reformation*, 125, 130. Jones argues that such tolerance disappeared after approximately 1580, although as the following example of John Hambly reveals, Catholic activity at the Inns continued.

4   See Edwin H. Burton, *London Streets and Catholic Memories* (London: Burns, Oates & Washbourne Ltd., 1925) 73.

5   SP Dom 12/192/46i; See Keith Thomas, *Religion and the Decline of Magic* (New York: Charles Scribner's Sons, 1971) 62–5, on the prohibition of public processions.

6   SP Dom 12/192/46i.

7   Michael de Certeau, *The Mystic Fable*, trans. Michael B. Smith (Chicago: University of Chicago Press, 1992) 97–8.

8   For another example of reconciliation to the Catholic Church at the Inns, see *CSP Dom* 12/217/38.

9   Geoffrey de C. Parmiter, *Edmund Plowden: An Elizabethan Recusant Lawyer* (Southampton: Hobbs the Printers of Southampton for the Catholic Record Society, 1987) 104–5, 163.

10   McGrath and Rowe, "The Imprisonment," 420; *A Tudor Journal: The Diary of a Priest in The Tower, 1580–1585*, ed. Brian A. Harrison (London: St. Paul's Publishing, 2000) appendix 4; Christine Kelly, *Blessed Thomas Belson: His Life and Times, 1563–1589* (Gerrards Cross: Colin Smythe, 1987) 23; J. H. Pollen and William MacMahon, eds., *The Venerable Philip Howard, Earl of Arundel, 1557–1595: English Martyrs, vol. II* (London: Catholic Record Society, XXI, 1919).

11   SP Dom 14/21/48. For Pounde's interpretation of his experiences, see chapter 4.

12   McGrath and Rowe, "The Imprisonment," 425. See also *CSP Dom* 12/248/43.

13   For examples, see Stonyhurst MS, Angl. A, ii, 41, quoted in Tierney, *Dodd*, vol. 3, cxcv; Seccion de Estado, Archivo General de Simancas 2592/63, quoted in Albert Loomie, ed., *Spain and the Jacobean Catholics: vol. 2, 1613–1624* (London: Catholic Record Society, LXVIII, 1978) 28–33; *CSP Dom* 12/274/5, 14/91/20, 16/260/64.

14   For examples, see Ellesmere MS 2128, f. 51; Ellesmere MS 2129, f. 53; Ellesmere MS 2130, f. 55v; Ellesmere MS 2131, f. 57; Ellesmere MS 2134, f. 63v;

Ellesmere MS 2137, ff. 67–67v, all in Anthony G. Petti, ed., *Recusant Documents from the Ellesmere Manuscripts 1577–1715* (London: Catholic Record Society, LX, 1968); Christopher Devlin, *The Life of Robert Southwell: Poet and Martyr* (London: Longmans, Green and Co., 1956) 160, 289, 318; John Byrde to Cecil, from *Salisbury* XI, 363, 27 August 1601, quoted in McGrath and Rowe, "The Imprisonment," 424–5.

15   Henry Garnet to Claudio Aquaviva, 7 March 1595, Arch Rom SJ Anglia, 31 I, ff. 109–113, quoted in Devlin, *Life of Robert Southwell*, 298–9.

16   Devlin, *Life of Robert Southwell*, 91.

17   Richard Challoner, *Memoirs of Missionary Priests and Other Catholics of Both Sexes that have Suffered Death in England on Religious Accounts from the Year 1577–1684.* vol. 1 (Edinburgh: Thomas C. Jack, Grange Publishing Works, 1878) 69–71.

18   *CSP Dom* 12/283/70. See also Devlin, *Life of Robert Southwell*, 91; Weston, *William Weston*, 176; Challoner, *Memoirs* (1878 ed.) 69–71, for further examples.

19   SP Dom 14/80/79, 83. Occasionally, a prisoner might petition to be allowed to possess certain religious books, as Robert Southwell did in 1592. See Devlin, *Life of Robert Southwell*, 289. See also SP Dom 12/158/9, 12/248/36, 14/111/91–2; *CSP Dom* 12/248/116; BL, Lansdowne MS 153, f. 123; Connelly, *Women*, 54.

20   BL, Lansdowne MS 153, f. 123.

21   BL, Lansdowne MS 153, f. 123. Based on Allison and Rogers, the Broughton and Granada titles received by Brunele and Wigges are most likely the titles referred to.

22   SP Dom 16/22/111. See also Nancy Pollard Brown's descriptions of prison copying and distribution of Catholic literature from the Marshalsea and the Clink in "Paperchase: The Dissemination of Catholic Texts in Elizabethan England," in *English Manuscript Studies 1100–1700*, vol. I, eds. Peter Beal and Jeremy Griffiths (Oxford: Basil Blackwell, 1989) 121, 139.

23   Burton, *London Streets*, 27. The Pope's Head Tavern, for example, dated from the time of Edward IV. The tavern's sign still existed in the late eighteenth century. Thomas Esser mentions Paternoster Row and Ave Maria Lane in *Zur Archäologie der Pater-Noster-Schnur* (Fribourg: Paulus, 1898) 53, cited in Winston-Allen, *Stories*, 112.

24   See also Brown, "Paperchase," 125–140, for discussion of a Catholic network in Spitalfields.

25   SP Dom 12/192/46i; *CSP Dom* 12/242/121.

26   For examples, see SP Dom 12/97/27, 12/172/111; *CSP Dom* 12/192/35; Oscott MS, Kirk's Collection, i, 33 quoted in J. H. Pollen, ed., *Unpublished Documents Relating to the English Martyrs: vol. 1. 1584–1603* (London: Catholic Record Society, V, 1908) 182–4; Roger Manning, *Religion and Society in Elizabethan Sussex: A Study of the Enforcement of the Religious Settlement, 1558–1603* (Bristol: Leicester University Press, 1969) 157.

27   Burton, *London Streets*, 6.

28   Henry Foley, *Records of the English Province of the Society of Jesus*, 7 vols.
      (London: Burns & Oates, 1877) ii, 489.

29   For conceptual issues, see Benedict Anderson, *Imagined Communities:
      Reflections on the Origin and Spread of Nationalism* (London: Verso Books,
      1983).

30   See the descriptions of Edmund Campion's and Robert Southwell's executions in
      E. E. Reynolds, *Campion and Parsons: The Jesuit Mission of 1580–1581*
      (London: Sheed and Ward, 1980) 199–200, and Devlin, *Life of Robert Southwell*,
      319, respectively.

31   See descriptions of John Boste's walk to the gallows from chapter 2 and Margaret
      Clitheroe's walk in chapter 4.

32   For example, see Stonyhurst MS, Collectanea M, f. 160, quoted in Pollen,
      Unpublished Documents, 286.

33   For example, see Timothy J. McCann, "Some unpublished Accounts of the
      Martyrdom of Blessed Thomas Bullaker, OSF, of Chichester in 1642," *Recusant
      History* 19, no. 2 (1988): 174, 176, 179.

34   See chapter 1, regarding the bull.

35   Burton, *London Streets*, 52.

36   Anonymous by an English Catholic present at Thomas Holland's execution at
      Tyburn. Published in Portuguese in Lisbon on June 10, 1643, by Lourenço de
      Anveres. See Anonymous, "A Portuguese narration of the Martyrdom of the Ven.
      Thomas Holland, SJ, 1642," trans. Edward Robert James (London: Catholic
      Record Society, XIII, 1913) 147–9; For similar examples, see Seccion de Estado,
      Archivo General de Simancas 2587/140, quoted in Albert Loomie, ed., *Spain and
      the Jacobean Catholics: vol. 1, 1603–1612* (London: Catholic Record Society,
      LXIV, 1973) 166–7; Devlin, *Life of Robert Southwell*, 319.

37   SP Dom 14/80/84. See also Foley, *Records*, iv, 115; *CSP Rome* Ser. 38, v. 2,
      Appendix VII, 568; Dom F.O. Blundell, *Old Catholic Lancashire* (London:
      Burns, Oates & Washbourne, Ltd., 1925) 78–82; Burton, *London Streets*, 143–4.

38   SP Dom 12/153/78; Reynolds, *Campion and Parsons*, 205.

39   *English Martyrologe* (St. Omer: John Wilson, 1608).

40   BL, Lansdowne MS 153, ff. 28–9. See also BL, Lansdowne MS 350, ff. 6v–7v,
      9–13v, 15, 21–21v, 30; SP Dom 14/32/4.

41   Tyburn was certainly not the only execution site for Catholics in London. Areas
      such as Fetter Lane and the Conduit in the Fleet Street area were used as well.
      Tyburn, however, was the best known. See Burton, *London Streets*, 33; Pollen,
      Unpublished Documents, 182–4.

42   Burton, *London Streets*, 6; See also *CSP Dom* 14/69/67, 14/71/64–5 for examples.

43   Blanks are in the manuscript.

44   BL, Add MS 39288, f. 6.

45   John Jewel, *The Zurich Letters: Comprising the Correspondence of Several English Bishops and Others . . .* (Cambridge: Parker Society, L, 44–5) quoted by Rowse, *Tudor Cornwall*, 322.

46   See chapter 1 for an explanation of relics' roles in accessing the saints and martyrs as intercessors before the throne of God.

47   Challoner, *Memoirs*, 78. For further examples, see Archivo General de Simancas, Seccion de Estado 2572/31, in Loomie, *Spain and the Jacobean Catholics: vol. 2*, 15–23; Stonyhurst MS, Collectanae M 186, 7. JJ, 1600 printed in Pollen, *Unpublished Documents*, 205–7.

48   Devlin, *Life of Robert Southwell*, 320–4. For confirmations of the events from various sources, see appendix, 358.

49   SP Dom 16/61/13; Blundell, *Old Catholic Lancashire*, 131–3; Pollen, *Unpublished Documents*, 290.

50   Foley, *Records*, ii, 489, 492.

51   Foley, *Records*, ii, 497.

52   Executed in London, May 3, 1606, in connection with the Gunpowder Plot.

53   BL, Add MS 21203, Plut. Clii. F, quoted in Foley, *Records*, iv, 129–30. For a similar description of martyrs' relics that refused to decompose, see Morris, *The Troubles*, iii, 52.

54   Foley, *Records*, iv, 121–3.

55   Foley, *Records*, iv, 133.

56   SP Dom 14/21/5; 14/216/218 a & b.

57   Cawood's shop in St. Paul's Churchyard, for example, appears to have been well known to Catholics as an outlet for books and Catholic items. See SP Dom 12/248/36.

58   SP Dom 14/80/107, for example, reported that Catholic books were on sale in St. Paul's Churchyard, possibly at Cawood's shop mentioned above. The bookseller's policy evidently was that his books were "not to be sold to any but to such as are known most to read them."

59   HMC, 12th Report, *The MSS of the Earl of Cowper*, Appendix, vol. II (1888) 216, quoted in J. M. Blom, *The Post-Tridentine English Primer* (London: Catholic Record Society, 1982) 40. See discussion of Bantre in chapter 3.

60   *CSP Dom* 16/450/94.

61   Ellesmere MS 2125, f. 47; See also Catholic Record Society, XL, 51, quoted in McGrath and Rowe, "Imprisonment", 420.

62   *CSP Dom* 14/20/7, 16.

63   *CSP Dom* 16/261/1; *Book of Acts of Court of High Commission*, February 1633/4, ff. 3, 6b, 15a, b.

64 Haus Hof Und Staats archiv, Vienna, PC 53, f. 34–35v, quoted in Loomie, *Spain and the Jacobean Catholics: vol. 2*, 74. Again, this is possibly Cawood's shop in St. Paul's.

65 Pierrepont would later be under the patronage of Sir William Howard of Naworth. See SP Dom 12/178/11; *Selections from the Household Books of Lord William Howard of Naworth Castle* (Durham: Surtees Society, LXVIII, 1878) 251, 508; BL, Lansdowne MS 50, f. 156; Pollen, *Unpublished Documents*, 182–4. During the 1590 examination/trial of Edward Jones, priest, it was entered into evidence that Protestant authorities apprehended Jones at a grocer's house on Fleet Street. This is likely Tailor as well.

66 For a more complete discussion of John Hambly, see chapter 6.

67 SP Dom 12/192/46.

68 BL, Lansdowne MS 153, f. 30.

69 *CSP Dom Add* 12/29/39.

70 *CSP Dom Add* 12/32/45.

71 BL, Lansdowne MS 50, f. 156.

72 Cecil Papers 168/110, HMC, vol. IV, 198, quoted in Clare Talbot, ed., *Miscellanea Recusant Records* (London: Catholic Record Society, LIII, 1961) 122.

73 SP Dom 12/172/8.

74 SP Dom 12/172/114. Interestingly, Edmund Campion, the first English Jesuit martyr, was the son of "an eminent member of the Grocers' Company" in London. See Jones, *English Reformation*, 22.

75 A physician, such as the Catholic Thomas Vavasour of York, could also serve as the crux of a Catholic network, since a good deal of traffic in people and books would not arouse much notice in a physician's office. Using the York City archives, Roland Connelly has also noted the importance of butchers, most notably butchers' wives, within Catholic networks in York in the 1570s. See *Women*, 62.

76 *CSP Dom* 12/29/39, 62, 12/32/45, 12/235/22.

77 *CSP Rome* ser. 38, v. 2, appendix VII, 568.

78 *CSP Dom* 16/464/31.

79 For examples, see SP Dom 12/178/11; *Selections from the Household Books of Lord William Howard of Naworth Castle*, 508.

80 In 1563, the Protestant government prohibited travelers or foreigners from attending Mass. See Spencer Hall, ed., *Documents from Simancas Relating to the Reign of Elizabeth, 1558–1568*, trans. Don Tomas Gonzalez (London: Chapman and Hall, 1865) 84, 100. See also Benjamin J. Kaplan, "Fictions of Privacy: House Chapels and the Spatial Accommodation of Religious Dissent in Early Modern Europe," *American Historical Review* (October 2002): 1052–4.

81   Hall, *Documents*, 77.

82   Hall, *Documents*, 82–3.

83   For examples, see SP Dom 14/119/90; BL, Lansdowne MS 23, ff. 110–1.

84   Sir Richard Grosvenor, *The Papers of Sir Richard Grosvenor, 1st Bart. (1585–1645)*, ed. Richard Cust (Stroud: Record Society of Lancashire and Cheshire, CXXXIV, 1996) 3.

85   BL, Lansdowne MS 23, f. 117; SP Dom 14/7/89, *CSP Dom* 14/61/103, 14/67/118, 14/68/60, 14/70/33, 14/76/48, 14/163/32–34, 14/164/46; Seccion de Estado, Archivo General de Simancas 2513 n. fol., quoted in Loomie, *Spain and the Jacobean Catholics: vol. 1*, 179.

86   Alexandra Walsham analyzes the place of this event in Catholic and Protestant propaganda and worldview in "'The fatall vesper': Providentialism and Anti-popery in Late Jacobean London," *Past and Present* (August 1994): 36–52.

87   BL, Add MS 4177, ff. 56–59.

88   Seccion de Estado, Archivo General de Simancas 2603/102, quoted in Loomie, *Spain and the Jacobean Catholics: vol. 2*, 160.

89   *CSP Dom* 14/154/17.

90   For examples, see BL, Lansdowne MS 23, ff. 110–1; *CSP Dom* 14/72/77; Hall, *Documents*, 82–3.

91   Sir John Mason to Sir Thomas Chaloner, 22 February 1562/3, quoted in Wright, *Queen Elizabeth and her Times* (1838) i, 128; SP Dom 14/119/90; *CSP Dom* 14/88/134.

92   Seccion de Estado, Archivo General de Simancas 2592/63, quoted in Loomie, *Spain and the Jacobean Catholics: vol. 2*, 28–33.

93   Salisbury MS, vol. 113, no. 90; Julian Sanchez de Ulloa to Philip III, Seccion de Estado, Archivo General de Simancas, 2598/101, in Loomie, *Spain and the Jacobean Catholics: vol. 2*, 39.

94   Diego de Sarmiento de Acuña to Philip III, Seccion de Estado, Archivo General de Simancas 2592/77, in Loomie, *Spain and the Jacobean Catholics: vol. 2*, 39. English Catholics also took their children to the embassies for baptism. See HMC Salisbury MS XVI, 374

95   BL, Lansdowne MS 153, f. 30.

96   *CSP Dom* 14/148/31 i–iv, 32; See also *Miscellanea VII* (London: Catholic Record Society, IX, 120–1.

97   P. R. Harris, "The Reports of William Udall, Informer, 1605–1612, part I," *Recusant History* 8, no. 4 (1966): 203–4. See also BL, Lansdowne MS 153, f. 6.

98   BL, Lansdowne MS 153, f. 68

99   See chapter 1 for a discussion of the penal laws.

100   Salisbury MS, vol. 113, no. 90.

101   *CSP Dom* 14/168/22; See also *CSP Dom* 14/90/68, 16/12/12, 18, 74; Salisbury
      MS, vol. 115, no. 3, February 1605/6.

102   *CSP Dom* 14/90/57.

103   *CSP Dom* 14/168/64. See also *CSP Dom* 16/21/11, 16/33/20.

104   *CSP Dom* 14/18/94, 16/12/58.

105   *CSP Dom* 16/239/24.

106   SP Dom 14/81/36.

107   SP Dom 14/83/25.

108   *CSP Dom* 14/97/95, 113, 114, 135, 136, and 14/104/6.

109   *CSP Dom* 16/18/19.

110   *CSP Dom* 16/23/59.

111   *CSP Dom* 14/155/21, 61–3.

112   *CSP Dom* 14/177/23.

113   *CSP Dom* 14/177/25, 27–8.

114   Seccion de Estado, Archivo General de Simancas 2590/8, 10; 2572/31 quoted in
      Loomie, *Spain and the Jacobean Catholics: vol. 2*, 15–23; Thomas McCoog,
      English and Welsh Jesuits, 1555–1650 (London: Catholic Record Society, LXXIV,
      1994) 15; *CSP Dom* 14/61/99.

115   SP Dom 16/255/33. See also *CSP Dom* 14/168/22, 16/21/34, 59.

116   Burton, *London Streets*, 64.

117   One of these priests was probably the Benedictine John Roberts executed in
      January 1611. Seccion de Estado, Archivo General de Simancas 2587/140, quot-
      ed in Loomie, *Spain and the Jacobean Catholics: vol. 1*, 166–7.

118   SP Dom 14/61/88, 91; Seccion de Estado, Archivo General de Simancas 2590/8,
      10, quoted in Loomie, *Spain and the Jacobean Catholics: vol. 2*, 20.

119   Seccion de Estado, Archivo General de Simancas 2590/8, 10, quoted in Loomie,
      Spain and the Jacobean Catholics: vol. 2, 15–23; Burton, *London Streets*, 64.

120   See chapter 4 where such issues are discussed in more detail.

121   McCoog, *English*, 15.

122   Many English Catholic women desired to become nuns or lead a communal reli-
      gious life in a lay order but either lacked the means to emigrate to the continent
      to join an order or wanted to remain in England to serve the Catholic cause.
      There were secret female monasteries in both London and York. Their innova-
      tions and relationship to the more formal, male-oriented mission await examina-
      tion in further depth, although see, for example, Colleen Marie Seguin, *Addicted
      unto Piety: Catholic Women in England, 1590–1690* (PhD Dissertation, Duke
      University, 1997) chap. 5. For examples of women involved in such activities, see
      Connelly, *Women*, 55, 102–3, 156–7, 162, 171, and particularly 208 in which

Mary Ward, founder of the Institute of the Blessed Virgin Mary, felt she was called not just to religious life but to "a new way of religious life."

123 Seccion de Estado, Archivo General de Simancas 2590/8, 10, 2572/31, quoted in Loomie, *Spain and the Jacobean Catholics: vol. 2*, 15–23.

NOTES TO CHAPTER 6

1 Richard Davies, *New Cornwall* 13, no. 3, quoted in P. Berresford Ellis, *The Cornish Language and its Literature* (London: Routledge and Kegan Paul, 1974) 1. My thanks to Deborah Bennetts of Ponsanooth, Cornwall, for directing me to this poem.

2 A. L. Rowse, *Tudor Cornwall: Portrait of a Society* (New York: Charles Scribner's Sons, 1969) 32.

3 A. K. Hamilton-Jenkin, *Cornwall and Its People: Cornish Seafarers, Cornwall, and the Cornish Homes and Customs* (London: J. M. Dent & Sons Ltd., 1946) 135–7.

4 John Norden, *Speculi Britanniae Pars; a Topograph and chorograph. description of Cornwall* (London, 1728) 3–4, quoted in Anne Duffin, *Faction and Faith: Politics and Religion of the Cornish Gentry before the Civil War* (Exeter: University of Exeter Press, 1996) 1.

5 Rowse, *Tudor Cornwall*, 320, 342, 378, for example, does not see the purpose in examining religious practices themselves, since most Catholics simply followed their betters in matters of religion and since the "struggle between Protestants and Catholics was in the main a struggle between two parties over the body of a mentally passive people, for the possession of power. Which ever side won, they [the people], with variations, would follow." Rowse describes Catholic efforts to maintain their religion as "their pathetic resistance," albeit maintained by Catholics he terms courageous. Alternatively, Duffin, *Faction and Faith*, describes the importance of religion to the Cornish (whether Catholics or Protestants) but does not examine whether Cornish understanding or experiencing of either religion changed during this period so that what each side perceived they were fighting for evolved over time.

6 Rowse, *Tudor Cornwall*, 344–5, 367, 370; For examples, see P. A. Boyan and G. R. Lamb, *Francis Tregian, Cornish Recusant* (London: Sheed and Ward Ltd., 1955); Helen Whelan, *Snow on the Hedges: A Life of Cuthbert Mayne* (Leominster, Herefordshire: Fowler Wright Books, 1984); Cecil Kerr, *The Life of the Venerable Philip Howard, Earl of Arundel and Surrey* (London: Longmans, Green, 1926); Duke of Norfolk, E.M., ed., *The Lives of Philip Howard, Earl of Arundel, and of Anne Dacres, His Wife* (London: Hurst and Blackett, 1857).

7 Richard Carew, *Survey of Cornwall* (1602) 127, quoted in and with translation from Cornish to English by Philip Payton, *The Making of Modern Cornwall* (Redruth: Dyllansow Truran, 1992) 152.

8 Rowse, *Tudor Cornwall*, 78.

9   Carew, *Survey*, in *Richard Carew of Antony, 1555–1620*, ed. F. E. Halliday (London: Andrew Melrose, 1953) 64. Despite its geographic and cultural isolation from the rest of England, Cornwall was politically tied to the English crown as a royal duchy. See Rowse, *Tudor Cornwall*, 50, 60–1, 77; John Doddridge, *History of Wales, Cornwall and Chester* (1630; reprint, Amsterdam: Theatrum Orbis Terrarum, 1973) 3; Duffin, *Faction and Faith*, 3–5. The crown increased the duchy's presence in Cornwall during the early Tudor period by annexing Cornish land formerly belonging to the Catholic Church during the Dissolution of the Monasteries.

10   For examples, see Mary Coates, *Cornwall in the Great Civil War and Interregnum, 1642–1660* (1933; reprint, Truro: Bradford Barton, 1963); Payton, *The Making*, 150; Payton, "'a . . . concealed envy against the English': a Note on the Aftermath of the 1497 Rebellions in Cornwall," in Philip Payton, ed., *Cornish Studies One* (Exeter: University of Exeter Press, 1993) 8–9; Duffin, *Faction and Faith*, 2; Rowse, *Tudor Cornwall*, 23, 139.

11   Rowse, *Tudor Cornwall*, 121, 139.

12   Quoted in Hamilton-Jenkin, *Cornwall and its People*, 166–7. Of course, most Cornish could not understand the Latin of the Catholic service either, however parts of this service were performed in Cornish in some communities.

13   See Thomas Cranmer, *Remains and Letters* (Parker Society, 163 foll.) in Rowse, *Tudor Cornwall*, 271. In punishment for his role in the rebellion and to send a powerful message to other rebels, the authorities executed the vicar of St. Thomas upon a gallows erected on top of his church tower. He was hanged dressed in his Massing vestments with rosary beads, a sacring bell, and a holy water bucket and sprinkle draped about his body.

14   Norden, *Speculum*, described how both the Cornish and the English still viewed the Cornish as a people separate from the English in 1584. Quoted by Ellis, *Cornish Language*, 74.

15   Duffin, *Faction and Faith*, xiv.

16   SP Dom 12/119/20. See also Rowse, *Tudor Cornwall*, 342.

17   Terms are defined in chapter 1.

18   SP Dom 16/11/52, 52i. It is not clear that the deputy lieutenants were restricting their count to heads of household, although given the purpose of their commission (to disarm Cornish Catholics who threatened to become a fifth column in case of invasion by Spain) it is likely that women and children were not included in this count.

19   PRO E179/89/324–339 cited in Duffin, *Faction and Faith*, 38–9.

20   Bossy, *ECC*, 404–5.

21   Hamilton-Jenkin, *Cornwall and its People*, 131–2, 167–8; Albert Peel, ed., *The Second Part of a Register*, 2 vols. (London: Cambridge University Press, 1915) ii, 88–9, 98–110, quoted in Rowse, *Tudor Cornwall*, 338. See also Rowse, *Tudor Cornwall*, 27–8, 222, 229–31, 321–2; Carew, *Survey*, 140–4.

22   For examples of clerical pluralism, absenteeism, non-residency or long-standing vacancies in Cornish parishes, see Hamilton-Jenkin, *Cornwall and its People*, 167–9. See also Rowse, *Tudor Cornwall*, 322, 338–9.

23   In the fifteenth century, for example, the Cornish rebuilt many of their churches with a distinctive Cornish design, characterized by three-stage towers, Norman fonts, and barrel roofs. I explore this phenomenon in more detail in *As One in Faith: The Reconstruction of Catholic Communities in Protestant England, 1559–1642* (PhD Dissertation, University of Texas, Austin, 2000) 450–3.

24   This may have been true in pre-reform Cornwall as well. L. E. Elliott-Binns, *Medieval Cornwall* (London: Methuen & Co. Ltd., 1955) 286–313, argues that the medieval diocese of Exeter was one of the largest in England and consequently more difficult to administer. Bishops of Exeter frequently were "often men busy with other affairs, so that their visits to the distant parts under their jurisdiction were necessarily infrequent." When bishops did journey into Cornwall, their time was typically taken up with "business of a secular nature, such as the inspection of manors; the rest was occupied by confirmations, church dedications, and other routine duties that left little opportunity for getting to know their clergy, still less the people to whom they ministered." Cornish administration was typically left to the archdeacons of Cornwall, "some of whom found it hard to hold their own with local magnates and officials, or to cope with the stubborn Cornishmen whose speech they might not understand."

25   Elliott-Binns, *Medieval Cornwall*, 292; Muriel E. Curtis, *Some Disputes Between the City and the Cathedral Authorities of Exeter*, History of Exeter Research Group., no. 5 (Manchester: Manchester University Press for the University College of the South-West of England, 1932).

26   Duffin, *Faction and Faith*, 38. Duffin appears to be arguing that Cornwall is distinctive in the relative freedom with which the archdeaconry of Cornwall operated when she postulates that this could explain why "Cornwall was affected rather less by the major religious upheavals of the period than other counties."

27   Rowse, *Tudor Cornwall*, 322.

28   For examples in other counties, see Christopher Haigh, *Reformation and Resistance in Tudor Lancashire* (Cambridge: Cambridge University Press, 1975).

29   Only six Cornish priests of the lower ranks were deprived of their posts after Elizabeth's Act of Supremacy despite clear evidence that clerics maintained traditional rituals and doctrine in the parishes. Similarly, in later years, few deprivations occurred although the traditional practices continued. Speech of Leonard Lockwood quoting Peel, *The Second Part of a Register*, ii, 88–9, 98–110, which includes the 1586 returns of clergy by the Puritans for a Supplication to be presented to Parliament.

30   During the Dissolution of the Monasteries, the Cornish laity negotiated with the crown to preserve such celebrations which the Protestant clergy generally disparaged. *L.P.*, XI, 405, and XII, I, 1001, quoted in Rowse, *Tudor Cornwall*,

188–9, 230–1. Following Elizabeth's Act of Uniformity, traditionally inclined Cornish continued to preserve many of the feast days of their Celtic saints in spite of Protestant efforts to discourage such celebrations and despite the Council of Trent's efforts to decrease devotion to locally or regionally popular saints not necessarily recognized by Rome. See Hamilton-Jenkin, *Cornwall and Its People*, 452.

31   Carew, *Survey*, 140–4; See also Hamilton-Jenkin, *Cornwall and Its People*, 131–2; Rowse, *Tudor Cornwall*, 27–8.

32   Nicholas Orme, *The Saints of Cornwall* (Oxford: Oxford University Press, 2000) 41.

33   For evidence of continuity in the reverence of such saints between the early seventeenth century and the present day, see CRO, DD/CY/5232; Brian Webb, *Kemsyk sen Perran, a St. Piran Miscellany* (Redruth: Dyllansow Truran, 1982) 12; Gilbert H. Doble, *The Saints of Cornwall*, 5 vols. (Chatham: Parrett & Neves, Ltd., 1960–1970) i, 131–2, ii, 16–17, and iv, 25–6; Hamilton-Jenkin, *Cornwall and Its People*, 452, 466–70; Rowse, *Tudor Cornwall*, 29.

34   Some feast day celebrations contained nominal concessions to the Protestant faith, yet still continued to exhibit most qualities of their late medieval antecedents. For an example, see Richard Carew's description of Lostwithiel's election of a mock mayor upon Easter Sunday cited by Hamilton-Jenkin, *Cornwall and its People*, 470. See also Natalie Zemon Davis, "The Reasons of Misrule," in *Society and Culture in Early Modern France: Eight Essays by Natalie Zemon Davis* (Stanford: Stanford University Press, 1975).

In addition to reverencing their traditional saints on their feast days, Cornish Catholics continued to worship them in a myriad of other ritual, gestural, or immanentist ways. The Cornish continued to name their children after traditional Celtic saints. See, for example, CRO, FP 133/1/1; Nicholas Roscarrock, *Lives of the Saints: Cornwall and Devon*, ed. Nicholas Orme (Devon and Cornwall Record Society, new series, XXXV, 1992) f. 298v. And they preserved their saints' relics when possible. See CRO, DD RS 76/1; A casket once containing the remains of St. Petroc, for example, is still displayed at Bodmin parish church. See also Payton, *The Making*, 112.

35   Also known as Meriadoc, Meriadek, Marazaack, or Maradzock.

36   Doble, *Saints*, i, 131–2, cites eighteenth-century historians Edward Lhuyd and Hals that this well was still maintained and visited by the faithful in the eighteenth century "in order to besprinkle themselves, out of an opinion of its great virtue and sanctity." Hals added that the locals called the visitors to the well "Merrasicks."

37   *Beunans Meriasek: the Life of St. Meriasek*, ed. and trans. Whitley Stokes (1872); See also Hilary Shaw, "Our Lady of Cornwall," *Katholik Kernow* 5 (Summer 1990): 5; Payton, "'a . . . concealed envy,'" 9–12.

38   Letter of deputy lieutenants of Cornwall to the Earl of Pembroke, 17 Dec 1625, PRO E 179/89/324–39, quoted by Duffin, *Faction and Faith*, 39. According to

Bossy, *ECC*, 419, there were only five Jesuits in Cornwall (the Jesuit district of St. Stanislaus) in both 1621 and 1632. Perhaps this incident is extremely illustrative of the common desire among neighbors to preserve peace which is analyzed by Bossy in *Peace in the Post-Reformation: The Birkbeck Lectures, 1995* (Cambridge: Cambridge University Press, 1998) 88–91.

39   See Elliott-Binns, *Medieval Cornwall*, 264, 279, who argues that the lag time between the re-introduction of Roman Christianity in the southeast and the arrival of the Saxon occupation in Cornwall in the ninth century allowed Celtic Christianity the opportunity to establish itself so firmly in Cornwall that it could not be dislodged.

40   CRO, RS 78/11; Exeter Chapter MS 3518; Cambridge University, Corpus Christi College, Parker MS 93.

41   University Library, Cambridge, Add MS 3041.

42   See CRO, FS 3/773 and AR/21/20.

43   Richard Challoner, *Memoirs of Missionary Priests and Other Catholics of Both Sexes that have Suffered Death in England on Religious Accounts from the Year 1577–1684*, vol. 1 (London: Burns, Oates & Washbourne, Ltd., 1924) 38; E. E. Reynolds, *Campion and Parsons: The Jesuit Mission of 1580–1* (London: Sheed and Ward, 1980) 154; CRO, FS 3/773; SP Dom 12/187/19; Rowse, *Tudor Cornwall*, 368.

44   Roscarrock likely had difficulty supporting himself since he had surrendered most of his Roscarrock land in Cornwall to the state in recusancy fines over the decades. See CRO, AR 28/3.

45   Rowse, *Tudor Cornwall*, 28, 367. A. L. Rowse, "Nicholas Roscarrock and His *Lives of the Saints*," in J. H. Plumb, ed., *Studies in Social History: A Tribute to G. M. Trevelyan* (London: Longmans, Green, 1955) 3–31.

46   Roscarrock supported his saints' lives with evidence from respected medieval authors and challenged those who would disbelieve to refute such respected, learned sources. For example, see Roscarrock, *Lives*, ff. 412–4, 361.

47   Although undated, the letter's references to Howard's son as the probable conservator of Roscarrock's writings place its authorship most likely in the decades of the 1640s or 1650s. Lord William Howard died in 1640.

48   Trevennor Roscarrock, Nicholas's brother, also a recusant.

49   Probably St. Brechanus and his family

50   Original letter published in S. Baring-Gould, *Cornish Characters and Strange Events*, 2 vols. (London: John Lane The Bodley Head Ltd., 1925) ii, 183–4. The letter is also included in the manuscript volume of Roscarrock's *Lives of the English Saints* at University Library, Cambridge, Add MS 3041. The careful manner in which Roscarrock organized his book and his comments to intended readers suggest he meant it for publication and distribution to a wider audience. Many of Roscarrock's comments to intended readers indicate this as well. For example, see Roscarrock, *Lives*, f. 25.

51   As Nicholas Orme argues, English reform failed to destroy such cults, particularly the cults based outside of parish churches, and people of all social classes continued to venerate Celtic saints. He places the number of church and chapel sites of Celtic saints in Cornwall at 185 today with many having ties to pre-reform and Reformation years. Orme, *Saints*, ix, 22, 37–45.

52   CRO, FS 3/45, particularly Ellis's notation on f. 105b. See also, F. Wormald, "The Calendar of the Augustinian Priory of Launceston Cornwall," *Journal of Theological Studies* 39, no. 153 (1938): 1–21.

53   CRO, FS 3/45, ff. 9–20b, 46b–60b. Celtic-Cornish saints lives were also preserved in post-reform years for private liturgical study, such as the excerpts from the Life of St. Meriasek copied in the seventeenth century from a fourteenth-century manuscript. See Orme, *Saints*, 188–9.

54   Roscarrock, *Lives*, ff. 202v, 323v, 359v–361. In Orme's notes upon Roscarrock, he refers to evidence of strong devotion to St. Keyna in St. Martin-by-Looe in 1535, immediately prior to Henry VIII's reforming efforts (146). See also, CRO, FS 3/45, Calendar of the Augustinian Priory at Launceston, and Exeter Chapter MS 3518, Exeter Martyrology, for evidence of continued devotion to Cornish saints during the late medieval period; Rowse, *Tudor Cornwall*, 27–8.

55   Rowse, *Tudor Cornwall*, 163, 183; Elliott-Binns, *Medieval Cornwall*, chapter 16.

56   Roscarrock, *Lives*, ff. 102r, 111r; John Whitaker, *The ancient cathedral of Cornwall historically surveyed* (London: Printed for John Stockdale, 1804) i, 327–8; ii, 1–5; Webb, *Kemsyk*, 2; Orme, *Saints*, 18. Additionally, Cornish Christians enjoyed strong links with Celtic Christians from Brittany. See Doddridge, *History*; *Kalendar of the Breviary of Leon and Treguier* and the Breton book of hours printed for the parish of Leon in the fifteenth or sixteenth centuries, cited in Webb, *Kemsyk*, 6–8.

57   Elliott-Binns, *Medieval Cornwall*, 279–80. Elliott-Binns also cites Henderson et al., *The Cornish Church Guide*, wherein it is estimated that of 212 parishes, 174 were of Celtic origin, 28 were of Saxon or Norman origin, and the remaining 10 were founded by townspeople.

58   Roscarrock, *Lives*, ff. 111v, 128; See also the lineages from Brechanus developed for St. Eneda (f. 203r), St. Etha (f. 207r), St. Gwen (f. 244r), St. Gwladhus (f. 244v), St. Helye (f. 247v), St. Jona (f. 270v), St. Isye (f. 272r), St. Keby (ff. 276v, 280v), St. Keneder (f. 278), St. Kerye (f. 280), St. Keyna (f. 280v), St. Maben (f. 296).

59   Celtic-Cornish Christians worshipped Roman-recognized saints as well as homegrown Celtic ones but often at a "lower level," described by Orme. Church dedications, for example, would be made in honor of Celtic saints while most "international" saints were venerated more modestly through images, altars, holy wells, etc. Orme, *Saints*, 33.

60   Roscarrock, *Lives*, f. 107.

61 Orme's notes in Roscarrock, *Lives*, f. 166. For a full discussion of Piran, see Orme, *Saints*, 220–3.

62 Roscarrock, *Lives*, ff. 359v–361r. For more Christ-like miracles of Cornish saints, see f. 101v (St. Brannoc), f. 111v (St. Cadoc), ff. 357v–358v (St. Petroc); f. 298v (St. Madern).

63 *Mark* 15:39.

64 It does not appear that the pre-reform lives of Piran that Roscarrock used as sources drew these strong parallels. While Roscarrock's sources may have chronicled certain of Piran's miracles, it was Roscarrock who drew together these threads into a legend that displays the striking similarities to Christ's life, death, and miracles.

65 Orme's notes in Roscarrock, *Lives*, 160–1, Orme, *Saints*, 202–3.

66 Stories of the early ascetics are chronicled in *The Desert Fathers: Translations from the Latin*, trans. Helen Waddell, reprint ed. (New York: Vintage Books, 1998); Laura Swan, *The Forgotten Desert Mothers: Lives and Stories of Early Christian Women* (New York: Paulist Press, 2001).

67 See Orme, *Saints*, 200–3, for a discussion of various cult traditions of St. Neot, not all in Cornwall. Orme concludes, however, that the evidence is stronger that Neot was Cornish than otherwise.

68 Roscarrock, *Lives*, ff. 323v–324v.

69 Roscarrock, *Lives*, ff. 131–131v, uses the term "desert" again in his life of St. Columba, a virgin saint.

70 CRO, RS 76/9.

71 For a detailed discussion of iconoclasm in England, see Margaret Aston, *England's Iconoclasts: vol. 1, Laws against Images* (Oxford: Clarendon Press, 1988). Also see Orme, *Saints*, 40, for discussion of the survival of traditional imagery on bench ends, rood screens, saints' paintings, and windows in Cornish churches.

72 Although images were removed in some Cornish churches, Cornwall appears to have been spared serious, violent bouts of iconoclasm. According to M. Quiller-Couch and L. Quiller-Couch, *Ancient and Holy Wells of Cornwall* (London: Charles J. Clark, 1894) 167–70, parents continued to bring weak children to Neot's well long after Protestant reforms. See also CRO, CN/1606/1–3.

73 For example, see Margaret Deanesly, *Augustine of Canterbury* (London: St. Augustine's Press, 1999) and Eddius Stephanus, "Life of Wilfrid," in D. H. Farmer, ed., *The Age of Bede*, trans. J. F. Webb (London: Penguin Books, 1988).

74 Whitaker, *The ancient cathedral*, ii, 27.

75 Roscarrock, *Lives*, ff. 323v–324v; Quiller-Couch and Quiller-Couch, *Ancient*, 167–70.

76 See also Roscarrock, *Lives*, ff. 264v (St. Indractus), 357v–358v (St. Petroc).

77   Robert Stephen Hawker, *Cornish Ballads and Other Poems* (orig. 1869) (Delmar, NY: Scholar's Facsimiles and Reprints, 1994) 158.

78   See chapter 1's discussion of immanence.

79   BL, Stowe MS 53, ff. 27v–28r, possibly from John of Tynemouth's *Nova Legenda Anglie*. For further evidence of holy wells associated with desert-father-type Cornish saints or other evidence of saints' close ties to the natural world, see CRO, DD RS 76/1 (St. Guron); Quiller-Couch and Quiller-Couch, *Ancient*, 89–91 (St. Jesus); BL, Stowe MS 53, ff. 27v–28v (St. Keyna); Roscarrock, *Lives*, ff. 264v (St. Indractus), 111v (St. Cadoc), 280v (St. Keyna), 298v (St. Madern), 357v–358v (St. Petroc); See also Orme, *Saints*, 162–3.

80   "Keyne" was a variant of Keyna. Carew, *Survey*, ii, 126v–127, 203. See also William Borlase, *Observations on the antiquities historical and monumental, of the county of Cornwall* (Oxford: W. Jackson, 1754) 351.

81   CRO, DD/CY/6673, EN 2472C, and FS 3/944/1–2; See also, Webb, *Kemsyk*, 12.

82   Geoffrey Grigson, reprinted in Peter Redgrove, ed., *Cornwall in Verse* (London: Secker and Warburg, 1982) 49.

83   For example, see CRO, DD/CY/80.

84   For examples, see CRO, RS/76/1, 7 and CN 1606/1–3; Quiller-Couch and Quiller-Couch, *Ancient*, 36–41. For a different argument, that holy wells were "de-Catholicized" as part of reform (at least in the northern shires), see Alexandra Walsham, "Reforming the Waters: Holy Wells and Healing Springs in Protestant England," in *Life and thought in the northern church, c. 1100–1700: essays in honour of Claire Cross*, ed. Diana Wood (Woodbridge, Suffolk: Boydell Press for the Ecclesiastical History Society, 1999) 227–55.

85   Holy wells at Dupath near Callington, and one dedicated to St. Cleer, for example, continued to be used, as did St. Madern's well which was associated with miracles on the feast of Corpus Christi. See Payton, *The Making*, 113; Roscarrock, *Lives*, f. 298v.

86   For example, St. Constantine's well in St. Merryn's parish. See Doble, *Saints*, ii, 16–17; Or St. Madern's well, described in Roscarrock, *Lives*, f. 298v. See also CRO, EN 2472C; Doble, *Saints*, i, 131–2; Hamilton-Jenkin, *Cornwall and its People*, 308; Quiller-Couch and Quiller-Couch, *Ancient*, 89–91.

87   Orme, *Saints*, 41. For a discussion of Cornish pilgrimage habits prior to reform, see Elliott-Binns, *Medieval Cornwall*, 272.

88   Hamilton-Jenkin, *Cornwall and its People*, 309; William Bottrell, *Traditions and Hearthside Stories of West Cornwall*, 2 vols. (Penzance: W. Cornish, 1870) ii, 239–42.

89   See Carew, *Survey*, 203.

90   Carew, *Survey*, ii, 144r–v. In an exception, Protestant authorities closed down Scarlet's Well near Bodmin due to its profound popularity in the 1580s, as reported by Carew. Evidently, even the authorities could only be pushed so far when

"huge numbers" flocked to a well on what appeared to be traditional religious pilgrimage. Orme, *Saints*, 41.

91   Also known as St. Selevan.

92   Doble, *Saints*, i, 3–9. For examples of other such sites associated with other saints and their use in this period, see Carew, *Survey*, 138v (St. Roche); Roscarrock, *Lives*, f. 323v (yard outside St. Neghton's chapel); Webb, *Kemsyk*, 12 (St. Piran).

93   Rowse, *Tudor Cornwall*, 364. See also Whitaker, *The ancient cathedral*, i, 156–7, for what may be an example of a private cell in which personal discipline could be practiced.

94   See Caroline Walker Bynum, *Holy Feast and Holy Fast: The Religious Significance of Food to Medieval Women* (Berkeley: University of California Press, 1988) and "Women Mystics and Eucharistic Devotion in the Thirteenth Century," *Women's Studies* 11 (1984): 179–214.

95   English reformers scorned popular belief in fairies, hobgoblins, ghosts, and other spirits. See Keith Thomas, *Religion and the Decline of Magic* (New York: Charles Scribner's Sons, 1971) 724–35; Alexandra Walsham, *Providence in Early Modern England* (Oxford: Oxford University Press, 2001) 28.

96   Oxford University, Bodleian Library, Clarendon MS 2443, f. 102, quoted in Hamilton-Jenkin, *Cornwall and its People*, 277. Also, Jeffries appears to have been clearly a Royalist which could also imply her supporting a more Catholic form of religion. See Clarendon MS 2478, f. 165.

97   Oxford University, Bodleian Library, Clarendon MS 2443, f. 102, and MS 2478, f. 165. See also Baring-Gould, *Cornish Characters*, ii, 164–5; Hamilton-Jenkin, *Cornwall and its People*, 276.

98   Humphrey Martyn to Moses Pitt, (Jeffries worked for the Pitt family when she had her first vision), 31 Jan 1693, quoted in Baring-Gould, *Cornish Characters*, ii, 157.

99   Moses Pitt of St. Teath, Cornwall, presently a publisher in London, to the Bishop of Gloucester, 1696, in Baring-Gould, *Cornish Characters*, ii, 157. Letter was based upon earlier reports of Humphrey Martyn who actually visited Jeffries to induce her to discuss her past.

100   Letter of Moses Pitt, quoted by Baring-Gould, *Cornish Characters*, ii, 164–5.

101   Letter of Moses Pitt, quoted by Baring-Gould, *Cornish Characters*, ii, 160–3.

102   Oxford University, Bodleian Library, Clarendon MS 2443, f. 102, quoted in Hamilton-Jenkin, *Cornwall and its People*, 276–7.

103   During this period, various Puritans and radical sectaries throughout England were also claiming to receive visions from God or to enjoy direct relationships with God. See J. F. McGregor, "Seekers and Ranters," in J. F. McGregor and B. Reay, eds., *Radical Religion in the English Revolution* (Oxford: Oxford University Press, 1988) 122–3, 129, 134, 179, 183–5. See also Paul Christianson, *Reformers and Babylon: English apocalyptic visions from the reformation to the eve of the civil war* (Toronto: University of Toronto Press, 1978). An important distinction

between Puritan or sectarian visions and Anne Jeffries's experiences is that the majority of the Puritan or sectarian visionaries typically advertised their abilities and used them to further spiritual or political causes. Their visions typically centered on the monarchy, war, denunciation of worldliness, and the apocalypse. Anne Jeffries, on the other hand, spoke of none of these issues and apparently would have preferred to have been left alone. Moreover, while Puritan and sectarian seers received revelations from the divine, they do not appear to have had a personal relationship with the divine in the way Jeffries did—meeting, talking with, and being fed by the divine. I have been unable to locate any evidence of Puritan or sectarian visionaries who were fed by God or who claimed to heal physical illness particularly without the aid of medicines through the power of God.

104   Letter of Moses Pitt, quoted by Baring-Gould, *Cornish Characters*, 159; Letter of Moses Pitt, quoted by Hamilton-Jenkin, *Cornwall and its People*, 276–7.

105   Letter of Moses Pitt, quoted by Baring-Gould, *Cornish Characters*, ii, 164–5.

106   Baring-Gould, *Cornish Characters*, ii, 166–7.

107   Letter of Moses Pitt, quoted by Baring-Gould, *Cornish Characters*, ii, 163.

108   For examples of possession of or regard for the efficacy of sacramental items by Cornish Catholics, see CRO, AD 37/50/19, 20 (index incorrectly lists these as 11, 12), CRO, DD/CY/1694, 1713; SP Dom 12/155/27, 16/250/19; Whitaker, *The ancient cathedral*, ii, 121–3; See also Hamilton-Jenkin, *Cornwall and its People*, 432–4; Ellis, *Cornish Language*, 67–8; SP Dom 12/248/99; Record Office, Castle of Exeter, Order from magistrate at Exeter to High Constable and Petty Constables of St. Mary Ottery to search houses looking for relics, Easter sessions 1605, in George Oliver, *Collections Illustrating the History of the Catholic Religion in the Counties of Cornwall, Devon, Dorset, Somerset, Wiltshire and Gloucester, in two parts, Historical and Biographical. With notices of the Dominican, Benedictine, & Franciscan Orders* (London: Charles Dolman, 1857) 9.

109   SP Dom 12/118/46; Whelan, *Snow*, 164–5; Oliver, *Collections*, 4–6.

110   SP Dom 16/250/19.

111   Many churches and chapels had been dedicated to Mary in the medieval years, for example, at Truro, Penzance, Mousehole, Camborne, Helston, Penryn, East Looe, Liskeard (a chapel of pilgrimage), Botus Fleming, Braddock, Callington, Sheviock, and Week St. Mary. Additionally, in one of the most popular Cornish miracle plays, *Beunans Meriasek*, the saint arrives in Camborne searching for a chapel of Mary so that he could establish an oratory near it. The play, still popular in the late sixteenth and early seventeenth centuries, includes special prayers to Mary to help the protagonist with his studies. See Shaw, "Our Lady of Cornwall," 5. There also existed in the fourteenth and fifteenth centuries guilds and confraternities dedicated to Mary, for example, the Guild and Fraternity of St. Mary of Portal in Truro. See Margaret Pollard and Faith Godbeer, *The Guild of Our Lady of the Portal* (Redruth: Dyllansow Truran, 1985) 9–10; Holy wells

dedicated to Mary were still recognized by the Cornish during our period. See CRO, DD/CY/80. The continued devotion of Celtic Christians of Cornwall and Wales to Mary can be seen in a Carol of the Rosary, written c.1577–84, Llanover MS, Welsh MS 23, Ph.2954, i, 255, and still in use at least until 1670, published in J. H. Pollen, ed., *Unpublished Documents Relating to the English Martyrs*, vol. 1. *1584–1603* (London: Catholic Record Society, V, 1908) 92–3; SP Dom 12/192/46; See CRO, AD 37/50/27 (index incorrectly lists item as 15), AR 21/15/1,2, DD/CY/1713, RS 76/9; BL, Arundel MS 318, see especially ff. 152–3.

112   For examples, see CRO, AD 37/50/20 (index incorrectly lists this item as 12), AR 21/15/1,2.

113   Whelan, *Snow*, 119, 130; Baring-Gould, *Cornish Characters*, ii, 281–2.

114   For example, SP Dom 12/164/48.

115   Ref. no. M. 30–1934.

116   See Whitaker, *The ancient cathedral*, ii, 91–2; Roscarrock, *Lives*, f. 202v; Orme's notes in Roscarrock, *Lives*, 11–2, plate 5, plate 14; Rowse, "Nicholas Roscarrock," 22.

117   V. H. H. Green, *A History of Oxford University* (London: B.T. Batsford, Ltd., 1974) 48, describes Exeter as one of the Catholic-inclined colleges of Oxford, along with Trinity, Lincoln, and New Colleges; Miles Jebb, *The Colleges of Oxford* (London: Constable & Co., Ltd., 1992) 75, agrees with this characterization of Exeter, as does John Richard Thackrah, *The Universities and Colleges of Oxford* (Lavenham, Suffolk: Terence Dalton, Ltd., 1981) 25. Colleges such as Exeter ejected few Catholic fellows following Protestant reform. They failed to enforce the required examinations of students to ensure Protestant conformity. They continued to accept Catholic students into the college, offering them Catholic-inclined tutors and the companionship of other Catholics within the college.

118   Duffin, *Faction and Faith*, 26.

119   Rowse, *Tudor Cornwall*, 356.

120   Duffin, *Faction and Faith*, 26: 44% of Cornishmen belonged to the Middle Temple; 27% to Lincoln's Inn, 22% to the Inner Temple, and 7% to Gray's Inn.

121   For a further example, see Rowse, *Tudor Cornwall*, 356.

122   SP Dom 12/118/46.

123   BL, Lansdowne MS 153, f. 123. Based on Allison and Rogers, the titles received by Wigges are most likely Richard Broughton's *Resolution of Religion* and Luis de Granada's *Memorials of a Christian Life*.

124   For examples, SP Dom 12/155/27, 12/248/118.

125   *CSP Dom* 12/248/94, 95, 116.

126   SP Dom 12/118/47; BL, Lansdowne MS 153, f. 123.

127   Ellis, *Cornish Language*, 72.

128   Godfrey Anstruther, *The Seminary Priests: A Dictionary of the Secular Clergy in England and Wales, 1558–1850*, 4 vols. (Ware, Herts.: St. Edmund's College, 1969–) i, 360, 367; Oliver, *Collections*, 4–5; Rowse, *Tudor Cornwall*, 356; Dominic Aidan Bellenger, *English and Welsh Priests, 1558–1800* (Bath: Downside Abbey, 1984).

129   There is no evidence that either Canterbury or Rome led these efforts. It appears that the Cornish clergy in Cornwall acted with relative independence in allowing the Cornish language to be used.

130   Rowse, *Tudor Cornwall*, 356–7; Bellenger, *English and Welsh Priests, 1558–1800*; Anstruther, *The Seminary Priests*, vols. 1 and 2. Unfortunately, little is known about many of the Cornish priests other than their places of birth and dates of profession and ordination from the registers of the English Colleges. Although some information exists as to when they were sent into England, their ultimate destinations are frequently unknown. Of those priests who returned to England for whom we have information (10 priests), eight can be linked to other Cornish networks, either in Cornwall or in London: John Brushford, John Cornelius, John Hambly, David Kemp, John Neale, Christopher Small, Francis Victor, and John Vivian.

131   Carew, *Survey*, 56. Prior to Protestant reform, some Cornish churches had conducted parts of their services in the Cornish language. See Ellis, *Cornish Language*, 59.

132   John Davies, rector of Mallwyd, translated Person's work in 1632 and entitled it *Llyfr y resolution . . . wedi ei gyfiefthu yn Gymraeg*. According to Ellis, *Cornish Language*, 75–6, subsequent editions were published in 1684, 1711, 1720, and 1802.

133   For this and other examples, see Oliver, *Collections*, 4–5; Boyan and Lamb, *Francis Tregian*, 35, 44, 49; Rowse, *Tudor Cornwall*, 355; J. H. Pollen and William MacMahon, eds., *The Venerable Philip Howard, Earl of Arundel, 1557–1595: English Martyrs*, vol. *II* (London: Catholic Record Society, XXI, 1919) 75; SP Dom 12/118/46, 47; *CSP Dom* 12/248/116; CRO, DD EN 2035.

134   Oliver, *Collections*, 9; Record Office, Castle of Exeter; Order from the magistrate at Exeter to search houses for relics, Easter Sessions, 1605.

135   Austin Woolrych, *Battles of the English Civil War: Marston Moor, Naseby, Preston* (New York: MacMillan Co., 1961) 14, 81–2; Also Duffin, *Faction and Faith*, 210–2; Letter of 21 Oct 1642, quoted in Oliver, *Collections*, 17, 24.

136   SP Dom 12/192/46.

137   As mentioned above, these meetings in either private homes or prison cells appear to have been predominately Cornish but rarely exclusively so.

138   SP Dom 12/192/46i.

139   Rowse, *Tudor Cornwall*, 359.

140   Oliver, *Collections*, 2, claims that Hambly was executed on 20 July 1587 at Chard.

141 Inscription written by the artist, John Miller.

NOTES TO CHAPTER 7

1 Howard supported many Catholic causes and maintained many recusants and church papists, such as the Cornish recusant and author Nicholas Roscarrock. The probability is very high that these tenants and servants were Catholics.

2 This is a continuation of the pre-reform Feast of Fools traditionally held near Christmas. A congregation typically elects a boy bishop to "rule" the congregation. The election, however, was not usually performed in the midst of divine service. See Natalie Zemon Davis, *Society and Culture in Early Modern France: Eight Essays by Natalie Zemon Davis* (Stanford: Stanford University Press, 1975) 98.

3 SP Dom 14/40/11. Allegedly the minister tolerated the misrule because he received much of his maintenance from Lord Howard. See Walsham, *Church Papists*, 89, who discusses Protestant churches as one of the most appropriate forums for Catholics to repudiate the reformers and their rituals, however not in the forms I discuss here. Ann W. Ramsey discusses the potential for the performance of rituals to defend alternative visions of order, which is what I argue is occurring in Westmoreland. See Ramsey, "The Reformation of Popular Culture," in *The Encyclopedia of European Social History from 1350 to 2000*, ed. Peter Stearns (Detroit: Charles Scribner's Sons, 2001) v, 53–66.

4 Cheshire Record Office, EDC 1/17/88v; EDV 1/4/13v, 1/12a/117; Haigh, *English Reformations*, chapter 15; SP Dom 12/223/47 discussed in Scarisbrick, *The Reformation*, 176.

5 A similar incident in the northern shires that bears further analysis is Walsham's description of the disruptions on Twelfth Night during which parishioners disrupted Protestant services and celebrated "the Flower of the Well" by bringing a "Mawmet" into church (which Walsham identifies as "perhaps a statue or image garlanded with foliage"), accompanied by piping, horn blowing, shouting, and ringing and beating on basins. See Walsham, "Reforming the Waters: Holy Wells and Healing Springs in Protestant England," in *Life and thought in the northern church, c. 1100–1700: Essays in Honour of Claire Cross*, ed. Diana Wood (Woodbridge, Suffolk: Boydell Press for the Ecclesiastical History Society, 1999) 235, drawing from information in J. S. Purvis, ed. *Tudor Parish Documents of the Diocese of York* (Cambridge: Cambridge University Press, 1948) 169 and cf. 179.

6 Identity and community in the northern shires appear to be regional in character. The evidence below does not suggest that this was one of the few contexts in which a British national character began to emerge.

7 Scarisbrick, *The Reformation*, 137.

8 Moreover, Bossy's estimates do not count communicating church papists or dissimulators, which would have raised the count of Catholic households in these

shires. Bossy, *ECC*, 404–5. No data were available to make accurate estimates for
Cumberland and Westmoreland.

9   BL, Cotton Titus MS F, xiii, 249, quoted in S.J. Watts, *From Border to Middle
Shire: Northumberland 1586–1625* (Bristol: Leicester University Press, 1975)
78–9. See also SP Dom 12/74/22.

10   See J. C. H. Aveling, "Catholic Households in Yorkshire, 1580–1603," *Northern
History* 16 (1980): 85, for evidence from Yorkshire; Watts, *From Border*, 85, for
Northumberland; SP Dom 12/184/33, 33i, 33ii, 14/86/113; *CSP Dom* 14/80/116,
14/87/94 and A. D. Wright, "Catholic History, North and South, Revisited,"
Northern History 25 (1989): 132, for Durham; Haigh, *Lanc*, 269, 317–9, for
Lancashire. SP Dom 12/245/131 provides evidence that Catholics in
Westmoreland and Cumberland were of significant number and that the Catholic
population was growing at this time. J. A. Hilton, "The Cumbrian Catholics,"
Northern History 16 (1980): 40–58, disagrees, however his conclusions are pri-
marily drawn from the fact that few Cumbrian Catholics appeared on recusancy
roles; See also J. A. Manning, ed., *Memoirs of Sir Benjamin Rudyard* (1841)
135–6, quoted by Lawrence Stone, *Causes of the English Revolution, 1529–1642*
(London: Routledge and Kegan Paul, 1972) 80–1; SP Dom 14/92/17; Haigh,
Lanc, 263; Ralph Sadler, *The State Papers and Letters of Sir Ralph Sadler*, ed.
Arthur Clifford (Edinburgh: A. Constable, 1809) ii, 55.

11   Exceptions occurred in the years 1592–1595, 1599–1600 (after Essex's departure
for Ireland), and 1610, when the brunt of the Oath of Allegiance controversy was
felt in the north. See Watts, *From Border*, 79–80.

12   *CSP Dom* 13/2/646. See SP Dom 12/155/1, 12/155/76; W. E. Rhodes, ed., *The
Apostolical life of Ambrose Barlow*, Chetham Miscellanies (Manchester:
Chetham Society, new series, II, 1909) 12; Watts, *From Border*, 79; Wright,
"Catholic History," 133; Haigh, "Continuity," 45.

13   *Calendar of Border Papers* 13/2/631; *Malachi* 1:4. See also Howard S. Reinmuth,
Jr., "Border Society in Transition," in *Early Stuart Studies: Essays in Honor of
David Harris Willson*, ed. Howard S. Reinmuth, Jr. (Minneapolis: University of
Minnesota Press, 1970) 239–41; SP Dom 12/32/50, 59, 12/33/19, 12/241/25,
12/243/59, 71, 12/245/131, 14/92/17, 15/30/17, 15/30/61, 15/32/50; Watts, *From
Border*, 78; See also Reinmuth, "Border Society," 231–50; B(orthwick) I(nstitute)
Y(ork), H(igh) C(ommission) A(ct) B(ooks) 15/1606/7–12, ff. 139–142; Privy
Council to the Earl of Huntingdon, transcribed in Francis Peck, *Desiderata
Curiosa: Or, a collection of divers scarce and curious pieces relating chiefly to
matters of English history* (1732–5), I, lib. iii, 8, quoted in Geoffrey de C.
Parmiter, "The Imprisonment of Papists in Private Castles," *Recusant History* 19,
no. 1 (1988): 24; *Acts of the High Commission Court within the Diocese of
Durham* (Durham: Surtees Society, XXXIV, 1858) 77.

14   Questier, *Conversion*, chaps. 5–6, and "Conformity," *Conformity and Orthodoxy*,
244.

15   *CSP Dom* 12/281/28. This revolt, also called the Northern Rebellion or the Revolt of the Northern Earls, was instigated by powerful Catholic lords of the northern shires. See Scarisbrick, *The Reformation*, 89, 107, 145–6.

16   J. H. Pollen, ed., *Unpublished Documents Relating to the English Martyrs, vol. 1. 1584–1603* (London: Catholic Record Society, V, 1908) 213; Dom F.O. Blundell, *Old Catholic Lancashire* (London: Burns, Oates & Washbourne, Ltd., 1925) 67; *CBorderP* 13/1/556.

17   Michael Questier, in "Practical Antipapistry during the Reign of Elizabeth I," *Journal of British Studies* 36 (1997): 371–96, discusses fears of a repeat of the 1569 Northern Rising. Even after the revolt, some powerful northern Catholics such as the Earl of Westmoreland continued to plot in the northern shires. This perhaps explains James's toleration and support of certain other northern Catholic lords who could help secure the region.

18   SP Dom 14/40/11; Reinmuth, "Border Society," 237, 244.

19   James I to Robert Cecil, 22 February 1607, HMC, *Cal. Salisbury MSS*, XIX, 52–3, quoted in Reinmuth, "Border Society," 237. For a further such example of the Lancashire Catholic Sir Richard Molyneux, see Pauline Croft, "The Catholic Gentry, the Earl of Salisbury and the Baronets of 1611," in *Conformity and Orthodoxy*, 271–2.

20   19 January 1607, Crawford MS, f. 195, quoted in Reinmuth, "Border Society," 243.

21   For further examples, see SP Dom 12/245/131; *CSP Dom* 12/240/138; BIY, HCAB 15/1606/7–12, ff. 139–142; Privy Council to the Earl of Huntingdon, transcribed in Peck, *Desiderata Curiosa*, i, lib. iii, 8, quoted in Parmiter, "The Imprisonment," 24; *Acts of the High Commission Court*, 77.

22   As Kenneth Fincham argues in "Clerical Conformity from Whitgift to Laud," in *Conformity and Orthodoxy*, 127, clergy and secular authorities in some areas "usually regarded issues of ceremonial conformity as a distraction from the imperative need to expand the narrow base of Protestantism and raise the preaching strength of the ministry . . ."

23   See SP Dom 12/152/48, 12/153/6, 12/153/45, 12/155/75, in Pollen, *Unpublished Documents*, 23–4. For more on shortages of Protestant ministers in the north, see Peter Marshall, *The Face of the Pastoral Ministry in the East Riding, 1525–1595* (York: University of York, Borthwick Paper 88, 1995) 4–6.

24   SP Dom 14/92/17. See also *CSP Dom* 12/240/138. *CBorderP* 13/2/171; Haigh, *Lanc*, 243.

25   SP Dom 12/243/223; Haigh, *Lanc*, 211–2, 237, 255.

26   Haigh, *Lanc*, 217–8.

27   William Palmes, SJ, *The Life of Mrs. Dorothy Lawson* (1646) 12, quoted in Connelly, *Women*, 189–90.

28   See SP Dom 12/243/223; BIY, RVII, HCAB 6, f. 86v; *Victoria County History*, v,
      125; *Victoria County History*, vi, 31; Haigh, "Continuity," 41, 67–8; Haigh, *Lanc*,
      212, 217.

29   BIY, HCCP 1624/5; ChRO, EDV 1/12b/158v, 1/13/102v, 1/17/23, 1/17/103,
      1/25/21–21r, 1/25/42; SP Dom 12/69/14, 12/138/18, Cecil Papers 144/184–88,
      HMC , vol. 17, 216, quoted in Clare Talbot, ed., *Miscellanea Recusant Records*
      (London: Catholic Record Society, LIII, 1961) 129–32; Henry Foley, *Records of
      the English Province of the Society of Jesus*, 7 vols. (London: Burns & Oates,
      1877) vii, 1108; Rhodes, *Apostolical life*, iii–iv; Quarter Sessions Roll 32 Eliz
      (1590) in *Lancashire Quarter Sessions Records*, vol. I., 1590–1606, ed. James Tait
      (Manchester: Chetham Society, new series, LXXVII, 1917) 12; *Acts of the High
      Commission Court*, 74, 113–4, 140–1; Lady Margaret Hoby, *Diary of Lady
      Margaret Hoby 1599–1605*, ed. Dorothy M. Meads (London: George Routledge
      and Sons Ltd., 1930) 247 (note #200); *Selections from the Household Books of
      Lord William Howard of Naworth Castle* (Durham: Surtees Society, LXVIII,
      1878) liv, 354; Haigh, *Lanc*, 217–9.

30   NRA Lancashire, Hornby Roman Catholic Mission, RCHy 1/3/1, 2/3/38; Fred H.
      Crossley, "The Post-Reformation Effigies and Monuments of Cheshire
      (1500–1800)" (Liverpool: Historic Society of Lancashire and Cheshire, XLI,
      1940) 33; *Selections from the Household Books*, xl (note); James L. Thornely, *The
      Monumental Brasses of Lancashire and Cheshire with Some Account of the
      Persons Represented* (Hull: William Andrews & Co. and The Hull Press, 1893)
      233–4, 239.

31   *Selections from the Household Books*, 135, 207, 215, 227, 234, 236, 247, 262–3,
      313–9.

32   Wright, "Catholic History," 133; See also R.C. Richardson, *Puritanism in North-
      West England* (Manchester: Manchester University Press, 1972) 162–3.

33   See chapter 3. Also see ChRO, EDA 12/2/82–82r, 12/3/4–4v, EDC 1/17/88v,
      EDV 1/4/13v, 1/10/122v, 1/10/155r, 1/12a/117r, 1/13/102v, 1/13/163–4, 1/25/29;
      Cecil Papers 141/282 in Talbot, *Miscellanea*, 147, 150; *Selections from the
      Household Books*, lxix–lxxi, 48, 96, 222, 267, 296, 300, 320–1, 356; Haigh, *Lanc*,
      217, 219, 222; Haigh, "Continuity," 60; J.A. Twemlow, ed., *Liverpool Town Books:
      vol. 2, 1571–1603: Proceedings of Assemblies, Common Councils, Portmoot
      Courts, etc.* (Liverpool: University Press of Liverpool, 1935) 186; "Rosary
      Confraternity Lists," contrib. Bede Jarrett, OP, in *Miscellanea IX* (London:
      Catholic Record Society, XIV, 1914) 205, 217, 222; *Acts of the High Commission
      Court*, 77.

34   R. S. Ferguson and W. Nanson, *Some Municipal Records of the City of Carlisle
      viz. the Elizabethan Constitutions, Orders, Provisions, Articles, and Rules from
      the Dormant Book, and the Rules and Orders of the Eight Trading Guilds*
      (Carlisle: C. Thurnam and Sons, 1897) 26, 93–4, 169–72, 176; Hoby, *Diary*, 247
      (note #200); SP Dom 14/40/11; BIY, HCCP 1596/7; Twemlow, *Liverpool Town
      Books*, 168–9, 243; Blundell, *Old Catholic Lancashire*, 135.

35   *Acts of the High Commission Court*, 77–8; SP Dom 12/240/138.

36   Haigh, "Continuity," 45; Aveling, "Catholic Households," 96; Hilton, "Cumbrian Catholics," 57–8.

37   SP Dom 12/120/21; 12/167/125; Laurence Vaux, *A catechisme*, lxxvii; Pollen, *Unpublished Documents*, 46; Haigh, *Lanc*, 256–7; Watts, *From Border*, 86; SP Dom 59/30/171; Philip Caraman, ed., *The Other Face: Catholic Life Under Elizabeth I* (London: The Camelot Press Ltd., 1960) 216; Aveling, "Catholic Households," 89–90; Stonyhurst MS, Angl. A, ff. 41–48, quoted in John Morris, ed., *The Troubles of Our Catholic Forefathers Related by Themselves*, 3 vols. (London: Burns & Oates, 1877) iii, 270–1; BL, Add MS 30262, E.2, quoted in Katharine M. Longley, "Blessed George Errington and Companions: Fresh Evidence," *Recusant History* 19, no. 1 (1988): 39–46; Richard Challoner, *Memoirs of Missionary Priests and Other Catholics of Both Sexes that have Suffered Death in England on Religious Accounts from the Year 1577–1684*. vol. 1 (Edinburgh: Thomas C. Jack, Grange Publishing Works, 1878) 75, 78, 80.

38   *CSP Dom* 14/17/31, 14/19/35; William Brereton, *Journal of Sir William Brereton 1635* (Durham: Surtees Society, CXXIV, 1915) 21–3.

39   SP Dom 12/216/153; Connelly, *Women*, 167; Walsham, "Reforming," 233–4. For evidence of other pilgrimages, see SP Dom 16/61/13; *Selections from the Household Books*, 246; E.B. Saxton, "A Speke Inventory of 1624" (Liverpool: Historic Society of Lancashire and Cheshire, XCVII, 1945) 109; John Aston, "Journal of John Aston 1639" (Durham: Surtees Society, CXVIII, 1910) entry for May 28, 1639; Brereton, "Journal," entry for June 25, 1635, 21–3; David Shorney, *Protestant Non-Conformity and Roman Catholicism: a guide to sources in the Public Record Office* (London: PRO Publications, 1996) 74; Connelly, *Women*, 201.

40   Rev. Daniel O'Hare, "An Old Lancashire Mission," *Upshaw Magazine* (December 1892) reprinted in Blundell, *Old Catholic Lancashire*, Appendix I, 169–70. See Blundell, *Old Catholic Lancashire*, 135, and Henry Taylor, *Ancient Crosses and Wells in Lancashire* (Manchester: Sherratt & Hughes, 1906).

41   Blundell, *Old Catholic Lancashire*, 32–7.

42   Frank Tyrer, "A Star Chamber Case: Asheton v. Blundell, 1624–31" (Liverpool: Historic Society of Lancashire and Cheshire, CXVIII, 1966) 32–3.

43   His land had not, to anyone's recollection, been used for any burials prior to this time. In a 1631 decision, Star Chamber decreed that the walls, graves, and land of Harkirke be destroyed by the local sheriff (PRO Star Chamber 9/1/2) quoted by Tyrer, "A Star Chamber Case," 37; Thomas Ellison Gibson, ed., *Crosby Records: A Chapter of Lancashire Recusancy* (Manchester: Chetham Society, new series, XII, 1887) xv.

44   BIY, HCCP 1596/7. For further examples, see SP Dom 14/40/11, 14/86/34; BIY, HCCP ND/11.

45   An excellent illustration of traditional religion perhaps *ultimately* shaping the
      early Anglican Church from the inside, as Walsham discusses in *Church Papists*,
      but was this how the rushbearers saw their activities at the time?

46   BIY, HCCP 1624/11.

47   Walsham, *Church Papists*, 81.

48   BIY, HCCP 1597/9.

49   Thanks to archivist Christopher Webb at BIY for supplying information on the
      proper administrative jurisdiction of Boroughbridge and its chapel.

50   The dean and chapter of the Cathedral Church at York never heard the case.
      Source: Katherine M. Longley, *Ecclesiastical Cause Papers at York: Dean and
      Chapter's Court 1350–1843* (York: University of York, 1980).

51   Peter Marshall suggests that the over-abundance of Roman priests in pre-reform
      years may have led to laypeople expecting some choice in similar matters. See
      Marshall, *Face*, 7. Judith Maltby discusses similar expectations and efforts among
      Protestants in *Prayer Book*, 230.

52   J. E. Bamber, "The Venerable Christopher Robinson," *Recusant History* 4, no.1
      (1975): 28 quoted in Hilton, "Cumbrian Catholics," 45.

53   *CSP Dom* 12/283/86.

54   BIY, HCCP 1624/7, 22. Harrison was later arrested. He admitted to recusancy,
      refused the Oath of Allegiance, and admitted escaping from Blanchard. Barton,
      in his deposition told a different and less likely version of events. For a similar
      episode, see Letter of Tobias Matthews, Bishop of Durham, to Sir Robert Cecil,
      27 June 1600, quoted in Connelly, *Women*, 112–3, describing violent resistance
      to the arrest of a priest in the Norton household in Durham.

55   BL, Lansdowne MS 153, f. 108. In a similar incident, approximately 50 Catholics
      in the North Riding of Yorkshire armed themselves with "staves, pitchforks, bows
      and arrows . . . halberds, fowling pieces, callviers, javelins, . . . swords and dag-
      gers" and attempted to halt sheriff's deputies from seizing cattle in payment for
      recusancy fines. The armed men wounded some of the sheriff's men, disarmed
      them, and took them to the recusant's home for "examination." See Connelly,
      Women, 151.

56   Vienna, Haus Hof und Staats archiv, PC 56 ff. 399–99v, in Albert Loomie, ed.,
      Spain and the Jacobean Catholics: vol. 2, 1613–1624 (London: Catholic Record
      Society, LXVIII, 1978) 140.

57   J. Gee, *Foot out of the Snare* (London, 1624) 34, quoted in Loomie, *Spain and
      the Jacobean Catholics: vol. 2, 1613–1624*, 140–1n.

58   See Davis, *Society and Culture*, especially chapters 4 and 6.

59   SP Dom 14/40/11.

60   Leonard, Lord Dacre, had been a prominent leader of the Northern Rising of
      1569. After the collapse of the rebellion, Dacre fled first to Scotland and then to
      Flanders where he received a pension from Philip II.

61   *CSP Rome* 38/2/43.

62   *CSP Rome* 38/2/44.

63   State Papers Scotland 52/47/51, 75, 52/48/24, 52/49/27, 43, 52/57/11, 52/58/108, 52/61/24, 52/64/83, 52/67/44; SP Dom 12/32/39, 66; Cumberland RO Percy Survey, D/Lec 169/1593, 1603; *CSP Dom* 16/452/22, 16/457/48i, 16/460/18i, 16/465/27.

64   *CBorderP* 13/2/853.

65   BIY, HCCP 1572/1; Hilton, "Cumbrian Catholics," 57–8, challenges this interpretation. The difficulties with Hilton's analysis were discussed above.

66   SP Dom 12/245/131. See also Robert Carey, *The Memoirs of Robert Carey*, ed. F.H. Mares (Oxford: Clarendon Press, 1972) 52–3; *CSP Dom* 12/243/71.

67   Carey, *Memoirs*, 8–9, 45–6; *CSP Dom* 12/248/9.

68   *CBorderP* 13/1/197.

69   As were political rebels. See SP Scot 52/49/35, 43, 47; *CBorderP* 13/1/766, 769.

70   SP Dom 12/245/131; *CSP Dom* 12/240/138. See also Pollen, *Unpublished Documents*, 143, 146–7, 149; Fr. John Hay, SJ, to Edward Mercurian, General of the SJ, 29 June 1579, in William Forbes-Leith, *Narratives of Scottish Catholics under Mary Stuart and James VI, Now First Printed from the Original Manuscripts in the Secret Archives of the Vatican and Other Collections* (Edinburgh: William Patterson, 1885) 141–165, 175–80; *CSP Rome* 38/2/812, 1020; *CSP Dom* 12/32/8, 12/242/121, 12/244/5; Watts, *From Border*, 76.

71   SP Dom 14/86/113.

72   *CSP Dom Add* 12/29/62, 156; SP Dom Add 12/28/59ii, in Pollen, *Unpublished Documents*, 36–7; *CBorderP* 13/1/494; SP Dom 12/28/58, 12/30/61, 12/286/15, 16/451/70, 16/451/71, 16/452/33, 16/457/104, 16/460/18i; SP Scot 52/47/107; *CSP Rome* 38/2/43, 44; *CBorderP* 13/1/776, 834 and 2/129, 211, 652; See also *CSP Dom Add* 12/32/39. 12/32/66; Peter Sahlins, *Boundaries: The Making of France and Spain in the Pyrenees* (Berkeley: University of California Press, 1989) for a discussion of the dynamics of divided loyalties in border regions.

73   *CBorderP* 13/2/171.

74   Stonyhurst MS, Angl. A, vii, 8, quoted in Pollen, *Unpublished Documents*, 278–84; SP Dom 12/248/24.

75   *CSP Dom* 16/25/81, 16/38/15, 16/44/84; See also *CSP Rome* 38/2/812, Appendix II.

76   Forbes-Leith, *Narratives*, 175–8.

77   SP Scot 52/48/30. Also SP Scot 52/47/103, 52/64/67; *CBorderP* 13/1/367, 461; Forbes-Leith, *Narratives*, 172–4.

78   His mother, Mary Queen of Scots.

79   *CBorderP* 13/1/417.

80   W. King, "The Public Fairs of Blackburn Hundred" (Liverpool: Historic Society of Lancashire and Cheshire, CXXXVIII, 1989) 19, 22.

81   *CBorderP* 13/1/494.

82   *CSP Dom Add* 12/32/39.

83   SP Dom 16/451/70, 71.

84   *CBorderP* 13/1/458; SP Scot 52/49/47.

85   Carey, *Memoirs*, 52–3.

86   *CBorderP* 13/1/458; for further examples, see *CBorderP* 13/2/652; *CSP Dom Add* 12/30/61, 12/32/8.

87   SP Dom 14/86/34, 14/87/14–5, 14/89/96, 14/90/156–7, 14/92/17, 16/12/64, *CBorderP* 13/2/452; *Selections from the Household Books*, 109, 131; Carey, *Memoirs*, 23; Ann M.C. Forster, "The Real Roger Widdrington," *Recusant History* 11, no. 4 (1977): 198; *Calendar of Acts of the Privy Council* 1625–6, 281, quoted in Forster, "The Real," 199.

88   SP Dom 14/87/14, 15; Forster, "The Real," 198.

89   SP Dom 14/40/11, 14/86/34; See also SP Dom 16/10/42; Henry Fishwick, "History of the Parish of Garstang in the County of Lancashire, Part II" (Manchester: Chetham Society, CV, 1879) 150–1.

90   SP Dom 12/153/62, 14/40/11, 14/86/34.

91   *Register of the Privy Council of Scotland*, vol. 7, 67–8, Acta May 1636–Nov 1639, ff. 164b–165b.

92   Scots Catholics do not appear to have been harshly persecuted according to John Coffey, *Persecution and Toleration in Protestant England, 1558–1689* (Harlow, England: Longmans, 2000) 103, citing Michael Mullett, *Catholics in Britain and Ireland, 1558–1829* (London: Palgrave-Macmillan, 1998) 33–54. See also Forbes-Leith, *Narratives*, 141–65; Alexander Peterkin, ed., *Book of the Universalle Kirke* (1839) ii, 429; iii, 451; And as evidence, SP Dom 14/89/24; SP Scot 52/47/107; *CBorderP* 13/1/13, 13/2/594, 600, 641, 728, 745.

93   SP Scot 52/47/34, 52/49/45; John Chamberlain, *The Letters of John Chamberlain*, vol. 1, Memoirs XII, Part 1, ed. Norman Egbert McClure (Philadelphia: The American Philosophical Society, 1939) 171; *CSP Rome* 38/2/142; *CSP Scot* 52/49/45; *Register of the Privy Council of Scotland*, vol. 7, Acta Nov 1641–Oct 1646, ff. 51b–52b; *BUK*, iii, 425–6, 458, 469; *CBorderP* 13/2/579.

94   *BUK*, iii, 457.

95   Fr. Robert Abercromby to Fr. Claudio Aquaviva, 9 June 1596, quoted in Forbes-Leith, *Narratives*, 226–9; *BUK*, iii, 451, 462; Fr. John Hay to Edward Mercurian, 29 June 1579, quoted in Forbes-Leith, *Narratives*, 161–2; Forbes-Leith, *Narratives*, 175–80, 191–2; Richard Verstegan, *The letters and despatches of Richard Verstegan*, ed. Anthony G. Petti (London: Catholic Record Society, LII, 1959) 75; *CBorderP* 13/1/247, 367, 393, 586; *Register of the Privy Council of Scotland*, vol. 7, Acta Nov. 1641–Oct 1646, ff. 51b–52b.

96 In 1602, just prior to the elimination of the border, it was estimated that one-third of the Scots nobility was still Catholic. See Charles Rogers, ed., *Estimate of the Scottish Nobility during the Minority of James VI* (Grampian Club, 1873) 77–80; Jenny Wormald, "'Princes' and the regions in the Scottish Reformations," in Norman MacDougall, ed., *Church, Politics and Society: Scotland 1408–1929* (Edinburgh: John Donald Publishers Ltd., 1983) chapter 4 and Forbes-Leith, *Narratives*, 63–81 (Letters from Jesuits working in Scotland back to their General) quoted by Wormald. See also Michael Lynch, *Edinburgh and the Reformation* (Edinburgh: John Donald, 1981) cited in Michael Lynch, "From privy kirk to burgh church: an alternative view of the process of Protestantism" in MacDougall, *Church*, chapter 5.

97 Seccion de Estado, Archivo General de Simancas 2513 n. fol., in Albert Loomie, ed., *Spain and the Jacobean Catholics: vol. 1, 1603–1612* (London: Catholic Record Society, LXIV, 1973) 181. In particular, while not necessarily insisting upon the eradication of Catholic belief and practice, James did insist that English Catholics take an Oath of Allegiance, swearing loyalty to the English monarch above all other leaders, including the Pope.

98 BL, Lansdowne MS 75, ff. 44–44v; Cardinal William Allen to Cardinal of Como, 8 February 1582, in Forbes-Leith, *Narratives*, 175–80; SP Dom 12/248/24; SP Scot 52/47/103, 52/53/86; *CSP Scotland* 52/50/4, 52/55/112; *CSP Dom* 12/28/57, 58, 12/29/62, 156, 12/32/8, 12/245/131; *CBorderP* 13/1/464, 465, 492, 494, 766, 919; 13/2/171; Stonyhurst MS, Angl. A, vii, no. 8 quoted in Pollen, *Unpublished Documents*, 278–84; *Acts of the High Commission*, 68; Watts, *From Border*, 86; For an opposing view, see Hilton, "Cumbrian Catholics," 45.

99 SP Dom 12/153/78, 12/158/17, 12/178/67, 12/175/110; SP Dom Add 12/28/58i, 12/28/59ii; *CSP Dom* 12/275/83; Pollen, *Unpublished Documents*, 35–7; Challoner, *Memoirs*, 66, 74–6, 78–80; Christopher Devlin, *The Life of Robert Southwell: Poet and Martyr* (London: Longmans, Green and Co., 1956) 226; Hilton, "Cumbrian Catholics," 44–5; E. E. Reynolds, *Campion and Parsons: The Jesuit Mission of 1580–1* (London: Sheed and Ward, 1980) 154; Christine Kelly, *Blessed Thomas Belson: His Life and Times, 1563–1589* (Gerrards Cross: Colin Smythe, 1987) 74; Blundell, *Old Catholic Lancashire*, 131–3; Rhodes, *Apostolical life*, iii–iv.

100 *CBorderP* 13/1/464, 465, 492, 494; Kelly, *Blessed Thomas Belson*, 74.

101 Gordon Donaldson, *The Scottish Reformation* (Cambridge: Cambridge University Press, 1960) chap. 2.

102 *BUK*, 429; SP Scot 52/64/67; *CBorderP* 13/1/393, 458.

103 *CBorderP* 13/1/417.

104 SP Scot 52/64/67.

105 SP Scot 52/47/103.

106 McGrath and Rowe, "The Elizabethan Priests," 215.

107   SP Dom Add 12/29/156, 157; SP Dom 12/178/11, 14/40/11; *CSP Scotland* 52/49/43, 55/112; Cardinal William Allen to Cardinal of Como, in Forbes-Leith, *Narratives*, 175–80; Watts, *From Border*, 76; McGrath and Rowe, "The Elizabethan Priests," 210–11.

108   *CSP Dom Add* 12/32/8. In a similar situation, the Catholic Richard Hargrave, servant to one of the doctors at the seminary at Rheims, traveled annually from the continent to London to the northern counties to collect "benevolences" for the continental seminaries. Having one or two brothers who were clothiers, he posed as a buyer of clothes as he made the rounds of northern Catholic households. See SP Dom 12/153/78.

109   John Chamberlain to Dudley Carleton, 29 February 1600, in Chamberlain, *Letters*. See also SP Dom 12/153/78, 12/168/30; *CSP Dom* 12/271/105, 14/72/77; *CSP Dom Add* 12/28/57.

110   *CSP Dom* 12/242/121, 122.

111   SP Dom 12/164/48

112   *CSP Dom* 12/242/121, 122.

113   SP Scot 52/45/1, 2, 52/48/30; *CSP Dom Add* 12/29/62.

114   BIY, HCCP 1567/2; Haigh, *Lanc*, 253.

115   *CBorderP* 13/2/1265, 1281. For similar example of Robert Carr (Kerr), Warden of the Middle March for Scotland, see Carey, *Memoirs*, 40–1; *CBorderP* 13/1/347, 390, 13/2/452, 465, 485, 853, 1276.

116   SP Dom 14/92/17. The writer is either William Morton or Sir Henry Anderson.

117   SP Dom 14/89/96, 14/90/156, 157. See also SP Dom 14/86/34, 14/87/14, 15; *CBorderP* 13/2/452. Details of the Howards' aid to outlaws can be found in *Selections from the Household Books*, 109, 131; Carey, *Memoirs*, 23, discusses the Graemes' resources to aid outlaws.

118   Forster, "The Real," 198; G.N. Taylor, "The Story of Elsdon," 16.

119   *Cal APC* 1625–6, 281 quoted in Forster, "The Real," 199. See also SP Dom 16/12/64.

120   Forster, "The Real," 202–3; SP Dom 16/409/207, 16/410/4, 29, 62, 16/413/32, 16/414/102, 16/415/11.

NOTES TO CHAPTER 8

1   *OED*, 1989 ed. This is likely a variant of "lange," which means to launch.

2   York Minster Library, Add MS 151, f. 58r.

3   Arthur Crowther and Thomas Vincent, *Jesus, Maria, Joseph, or, The Devout Pilgrim, of the Ever Blessed Virgin Mary, in His Holy Exercises, Affections, and Elevations* (Amsterdam, 1657) 83–4.

4   Garnet, "An epistle consolatory . . ." in *The societie*, 8–9; Ramsey. *Liturgy*, 214–5, suggests that "affective investment in liturgical ritual can, under specific histori-

cal conditions, generate the most fundamental bonds of community . . ." I argue that such conditions existed in England at this time.

5   Wooding, *Rethinking*, 127, argues that the Marian church, like the Henrician, had little use for papal authority but that the early Elizabethan Catholic intellectuals and theologians renewed their loyalty to the papacy.

6   Protestants, of course, also saw themselves as heirs to the ancient church but in a different context. Protestants viewed their church as a return to the perfection of the gospels before layers of Roman Church tradition obscured the earlier church's message. See Jones, *English Reformation*, 156–7.

7   Walsham and Wooding argue that Rome and English Catholic writers on the continent engaged in a propaganda campaign to popularize this brand of Catholic identity. I argue that the laity consciously participated in the creation of such an identity because, unlike many ideas emanating from the continent, this one met their needs. See Walsham, "'Yielding to the Extremity of the Time': Conformity, Orthodoxy and the Post-Reformation Catholic Community," in *Conformity and Orthodoxy*, 232–3; Wooding, *Rethinking*, 262–3.

8   For example, see will of Philip, Earl of Arundel, d. October 1595/6, quoted in David Mathew, *Catholicism in England 1535–1935: Portrait of a Minority: Its Culture & Tradition* (London: Longmans, Green & Co., 1936) 50.

9   *Selections from the Household Books of Lord William Howard of Naworth Castle* (Durham: Surtees Society, LXVIII, 1878) lxi, 363; BL, Stowe MS 53; Letter from W. Webbe to unknown, inserted in Nicholas Roscarrock, *Lives of the English Saints*, at University Library, Cambridge, Add MS 3041, quoted in S. Baring-Gould, *Cornish Characters and Strange Events*, 2 vols. (London: John Lane The Bodley Head Ltd., 1925) ii, 183–4; Margaret Pollard and Faith Godbeer, *The Guild of Our Lady of the Portal* (Redruth, Cornwall: Dyllansow Truran, 1985) 7–9, 19–23; A.L. Rowse, *Tudor Cornwall: Portrait of a Society* (New York: Charles Scribner's Sons, 1969) 27–8; CRO, RS/76/9; Robert Stephen Hawker, *Cornish Ballads and Other Poems* (1869; reprint, Delmar, NY: Scholar's Facsimiles and Reprints, 1994) 158, 161–3, 173–6, 177.

10   BL, Stowe MS 53, ff. 10–20; BL, Arundel MS 321, f. 5; William Stanney, *A treatise of penance, with an explication of the rule, and maner of living, of the brethren and sisters, of the Third Order of St. Frauncis, comonli called the Order of Penance, ordained for those which desire to leade a holy life, and to doe penance in their owne houses*, Part I (Douai: John Heigham, 1617) 361; Henry Garnet, *The societie of the rosary* (n.p.d., 1596/7) 169, 179–81.

11   Cornish Catholics, in particular, remembered the tribulations and deaths of these early British confessors and martyrs such as St. Albanus and the battles against heresies such as Pelagianism. John Whitaker, *The ancient cathedral of Cornwall historically surveyed* (London: Printed for John Stockdale, 1804) i, 87–8, 263–70.

12   Crowther and Vincent, *JMJ*, 5–6; W. E. Rhodes, ed., *The apostolical life of Ambrose Barlow*, Chetham Miscellanies (Manchester: Chetham Society, new series, II, 1909) 10.

13   Robert Persons to Fr. Alfonso Agazzari, Rector of the English College at Rome, July 1582, quoted by Michael Hodgetts, "*Loca Secretiora* in 1581," *Recusant History* 19, no. 4 (1989): 387.

14   Richard Broughton, *A new manual of old Christian Catholick meditations & praiers faithfully collected and translated, without any word altered, or added* (n.p., 1617); Broughton, *A Manual of Praiers vsed by the Fathers of the Primitive Church, for the most part within the foure first hundred years of Christ, and all before the end of the sixt hundred yeare* (n.p., 1618); Garnet, *The societie,* 169–71, 177–8; Anthony Batt, *A Poore mans mite. A letter of a religious man of the Order of St. Benedict vnto a Sister of his, concerning the rosarie or psalter of our blessed Ladie, Commonly called the Beades* (Douai: Widow of Mark Wyon, 1639) 14.

15   *Selections from the Household Books,* 246, 462; SP Dom 12/216/153, 16/61/13.

16   BL, Arundel MS 321, ff. 1v–2.

17   Garnet, *The societie,* 233–.

18   1615 translation of *Rex gloriose martyrum* by Richard Verstegan, printed in J. M. Blom, *The Post-Tridentine English Primer* (London: Catholic Record Society, 1982) 89.

19   As Brad S. Gregory has noted, "The historical community of the unjustly killed was alive, reborn, and thriving with the modern witness of fellow believers." Protestant, Anabaptist, and Catholic martyrs throughout early modern Europe all identified with the older traditions of Christian martyrdom. Gregory describes a "renaissance of Christian martyrdom" in which "historical community" of the martyrs was revivified and reinterpreted to meet the needs of early modern Christians of varying faiths. "Their respective accents varied within a framework of a common language" and included varied couplings of ancient tradition and modern reenactment. Gregory, *Salvation at Stake: Christian Martyrdom in Early Modern Europe* (Cambridge: Harvard University Press, 1999) 119–26.

20   For definitions and discussions of ancient Christian martyrdom and the revival and reinterpretation of traditions of martyrdom across faiths (particularly in societies where political circumstances are in flux), see Margaret Cormack, ed., *Sacrificing the Self: Perspectives on Martyrdom and Religion* (Oxford: Oxford University Press, 2001) especially the introduction and chapters 3 and 7.

21   Stanney, *A treatise,* 184. See also Garnet, *A treatise of Christian Renunciation . . . Whereunto is added a shorte discourse against going to the Hereticall Churches with a Protestation* (n.p.d., 1593) 5.

22   BL, Harleian MS 4149, ff. 37v–38, also 41v–42.

23   Either Richard or William Wallis, both discovered in the house on Golden Lane rented by William Wiseman.

24   *CSP Dom* 12/248/31, 36, 38. Also see SP Dom 14/21/48.

25 Westminster Archives, vols. 287 & 321, Colim-Collectanea B, 31 & 65, quoted in J. H. Pollen, ed., *Unpublished Documents Relating to the English Martyrs, vol. 1. 1584–1603* (London: Catholic Record Society, V, 1908) 200.

26 See York Minster Library, Add MS 151, ff. 27–27v.

27 *Mark* 14:36.

28 See chapters 2, 4, and 5 in which such attempts to bond with Christ are discussed in more detail.

29 Protestants believed their martyrs were following in the footsteps of the apostles and ancient martyrs and confessors as well. See John Foxe, *Actes and Monuments* (London: Company of Stationers, 1684).

30 John Ingram to fellow prisoners, July 1594, quoted in Pollen, *Unpublished Documents*, 203.

31 Robert V. Caro, SJ, "William Alabaster: Rhetor, Mediator, Devotional Poet-1,"*Recusant History* 19, no. 1 (1988): 67. See also Stanney, *A treatise*, 184, and chapter 1, where Stanney quotes the "Order of Penance for Third Order of St. Francis instituted in a breve of Nicholas IV."

32 *CSP Dom* 12/27/93.

33 Henry Foley, *Records of the English Province of the Society of Jesus*, 7 vols. (London: Burns & Oates, 1877) ii, 1108. From SJ Collectanea, pt. i, 1108. from Annual Letters SJ, 1624, RE Rev. John Layton, alias Port, SJ, buried at Halkirke, 19 Feb 1624.

34 Stonyhurst MS, Collectanea M, f. 160, in Pollen, *Unpublished Documents*, 285–6. For a more in depth analysis of this event, see chapter 2.

35 James Tailor, a grocer living on Fleet Street, was discussed in detail in chapter 5.

36 Oscott MS, Kirk's Collection, i, 33, quoted in Pollen, *Unpublished Documents*, 182–4. See also the prison writings of the missionary priest John Nelson and of Ralph Sherwin who equated their impending martyrdoms with the ancient martyrs', as chronicled by Gregory, *Salvation at Stake*, 122–3.

37 BL, Lansdowne MS 350, ff. 7–8

38 For example, see portrayal of Margaret Clitheroe's appearance before Yorkshire magistrates in York Minster Library, Add MS 151, ff. 50v–56.

39 *CSP Rome* 38/2/Appendix VII.

40 *CSP Dom Add* 12/27/93.

41 SP Dom 14/216/218b; Also see ChRO, CR 63/2/694/19.

42 Rowse, *Tudor Cornwall*, 207. See also Thomas Wright, *The Passions of the Mind in General*, ed. William Webster Newbold (New York: Garland Publications Inc., 1986) 200–1.

43 Catholics such as the Cornish layman Nicholas Roscarrock carefully distinguished their new martyrs from those created by the Protestants. Roscarrock called the Protestant martyrs "false and counterfeit" and remarked that the

Protestant John Foxe's *Actes and Monuments* "in truth doth rather serve the title of Miniments." Many of Foxe's martyrs, Roscarrock claimed were "a huge heap of saints and martyrs of his own making; whereof some were long after living . . . some that were never in being . . . some never put to death, nor so much as imprisoned. . . ." See Rowse, "Nicholas Roscarrock and his *Lives of the Saints*," in J. H. Plumb, ed., *Studies in Social History: a Tribute to G. M. Trevelyan* (London: Longmans, Green, 1955) 19.

44   For examples, see John Morris, ed., *The Troubles of Our Catholic Forefathers Related by Themselves*, 3 vols. (London: Burns & Oates, 1877) iii, 52; BL, Add MS 21203, Plut. Clii. F, quoted in Foley, *Records*, iv, 129–30.

45   Perhaps the appeal of antiquity to English Catholics can, in part, be explained by English belief in the power of their own ancient constitution. See F.M. Stenton, *Anglo-Saxon England*, 3rd ed. (Oxford: Clarendon Press, 1971) particularly chapters 15 and 17; Bruce Lyon, *A Constitutional and Legal History of Medieval England* (New York: Harper and Brothers, 1960) particularly chap. 38; Peter Spufford, *Origins of the English Parliament* (London: Longmans, Green and Co., Ltd., 1967) chap. 4; A. L. Brown, *The Governance of Late Medieval England 1272–1461* (Stanford: Stanford University Press, 1989).

46   Alternatively, Protestants had no such need. Protestants looked to the ancient church to define their beliefs and maintained that their clergy traced its authority back to Peter too. (Catholics, however, disputed these claims, arguing that the excommunication of the English Protestant clergy and Protestant denial of the sacramental nature of clerical ordination broke the chain.) Protestants, however, denied the *need* for a visible, unbroken chain of authority. They preached that Rome severed connections with Christ's teachings and the true church centuries ago. Protestants merely attempted to reclaim what had been lost.

47   William Hunt, *The Puritan Moment: The Coming of Revolution in an English County* (Cambridge, MA: Harvard University Press, 1983) 131.

48   Bossy, *ECC*, 77, 108, 144, characterizes the separation of Catholics into their own sect as a gradual diminishment of the bonds of collective behavior. Alexandra Walsham, *Church Papists*, 73, on the other hand, suggests that church papistry continued to integrate many Catholics back into their overarching communities although she is discussing Protestant-structured communities rather than Catholic-defined ones.

49   The authors of the petition signed it "The Catholics of England." No copy of the petition survives so it is impossible to know who the authors were, yet the content appears to reflect a growing desire of many English Catholics for some sort of accommodation with the English government. The text survives, preserved in Anglican documents that sought to respond to the Catholic demands. See A.F. Allison and D,M. Rogers, eds., *The Contemporary Printed Literature of the English Counter-Reformation between 1558 and 1640. Vol. II: Works in English* (Aldershot, Hants.: Scolar Press, 1994) 44–5.

50 "The Catholics' Supplication unto the King's Majesty for toleration of Catholic religion in England," quoted in M. A. Tierney, *Dodd's Church History of England from the Commencement of the Sixteenth Century to the Revolution in 1688*, 5 vols. (London: Charles Dolman, 1839) vol. 4, lxxii–lxiv.

51 "Substance of a Petition presented to King James I by the English Catholics in 1604," quoted in Tierney, *Dodd's Church History*, vol. 4, lxxxiii.

52 In 1623, William Bishop was appointed Bishop of Chalcedon and enjoyed full jurisdiction over English Catholics. The appointment of Bishop marked the papacy's abandonment of the "archpriest" system, wherein Rome, beginning in 1598, had appointed a resident archpriest in England to oversee English Catholic clergy and laity. Although the archpriest enjoyed jurisdiction and powers similar to those of a bishop, many Catholics resented the archpriest system saying that it denied English Catholics a proper place within the hierarchy of the church.

53 William Bishop, Bishop of Chalcedon, to his agent Thomas Rant, 25 September 1623, quoted in Tierney, *Dodd's Church History*, vol. 4, cclxxxiii.

54 Bossy, *ECC*, 108–10, wrote of his reconsideration of the idea of Catholic separation from the Church of England into a "small, non-conforming community." He wrote, ". . . it has been borne upon me that the word 'separation' has another and perhaps a deeper meaning here than the one which was first intended: a ritual, as well as a social signification. To be separate, or set apart, is one of the attributes of the holy. . . . [I]t has dawned on me that fasting and abstinence, before they are anything else, are acts of ritual separation . . . and are as such perhaps inherently better adapted to the circumstances of a sectarian community than to that of a religious multitude." Bossy continues by investigating certain practices of feasting and fasting. In previous chapters of this book, I have expanded upon this idea of ritual separation to include many more sets of traditional activities and beliefs practiced by *and altered by* English Catholics. Additionally, I argue that such ritual separation helped create a larger sense of religious community.

55 See chapters 2, 3, and 4. For examples of this type of direct interaction with God and the saints, see BL, Sloane MS 4035, ff. 9v–13; BL, Sloane MS 3785.

56 See chapter 1 for explanation of the difference between mediation *via* a priest and intercession *via* the saints.

57 For examples, see York Minster Library, Add MS 151, ff. 33v–34; BL, Sloane MS 3785.

58 See Benedict Anderson, *Imagined Communities: Reflections on the Origin and Spread of Nationalism* (London: Verso Books, 1983).

59 Broughton, *A new manual*, 25–6.

60 See, for example, SP Dom 12/235/40; William Moore to Lords of the Council, c. 18 October 1570, in Alfred John Kempe, ed., *The Loseley Manuscripts* (London: John Murray, 1836) 234.

61 Christopher Devlin, *The Life of Robert Southwell: Poet and Martyr* (London: Longmans, Green and Co., 1956) 294.

62   Batt, *A Poore mans mite*, 36–7.

63   Crowther and Vincent, *JMJ*, 84.

64   Garnet, *The societie*, 12–3; See also Crowther and Vincent, *JMJ*, 5–6, 83–4. The Society is discussed in chapter 3.

65   Stanney, *A treatise*, 298.

66   For example, see CRO, AR 21/36.

67   Foley, *Records*, iv, 115–9. See also SP Dom 14/80/84.

68   For a similar incident, see Challoner, *Memoirs*, 1924 ed., 276.

69   For example, see Garnet, *The societie*, 12–3, Crowther and Vincent, *JMJ*, 5–6, 10–12.

70   For a discussion of the emergence and creation of textual communities, see Brian Stock, *The Implications of Literacy: Written Language and Models of Interpretation in the Eleventh and Twelfth Centuries* (Princeton: Princeton University Press, 1983) particularly part II.

71   John Gerard, *The Autobiography of a Hunted Priest*, trans. Philip Caraman (Garden City, NY: Image Books, 1955) 32, quoted by Connelly, *Women*, 89.

72   For examples of such schools, see Connelly, *Women*, 50, 55, 115, 153, 157, 211.

73   SP Dom 14/80/83. See also, SP Dom 12/152/39, 12/154/75, 12/167/47, 12/172/105, 107, 111, 113, 114, 12/184/33i–ii, 12/195/77, 12/248/36, 14/118/24ii, 14/151/83; *CSP Dom* 12/245/33; ChRO, EDA 12/2/81v, 132–132v; Morris, *The Troubles*, iii, 40; BL, Lansdowne MS 42, f. 174; BL, Lansdowne MS 153, f. 123; *Miscellanea VII* (London: Catholic Record Society, IX, 1911) 116–7, 120–1; Blom, *Post-Tridentine*, 19–20, 113–5, 121, 127; Ann M.C. Forster, "The Real Roger Widdrington," *Recusant History* 11, no. 4 (1977): 203; Nicholas Roscarrock, *Lives of the Saints: Cornwall and Devon*, ed. Nicholas Orme (Devon and Cornwall Record Society, new series, XXXV, 1992) 181.

74   SP Dom 12/167/47. For an example of another such book-based community, see Nancy Pollard Brown, "Paperchase: The Dissemination of Catholic Texts in Elizabethan England," in *English Manuscript Studies, 1100–1700*, vol. I, eds. Peter Beal and Jeremy Griffiths (Oxford: Basil Blackwell, 1989) 125–40.

75   Blom, *Post-Tridentine*, 19–20.

76   Kelly, *Blessed Thomas Belson*, 130; Haigh, *Lanc*, 214, 249. Former warden of the collegiate church at Manchester, Vaux emigrated to Louvain in 1559. He later visited England as Pius V's representative and became an arbiter of sorts of what was acceptable Catholic practice.

77   Allison and Rogers, *The Contemporary Printed Literature*, 148–9.

78   For example, see Laurence Vaux, *A catechisme*, especially regarding the form of confession, adherence to the first commandment on professing true faith, hearing of Mass, and reception of the Eucharist.

79   For examples, see ChRO, EDA 12/2 ff. 130–32v; SP Dom 12/162/14; 12/172/107, 113; *Miscellanea VII*, 116–7; Haigh, *Lanc*, 253, 292.

80   SP Dom 14/151/83. Protestants even caught church papists using Vaux's *Catechism* during Protestant services. See SP Dom 12/164/59–61.

81   See chapter 1 for a more detailed discussion of printing and transporting books.

82   SP Dom 12/172/105.

83   SP Dom 14/17/47; See also *Miscellanea VII*, 120–1.

84   Michel Vovelle, *La mort et l'Occident de 1300 a nos jours* (Paris: Gallimard, 1983) 209, calls the Reformation a "revolution in death." Protestants rejected the notion of a Purgatory since there is no scriptural justification for it and because a belief in Purgatory was contradictory to the Protestant tenet of salvation through faith alone. As a result, Masses, indulgences, and prayers to aid the soul in Purgatory become unnecessary and even sinful as chronicled in Nancy Beaty, *The Craft of Dying: A Study in the Literary Tradition of the* Ars Moriendi *in England* (New Haven: Yale University Press, 1970) 133. Instead, souls were believed to lie in latency until the Last Judgment. Robert Watson, *The Rest is Silence: Death as Annihilation in the English Renaissance* (Berkeley: University of California Press, 1994) 5–6, argues that Calvinism placed "a blank wall between the living and the dead."

85   For contrasting Protestant views on the issues, see Edmund S. Morgan, *Visible Saints: The History of a Puritan Idea* (Ithaca: Cornell University Press, 1971) chapter 1, and J. F. H. New, *Anglican and Puritan: The Basis of Their Opposition, 1558–1640* (London: Adam and Charles Black, 1964) 40–5.

86   For more detail, see Diarmaid MacCulloch's analysis of the changes in English funerary theology in *Thomas Cranmer, A Life* (New Haven: Yale University Press, 1996) 508–9, 614.

87   Although it did remain critical to many Catholics to be buried on holy ground. See CRO, AD 37/50/19, 20 (index mislabels these as 10–12).

88   Star Chamber 9/1/2; *CSP Dom* 14/154/17; BL, Add MS 4177, ff. 56–58v; See also Frank Tyrer, "A Star Chamber Case: Asheton v. Blundell, 1624–31" (Liverpool: Historic Society of Lancashire and Cheshire, CXVIII, 1966) 19–37.

89   Tyrer, "A Star Chamber Case," 32–3.

90   For example, see ChRO, EDV 1/17/103; *Acts of the High Commission Court within the Diocese of Durham* (Durham: Surtees Society, XXXIV, 1858) 142. English Protestants maintained that burial rites and the Catholic sacrament of the last rites were unnecessary. The burial rite in the 1552 Book of Common Prayer had been purged of much of the medieval ceremony, such as the tolling of the bells, the sprinkling of holy water, and traditional prayers for the souls of the dead. In 1649, an Englishman complained that funerals were "in a manner profane, in many places the dead being thrown in the ground like dogs, and not a word said." But the traditional rituals were often considered optional, not prohibited. See N. Strange in Preface to (R. Carier), *A Missive to his Majesty of*

Great Britain (1649) 12, and D. Person, *Varieties* (1635) 164–5, both quoted in Thomas, *Religion*, 604–5; See also Duffy, *Stripping*, 474–5; R.S. Guernsey, *Ecclesiastical Law in* Hamlet: *The Burial of Ophelia* (New York: AMS Press for the Shakespeare Society of New York, 1885).

91   BL, Add MS 4177, ff. 56–58v; Seccion de Estado, Archivo General de Simancas 2603/102 quoted in Loomie, *Spain and the Jacobean Catholics: vol. 2, 1613–1624*, 160.

92   Haigh, *Lanc*, 217–8, 220; See also SP Dom 12/69/14, ChRO, EDA 12/2/80, 81v, 132v; EDA 12/3/28–28v; EDV 1/12b/158v; EDC 5, 1596.

93   R.C. Richardson, *Puritanism in North-West England* (Manchester: Manchester University Press, 1972) 159, 161, 169; A. D. Wright, "Catholic History: North and South Revisited," *Northern History* 25 (1989): 132.

94   SP Dom 14/14/53. See also *Selections from the Household Books*, 354, when bells and candles are used at burial.

95   The House of Commons had denounced Courtenay as a recusant in 1624. Courtenay died six years later in London and was buried in his family's tomb. George Oliver, *Collections Illustrating the History of the Catholic Religion in the Counties of Cornwall, Devon, Dorset, Somerset, Wiltshire and Gloucester, in two parts, Historical and Biographical. With notices of the Dominican, Benedictine, & Franciscan Orders* (London: Charles Dolman, 1857) 18. See also p. 20, for the example of a cross erected to honor Catholic members of the Risdon family.

96   Northumberland was executed for his role in the 1569 Northern Rising. *Chronicles of the Canonesses of Saint Augustine at Saint Monica's in Louvain*, i, 169, quoted in Connelly, *Women*, 39.

97   For example, see University Library Cambridge, Add MS 3041, letter, undated, of W. Webbe quoted in Baring-Gould, *Cornish Characters*, ii, 183–4.

98   Exceptions include wealthy Catholics who would pay continental orders to say Masses and prayers for English loved ones. See Colleen Marie Seguin, *Addicted unto Piety: Catholic Women in England: 1590–1690* (Ph.D. Dissertation, Duke University, 1997) 297–8.

99   Scarisbrick, *The Reformation*, 60, quoted in Doreen Rosman, *From Catholic to Protestant: Religion and the People in Tudor England* (London: UCL Press, 1996) 35.

100   Ralph Brentano, *Two Churches: England and Italy in the Thirteenth Century* (Berkeley: University of California Press, 1988); Scarisbrick, *The Reformation*, 56–64; A. G. Dickens, *The English Reformation*, 2nd ed. (University Park, PA: Pennsylvania State University Press, 1989) chaps. 2–4; Wooding, *Rethinking*, chaps. 2–5.

101   *CSP Rome* 38/2/373; For a representative example, see Gerard, *Autobiography*.

102   Baring-Gould, *Cornish Characters*, ii, 279–85; SP Dom 12/167/47, 12/206/53; Richard Verstegan, *The Letters and Despatches of Richard Verstegan*, ed. Anthony G. Petti (London: Catholic Record Society, LII, 1959) 79; Haigh, *Lanc*,

253; Edwin H. Burton, *London Streets & Catholic Memories* (London: Burns, Oates & Washbourne Ltd., 1925) 52.

103 SP Dom 12/245/131; Charles Spinola to Claudius Aquaviva, in *The Life of Charles Spinola* (Antwerp, 1630) quoted in Oliver, *Collections*, 3.

104 See BL, Add MS 30262, E2, quoted in Katharine M. Longley, "Blessed George Errington and Companions," *Recusant History* (GB) 19, no. 1 (1988): 41–3; Rowse, *Tudor Cornwall*, 350; *CSP Dom Add* 12/27/93; *CSP Rome* 38/2/568.

105 SP Dom 12/48/34, 71, 72; Haigh, *Lanc*, 250.

106 Burton, *London Streets*, 52. The authorities arrested Felton for nailing a copy of the papal bull excommunicating Elizabeth to the door of the palace of the Bishop of London.

107 *CSP Dom* 12/27/93.

108 Vaux, *Catechism*, ccciii–iv, quoted in Haigh, *Lanc*, 249. See also Henry Garnet to Claudio Aquaviva from the Archives of the Society of Jesus, Rome, in Philip Caraman, *Henry Garnet 1555–1606 and the Gunpowder Plot* (London: Longmans, 1964) quoted in Walsham, *Church Papists*, 21.

109 SP Dom 12/118/46; Rowse, *Tudor Cornwall*, 350. See Walsham, *Church Papists*, chapter 2, for a discussion of early polemics against attendance at Protestant services, such as Gregory Martin's *Treatise of Schisme* (1578) and Robert Persons's *Brief Discourse contayning certayne reasons why Catholiques refuse to goe to Church* (orig. 1580).

110 Seccion de Estado, Archivo General de Simancas 2593/72, in Loomie, *Spain and the Jacobean Catholics: vol. 2, 1613–1624*, 48.

111 E. E. Reynolds, *Campion and Parsons: The Jesuit Mission of 1580–1* (London: Sheed and Ward, 1980) 18, has suggested that Rome is not entirely to blame for its failure to aid English Catholics more vigorously. At the beginning of Elizabeth's reign, Pope Paul IV attempted to send envoys to the new queen, hoping to protect Catholic interests, but Philip II of Spain prevented their departure from the Low Countries. According to Reynolds, Philip II was trying to ensure that England did not ally with France, his enemy. He wanted to keep Elizabeth firmly within his own political grasp. Most of the decline in loyalty to Rome, however, occurred decades later.

112 William Allen in William Allen and Richard Barrett, *Letters of William Allen and Richard Barrett 1572–1598*, ed. P. Renold (London: Catholic Record Society, LVIII, 1967) 31. See also Walsham, *Church Papists*, 22–3, 50–1.

113 Garnet, *Treatise*, 160–1, in Allen and Barrett, *Letters*, 31 fn. Ironically, Jesuits working in Scotland took a different stance, claiming there was no sin in Catholic attendance at reformed services as long as Catholics did not participate in prayers or rituals. See Walsham "Yielding," *Conformity and Orthodoxy*, 232.

114 SP Dom 12/243/80. See Walsham's analysis of Allen's agenda in *Church Papists*, 1999 reprint, 69.

115 See Walsham, *Church Papists*, 2–3, 51–6, particularly her analysis of an anony-
     mous manuscript attributed to Dr. Alban Langdale that maintained it was no
     mortal sin to outwardly conform. Also valuable is Walsham's treatment of the
     priest Thomas Bell who suggested that mere attendance at Prayer Book services
     did not endanger Catholic souls as long as Catholics engaged in no Protestant
     worship, "Yielding," *Conformity and Orthodoxy*, 218–36.

116 Certain Catholics drew such distinctions between what was God's and what was
     the monarch's during Elizabeth's reign, but such efforts did not become wide-
     spread until James's reign. During the threat of the Spanish Armada in 1588,
     some Catholics issued statements of allegiance, promising not to attempt to over-
     throw Elizabeth. See also Roger Manning, *Religion and Society in Elizabethan
     Sussex: A Study of the Enforcement of the Religious Settlement, 1558–1603*
     (Bristol: Leicester University Press, 1969) 161, treatment of the Montagues.

117 Tierney, *Dodd's Church History*, vol. 3, clxxxvii–cxci.

118 Arnold Oskar Meyer, *England and the Catholic Church under Queen Elizabeth*,
     trans. J.R. McKee (New York: Barnes & Noble, 1967) 420, 456f, has interpreted
     this Protestation as evidence of the emerging modern state. It is not my intention
     to address such implications. John Bossy, *ECC*, chap. 2, addresses these issues
     more fully.

119 Tierney, *Dodd's Church History*, vol. 3, clxxxvii–cxci. The protestation was made
     in the midst of the appellant priest controversy. In November 1602, Elizabeth
     issued *A Proclamation against Jesuits and others* ordering all Jesuits and their fol-
     lowers out of England. She ordered the appellant priests to leave within 3 months
     unless they swore their duty and allegiance to her.

120 There had never been broad-based support among English clerics for this claim.

121 Tierney, *Dodd's Church History*, vol. 3, clxxxviii–cxci; vol. 4, lxxxiii.

122 *CSP Dom* 12/282/74.

123 *Statutes of the Realm*, IV, 1071–7, quoted in J.P. Kenyon, ed., *The Stuart
     Constitution 1603–1688*, 2nd ed. (Cambridge: Cambridge University Press,
     1986) 170–1.

124 Papal bull of Paul V prohibiting English Catholics from taking the Oath or going
     to Church of England services, see SP Dom 14/23/15.

125 Extracts from the examinations of twenty-two priests in 1615, in Tierney, *Dodd's
     Church History*, vol. 4, cxcviii–ccv; See also Father Holtby to Robert Holtby, 26
     June 1611, in Tierney, *Dodd's Church History*, vol. 4, cxcii; Foley, *Records*, ii,
     492.

126 Examination of Oswald Needham, priest, September 27, 1609, in Tierney,
     Dodd's Church History, vol. 4, cxciii. Oswald Needham was one of the thirteen
     priests who signed the 1603 "Protestation of Allegiance." (vol. 3, clxxxviii–cxci)

127 Foley, *Records*, ii, 491.

128 Supplication of Eight Priests, prisoners in Newgate, to Pope Paul V translated in Tierney, *Dodd's Church History*, vol. 4, ccv–ccviii. Such priests, according to Walsham, "mounted a powerful challenge" to Rome's official position and were representative of a large segment of the English priesthood. "Yielding," *Conformity and Orthodoxy*, 233.

129 James I, *Apologie for the Oath*, 7, 8, in Tierney, *Dodd's Church History*, vol. 4, ccv–ccviii.

130 John Mush to More, 19 August 1611, in Tierney, *Dodd's Church History*, vol. 4, clxxix–xxx.

131 *CSP Dom* 14/89/24. As Walsham argues, such an approach was a signal of neither political or religious apathy but an active negotiation of one's Catholicism. Walsham, "Yielding," *Conformity and Orthodoxy*, 213.

132 John Nelson to Dr. More, 8 June 1611, in Tierney, *Dodd's Church History*, vol. 4, clxxiii–v; See also George Birkhead to Dr. Thomas More, agent in Rome, March 1611, in Tierney, *Dodd's Church History*, vol. 4, clxv fn.

133 Extracts from the examinations of twenty-two priests in 1615, in Tierney, *Dodd's Church History*, vol. 4, cxcviii–ccv. As Walsham argues in *Church Papists*, chapter 3, there was little clerical agreement over issues of degrees of conformity, ranging from churchgoing to oathtaking.

134 See also William Warmington's *A Moderate Defense of the Oath of Allegiance* (1612) and Barclay's *De Potestate Papae, quatenus in Regis et Principes saeculares jus et imperium habeat* (France, 1609) mentioned by George Birkhead, in letters to his agent in Rome, Dr. More, 3 May and 6 October 1611, in Tierney, *Dodd's Church History*, vol. 4, clxvii–ix, clxxxiii. Richard Sheldon was a Clinker in 1611.

135 Cecil Papers, Petitions, No. 1101 (no date or signature) in Clare Talbot, ed., *Miscellanea Recusant Records* (London: Catholic Record Society, LIII, 1961) 172–3.

136 Jesuits, seminarians, Franciscans, and Benedictines began accusing each others' orders of disloyalty to Rome, heating up the controversy further and contributing to suspicions and disunity among the English clerics. See Tierney, *Dodd's Church History*, vol. 4, clxiii–v for more information. Also see Bossy, *ECC*.

137 George Blackwell to his clergy, 7 July 1607, in Tierney, *Dodd's Church History*, vol. 4, cxlvii–viii.

138 Tierney, *Dodd's Church History*, vol. 4, clxxx.

139 *CSP Dom* 14/31/11.

140 Birkhead to Priests in the Clink, 2 May 1608, in Tierney, *Dodd's Church History*, vol. 4, clx–xi.

141 Birkhead to Dr. Smith, agent in Rome, 16 May 1609, John Mush to More, 19 August 1611, and Birkhead to More, 6 October 1611, in Tierney, *Dodd's Church History*, vol. 4, clxi–ii, clxxx, clxxxiii.

142   Birkhead to Priests in the Clink, 2 May 1608, Birkhead to Fr. Robert Jones, Superior of the Jesuits, 24 June 1610, Birkhead to Smith, 16 May 1609 and 5 June 1609, John Mush to More, 19 August 1611, and Birkhead to More, 6 October 1611, in Tierney, *Dodd's Church History*, vol. 4, clx–xv, clxxx, clxxxiii.

143   Birkhead to Dr. Thomas More, 3 May 1611, in Tierney, *Dodd's Church History*, vol. 4, clxvii–ix.

144   Birkhead to More, 30 May 1611, in Tierney, *Dodd's Church History*, vol. 4, clxxi.

145   Note how Mush describes Yorkshire Catholics' attempts to satisfy God, not the pope. John Mush to Dr. Thomas More, agent in Rome, 19 August 1611, in Tierney, *Dodd's Church History*, vol. 4, clxxvi–viii.

146   Mush to More, 19 August 1611, in Tierney, *Dodd's Church History*, vol. 4, clxxvii–viii.

147   Ibid, clxxvii–viii.

148   George Birkhead to Dr. Smith, agent in Rome, 26 July 1610, in Tierney, *Dodd's Church History*, vol. 4, clxvi–vii.

149   Tierney, *Dodd's Church History*, vol. 4, cxc–cxci. Such a statement was likely included in response to the assassination of the excommunicated Protestant French King Henri IV by a zealous Catholic monk in 1610.

150   Foley, *Records*, ii, 491.

151   Individual Protestants were also engaging in similar attempts to reconcile their consciences and "redefine sin and self" in light of competing and irreconcilable Protestant theologies and rituals, according to Jones, *English Reformation*, 199, 201. Such redefinitions, typically done without fears of excommunication or charges of treason, were performed in a different context than English Catholics' redefinitions of "sin and self."

NOTES TO CONCLUSION

1   York High Commission Book 1612–25, f. 10, quoted in Aveling, "Meynell," xxv.

2   See for example, Wooding's recent interpretation of Mary I's priorities in reestablishing Catholicism in England in *Rethinking*, chapters 4 and 5, as well as D. M. Loades's in-depth analysis of Mary's reign in *The Reign of Mary Tudor: Politics, Government, and Religion in England, 1553–1558* (New York: St. Martin's Press, 1979).

3   Jones, *English Reformation*, 165, 196–202.

4   See John Coffey, *Persecution and Toleration in Protestant England, 1558–1689* (Harlow, England: Longmans, 2000) introduction, for a persuasive comparison.

5   Catholics were judicially labeled as traitors and officially executed for treason, not for religion. See Walsham, *Church Papists*, 1999 reprint ed., 11–12.

Select Bibliography

PRIMARY SOURCES: ARCHIVAL DEPOSITORIES

Borthwick Institute, York

 High Commission Act Books

 High Commission Cause Papers

 Visitation Acts Books

British Library

 Add 4177: ff. 56r-58v

 Add 32092, ff. 218-219v

 Add 39288, f. 6

 Arundel 318: ff. 152-153

 Arundel 321

 Cotton Titus C VII, f. 60r

 Harleian 367, f. 79

 Harleian 494, ff. 105-106v

 Harleian 791, ff. 43-44

 Harleian 1619, ff. 3-4

 Harleian 2277

 Harleian 4149

 Harleian 6211

 Harleian 6624

 Lansdowne 23, ff. 110-111, 117

Lansdowne 25, f. 167

Lansdowne 42, f. 174

Lansdowne 50, f. 156

Lansdowne 72, ff. 133-135v

Lansdowne 75, ff. 44-44v

Lansdowne 153, ff. 9, 30, 67, 68, 70, 73, 108, 123, 152

Lansdowne 350, ff. 2-37

Sloane 3785

Sloane 4035, ff. 2-34

Stowe 53

Stowe 423, ff. 150v-153

Cornwall Public Record Office, Truro

Additional/Miscellaneous Accessions

Arundel

Bullar Family of Morvel

Carlyon of Trehegan

Coryton Muniment

Enys

Rashleigh Family of Menabilly

Rashleigh Family of Stoketon

Rogers Family of Penrose

Tremayne of Heligan

Cheshire Public Record Office, Chester

Diocesan Records Consistory Court

Proceedings of the Royal Commissioners

Visitation Correction Books

Chester City Archive, Chester

CR 63/2/697

Public Record Office, Kew

State Papers, Domestic

State Papers, Scotland

York Minster Library, York

Add 151

PUBLISHED PRIMARY SOURCES-CALENDARS

Calendar of State Papers, Domestic Series, of the reign of Charles I, 1625–1649. Public Record Office, series 3. London: Longman, Brown, Green, Longmans & Roberts, 1964.

Calendar of State Papers, Domestic Series, of the reign of Elizabeth I. Public Record Office, series 2. London: Longman, Brown, Green, Longmans & Roberts, 1856–72.

Calendar of State Papers, Domestic Series, of the reign of James I, 1603–1625. Public Record Office, series 2. London: Longman, Brown, Green, Longmans & Roberts, 1856–72.

Calendar of State Papers relating to Scotland. Public Record Office, series 10. London: Longman, Brown, Green, Longmans & Roberts, 1858–.

Calendar of State Papers, Rome. Public Record Office, series 38. London: H.M.S.O., 1916–.

Register of the Privy Council of Scotland. 14 vols. Edinburgh: H.M. General Register House, 1877.

Statutes of the Realm. 11 vols. London: Dawson's of Pall Mall, 1810–1828.

PUBLISHED PRIMARY SOURCES-TREATISES, LETTERS, COLLECTIONS, ETC.

Acts of the High Commission Court within the Diocese of Durham. Durham: Surtees Society, XXXIV, 1858.

Allen, William. *A defense and declaration of the Catholike Churchies doctrine, touching purgatory, and prayers for the soules departed.* Antwerp: Iohn Latius, 1565.

———. *A treatise made in defence of the lauful power and authoritie of Priesthood to remitte sinnes: of the peoples duetie for confession of their sinnes to Gods ministers: and of the Churches meaning concerning indulgences.* Louvain: Joannem Foulerum, 1567.

———. *A true, sincere, and modest defence of English Catholiques that suffer for their faith both at home and abrode: against a false, seditious and slanderous libel.* n.p., 1584.

———. *An apologie and true declaration of the institution and endeuours of the two English colleges, the one in Rome, the other now resident in Rhemes.* Mons, Hainault, 1581.

————— and Barrett, Richard. *Letters of William Allen and Richard Barrett 1572–1598.* ed. P. Renold. London: Catholic Record Society, LVIII, 1967.

Androzzi, Fulvio. *Certaine deuout considerations of frequenting the Blessed Sacrament.* trans. Thomas Everard. St. Omer: John Heigham, 1618.

Anonymous. "A Portuguese narration of the martyrdom of the Ven. Thomas Holland, S.J. 1642." trans. Edward Robert James. London: Catholic Record Society, XIII, 1913.

Arias, Francisco. *The little memorial, treating of the good, & fruitfull vse, of the holy sacraments, of pennance and communion.* trans. Henry Garnet. 2nd edition. St. Omer: English College Press, 1620.

Batt, Anthony. *A Poore mans mite. A letter of a religious man of the Order of St. Benedict vnto a Sister of his, concerning the rosarie or psalter of our blessed Ladie, Commonly called the Beades.* Douai: Widow of Mark Wyon, 1639.

Bellarmino, Roberto Francesco Romolo. *The Art of Dying Well.* trans. Edward Coffin. n.p., 1621.

Borgia, St. Francis. *The Practice of Christian Workes.* trans. John Wilson (orig. 1620). Menston, Yorkshire: Scolar Press, 1970.

————. *Three & Thirty Most Godly and Devout Prayers or Salutations to be Recited in honour of the Sacred Life & Passion of Our Beloved Saviour Sweet Jesus, for Faithful Soules departed: After ech wherof, must be said the Psalme Miserere* (orig. 1641?). Menston, Yorkshire: Scolar Press, 1970.

Brereton, William. *Journal of Sir William Brereton 1635.* Durham: Surtees Society, CXXIV, 1915.

Bristow, Richard. *A Briefe Treatise of diverse plaine and sure wayes to finde out the truthe in this doubtful and dangerous time of Heresie: conteyning sundry worthy Motives unto the Catholicke faith.* Antwerp, 1574.

Broughton, Richard. *A Manual of Praiers vsed by the Fathers of the Primitive Church, for the most part within the foure first hundred years of Christ, and all before the end of the sixt hundred yeare.* n.p., 1618.

————. *A new manual of Old Christian Catholick meditations, & praiers faithfully collected and translated, without any word altered, or added.* n.p., 1617.

Bucke, John. *Instructions for the use of the beades* (orig. 1589). Menston, Yorkshire: Scolar Press, 1971.

Canisius, St. Peter. *Certayne Necessarie Principles of Religion which may be entitled A Catechisme conteyning all the partes of the Christian and Catholique Fayth.* trans. T. I. Douai: Joannem Bogardum, 1578–9.

———. *A summe of Christian doctrine.* trans. Henry Garnet. n.p., 1592.

Carew, Richard. "The Survey of Cornwall" (orig. 1602) in *Richard Carew of Antony 1555–1620.* ed. F. E. Halliday. London: Andrew Melrose, 1953.

Chamberlain, John. *The Letters of John Chamberlain.* vol. 1. Memoirs XII, Part 1. ed. Norman Egbert McClure. Philadelphia: The American Philosophical Society, 1939.

Crowther, Arthur. *A daily exercise of the devout Christian: Containing several most pithy practices of piety; in order to live holily and dye happily.* n.p., 1657.

——— and Vincent, Thomas. *The Dayly Exercise of the Devout Rosarists Containing several most pithy Practices of Devotion: profitable not only for such as are members of the sacred Rosary, but also for all pious Christians.* Amsterdam, 1657.

——— and Vincent, Thomas. *Jesus, Maria, Joseph, or, The Devout Pilgrim, of the Ever Blessed Virgin Mary, in His Holy Exercises, Affections, and Elevations.* Amsterdam, 1657.

Decrees of the Ecumenical Councils, vol. 2, *Trent to Vatican II*, ed. Norman P. Tanner, original text established by G. Albergio, J. A. Dossetti, P.-P. Joannou, C. Leonardi, and P. Prodi, in consultation with H. Jedin. London: Sheed and Ward, Ltd., and Washington, DC: Georgetown University Press, 1990.

de Sales, St. Francis. *Delicious Entertainments of the Soule.* trans. Pudentiana Deacon. Douai: Gheerart Pinson, 1632.

Dodd, Charles. *The History of the English College at Douay: from its First Foundation in 1568, to the Present Time.* London: Bernard Lintott, 1713.

Doddridge, John. *History of Wales, Cornwall and Chester* (orig. London, 1630) Amsterdam: Theatrum Orbis Terrarum, 1973.

D'Oultreman, Phillip. *The True Christian Catholique or the Maner how to Live Christianly.* trans. John Heigham. St. Omer, 1622.

E.I. *A New-Year Gift for English Catholikes or A Brief and cleare Explication of the New Oath of Allegiance.* n.p., 1620.

E.W. *A brief explication of the Office of the Blessed Virgin Marie* . . . . Douai, 1652.

Fitzsimon, Henry. *The iustification and exposition of the divine sacrifice of the masse.* Douai: L. Kellam, 1611.

Floyd, John. *An apology of the Holy Sea Apostolicks proceedings for the government of the Catholicks of England during the time of persecution.* Rouen, 1630.

Foley, Henry. *Records of the English Province of the Society of Jesus.* 7 vols. London: Burns & Oates, 1877.

Forbes-Leith, William. *Memoirs of the Scottish Catholics during the Seventeenth and Eighteenth Centuries, selected from hitherto unedited manuscripts.* London: Longmans, Green, 1909.

———. *Narratives of Scottish Catholics under Mary Stuart and James VI, Now First Printed from the Original Manuscripts in the Secret Archives of the Vatican and Other Collections.* Edinburgh: William Patterson, 1885.

Garnet, Henry. *A treatise of Christian Renunciation . . . Whereunto is added a shorte discourse against going to the Hereticall Churches with a Protestation.* n.p., 1593.

———. *An Apology against the defense of schisme. Lately written by an English divine at Doway, for answere to a letter of a lapsed Catholicke in England to his frend: who having in the late Commission gone to the Church, defended his fall. Wherin is plainely declared, and manifestly proved, the generall doctrine of the Divines & of the Church of Christ, which hiterto hath bene taught and followed in England concerning this pointe.* n.p., 1593.

———. *The societie of the rosary.* n.p., 1596/7.

Gennings, John. *The Life and Death of Mr. Edmund Geninges, priest, crowned with Martyrdom at London.* St. Omer: Charles Boscard, 1614.

Gerard, John. *The Autobiography of a Hunted Priest.* trans. Philip Caraman. Garden City, NY: Image Books, 1955.

Gifford, George. *A dialogue between a papist and a Protestant: applied to the capacity of the unlearned.* n.p., 1583.

Gordon, James. *A summary of controversies.* trans. William Wright. St. Omer, 1618.

Hall, Spencer, ed. *Documents from Simancas Relating to the Reign of Elizabeth, 1558–1568.* trans. Don Tomas Gonzalez. London: Chapman and Hall, 1865.

Heigham, John. *A devout exposition of the holie Masse.* Douai, 1614.

Hill, (Edmund) Thomas, *A Quarton of Reasons of Catholike Religion, with as many briefe reasons of refusall.* Antwerp, 1600.

Horae Eboracenses: The Book of Hours of the Blessed Virgin Mary with Other Prayers According to the Use of the Church of York with Other Devotions as they were used by the Lay Folk in the Northern Province in the XVth and XVIth Centuries, from the edition printed in 1536. ed. C. Wordsworth. Durham: Surtees Society, CXXXII, 1919.

Kempe, Alfred John, ed. *The Loseley Manuscripts.* London: John Murray, 1836.

Knox, T. F., ed. *The First and Second Diaries of the English College at Douai.* London: David Nutt, 1878.

Lewis of Granada. *A Treatise of the Love of God. Wherein consisteth the perfection of Christian Life.* Douai: John Heigham, 1611.

Little Office of the Blessed Virgin Mary: The primer according to the last edition of the Roman Breviarie. n.p., 1617.

Loarte, Gasparo. *Instructions and Advertisements How to Meditate upon the misteries of the Rosarie of the most holy Virgin Mary* (orig. 1613) trans. anonymous. Menston, Yorkshire: Scolar Press, 1970.

Loomie, Albert, ed. *Spain and the Jacobean Catholics, volume 1, 1603–1612.* London: Catholic Record Society, LXIV, 1973.

———, ed. *Spain and the Jacobean Catholics, volume 2, 1613–1624.* London: Catholic Record Society, LXVIII, 1978.

Martin, Gregory. *A Treatise of Schisme. Shewing, that al Catholikes ought in any wise to abstaine altogether from heretical Conventicles, to witt, their prayers, sermons, &.* Douai: Joannem Foulerum, 1578.

McCann, Justin and Connolly, Hugh, eds. *Memorials of Father Augustine Baker and Other Documents Relating to the English Benedictines.* London: Catholic Record Society, XXXIII, 1933.

Miscellanea VII. London: Catholic Record Society, IX, 1911.

Morris, John, ed. *The Troubles of Our Catholic Forefathers Related by Themselves.* 3 vols. London: Burns & Oates, 1877.

Perin, Wyllyam. *Spirituall Exercyses and Goostly Meditations, and a neare waye to come to perfection and lyfe contemplatiue, very profytable for Religyous, and generally for al other that desyre to come to the perfecte loue of God and to the contempte of the world.* Caen: Peter le Chandelier, 1598.

Persons, Robert. *Letters and Memorials of Father Robert Persons, SJ, Volume I (to 1588).* ed. L. Hicks. London: Catholic Record Society, XXXIX, 1942.

Peterkin, Alexander, ed. *The Booke of the Universall Kirke of Scotland*. Edinburgh: The Edinburgh Printing and Pub. Co., 1839.

Petti, Anthony G., ed. *Recusant Documents from the Ellesmere Manuscripts 1577–1715*. London: Catholic Record Society, LX, 1968.

Pinelli, Luca. *The Virgin Marie's life, faithfully gathered out of aunclent & holie fathers*. trans. Richard Gibbons. Douai: Laurens Kellam, 1604.

Pollen, J. H., ed. *Unpublished Documents Relating to the English Martyrs: vol. 1, 1584–1603*. London: Catholic Record Society, V, 1908.

Possevino, Antonio. *A Treatise of the Holy Sacrifice of the Altar, called the Masse*. trans. Thomas Butler. Louvain: Ioannem Foulerum, 1570.

Preston, Thomas (Roger Widdrington). *A Theologicall Disputation concerning the Oath of Allegiance*, n.p., 1613.

Radford, John. *A Directorie Teaching the Way to the Truth in a Briefe and Plaine Discovrse against the heresies of this time*. n.p., 1605.

Relatio incarcerationis et martyrii P. Ioannis Ogilbei natione Scoti e Societate Iesu Presbyteri. Doaui: Laurence Kellam, 1615.

Richeome, Lewis. *Holy pictures of the mysticall figures of the most holy sacrifice and sacrament of the Eucharist . . . translated into English for the benefit of those of that Nation as well Protestants as Catholikes*. trans. C.A. n.p., 1619.

Roscarrock, Nicholas. *Lives of the Saints: Cornwall and Devon*. Nicholas Orme, ed. Devon and Cornwall Record Society, new series, XXXV, 1992.

Selections from the Household Books of Lord William Howard of Naworth Castle. Durham: Surtees Society, LXVIII, 1878.

Somerset, Sir Charles. *The Travel Diary (1611–1612) of an English Catholic*. ed. Michael G. Brennan. Leeds: Leeds Philosophical and Literary Society Ltd., 1993.

Southwell, Robert. *An Epistle of Comfort, to the reverend priestes & to the honorable, worshipful, & other of the laye sort restrayned in durance for the Catholicke fayth*. Paris, 1587.

Stafford, Anthony. *The femall glory: or The life, and death of our Blessed Lady, the holy Virgin Mary, Gods owne immaculate mother*. London: Thomas Harper, 1653.

Stanney, William. *A treatise of penance, with an explication of the rule, and maner of living, of the brethren and sisters, of the Third Order of St. Frauncis, comon-li called the Order of Penance, ordained for those which desire to leade a holy life, and to doe penance in their owne houses*, Part I. Douai: John Heigham, 1617.

Talbot, Clare, ed. *Miscellanea Recusant Records*. London: Catholic Record Society, LIII, 1961.

Tierney, M. A. *Dodd's Church History of England from the Commencement of the Sixteenth Century to the Revolution in 1688*. 5 vols. London: Charles Dolman, 1839.

Vaux, Laurence. *A catechisme or a Christian doctrine, necessarie for children & the ignorant people*. Rotho Magi: Henricum Mareschalum bibliopolum, 1580.

Verstegan, Richard. *The letters and despatches of Richard Verstegan*. ed. Anthony G. Petti. London: Catholic Record Society, LII, 1959.

Weston, William. *William Weston, The Autobiography of an Elizabethan*. trans. Philip Caraman. London: Longmans, Green and Co., 1955.

Wiseman, Sir William. *The Christian Knight*. London: John Legatt, 1619.

Worthington, Thomas. *Rosarie of Our Lady*. Ingolstadii: Ederiana apud Andreas Angermarium, 1603.

Wright, Thomas, *The Passions of the Mind in General*. ed. William Webster Newbold. New York: Garland Publications Inc., 1986.

SECONDARY SOURCES-BOOKS OR PARTS OF BOOKS

Anstruther, Godfrey, *The seminary priests: a dictionary of the secular clergy in England and Wales, 1558–1850*. 4 vols. Ware, Herts.: St. Edmund's College, 1969–77.

Aston, Margaret. *England's Iconoclasts: vol. 1, Laws against Images*. Oxford: Clarendon Press, 1988.

Aveling, J. C. H. *The Handle and the Axe: The Catholic Recusants in England from Reformation to Emancipation*. London: Blond and Briggs Ltd., 1976.

———. *Northern Catholics: The Catholic Recusants of the North Riding of Yorkshire, 1558–1790*. London: Dublin Chapman, 1966.

Baring-Gould, S. *Cornish Characters and Strange Events*. 2 vols. London: John Lane The Bodley Head Ltd., 1925.

Beinert, Wolgang and Fiorenza, Francis Schussler, eds. *Handbook of Catholic Theology*. New York: Crossroads, 1995.

Blom, J. M. *The Post-Tridentine English Primer*. London: Catholic Record Society, 1982.

Blundell, Dom F. O. *Old Catholic Lancashire*. London: Burns, Oates & Washbourne, Ltd., 1925.

Borlase, William. *Observations on the antiquities historical and monumental, of the county of Cornwall*. Oxford: W. Jackson, 1754.

Bossy, John. *The English Catholic Community, 1570–1850*. London: Darton, Longman & Todd, 1975.

Bottrell, William. *Traditions and Hearthside Stories of West Cornwall*. 2 vols. Penzance: W. Cornish, 1870.

Bouyer, Louis. *Eucharist: Theology and Spirituality of the Eucharistic Prayer*. trans. Charles Underhill Quinn. Notre Dame: University of Notre Dame Press, 1968.

Boyan, P. A. and Lamb, G. R. *Francis Tregian, Cornish Recusant*. London: Sheed and Ward Ltd., 1955.

Bridgett, T. E. *Our Lady's Dowry: How England Gained that Title*. London: Burns & Oates Ltd., n.d.

Brown, Nancy Pollard. "Paperchase: The Dissemination of Catholic Texts in Elizabethan England," in *English Manuscript Studies, 1100–1700*, vol. I, eds. Peter Beal and Jeremy Griffiths. Oxford: Basil Blackwell, 1989, pp. 120–143.

Brown, William Eric. *John Ogilvie: An Account of His Life & Death with a Translation of Documents Relating Thereunto*. London: Burns, Oates & Washbourne, Ltd., 1925.

Burton, Edwin H. *London Streets & Catholic Memories*. London: Burns, Oates & Washbourne Ltd., 1925.

Caraman, Philip. *Henry Garnet, 1555–1606, and the Gunpowder Plot*. London: Longmans, 1964.

———, ed. *The Other Face: Catholic Life Under Elizabeth I*. London: The Camelot Press Ltd., 1960.

Challoner, Richard. *Memoirs of Missionary Priests and Other Catholics of Both Sexes that Have Suffered Death in England on Religious Accounts from the Year 1577–1684*. vol. 1. Edinburgh: Thomas C. Jack, Grange Publishing Works, 1878.

———. *Memoirs of Missionary Priests and Other Catholics of Both Sexes that Have Suffered Death in England on Religious Accounts from the Year 1577–1684.* vol. 1. London: Burns, Oates & Washbourne, Ltd., 1924.

Coffey, John. *Persecution and Toleration in Protestant England, 1558–1689.* Harlow, England: Longmans, 2000.

Collinson, Patrick. *The Religion of Protestants: The Church in English Society, 1559–1625.* Oxford: Clarendon Press, 1984.

Connelly, Roland. *The Women of the Catholic Resistance: In England, 1540–1680.* Edinburgh, The Pentland Press Limited, 1997.

Cormack, Margaret, ed. *Sacrificing the Self: Perspectives on Martyrdom and Religion.* Oxford: Oxford University Press, 2002.

Crawford, Patricia. *Women and Religion in England, 1500–1720.* London: Routledge, 1993.

Cressy, David. *Bonfires and Bells: National Memory and the Protestant Calendar in Elizabethan and Stuart England.* Berkeley: University of California Press, 1989.

Cunneen, Sally. *In Search of Mary: The Woman and the Symbol.* New York: Ballantine Books, 1996.

Devlin, Christopher. *The Life of Robert Southwell, Poet and Martyr.* London: Longmans, Green and Co., 1956.

Dickens, A. G. *The English Reformation.* 2nd ed. University Park, PA: Pennsylvania State University Press.

Dippel, Stewart A. *A Study of Religious Thought at Oxford and Cambridge, 1590–1640.* Lanham, MD: University Press of America, 1987.

Doble, Gilbert H. *The Saints of Cornwall,* 5 vols. Chatham: Parrett & Neves, Ltd., 1960–1970.

Donaldson, Gordon. *The Scottish Reformation.* Cambridge: Cambridge University Press, 1960.

Duffin, Anne. *Faction and Faith: Politics and Religion of the Cornish Gentry before the Civil War.* Exeter: University of Exeter Press, 1996.

Duffy, Eamon. *The Stripping of the Altars: Traditional Religion in England, 1400–1580.* New Haven: Yale University Press, 1992.

Ellington, Donna Spivey. *From Sacred Body to Angelic Soul: Understanding Mary in Late Medieval and Early Modern Europe.* Washington, DC: Catholic University of America, 2001.

Graef, Hilda. *Devotion to the Blessed Virgin.* London: Burns & Oates, 1963.

———. *Mary: A History of Doctrine and Devotion.* 2 vols. London: Sheed and Ward, 1987.

Green, V. H. H. *A History of Oxford University.* London: B. T. Batsford, Ltd., 1974.

Gregory, Brad S. *Salvation at Stake: Christian Martyrdom in Early Modern Europe.* Cambridge, MA: Harvard University Press, 1999.

Haigh, Christopher. *English Reformations: Religion, Politics, and Society under the Tudors.* Oxford: Clarendon Press, 1993.

———. *Reformation and Resistance in Tudor Lancashire.* Cambridge: Cambridge University Press, 1975.

Hamilton-Jenkin, A. K. *Cornwall and Its People: Cornish Seafarers, Cornwall and the Cornish Homes and Customs.* London: J. M. Dent & Sons Ltd., 1946.

———. *The Story of Cornwall.* London: Thomas Nelson and Sons, Ltd., 1936.

Hoff, Linda Kay. *Hamlet's Choice: Hamlet—A Reformation Allegory.* Studies in Renaissance Literature, vol. 2. Lewiston, NY/Queenston, Ont./Lampeter, Wales: The Edwin Mellon Press, 1988.

Holmes, P. J., ed. *Elizabethan Casuistry.* London: Catholic Record Society, LXVII, 1981.

Holmes, Peter. *Resistance and Compromise: The Political Thought of the Elizabethan Catholics.* Cambridge: Cambridge University Press, 1982.

Jebb, Miles. *The Colleges of Oxford.* London: Constable & Co., 1992.

John, Catherine Rachel. *The Saints of Cornwall.* Padstow: Lodenek Press and Redruth: Dyllansow Truran, 1981.

Jones, Norman. *The English Reformation: Religion and Cultural Adaptation.* Oxford: Blackwell Publishers Ltd., 2002.

Katz, Melissa R. and Orsi, Robert A., eds. *Divine Mirrors: The Virgin Mary in the Visual Arts.* Oxford: Oxford University Press, 2001.

Kelly, Christine. *Blessed Thomas Belson: His Life and Times 1563–1589.* Gerrards Cross: Colin Smythe, 1987.

Kennedy, W. P. M. *Elizabethan Episcopal Administration*. 3 vols. Milwaukee: Morehouse Publishing Co., 1924.

Lake, Peter and Questier, Michael, eds. *Conformity and Orthodoxy in the English Church, c. 1560–1660*. Woodbridge: The Boydell Press, 2000.

Latz, Dorothy. *Glow-worm Light: Writings of Seventeenth-Century English Recusant Women from Original Manuscripts*. Salzburg Studies in English Literature. Salzburg: Aus Institut fur Anglistik und Amerikanistik, Universitat Salzburg, 1989.

Loomie, Albert J., SJ. *The Spanish Elizabethans: The English Exiles at the Court of Philip II*. New York: Fordham University Press, 1963.

Lynch, Michael. "From privy kirk to burgh church: an alternative view of the process of Protestantism." in Norman MacDougall, ed. *Church, Politics and Society: Scotland 1408–1929*. Edinburgh: John Donald Publishers Ltd., 1983.

MacCulloch, Diarmid. *Thomas Cranmer: A Life*. New Haven: Yale University Press, 1996.

Maisch, Ingrid. *Between Contempt and Veneration . . . Mary Magdalene: The Image of A Woman through the Centuries*. Collegeville, MN: The Liturgical Press, 1998.

Maltby, Judith. *Prayer Book and People in Elizabethan and Early Stuart England*. Cambridge: Cambridge University Press, 1998.

Manning, Roger B. *Religion and Society in Elizabethan Sussex: A Study of the enforcement of the religious settlement 1558–1603*. Bristol: Leicester University Press, 1969.

Marotti, Arthur F., ed. *Catholicism and Anti-Catholicism in Early Modern English Texts*. New York: St. Martin's Press, 1999.

Marshall, Peter and Ryrie, Alec, eds. *The Beginnings of English Protestantism*. Cambridge: Cambridge University Press, 2002.

———. *The Catholic Priesthood and the English Reformation*. Oxford: Oxford University Press, 1994.

———. *The Face of the Pastoral Ministry in the East Riding, 1525–1595*. York: University of York, Borthwick Paper 88, 1995.

McClain, Lisa. *As One in Faith: The Reconstruction of Catholic Communities in Protestant England, 1559–1642*. Ph.D. Dissertation, University of Texas-Austin, 2000.

McConica, James, ed. *The History of the University of Oxford*. vol. 3. Oxford: Clarendon Press, 1986.

McGrath, Patrick. "Apostate Priests and Naughty Priests in England under Elizabeth I," in *Opening the Scrolls, Essays in Honor of Godfrey Anstruther*. ed. Dominic Aidan Bellenger. Bath: Downside Abbey Trustees, 1987.

Mendelson, Sara Heller and Crawford, Patricia. *Women in Early Modern England, 1550–1720*. Oxford: Clarendon Press, 1998.

Morris, Jan, ed. *The Oxford Book of Oxford*. Oxford: Oxford University Press, 1978.

Norman, Edward. *Roman Catholicism in England from the Elizabethan Settlement to the Second Vatican Council*. Oxford: Oxford University Press, 1985.

Oliver, George. *Collections Illustrating the History of the Catholic Religion in the Counties of Cornwall, Devon, Dorset, Somerset, Wiltshire and Gloucester, in two parts, Historical and Biographical. With notices of the Dominican, Benedictine, & Franciscan Orders*. London: Charles Dolman, 1857.

Olin, John. *Catholic Reform from Cardinal Ximenes to the Council of Trent, 1495–1563: An Essay with Illustrative Documents and a Brief Study of St. Ignatius Loyola*. New York: Fordham University Press, 1990.

O'Malley, John W. *The First Jesuits*. Cambridge, MA: Harvard University Press, 1993.

———. *Trent and All That: Renaming Catholicism in the Early Modern Era*. Cambridge, MA: Harvard University Press, 2000.

Orme, Nicholas. *The Saints of Cornwall*. Oxford: Oxford University Press, 2000.

Ozment, Steven E. *The Age of Reform, 1250–1550: An Intellectual and Religious History of Late Medieval and Reformation Europe*. New Haven: Yale University Press, 1980.

———. *Mysticism and Dissent: Religious Ideology and Social Protest in the Sixteenth Century*. New Haven: Yale University Press, 1973.

Page, William. *A History of the County of Cornwall*. vol. 2. Victoria County History. London: St. Catherine's Press, 1924.

Payton, Philip. *Cornwall*. Fowey: Alexander Associates, 1996.

———. *The Making of Modern Cornwall*. Redruth: Dyllansow Truran, 1992.

Pelikan, Jaroslav. *Mary through the Centuries: Her Place in the History of Culture*. New Haven: Yale University Press, 1996.

Prest, Wilfrid R. *The Inns of Court under Elizabeth I and the Early Stuarts, 1590–1640.* London: Longman Group Ltd., 1972.

Questier, Michael. *Conversion, Politics, and Religion in England, 1580–1625.* Cambridge: Cambridge University Press, 1996.

Quiller-Couch, M. and Quiller-Couch, L. *Ancient and Holy Wells of Cornwall.* London: Charles J. Clark, 1894.

Ramsey, Ann W. *Liturgy, Politics, and Salvation: The Catholic League in Paris and the Nature of Catholic Reform, 1540–1630.* Rochester: University of Rochester Press, 1999.

Reinmuth, Howard S., Jr. "Border Society in Transition," in *Early Stuart Studies: Essays in Honor of David Harris Willson.* ed. Howard S. Reinmuth, Jr. Minneapolis: University of Minnesota Press, 1970.

Reynolds, E. E. *Campion and Parsons, The Jesuit Mission of 1580–1.* London: Sheed and Ward, 1980.

Rhodes, W. E., ed. *The Apostolical Life of Ambrose Barlow.* Chetham Miscellanies. Manchester: Chetham Society, new series, II, 1909.

Rosman, Doreen. *From Catholic to Protestant: Religion and the People in Tudor England.* London: UCL Press, 1996.

Rowse, A. L. "Nicholas Roscarrock and His *Lives of the Saints*." in J. H. Plumb, ed., *Studies in Social History: a Tribute to G.M. Trevelyan.* London: Longmans, Green, 1955.

———. *Oxford in the History of the Nation.* London: Weidenfeld & Nicolson, 1975.

———. *Tudor Cornwall: Portrait of a Society.* New York: Charles Scribner's Sons, 1969.

Rubin, Miri. *Corpus Christi: The Eucharist in Late Medieval Culture.* Cambridge: Cambridge University Press, 1991.

Scarisbrick, J. J. *The Reformation and the English People.* Oxford: Basil Blackwell Ltd., 1984.

Scribner, Robert. *For the Sake of Simple Folk: Popular Propaganda for the German Reformation.* Oxford: Clarendon Press, 1994.

Seguin, Colleen Marie. *Addicted unto Piety: Catholic Women in England, 1590–1690.* Ph.D. Dissertation, Duke University, 1997.

Sullivan, Ceri. *Dismembered Rhetoric: English Recusant Writing, 1580–1603.* London: Associated Universities Press, 1995.

Thackrah, John Richard. *The University and Colleges of Oxford.* Lavenham, Suffolk: Terence Dalton Ltd., 1981.

Thomas, Keith. *Religion and the Decline of Magic.* New York: Charles Scribner's Sons, 1971.

Walsham, Alexandra. *Church Papists: Catholicism, Conformity and Confessional Polemic in Early Modern England.* Woodbridge, Suffolk: The Royal Historical Society, The Boydell Press, 1993.

———. *Providence in Early Modern England.* Oxford: Oxford University Press, 2001.

———. "Reforming the Waters: Holy Wells and Healing Springs in Protestant England," in *Life and thought in the northern church, c. 1100– c. 1700: essays in honour of Claire Cross*, ed. Diana Wood. Woodbridge, Suffolk: Boydell for the Ecclesiastical History Society, 1999.

Warner, Marina. *Alone of All Her Sex.* New York: Vintage Books, 1976.

Watts, S. J. *From Border to Middle Shire: Northumberland, 1586–1625.* Bristol: Leicester University Press, 1975.

Winston-Allen, Anne. *Stories of the Rose: The Making of the Rosary in the Middle Ages.* University Park, PA: Pennsylvania State University Press, 1997.

Wooding, Lucy E. C. *Rethinking Catholicism in Reformation England.* Oxford: Clarendon Press, 2000.

Wormald, Jenny. "'Princes' and the Regions in the Scottish Reformations," in Norman MacDougall, ed., *Church, Politics and Society: Scotland 1408–1929.* Edinburgh: John Donald Publishers Ltd., 1983.

SECONDARY SOURCES-ARTICLES

Aveling, J. C. H. "Catholic Households in Yorkshire, 1580–1603." *Northern History.* 16 (1980): 85–101.

———, ed. "Recusant Papers of the Meynell Family." in E. E. Reynolds, ed. *Miscellanea VI.* London: Catholic Record Society, 1964.

Bossy, John. "The Character of Elizabethan Catholicism." *Past and Present* 21 (1962): 39–59.

Brennan, Gillian E. "Papists and Patriotism in Elizabethan England." *Recusant History* (GB) 19, no. 1 (1988): 1–15.

Bynum, Caroline Walker. "Women Mystics and Eucharistic Devotion in the Thirteenth Century." *Women's Studies* 11 (1984): 179–214.

Caro, Robert V., SJ. "William Alabaster: Rhetor, Mediator, Devotional Poet-1." *Recusant History* 19, no. 1 (1988): 62–79.

Forster, Ann M. C. "The Real Roger Widdrington." *Recusant History* 11, no. 4 (1977): 196–205.

Haigh, Christopher. "The Continuity of Catholicism in the English Reformation." *Past and Present* (GB) 93 (1981): 37–69.

———. "From Monopoly to Minority: Catholicism in Early Modern England." *Transactions of the Royal Historical Society* 31 (1981): 129–147.

———. "Revisionism, the Reformation, and the History of English Catholicism." *Journal of Ecclesiastical History* 36 (1985): 394–408.

Harris, P. R. "The Reports of William Udall, Informer, 1605–1612, pt. I." *Recusant History* 8, no. 4 (1966): 192–249.

———. "The Reports of William Udall, Informer, 1605–1612, pt. II." *Recusant History* 8, no. 5 (1966): 252–297.

Hibbard, Caroline. "Early Stuart Catholicism: Revisions and Rerevisions." *Journal of Modern History* 52 (1980): 1–34.

Hilton, J. A. "The Cumbrian Catholics." *Northern History* 16 (1980): 40–58.

Kaplan, Benjamin J. "Fictions of Privacy: House Chapels and the Spatial Accommodation of Religious Dissent in Early Modern Europe." *American Historical Review* (October 2002): 1031–64.

McCann, Timothy J. "Some Unpublished Accounts of the Martyrdom of Blessed Thomas Bullaker, OSF, of Chichester in 1642." *Recusant History* 19, no. 2 (1988): 171–182.

McClain, Lisa. "Without Church, Cathedral, or Shrine: The Search for Religious Space among Catholics of England, 1559–1625," *The Sixteenth Century Journal* 33, no. 2 (2002): 381–399.

———. "Using What's at Hand: English Catholic Reinterpretations of the Rosary," *The Journal of Religious History* 27, no. 2 (2003): 161–176.

McGrath, Patrick. "Elizabethan Catholicism: A Reconsideration." *Journal of Ecclesiastical History* 35 (1984): 414–28.

——— and Rowe, Joy. "The Elizabethan Priests: Their Harbourers and Helpers." *Recusant History* (GB) 19, no. 3 (1989): 209–233.

——— and Rowe, Joy. "The Imprisonment of Catholics for Religion under Elizabeth I." *Recusant History* (GB) 20, no. 4 (1991): 415–435.

Questier, Michael C. "English Clerical Converts to Protestantism, 1580–1596." *Recusant History* 20, no. 4 (1991): 455–476.

———. "Practical Antipapistry during the Reign of Elizabeth I." *Journal of British Studies* 36 (1997): 371–96.

Reinburg, Virginia. "Liturgy and the Laity in Late Medieval and Reformation France." *The Sixteenth Century Journal* 23, no. 3 (1992): 526–546.

Scribner, Robert. "The Reformation, Popular Magic, and the 'Disenchantment of the World.'" *Journal of Interdisciplinary History* 23, no. 3 (1993): 475–494.

Walsham, Alexandra. "'The fatall vesper': Providentialism and Anti-Popery in Late Jacobean London." *Past & Present* 144 (August 1994): 36–52.

Wormald, F. "The Calendar of the Augustinian Priory of Launceston Cornwall." *Journal of Theological Studies* 39, no. 153 (1938): 1–21.

Wright, A. D. "Catholic History: North and South Revisited." *Northern History* 25 (1989): 120–134.

Index